ICTs for Health, Education, and Socioeconomic Policies:
Regional Cases

Ahmed Driouchi
Al Akhawayn University, Morocco

Forum Euroméditerranéen
des Instituts de Sciences Économiques

Information Science
REFERENCE

FEMISE EDITED VOLUME SERIES, 2013.

Managing Director:	Lindsay Johnston
Editorial Director:	Joel Gamon
Book Production Manager:	Jennifer Yoder
Publishing Systems Analyst:	Adrienne Freeland
Development Editor:	Austin DeMarco
Assistant Acquisitions Editor:	Kayla Wolfe
Typesetter:	Erin O'Dea
Cover Design:	Jason Mull

Published in the United States of America by
Information Science Reference (an imprint of IGI Global)
701 E. Chocolate Avenue
Hershey PA 17033
Tel: 717-533-8845
Fax: 717-533-8661
E-mail: cust@igi-global.com
Web site: http://www.igi-global.com

Library of Congress Cataloging-in-Publication Data

Driouchi, Ahmed, 1948-
  ICTs for health, education, and socioeconomic policies: regional cases / by Ahmed Driouchi.
     pages cm
  Includes bibliographical references and index.
  Summary: "This book discusses the benefits that can be gained from the interactions between health, education, and socioeconomic areas, particularly providing a regional focus on the Southern Mediterranean, Middle Eastern, and Arab economies"--Provided by publisher.
  ISBN 978-1-4666-3643-9 (hardcover) -- ISBN 978-1-4666-3644-6 (ebook) -- ISBN 978-1-4666-3645-3 (print & perpetual access) 1. Information technology--Economic aspects. 2. Information technology--Social aspects. 3. Information technology--Developing countries--Case studies. I. Title.
  HC79.I55D75 2013
  303.48'33091724--dc23
                                  2012045821

British Cataloguing in Publication Data
A Cataloguing in Publication record for this book is available from the British Library.

All work contributed to this book is new, previously-unpublished material. The views expressed in this book are those of the authors, but not necessarily of the publisher.

This book is produced with the financial support of the European Union within the context of the FEMISE, Edited Volume Series. The contents of this book can under no circumstances be regarded as reflecting the position of the European Union.

Table of Contents

Section 1
Fragmentation, Interdependencies, and Assessments

Chapter 1

Chapter 2

Chapter 3

Section 2
Interdependencies and ICTs per Sector

Section 3
Socioeconomic Issues and Policies

Preface

This book addresses the role of Information and Communication Technologies (ICTs) as a form of advanced technologies in promoting social and economic coordination of activities at the levels of individuals, groups, organizations, and countries. A major focus is placed on the coordination benefits that that take place between education, health, and other socioeconomic areas. The regional and national contexts for the empirical applications pursued are based on South Mediterranean Countries (SMC) with a focus on the Middle East and North Africa (MENA) and Arab economies.

The production and publication of this book is motivated by the increasing rate of convergence between technologies, economics, and social sciences in general. This book is devoted to showing how the new technologies and mainly ICTs play promising roles in accounting for both fragmentation and coordination and thus ensure further and enhanced coordination. Interdependencies and their implied coordination have been increasingly developing with the higher number of players, institutions, markets, as well as the large array of new needs. These trends are related to the increased globalization, the development of networks, and the multiplication of interdependent platforms. This motivation is related to the beliefs that are held by individuals and groups in relation to the daily interdependencies in which they live and also the large array of needs of and from others. Can these daily requirements be expressed and revealed at the aggregate levels of economies and regions? Can the available data reveal the importance of interdependencies? How could this exercise be conducted while focusing on health, education, and socioeconomic conditions? How can these elements enrich economic and social policies, and how could coordination be enhanced? What about specific world regions? What roles can be played by new technologies, including ICTs? How could the findings be used to enhance the overall understanding of interdependencies and coordination with a focus on local, national, and regional development?

POTENTIAL USERS OF THIS BOOK

Based on the above motivations and related series of questions, it appears that different types of uses and users can be predicted for this book.

Besides universities and research centers, public, private, and nongovernmental agencies can find helpful elements and issues in this book. As with the convergences discussed above, engineering and business students and other scholars willing to investigate the frontiers of their own fields are also targeted. Quantitatively oriented scholars and students as well as those that require more qualitative arguments may find promising pieces, methods, and empirical evidence in this book. The empirical content of each chapter and of the overall book is also attractive for policy makers at both national and international levels. General and university libraries may acquire copies for their community of readers and users of promising material. While countries in of the South Mediterranean countries, MENA, and the Arab region are specifically targeted, other economies could be interested in acquiring copies of this book. This is also an interesting addition to the knowledge base about Arab countries, even though this is not explicit from the book's title.

I do also recognize the need for such a book in the FEMISE network and its 80 institutes and research centers that have been generating a climate of scholarship and devotion to theoretical and applied questions that concern the Mediterranean area. Besides FEMISE, the Economic Research Forum (ERF), as it pursues complementary objectives and tasks, may identify the pertinence of the book.

I identify on the same occasion, universities in the Mediterranean region and outside it, where students and faculty are, on daily basis, struggling to further the frontier of knowledge. International organizations, as they are devoting efforts to promote research and development in different areas with a focus on human development, health, education, and socio-economic conditions, may find this book useful. These include organizations related to the United Nations in areas of food and agriculture, health, education, commerce, and development. The World Bank, the International Monetary Fund are seen as major and potential users of this book. As nongovernmental agencies, both at national and international levels, are largely discussed in the book chapters, they are also identified as major users that would benefit from access to the present book.

GENESIS OF THIS BOOK

As said earlier, there are trends in sciences and in development practices that push towards accounting for convergence between disciplines and sectors of the economy. When convergence imposes itself to a specific discipline and to a narrower area of knowledge, it often creates needs for investigations at the boundaries of the domain, generating interferences with other scientific areas. These scientific interdependencies lead to mutual enrichment and create material that could be of high benefit to scientific communities and developers.

The current book is generated in relation to the development of scientific convergence, to interdependencies, and to the multidisciplinary academic tradition as described in this short introduction. The genesis of this book relates initially to a simple research proposal submitted to FEMISE (Foundation of Euro-Mediterranean Institutes of Economic Sciences). The original proposal emphasizes the analysis of the relationships between health, education, and socioeconomic outcomes in the context of South Mediterranean Economies with a focus on economic and social policies, under the title of "Interdependencies of Health, Education, and Poverty with Policy Implications for Southern Mediterranean Countries." This led to the production of a scientific FEMISE report FEM-32-01, published in 2009.

This process was followed by a new competition launched in 2011 under "FEMISE Edited Volumes," where authors and FEMISE members were invited to submit proposals for producing books based on FEMISE scientific reports. My proposal to this competition was that FEM-32-01 could be a good basis for generating a book emphasizing health, education, and socioeconomic outcomes. Winning this competition with financial support from FEMISE led to a discussion with IGI with a final arrangement attained for a new book: *ICTs for Health, Education, and Socioeconomic Policies: Regional Cases*. This means that the new book needs to account for Information and Communication Technologies (ICTs) with a focus on interdependencies and coordination. Most of the work consisted of introducing the role and impacts of ICTs to the initial FEMISE scientific report FEM-32-01. Major transformations were then undertaken along with a large set of additions to ensure that the new topic is covered. It took a lot of time to add chapters, sections, and to establish the functional links needed for transforming the initial material. This resulted in a transformation of the initial document where most of the core features of FEM-32-01 are kept and updated to remind the reader of the initial report. Viewing coordination of health, education, and socioeconomic outcomes with the lens of ICTs has generated new needs for further understanding of coordination.

SCOPE OF THE BOOK

Coordination has been an important issue, at least in the social sciences, even though individuals and different organizations have been practically involved under one form or another in coordinating their activities. The development of different types of Information and Communication Technologies (ICTs) has played an important role in coordinating operations at different levels of organizations and governments. Such interconnections and the need for coordination is imposed by economic and social factors and driven by needs of individuals, groups, and organizations.

In opposition to coordination, fragmentation and scattered operations are often found to produce inefficiencies and thus lead to higher private and social costs. Some areas are interdependent, and lack of knowledge implies a lack of benefits from limited coordination. This happens when individuals, groups, and organizations are ignorant about the interdependencies existing between at least two areas of interest. This can be, for example, a situation where the effects of nutrition, education, and health are not known or ignored. At the level of a government, the ministry of health may not coordinate enough with the departments of education and social affairs. This leads to inefficiencies as some social benefits will not be utilized or possibly eliminated because of the absence of coordination. Similar examples can be provided in relation to the same sectors of health, education, and economic activities. They do generally have a series of components that need to be coordinated. Issues such as the economic and social problems related to the youngest segments of the population and matters related to the needs and situation of women provide more incentives for coordination. Research itself can benefit from further coordinated networks to produce higher outcomes in most cases. Technologies that are either specific or general can favor coordination, and ICTs are the best examples of drivers and engines for the enhancement of social benefits. There are of course major variations across countries and sectors, but the trend taking place appears to be promising in the sense of accruing benefits, ensuring coordination, and producing higher prospects.

LIMITATIONS OF THE BOOK

There are of course several limitations that still exist in relation to the issues raised in this book. Most of these limitations are linked with the multidisciplinary nature of the topics raised. In addition, the data used does not often cover recent years and is limited to covering up to 2006 and 2008 at best. Only a few chapters use recent data, covering 2010 and 2011. As ICTs develop and promise new instruments for coordination, some of the detailed benefits are not discussed, but readers are often invited to imagine the expected gains either for specific sectors or in general from the overall effects and impacts of the larger category called ICTs.

However, my hope is that these limitations lead to further investigations and research in some specific niches that are left untouched in this book.

ORGANIZATION OF THE BOOK

This preface introduces some conceptual and organizational matters devoted to showing the logic and approaches pursued throughout this book and its chapters. As explained in most of the chapters, the current book is written by an Applied Economist, who has been exposed to different interrelated developmental economic issues. These include the interdependencies between health, education, and economic factors as dimensions that require further policy coordination. In this sense, economic, social, and political transversal coordination and policies can have superior outcomes in comparison with sector-based policies. This also accounts for the progress taking place in technologies with the amazing role of Information and Communication Technologies (ICTs). Such technologies include not only telecommunication components but also the software and all the advances made in media and communication. The book attempts to discuss the above issues in the context of developing countries, but the accumulated information allows for further focus on South Mediterranean Countries (SMC). Within this context, North African and Middle Eastern (MENA) countries and more specifically the Arab countries are most of the time the countries chosen for illustration and representation of regional cases.

The above components constitute the core of the present book. Coordination, health, education, and economic outcomes form the most essential pillars discussed. In addition, ICTs are largely considered to show the high potential offered by the coordination of policies. The context of South Mediterranean Countries (SMC), MENA, and Arab countries is used interchangeably (depending on the availability of data and information) for regional applications.

STRUCTURE AND ORGANIZATION OF THE BOOK

The book is organized in three interdependent sections:

- **Section 1:** Fragmentation, Interdependencies, and Assessments
- **Section 2:** Interdependencies and ICTs per Sector
- **Section 3:** Socioeconomic Issues and Policies

These three sections are interdependent and devoted to guiding the reader in choosing the dimensions needed for the investigation and perusal of the role of ICTs and other related issues.

As indicated, the first section focuses on the introduction of the concepts, strategies, and applications to countries from the selected region. By the end of this section, the reader gains knowledge about fragmentation, coordination (chapters 1 and 2) and related models for assessment (chapter 3). The reader also becomes more familiar with the complexity of the analysis of interdependencies and the requirements for the mobilization of advanced software in these operations (chapter 4).

The second section has focuses more directly on the use of ICTs in coordinating health (chapter 5), education (chapter 6), women empowerment (chapter 7), and poverty alleviation (chapter 8). These presentations are more illustrative of the roles played by ICTs within the context of coordination of health, education, and economic outcomes. This prepares for the opening of some thematic discussion in relation to the interdependencies of health, education, and poverty. This is the central topic covered in section 3.

The third section of this book deals with special matters and socioeconomic policies that are in connection with the interdependencies and coordination as discussed in the two first sections. Chapter 9 introduces a framework that applies to the coordination of interdependent sectors. Social deficits, social cohesion, ICTs, and MDGs are, respectively, in chapters 10 and 11. Chapter 12 discusses the effects of risks on interdependencies and the implied socioeconomic policies. Chapter 13 is a concluding chapter that gathers most of the findings from the previous sections with a focus on the necessary strengthening of socioeconomic policies.

Ahmed Driouchi
Al Akhawayn University, Morocco

Acknowledgment

This book is produced and published with a great deal of help from a lot of people, including colleagues and institutions. It is a tough exercise for me to cite all those that are related to this production process. I will try to mention those that I can easily recognize as unforgettable contributors.

My wife, Fatima, and my sons, Amine, Ouassim, and Tarik, are directly recognized for their inputs to this book through allowing me to pursue the task of research and writing while providing me with the best material and immaterial conditions for my comfort and creativity. Their continuous encouragements and love are major inputs in this modest realization.

I want also to acknowledge the continuous support of the President of Al Akhawayn University, Professor Driss Ouaouicha, and the Vice-President for Academic Affairs, Professor Ahmed Legrouri. They have had supportive functions through their recognition of the outputs produced by the Institute of Economic Analysis and Prospective Studies (IEAPS). The continuous encouragements of these officers are recognized as major sources of inspiration and energy to the author and editor of the current book.

My deep thanks go also to the Foundation of the Mediterranean Institutes of Economic Sciences (FEMISE) for the continuous support provided and for the efforts of promoting economic research and applications in the Mediterranean region.

I recognize and appreciate the opportunity and confidence placed in me and in my laboratory to conduct the realization of this book. Special thanks are addressed to Professor Jean Louis Reiffers, who played a key role in conceiving and ensuring the scientific instruments and guidance of FEMISE. Professor Reiffers could not be acknowledged without referring to Dr. Frederic Blanc and Dr. Maryse Louis who have carried the academic, administrative, and financial load of FEMISE. Besides those, there are the members of the FEMISE scientific committee, who need to be congratulated for their wonderful accomplishments. My gratitude goes also to Professor Ahmed Galal, who has been instrumental in the promotion of the FEMISE and Economic Research Forum (ERF) networks in the Mediterranean and MENA region.

My deep acknowledgments go to IGI, who encouraged me to pursue this project under the continuous help and monitoring of Ms. Hannah Abelbeck and Mr. Austin DeMarco, respectively.

This work could not be achieved without the input from my colleagues and FEMISE collaborators to the research project FEM-32-01. I can cite here the example of Ms. Nada Zouag from the IEAPS, Professors Cristina Boboc from the University of Bucharest, and Ahmad Baijou from Al Akhawayn University,

Ifrane, Morocco, Professor Lahcen Oulhaj and Professor Mouna Cherkaoui from Mohammed V University, Rabat, Morocco. I also recognize that the contributions of Ms. Nada Zouag have continued beyond FEM-32-01, as her production process has also covered segments of the current book.

It is important to note at this stage the help of Mrs. Amale Achehboune with the editing and organization of different chapters and other editorial matters required under the standards of IGI. Her contributions to this book but also to the IEAPS are highly identified and recognized. The assistantships of Ms. Ghita Bentouila, Ms. Hajar Bousfiha, and of Mr. Youssef Chetioui are also well identified and acknowledged. Major inputs related to youth, poverty, and women are developed by Mr. Youssef Chetioui.

The contributions of different reviewers, including those selected by IGI for analyzing the full manuscript and those I selected for individual chapters, are highly appreciated. These include, besides the anonymous referees, Professors Daniel Sauers, Antonio Rodriguez, Karim Moustaghfir, and Andrew Canterbury, with the contribution of Dr. Khalid Mrabet. Inputs from Amine Driouchi, Noureddine Labied, Khadija Iraqi, and Nesrine Ouriaghli are also highly recognized. All these contributors are acknowledged here for their wonderful accomplishments, especially the input provided by Ms. Nesrine Ouriaghli in ensuring the APA style in the overall book.

I would like to thank each one of the above contributors for their confidence and for their generous input. All the mistakes and inconsistencies introduced while working on this book and ensuring the final output are my responsibility as the author and the editor.

Finally, special thanks are addressed to those individuals, groups, and institutions that will identify and use this book. In this set, I recognize the FEMISE network that has been over time generating a climate of scholarship and devotion to theoretical and applied questions that concern the Mediterranean area. I also identify ERF, which pursues complementary objectives and tasks. I identify the universities in the Mediterranean region and outside it, where students and faculty are, on daily basis, struggling for pushing further the frontier of knowledge. I also identify international organizations that are devoting efforts to promote research and development in different areas with a focus on human development, health, education, and socio-economic conditions. The organizations related to the United Nations in areas of food and agriculture, health, education, commerce, and development are seen as major and potential users of this book. Other organizations, such as the World Bank, the IMF, and others, besides nongovernmental institutions, are also acknowledged. They are all cited as important providers of knowledge for development but also acknowledged in advance for identifying and using this book.

Ahmed Driouchi
Al Akhawayn University, Morocco

Section 1
Fragmentation, Interdependencies, and Assessments

Chapter 1
Need of a Balance between Fragmented and Coordinated Decision-Making

ABSTRACT

This chapter looks at fragmentation and implications in different decision-making contexts with a focus on new technology and enterprise creation in developing economies. Coordination is introduced as the response to external effects of fragmented and scattered decisions. The most important features of this framework are captured under a simplified theoretical economic model. The evidence on economic sectors is provided in the literature review, but the data from "Doing Business" of the World Bank is used to test for the high costs implied by the implicit scattering and fragmentation of decisions related to enterprise creation. The attained results either from access to new technologies or from the empirical analysis of "Doing Business" data show the prevalence of anti-commons and fragmentation in developing economies. This points out how anti-commons and fragmentation can limit development through reducing business expansion and social benefits, even when national and international institutions exhibit clear intentions for coordination.

INTRODUCTION

Large arrays of empirical evidence about the high private and social costs related to scattered decisions (fragmented)[1] among different inter-related economic and social agents and units do exist. While the development of selfishness and individualistic behaviors are increasingly engines

for the promotion of market economies, it is shown that the effects of externalities and lack of recognition of interconnections may impose higher direct and indirect costs that could lead to market failures and misallocations of resources.

This chapter aims at addressing the role of coordination[2] by opposition to fragmentation, in promoting social and economic activities at the

DOI: 10.4018/978-1-4666-3643-9.ch001

levels of individuals, groups and organizations. The focus is placed on the implicit costs related to fragmentation. By opposition to coordination, fragmentation and scattered operations are often found to produce inefficiencies and thus lead to higher private and social costs. As some areas can be found to be interdependent such as markets and economies[3], the lack of knowledge about these links implies a lack of benefits from any type of coordination. This happens when individuals, groups, and organizations are ignorant about the existing interdependencies between at least two operations, two economic agents, markets, and economies[3]. This can be for example, a situation where the cross-effects of nutrition, education and health are not known or ignored. At the level of a Government, the Ministry of health may not coordinate enough with the departments of education and of social affairs. This leads to inefficiencies as some social benefits will not be captured and eliminated with this absence of knowledge followed by a lack of coordination. Similar examples can be provided in relation to health, education, and economic activities that exhibit series of components that need to be co-ordinated. Issues such as the economic and social problems related to the youngest segments of the population are also matters related to the needs and situation of women. It is also well known, that research itself can benefit from further coordinated networks. Technologies that are either specific or general can favor coordination and ICTs are the best examples of drivers and engines for the enhancement of social benefits at both individuals and global levels. There are of course major variations across situations, but the trend taking place appear to be promising for the enhancement of benefits through ensuring coordination and producing higher prospects.

Economics, as in other sciences, has been referring to the pool of knowledge and expertise scattered among different poorly connected decision making public and private agents as "anti-commons" with resources utilized in a sub-optimal

and inefficient way. As a result, transversal development policies and private business promotion can fail to gather all the necessary information, knowledge, resources, and capital, that diminish chances of success, leading to the tragedy of anti-commons and thus to failure to contribute to the enlargement of new economic and social opportunities (Heller, 1998; Kennedy & Michelman, 1980; Buchanan & Yoon, 2000). While in "common[4] pool" open access resources, no actor has the right to exclude another until full depletion of the resource, the anti-commons is the reverse as too many have the right to exclude (Aoki, 1998) creating thus the tragedy of anti-commons[5] that is the total under-use of the resource.

Economic and social policies in the developing world are today increasingly required to benefit optimally from transversal and coordinated actions in all areas and sectors. This includes also the bilateral and world relations.

The growing evidence and consensus has been showing that poverty is a complex and multidimensional phenomenon. It requires solutions at multiple levels such as in health, education and employment rather than accounting only for a single sector. The needed transversal policies necessitate the collaboration of an overlapping web of government bodies and private partners that control the relevant knowledge and expertise relative to each policy dimension. Besides that, new and diversified sets of inputs that are informational, technological, and institutional are continuously needed. Transversal policies and actions in developing countries are likely to be penalized by the scattering of expertise.

However, coordination is not easy to achieve as there is a diversity of interests, views, and levels of information, expertise, and knowledge among the participants. The following recent papers have highlighted some important features.

In the general literature, this is shown to be related to factors such as bureaucracy, institutional rigidity, and weak coordination channels besides the limited levels of transparency and lack of updated knowledge. The economic literature is showing that the tasks of gathering the required inputs are time consuming and leading most of the time to high transaction and very high social costs.

Kuziemsky, Weber-Jahnke, and Williams (2012) focus on healthcare provision as highly collaborative work. They consider that designing information and communication technologies to support collaboration is challenging due to the complex and dynamic nature of the healthcare collaboration space with multiplicity of tasks and team members. They introduce the method of 'collaboration engineering' as a method for developing the collaboration space that accounts for intentional modeling and "interaction design theory." The available contributions are used by the authors to identify a set of intentions that define the healthcare collaboration space. A case study is also used to illustrate how this method would be used for engineering the healthcare collaboration space. The selection of ICT tools is necessary in order to adjust to the diversity of situations faced in the healthcare systems of delivery in terms of knowledge uncertainties and risks. This chapter shows how coordination can be adapted to the situations faced by the operators of healthcare.

Lindhal (2012) discusses the role of environmental uncertainty that prevails in the common resource literature. The author relaxes the assumption of symmetric uncertainty to analyze how knowledge heterogeneity influences coordination. Knowledge asymmetry and heterogeneity can operate as coordinating devises. To the author, more different users with respect to knowledge lead to smaller coordination with higher probability of resource depletion. Furthermore, regulation can reduce the coordination problem further, but only by reinforcing the benefit from ignorance. Thus when analyzing and suggesting policies for reducing the inefficiencies associated with common resources where rivalry prevails, one should not only be concerned about the level of environmental uncertainty, but also the distribution, as it matters too.

Ranjay conceptually separate cooperation and coordination in the context of inter-organizational collaboration, and examine how the two phenomena play out in the partner selection, design, and post-formation stages of an alliance life cycle. As shown in the chapter, a coordination perspective helps resolve some empirical puzzles, but it also represents a challenge to received wisdom grounded in the salience of cooperation. What accounts for the high failure rate of inter-organizational collaborations? The overwhelming majority of sociological and economic studies assert that failure to cooperate is related to dissymmetric incentives of agents.

Boettke, Zakary, Caceres, and Martin (2012) introduce elements from behavioral economics to show the limitations of cognitive abilities of individuals. The conclusions of such inquiries call into question that the results from standard economic modeling depend on assumptions of strong rationality. Most conspicuously, behavioral economists have introduced a host of new potential causes for market failures. Gaps in individual rationality thus fail to provide adequate grounds for positing market failures. This essay situates behavioral economics in the market failure literature. Obviously, this is but one side of behavioral economics, whose origins also is closely connected with both experimental economics and economic psychology. Nonetheless, the authors argue that the idea of market failure is critical to the both the development and use of behavioral ideas. "If markets work because hypothetical agents are smart, markets must fail because real people are stupid." Market failure arguments are consequently related to welfare maximization ensured by competitive markets under absence of externalities and to the real world situation where these conditions do not often hold. Under these circumstances, markets fail to maximize welfare.

Zhang, Yang, Bolton, and Gary (2012) examine a coordination game with players engaging in exogenously connected subsets of the population to analyze the linkage between social network and coordination. Players know the number of local links they possess but otherwise have incomplete information about the global network structure. The authors investigate two potential network effects: the global network effect as represented by the density of the grand network, and the local network effect as represented by the number of local links an individual has. The results show that in high-density networks, coordination is consistent with the payoff-dominant pooling equilibrium. In the sparser networks, more connected players exhibit higher levels of coordination than those with fewer social links. This indicates that network density, individual connectivity, and economic return affect the amount of strategic risk in coordination.

The objective of this chapter is to underline the importance of fragmented and coordinated decisions. This chapter shows how a balance between fragmentation and coordination is often required. It prepares also for a better understanding of the role of Information and Communication Technologies (ICTs) in the enhancement of the economic and social outcomes expected from coordination.

This chapter shows also how anti-commons and fragmentation can implicitly contribute to reducing economic and social development where the positive effects of institutional and promising technological innovations for providing inputs to the population. This constrains development.

This research is undertaken in the context of developing economies where cases and practices are not often accounting for the extent and magnitude of anti-commons and fragmentation. This leads to series of failures that are hard to predict.

Three major steps are pursued to achieve the goals assigned to this chapter. The first one is a literature review addressing the main features related to fragmentation, commons, anti-commons, and semi-commons. The second step focuses on a simplified theoretical model that is mobilized to assess the effects of anti-commons. The last section is empirical and based on targeting examples and cases of anti-commons in developing economies. The limitations in the development of enterprises in relation to the fragmentation of the decision process is considered as an empirical example where developing economies do face higher costs related to anti-commons.

LITERATURE REVIEW

This review is intended to show how fragmentation besides commons and anti-commons are pervasive and do affect the performance of economic and social projects. While the first part looks at introducing an overview on the issue, the remaining parts are devoted to underlying the links between technologies that are promising for agriculture, health, and education and for social development. Focus on innovation and resource ownership emphasizes the issues related to property rights and procedures of use. New technologies and institutional innovations are assumed to be the means that can enhance access to further education, health and other resources that can help reduce social deficits and poverty. The type of property rights involved at the stage of new technologies is mainly related to intellectual ownership and use.

Overview about Old and New Forms of Fragmentation

Fragmentation can be observed in relation to goods, services, markets but also to the number and nature of the decision makers involved. An important asset that is land, has been all the time seen as fragmented and scattered or consolidated with respect to activities such as agriculture and construction. This is still a promising research area that is investigated by series of economists and social scientists but new forms of fragmentation are identified in relation to the development of new technologies. The following paragraphs introduce respectively old and new forms of fragmentation.

Old Forms of Fragmentation

The earliest contributions have focused mainly on land and its scattering within agricultural and urbanization processes. Johnston (1970), Hung et al. (2007), and more recently Neal et al. (2012) are examples of authors that discussed the issue of land fragmentation in relation to productivity, economies of scale and size but also to output specialization. Klerkx and Proctor (2012) have placed emphasis on the growing multi-functionality in agriculture, combined with privatization of previously public agricultural extension services in relation to fragmentation from previously consolidated land. Several publications related to urbanization and its economic implications have also stressed the issues related to fragmentation in an urban setting. Various issues have been discussed in this type of literature. Lewis and Plantinga (2007) focus on habitat fragmentation considered as a primary threat to biodiversity. They analyze incentive-based policies designed to reduce forest fragmentation in the coastal plain region of South Carolina. An econometric model of land use with simulations is used to show the spatial pattern of land-use change.

New Forms of Fragmentation

The development of new technologies has had an important impact on the identification of areas that need to be analyzed in relation to the pervasiveness of fragmentation.

The relatively recent research on the economics of patents by Hall and Harhoff (2012) covers theoretical and empirical evidence on patents as incentives to innovation. The effectiveness of patents for invention disclosure, patent valuation, and what is known about the design of patent systems are also discussed. The study looks also to what is known about some current policy areas, including software and business method patents, university patenting, and the growth in patent litigation. A

special attention is devoted to underlying the role of fragmented invention. The literature review observes that the increase in patent ownership under the complexity of modern technology implies that a single product may involve accessing the technologies in hundreds of patents. The author refers to Shapiro (2001) who mentions the role of ICTs and biotechnologies in this increase of fragmentation.

Besides that, globalization of businesses has been leading to further fragmentation mainly in multinational firms. D'Agostino and Santangelo (2012) refer to a form of fragmentation pursued by multinational corporations. "They increasingly disaggregate their value chain in finer slices across borders and locate each slice according to the competences and resources of the destination countries." Series of references are used to support the development of this trend (Mudambi, 2008; UNCTAD, 2010). This may have also an effect on R&D activities as fragmentation and geographical dispersion of R&D value chain has been poorly analyzed empirically.

Liao (2012) indicates how information technology have been facilitating the geographic separation of production tasks mainly when "offshoring" and "inshoring" are pursued respectively in international and domestic markets. Thus, fragmented production has been coordinated through ICTs on both local and international markets.

Chang (2012) is also a contribution to offshoring. It begins with a discussion of the factors that determine decisions to offshore and illustrates, with simple models, the cost saving of offshoring some stages of production and the advantages of specializing in some input production and engaging in other input trade. The chapter then examines the recent trend in offshoring with emphasis on the rise of ICT offshoring and also the characteristics in relation to offshoring and exporting. The effect of offshoring and national welfare is then discussed in light of numerous results in recent empirical studies.

However, international trade in relation to fragmentation has mainly benefited from the contributions of Deardorff (1998a). This work examines the effects of "fragmentation," defined as the splitting of a production process into two or more steps that can be undertaken in different locations but that lead to the same final product. Introducing the possibility of fragmentation into simple theoretical models of international trade, the chapter finds the effects of fragmentation on national welfare, on patterns of specialization and trade, and on factor prices. The same author Deardoff (1998b) examines the effects of fragmentation across cones of diversification using a model of international trade.

All the above contributions show that fragmentation does most of the time lead to coordination of actions towards higher levels of social efficiency at the level of firms, households and public organizations, but some other authors have emphasized the interactions between technologies and institutions. The introduction of the frameworks of commons, semi-commons, and anti-commons by institutional economists has been helpful in enhancing the required levels of contributions to attain higher social efficiencies. Otherwise, the ignorance of such interferences may lead to important social losses.

Commons, Semi-Commons, and Anti-Commons

The tragedy of commons as a concept is made popular by the Hardin (1968). The tragedy the author refers to emerges from the overuse of an open access and use of a common resource. Other publications on commons have been developed by different authors with a leading role of Ostrom (1990) and Ostrom and Schlager (1992) ensuring promising theoretical grounds and promising cases. In these studies, communities have developed institutional arrangements to durably manage common pool resources with more or less success in preventing resource exhaustion (Berge & Van

Laerhoven, 2011). The work of Fennell (2011) has also to be noted. These findings have shown that in real world commons are more complex than what some social scientists have tried to model. Further issues related to specificities of some commons expressed by Ostrom (1990) are discussed in Bergstrom (2010). The link between commons and private ownership with exclusion possibilities are also developed (Schlager & Ostrom, 2010).

However, the symmetrical image of this situation was later termed by Heller (1998) the tragedy of anti-commons where the resource is underused given that exclusion rights are added to the usage rights. Thus an anti-common situation occurs when more than one user of a resource are endowed with the right to exclude others from the usage of the resource, without none of them having a full privilege of usage unless authorized by all the others. The result is the suboptimal utilization of the resource and or even its idleness in extreme cases. All the agents in this case are said to act under individualistic competition and exclusion rights in form of veto power are likely to be exercised even when the use of the resource by one agent can yield a generalized social benefit (Coelho & Ferreira, 2009). Buchanan and Yoon (2000) suggest that the tragedy of anti-commons can be measured in terms of the non-realized economic value due the under-use of the resource and that the size of such forgone opportunity is proportional to the number of exclusion right-holders involved. The keyword here is obviously the inefficiencies imposed by each exclusion right holder on the others and thus on society in general. Accordingly, commons and anti-commons are symmetrical in the sense that for both situations, agents reduce each other's rents (including themselves) from the resource be it through resource depletion on the long run (tragedy of the commons) or through maintaining the resource idle (tragedy of anti-commons) (Buchanan & Yoon, 2000).

Parisi, Depoorter, and Schultz (2005) explain that understanding the working of either commons or anti-commons requires a departure from the intuitive comparison with unified property as in commons and anti-commons limits between rights of use and rights of exclusion is blurred. In the case of commons, the right to use is more emphasized than the right to exclude. In the case of anti-commons however, the right to use is eclipsed by the exclusion rights held by all other co-owners. Moreover, both commons and anti-commons situations imply some extent of forgone synergies between the co-owners. That is how the authors reach the conclusion that commons as anti-commons are characterized by a discrepancy between usage and exclusion rights and that the final result is a misalignment between the private and social incentives of the various owners.

Parisi, Depoorter, and Schultz (2005) go further in their explanation of anti-commons by underlining that the latter induce two types of externalities[6], static and dynamic. The static externalities result from the current exercise of a right of exclusion by one owner which nullifies the value of the similar rights held by others. Dynamic externalities occur throughout time and are due to the under-use of the productive assets in the present implying future penalties. In addition, Parisi, Depoorter, and Schultz (2005) distinguish between simultaneous and sequential cases of anti-commons. In simultaneous anti-commons, the different right-holder exercise exclusion at the same time and independently as they are all at the same level of the value chain. In sequential anti-commons, exclusion rights tend to be exercised at sequential levels of the value chain such as blockages follow a given pattern.

An insightful parallelism can be drawn between Parisi, Depoorter, and Schultz (2005) distinction between sequential and simultaneous anti-commons and the distinction between hierarchical and polyarchical types of decision-making architectures. Such convergence between the economics of property and the economics of decision-making helps broadening the understanding of how the tragedy of anti-commons can emerge in spheres other than physical property. It is exactly the

logic followed by Buchanan and Yoon (2000) who extend the concept to stand for an analytical framework applied to the study of the disparate and overlapping institutional structures. In this sense, the authors state that the tragedy of anti-commons captures the inefficiencies of overlapping bureaucracies. For instance, an entrepreneur has often to overcome series of obstacles embodied in different permits issued by different authorities that hold specific veto and hence, exclusion rights. The fragmented resource is here the authority and executive power held by multiple agencies and fragmented following an anti-common model. The on-going strategic game[7] may then lead to outcomes that are not socially desired.

Depoorter and Vanneste (2004) recently, referred to the risks related to the excessive propertization in the context of "anti-commons" property regimes. The authors looked at the deadweight losses in relation to the complementarily between ownership and fragmentation.

With the above characterizations of commons and anti-commons, some authors have been working on the framework of semi-commons[8]. In this sense, the Internet is itself a type of semi-commons (Grimmelmann, 2010, 2012). Depoorter, Bertacchini, and De Mot (2008) emphasize similar issues. This component of ICTs links strongly private and common rights. Private rights are expressed when accessing a computer and then a server but the server is part of a shared network. A shared communications platform links different private right owners. This combination is considered to be distinctive of ICTs feature that explains the Internet's success but illustrates some of its problems. This description of semi-commons is built on Henry Smith's theory based on the medieval open-field system (Smith, 2000) but that is still characterizing the use of natural resources in large areas of developing countries nowadays. The semi-commons framework explains the dynamic interplay between private and common uses of a given resource. While the Internet enables worldwide sharing and collaboration without collapsing under the strain of misuse, other resource may be used locally. These resources can include traditional as well as new ones and new services. Water is among the resources that can be used under local semi-commons (Smith, 2008). Other new types of platforms can related to television, information, and media where semi-commons can also be pervasive (Smith, 2005). The development of new technologies namely information and communication technologies besides biotechnologies have also been helping the identification of larger areas where semi-commons prevail.

A good illustration is provided by Sadowsky (2012) where the type and number of agents operating at each stage are identified in relation to different ICT components and mainly with the Internet. This is introduced on the occasion of discussing the Internet governance. The author refers to different types of agents and functions that are related to the Internet process. To the author, "a grouping of organizations by their general orientation suggests three groups." The first group includes intergovernmental organizations such as the International Telecommunication Union (ITU), national standards offices, and professional organizations, with formal and informal organizations IETF (Internet Engineering Task Force). The second group includes organizations dealing with management (regional Internet registries and the global and national domain registries). The last set is composed of organizations in charge of policy and regulation (UN, EU, OECD, and others). These generate interferences and interdependencies among the three groups.

Among the outcomes from the above description of the domain of ICTs, it appears clearly that the Web is also a potential source of interdependencies between large numbers of operators. Coordination is the best response to the existing complex set of relationships between different organizations.

These features as they relate to fragmentation, semi-commons and commons in almost every domain including the Internet and the Web, require further investigations in order to better capture their effects. A theoretical model is introduced first before the development of empirical analysis devoted to showing the higher costs from limited coordination.

A THEORETICAL ECONOMIC MODEL OF FRAGMENTATION, SEMI-COMMONS, COMMONS, AND ANTI-COMMONS

Following the simplified model developed by Canavese (2005), and in order to introduce anti-commons, different market structures are attempted under the hypothesis of a linear aggregated demand function for the good or service (Y). Profit maximization is also assumed under zero costs production. The first order conditions for profit maximization that are necessary and sufficient under this simple model lead to optimal prices and quantities that solve the profit maximization problem under each market structure. This is shown respectively for perfectly competitive, monopolist, duopolist, and oligopolist markets with focus on commons and anti-commons.

Gulati, Wohlgezogen, and Zhelyazkov (2012) introduce the distinction between cooperation and coordination as two facets of collaboration. Before that, only cooperation as commitment of partners is the key determinant of collaborative success. The critical role of coordination has not being emphasized (see Table 1).

Table 1's simplified model shows the difference between commons and anti-commons. While "commons" show overuse of the resource, "anti-commons" are characterized by under use and higher prices or higher costs that inhibit access and expansion of private activities. Empirical evidences are suggested in the following sections. Two steps are followed for the introduction of these evidences. The first step is mainly based on the literature introducing the empirical evidence related to new technologies with their negative impacts and limited adoption. The second set focuses on the analysis of "doing business data" in relation to enterprise creation.

EMPIRICAL EVIDENCE ABOUT FRAGMENTATION AND ANTI-COMMONS IN DEVELOPING ECONOMIES

The empirical evidence introduced here concern respectively the general trends taking place in both technological and institutional innovations and the related economic policies pursued by series of developing countries. While economies should develop further awareness about the negative effects of anti-commons and related tragedies, they are invited to the strengthening of their knowledge base and their economic foundations. This helps sustain different policy shifts and reforms, especially when accounting for access to promising technologies.

The pervasiveness of anti-commons appears at different levels of these economies and is not often perceived outside the existing legal frameworks. With the expansion of urbanization and the increase of the number of buildings where individuals and households own apartments in different floors, individualistic incentives show often the blockages taking place in the access to new technologies (Internet) and in the maintenance and repair of different facilities. This concerns the common areas, the overall environment besides some useful facilities (elevator, utilities besides others).

Anti-Commons, Health, and Agriculture in Developing Economies

After the elicitation of anti-commons problems by Heller (1998), many cases related mainly to patenting started rising from both developed and developing countries. Velho (2004) shows that the

North-South cooperation is vital for developing countries access to technology and research. This is due to the control that developed countries have on the technology and research in the crucial fields of heath and agriculture. Following the Bayh-Dole act in 1980, a massive patenting campaign, issued by US universities and non-profit institutions, took place. A study by Graff et al. (2003) shows that 2.5% of patents in all fields of technology are owned by the US public sector. In the agricultural field, this percentage is 25%. In the health sector, Kapczynski et al. (2003) state that major patents needed for HIV treatment are held by Yale University, University of Minnesota, Emory University and Duke University. This patenting wave from Bayh-Dole, helped in clarifying the ownership of intellectual properties and technologies; however, its implementation raised anti-commons problems.

A good example to illustrate the anti-commons problems related to patenting is the Golden Rice case. In late 1990s, a research team found that vitamin A can be introduced to rice through genetic manipulations. This discovery will be of great benefit to developing countries as 1 million of children are suffering A-vitamin deficiencies die every year while 350,000 become blind. When applying for the patent, Potrykus and Beyer found that their work involves 32 companies and universities in both public and private sectors. This is a case for anti-commons that would have caused this invention not to be launched, causing losses that would have dramatically affected the developing countries. In order not to lose this discovery, the world's largest agricultural biotechnology firm Syngenta intervened to help the inventors in contacting all the holders of the patents needed. In 2001, the Rockefeller Foundation announced that big companies donated their licenses free of charge to this project making it feasible. Golden Rice is a complicated patenting case that illustrates the anti-commons tragedy.

Another example in the agricultural and biological fields is the Xa21 Saga cited by Cantrell et al. (2004) and Graff et al. (2003). In 1977, the

Table 1. Simplified model

Perfectly competitive market (fully fragmented)	$p = \alpha - \beta.Y$; $\pi = p.Y$; $\pi^{'} = p = 0$; $p^{*} = 0$ And $Y^{*} = \dfrac{\alpha}{\beta}$
Under monopoly (sole agent):	$\pi = p.Y$; $\pi = \left(\alpha - \beta.Y\right)Y$; $\pi = \alpha.Y - \beta.Y^{2}$; $\pi^{'} = \alpha - 2\beta.Y = 0$; $Y^{*} = \dfrac{\alpha}{2\beta}$ and $p^{*} = \alpha/2$
Duopoly (2 agents):	$p = \alpha - \beta\left(Y_1 + Y_2\right)$; $\pi_1 = pY_1 = \left[\alpha - \beta\left(Y_1 + Y_2\right)\right]Y_1$ $\pi_2 = pY_2 = \left[\alpha - \beta\left(Y_1 + Y_2\right)\right]Y_2$; $\pi_1^{'} = \alpha - 2\beta.Y_1 - \beta.Y_2 = 0$ $\pi_2^{'} = \alpha - \beta.Y_1 - 2\beta.Y_2 = 0$; the reaction functions are: $Y_1 = \dfrac{\alpha}{2\beta} - \dfrac{Y_2}{2}$; $Y_2 = \dfrac{\alpha}{2\beta} - \dfrac{Y_1}{2}$; $\left(Y_1 + Y_2\right)^{*} = \dfrac{2\alpha}{3\beta}$ And $p^{*} = \alpha/3$
Three agents:	$p = \alpha - \beta\left(Y_1 + Y_2 + Y_3\right)$; $\pi_1 = pY_1 = \left[\alpha - \beta\left(Y_1 + Y_2 + Y_3\right)\right]Y_1$; $\pi_2 = pY_2 = \left[\alpha - \beta\left(Y_1 + Y_2 + Y_3\right)\right]Y_2$; $\pi_3 = pY_3 = \left[\alpha - \beta\left(Y_1 + Y_2 + Y_3\right)\right]Y_3$; $\pi_1^{'} = \alpha - 2\beta.Y_1 - \beta.Y_2 - \beta.Y_3 = 0$; $\pi_2^{'} = \alpha - \beta.Y_1 - 2\beta.Y_2 - \beta.Y_3 = 0$; $\pi_3^{'} = \alpha - \beta.Y_1 - \beta.Y_2 - 2\beta.Y_3 = 0$ The reaction functions are then: $Y_1 = \dfrac{\alpha}{2\beta} - \dfrac{Y_2}{2} - \dfrac{Y_3}{2}$; $Y_2 = \dfrac{\alpha}{2\beta} - \dfrac{Y_1}{2} - \dfrac{Y_3}{2}$; $Y_3 = \dfrac{\alpha}{2\beta} - \dfrac{Y_1}{2} - \dfrac{Y_2}{2}$; $\left(Y_1 + Y_2 + Y_3\right) = \dfrac{3\alpha}{2\beta} - \left(Y_1 + Y_2 + Y_3\right)$; So, $\left(Y_1 + Y_2 + Y_3\right)^{*} = \dfrac{3\alpha}{4\beta}$ and $p^{*} = \alpha/4$

continued on following page

International Rice Research Institute (IRRI) discovered genes for resistance in Mali. The institute included it into a variety of rice, which was later studied at University of California at Davis (UCD), between 1992 and 1995. UCD went further in isolating the genes and found the exact code to be replicated and called it "Xa21." The latter was patented exclusively under the UCD. This created an anti-commons problem as it prevented IRRI from using Xa21 and its related technology even if it was the first organism to characterize the gene. In addition, the patenting prevented from using it in further research that will be beneficial for developing countries. Xa21 can be inserted in all types of crops to increase their resistance. This international issue lasted about 25 years. It was

Table 1. Continued

Commons with n agents (open access):	$p = \alpha - \beta\left(Y_1 + Y_2 + Y_3 + \ldots + Y_n\right);$ $\pi_i = pY_i = \left[\alpha - \beta\left(Y_1 + Y_2 + Y_3 + \ldots + Y_n\right)\right]Y_i$ $\pi_i' = \alpha - 2\beta.Y_i - \beta(Y_1 + Y_2 + Y_3 + \ldots + Y_n) = 0$ $\pi_i' = \alpha - \beta.Y_i - \beta(Y_1 + Y_2 + \ldots + Y_i + \ldots + Y_n) = 0$ $Y_i = \dfrac{\alpha}{\beta} - (Y_1 + Y_2 + \ldots + Y_i + \ldots + Y_n);$ since $Y_1 + Y_2 + \ldots + Y_i + \ldots + Y_n = \bar{Y};$ then, $\displaystyle\sum_{i=1}^{n} Y_i = \sum_{i=1}^{n} \dfrac{\alpha}{\beta} - \sum_{i=1}^{n} \bar{Y};$ and since $\displaystyle\sum_{i=1}^{n} Y_i = \bar{Y};\ \bar{Y} = \dfrac{n\alpha}{\beta} - n\bar{Y};\ \bar{Y} = \dfrac{n\alpha}{(1+n)\beta}$ and $p^* = \dfrac{\alpha}{1+n}$ When $n \to \infty$ then, $\bar{Y} \to \dfrac{\alpha}{\beta}$ and $p \to 0$
Anti-commons with n agents:	$\displaystyle\sum_{i=1}^{n} p_i = \alpha - \beta.Y;\ Y = \dfrac{\alpha}{\beta} - \dfrac{1}{\beta}\sum_{i=1}^{n} p_i;$ given that $\displaystyle\sum_{i=1}^{n} p_i = \bar{p},$ then $Y = \dfrac{\alpha}{\beta} - \dfrac{1}{\beta}\bar{p};\ \pi_i = p_i.Y = p_i\left(\dfrac{\alpha}{\beta} - \dfrac{1}{\beta}\bar{p}\right);$ $\pi_i' = \dfrac{\alpha}{\beta} - \dfrac{2}{\beta}p_i - \dfrac{1}{\beta}\left(p_1 + p_2 + p_3 + \ldots + p_n\right) = 0$ $\pi_i' = \dfrac{\alpha}{\beta} - \dfrac{1}{\beta}p_i -$ $\dfrac{1}{\beta}\left(p_1 + p_2 + \ldots + p_i + \ldots + p_n\right) = 0$ $\alpha - p_i - \bar{p} = 0;\ p_i = \alpha - \bar{p};\ \displaystyle\sum_{i=1}^{n} p_i = n\alpha - n\bar{p} = \bar{p}$ $\bar{p} = \dfrac{n\alpha}{(1+n)}$ and $Y^* = \dfrac{\alpha}{(1+n)\beta};$ when $n \to \infty,$ then $\bar{p} \to \alpha$ and $Y \to 0.$

solved by the creation of the Genetics Resource Recognition Fund by UCD to distribute the license of Xa21 with part of the benefits devoted to support research in Mali.

The research and development in pharmaceutical products is full of examples and cases relating to anti-commons. The Program for "Appariâtes Technologies" in Heath (PATH) is a non-profit international institution providing help in the health field for developing countries. PATH was confronted to anti-commons when developing vaccine for certain form of Malaria in a program called "Malaria Vaccine Initiative." The initiators of the program discovered that the antigen MSP-1, produced by the Malaria parasite and crucial for the development of the vaccine, was subject to 22 licenses and patents. It took considerable time and resources for the PATH to negotiate with the different rights' holders and partnership were signed to allow the starting of this initiative.

Health and pharmaceutical domains are facing anti-commons from the changes and increasing rates of licensing and patenting. Nowadays, the patents are concerning fragments of genes and agents and this makes the work of researchers harder. Any initiative enclosing the acquisition of others patents gives the floor to complexities and high transaction costs.

Most of the development problems are of transversal nature and need contributions of scattered operators from public, private, national, and international economies. Most of the time, when transactions costs are high, and under restricted information, only limited solutions are implemented. This is an example of anti-commons where scattered operators and fragmented sources of information have difficulties providing timely knowledge to potential users. Under this situation, private and public actions can be blocked because of lack of information.

While information is diffused and used rapidly in the context of developed economies, it is not often the case in developing countries, as further steps are needed to spread the knowledge. Economic agents and households face difficulties of access and implementation. The information gap increases with the degree of integration characterizing the piece of knowledge. The health issues in relation to the effects of nutrition on non-communicable diseases have not all the time been considered in a large number of developing economies. While obesity is an issue for developing economies, it is not yet perceived as such in most of these countries. The need for both larger domestic and foreign investments has not been coupled with health and environmental standards. In these circumstances, private firms

are still and have been expanding in areas of fast food, sweeties and related products. This shows that both the enlargement of investments and of consumer choices is progressively becoming harmful illusions in the developing world.

Empirical Evidence of Anti-Commons in Developing Economies through Enterprise Creation

The process of enterprise creation requires compliance with a series of laws and regulations that are most of the time specific to each country and locations. Enterprise and business creation is thus subject to sets of authorizations and lengthy procedures. It is generally governed by an array of institutions that are likely to issue all the licenses needed for enterprise creation. These procedures usually reveal the existence of fragmented and scattered decision makers. Anti-commons are likely to exist and may lead to the limitation of the number of enterprises to be created.

These features and hypotheses are tested in this chapter using the quantitative information provided by "Doing Business Data" and mainly the component that relates to starting a business.

Variables, Data, and Observations

Three sources of data are used. They include "Doing Business Report" (DBR), Transparency International and United Nations Development Program. These sources have provided respectively business data, corruption data, and information on human development index. All these data pertain to 2010.

Three variables are extracted from DBR. The first one relates to the number of procedures needed for enterprise creation. The second variable is "time" for the completion of the above procedures. The cost related to the creation of enterprises as a percentage of the country's income per capita is the last variable considered.

The Corruption Perception Index (CPI) of 2010 is also used in this analysis. The Human

Development Index (HDI) of 2010 has been useful in characterizing the level of development of countries (countries with larger HDI are more developed than the ones with lower HDI). The overall sample includes 154 countries that have data on starting a business, CPI and HDI.

Descriptive Statistics

As shown in the 2010 DBR, the average number of procedures, time and cost are higher for different groups of developing countries in comparison with the data of the OECD economies (Table 2).

The above observations are confirmed through the overall descriptive analysis of the detailed data. Tables 3, 4, and 5 show the summary statistics for the variables "procedures," "time," and "cost" for the starting of business topic. These tables are based on the overall data (Table 3) with the division of the overall sample in two equal size groups where developed countries have the highest HDI (Table 4) and developing economies with the lowest HDI (Table 5). The following

graph introduces a box-plot representation of the overall observations by variable. It provides information about the mean and the presence of outliers (see Figure 1).

When accounting for both the means and the standard deviations related to each variable and under a t-statistics test, high and low HDI countries exhibit statistically significant differences as shown in Table 6. This implies that high HDI or developed countries exhibit statistically significant differences in the number of procedures, in time and costs relative to lower HDI or developing countries. Given the direction of these t-statistics values, developing economies show higher number of procedures, time, and costs for enterprise creation.

Regression Analysis

Regression analysis is conducted using the cost of enterprise creation as dependent variable. The independent variables are the number of procedures, the time required for business creation, the

Figure 1. Graph

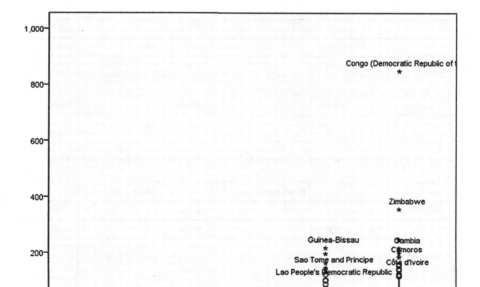

Table 2. Number of procedures, time, and cost to start a business by region (source: DBR, 2010)

	Procedures (number)	Time (days)	Cost (% of income per capita)
Latin America & Caribbean	9.3	56.7	36.2
Sub-Saharan Africa	8.9	45.2	95.4
Middle East & North Africa	8.1	20	38
East Asia & Pacific	7.8	39	27.1
South Asia	7.1	24.6	24.5
Eastern Europe & Central Asia	6.3	16.3	8.5
OECD	5.6	13.8	5.3

Table 3. Descriptive statistics of starting a business variables concerning all the countries

	N	Minimum	Maximum	Mean	Std. Deviation
HDI 2010	154	.14	.9375	.6305	.1893
CPI 2010	154	1.4	9.3	4.038	2.1304
Procedures (number)	154	1	20	7.97	3.576
Time (days)	154	1	216	31.98	35.671
Cost (% of income per capita)	154	.0	847.6	44.451	88.7243

Table 4. Descriptive statistics of starting a business variables concerning high HDI countries

	Procedures	Time	Cost
Mean	6.58	19.50	5.58
Median	6.00	13.00	5.00
Mode	6.00	6.00	0.70
Standard Deviation	3.09	20.83	4.15
Minimum	1	1	0
Maximum	18.00	120.00	14.70

Table 5. Descriptive statistics of starting a business variables concerning low HDI countries

	Procedures	Time	Cost
Mean	9.17	50.36	77.67
Median	9.00	34.00	45.00
Mode	6.00	12.00	17.50
Standard Deviation	3.30	78.05	97.43
Minimum	4	5	15
Maximum	20.00	694.00	847.60

Table 6. T-tests of the 3 variables between high and low HDI countries

	Procedures	Time	Cost
t-test	3.54	7.95	18.86

Corruption Perception Index (CPI) and HDI. All the variables are under their logarithmic forms with the regression run on the overall available data and variables. Under this regression, a statistically non-significant coefficient for time is exhibited. Procedures and time have shown significant correlation (procedures=0.804+0.385*time with R^2=0.541 and t-stat respectively of 8.869 and13.390). This has motivated the non-inclusion of time in the final regression.

The results of this regression are introduced in Table 6. This table accounts also for testing for multicollinearity through showing the values of the level of tolerance (tolerance) and the Variance Inflation Factor (VIF) as in O'Brien (2007).

Table 7 shows that with $R^2 = 0.669$ and an overall high level of the F test, the statistically significant coefficients (or elasticities) at the 1% level are those for HDI 2010 (-2.831) and Procedures (1.140) while CPI 2010 (-0.593) has a statistically significance only at 5%. No multicollinearity is observed as the tolerance is between 0.4 and 0.5 and VIF between 1.27 and 2.20 (tolerance less than

0.20 or 0.10 and/or VIF of 5 or 10 and above for the existence of multicollinearity (O'Brien, 2007).

These results show that the costs of creating enterprises are sensitive to HDI and to the number of procedures. The higher (respectively lower) is HDI, the lower (respectively higher) is the cost of enterprise creation. This implies that developed countries benefit from lower costs relative to developing economies that have higher costs. A 1% increase (respectively decrease) in HDI generates 2.831% cost decrease (respectively increase). Besides that, a 1% increase (decrease) in procedures generates a 1.140% increase (decrease) in costs. Besides that, a 1% decrease (increase) in CPI implies a 0.593% increase (decrease) in costs of enterprise creation. Furthermore, when comparing the coefficients of HDI and procedures (t-test=-1587.86), the driving power of HDI appears to be higher. This confirms the role of development in the determining the costs.

The higher costs in developing countries are indications of the existence of more fragmentation and that the probability of existence of anti-commons is higher in these countries in comparison with developed economies. This might be a signal of blockage for the creation of larger numbers of enterprises in the developing world. The access to market economies is thus lowered by the likely existence of anti-commons in less developed economies.

Table 7. Regression results from the stage of "creating a business"

R-Square	0.669					
R-Square Adj	0.662					
Standard Error of Estimate	1.069					
F-test	101.1					
	Coefficient	Std Error	t Ratio	Prob>ltl	Tolerance	VIF
Intercept	-0.431	0.693	-0.622	0.534		
HDI 2010	-2.831	0.335	-8.431	0.001	0.533	1.876
CPI 2010	-0.593	0.269	-2.204	0.029	0.450	2.198
Procedures	1.140	0.190	5.978	0.001	0.787	1.270

The Example of One Country: Morocco

In Morocco, enterprise creators can submit their requests either to the Regional Investment Centers (RIC) or directly to other institutions to initiate the creation of enterprises. There is a RIC for each of the 16 regions of Morocco. Each RIC gathers all the processes and administration that is needed for the authorization of the enterprise. However, even under this high level of integration, the number of enterprises created within the RIC and outside it is still limited. The costs of creation as provided by data on "Doing Business" are still high. This shows that fragmentation is still underway with the prevalence of anti-commons. Tables 8, 9, and 10 are devoted to showing the prevalence of anti-commons while dealing with enterprise creation in Morocco.

Table 8 introduces data on enterprise creation in different regions of Morocco before and after the creation of the Regional Investment Centers in 2002. The computed t-test shows that the number of enterprises initiated after 2002 is slightly higher. This implies that RICs have been capturing the flows of created enterprises but even with further integration of the operations for starting a new business, possibilities of fragmentation are still prevailing.

Data for the period 2006-2010 show that enterprise creation in Morocco has known a general increasing trend over these years (Table 9). As these data include enterprises created within and outside RIC, they are higher than those shown under RIC. But, this increase within or outside the RIC, is limited by the bureaucratic process of starting a business in terms of number of procedures and time. This is confirmed also through the larger costs of enterprise creation in Morocco relative to other countries. As of Doing Business Report 2010, the cost of creating an enterprise in Morocco is 15.8% of the income per capita while neighboring countries like Algeria have 12.9%, Egypt 6.3% and Tunisia 5%. Those costs are even lower in developed countries such as France, Finland and United States with only around 1% of income per capita needed to start a business. These higher costs are mainly related to the series of steps and procedures that need to be pursued by applicants for enterprise creation. Most of the time, each step is related to an independent institution, even if RIC gathers most of the administrations (Table 10). This is again a high indication of the existence of fragmentation and anti-commons.

Discussion of Results

Based on the outputs from the above regressions, the number of procedures besides the time required appears to have significant effects on the costs at each stage of the enterprise creation in both developed and developing economies. However, given the high costs of creation exhibited by developing economies, it clearly appears that the number of procedures and the time required are leading to implicit high level of costs for business creation. This shows how large numbers of procedures besides the time required are important signals for fragmentation and scattered decision makers, even under efforts of reduction of procedures and time. Fragmentation and high costs are consequently leading to the lowering of the probabilities of enterprise creation in developing economies. A different situation is observed in developed economies where the costs are lower in relation to lower levels of fragmentation, meaning that lower probabilities of enterprise failure are expected relative to economies with higher costs. Fewer enterprises are consequently created as the consequence of fragmentation and anti-commons related to the processes of authorizations and licensing. This is another difficulty that adds to the initial process of licensing and accessing to business ideas and technologies and also to the required patenting processes.

These results require that developing economies have to develop further awareness about

Table 8. Average number of yearly creation of enterprises before and after RIC

Regions	Average number of Enterprises created before RIC	Average number of enterprises created After RIC
Grand-Casablanca	4695	5255
Marrakech-Tensift-Al haouz	2226	3101
Meknès-Tafilalt	3034	2610
Rabat-Salé-Zemmour	2834	2836
Doukala-Abda	1542	2264
Tanger-Tétouan	2684	4025
Guelmim-Es Smara	1163	1173
Région de l'Oriental	2764	3134
Souss-Massa-Drâa	3067	4078
Fès-Boulmane	2061	1825
Lâayoune-Boujdour	1552	1337
Gharb-Chrarda Beni Hssen	1279	1755
Chaouia-Ouardigha	1378	1607
Taza-Al Houceïma-Taounate	779	823
Tadla-Azilal	991	1357
Oued Eddahab-Lagouira	655	641
Average	2044	2363.8125
Standard Deviation	1082.506597	1305.094797
Count	16	16
t-stat (comparing average number before and after)	3.02	

Source: Rajae Berjal (2005), MBA qualifying exam, SBA, Al Akhawayn University, Ifrane.

Table 9. Total yearly number of enterprises created 2006-2010

Regions	2010	2009	2008	2007	2006
Grand Casablanca	8408	7958	7941	8573	6607
Tanger-Tétouan	2416	2603	2937	3240	2236
Marrakech-Tensift-Elhouz	2149	2140	2336	2929	2173
Rabat-Salé-Zemmour	2871	2506	2407	2873	1929
Meknes- Tafilalet	1307	1356	1147	1201	729
Sous Massa Draa	1370	1463	1400	1627	1163
Fes-Boulmane	1065	1074	954	1049	726
Oriental	1030	1007	1035	990	680
Other Regions	3944	3703	3395	2991	2460
Total	**24560**	**23810**	**23552**	**25833**	**18703**

Source: OMPIC, Annual Reports 2006, 2007, 2009, and 2010

Table 10. List of procedures, time to complete, and costs to start a business in Morocco in 2010

	Procedure	Time to Complete	Complete
1	Obtain a negative certificate, which registers the company name at the "Centre Regional d'Investissement" (CRI)	1 day	MAD 190 (MAD 170 + MAD 20 droits de timbres)
2	Deposit paid-in capital in a bank and obtain an attestation de depot	1 day	no charge
3	Legalize statutes at Mayor's office (Commune)	1 day	DH 20/page + DH10
4	File documents with CRI to register with the Ministry of Finance for patente tax, with the Tribunal of Commerce, and for social security and taxation		7 days for registration, 30 days for publication
5	File a declaration with the economic office of the Prefecture (Service Economique de la Commune)	1 day	no charge
6	Make company stamp	1 day	MAD 200

Source: World Bank and IFC, Doing Business Report 2010

fragmentation and anti-commons besides issuing the needed remedies to reduce the negative effects of new technologies and new institutional reforms.

FURTHER DISCUSSION: IS A BALANCE BETWEEN FRAGMENTATION AND COORDINATION NEEDED?

The above examples and cases have revealed that they are instances where fragmentation could lead to lower private and social benefits if pursued. The real situations involve fragmentations as expressed by private self-interests, specific stages in a given chain and other matters. These situations often involve externalities, as there are effects of one agent on the other and one stage on the other with multiple levels of interferences. These increase with the number of agents and with the prevailing interests. This means definitely that the interdependencies and externalities need to be identified and their magnitudes assessed in order to ensure higher levels benefits from coordination. This can happen with scattered individuals, dispersed resources as well as in groups and resources that are under commons, semi-commons, and anti-commons. Even collective resources and the use of public goods, club-goods and others, require

coordination in order to enhance efficiency for private users as well as for the group. For that, rules are needed based on the knowledge of the external effects, the interactions, and the interdependencies. Under perfectly competitive markets, integration is ensured through the operations of the economy and prices are means that account for independencies. Otherwise, any source of imperfection requires the use of non-market instruments where regulatory agencies, courts and other intermediation mechanisms become necessary. Government intervention is an important means to ensure market regulation where series of instruments can be used at the level of enterprises, agents, and markets. The same trend exists outside integrated markets where NGOs and intermediation can help coordinate or self-coordinate.

This implies that both private and public institutions as well as markets and Governments are necessary in any economy so that each party can help alleviate inefficiency. However, the excess of one party relative to other may not be desirable unless justified on economic and social grounds. The existence of large number of players with several sectors, goods, and services increase the demand for further coordination. This complicates the tasks of intermediation and coordination where sophisticated tools such as those provided under ICTs are needed. Similarly, innovative attitudes and outcomes have generated new challenges where the need for satisfying the interests of innovation producers and those of users, require special attention devoted to new rights such as intellectual property rights. This has been adding new burdens and new challenges to each economy and especially those of developing countries. Further coordination is thus increasingly necessary.

CONCLUSION

As this chapter looked to the social costs of fragmentation and anti-commons from the standpoint of developing economies, an important emphasis has been initially placed first on showing how different authors have dealt with this question. Furthermore, cases have been used to underline the impacts of fragmentation and anti-commons on economic and social development. A special focus is placed on the situation of developing economies, mainly in relation to the new issues raised by the new technologies and institutions that are highly desired in developing economies. Health and agriculture with the needs of the poorest segments of the population are chosen to illustrate the effects of fragmentation and scattering. A simplified theoretical model is used to underline the differences between commons, anti-commons and different market structures. The "Doing Business" data are also mobilized to test empirically for the effects of fragmentation and anti-commons on enterprise creation. The results show that, in developing countries, as the number of procedures and the required time for enterprise creation increase the costs related to the stages considered by the dataset. The attained results confirm the validity of the theoretical model used but also the likelihood of the effects of fragmentation and anti-commons on developing economies. The need of a balance between fragmentation and coordination is definitely in favor of coordination but such a balance resides in the continuous awareness about the monitoring of economies and society in order to identify areas where interventions are necessary. The identification of the types of coordination requires also that research be continuously mobilized with instruments requiring continuous updates.

The flowing chapters address coordination and interdependencies between different facets of the same problem. This problem is related to the interactions between health, education and the economy in local and regional contexts of the South Mediterranean and Arab countries. Through these first chapters, readers are prepared to the demand for coordination and tools to contribute to ensure it. Information and Communication Technologies (ICTs) as a set of means devoted to the enhancement of the management and coordination of interfaces between large series of functions and players are then introduced.

REFERENCES

Aoki, K. (1998). Neocolonialism, anticommons property, and biopiracy in the (not-so-brave) new world order of international intellectual property protection. *Indiana Journal of Global Legal Studies, 6*(1), 11–38.

Berge, E., & Van Laerhoven, F. (2011). Governing the commons for two decades: A complex story. *International Journal of the Commons, 5.* Retrieved from http://www.thecommonsjournal. org/index.php/ijc/article/view/325/230 accessed 03 sept 2012

Bergstrom, T. (2010). The uncommon insight of Elinor Ostrom. *Scandinavian Journal of Economics.* Retrieved August 10, 2012, from http://works. bepress.com/ted_bergstrom/107

Boettke, P. Z., Caceres, W., & Martin, A. G. (2012). *Error is obvious, coordination is the puzzle.* Retrieved August 12, 2012, from http:// ssrn.com/2004362

Buchanan, J. M., & Yoon, Y. J. (2000). Symmetric tragedies: Commons and anti-commons. *The Journal of Law & Economics*, *43*, 1–13. doi:10.1086/467445

Canavese, A. (2005). *Commons, anti-commons, corruption, and behavior*. Retrieved August 12, 2012, from http://escholarship.org/uc/item/09p2972h

Cantrell, R., Hettel, G., Barry, G., & Hamilton, R. (2004). Impact of intellectual property on nonprofit research institutions and the developing countries they serve. *Minnesota Journal of Law. Science & Technology*, *6*, 253–276.

Chang, W. W. (2012). *The economics of offshoring*. Retrieved from.

Coelho, M., Filipe, J., & Ferreira, M. (2009). *Tragedies on natural resources a commons and anti-commons approach*. Working Papers 2009/21. Lisbon, Portugal: Technical University of Lisbon.

D'Agostino, L. M., & Santangelo, G. D. (2012). *Does the global fragmentation of R&D activities pay back? The home region perspective*. Paper presented at the DRUID Academy. Cambridge, UK.

Deardorff, A. V. (1998). *Fragmentation in simple trade models*. Discussion Paper No. 422. Paper presented in a Session on Globalization and Regionalism: Conflict or Complements? Chicago, IL.

Deardorff, A. V. (1998). *Fragmentation across cones*. Discussion Paper No. 427. Paper presented at a Conference on Globalization and International Trade. Bürgenstock, Switzerland.

Depoorter, B., Bertacchini, E., & De Mot, J. (2008). Never two without three: Commons, anticommons and semicommons. *Social Science Research Network Electronic Paper Collection*. Retrieved August 12, 2012, from http://ssrn.com/abstract=1162189

Depoorter, B., & Vanneste, S. (2004). *Putting humpty dumpty back together: Experimental evidence of anticommons tragedies*. Research Paper No. 04-53. Washington, DC: George Mason Law & Economics.

Fennell, L. A. (2011). Ostrom's law: Property rights in the commons. *International Journal of the Commons, Anti-Commons. Semi-Commons*, *5*(1), 9–27.

Gollock, A. (2008). *Les implications de l'Accord de l'OMC sur les aspects de droits de propriété intellectuelle qui touchent au commerce (ADPIC) sur l'accès aux médicaments en Afrique subsaharienne*. (Thesis). Université Grenoble II. Grenoble, France.

Graff, G., Cullen, S., Bradford, K., Zilberman, D., & Bennett, E. (2003). The public and private structure of intellectual property ownership in agricultural biotechnology. *Nature Biotechnology*, *21*, 989–995. doi:10.1038/nbt0903-989

Grimmelmann, J. (2010). The internet is a semicommons. *Fordham Law Review*, *78*, 2799–2842.

Grimmelmann, J. (2012). *Three theories of copyright in ratings*. Retrieved from http://ssrn.com/2094523

Hall, B. H., & Harhoff, D. (2012). *Recent research on the economics of patents*. NBER Working Papers 17773. Washington, DC: National Bureau of Economic Research, Inc.

Hardin, G. (1968). The tragedy of the commons. *Science*, *162*, 1243–1248. doi:10.1126/science.162.3859.1243

Heller, M., & Eisenberg, R. (1998). Can patents deter innovation? The anticommons in biomedical research. *Science*, *280*(5364), 698–701. doi:10.1126/science.280.5364.698

Heller, M. A. (1998). The tragedy of the anti-commons: Property in the transition from Marx to markets. *Harvard Law Review, 111*(3), 621–688. doi:10.2307/1342203

Hung, V. P., Macaulay, T. G., & Marsh, S. P. (2007). The economics of land fragmentation in the north of Vietnam. *The Australian Journal of Agricultural and Resource Economics, 51*(2), 195–211. doi:10.1111/j.1467-8489.2007.00378.x

Johnson, O. E. G. (1970). A note on the economics of fragmentation. *The Nigerian Journal of Economic and Social Studies, 12*, 175–184.

Kapczynski, A., Crone, E., & Merson, M. (2003). Global health and university patents. *Science, 301*, 1659. doi:10.1126/science.301.5640.1629

Kennedy, D., & Michelman, F. (1980). Are property and contract efficient? *Hofstra Law Review, 8*(711), 712–737.

Klerkx, P. (2012). Beyond fragmentation and disconnect: Networks for knowledge exchange in the English land management advisory system. *Land Use Policy, 3*, 13–24.

Kuziemsky, C., Weber-Jahnke, J., & Williams, J. (2012). Engineering the healthcare collaboration space. In *Proceedings of IEEE SEHC*, (pp. 51-57). Zurich, Switzerland: IEEE Press.

Lewis, D. J., & Plantinga, A. J. (2007). Policies for habitat fragmentation: Combining econometrics with GIS-based. *Land Economics, 83*, 109–127.

Liao, W.-C. (2012). *Inshoring: The geographic fragmentation of production and inequality*. Singapore, Singapore: National University of Singapore.

Lindhal, T. (2012). Coordination problems and resource collapse in the commons — Exploring the role of knowledge heterogeneity. *Ecological Economics Ecological, 79*, 52–59. doi:10.1016/j.ecolecon.2012.04.016

Mudambi, R. (2008). *Location, control and innovation in knowledge-intensive industries*. Discussion Paper 08-0430. Philadelphia, PA: Temple University Fox School of Business.

Nash, M. (2001). Grains of hope. *Time*. Retrieved from www.time.com/time/asia/biz/magazine/0,9754,98034,00.html

Neal, K., Doye, D., & Brorsen, B. W. (2012). *Fragmentation of agricultural land parcels*. Paper presented at the Southern Agricultural Economics Association Annual Meeting. Birmingham, AL.

Ostrom, E. (1990). *Governing the commons: The evolution of institutions for collective actions*. Cambridge, UK: Cambridge University Press. doi:10.1017/CBO9780511807763

Ostrom, E., & Schlager, E. (1992). Property rights regimes and natural resources. *Land Economics, 68*, 249–262. doi:10.2307/3146375

Parisi, F., Depoorter, B., & Schulz, N. (2005). Duality in property: Commons and anticommons. *International Review of Law and Economics, 25*, 4–10. doi:10.1016/j.irle.2005.12.003

Ranjay, G., Franz, W., & Pavel, Z. (2012). The two facets of collaboration: Cooperation and coordination in strategic alliances. *The Academy of Management Annals, 6*, 531–583. doi:10.1080/19416520.2012.691646

Sadowsky, G. (2012). Introduction. In Sadowsky, G. (Ed.), *Accelerating Development using the Web: Empowering Poor and Marginalized Populations*. New York, NY: World Wide Web Foundation.

Schlager, E., & Ostrom, E. (2010). Property-rights regimes and natural resources: A conceptual analysis. *Land Economics, 68*, 249–262. doi:10.2307/3146375

Shapiro. (2001). Navigating the patent ticket: Cross licenses, patent proofs and standard setting. In *Innovation Policy and the Economy*, (vol. 1, pp. 119-150). Cambridge, MA: MIT Press.

Smith, H. E. (2000). Semi-common property rights and scattering in the open fields. *The Journal of Legal Studies*, *29*, 131–169. doi:10.1086/468066

Smith, H. E. (2005). Governing the tele-semi-commons. *Yale Journal on Regulation*, *22*, 289–314.

Smith, H. E. (2008). Governing water: The semi-commons of fluid property rights. *Arizona Law Review*, *50*, 445. Retrieved from http://nrs.harvard.edu/urn-3:HUL.InstRepos:dash.current.terms-ofuse#OAP

The World Bank Group. (2012). *Doing business home*. Retrieved from http://www.doingbusiness.org/

UNCTAD. (2010). *Information and communication report, 2010*. New York, NY: UNCTAD.

Velho, L. (2004). Agricultural biotechnology research partnerships in sub-saharan Africa: Achievements, challenges and policy issues. *Technology Policy Briefs*, *4*, 1–12.

Zhang, Y., & Bolton, G. E. (2012). *Social network effects on coordination: A laboratory investigation*. Retrieved from http://ssrn.com/102139/ssrn.2000974

ENDNOTES

[1.] Fragmentation: From a marketing stand point, fragmentation occurs when in market conditions, there exist no dominant group of buyers or suppliers. It also refers to the emergence of new segments (in a previously homogeneous market) which have their own distinct needs, requirements, and preferences. However, the concept can be found in series of physical and socio-economic conditions. The best representation is provided in Enthoven (2009) when dealing with "Integrated Delivery Systems: The Cure for Fragmentation." The author says that "Our healthcare system is fragmented, with a misalignment of incentives, or lack of coordination, that spawns inefficient allocation of resources. Fragmentation adversely impacts quality, cost, and outcomes."

[2.] Coordination: Coordination in economics refers to the problems associated with making diverse economic activities mesh together seamlessly to produce economic value. Historically, economic coordination referred to the coordination of activities and processes within an organization. More recently, it has been used to address the co-ordination of all economic activities across an economic sector and how this takes place in the absence of a coordinating authority. These concepts can also be applied to the global marketplace. A lack of coordination results in lower benefits to the participants in the economic activity.

[3.] Integration: Economic integration is term used in different contexts but refers but can refer basically to market integration as well as to the links between economies. In international economics and trade, integration describes how different aspects of each participating economy are inter-related. As economic integration increases, barriers of trade between markets disappear. The most integrated economy today, between independent nations, is the European Union and its euro zone. The degree of economic integration can be categorized into stages: Preferential trading are, Free trade area, Customs union, Common market, Economic and monetary union, and Complete economic integration. Otherwise, market integration in industrial economics refer to the relationships between markets. Markets may be based on technological relationships but generally on input-output linkages. Vertical integration is used for a market chain where different goods entertain technological relationships and where prices are easily transmitted under these market interdependencies. In this type of integration, the output of the previous market is used as an input in the following market in the marketing chain. Horizontal integration focuses on the markets that relate to the same good and where several inputs are used to produce a single output.

4. Commons: This is an institutional arrangement where resources are owned or used in common. These resources can be natural, land, software, culture, and values that are publically or privately owned but used according to an established set of rules. Under full open access, the situation refers to common pool resources. With restricted access (only to members), commons can become "clubs" where the rights of use are limited to members only. The tragedy of commons is defined by the existence of several owners with no one having the right to exclude the others. This implies an excess use of common resources due to the existence of multiple users. The result of this non-exclusion is the overuse of the given resource that leads to a "tragedy of the commons" as introduced in Hardin (1968).

5. Anti-commons: The tragedy of "anti-commons" as explained by Heller (1998) and Heller and Eisenberg (1998), is a mirror of "commons." In the situation of anti-commons, owners have the right to exclude others from a scarce resource while no one is allowed to use it effectively. This situation leads to the under use of the scarce resource and thus, to the "tragedy of the anti- commons" (Heller, 1998). This phenomenon was first described by the latter author in relation to the reforms that took place in ex-socialist economies. This was related to the "storefronts that remained empty

while small kiosks were full of goods and mushroomed on the streets" (Osterloh & Rota, 2004). Heller (1998) suggested then, that the root of the problem was the way property rights were distributed and not only the ambiguity of their definition or scope, corruption or defiance of the rule of law. The issue with the way intellectual property rights are distributed is closely related to how intellectual property rights, over a given idea, impacts the possibility to build upon that piece of knowledge for future research and development activities. In practice, because of high levels of IPRs protection, the domain of ideas is largely segmented with high levels of exclusion of others leading to higher probability of social welfare loss. A large number of cases have been reported in the literature where segmented intellectual property rights, in biomedical research and in the software industry have been serious constraints to the generation of further positive effects on the economy (Heller, et al., 1998). Therefore, intellectual property rights or patents, if largely distributed, may decrease social welfare by limiting future inventions, creating anti-commons and encouraging non-competitive behavior (Heller, et al., 1998; Jensen, et al., 2004). However, if they are granted carefully, this may reduce enterprise willingness to invest in imitated and differentiated inventions. The issue is to find a balance between social and inventors' interests (Jensen, et al., 2004). Gollock (2008) provides also important arguments to investigate the roles of IPRs.

6. Externalities: An externality, or transaction spillover, is a cost or benefit that is not easily revealed or transmitted through markets. A negative externality leads to costs that are supported by individuals or groups (pollution leads to negative externalities). A positive externality is based on a beneficial interdependency that could lead to positive benefits

to the parties involved (a bee producer and apple grower do both benefit from being neighbors). For both negative and positive externalities, prices in a competitive market do not reflect the full costs or benefits of producing or consuming a product or service. Also, producers and consumers may neither bear all of the costs nor reap all of the benefits of the economic activity, and too much or too little of the goods will be produced or consumed in terms of overall costs and benefits to society.

7. Game theory: Game theory is a method for studying strategic decision making. It is "the use of mathematical models of conflict and cooperation between rational decision-makers. It is also referred to as interactive decision theory with large number of agents and different objectives. This approach is largely used in economics, political science,

and psychology and other disciplines. Different games have been identified to include the zero-sum games where one person's or group gains exactly the losses of the other participant(s) and positive sum games when resources are growing. There are many publications that introduce to game theory starting with the classical one by Nash (2001).

8. The best example of semi-commons can be provided by the users of a common pool resource that can be used collectively to graze animals. Animals are privately owned while the land is collectively used. In this type of framework, it is hard to control that all those having the right to use the common pool are having similar herd size. Private incentive pushes individual to own larger herds in other to increase their individual benefits from the common resource.

Chapter 2
Insights to the Interconnections of Health, Education, and Other Wealth Components

ABSTRACT

This chapter is devoted to showing the levels of manifestation of interconnections in the area of economic and social development with a focus on health, education, and other wealth components. It describes the existing interconnections between different assets, which are health, education, and social capital, besides traditional economic factors owned by individuals, groups, and economies. The chapter is mainly based on a review of the previous literature that has looked at one or several dimensions of these interconnections. This covers the interdependencies that have been described in the context of specific world regions. The outcomes from this chapter prepare one for the coming chapters on the role of ICTs in coordination.

INTRODUCTION

The aim of this chapter is to show how interdependencies are expressed in the areas of health, education and economic outcomes. It also prepares to a better perception of the roles of coordination with where Information and Communications Technologies (ICTs) play an important role.

Insights into the likely relationships of health, education, and economic performance have been explicitly discussed in series of social science, public health publications, and reports. Different approaches have been used to tackle the extent and magnitude of these relationships. It is obvious that these linkages are well known but their magnitude and extent with their utility for economic and social policies are not obvious. During these last years, evidence about the magnitude and extent of the policy impacts of more than one socioeconomic sector, has been increasing. This review deals with the importance of interdependencies between health, education and different wealth measures and the major findings accumulated in the socio-economic literature.

DOI: 10.4018/978-1-4666-3643-9.ch002

The present chapter is composed of two parts. The first one discusses the theoretical aspects related to different wealth components with focus on health, education, social capital and traditional economic factors. The second part of this chapter introduces the empirical evidence that has been reported in the literature with insistence on South Mediterranean Economies.

THEORETICAL APPROACHES AND INTERDEPENDENCIES

The main publications that have been reviewed are those that contribute to the assessment of the relationships involving health. Two major types of approaches have been identified in relation to the number of variables affecting health. These relationships are respectively reviewed with emphasis placed on different socioeconomic factors. The first set introduces a more general view about the variables and their levels of interactions. The second is based on few socioeconomic variables and their relationships to health. This refers to the relationships of health and nutrition, health and education, health and governance and health and labor markets.

Relationships of Health and Other Socioeconomic Variables

Bernard (2006) describes life as a multi-faceted process. This is explained by the fact that individuals use, gather, or lose various interdependent forms of capital throughout their lifespan. Three basic resources (health, education, and economic) can be seen as interdependent causes and consequences of one another over the lifetime of an individual[1]. The social capital[2] could be considered as an important factor as individuals can accumulate other useful resources for themselves, their families, and their communities through social networks.

The variables introduced by the authors underline the existence of inter-relations both in static and dynamic terms. These account not only for economic variables but also all the other socioeconomic factors including education (Hurd & Kapteyn, 2003). These authors have integrated most of the variables that may have relationships to health to explore the causality among all these factors. Adams, Hurd, McFadden, Merril, and Riberiro (2003) identified causal relationships between "Socioeconomic Status" and health conditions. While empirical evidence is established between socio-economic factors and health, no clear opposite causality is found.

Lee and Kim (2007) conducted a longitudinal analysis to detect a long-term effect of health shocks on wealth and compared that with its short-term effect on the elderly, which goes along with the previous studies including that of Adams et al. (2003). New health events have negative impacts on wealth but tend to disappear over time (Lee & Kim, 2007). The results have also shown that severe health conditions (existing and new) significantly influence wealth depletion mainly when shocks happen later in life. Besides, health capital (existing severe chronic conditions) has a persistent negative impact on wealth changes over time. However, these results are subject to variations with the level of education, the family status, and other factors.

Longer term effects have been also investigated using panel data by Adams et al. (2002) and by Cutler, Miller, and Norton (2007), however only limited evidence is attained. The same results are found in the study of Culter, Miller, and Norton (2007). Mayer-Foulkes, Aghion, and Howitt (2004) addressed the long-term impact of health by including the intergenerational and life-long dimensions.

The relationships between health and each of the components that define the wealth of an individual, a group, and a country are examined through different publications.

Cutler, Lleras-Muney, and Vogl (2008) show the existence of a clear link between socioeconomic status and health, which are identified by a number of studies covering both the United States and European Countries. A number of socioeconomic variables such as education, income, occupation, race, and ethnicity used as measures of socioeconomic status have been associated with poor health and increased mortality risk. For example, mortality risk rises when individuals do not reach upper secondary education in the United States and in some European Countries. Each of the measures of socioeconomic status would influence health through different mechanisms. This has important implications for the choice of public policies aiming at improving the health of individuals under specific conditions (Sen, 1998).

Cutler, Lleras-Muney, and Volg (2008) have reviewed research of the last two decades on the SES (Socioeconomic Status) health gradient by paying particular attention to the mechanisms through which each of the SES measure affects the health status. They have divided the SES into four domains: education, financial resources, rank race, and ethnicity. The studies reviewed have explored and have analyzed the contributions from different fields including not only economics but also sociology, demography, epidemiology, psychology, and evolutionary biology and others. The authors cited above, have recognized that the characteristics of the developing countries which are the interest of the present report are such that the "SES health gradient and its underlying mechanisms require further attention in poor countries."

To study the link between SES and health the authors start by looking at some facts using the National Health interviews survey of 1986 through 1995. They use two measures of health: Self Reported Health Status (SRHS) and mortality and four measures of SES (education, income, occupation, race, and ethnicity). Those with more than 16 years of school have lower mortality rates than those with less than 8 years of school and

more education is also associated with better SRHS. When household income is used to replace education as an indicator of SES, the results are similar in the sense that as SES improves, mortality decreases and there is an amelioration of SRHS. When occupation is used, lower occupational status increases mortality.

The literature based on quasi experiments such as the enforcement of compulsory education or the existence of high unemployment forcing individuals to stay at schools, reveals that education affects health positively (Sandra, Devereux, & Salvanes, 2005). The reverse effect holds as well. The positive link between education and health is shown to hold in developing countries as well. Randomized experiments in India and Kenya (Bobonis, 2006; Miguel & Kremer, 2004) as well as quasi experiments from developing countries (Lucas, 2005; Bleakley, 2007) confirm these results. These studies seem to imply that schooling improves health because it reduces morbidity and improve cognitive development. However, this could be an expectation of longer life that increases human capital investment.

The link between income and health is first, perceived in the literature as running from income to health. More recent work shows that the relationship is more complex and varies with the population age. Income improves access to health inputs but a better health allows one to earn a better income. Poor health increases spending and reduces wealth through a decline in labor earnings and some factors such as education affects both health and income. The study about the elderly in developed countries indicates that income is not a factor, which is associated with a better health. However, it is found that family income affects children's health. The early health status of children affects their later health status when older and thus their ability to earn income. If this is true, then children's health plays an important role in the intergenerational transmission of socioeconomic status.

These results hold also in developing countries as shown by some case studies. Exposure to malaria eradication in the Americas (Bleakley, 2007) and being born during years of good rainfall in rural Indonesia (Maccini & Yang, 2008) seem to improve SES in later life.

Low social status through membership in a disadvantaged racial group or through low rank in a hierarchy may also cause poor health in adulthood.

One of the important findings of this literature review is the importance of the lifecycle. Parent's resources (education, income) have an effect on the health of children.

Health, Wealth, and Income

The approaches included in this part consider health as the most critical source of wealth. Sommestad (2001) emphasizes the role of investment in human capital with health being the major engine of economic growth based on the some empirical evidence "a 5-year gain in life expectancy resulted in 0.3 to 0.5 per cent economic growth." This evidence supports the work of Bloom, Canning, and Sevilla (2004) about the effect health status on productivity, education, investment in physical capital and the demographic dividend. Poverty and poor health penalize economic growth (Bloom, Canning, & Sevilla, 2004). In *The Health and Wealth of Nations,* Bloom and Canning (2000) acknowledged the relationship between health and income, which indicates higher income and leads to a longer life expectancy. A healthier population works more efficiently with higher chances of improving its skills, generating, and attracting more investments, and benefits from a higher resource allocation. This causality between health and income lead to health improvement and then to further income increase. Various examples of this "Virtual Spiral" are from East Asia and Ireland (Bloom & Canning, 2000). In the previous cited publication Bloom, Canning, and Sevilla (2004), the authors have stressed that investing in health, leads to higher economic and

social performance, under sound macroeconomic policies and governance. The same study showed that initial beneficiaries of health improvements are often the most vulnerable groups (children) with healthier children having better school attendance and improved performance. This shows how health and income have been identified to be highly related.

When introducing health in the budget constraint, Hoel (2003) found that the budget should be allocated in such a way that the marginal cost per unit of health improvement in the optimal outcome, is equalized across health states.

Bridges and Haywood (2003) provided a detailed analysis of the methodological differences that exist in health economics and the expected changes that have been taking place especially between theoretical and empirical contributions. Hurd and Kapteyn (2005) have also analyzed the relationship between health and income. They find large variations in wealth in some countries as associated with large variations in health. Further techniques and analyzes have shown the importance of the link between health and expenditures. Xu, Evans, Kawabata, Zeramdini, Klavus, and Murray (2003) demonstrate the existence of an overall positive relation between the proportion of households with catastrophic health expenditures and the share of out-of pocket payments in total health expenditure. The results confirm that countries with a higher share of out-of-pocket payments in total health expenditures are more likely to have a higher proportion of households facing catastrophic expenditures. Gerdtham and Thgren's (2002) tested for co-integration between health expenditure and GDP and found that health expenditure and GDP are co-integrated around linear trends. Acemoglu and Johnson (2006) establish the links between diseases, health problems, and economic growth.

Other studies like the one by Doyle, Harmon, and Walker (2005) explore the robustness of the presumed effect of parental background, mainly education and income, on child health. Children of poorer households tend to enter adulthood in worse health and with more serious chronic conditions. This is referred to as a "gradient" in health status. The authors however suspect the possibility that unobservable factors might still account for these results. Other important relationships have been investigated in the literature.

Health, Nutrition, Education, and Labor

Knapp (2007) dealt with the links between nutrition, labor productivity and a health variable that is height. The net role of nutrition on labor productivity was shown to be highly significant. Muysken, Yetkiner, and Ziesemer (1999) show the higher is the scarcity of physical capital, the higher are the expenditures on health and consumption are higher. In addition, consumption is no longer likely negatively related to population growth because it enhances the percentage of health workers.

Wichmann (1995) investigate the nutrition-productivity relationship and show the existence of a strong link between the state of nutrition, health and labor productivity, at low levels of income. The dynamic version did show that better nutrition increases the productivity of the learning by doing process. The empirical evidence gathered confirmed the above findings but revealed that, children with good nutrition and health start school at an earlier age, progress further, and repeat fewer grades (Yamauchi, 2006). However, the analysis of long panel of data (11 years) suggests that good health may discourage further investments in schooling at the stage of transition from primary to secondary school and that better health status may reinforce incentives to go to work.

The relationship between health and education has been also stressed in series of publications such as the one of Freudenberg and Ruglis (2007). The findings show that poor health is a causal effect of poor education and dropout. In addition, health professionals and educators would be better off bringing their efforts together in reducing dropout rates and developing health awareness, as both their sectors (health and education) would obtain considerable benefits from such a cooperation.

Regarding the relationship to labor, health is one of the strongest determinants of labor supply (Lambrinos, 1980) and thus the relation between health and labor is clearly important. Arayssi, Sarkis, and Uwaydah Mardini (2006) demonstrate that individuals place a positive value on job risk insurance because they demand higher earnings and work longer hours for riskier jobs. Therefore, insurance companies may charge people with different willingness to pay, particularly those in different income brackets, different premiums. The value of a small reduction in mortality risks is subject to the views of the individual. It is also based on the idea that only a person is able to assign an accurate dollar value to his/her own life. According to Arayssi et al. (2006), the message from this study indicates that there is room for policymakers to provide incentives for voluntary self-protection as well.

Further series of publications have produced major inputs into how interdependencies could be used to support more realistic policies.

Anderson, Foster, and Frisvold (2004) showed how to account for evidence about early childhood socioeconomic conditions that have long-term health consequences on health disparities over the life course in relation to early investments in education. These have lasting effects on health outcomes later in life. Aging populations in the developed world are currently posing a serious threat to the cost of pensions and health care. The authors explain why these countries cannot expect to grow themselves out of the problem using measures such as increasing immigration, raising the retirement age, and encouraging households to have more children.

According to Farrell, Ghai, and Shavers (2005), the only effective measures are for households and governments to increase their savings rates and to allocate capital more efficiently in order to earn higher returns on the assets they have.

Grimm and Harttgen (2007) look at the role of dependency ratio in relation to population growth in connection to health. They also find that a low life expectancy reduces substantially welfare despite the related economic feedback effects.

Health and Governance

Some authors have been pointing out to the role of political institutions in supplying better health. Rationally, better governance leads to better supplies of both private and public goods and services. However, there are paradoxes and dilemmas that have been reported in the literature. Evans (2008) is convinced that the famous drop in the main killer diseases is not the result of medical advance or this has been at least a little influenced by this progress. To demonstrate this result, McKeown (1979) uses the example of Cuba (WHO, 2006) in the paper "Thomas McKeown, Meet Fidel Castro: Physicians, Population Health, and the Cuban Paradox." Cuba has the lowest GDP per capita among the countries studied—St. Lucia, Uruguay, Argentina, United States, Canada, Mexico, and Chile. At the same time, the country registers the highest number of physicians per 1000 people in the sample. Cuban life expectancy at birth (78) is among the highest in the sample, which is similar to the value in the United States and close to the

value in Canada (80). Besides that, the mortality under age 5 is the lowest (7) in the sample after the value for Canada (6). This Cuban Paradox results from the fact that even though Cuba has poor economic achievements, it has a good health performance that is comparable to developed countries (see Figure 1).

Evans (2008) find out that according to the Cuban experience, increased wealth is not an important factor for health improvement. He explains the Cuban health improvement by a political determination that recognizes the importance of social actions and health determinants other than medical. However, the above papers do not discuss how health performance is transferred to education and to other economic factors?

INTERDEPENDENCIES OF HEALTH, EDUCATION, AND POVERTY IN SOUTHERN MEDITERRANEAN ECONOMIES

This part of the chapter is mainly based on publications and reports related to the South Mediterranean region and that have covered issues related to the topic of this research. The objective of this part is to identify the state of knowledge to date about the interdependencies of health, education,

Figure 1. Health indicators and GDP per capita for the Americas countries in the sample

Country	Physicians per 1,000 population	Life expectancy at birth	Mortality under age 5	GDP per capita
Cuba	5.91	78	7	$3,438
St. Lucia	5.17	74	14	$5,880
Uruguay	3.65	75	14	$8,408
Argentina	3.01	75	18	$11,989
United States	2.54	78	8	$37,572
Canada	2.14	80	6	$30,192
Mexico	1.98	74	28	$9,387
Chile	1.09	77	9	$11,590

Source: WHO 2006, Statistical Annex, Tables 1 and 4.

and poverty in the context of the region. Besides reviewing the publications of different authors, inputs from different international and regional organizations have been widely used. In this context, interdependencies are analyzed through the relationships between two sets of variables and through the links between several components that relate to health, education and poverty in the region. As it can be seen from chapter, three promising models have been developed to assess the levels of interdependencies of health, education and income (Gan & Gong, 2007; Chakraborty & Das, 2005).

Health, Nutrition, and Population

Based on Demographic and Health Surveys (DHS), important series of reports are produced about the links between health, nutrition, and population. Among the South Mediterranean Countries) with the inclusion of Morocco, Egypt, Jordan, Turkey, and Yemen are covered. The related publications (Gwatkin, Rutstein, Kiersten, Eldaw, Wagstaff, & Amouzou, 2007) provide the most important links between health, nutrition, and demographic issues.

The comparison of 1992 and 2004 data show that Morocco suffers from disparities in both health conditions and health service use with a high infant mortality rate especially for children aged 5 or less. Female maternal mortality is found also to be high with other health problems prevalent among children (fever, diarrhea, and acute respiratory infection). Education is also as critical in relation to series of areas among which, the disadvantage against women regarding school completion and participation.

For Egypt, children under the age of 5 suffer from mortality with a high prevalence of fever, diarrhea, respiratory infection, bad nutrition, severe stunting, severe underweight, and severe anemia. Large segments of women in rural areas, suffer from malnutrition as well as anemia among

others. However, major improvements have identified between 1995 and 2000.

The 1997 DHS data for Jordan (Gwatkin, et al., 2007) showed higher fertility rate for poor households as compared to those with higher income. Besides that, the poorer segments are in rural areas. Problems related to health, nutrition and other demographic problems are consequently mainly concentrated in rural areas. Women and children are again the highly vulnerable segments.

The comparison of the 1993 and 1998 data from DHS (Demographic and Health Surveys) for Turkey show improvements in health, nutrition and other related socioeconomic components. Women and children have benefited from these major improvements but important gaps are still prevailing between rural and urban areas. These changes include reduction of the prevalence of underweight besides the decrease of infant mortality besides increasing health services that can explain the high rate of school completion.

The report about Yemen confirms the links among poverty, bad health, and low education. These links are supported by 1997 data and showed that rural areas suffer more than urban areas with women being those that do not benefit from health, education and economic services (Gwatkin, et al., 2007).

The above results have been consistently confirmed by other studies. Akala and Saharti (2006) assert that while the region benefits from health improvements, more effective and structured commitment toward health service is required. The authors suggest that this limited engagement, is directly related to the levels of investments devoted to the health area. The population of the region is identified to be suffering from the lack of reforms and changes in the healthcare system (Schieber, Maeda, & Klingen, 2007). These issues have been developed earlier by Roudi-Fahimi (2005). To this latter, reforms that would place the reproductive health of women at the center, could help promote further the illiteracy rate and other social obstacles.

This is supported also by other studies such as that of Roudi-Fahimi (2007) who highlights the considerable lack in women's health awareness. There exist alarming gender disparities in the access to public health services that are usually justified by cultural matters. Further details are provided in Schultz (2005).

The Relationship between Health and Productivity

There is increased evidence that health has a positive impact on productivity for both developed and developing countries. In her study, Tompa (2002) found that health increases output at both the personal and the aggregate levels. "At the personal level, health can directly increase general output (e.g., through enhanced physical energy and mental acuity), yearly output (e.g., through reduced sickness absence), and career output (e.g., through decreased morbidity or increased longevity, resulting in a longer career)." The sum of individual increases in output translates to an aggregate increase in productivity expressed by an increase in the output per hour and the output per worker. Bloom et al. (2001) confirmed the positive and significant impact of health on economic growth, measured by productivity. They suggested that "a one year improvement in a population's life expectancy contributes to a 4 percent increase in output." Studies conducted by Rivera et al., found that "between 21 and 47.5 percent of GDP growth per worker (working-age person) over the last 25 to 30 years can be explained by improvements in the health of populations (defined as health-care expenditures and life expectancy) at the country level." Furthermore, a decrease in child mortality in the recent decades has led to reduced fertility rates, which in turn can cause an increase in workforce participation and productivity (Bloom & Canning, 2000). The effects of child mortality are also discussed in Bozzoli, Deaton, and Quintana-Domeque (2007). Weichun, Engineer,

and King (2006) analyze longevity in relation to overlapping generation frameworks.

According to Bloom et al. (2001), a healthy workforce is more energetic and robust, thus it is more productive and can earn higher wages. Firms with a healthy workforce have lower absenteeism rates. It could be added that Strauss and Thomas (1998) found that in developing countries, low levels of health have a greater impact on the poor because they are more likely to suffer from serious health problems as they have jobs that require much physical effort. Another finding of their study was that men with higher weights (anthropometric indicator of status of nutrition in adulthood) and heights (anthropometric indicator of status of nutrition in childhood) earned higher wages as their productivity is greater. Indeed, "a 1 percent increase in height is associated with 8 percent increase in wages." Tompa (2002) identified a spillover effect from increased levels of human capital and from health particularly. Higher levels of health can increase not only a worker's own productivity, but also the productivity of co-workers and on society as a whole.

Based on Aguayo-Rico, Guerra-Turrubiates, and Montes (2005), investment in health should be included as one of the macroeconomic policy factor. Studies have found that differences in economic growth rates among countries are significantly explained by health levels. Besides, investments in health have proven to increase labor productivity and, thereby, economic growth. However, diminishing marginal returns to investment in health are well recognized.

The Southern Mediterranean region has accomplished remarkable improvement in the health sector over the last two decades. The average life expectancy has increased by 10 years (from 59 years in 1980 to 69 years in 2003) and infant mortality rate decreased by half (from 90 deaths per 1,000 live births to about 40). Active population policies have been put in place, which contributed to great reductions in total fertility rates (from an average of 6 births per women in 1980 to just below 4 births per women in 2003). However, the decline in fertility rates is lagging behind the decline in mortality rates, which causes a rapidly expanding youth population. This "youth bulge" represents both an opportunity and a challenge to social and economic growth in the region (El Naggar, 2007).

Most countries face the problem of inefficient management of the health system. According to the same report, "efficiency gains in health services would translate into improved fiscal sustainability, better labor market incentives and labor productivity, and overall higher social welfare." In fact, inefficient spending on health will negatively affect the economic and human development of the region. "It could act as a drag on labor productivity, add fiscal pressure on a limited government budget, and reduce governments' ability to target public resources for the vulnerable groups" (World Bank, 2006). Another World Bank (1999) report states that public expenditure in health and education provisions helps improve labor force productivity. Finally, improving health level enhances individual security and capabilities, which leads to improved productivity, national income, and development prospects (Roudi-Fahimi & Ashford, 2005).

In fact, the relationship between health and productivity is a two-way causality relationship. As described by Smith (1999) "a lot of people who otherwise wouldn't be poor are simply because they are sick; however, few people who otherwise would be healthy are sick because they are poor" (Aguayo-Rico, et al., 2005). Strauss and Thomas (1998) suggest that as workers' productivity increases, their earnings increase allowing them to invest more in their health. Smith (1999) believes that the impact of productivity, translated into earnings, on health exists albeit it is lower than the impact of health on productivity/earnings. According to Chatterjee (1990), productivity has a direct positive impact on education, which

is expressed through an increase in wages and household nutrition. Still, there are many factors that mediate this relationship such as wage, nature, and seasonality of employment.

Further research needs to investigate which population groups and under what labor market conditions health/productivity relationship is most significant (Strauss & Thomas, 1998). Aguayo-Rico et al. (2005) add that one of the major shortcomings in the empirical studies in this field is the use of life expectancy as a proxy variable of health. They believe that to assess the true value of health, all health dimensions should be included: mortality, morbidity, disability, and discomfort.

Relationship between Health and Education

Health conditions are strongly associated with educational achievement of the child. Health is believed to be a factor for better performance in education. At the same time, education is considered to have a significant impact on the level of health of the person or the person's children.

According to Hoxby (2007), the most important part of the relationship between health and education is associated with infancy and early childhood. In this context, health, nutrition, and the environment have disproportionate effects on cognitive development.

Through the study of Ding, Lehrer, Rosenquist, and Audrain-McGovern (2007), poor health, represented by obesity and depression, has a substantial impact on academic achievement. First, it may affect the child's physical energy level which determines the time that can be used for learning (attendance and after school educational activities). Indeed, obesity has been found to be the largest determinant of absenteeism. Secondly, poor health influences the child's mental status, which has a direct impact on academic performance. For instance, obesity reduces self-esteem, which leads to classroom disengagement, thereby reducing academic performance. In addition, clinical depression can affect a child's attention span, which negatively impacts her academic achievements. A student suffering from obesity or depression has a lower GPA than average by 0.45 points, equivalent of one standard deviation. However, the relationship between health and education is significantly influenced by gender. The academic performance of female students is strongly and negatively affected by poor physical and mental health conditions while the academic performance of males is less impacted by health factors.

Besides that, lower birth weight babies have lower educational attainment and earnings. To examine this relationship, research uses within-twin estimates of the effect of birth weight on long-run outcomes. In fact, birth weight has a great effect on longer-run outcomes such as height, IQ at age 18, earnings, and education. Black, McTear, Black, Harper, and Lemon (2005) associate increase a 10% increase in birth weight with a 1% probability increase of high school completion.

Using data on monozygotic twins, Behrman and Rosenzweig (2004) suggest that there are real payoffs to increasing body weight at birth. Increasing birth weight increases adult educational performance and adult height but has no effect on adult body mass. The heavier twin is more likely to be taller, achieve higher educational performance, and receive higher wage.

Case, Fertig, and Paxson (2003) add that children with low birth weight and poorer childhood health indicators have significantly lower educational attainment: "However, it is possible that there is no causal relationship underlying these correlations, as low birth weight may be correlated with many difficult-to-measure socio-economic background and genetic variables."

Evidence also exists that education plays an important role in determining health level of adults as well as the health of their children (Hoxby, 2007). This later relationship is more observed in the case of women. They have a substantial

influence on the health of their children both at the pre-natal and post-natal phases.

As in Hoxby (2007, p. 53) "...the years of mother's education rise, child mortality falls linearly with no lower educational threshold. Mothers with some secondary education lose half as many infants and a fifth as many toddlers as do women with no education." Although the education of the father has some impact over children's health, this impact does not exceed half of the mother's. Educated mothers prevent accidents or sickness and prevent minor health problems from becoming major ones. Moreover, more educated mothers interact better and easier with modern health services which enables them to optimize their outcomes (Australian Medical Association, 2002).

In the region of the SMC, low levels of education, especially for females, hamper health development. According to Sarbib (2002), girls' education improves family health and nutrition. Their education can also lead to birth spacing, health care seeking behavior, and lower infant mortality and morbidity rates. "A ten-percentage point increase in girls' primary school enrolment has been shown to decrease infant mortality by 4.1 deaths per 1000 live births, and a similar 10 percent rise in secondary enrollment by another 5.6 deaths per 1000 live births." Besides, gender discrimination and inadequate access to education in the region lead to poor mental and family health.

Many limitations have been observed in the existing literature about the relationship between health and education. First, due to data limitations, much of the literature focuses on a single measure or proxy of an individual's health such as birth weight. Other measures of physical and mental health include standing heart rate, blood pressure, and mental clarity.

Another restriction in the previous studies concerns the categorization of adolescents. Some models exclusively treat adolescents as "children" whose parents make all their health and education choices while other models treat them as "adults" who make all the decisions by themselves. Future research need to treat teenagers as "teenagers" who make a subset of all the decisions. Examples of decisions that teenagers make independently are smoking and having sex and examples of decisions made by the parents are the number of visits to health care providers (Ding, et al., 2007).

Finally, future research needs to focus on why females and not males are so adversely affected by poor health outcomes.

In a most recent contribution, Cutler and Lleras-Muney (2012) provide a synthesis of about the relationship between education and health. The authors underline the large set of interactions between education and health. They also emphasize the links between education and health with the ambiguities about the directions of causality. Furthermore, the authors recognize that large arrays of questions need further answers. They consider that a review written "a decade from now will ideally have many more specific conclusions to draw."

Relationship between Health and Income

The National Longitudinal Mortality Survey in 1980 indicated that people in the top 5% of income (greater than $50,000) have a life-expectancy, at all ages, 25% longer than that of people in the bottom 5 percent (less than $5,000) (Deaton, 2003, 2006).

Lynch, Smith, Kaplan, and House (2002) found out that there are three interpretations of the relationship between income and health. The Individual Income interpretation assumes that "determinants of population health are completely specified as attributes of independent individuals and that health effects at the population level are merely sums of individual effects." The second interpretation of the health-income linkage is the Psychosocial Environment Interpretation. It suggests that poor people have a negative perception about their socioeconomic status especially when comparing themselves to the rich.

In the South Mediterranean region, important changes have been recorded in health patterns. Indeed, fertility rates, mortality rates, and communicable diseases have decreased while life expectancy and non-communicable diseases have increased. This increase in non-communicable diseases has been related to changing lifestyles (smoking and decreased levels of physical activity) due to increased income. Although most studies suggest that generally, rich countries have healthier population, there are many countries in the region of study that contradict these findings. For instance, while Oman is an upper-middle-income country, the health conditions of its population (in terms of child malnutrition, low birth-weight, and maternal anemia) are as low as those found in some lower-middle income countries such as Egypt and Morocco (Disease Control Priorities Project, 2006).

In fact, the causality between income and health flows in both directions. Empirical evidence has found that health has an impact on income too. A study done on Britain has shown that 30% of the country's economic growth between 1780 and 1979 is attributed to improved nutrition leading to increased longevity. Better health is also believed to create the optimism needed for long-term economic planning. The impact of health on economy can also be viewed from the following perspective: improved health conditions imply increased savings, which leads, relatively, to increased income. Based on a research conducted in USA, health (measured by life expectancy, death rate, infant mortality, medical research) has a significant impact on income level. Hence, government policies need to be directed towards improving the health system and increasing expenditures for health care as a means to increase productivity and income (Brinkley, 2011).

According to Weil (2006, p. 16), "eliminating health gaps between countries would reduce the variance of log GDP per worker by 9.9%." This finding was reached by using Adult Survival Rate for males as a measure of health. Using historical data, the research shows that the share of the population unable to work, due to its malnutrition, drops from 20% to zero with an increase in labor input by a factor of 1.25. In addition, for people working, "increased caloric consumption allowed for a 56 percent increase in labor effort." The combination of these two effects show that improved nutrition increased labor input by 1.95. It is also important to note the indirect impact of health on income that is made through education. Better health results in an increased level of education that a person can attain. In addition, healthier people have an incentive to get more education since their investment can be amortized over more working years.

However, one should take into account how improved health can have a negative impact on income. This is actually true if we consider how better health leads to population growth which, in turn, lowers the GDP per capita. Lowering the GDP per capita is done through raising the ratio of children to adults or through reductions in the quantities of physical capital and land per worker (Weil, 2006).

Future research needs to investigate how the relationship between health and income differs with gender.

The Relationship between Health and Employment

"Employment and health are positively correlated, but is employment a cause or a consequence?" (Mirowsky & Ross, 1995, p. 24). The relationship between health and employment is a two-ways relationship. Studies all over the world have proven that employment has an impact on health and health has an impact on employment.

According to the London Health Commission (2004) employment is considered to be one of the strongest determinants of health. The nature of the job and its status affect the worker's physical and mental health as well as her life expectancy. In fact, the impact of employment on health is made through income. In other words, it is mainly the generated income through employment that affects a person's health conditions. Other researchers believe that employment affects health through both economic and non-economic rewards. The economic rewards include status, power, and economic independence while the non-economic rewards are mainly social support and recognition. These benefits translate both directly and indirectly to improved health (Mirowsky & Ross, 1995).

Unemployment can be the cause of many health problems but its consequences can be different from males to females. Jobless men tend more to experience serious mental problems or substance abuse while unemployed women are more likely to suffer from higher rates of diagnosed disorders. However, it is important to note that not all employment is good. A study done in UK indicates that "over 2 million people in the UK suffer from illness caused or made worse by their work" (London Health Commission, 2004).

A study about "a positive association between job insecurity and adverse psychological changes for a cohort of white-collar British civil servants" indicates that, currently, there is a significant relationship between feelings of job insecurity and stress. This relationship becomes even stronger as the insecurity increases (Burchell, Lapido, & Wilkinson, 1999). However, when studying the relationship between individual's mental health and atypical employment (temporary and part-time). Bardasi and Francesconi (2003) failed to prove any relationship. In addition, Rodriguez (2002) could not prove a significant association of poor health status with marginal employment in Britain.

On the other hand, good health can be a predictor for getting or keeping a paid-job. There are many instances where individuals cannot get a job because of a disability or a disease. The chances to not get a job become stronger when the disease/disability is visible (Mirowsky & Ross, 1995). A study done on Jamaica found that poor health has a significant negative impact on employment (both for entry and retirement). This impact seems to be higher for males than for females although these latter suffer from poorer health conditions. "While any limitation affects the employment behavior of males, only severe limitations affect the behavior of females." In an attempt to explain this differential in the impact of health on employment, the authors fail to relate it to the hypothesis that men's jobs require more health inputs than women's. The remaining, unchecked, hypothesis is that "poor women may have little choice to continue working unless health diminishes to extremely severe levels" (Handa & Neitzert, 1997).

Besides that, the relationship between health and employment tends to vary depending on the stages of an individual's lifecycle. This relationship is stronger during the very early and late stages of lifecycle. For young adults, poor health limits market work activity while for old workers poor health becomes the main determinant for retirement decisions (Handa & Neitzert, 1997). Schuring (2006) confirms the same trend amongst European workers. "A poor health was a risk factor for remaining unemployed among men, but had less effect among women. A poor health was also a risk factor for becoming unemployed or retiring, especially among highly educated workers. In fact, workers in poor health retire between one to three years earlier than those in good health with the same economic and demographic characteristics. Moreover, health shocks have a considerable effect on labor supply decisions of workers aged between 50 to 69 years old. A heart attack or a stroke, for example, reduces the number of work hours supplied by a male (female) worker by 1,030 (654) per year and increases the probability of quitting the job by 42% (31%) (Suhrcke, 2005).

Further research must be conducted to investigate how the linkage health-employment is affected by gender, social status, and education level.

The contribution of Farrukh (2006) strengthens the outcomes attained so far about the region. According to the above study, direct estimates of poverty for the Middle East and North Africa

region are mostly available from the mid-1980s onward. For the period before the 1980s, comparable estimates of poverty based on per capita consumption expenditure are only available for Tunisia (in 1965) and Egypt (in 1975). Based on the latter data, the poverty rate was as high as 51.3 percent in Tunisia in 1965 and 82.2 percent in Egypt in 1975 (at the $2 line). Comparing these statistics to those achieved by the mid-1980s showed that considerable poverty reduction was achieved during the early period. Yet, average poverty rates for the Middle East and North Africa have fluctuated since 1987 as they first decreased for about six years and then they increased by the mid-1990s before declining again toward the turn of the decade. It is worth mentioning that although poverty rates were slightly lower on average in 2001 than in 1987 (regardless of whether they are measured at the $1 or $2 level), the general picture is one of stagnation. In effect, after having reached the lowest levels of absolute poverty among developing regions by the late 1980s, the region failed to make further progress in the period thereafter. In addition, when looking at whether the region performed better or worse in poverty reduction than did other comparable developing regions, the patterns suggest that the Middle East and North Africa performed worse than most. While East Asia and South Asia showed clear gains over the 1990s, and Latin America showed modest gains, the Middle East and North Africa stagnation was similar to that of Sub-Saharan Africa.

Concerning the determinants of these poverty patterns, two main factors are to be pointed out. First, the high levels of public sector employment in most of the countries in the region. The report mentions the statistically significant negative relationship between government employment (as a share of total employment) and the poverty rate (measured at the $1 line) while controlling for per capita Gross Domestic Product (GDP) and inequality (measured by Gini coefficient). It is also reported that the link between government employment and poverty is stronger in Middle

Eastern and North African countries compared to other regions. This finding supports their assertion that "since the early 1970s, a number of South Mediterranean Countries have used public sector employment (including government work) as a kind of blunt policy instrument for providing welfare employment to an ever-increasing proportion of the labor force" (Adams & Page, 2003, p. 2031). The second factor is related to private transfers via remittances as an important source of poverty reduction in the region. The region experienced an economic boom between 1975 and 1985 on the basis of high oil prices. This boom spread throughout the region as workers from countries with large labor forces and/ or low oil resources (such as Egypt and Jordan) migrated to work in the oil-producing countries of the Persian Gulf. At the same time, waves of poor workers from the Maghreb countries began migrating to Western Europe in search of jobs. Thus, large volumes of remittances were generated during 1975–1990 and these are most likely to have accrued to relatively poor families in the labor-exporting countries.

It could be noticed that the way these factors have evolved over time and especially during the 1990s is consistent with growth and poverty trends in the region during the same period. As a matter of fact, during the 1990s both public sector employment and remittances declined on average in the Middle East and North Africa Region, and may have contributed to the relative stagnation of income growth, for instance, public sector employment declined in the 1990s in four of five Middle Eastern and North African countries for which suitable data are available, namely, Algeria, Jordan, Morocco, and Tunisia (World Bank, 2004h, Figure 4.6). The involvement of many of the region's countries in structural adjustment programs explains partially this decline. Similarly, there was a decline in the ratio of workers' remittances to GDP in all the main remittance-receiving countries during the 1990s as in Egypt for instance

remittances declined from around 15 percent of GDP in 1992 to less than 5 percent by 2003.

Last but not least, household survey data make it possible to investigate the relationship between poverty and other household characteristics for which information is typically available: geographic location of the household and the education, employment, occupation, and gender of the head of household. Three observations may be made with respect to the link between poverty and location on the basis of analysis of Middle East and North Africa data. First, there is a clear pattern of poverty rates being higher in rural areas than in urban areas. Second, there is also a clear pattern of some regions being relatively poorer than other regions. Nevertheless, and third, where sufficient data are available and have been analyzed, more complex patterns may also be detected where pockets of high poverty coexist with low poverty in both urban and rural areas and within geographic regions.

Further, the link between employment and poverty extends across three dimensions: sector of employment, nature of occupation, and status of employment. With regard to the sector of employment, the chance of being poor is typically higher for those in the private sector and much lower if one were employed in the public sector. For occupation or nature of economic activity, the chance of being poor is typically highest for those in agriculture and much lower for those in manufacturing or services. Finally, with regard to work status, unpaid workers are more likely to be poor than are paid or self-employed workers, but being unemployed does not necessarily raise the probability of being poor.

Poverty assessments for several countries in the region show that female-headed households are not likely to be poorer than male-headed households at the national level, yet differences in gender-specific poverty rates by geographic region (rural/urban) are notable in the case of many countries in the region.

Poverty and Education

The most recent reports highlight that the region has made improvements in education at a faster rate than other zones; however, the improvements during the period of 1980–2000 have been faster, mainly due to its initial levels of income and education and to its income growth and public spending profile. Primary enrolment data show an increasing trend that provides evidence of improving access to education among the poor. The data concerning education improvements about the countries of the region make it very clear with regard to gross primary enrollment, which has risen rapidly since 1970. Precisely, the rate of increase has been above 95 percent since 1990. Further, enrollment rates have been rising steadily for secondary schooling as well. Yet, despite these substantial improvements in access to education over the past four decades, challenges remain with differences from one country to another in the region. The paramount of these differences is mainly due to the nature of geographic pockets of low access in addition to groups who are still excluded, or who drop out before completing primary education, typically the poor and girls in remote rural areas, the disabled in all income groups, and working and street children in urban areas. Other constraints to access of the poor and girls in rural areas include distance to school and the direct and indirect user costs of schooling. Dropping out of school is attributed to increasing opportunity costs for the poor as children get older, to lack of acceptable facilities and security for girls, and to perceived poor quality and low value of the education provided.

With regard to education and income growth among poor people, most poverty assessments find a high correlation between education status and income status. The Middle East and North Africa Region present the same general pattern. In all cases where detailed analysis of household data has been carried out, poverty rates are the highest for households headed by illiterate people and decline with increased education of the household head. Rationally, poverty and education are negatively correlated. However, are well-off people better educated because they can afford to pay for education? Or are they better off because they are well educated? By looking more closely at the channels through which education reduces poverty some answers can be reached. In this sense, it is believed that education can help a family overcome poverty directly by increasing household income, through increasing the productivity of self-employed workers, or by enabling access to higher-paid jobs. Yet, the report mentions a recent analysis by the World Bank which provided estimates on the return on education for four countries (Egypt, Jordan, Morocco, and the Republic of Yemen) using a common methodology. Generally, the results reflect low rates of return on education, for example, in Morocco the rates of return for males in public employment were 12.4 percent for primary education in 1991, and fell to 6.1 percent in 1999. By way of comparison, Psacharopoulos and Patrinos (2002) reported average returns on investment in education of 20 percent for Asia, 27 percent for Latin America and the Caribbean, and 38 percent for Sub-Saharan Africa. The general impression from these statistics is that education was not a high-yielding investment in Middle Eastern and North African countries during the 1990s. In addition, Morrisson (2002) shows the links between health, education, and poverty reduction. The relationship to government spending is better described in Gupta, Verhoeven, and Tiongson (1999).

Concerning the trends in education spending (for all three levels—primary, secondary, and tertiary) in SMC shows a very clear two-part trend since 1965. In the first part, between 1965 and 1980, education spending per capita rose more than fivefold, from less than $50 to more than $250, corresponds roughly to an increase in the ratio of spending to GDP from 4 percent to

6.5 percent. At this level, SMC, 10 countries not only were spending more on education than their middle-income comparators, but also spending more than OECD countries on average. The second part of the trend, between 1980 and 2000, shows a sharp decline in the 1980s and a slow rise during the 1990s such that the level of spending was just below $200 per capita by the year 2000. The first phase of the trend helps explain the region's strong performance in raising education attainments prior to 1980. The second phase suggests that the region's continued strong performance in education attainment since 1980 must have been due in part to other sources, including improvements in the efficiency of the education delivery system.

More importantly, the poverty impact of public spending on education depends in part on its incidence among income groups. The benefit incidence of expenditure on education in the Middle East and North Africa Region follows the typical pattern of being pro-poor at the basic level, and pro-rich at the tertiary level. Because the poor tend to drop out of the education system earlier than the less poor, and are much less likely to continue to the tertiary level of education, expenditure at the tertiary level inevitably favors those who are better off.

Poverty and Health

The Middle East and North Africa Region have made significant progress in improving the average health status of its citizens. During the last two decades, the rates of progress have been above and beyond what can be explained by its initial levels of income and health in 1980 and subsequent income growth. Measures such as child mortality life expectancy or infant mortality all converge to show a clear-cut and steady health status improvement in most of the region. The question that arises is whether the gains in average health status have also redounded to the benefit of the poor.

Health and wealth are frequently correlated. A sense of the extent of the correlation in this region can be obtained from recent Demographic and Health Survey (DHS) data for Egypt, Jordan, Morocco, and the Republic of Yemen. Across the four countries, on average, health outcomes among the poorest are worse than among the richest, that is, the children of the poorest 20 percent of the population are more than twice as likely to die before they reach their fifth birthday, compared to the children of the richest group; furthermore more four times as many mothers in the poorest group are malnourished with respect to the mothers in the richest group. Thus, while acknowledging the improvements that have occurred to date, it is necessary to pay attention once again to the health inequality challenges that remain. Decision makers in health policies in the region must continue to take into consideration the actions and measures that should be reducing the large disparities that remain between rich and poor people. Through such measures an extension of health insurance coverage to the poor, an allocation of more health resources (such as, hospitals doctors, nurses, and clinics) to rural and poor areas, and implementation of multifaceted community-level interventions to reach the poor.

Fifty percent of health spending in the region accounts for private sector in which insurance accounts only for small fraction. In other words, most private spending represents out-of-pocket outlays. The significant reliance on out-of-pocket spending means that many households have little or no financial protection in the event of a catastrophic illness or injury. Such vulnerability is higher among lower-income households. In general, such households allocate higher proportions of their budgets to health care services. Accordingly, a high priority should be given to the design of sustainable health insurance of those schemes to mitigate the risks among the poor and the near-poor.

Future challenges in health are likely to be different partially from those in the past because of an ongoing demographic and epidemiologic transition. In 1980s and early 1990s the Middle East and North Africa had the highest population growth rate worldwide. In addition, by 2015 it is expected that the number of adults in the region will have increased by 140 percent, representing the highest adult population growth in the world after Sub-Saharan Africa. Further, over the next two decades, health patterns in the Middle East and North Africa will be profoundly influenced by continued declines in fertility and mortality as countries go through the demographic transition. The overall effect of the declines in fertility and mortality is a dramatic shift in the age structure and causes of morbidity and mortality.

The challenges of an aging population include a substantial rise in non-communicable diseases and increasing demand for costly long-term care. In addition to the impact of the demographic transition, rapid urbanization and changing lifestyles have contributed to an increase in non-communicable diseases and injuries in the region. Dealing with these challenges may have implications for the poor. The emerging disease patterns require individual-oriented and technology-intensive treatment regimes that are expensive. Thus, an increasing share of health budget resources is likely to be pulled toward the treatment of such cases. This may put the poor at a disadvantage if the needed resources are taken from services that address their needs. Indeed, there is some evidence that such a shift in resources is already occurring. In recent years, governments in the region have been investing in expensive medical technology to cope with the rising demand from urban middle-class populations. Finding a balance between competing demands to address the demographic and epidemiologic transition and improve access to quality health services for poor people represents a major challenge for the countries in the Middle East and North Africa.

Overall, the key conclusions of this chapter on the issue of poverty and health are (a) despite substantial gains, health disparities continue to exist between the poor and the rich, albeit to different extents in different countries; (b) health spending and outcomes vary among Middle Eastern and North African countries, reflecting different degrees of system efficiency; and (c) coping with the disease patterns emerging from the ongoing demographic transition will require new approaches to health care financing that should aim at protecting budget resources to address the needs of the poor.

An important study about *Public Policy and Poverty Reduction in the Arab Region* edited by Ali Abdel Gadir Ali and Shenggen Fan (2007) includes the contribution of several authors in clarifying the link between public policies and poverty reduction. All Arab countries are identified to have strategic plans for poverty alleviation even though not all countries are suffering from this problem but all countries can be concerned with the poverty reduction.

CONCLUSION

Even if interconnections between health, education, and economic outcomes are intuitively well known by individuals and households, these interdependencies need to be identified and assessed at different levels of aggregation. The expression of these interdependencies helps for a better perception of the role of ICTs in coordinating the interferences of health, education, and economic outcomes.

The empirical applications as underlined in this document are showing the importance of the magnitude of these interdependencies in different economic and social contexts. The central role of the theory that accounts for the different types of assets such as health, knowledge, social capitals, and traditional economic wealth appears to be promising. It introduces a framework that helps understand the foundations of deficits in relation to different wealth components of. This includes the definitions and expressions of poverty. This has also shown how health is a major component in the wealth of individuals and countries as a whole, that is, health can be a major source that ensures economic activities through labor productivity. This relationship can then be enhanced with the other types of assets such as knowledge and social capital.

Attempts to test empirically for interdependencies have been also discussed. They indicate that major steps have been made to investigate the magnitude of the likely gains to be attained when accounting for interdependent and integrated policies. While causality has not yet been established, major progress is expected in this area.

The assessments that have been achieved so far have been expanded through the works of international organizations as well as through the inputs of some individual pioneers. But further investigations are needed, given the deficit of knowledge existing on series of related issues and the types of specialists needed to cover the missing dimensions.

REFERENCES

Acemoglu, D., & Johnson, S. (2006). *Disease and development: The effect of life expectancy on economic growth.* Cambridge, MA: MIT Press. doi:10.3386/w12269

Adams, P., Hurd, M., McFadden, D., Merril, A., & Ribeiro, T. (2003). Healthy, wealthy and wise? Tests for direct causal paths between health and socioeconomic status. *Journal of Econometrics, 112*(1), 3–56. doi:10.1016/S0304-4076(02)00145-8

Aguayo-Rico, A., Guerra-Turrubiates, I., & Montes, R. (2005). Empirical evidence of the impact of health on economic growth. *Issues in Political Economy, 14.* Retrieved from http://org.elon.edu/ipe/aguayorico%20final.pdf

Ali Abdel Gadir, A. (2007). Poverty in the Arab region: A selective review. In Ali Abdel Gadir, A., & Shenggen, F. (Eds.), *Public Policy and Poverty Reduction in the Arab Region.* Safat, Kuwait: The Arab Planning Institute.

Anderson, K., Foster, J., & Frisvold, D. (2004). *Investing in health: The long-term impact of head start.* Working Paper No. 04-W26. Nashville, TN: Vanderbilt University.

Arayssi, M., Sarkis, J. K., & Mardini, R. U. (2006). The value of life: A new labor theory-based model. *Journal of Business Valuation and Economic Loss Analysis, 1*(1). doi:10.2202/1932-9156.1004

Australian Medial Association. (2002). *The links between health and education for indigenous Australian children.* Retrieved from http://ama.com.au/node/508

Ayodeji, A. F., & El-Saharty, S. (2006). Public-health challenges in the Middle East and North Africa. *Lancet, 367,* 961–964. doi:10.1016/S0140-6736(06)68402-X

Bardasi, E., & Francesconi, M. (2003). The impact of a typical employment on individual wellbeing: Evidence from a panel of British workers. *Institute for Social and Economic Research.* Retrieved from http://www.iser.essex.ac.uk/pubs/workpaps/pdf/2003-02.pdf

Behrman, J. R., & Rosenzweig, M. R. (2004). Returns to birth weight. *The Review of Economics and Statistics, 86*(2), 586–601. doi:10.1162/003465304323031139

Bernard, P. (2006). *The lifecourse paradigm in research and in policy*. Paper presented at the First Symposium of the Population, Work and Family Collaboration. Ottawa, Canada. Retrieved from http://policyresearch.gc.ca/doclib/LC/PS_LC_Bernard_200603_e.pdf

Black, L., McTear, M., Black, N., & Harper, R., & Lemon. (2005). Evaluating the DI@l-log system on a cohort of elderly, diabetic patients: Results from a preliminary study. [Lisbon, Portugal: InterSpeech.]. *Proceedings of InterSpeech, 2005*, 821–824.

Bleakley, H. (2007). disease and development: evidence from hookworm eradication in the American south. *The Quarterly Journal of Economics, 122*(1), 73–117. doi:10.1162/qjec.121.1.73

Bloom, D. E., & Canning, D. (2000). The health and wealth of nations. *American Association for the Advancement of Science, 287*(5456), 1207–1209. doi:10.1126/science.287.5456.1207

Bloom, D. E., Canning, D., & Sevilla, J. (2004). The effect of health on economic growth: A production function approach. *World Development, 32*(1), 1–13. doi:10.1016/j.worlddev.2003.07.002

Bobonis, G. J., Miguel, E., & Sharma, C. P. (2006). Anemia and school participation. *The Journal of Human Resources, 41*(4), 692–721.

Bozzoli, C., Deaton, A., & Quintana-Domeque, C. (2007). *Child mortality, income and adult height*. Retrieved from http://papers.nber.org/papers/w12966.pdf

Bridges, J. F. P., & Haywood. (2003). Theory verses empiricism in health economics. *The European Journal of Health Economics, 4*, 90–95. doi:10.1007/s10198-002-0162-1

Brinkley, G. L. (2011). *The macroeconomic impact of improving health: Investigating the causal direction*. Retrieved from http://trc.ucdavis.edu/glbrinkley/Docs/Causal.pdf

Burchell, B., Lapido, D. K., & Wilkinson, F. (1999). Job insecurity and work intensification: Flexibility and the changing boundaries of work. *Joseph Rowntree Foundation*. Retrieved from http://www.jrf.org.uk/knowledge/findings/socialpolicy/849.asp

Case, A., Fertig, A., & Paxson, C. (2003). *From cradle to grave? The lasting impact of childhood health and circumstance*. Retrieved from http://www.nber.org/papers/w9788

Chakraborty, S., & Das, M. (2005). Mortality, human capital and persistent inequality. *Journal of Economic Growth, 10*(2), 159–192. doi:10.1007/s10887-005-1670-5

Chatterjee, M. (1990). *Indian women, their health, and economic productivity*. Discussion Paper 109. Washington, DC: The World Bank.

Chen, W., Engineer, M., & King, I. (2006). *Choosing longevity with overlapping generations*. Dunedin, New Zealand: University of Otago and University of Victoria.

Cutler, D. & Lleras-Muney. (2012). *Education and health: Insights from international comparisons*. NBER Working Paper No. 17738. Washington, DC: NBER program.

Cutler, D., Lleras-Muney, A., & Vogl, T. (2008). *Socio economic status and health: Dimensions and mechanisms*. NBER Working Paper 14333. Washington, DC: NBER.

Cutler, D., Miller, G., & Norton, D. (2007). *Evidence on early-life income and late-life health from America's dust bowl era*. Rochester, NY: University of Rochester. doi:10.1073/pnas.0700035104

Deaton, A. (2003). Health, income, inequality and economic development. *Journal of Economic Literature, 41*(1), 113–158. doi:10.1257/002205103321544710

Deaton, A. (2006). *Global patterns of income and health: Facts, interpretations and policies.* 2006 WIDER Annual Lecture. Retrieved from http://www.wider.unu.edu/events/wider-annual-lecture-2006-announcement.htm

DeJong, J., Shepard, B., Roudi-Fahimi, F., & Ashford, L. (2005). *Young adolescents' sexual and reproductive health and rights: Middle East and North Africa.* Washington, DC: Population Reference Bureau.

Ding, W., Lehrer, S. F., Rosenquist, J. N., & Audrain-McGovern, J. (2007). *The impact of poor health on education: New evidence using genetic markers.* Retrieved from http://post.queensu.ca/~lehrers/genes.pdf

Doyle, O., Harmon, C., & Walker, I. (2005). *The impact of parental income and education on the health of their children. Institute for the Study of Labor, IZA DP No. 1832.* Washington, DC: Institute for the Study of Labor.

El Naggar, D. (2007). Overview: Health sector brief. *The World Bank.* Retrieved from http://web.worldbank.org/Website/External/Contries/MENA/Extmnaregtophealth/0,contentMD K:20 510402~menuPK:583116~pagePK:34004173~pi PK:34003707~theSitePK:583110,00.html

Evans, R. G. (2008). The undisciplined economist. *Health Policy (Amsterdam), 3*(4), 21–32.

Farrell, D., Ghai, S., & Shavers, T. (2005). *The coming demographic deficit: How aging population will reduce global wealth.* Retrieved from http://mkqpreview1.qdweb.net/PDFDownload.aspx?ar=1588

Farrukh, I. (2006). *Sustaining gains in poverty reduction and human development in the Middle East and North Africa.* Portland, OR: Book News, Inc.

Freudenberg, N., & Ruglis, J. (2007). Reframing school dropout as a public health issue. *Preventing Chronic Disease, 4*(4). Retrieved from http://www.cdc.gov/pcd/issues/2007/oct/07_0063.htm

Gan, L., & Gong, G. (2007). *Estimating Interdependence between health and education in a dynamic model.* NBER Working Papers: 12830. Washington, DC: National Bureau of Economic Research, Inc.

Gerdtham, U. G., & Thgren, M. L. (2002). New panel results on co-integration of international health expenditure and GDP. *Applied Economics, 34,* 1679–1686. doi:10.1080/00036840110116397

Grimm, M., & Harttgen, K. (2007). Longer life, higher welfare? *Oxford Economic Papers, 60*(2), 193–211. doi:10.1093/oep/gpm025

Gupta, S., Verhoeven, M., & Tiongson, E. (1999). *Does higher government spending buy better results in education and health care?* Washington, DC: International Monetary Fund, Fiscal Affairs Department.

Gwatkin, D. R., Rutstein, S., Kiersten, J., Eldaw, S., Wagstaff, A., & Amouzou, A. (2007a). *Socio economic differences in health, nutrition, and population, Morocco (1992-2003/04).* Washington, DC: The World Bank.

Gwatkin, D. R., Rutstein, S., Kiersten, J., Eldaw, S., Wagstaff, A., & Amouzou, A. (2007b). *Socioeconomic differences in health, nutrition, and population, Egypt (1995-2000).* Washington, DC: The World Bank.

Gwatkin, D. R., Rutstein, S., Kiersten, J., Eldaw, S., Wagstaff, A., & Amouzou, A. (2007c). *Socioeconomic differences in health, nutrition, and population, Jordan (1997).* Washington, DC: The World Bank.

Gwatkin, D. R., Rutstein, S., Kiersten, J., Eldaw, S., Wagstaff, A., & Amouzou, A. (2007d). *Socioeconomic differences in health, nutrition, and population, Turkey (1993, 1998)*. Washington, DC: The World Bank.

Gwatkin, D. R., Rutstein, S., Kiersten, J., Eldaw, S., Wagstaff, A., & Amouzou, A. (2007e). *Socioeconomic differences in health, nutrition, and population, Yemen (1997)*. Washington, DC: The World Bank.

Handa, S., & Neitzert, M. (1997). *Gender and life-cycle differentials in the impact of health on employment in Jamaica*. Outreach Division Discussion Paper No.16. Washington, DC: International Food Policy Research Institute. Retrieved from http://www.ifpri.org/divs/cd/dp/papers/commdp16.pdf

Hoel, M. (2003). Efficient use of health care resources: The interaction between improved health and reduced health related income loss. *International Journal of Health Care Finance and Economics*, 2, 285–296. doi:10.1023/A:1022308217947

Holmes, C. C., & Adams, N. M. (2002). A probabilistic nearest neighbor method for statistical pattern recognition. *Journal of the Royal Statistical Society. Series B. Methodological*, 64, 295–306. doi:10.1111/1467-9868.00338

Hoxby, C. (2007). Child mortality, income and adult height. *National Bureau of Economic Research*. Retrieved from http://www.nber.org/programs/ed/

Hurd, M., & Kapteyn, A. (2003). Health, wealth, and the role of institutions. *The Journal of Human Resources*, 38(2), 386–415. doi:10.2307/1558749

Hurd, M., & Kapteyn, A. (2005). Health, wealth and the role of institutions. In *Multidisciplinary Economics* (pp. 307–332). Washington, DC: RAND. doi:10.1007/0-387-26259-8_28

Knapp, D. (2007). *The influence of health on labor productivity: An analysis of European conscription data*. (Thesis). The Ohio State University. Columbus, OH.

Lambrinos, J. (1980). Health: A source of bias in labor supply models. *The Review of Economics and Statistics*, 63(2), 206–216. doi:10.2307/1924091

Lee, J., & Kim, H. (2007). A longitudinal analysis of the impact of health shocks on the wealth of elders. *Journal of Population Economics*, 21(1), 217–230. doi:10.1007/s00148-007-0156-5

London Health Commission. (2004). *Sustainable local economies for health project*. Retrieved from http://www.londonshealth.gov.uk/RTF/SLEHP_guidance.doc

Lucas, A. O. (2005). International collaboration in health research. *Bulletin of the World Health Organization*, 83(7), 481–560.

Lynch, W. J., Smith, G. D., Kaplan, G. A., & House, J. S. (2002). Income inequality and mortality: Importance to health of individual income, psychosocial environment, or material conditions. *British Medical Journal*, 320(7243), 1200–1204. doi:10.1136/bmj.320.7243.1200

Maccini, S., & Yang, D. (2008). *Under the weather: Health, schooling, and economic consequences of famines on survivors: Evidence from China's great famine*. IZA Discussion Paper. Washington, DC: IZA.

Mayer-Foulkes, D. (2004). *The intergenerational impact of health on economic growth*. Paper presented at the Global Forum for Health Research, Forum 8. Mexico City, Mexico.

Mayer-Foulkes, D., Aghion, P., & Howitt, P. (2004). *The effect of financial development on convergence: Theory and evidence*. NBER Working Papers 10358. Washington, DC: National Bureau of Economic Research, Inc.

McKeown, T. (1979). *Medicine; health; diseases; public health; philosophy, medical; philosophy; causes and theories of causation.* Princeton, NJ: Princeton University Press.

Miguel, E., & Kremer, M. (2004). Worms: Identifying impacts on education and health in the presence of treatment externalities. *Econometrica, 72,* 159–217. doi:10.1111/j.1468-0262.2004.00481.x

Morrisson, C. (2002). *Health, education and poverty reduction. OECD Development Centre Policy Brief No. 19.* Paris, France: OECD Development Centre.

Muysken, J., Yetkiner, I. H., & Ziesemer, T. (1999). *Health, labour productivity and growth.* CCSO Working Papers 200015. Groningen, The Netherlands: University of Groningen.

Psacharopoulos, G., & Patinos, H. P. (2002). *Returns to investment in education.* Policy Research Working Paper 2881. Retrieved from http://siteresources.worldbank.org/EDUCATION/Resources/278200-099079877269/547664-1099079934475/547667-1135281504040/Returns_Investment_Edu.pdf

Rodriguez, E. (2002). Marginal employment and health in Britain and Germany: Does unstable employment predict health? *Social Science & Medicine, 55,* 963–979. doi:10.1016/S0277-9536(01)00234-9

Ross, C., & Mirowsky, J. (1995). Does employment affect health? *Journal of Health and Social Behavior, 36,* 230–243. doi:10.2307/2137340

Roudi-Fahimi, F. (2005). *Achieving the MDGs in the Middle East: Why improved reproductive health is key.* Washington, DC: Population Reference Bureau.

Roudi-Fahimi, F. (2007). *Gender and equity in access to health care services in the Middle East and North Africa.* Washington, DC: Population Reference Bureau.

Roudi-Fahimi, F., & Ashford, L. (2005). *Investing in reproductive health to achieve development goals, The Middle East and North Africa.* Washington, DC: Population Reference Bureau.

Sandra, E. B., Devereux, P. J., & Salvanes, K. J. (2005). *From the cradle to the labor market? The effect of birth weight on adult outcomes.* Working Paper 11796. Washington, DC: NBER. Retrieved from http://www.nber.org/papers/w11796.pdf?new_window=1

Sarbib, J. L. (2002). *Meeting the public health challenges in the 21st century in the MENA/EM region.* Washington, DC: World Bank.

Schieber, G., Maeda, A., & Klingen, N. (2007). Health reforms in the MENA region. *The World Bank Research Observer, 13*(1), 123–131.

Schultz, T. P. (2005). *Productive benefits of health: Evidence from low-income countries.* New Haven, CT: Yale University.

Schuring, M., Burdorf, L., Kunst, A., & Mackenbach, J. (2006). *The effects of ill health on entering and maintaining paid employment: Evidence in European countries.* Rotterdam, The Netherlands: Department of Public Health, Erasmus MC. Retrieved from http://jech.bmj.com/cgi/content/full/61/7/597

Sen, A. (1998). Mortality as an indicator of economic success and failure. *Economic Journal. Revue Economique et Sociale, 108*(446), 1–25.

Smith, E. R. (1999). *Social identity and social cognition.* Oxford, UK: Blackwell Publishers.

Sommestad, L. (2001). Health and wealth: The contribution of welfare state policies to economic growth. In *Proceedings of the Expert Conference Best Practices in Progressive Governance, 2001.* Institute for Futures Studies.

Strauss, J., & Thomas, D. (1998). Health, nutrition, and economic development. *Journal of Economic Literature, 36*(2), 766–817.

Suhrcke, M., McKee, M., Sauto Arce, R., Tsolova, S., & Mortensen, J. (2005). *The contribution of health to the economy in the European Union*. Retrieved from http://ec.europa.eu/health/ph_overview/Documents/health_economy_en.pdf

Tompa, E. (2002). The impact of health on productivity: Empirical evidence and policy implications. In *The Review of Economic Performance and Social Progress 2002: Towards a Social Understanding of Productivity, 2002*, (pp. 181-202). Retrieved from http://www.csls.ca/repsp/2/emiletompa.pdf

United Nations Development Programme. (2002). *Arab human development report*. New York, NY: UN.

United Nations Development Programme. (2003). *Arab human development report*. New York, NY: UN.

United Nations Development Programme. (2004). *Arab human development report*. New York, NY: UN.

United Nations Development Programme. (2005). *Arab human development report*. New York, NY: UN.

Weil, D. N. (2006). *Accounting for the effect of health on economic growth*. Retrieved from http://weblamp.princeton.edu/chw/papers/Weil_David_Accounting_for_the_Effect_of_Health_on_Economic_Growth_Oct_2006.pdf

Wichmann, T. (1995). *Food consumption and growth in a two sector economy*. Berlin, Germany: Technical University Berlin.

Xu, K., Evans, S. B., Kawabata, D., Zeramdini, R., Klavus, J., & Murray, C. (2003). Household catastrophic health expenditure: A multicounty analysis. *Lancet, 362*, 111–117. doi:10.1016/S0140-6736(03)13861-5

Yamauchi, F. (2006). *Early childhood nutrition, schooling, and sibling inequality in a dynamic context: Evidence from South Africa*. FCND Discussion Paper 203. Washington, DC: FCND.

ENDNOTES

1. Individuals and groups recognize that there are interconnections between different components of wealth and that wealth include health status, knowledge, social capital and economic components. They also recognize that there are material and immaterial sources that are important assets in life. However, these feelings and recognitions are not most of the time considered at the aggregate levels (countries, regions, and other levels of aggregation).

2. Social capital is an important source of wealth to individuals and groups. It accounts for all the relationships recognized and developed by individuals, groups, and society. They include also the professional networks. It starts generally with the family ties without which most societies recognize the likely deficits implied by the loss of one or both parents (orphans). This social capital can be expanded to cover larger networks and relationships.

Chapter 3
Theoretical Model and Foundations for Assessing Interactions of Health, Education, and Economic Outcomes

ABSTRACT

The statistical technique of variance and covariance analysis is widely used in the physical sciences to identify and test inter-relations and interactions. While this technique is also used in the social sciences context, especially in behavioral and experimental economics, it cannot always be directly employed on aggregate economic and social data. This chapter shows how a theoretical framework can be used to guide the empirical analysis of interconnections. The authors introduce the main analytical tools, the key variables, and the datasets needed to assess health and education interdependencies. This chapter sets the grounds for a better understanding of how ICTs that also include analytical software can provide important support for this kind of analysis.

INTRODUCTION

This chapter has two main objectives. The first is to show how health, education, and income can be linked in a theoretical model with empirically testable implications. The second is to use the theoretical model to relate health and education variables to other economic and social indicators.

While a number of empirical studies have identified interdependencies between many variables that underpin human development, there are still controversies in relation to the extent of data and their use in empirical work.

The empirical literature that tackles the issue of health and education as main drivers of human development in the South Mediterranean Region

DOI: 10.4018/978-1-4666-3643-9.ch003

is scant. This is despite it being widely known that the region suffers from a large deficit in both education and health, and a significant part of the population lives in poverty (Arab Human Development Reports, 2002, 2003, 2004, 2005). Furthermore, theoretical models that highlight the channels through which these variables influence each other are limited in scope. Developing theoretical models is desirable because it would enhance the likelihood of empirically sound investigations. Furthermore, focusing on this region of the world would afford a unique opportunity to better understand how the above-mentioned interdependencies operate.

With this objective in mind, we propose a theoretical model and lay out its empirically testable implications. Our main data sources include databases from international organizations. We employ both descriptive and regression analysis to test for interdependencies between health, education, earnings, and other socio-economic variables. Tests are also conducted to examine the roles of gender, socio-economic status, and public policies. The empirical work and the hypothesis testing are pursued in the following chapter. The present one introduces only the bases for the empirical investigations.

LITERATURE REVIEW AND STYLIZED FACTS

This section is devoted to showing the most important findings from previous literature and to supporting the need for further empirical analysis about the interdependencies of health and education.

Literature Review

The relationships between health, education, and poverty have been recently recognized as important sources for major gains in the improvement of public policies, mainly those devoted to poverty reduction. Both theoretical and empirical studies have been providing evidence for these interdependencies. The available literature on this issue, however, provides more empirical studies than theories. The recent contribution of Cutler and Lleras (2006) attempts an evaluation of the theories about and evidence for the relationship between health and education. These authors have noted that the different conclusions reached by different contributors are mainly due to data limitations. Furthermore, this study recognized that not all the related theories have been tested. Using a regression model, the authors found that there is a large magnitude in the relationship between both education and health. Bozzoli, Deaton, and Climent Quintana-Domeque (2007) in their work on child mortality, income, and adult height looked at the effect of income and disease in childhood on adult height. They developed a model of selection and scarring, where childhood disease and lack of nutrition does not necessarily lead to death but could have a long-term effect on adults as expressed in terms of adult height and late-life diseases. The authors found, among other things, that post-neonatal mortality rates predict adult height and late-life diseases. In countries with the highest mortality rates, food availability (measure of income) was added to disease indicators to explain the adult height. The research showed strong evidence that selection is the dominant factor for adult heights over scarring in high mortality and low-income countries, since a harsh health environment leads to survival through selection.

Deaton (2006), in his work "Global Patterns of Income and Health: Facts, Interpretations, and Policies," questioned the benefit of using life expectancy and economic growth to assess the health improvements of different countries. The author considered that life expectancy is a summary measure of overall population health and heavy weighting does not identify the health changes within countries. In addition, the worldwide convergence of life expectancy that was observed during the last decades differs, since gains in longevity in low-life-expectancy countries is caused by the reduction of the infant mortality ratio, while in high-life-expectancy countries it is caused by the reduction of mortality among the middle-age and elder population. Economic growth was also dismissed as a good measure, since its increase does not necessary lead to health improvements.

In response to the question of the effect of increasing life expectancy on economic growth, Acemoglu and Johnson (2006) provided an answer that "there is no evidence that the large exogenous increase in life expectancy led to a significant increase in per capita economic growth." Furthermore, Acemoglu et al. (2006) maintained that these results confirm that global efforts to combat poor health conditions in less developed countries can be highly effective, but also shed doubt on claims that unfavorable health conditions are the root cause of the poverty of some nations. Due to the fact that past studies have not established a causal effect of health and disease environment on economic growth but only cross-country regression between health indicators and economic development, the authors investigated the effect of life expectancy at birth—through the use of epidemiological indicators—on economic growth.

A study conducted by Morrisson (2002) on health, education, and poverty reduction underlined the fact that the 1990 World Development Report did not consider health performance in relation to education and income. The research projects of the OECD Development Centre on "Health, Education, Spending, and Poverty" resulted in a number of findings. They included the expansion of access to public services, meeting the demand for services for the poor, evaluating policies by outcomes rather than through resources, and long-term strategies to overcome poverty with the participation of all stakeholders. The paper also identified avenues for reducing poverty. Measures include subsidies of education expenditures and provision of free health care services in addition

to the reduction of public intervention and the targeting of primary education.

Gupta, Verhoeven, and Tiogson (1999) analyzed public spending and its relation to education and health care. This study showed that the statistical correlation between public spending and education is stronger than it is between public spending and health. It provided an empirical support that indicated that the amount and efficiency of allocations are important for the improvement of education and health care in developing and transitioning countries.

Schultz (2005) focused on the productive benefits of health in low-income countries. Many reasons lead to the lack of consensus on the best way to quantify the cost/benefit of health improvements.

More recently, Gan and Gong (2007), using a theoretical dynamic model, investigated the positive relationships between education using dynamic programming techniques. They concluded that better education leads to better health and better health leads to better education when implementing their model for children under 16 years of age with the introduction of schooling, work, health expenditure, work, and savings as decision variables. The authors performed two policy experiments based on the estimated dynamic model. The first policy experiment concerned a direct college tuition subsidy. The second focused on a high-school health expenditure subsidy. The direct college tuition would favor healthy and people of low academic achievement, while the high-school health expenditure subsidy would favor the unhealthy and people of high academic achievement. The outcome of the policy experiments showed that there is a stronger impact on education attainment when opting for the first policy rather than the second.

Chakraboty and Das (2004) looked at the interaction between health and income in a static two-period model. The authors argued that poverty does not represent a burden for a single generation but that it is accumulated and inherited throughout generations. Initial health inequality can be a measure of the persistence of income inequalities across generations. The authors showed that health status alters individual mortality risk, leading to a change in a person's incentives. Furthermore, with the provision of an efficient public health system, income is not the only determinant of adult mortality risks. The provision of health care services plays a role as well, leading to the reduction of intergenerational inequality and poverty.

Chen, Engineer, and King (2006) used a two-period, overlapping-generations model with production to illustrate the choices individuals make about whether to stay alive in the second period of their lives. Using steady state to get analytical solutions, the authors came up with the observation that within low-income countries, agents in the second-period generation may choose not to live. The higher the income per capita and the growth of the economy are, the lower the fraction of those agents is.

Thus, there is a positive relationship between per capita income and life expectancy. The first observation raised by the authors was the agents' value perceptions of exiting life early. In fact, there would always be a low capital stock value that would not be in favor of staying alive.

Stylized Facts

These are data and statements recovered from a series of publications focusing on the South Mediterranean and MENA countries.

The Infant Mortality in the Arab World

In the 1960s the infant mortality rate in the Arab countries was very high; it was above 157 per 1000 live births, while the world average was around 82 per 1000 live births. During the last 25 years, the urban infant mortality rate decreased by 60% to 80% in the majority of Arab countries. It is in the countries of the Persian Gulf that the changes were the most remarkable. The infant mortality rate

moved back by 91.3% in Qatar, 86.2% in Oman, and 85.5% in Saudi Arabia. However, not all the Arab countries—mainly the Arab sub-Saharan African countries—have been able to decrease significantly their infant mortality rates. The urban infant mortality rate moved back by only 50.4% in Sudan, 48.1% in Mauritania, and 33.3% in Somalia.

Iraq is the single country that faced stagnation in terms of the infant mortality rate (104% in 1979 and 103% in 2003) for reasons that we know. More than half of the infant mortalities in Morocco, in Egypt, and in Palestine take place after the first month after birth (exogenous mortality), while a small proportion of those deaths take place during the first day (endogenous mortality).

It is difficult to fight against this type of premature mortality, which is caused by genetic pathologies (called infant mortality of rich people). Nevertheless, the deaths which take place after the first month of life are related to the environment (e.g., lack of hygiene, unhealthy food, cold) and to the parent's inaction or actions (negligence, violence). It is relatively easy to fight against this "infant mortality of the poor people" by organizing vaccine campaigns and by improving the availability of drinkable water and better sanitation.

For example, in Morocco only 71% of the population has a sustainable access to improved water sources, and 76% have access to improved sanitation. In Bahrain, Qatar, and Kuwait less than one-third of infant deaths occur beyond the first month of life. Seventy-three percent of Bahraini newborns die during their first week of life. This proportion is 53% in Kuwait and 49% in Qatar. Conversely, the percentage of newborn dead beyond the first month of life is, respectively, 20%, 32%, and 3%.

This profile of infant mortality reflects the relatively better capacity of the municipal and sanitary local authorities to fight the avoidable causes of death such as infectious and parasitic diseases, malnutrition, or trauma.

The challenge which arises at the moment in these countries is the fight against the endogenous infant deaths that are caused by deformities, difficult deliveries, or genetic pathologies (e.g., congenital heart diseases, and trisomies). Three major groups of countries can be identified. The first group includes the oil states of the Persian Gulf as well as Tunisia. In this group of countries, there is a dominance of congenital abnormalities: 44.8% of the deaths in Bahrain, 43.8% in Kuwait, and 34.2% in Qatar. There is a low rate of infant mortality from infectious or parasitic diseases and malnutrition.

This structure of infant mortality shows a very favorable sanitary situation, because those newly born who do die essentially for endogenous reasons that are independent of the environment.

The second group is composed of Morocco, Palestine, and Egypt. In these countries there is a dominance of infant mortalities which are due to infectious and parasitic diseases. In Morocco 80% of the infant deaths happen after the first month of life; this rate is 55% in Egypt and 52% in Palestine.

It is possible to fight against this type of infant mortality by improving vaccine coverage and encouraging good habits of hygiene and nutrition. In this second group of countries, the local authorities and, in particular, the municipalities and the local clinics are on the front line and have a big responsibility in the reduction of the risks incurred by children. Between these two groups of extreme countries are situated the other Arabic nations, at diverse points along the scale of completion of the infant epidemiological transition. In this third category of countries, the local authorities can also play a significant role in the minimization of infant risk.

The Arab countries have the lowest level of freedom for their population. Women remain marginalized, and the participation of Arab women in their countries' political and economic life is the lowest in the world. In nearly all Arab countries, women suffer from unequal citizenship and lack of legal entitlements. Only four Gulf countries—Bahrain, Qatar, Oman, and Kuwait—have given voting rights to women. The proportion of women in parliament in Arab countries is extremely low. They occupy 3.5% of all seats in parliaments compared to 4.2% in East Asia, 11% in sub-Saharan Africa, 12.7% in South East Asia and the Pacific, and 12.9% in the Latin American and Caribbean countries. Rapid improvements before 1990 raised hopes that mortality rates for infants and children under five could be cut by two-thirds in the following 25 years. However, progress slowed almost everywhere in the 1990s. No region except possibly Latin America and the Caribbean is on track to achieve that target.

Progress has been particularly slow in Sub-Saharan Africa, where civil disturbances and the HIV/AIDS epidemic have driven up rates of infant and child mortality in several countries.

Child mortality is closely linked to poverty. In 2001, the average rate of under-five mortality was 121 deaths per 1000 live births, 41 in lower-middle income countries, and 27 in upper-middle income countries. In high-income countries the rate was less than 7. For 70% of the deaths before the age of five, the cause is a disease or a combination of diseases and malnutrition that would be preventable in a high-income country: acute respiratory infections, diarrhea, measles, and malaria.

Improvements in infant and child mortality have come slowly in low-income countries (such as Yemen and Mauritania), where mortality rates have fallen by only 12% since 1990. Upper-middle income countries have made the greatest improvement, reducing average mortality rates by 36%. Unfortunately, even this falls short of the rate needed to reach the target.

Just as child deaths are the results of many causes, reducing child mortality will require multiple, complementary interventions. Raising incomes will help increase public spending on health services. However, more is needed. Access to safe water, better sanitation facilities, and improvements in education especially for girls and mothers are closely linked to reduced mortality. Also needed are roads to improve access to health facilities and modern forms of energy to reduce dependence on traditional fuels, which cause damaging indoor air pollution.

Maternal Mortality

According to the World Bank (2003), about 500,000 women died during pregnancy and childbirth in 2000, most of them in developing countries. What makes maternal mortality such a compelling problem is that it strikes young women undergoing what should be a normal process. The difference in outcomes is enormous between those who live in rich countries, where the average maternal mortality ratio is around 21 deaths per 100,000 live births, and those who live in poor countries, where the ratio may be as high as 1,000 deaths per 100,000 live births.

The Millennium Development Goal (MDG) calls for reducing the maternal mortality ratio by three-quarters between 1990 and 2015. For this to be possible, women need access to modern health services. The share of births attended by skilled health staff provides a great index of where the need is greatest. Only 58% of women in developing countries give birth with the assistance of a trained midwife or doctor.

Significant progress in reducing maternal mortality will require a comprehensive approach to health care: deaths in childbirth often involve complications such as hemorrhaging that require fully equipped medical facilities. Causes of complications during pregnancy and childbirth include inadequate nutrition, unsafe sex, and poor health care. Gender inequalities in controlling household resources and making decisions also contribute to poor maternal health. Early childbearing and closely spaced pregnancies increase the risks for mothers and children. Access to family planning services, helps women plan whether and when to have children.

Education

A major mismatch exists between the output of educational systems and labor market needs. The mismatch is compounded by the increasingly rapid change in these needs brought about by globalization and the needs of accelerating technology.

About 65 million adult Arabs are illiterate. Two out of three are women. These illiteracy rates are much higher than in much poorer countries. This challenge is unlikely to disappear quickly. Ten million children between 6 and 15 years of age are currently out of school; if current trends persist, this number will increase by 40% by 2015.

There is a low quality of education associated with the lack of mechanism for intellectual. Arab countries' access to and use of cutting-edge technology, exemplified by Information and Communication Technology (ICT), is very limited; only 0.6% of the population uses the Internet, and the personal computer penetration is only 1.2%.

More generally, investment in research and development does not exceed 0.5% of the GNP, well below the world average. Three major deficits in the Arab world today are freedom, knowledge, and women's rights.

The Arab human development report reveals that illiteracy rates in the Arab world are still higher than the international average and even higher than the average in the developing countries; even though MENA countries invest a high proportion of their GDP in education compared to other regions.

The education of females has a particular bearing on nutrition, health care, and hygiene. Several studies suggest that the education of females is positively correlated with a significant increase in immunization and children mortality rates. It has been estimated that the children of mothers who have completed their primary school have 20% less malnutrition than those of illiterate mothers.

Education is the key to human development, progress, and competitiveness. No country can hope to improve without making a heavy investment in human development, especially in education. AHD 2003 concludes that the status of knowledge in the Arab world in terms of demand, production, and dissemination is grossly inadequate and ineffectual. AHD 2004 points out that scientific research in the Arab countries is less than 1/7 of the world average (0.5% in Arab countries). There is a weak basic research and almost a total absence of advanced research fields such as IT and molecular biology. These countries have one of the lowest levels of research finding in the world.

The average number of scientists and engineers working in research and development in Arab countries 371 per million people while the world average – including countries in Asia, Africa, and Latin America—is 979 per million people. The number of books published in the Arab world does not exceed 1.1% of world production; the number of books translated from foreign languages into Arabic is negligible.

The global economy is a knowledge economy, one that uses the Internet, various media, and ICT. The economic and social scenario in most Muslim countries is defined by low or stagnant growth, low productivity, wide income disparities, injudicious use of most resources, a heavy burden of debt, escalating employment rates, rising inflation, and insensitive administration. The GDP of all Arab states combined was $531.2 billion, less than that of a single middle-sized European country.

There are 22 Arab states with 280 million people, who constitute about 5% of the global population. The AHD reported in 2002 that 20% of the population, still lives on less than $2 a day. Nearly 50% of labor force is unemployed. According to an internal labor organization study, of the 88 million unemployed males between 15 and 24 years, almost 26% are in the Middle East and North Africa. According to the AHD report of 2002, the number of the telephone lines in the Arab world is barely one-fifth of that in developed countries. Access to digital media in the Arab

world is among the lowest in the world. There are just 18 computers per 1000 people in the region, compared to the global average of 78.3 per 10,000 people. Only 1.6% of the Arab world has Internet access. The AHDR reports of 2002, 2003, and 2004 tell a sad story of failed planning, lack of vision, and poor strategy. One inescapable conclusion that emerges from the reports is that the Arab world is in deep decline, even when it is compared to the developing countries.

The Economic Situation

Low productivity in the Arab world does not stem from lack of natural resources or low domestic investment rates. There is plenty of skilled labor and plenty of capital. The problem is that financial markets in the Arab world do not channel capital into its most productive and efficient uses. Most capital is controlled by a small number of financial institutions that cater to a select, privileged cohort. Those who have capital are not competing vigorously to find productive projects, while credit-worthy entrepreneurs and small business that need capital cannot find it.

Stock markets in the Arab world are very small, illiquid, and poorly regulated with annual reports are not published in a timely manner.

Population Challenges and Unemployment

Over the past 50 years, this region experienced the highest rate of population growth of any region in the world. The total population increased from around 100 million in 1950 to around 380 million in 2000. During this period, the population of the MENA region increased 3.7 times more than any other major region. Regardless of the economic development or national income, MENA governments are increasingly challenged to provide the basic needs—adequate housing, sanitation, health care, jobs, and education—for a growing number of citizens and to combat poverty, narrow the gap between the rich and the poor, and generally improve the standard living. In addition, the region's scarce water resources need to be managed in the face of growing demand where the water reserves in this region represent 1%. A third of the MENA population is under 15.

Over the next 15 years, these children and the adolescents will reach their childbearing years and enter the job market. In most MENA countries, the number of women of childbearing age (15 to 49 years) will at least double in the next 30 years. Providing quality reproductive health services to a growing number of women is a challenge and a key to slowing population growth. As MENA's total population increases, so does its elderly population and with it a health burden that has important implications for the cost and configuration of health systems. For example, the elderly population of Egypt (60 years and older) is expected to grow from 1 million in 2000 to 7.7 million in 2050.

MENA's working-age population is growing rapidly. In Jordan, five Jordanians under the age of 15 are poised to enter the labor market for every Jordanian aged 45 to 60 nearing retirement age; in Saudi Arabia, that ratio was 8 to 1 in 1996. The ratio of the economically inactive to the economically active population is the highest in the world.

Because of its young age structure and low level of female labor force participation, the proportion of the population that is economically active is lower in MENA than in all other regions. According to the International Labor Organization (ILO) are found in MENA.

MENA countries are currently more likely to experience "brain drain," as large numbers of educated people leave the region for Europe, North America, and other parts of the world. The MENA unemployment rate is the highest in the world. The Egyptian economy, for example, needs to create an additional 500,000 new jobs each year to absorb new entrants into its job market. Given

some of the oil rich countries in the Gulf such as Saudi Arabia, which have traditionally had no employment, are faced with youth unemployment.

Women in MENA have the highest rate of unemployment in the world. According to the ILO, the largest gender gaps in unemployment are found in MENA. Unemployment rates in Egypt were reported to be 24% for women and 7% for men in 1995.

The human development reports (2002, 2003, 2004, 2005) have shown large deficits in different aspects of human development in the region. The areas of health and knowledge have shown large deficits and are key factors in limiting people's access to better lives.

The importance of health and education has been recognized since the early work of Sen (1998, p. 19). This author said that the "quality of life depends on various physical and social conditions, such as the epidemiological environment in which a person lives. The availability of health care and the nature of medical insurance (public as well as private) are among the important influences on life and death. Besides that, the international community has embarked since 2000 in achieving Millennium Development Goals (MDGs). These goals cover poverty, illiteracy, health, education, and environment among others. Furthermore, since the publication of the first world human development report in 1990, more emphasis has been placed on the monitoring of human development as it is annually covered under world, regional, and country reports. These trends imply that most developing countries, including those in the South Mediterranean region, have been involved in policies and actions aimed at promoting better livelihoods for their populations.

As different empirical reports and studies suggest, human development policies do have important interdependencies that should be better identified. These identifications would help in refining the knowledge and the directions of policy actions that could enhance the level of promotion of the attainment of the MDGs as well as the enhancement of living conditions for the population.

THEORETICAL MODEL[1]

In relation to economic development theories and as shown by earlier works in economics and the publications related to human development, individuals own different types of assets that are inter-related in a given environment (economic, political, social, and natural). The major assets considered are economic, health, knowledge, and social capital. While it is easy to show that economic capital includes assets and liabilities besides the flows of income and returns generated from economic activities, it is more difficult to show how other assets are formed. It can be underlined, though, that, in terms of capital, health capital refers to all the physical and mental characteristics of an individual during his or her lifespan. Knowledge capital includes the experience of and mainly the level of education of an individual. The network or social capital refers to the gains and external effects obtained from being a member of a group, which can be family and/or professional and social group or club. These levels of capital do change throughout the lifespan of any individual. Different levels of capital can be related to different stages of the human growth curve. The levels of different capitals at different stages of life define also the levels of vulnerability of any individual. While generally economic and knowledge capitals can be lacking at the beginning of life; health and social capitals do determine the level of vulnerability of children. For example, orphans do suffer from the absence of parents and thus are socially vulnerable. Bad health during the early years leads also to a vulnerable existence with negative impacts on a person's growth curve. Orphans with health limitations are more vulnerable than orphans with better health. At the other extreme, when older,

individuals can suffer mainly from limitations in their health and social capital, but those who have the knowledge and the economic capital can suffer less than their poorer counterparts in the effort to attain the highest stages of their growth curve.

Despite the existence of a large body of investigative studies (see literature review), as noted above, most are empirical and only a few have offered theoretical models recently (2004-2007) to support the existence of interdependencies between development variables and (mainly) those relating to health, education, and income. These contributions have notably come from Gan and Gong (2007), Chakraborty and Das (2004), and Chen, Engineer, and King (2006). However, as noted by Cutler and Lleras-Muney (2006), not all the existing theories have been tested, and most of the empirical work is not supported by theory.

The theoretical models appear to be converging with regard to the identification of the likely interdependencies between health, education, and income, especially in the context of developing economies. Based on these frameworks, a new model is established to unify the above theoretical frameworks and strengthen their validity. This new model follows mainly the assumptions and the most important steps of Chakraborty and Das (2004) but introduces expenditures on education instead of savings. But the new model accounts also for features shown in Chakraborty and Bhattacharya (2012) and in Chakraborty (2004).

This is a static framework where individuals live for two periods, a first period as "young" with certainty and a second period as "old" with a given probability that depends on health status. The individual is assumed to work in both periods of life and earn an income (ω). In the first period, the individual also receives as inheritance from the older generation a certain amount of wealth (W). Out of this income the agent consumes (c_1) and invests in education (e) and in health (h). At the beginning of the second period of life, the individual is faced with a mortality shock with the probability $[1 - m_s(h)]$. If the agent survives till the next period, he will earn a given gross return on his investment in education (R) in the form of an increase in salary. The agent who survives uses his wealth (wage + return on education) for consumption in the second period (c_2) and as an amount of wealth left for his children as inheritance (I).

Under these assumptions, the budget constraints are:

$$c_1 + e + h = \omega + W \qquad (1)$$

$$c_2 + I = \omega + \mathrm{Re}. \qquad (2)$$

Assuming a zero utility from death and that both u and v are concave utilities, the expected utility of this agent during his lifetime is:

$$U = u(c_1) + m_s(h)[u(c_2) + a.v(I) \qquad (3)$$

The individual maximizes this utility subject to (1) and (2).

The agent's survival beyond the first period depends on health investment during youth (h) given the following assumed definitions:

$$m_s = m_s(h) \in [0,1]$$

$$m_s(0) = 0, m_s' > 0, m_s'' \leq 0 \text{ and}$$
$$\lim_{h \to \infty} m_s(h) = \bar{m}_s \leq 1$$

$$m_s(h) = \begin{cases} ah^\gamma, if \ h \in [0,\hat{h}] \ where \\ \hat{h} \equiv (\bar{m}_s / a)^{1/\gamma} \\ \bar{m}_s, \ otherwise \end{cases} \qquad (4)$$

The utility functions are defined as follows for more convenience:

$$u(c) = \frac{c^{1-\delta}}{1-\delta} \text{ and } v(I) = \frac{I^{1-\delta}}{1-\delta} \text{ given that}$$
$$\delta \in (0,1). \qquad (5)$$

An additional assumption is made about the following parametric restriction: $\delta > \gamma$.

The first order necessary conditions linked to e, h and I are (see Appendix):

Therefore, the necessary condition associated with e is the following:

$$\frac{\partial U}{\partial e} = u'(c_1) + m_s(h)u'(c_2) =>$$
$$(c_1)^{-\delta} = R.m_s(h).(c_2)^{-\delta} \qquad (6)$$

$$\frac{\partial U}{\partial h} = u'(c_1) + m_s'(h)[u(c_2) + a.v(I)] =>$$

$$(1-\delta)(c_1)^{-\delta} = m_s'(h)[(c_2)^{1-\delta} + \alpha I^{1-\delta}] \qquad (7)$$

$$\frac{\partial U}{\partial I} = m_s(h)[u'(c_2) + a.v'(I)] =>$$
$$I = \alpha^{1/\delta}.c_2. \qquad (8)$$

So, $c_2 = \beta R h \qquad (9)$

where $\beta = \dfrac{(1-\delta)}{\gamma(1+\alpha^{1/\delta})}$ (see Appendix).

Using the two budget constraints (1) and (2), the two-period budget constraint is the following:

$$c_1 + h + \frac{c_2}{R} + \frac{I}{R} = y \text{ (see Appendix)},$$

where $y = (1 + 1 / R)\omega + W$ is the present discounted value of lifetime income.

Using Equations (6), (8), and (9), the following expression results:

$$f(h) = h + \beta h[1 + a^{1/\delta} + \frac{R^{1-1/\delta}}{[m_s(h)]^{1/\delta}} = y,$$

$$(10)$$

where the concavity of $f(h)$ is ensured only when $\delta > \gamma$ meaning that $f(h)$ is increasing.

Equation (10) implicitly defines health expenditure as a function of income, $h = \eta_0(y)$.

When $y > \hat{y}$, given that $\eta_0(\hat{y}) = \hat{h}$, the survival probability doesn't increase with health investment beyond $\hat{h}$, so health investment is kept at the level $\hat{h}$ for all income levels.

The associated first order conditions, when $\hat{h}$ is considered, are:

$$(c_1)^{-\delta} = \bar{m}_s . R . (c_2)^{-\delta}$$

$$(c_2)^{-\delta} = \alpha . I^{-\delta}.$$

This gives the following results (see Appendix):

$$c_1 = \left[\frac{1}{1 + \rho(1 + a^{1/\delta})}\right](y - \hat{h}),$$

$$c_2 \left[\frac{\rho}{1 + \rho(1 + a^{1/\delta})}\right] R(y - \hat{h})$$

$$I = \left[\frac{a^{1/\delta}\rho}{1 + \rho(1 + a^{1/\delta})}\right] R(y - \hat{h}),$$

$$e = \left[\frac{\rho(1 + a^{1/\delta})}{1 + \rho(1 + a^{1/\delta})}\right](y - \hat{h}) - \frac{\omega}{R}, \qquad (11)$$

where $\rho \equiv (\bar{m}_s)^{1/\delta} R^{1/\delta-1}$.

From the results (11), it is clear that interdependencies exist in this theory between health, education and the level of income (poverty) of individuals. While these theoretical results can be intuitive and show how economic, education, and health variables are interconnected, they need to be empirically confirmed in real contexts us-

ing appropriate data. The context selected in this study and in the following chapters is the South Mediterranean countries. The above equations show that there are both simultaneous equations to be estimated for different variables with specific hypotheses and tests to be conducted both at the country and at the regional levels. It is obvious that, when aggregating the above decision rules on individuals in a given economy and over countries, the simultaneous equations framework is preserved.

EMPIRICAL METHODS

The study of interdependencies of health, education, and poverty within the theoretical framework underlined above requires empirical evidence based on the available and accessible data. This section introduces the empirical methods and the variables and data used in this study.

While the most relatively complete work cited in the literature review integrates not only the economic variables with health but also all the other socioeconomic factors including education (Hurd & Kapteyn, 2003), similar methods are used in the current report. While attempts at identification of directions of causality were made by Hurd and Kapteyn (2003), the on-going analysis is only devoted to showing the relationships between different sets of variables as in Bernard (2004). The procedure set in Adams, Hurd, McFadden, Merril, and Ribeiro (2003) between socioeconomic status and health conditions is also adopted herein.

As in Cutler and Lleras-Muney (2006), linear models are specified as:

$$H_i = c + \beta E_i + \delta X_i + \varepsilon_i$$

where H_i measures an individual's, i, health or health behavior, E_i measures i's educational achievement, X_i is a vector of individual characteristics that includes race, gender and age; c is a constant term; and ε_i is the classical error term. β

is the education gradient and measures the impact of one more year of education on health. In the above contribution, the first estimation evaluates the relationship between the years of schooling and the five-year morbidity (that is, whether an individual died within five years of the interview) and between the years of schooling and self-reported health status. Following the above authors, the relationships between education and health apply to developed and developing countries taken individually. It applies also across countries.

Grossman (2005) analyzed the impact of education on non-market outcome. The outcomes he discussed include general consumption; savings; the rate of growth of consumption over time; a subject's own health; and inputs into the production of a person's own health and fertility, a child's health, and cognitive development.

Clearly, there are higher earnings and wages to be gained by higher education, but the non-market outcomes that the author considered are those associated with the time that the consumer spends outside the labor market.

The author presented several conceptual frameworks that generate the effects of education on non-market outcomes and summarize and criticize empirical evidence related to these effects. He focuses on health outcome.

He considered models in which education has productive and allocative efficiency effects. The models are modified to take into account the fact that the nature of schooling decisions is endogenous. The schooling effect can be attributed to omitted variables. One possible variable here is the orientation toward the future. This is complicated by the fact that education affects this orientation.

In an earlier effort, Strauss and Duncan (1998) looked at the relationship between health, nutrition, and development. In this study, the authors focused on education and health, both as related to labor market successes. While the link between education and labor market has been largely studied, that of health and labor market, has received less attention. This latter link is particularly important for developing economies.

For the above authors, various models related nutrition, productivity, and wages with marginal productivity of health higher in the developing countries because the health levels were lower and the nature and prevalence of diseases such as malnutrition higher in developing countries. Children in developing countries are more likely to be ill, and the health of adults is more likely to depend on early life conditions. In the context of the developing world, the consequences of a lower level of health will be more pronounced for the poor.

In the developing countries, the credit constraints imply that the health investment might be below efficient levels in poor households. In addition, the allocation of health-related inputs within the household is likely to depend on the activity.

The authors' review in the chapter presents correlations between health and labor outcomes. If better health is associated with better productivity and income, then more income will be invested in health care. As productivity increases, income increases and that additional income can be invested in matters of health. The direction of causality here will need to be identified.

Health status has to be distinguished from other human capital measures, but it is multidimensional and difficult to measure.

Studying the stature of individuals in the United States, Brazil, Vietnam, and Ivory Cost, the author finds that changes over time in the stature of individual men and women give information on health and development over the long term. In all four populations, the gains in height have been substantial. These gains were important for all the countries except Vietnam during the war. There are differences between men and women. Within countries, there are also differences by regions. Using household data makes it clear that there is evidence that income and health are related.

The authors present non-parametric estimates of the bivariate relationship between height and log hourly wages. There is a strong association between height and wages in Brazil and the United States, the effect being higher in Brazil.

The authors have also shown that health and education are related. Here height is used as an indicator of investment in health during childhood. The correlation between adult stature and years of schooling indicates that taller men tend to be better educated in both countries. This correlation is substantially larger in Brazil.

The authors described in detail the theoretical developments allowing a better understanding of the behaviors that underlie associations between health and labor market decisions. They also reviewed the efforts made by physicians and epidemiologists in measuring health. They pointed out that health is difficult to measure because health is multidimensional. In addition, different measures of health will have different impacts on labor outcomes.

The different measures of health which they discussed are self-reported health status, self-reported morbidities, limitations to normal activities, measures of physical functioning, and nutrition-based health measures. They present the nature of the information imbedded in each measure and the measurement error it may include.

One point that seems important, given the results of the study, is the result that self-evaluations reflect perceptions of health. These perceptions are related to values background, beliefs, and information, which are all related to socio-economic status including income and wages. The information of health status is necessarily linked to the use of the health care system. If health facilities are not available and since most people assume that they are in good health unless informed to the contrary, it is likely that those with lower access to the health system are more likely to report better health. Various experiments show evidence of this phenomenon.

The authors concluded that substantial progress has been made in documenting the link between health and productivity and wages in low-income economies using both experimental and non-experimental methods. A small number of studies have shown that an improvement in health has a larger return at very low levels of health and for specific types of jobs. Health and income are clearly linked one to the other but also to other factors where the relationship is ambiguous.

Based on the above modeling efforts and on types of data available, two approaches have been pursued. The first one is based on the analysis of country data as supported by existing international data and local information. The second approach is achieved using regional data that uses panels covering some or all countries included in the study. The results related to each approach are introduced respectively in the following chapters.

The methods used for the analyses and testing of interdependencies of health, education, and economic performance of the economies of the South Mediterranean Countries (SMC) include mainly descriptive statistics and regression analysis based on the theoretical simultaneous equation models.

Descriptive analysis accounts for principal component analysis and factor determination used when dealing with panels of data covering several countries. The aim of this analysis is to identify the most important variables among those covered under health, education, and socio-economic variables. It is also used to compare countries in relation to their performance in relation to the chosen variables. Grouping of countries is then achieved through this analysis that is completed with correlation and regression analyses. The correlation analysis of the different clusters is mainly used to complete the regression analysis in the evaluation of the relationships. Since correlation does not necessarily imply causation between two variables (e.g., health and income, education and income), the assessment of a potential relationship can only be determined with the regression analysis of the clusters.

In addition, the correlation is likely to show the strength and direction of a linear relationship. Regression analysis consisted in running ordinary linear least square estimation on different sets of dependent and explanatory variables. This technique has been used in different sections of this report where variables are logarithmic most of the time to ensure a better interpretation of the results.

Simultaneous equation estimations have been used on systems of independent relationships where ordinary linear least square estimation has been useful to assess the parameters related to each single equation. The underlying approach here is that the aggregate economy of the region is under the effects of a system of relationships that relate health, education, and socio-economic variables. Given that each sub-set of variables includes series of variables, different dependent and explanatory variables have been selected to ensure the independency of the error related to each equation in the system.

VARIABLES

The variables include education, health, and economic dimensions that are explained below.

Education

Education indicators used relate to three main fields: education outcomes, participation in education, and education inputs.

The education outcomes variables are assessed by the total adult literacy rate (age 15 and above), the total youth literacy rate (from age 15 to age 24). The two measures of education outcomes only cover the year 2004. The total adult literacy rate is the percentage rate of people aged from 15 years and older who can understand while reading and writing sentences from their everyday life, while the calculation of the total youth literacy rate only differs from the adult literacy rate by the age range (15 years to 24 years).

Measures of participation in education include the number of children out of school in primary education in 2000, the mean years of schooling

(age 15 and above) in 2000, the pre-primary school life expectancy in years (from 1999 to 2004), and the primary to tertiary school life expectancy in years (from 1999 to 2004). The children out of school indicator concerns the number of children who are out of primary school education while they are still of primary school age. The mean years of schooling provide an indication of skills acquired during an estimated average period of schooling. The pre-primary school life expectancy represents the number of years that a pre-primary-school-age child should expect to spend in his/her pre-primary school. The primary to tertiary school life expectancy predicts the expected number of years that an enrolled student should spent from primary to tertiary education.

Education inputs were only illustrated by the pupil-teacher ratio from 1999 to 2004. They represent the number of students enrolled in primary schools over the number of primary education teachers.

Adult Literacy Rate

From the correlation analysis table, we can observe the variability of the results from cluster to cluster. The high as well as the low human development countries show a complete independence from the adult literacy rate and the GDP per capita. The European Union obtains a small negative correlation, while both the medium human development and major oil net exporters have average positive correlations. By exceeding 50%, world and SMC clusters prove that there is a large positive linear dependency between respective adult literacy rates and GDP per capita.

Children out of Primary School

Concerning the children out of primary school and their potential linear dependence with GDP per capita, this measure generally displays reverse correlations. Both oil exporting countries and the EU clusters show great disparity in their results. The oil exporters' correlation moved from no dependence from 1999-2001 to small positive dependence in 2002 and 2003. In 2004, the oil-exporting cluster even got a correlation that equals 30%. European Union countries also moved from a small positive linear dependence in 1999 to medium negative correlation in 2004. For the high human development countries, the correlation table indicates a regular, positive, and small linear dependence between the number of children out of primary school and the GDP per capita. All the remaining clusters demonstrate a reverse linear dependency between the two variables; the difference consists in their respective degree of dependence. The world cluster tends to present a decreasing correlation that changed from -24% in 1999 to -16% in 2004. The SMC region keeps the range of the correlations between 30% and 40%. Regarding the low human development countries, they have very high linear dependencies since their correlations exceed 70% in all the covered years.

Mean Years of Schooling

The correlations of the mean years of schooling and the GDP per capita can be divided among three main groups. The first group includes the European Union, which almost proved independence between the two variables, with its score of 8%. The second group comprises the low and medium human development countries, with scores of interdependencies of 36% and 47%, respectively. The last group contains world, SMC, oil exporters, and high human development countries that demonstrated a strong linear dependence between the mean years of schooling and the GDP per capita.

Pre-Primary School Life Expectancy

The correlation analysis of the pre-primary school life expectancy reveals various inconsistencies, especially for the low human development and EU clusters. The European Union had correlations displaying no linear dependence except for 2004.

In that year the correlation equals -16%, implying a relatively small linear dependence. In 1999 and 2000, the correlation results of low human development countries were nearly equal to zero. Starting from 2001, the correlation jumped to 22% and then remained approximately stable at 15%. Both high and medium human development countries had relatively stabilized correlations from 1999 to 2002. Starting from 2003, their degrees of linear dependence started to drop drastically. The three remaining clusters (world, SMC, and oil exporting countries) have a strong positive linear dependence.

Primary to Tertiary School Life Expectancy

While observing the correlations obtained from primary to tertiary school life expectancy and the GDP per capita variables, we notice that a large majority of clusters display a positive linear dependence. The disparity between those positive dependencies relies on their strength. Besides the low human development countries that show large negative correlations, the remaining clusters' correlations are all positive. The medium human development countries illustrate irregular trends in their correlations. From 1999 to 2003, the correlations of medium human development countries dropped by 9%, and in 2004, it returned back to the 1999 rate. For the European Union, there is a clear decreasing trend with a correlation that moves from 42% in 1999 to 17% in 2004. The remaining clusters (SMC, oil exporters, world, and high human development countries) obtained significant degrees of linear dependence between primary to tertiary school life expectancy and the GDP per capita.

Pupil-Teacher Ratio

The correlation analysis of the pupil-teacher ratio shows a more uniform set of results than the other education indicators. The European Union made the exception, compared to the rest of clusters, by showing independence of its pupil-teacher ratio and the GDP per capita. The remaining clusters have medium to large negative correlations that vary from -39% to -70%.

Youth Literacy Rate

From the correlations of the different clusters that concern the youth literacy rate and the income indicator, we can identify three sets. The first set comprises the low human development countries, with a small negative correlation (-20%). The second group is composed of the European Union countries. The latter has a small correlation percentage of 22%. The last group includes SMC, world, major oil net exporters, and high and medium human development countries.

Health

Health measurements presented in the database cover three major topics: population dynamics, mortality, and reproductive health. The population dynamics are drawn from the crude death rate per 1,000 people. Due to the lack of continuous death rate data across countries, only the years 1995, 1997, 2000, 2002, 2003, and 2004 are registered. The death rate gives the estimated number of deaths per 1,000 people in a country at mid-year.

Mortality is illustrated with the following indicators: infant mortality rate per 1,000 live births, under-five mortality rate per 1,000, and total life expectancy at birth in terms of years. Both infant and under-5 mortality rates have available statistics for 1995, 2000, and 2004. The figures for life expectancy at birth cover the same years as the death rate. The infant mortality rate represents the number of children dying before their first year among 1,000 live births per year. The under-five mortality rate represents the probability that a child would die before reaching his/her fifth year, knowing that the child is subject to the actual, age-specific mortality rates. Life expectancy at birth embodies the probability that a born infant would live, giving that the mortality conditions

stay the same from the day of the child's birth to his/her death.

Reproductive health is shown by the maternal mortality ratio per 100,000 live births. This latter only covers 1995 and 2000, and it shows the number of mothers who died because of pregnancy and childbirth over 100,000 live births.

Death Rate

While analyzing the correlations between the death rate and the income per capita, we noticed that the human development clusters have distinguishing characteristics. High, medium, and low human development countries have correlations approximately equaling zero, with few exceptions. Those exceptions concern the medium human development that had a zero correlation starting from 2000, while the low human development had zero correlation starting from 2002. In other words, human development clusters' death rate is independent of the GDP per capita. Distinguished by their degree of independence, regional and oil-related clusters have negative correlations. The major oil net exporters showed a stable and small negative linear dependence that ranged from -20% to -23%. The world cluster displays, in general, a trend that departs from linear dependence. Only the two regional clusters (SMC and EU) had large correlations, implying a significant linear dependence between death rate and GDP per capita.

Infant Mortality Rate

The results obtained from the correlation of the infant mortality rate and GDP per capita illustrate some kind of homogeneity. Besides the irregularity that can be observed with the correlation of low human development countries (declining from -0.4 in 1995 to -0.13%), the remaining clusters have significant degrees of dependence. In fact, their correlations are larger than 40% for the three covered years (1995, 2000, and 2004). In addition, for all the clusters we can notice negative correlations between the rate of infant mortality and the GDP per capita.

Life Expectancy at Birth

Two main remarks can be raised from the analysis of the clusters' correlations. First, the low as well as medium human development countries demonstrated clear downward trends. Actually, low and medium human development clusters displayed positive medium linear dependence between the two studied variables in 1995, but the dependency started to decline until reaching nearly zero. Similarly, the dependence between life expectancy at birth and GDP per capita shrunk from 1995 to 2004. The second remark relates to the large correlations (more than 62% in all the covered years) demonstrated by the regional (SMC and EU), oil-related, and high human development clusters.

Maternal Mortality Ratio

The following illustrate the different observations that could be obtained from the analysis of the different correlations. In general, the clusters show medium to large linear dependence between the ratio of maternal mortality and the GDP per capita. The only exception concerns the 2000 medium human development countries' correlation of -15%. In addition, in 2000 the European Union demonstrated a noteworthy drop in its correlations compared to the 1995 results. SMC, major oil net exporters, world, and high human development countries, with downsizing tendencies, have shown a significant departure of the two variables from independence.

Under-Five Mortality Rate

Regarding the under-five mortality rate and GDP per capita's correlations, we drew the following observations. First, the low human development countries demonstrated a decreasing trend with correlations that declined from -49% in 1995 (a large correlation) to -22% in 2004 (a small cor-

relation). The remaining clusters presented large correlations, except for medium human development countries that came in at -40% in 2004.

Income

Due to the inconsistency and unavailability of income indicators for a period of eleven years and for 216 countries, only the GDP per capita was taken into account as a measurement of income. It covers a range of 11 years from 1995 to 2005. The GDP per capita indicator is based on the purchasing power parity rates converted to current international dollars.

DATA

Sources of Data

The databases comprise three main axes: political, socio-economic, and technological indicators. Each axis includes data from major indices, surveys, rates, ratios, percentages, and total amounts from various research centers, institutions, statistical divisions, and organizations. The World Bank Indicators, the World Economic Outlook from the International Monetary Fund, the Common Database of the United Nations Statistics Division, Human Development Reports, the Worldwide Governance Indicators, the Energy Information Administration of the United States Department of Energy, the Organization of the Petroleum Exporting Countries, the United Nations Organization for Education, the Science and Culture Institute for Statistics, the United Nations Children's Fund Global Database, the International Labor Organization Statistics, the World Health Organization Statistical Information System, the "Centres d'Etudes Prospectives et d'Informations Internationales," the International Country Risk Guide, the Greater Zurich Area AG, the Heritage Foundation, the Environmental Performance Index

Centers, the Transparency International Indices, and the Reporters Without Borders are the sources of the different indicators used for elaborating the databases.

Clusters and Years Range

The databases used cover a range of 216 countries. These set of countries are classified in three different clusters: geographical, human development, and oil export. The geographical cluster includes the European Union and the Middle East and North Africa. The studies based on the databases give a particular attention on the two cited regions. In addition, all countries with available data are part of the World cluster. The human development cluster is based on the 2006 Human Development Index. In other words, only countries categorized within the high human development, medium human development, and low human development countries are part of the three human development clusters. The final group of clusters includes the major oil net exporting countries, mainly nations that have net oil exports of more than 100,000 barrels per day.

The range of years that is used within the three databases runs from 1995 to 2006. Those indicators that lack continuity in terms of countries and years are considered null, and they are not included within the different clusters cited above.

Three subsets were made in order to identify and compare major differences and relationships among human development, oil exporting, and geographical clusters. The human development cluster is based on the 2006 Human Development Index rank, which identifies three groups of countries. The first group of countries represents the high human development countries with 63 countries. The medium human development countries group includes 83 countries. The third subset of countries is the low human development countries, that cover 31 countries. Countries that are not categorized by the 2006 Human Devel-

opment Report are included within the World category of the geographical cluster.

The second cluster concerns the major oil net exporting countries. The list of countries is based on the current OPEC membership. In addition, data on the major non-OPEC oil exporters are provided by the Energy Information Administration of the United States Department of Energy. Only net exporters of more than 100,000 barrels per day were considered. Because the reporting system differs from country to country, only the most recent data were taken into account in the oil exporters' cluster.

The final cluster is related to geographical location. The focus was on the Middle East and North Africa (SMC), the European Union (EU), and the World. The list of SMC countries is based on the World Bank regional categories. Only the West Bank and Gaza region (Palestinian Occupied Territories) was not included in the cluster because of the complete lack of statistical indications in any of the health, education, and income indicators used. For the EU region, the 27 member countries are grouped within the second geographical cluster. The World cluster includes all the 216 countries that are part of the database.

CONCLUSION

This chapter is mainly based on a description of the general methodological guidelines that are used in some of the following chapters and sections. It also shows how a theoretical model is often needed to guide the empirical analysis, the inclusion of relevant variables besides the types of data needed. This chapter includes the introduction of a theoretical model that indicates how empirical investigations need to be carried out. It also introduces the empirical methods that are likely to be applied. Variables and data are also discussed with focus on the SMC countries. The methodologies underlined mobilized also account for simple regression analysis besides the introduction of simultaneous equations with seemingly unrelated errors.

Different types of variables and sub-variables are described depending on the sources of the information used. Data are mainly related to cross-sections of countries in the region as published in alternative sources. This clearly establishes the need for software, databases, and other information as necessary ICT components for the conduct of the analysis of interdependencies among health, education, and other wealth variables.

REFERENCES

Acemoglu, D., & Johnson, S. (2006). *Disease and development: The effect of life expectancy on economic growth*. Cambridge, MA: MIT Press. doi:10.3386/w12269

Adams, P., Hurd, M., McFadden, D., Merril, A., & Ribeiro, T. (2003). Healthy, wealthy and wise? Tests for direct causal paths between health and socioeconomic status. *Journal of Econometrics*, *112*(1), 3–56. doi:10.1016/S0304-4076(02)00145-8

Bernard, P. (2006). *The lifecourse paradigm in research and in policy*. Paper presented at the First Symposium of the Population, Work and Family Collaboration. Ottawa, Canada. Retrieved from http://policyresearch.gc.ca/doclib/LC/PS_LC_Bernard_200603_e.pdf

Bozzoli, C., Deaton, A., & Quintana-Domeque, C. (2007). *Child mortality, income and adult height*. Retrieved from http://papers.nber.org/papers/w12966.pdf

Chakrabarty, R. P. (1989). *Multivariate analysis by users of SIPP micro-data files*. Washington, DC: U.S. Bureau of Census.

Chakraborty, S., & Bhattacharya, J. (2012). *Fertility choice under child mortality and social norms. Staff General Research Papers 34911*. Ames, IA: Iowa State University.

Chakraborty, S., & Das, M. (2005). Mortality, human capital and persistent inequality. *Journal of Economic Growth*, *10*(2), 159–192. doi:10.1007/s10887-005-1670-5

Chen, W., Engineer, M., & King, I. (2006). *Choosing longevity with overlapping generations*. Dunedin, New Zealand: University of Victoria and University of Otago.

Cutler, D. M., & Lleras-Muney, A. (2006). *Education and health: Evaluating theories and evidence*. Washington, DC: National Bureau of Economic Research. doi:10.3386/w12352

Deaton, A. (2006). *Global patterns of income and health: Facts, interpretations and policies*. Retrieved from http://www.wider.unu.edu/events/wider-annual-lecture-2006-announcement.htm

Gan, L., & Gong, G. (2007). *Estimating interdependence between health and education in a dynamic model*. Washington, DC: National Bureau of Economic Research.

Grossman, M. (2005). *Education and nonmarket outcomes*. Washington, DC: National Bureau of Economic Research. doi:10.3386/w11582

Gupta, S., Verhoeven, M., & Tiongson, E. (1999). *Does higher government spending buy better results in education and health care? International Monetary Fund, Fiscal Affairs Department, WP/99/21*. Washington, DC: International Monetary Fund.

Hurd, M., & Kapteyn, A. (2003). Health, wealth, and the role of institutions. *The Journal of Human Resources*, *38*(2), 386–415. doi:10.2307/1558749

Morrisson, C. (2002). *Health, education and poverty reduction. OECD Development Centre Policy Brief No. 19*. Paris, France: OECD Development Centre.

Schultz, T. P. (2005). *Productive benefits of health: Evidence from low-income countries*. New Haven, CT: Yale University.

Sen, A. (1998). Mortality as an indicator of economic success and failure. *Economic Journal . Revue Economique et Sociale, 108*(446), 1–25.

Strauss, J., & Duncan, T. (1998). Health nutrition and economic development. *Journal of Economic Literature, 36*(2), 766–817.

ENDNOTES

[1.] The selected theoretical model leads to the generation of two simultaneous decision rules.

APPENDIX

$$U = u(c_1) + m_s(h)[u(c_2) + a.v(I)]$$

The first order necessary conditions related to $e, h,$ and I :

- For e, we have: $\dfrac{\partial U}{\partial e} = u'(c_1) + m_s(h).u'(c_2)$

Given that: $u'_e(c_1) = u'_e(\omega + W - e - h)$ and $u'(c_1) = (c_1)' \cdot (c_1)^{-\delta} => u'_e(c_1) = -(c_1)^{-\delta}$

$u'_e(c_2) = u'_e(\omega + R.e - I)$ and $u'(c_2) = (c_2)' \cdot (c_2)^{-\delta} => u'_e(c_2) = R.(c_2)^{-\delta}$

So, $\dfrac{\partial U}{\partial e} = -(c_1)^{-\delta} + m_s(h).R(c_2)^{-\delta} = 0 =>$

$\quad (c_1)^{-\delta} = R.m_s(h)(c_2)^{-\delta}$

- For h : $\dfrac{\partial U}{\partial h} = u'(c_1) + m_s{}'(h)[u(c_2) + a.v(I)]$

$u'_h(c_1) = u'_h(\omega + W - e - h) = -(c_1)^{-\delta}$ then: $\dfrac{\partial U}{\partial h} = -(c_1)^{-\delta} + m'_s(h)\left[\dfrac{(c_2)^{1-\delta} + \alpha.I^{1-\delta}}{(1-\delta)}\right] = 0$

$=> (1-\delta)(c_1)^{-\delta} = m'_s(h)[(c_2)^{1-\delta} + a.I^{1-\delta}]$

- For I : $\dfrac{\partial U}{\partial I} = m_s(h)[u'(c_2) + a.v'(I)]$

$u'_I(c_2) = u'_I(\omega + R.e - I) = -(c_2)^{-\delta}$ and $v'_I(I) = I^{-\delta}$, then:

$$\dfrac{\partial U}{\partial I} = m_s(h)\left[-(c_2)^{-\delta} + \alpha.I^{-\delta}\right] =$$
$$0 => I = \alpha^{1/\delta}.c_2$$

Definition of c_2 :

$(1-\delta)(c_1)^{-\delta} = m_s{}'(h)\left[(c_2)^{1-\delta} + \alpha.I^{1-\delta}\right]$ and $I = \alpha^{1/\delta}.c_2$

So, $m_s{}'(h) = \dfrac{(1-\delta)(c_1)^{-\delta}}{(c_2)^{1-\delta}(1+\alpha^{1/\delta})} =$

$$\dfrac{(1-\delta)}{(1+\alpha^{1/\delta})c_2} \cdot \left(\dfrac{c_1}{c_2}\right)^{-\delta}$$

Since $\left(\dfrac{c_1}{c_2}\right)^{-\delta} = R.m_s(h)$, then: $\dfrac{m_s'(h)}{m_s(h)} = \dfrac{(1-\delta)}{(1+\alpha^{1/\delta})} \cdot \dfrac{R}{c_2}$

$m_s'(h) = \gamma.a.h^{\gamma-1}$ and $m_s(h) = a.h^{\gamma}$, so: $c_2 = \dfrac{(1-\delta)}{\gamma(1+\alpha^{1/\delta})} Rh$

Given that $\beta = \dfrac{(1-\delta)}{\gamma(1+\alpha^{1/\delta})} => c_2 = \beta Rh$

Definition of $f(h)$:

From the budget constraints (1) and (2), $e = \dfrac{c_2}{R} + \dfrac{I}{R} - \dfrac{\omega}{R} =>$

$c_1 + h + \dfrac{c_2}{R} + \dfrac{I}{R} = \left(1 + \dfrac{1}{R}\right)\omega + W = y$, where $y = (1 + 1/R)\omega + W$

Then, by introducing the values of c_1 and c_2, the following equation results:

$$y = \dfrac{R^{1-1/\delta}}{\left[m_s(h)\right]^{1/\delta}} \beta h + h + \beta h + \alpha^{1/\delta}\beta h$$

So, $y = h + \beta h\left[1 + \alpha^{1/\delta} + \dfrac{R^{1-1/\delta}}{\left[m_s(h)\right]^{1/\delta}}\right]$

Definition of the variables $c_1, c_2, I,$ and $e,$ as function of y and $\hat{h}$:

Given that $c_1 = (\bar{m}_s)^{-1/\delta}.R^{-1/\delta}.c_2$ and $c_2 = \beta R\hat{h} => c_1 = \beta\hat{h}\dfrac{R^{1-1/\delta}}{(\bar{m}_s)^{1/\delta}}$

$y = \hat{h} + \beta\hat{h}\left[1 + \alpha^{1/\delta} + \dfrac{R^{1-1/\delta}}{(\bar{m}_s)^{1/\delta}}\right] =$

$\hat{h} + \beta\hat{h}(1 + \alpha^{1/\delta}) + \beta\hat{h}\dfrac{R^{1-1/\delta}}{(\bar{m}_s)^{1/\delta}}$

$y - \hat{h} = \dfrac{c_2}{R}(1 + \alpha^{1/\delta}) + c_1 =$

$c_1(\bar{m}_s)^{1/\delta}.R^{1/\delta^{-1}}(1 + \alpha^{1/\delta}) + c_1$

So, $c_1 = \left[\dfrac{1}{1 + (\bar{m}_s)^{1/\delta}R^{1/\delta^{-1}}(1 + \alpha^{1/\delta})}\right](y - \hat{h})$

Or, $c_1 = \left[\dfrac{1}{1 + \rho(1 + \alpha^{1/\delta})}\right](y - \hat{h})$ where $\rho = (\bar{m}_s)^{1/\delta}.R^{1/\delta^{-1}}$

$$y - \hat{h} = \frac{c_2}{R}(1 + \alpha^{1/\delta}) + \frac{c_2}{R^{1/\delta}(\bar{m}_s)^{1/\delta}} =$$

Also,

$$\frac{c_2}{R}\left[1 + \alpha^{1/\delta} + \frac{1}{R^{1/\delta - 1}(\bar{m}_s)^{1/\delta}}\right]$$

So, $c_2 = \left[\dfrac{\rho}{1 + \rho(1 + \alpha^{1/\delta})}\right] R(y - \hat{h})$ where $\rho = (\bar{m}_s)^{1/\delta}.R^{1/\delta - 1}$

Given that $\beta\hat{h} = \dfrac{I}{\alpha^{1/\delta}R}$ and $I = \alpha^{1/\delta}(\bar{m}_s)^{1/\delta}R^{1/\delta}.c_1 =>$

$$y - \hat{h} = \frac{I}{R}\left[\frac{(1 + \alpha^{1/\delta})}{\alpha^{1/\delta}} + \frac{1}{\alpha^{1/\delta}(\bar{m}_s)^{1/\delta}R^{1/\delta - 1}}\right]$$

Thus, $I = \left[\dfrac{\rho\alpha^{1/\delta}}{1 + \rho(1 + \alpha^{1/\delta})}\right] R(y - \hat{h})$

Replacing $I = \alpha^{1/\delta}.c_2$ in (1) => $e + \dfrac{\omega}{R} = (1 + \alpha^{1/\delta})\dfrac{c_2}{R}$

$$y - \hat{h} = \frac{c_2}{R}(1 + \alpha^{1/\delta}) + \frac{c_2}{R^{1/\delta}(\bar{m}_s)^{1/\delta}} = y - \hat{h} = \left(e + \frac{\omega}{R}\right)\left[\frac{1 + \rho(1 + \alpha^{1/\delta})}{\rho(1 + \alpha^{1/\delta})}\right]$$

Since

$$\frac{c_2}{R}(1 + \alpha^{1/\delta})\left[1 + \frac{1}{\rho(1 + \alpha^{1/\delta})}\right]$$

Hence, $e = \left[\dfrac{\rho(1 + \alpha^{1/\delta})}{1 + \rho(1 + \alpha^{1/\delta})}\right](y - \hat{h}) - \dfrac{\omega}{R}$

Chapter 4

Descriptive Statistics, Regression Analysis, and Tests of Hypotheses of Interdependencies of Health, Education, and Economic Outcomes

ABSTRACT

This chapter is composed of two major parts. The first one measures interactions and interconnections between health and education using aggregate data on South Mediterranean countries. It focuses on Principal Components Analysis (PCA), descriptive statistics, and regression analysis. This latter is based on different clusters concerning the likely potential links between education, health, and income. The results attained show how different series of results are obtained. The inter-relations identified do account for health, education, and income variables, and are sensitive to the type of data mobilized. This illustrates how ICTs can be used to respond to the analysis required in this type of situation. The second part addresses the directions of links between health, education, and income, and introduces causality tests. This is established in the context of the regional data on South Mediterranean countries. The analysis is consequently conclusive about the role of education based on the data used. Coordination of actions can then target education as the main source of causal relationships. This type of analysis has the merit of facilitating the use of ICTs in the coordination process.

DOI: 10.4018/978-1-4666-3643-9.ch004

INTRODUCTION

This chapter assesses interdependencies between health, education, and income. This is achieved first through techniques that are mainly *descriptive* in nature including the use of *principal component analysis*. The following type of analysis focuses on the mobilization of *multivariate regression* on different datasets besides using *causality tests*.

A DESCRIPTIVE ASSESSMENT OF WEALTH COMPONENTS

The main objective of this part[1] is to check the interdependencies between different sources of wealth (education, health and economic wealth). The analysis is based on datasets made of World Bank and United Nations.

The first section uses descriptive statistics, and simple regressions to make a comparative analysis between South Mediterranean countries and countries of the European Union about the levels of education, health and economic wealth, taking also into consideration the evolutions during the last 10 years, the classification of countries (developed, developing, underdeveloped countries), or membership in different organizations (OPEC or oil exporters). The second section uses factorial methods to detect the interdependencies between the selected indicators of education, health, and economic development (GDP per capita, literacy rate, school life expectancy, life expectancy, and infant mortality rate).

Using these variables, three wealth patterns are observed and are analyzed for SMC and EU countries.

The last section is an econometric analysis of the relation between education, health and economic development. To obtain better results, a dummy variable is introduced to account for country wealth (if a country is rich or with medium wealth dummy=1 or if it is poor dummy=0).

The main conclusion is that all the components of human welfare are strongly interdependent. For SMC countries, the impact of any change in the level of education or health on the level of economic development depends on the wealth patterns. There are some differences between SMC and EU countries. No direct relationship between the level of education and economic development could be seen for EU countries, and the relationship between health and economic development is different from South Mediterranean countries.

Descriptive Statistics

Economic Development

Per capita economic development in the SMC region has been relatively low over the past 20 years, partly because of high population growth rates and partly because many countries still depend on oil exports and oil prices remained relatively low during this period. Under this situation, human capital (health and education) and economic development are not expected to show meaningful relationships.

The Gross Domestic Product (GDP) per capita shows that the SMC region is of medium wealth. The GDP per capita in 2004 was 10881.22 (PPP) current international $ compared to the overall mean of 10390.66 (PPP) current international $. The GDP growth during the period 1995-2004 for MENA countries was 34%, much lower than the growth of 57% for EU countries during the same period (Table 1).

Health and Education

Many scientists consider that literate people have a better health and a higher socio-economic status. The general measure used to describe the educational level of a country is the literacy rate, calculated as the percentage of the population 15 years and older who are literate (can read and write).

Table 1. Wilks' lambda

Wilks' Lambda

Test of Function(s)	Wilks' Lambda	Chi-square	df	Sig.
1 through 2	.065	169.466	10	.000
2	.872	8.505	4	.075

The variation of literacy rate across countries is very high, ranging from 52% for underdeveloped countries to 94% for developed ones.

The region has invested heavily in education over the past few decades. Consequently, the mean of the literacy rate increased from 68% in 1995 to 79% in 2004. Nevertheless, disparities between countries are very high. For example, in the Arab Republic of Egypt, the literacy rate increases from 51% in 1995 to 71% in 2005, while it remains relatively stable in other countries (e.g., in Bahrain the literacy rate remains stable at 85%-86% during the analyzed period) (see Table 2).

Life expectancy at birth is one of the most important indicators of health. For much of human history, life expectancy was between 20 to 35 years (Preston, 1996). In 2004, it was 72 years for the region under study, compared to 66 years worldwide. Life expectancy at birth has increased with the level of development from 47 years for the underdeveloped countries to 77 years for the developed countries. While the variations of life expectancy across regions and level of development are significant, the variation across organization (oil exporters, OPEC) is not significant. For oil exporting countries and OPEC countries, it has been 68 years (Table 2).

The impact of health on literacy rate is much higher for SMC countries than for the other regions. An increase of 1 year in life expectancy corresponds to an increase of 2.44% in literacy rate. Sixty-three percent of the variation of literacy rate is explained by the variation of life expectancy (see Table 3).

Table 2. Parameter estimates of the regression models that describe the relationship between health and GDP per capita taking into account the initial level of wealth of the country

Variables**	N	R^2	F	Model
SMC countries				
Dependent variable: GDP Independent variables: LEB Dummy variable	29	0.968	252.99	GDP = -23011.7 + 401.749·LEB – (-4.457) (5.317) – 69781.1·Dummy + 1068.254·LEB·Dummy (-5.927) (6.678)
Dependent variable: GDP Independent variables: IMR Dummy variable	29	0.93	120.85	GDP = 8243.643 - 87.444·IMR + (-7.051) (-3.707) +15907.915·Dummy – 450.125·IMR·Dummy (9.662) (-5.181)
EU countries				
Dependent variable: GDP Independent variables: LEB Dummy variable	38	0.873	120.28	GDP = -74752.2 + 1162.2·LEB + (-6.087) (6.659) + 48.93·LEB·Dummy (2.685)
Dependent variable: GDP Independent variables: IMR Dummy variable	38	0.756	54.353	GDP = 17175.362 – 719.152·IMR + (5.754) (-3.535) + 5142.729·Dummy (2.563)

* The corresponding t-value is written under each regression coefficient.

**Dummy=1 if rich or with medium wealthy country and Dummy=0 if poor country; GDP = GDP per capita, PPP (current international $); LEB = Life expectancy at birth, total (years); Mortality rate, infant (per 1,000 live births) (IMR)

Recent studies argue that correlations of education with health and socio-economic status may have more to do with the effects of schooling rather than literacy in general.

School life expectancy shows the overall level of development of an educational system in terms of the number of years of education that a child can expect to achieve. Special attention is required in the interpretation, as long as relatively higher school life expectancy indicates greater probability for children to spend more years in education but also higher overall retention within the education system. The overall mean of school life expectancy is 12 years, much higher in developed countries than in developing or underdeveloped ones (15 years in developed countries versus 7 years in underdeveloped countries). In the region, school life expectancy increased from 11 years in 1995 to 12 years in 2004. Between countries, there are large disparities. For example, school life expectancy in Djibouti was 4 years in 2004 compared to 15 year in Israel (see Table 2).

Factor Analysis of Wealth Patterns

How Education, Health, and Economic Development are Interrelated

In order to have a suggestive representation of the interrelations between education, health and economic development, Principal Component Analyze (PCA)[2] is applied. It is a technique used to reduce multidimensional data sets to lower dimensions for analysis. PCA is mathematically defined as an orthogonal linear transformation that projects the data to a new coordinate system (which are called principal components) in order to obtain the greatest variance by any projection of the data.

The variables used in this analysis are: GDP per capita PPP (current international dollars), life expectancy at birth (years), adult literacy rate, mortality rate, infant (per 1000 live births), and school life expectancy (years)—primary to tertiary, for SMC and EU countries, for three years 1995, 2000, and 2004. As long as Adult literacy rate is available only for the year 2004, we have considered it constant all these years. Most of the information is preserved (92%) by the projection of the variables on the plan determined by the first two principal components.

On the first axis, the best-represented variables are on one side School life expectancy (Years)—Primary to tertiary and Adult literacy rate and on the other side Mortality rate, infant (per 1000 live births). Therefore, the first axis summarizes the educational and health components of wealth. School life expectancy (Years)—Primary to tertiary and Adult literacy rate are strongly positively correlated but have negative relationship

Table 3. Parameter estimates of the regression models that describe the relationship between education and GDP per capita taking into account the initial level of wealth of the country

Variables* (SMC countries)	N	R²	F	Model **
Dependent variable: GDP Independent variables: LR Dummy variable	29	0.86	76.45	GDP = -5672.798 + 155.483·ALR + (-1.982) (3.635) +10309.03·Dummy (7.721)
Dependent variable: GDP Independent variables: SLE Dummy variable	29	0.90	119.35	GDP = -8698.406 + 1193.866·SLE + (-3.452) (5.357) +11503.689·Dummy (11.942)

*Dummy=1 if a rich or medium wealthy country and Dummy=0 if a poor country; GDP = GDP per capita; PPP (current international $); LR = Adult literacy rate (%), Total; SLE = School life expectancy (years), Primary to tertiary, Total.

**The corresponding t-value is written under each regression coefficient.

with Infant mortality rate. The countries on the positive side of the first axis have the values of educational indicators higher than the average and the values of Infant Mortality rate lower than the average. The farther the country is from the center of the axis on the positive side, the wealthier in education and the healthier the country. The farther the country is from the center of the axis on the negative side, the lower the education and health of the country. The SMC countries with the highest levels of education and lowest levels of Infant mortality rates are Israel and Jordan, and the countries with the lowest levels of education and highest levels of Infant mortality rates are Yemen and Morocco. Countries like Morocco, Yemen, Jordan, and Tunisia became richer in education and health during the last ten years and Israel, Saudi Arabia, Iran, Oman, and Kuwait became poorer in education and healthier during the last ten years.

On the second axis the best-represented variables are on one side GDP per capita, PPP (current international $) and Life expectancy at birth, total (years) and on the other side Mortality rate, infant (per 1000 live births). Therefore, the second axis summarizes the economic and health components of wealth. School GDP per capita is strongly positively correlated, while life expectancy at birth negatively correlated with Infant mortality rate. The countries on the positive side of the second axis have the values of GDP per capita and Life expectancy at birth higher than the average and the values of Infant Mortality rate lower than the average. Farther is the country from the center of the axis on the positive side, richer and healthier is the country. The farther a country is from the center of the axis on the negative side, the poorer it is. The richest and healthiest SMC countries are Israel and United Arab Emirates and the poorest is Yemen. During the last ten years, all the countries became richer and healthier.

Taking into consideration all the variables, the wealthiest countries in health, in education and economically will be represented in the first

dial, far from the axis center and the poorest will be represented in the third dial, far from the axis center. Therefore, the richest SMC country from all points of view is Israel and the poorest SMC country from all points of view is Yemen.

The main differences between SMC countries and EU countries are in education. Almost all SMC countries are on the negative side of the first axis, and almost all EU countries are on the positive side of the first axis, which is determined by educational wealth and infant mortality rate. The general time trend is the translation of countries to higher values of education, health, and GDP. As long as for many of SMC countries the improvement in education is more visible, for most of EU countries the improvement in GDP per capita and health is more important. The homogeneity on the first axis is much higher for EU countries than for SMC countries, so EU countries are much more homogenous in Education and Infant mortality rate than SMC countries (see Figure 1).

Wealth Patterns by Education, Health, and Economic Development

To determine the wealth patterns by education, health and economic development for SMC countries (and compare them with wealth patterns for EU countries) data clustering methods are used. Data clustering means the classification of objects into different groups (clusters), so that the data in each cluster share some common attributes—often proximity according to some defined distance measure. In our case, the distance measure is the Euclidean distance and the methods used are "Ward method and k-means clustering."

Three groups are identified having the following characteristics.

Cluster 1 includes countries with medium wealth:

- **SMC countries:** Bahrain, 1995; Kuwait, 1995; Saudi Arabia, 1995, 2000, 2004; Oman, 2000, 2004;

- **EU countries:** Cyprus, 1995; Greece, 1995, 2000; Portugal, 1995; Slovenia, 1995, 2000; Slovak Republic, 2000, 2004; Spain, 1995; Estonia, 2004; Latvia, 2004; Malta, 2000, 2004; Portugal, 2000; Lithuania, 2004.

School life expectancy (primary to tertiary) in mean is 13.6 years and adult literacy rate in mean is 92%. Therefore, the countries from this group have average levels of education. Life expectancy at birth in mean is 74.6 years and Infant mortality rate in mean is of 9.8 dead infants for 1000 live births. Therefore, this cluster contains countries with an average level of health. The GDP per capita, PPP in mean is 14663 current international $.

The SMC countries from this cluster are on the left side of the graph and the EU countries from this cluster are on the right side of the graph. Thus, the SMC countries in this cluster are different from EU countries in education level (have lower education level) and Infant mortality rate (have higher Infant mortality) (see Figures 2 and 3).

Cluster 2 includes poor countries from all points of view:

- **SMC countries:** Algeria, 2004; Iran, 1995, 2000, 2004; Jordan, 2000, 2004; Morocco, 1995, 2000, 2004; Tunisia, 1995, 2000, 2004; Yemen, 1995, 2000, 2004;
- **EU countries:** Bulgaria, 1995, 2000, 2004; Estonia, 1995, 2000; Latvia, 1995, 2000; Lithuania, 1995, 2000; Romania, 1995, 2000, 2004; Slovak Republic, 1995.

School life expectancy (primary to tertiary) in mean is 12.13 years and adult literacy rate in mean is 82%. Therefore, the countries from this group have low levels of education. Life expectancy at birth in mean is 69.2 years and Infant mortality rate in mean is of 30.2 dead infants for 1000 live births. Therefore, this cluster contains countries with low level of health. The GDP per capita, PPP in mean is 5649 current international $.

As for the first cluster, the SMC countries differ from EU countries in education level (have lower education level) and Infant mortality rate (have higher Infant mortality).

Cluster 3 includes rich countries:

Figure 1. Variable representation on factorial plan

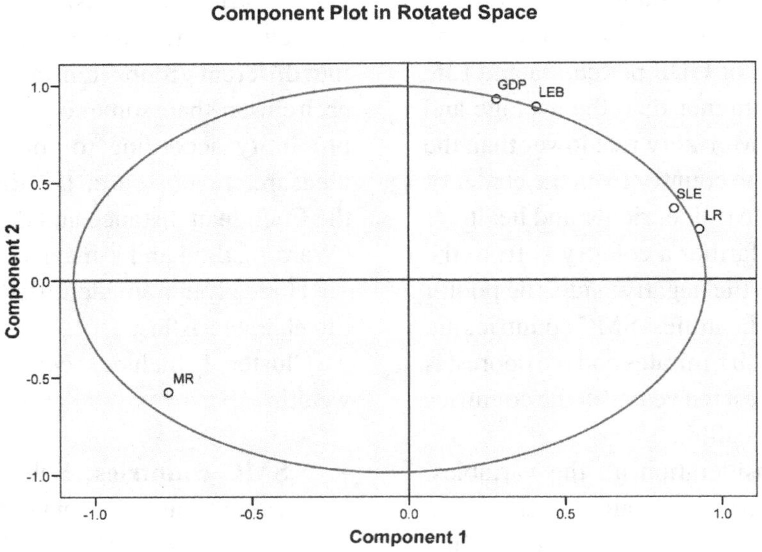
Component Plot in Rotated Space
GDP
LEB
SLE
LR
MR
1.0
0.5
0.0
-0.5
-1.0
-1.0
-0.5
0.0
0.5
1.0
Component 2
Component 1

- **SMC countries:** Bahrain, 2004; Israel, 1995, 2000, 2004; Kuwait, 2004; United Arab Emirates, 1995, 2000;
- **EU countries:** Cyprus, 2000, 2004; Italy, 1995, 2000, 2004; Greece, 2004; Portugal, 2004; Slovenia, 2004; Spain, 2000, 2004.

School life expectancy (primary to tertiary) in mean is 14.46 years and adult literacy rate in mean is 95%. Therefore, the countries from this group have average levels of education. Life expectancy at birth in mean is 78 years and Infant mortality rate in mean is of 5.9 dead infants for 1000 live births. Therefore, this cluster contains countries with an average level of health. The GDP per capita, PPP in mean is 22171 current international $.

In this cluster, there are not big differences between SMC and EU countries.

In time, there are changes from a cluster to another. Kuwait and Bahrain passed from the cluster 1 to cluster 3, so from medium wealthy countries to rich countries. Many of new entrants in EU passed from cluster 2 of countries with low level of wealth indicators to cluster 1 of countries with medium level of wealth indicators. The classification of countries and the changes in time, confirm the interdependencies between the wealth components. The increase in GDP is correlated with the improvement in health and in education. SMC countries have lower education level and lower level of health then EU countries for the same level of GDP per capita.

What are the Main Determinants of Wealth Patterns?

In order to answer to that question it is used a discriminant function analysis. The results obtained are significant, with a probability of 95%.

Discriminant analysis determines some optimal combination of variables (called discriminant functions) so that the first function provides the highest overall discrimination between groups; the

Figure 2. SMC countries representation on factorial plan and wealth clusters

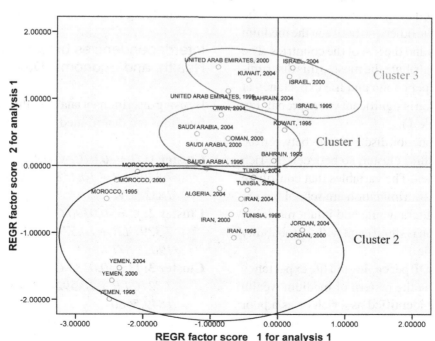

Figure 3. EU countries representation on factorial plan and wealth clusters

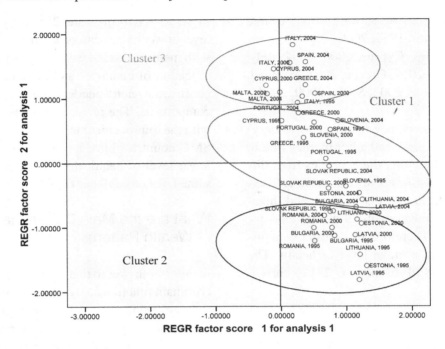

second provides second most, and so on. Moreover, the functions will be independent or orthogonal, that is, their contribution to the discrimination between groups will not overlap.

The first function discriminates between the first cluster and the others, so between the medium wealth countries and the rest of the countries. The variables that contribute the most to this discrimination are GDP per capita and life expectancy at birth. This function is significant with a probability of 99% (see Table 1).

The second function discriminates between the second and the third cluster, so between the rich and poor countries. The variables that contribute the most to this discrimination are school life expectancy, adult literacy rate and infant mortality rate. This function is significant with a probability of 90% (see Table 1).

Therefore, GDP per capita and life expectancy at birth determine the pattern of medium wealth countries. To be identified as a rich or as a poor

country, the other variables as school life expectancy, adult literacy rate, and infant mortality rate are important. So, the economic and health components of wealth are used in the first time in identifying the wealth patterns of a country.

Interdependencies between Education, Health, and Economic Development

By using discriminant analysis, three classification functions are determined:

Cluster 1: $f1 = -0.0161 \cdot GDP + 41.5181 \cdot LExp + 7.2403 \cdot LR + 10.4329 \cdot MRI + 2.3753 \cdot SLE - 1832.5091$

Cluster 2: $f2 = -0.0190 \cdot GDP + 42.5590 \cdot LExp + 7.3291 \cdot LR + 10.5740 \cdot MRI + 3.5402 \cdot SLE - 1903.3871$

Cluster 3: $f3 = -0.0135 \cdot GDP + 41.1570 \cdot LExp + 7.3210 \cdot LR + 10.5920 \cdot MRI + 1.5637 \cdot SLE - 1849.5680$

The country it is classified into the group with the highest value of the classification function. By using these classification functions, 100% of the cases used into the analysis are correctly classified.

Some *simulations* for the SMC countries were done to check if there is any possibility to pass from one group of countries to another (e.g., from a medium wealthy country to a rich country or from a poor to a medium wealthy country) improving only one component of wealth, or it is necessary to improve more or less all the components of wealth. For four SMC countries (Kuwait, Jordan, United Arab Emirates, Morocco) there are calculated the values for the classification functions, varying one by one the indicators from the minimum to the maximum observed value in the database and maintaining constant all the other indicators at 2004 observed level. Improvements in GDP per capita involve the revision of country classification. The speed of change depends on the level of all the other wealth components. The higher are levels of health and education the faster is the adjustment to a better group of countries (see Figure 4).

The main conclusion of this analyze is that all the wealth indicators are interdependent. Modifying or improving only one indicator, it is not sufficient in general for a country to become wealthier.

However, a better health of population determines a better human capital, so more productivity and in conclusion a better economic result at country level. More educated people will determine an improvement in human capital, so a greater level of GDP per capita. Furthermore, a richer country from economically point of view will invest more in education and in health of people but the response is not so quickly as for the other implications.

The next two sections give some measurable results of these two statements.

Econometric Analysis of the Relationship between Education, Health, and Economic Development

The main question is, "Does the quality of human capital (health and education) enhance economic

Figure 4. Changes in classifications by GDP per capita

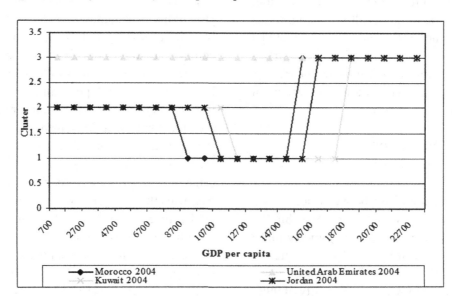

development?" There are compelling reasons to believe that education and health contributes positively to economic growth. However, empirical studies show that this relationship is not always significant. Barro (1990) show that for a given level of wealth, the economic growth rate was positively related to the initial level of human capital of a country, whereas for a given level of human capital the growth rate was negatively related to the initial level of GDP per capita. Azariadis and Drazen (1990) assume that economic growth is not a linear process. Their results show that literacy is correlated with the variation of growth in the least advanced countries, but it does not seem to be related to the growth of the most developed countries. Furthermore, they show that the coefficient of human capital in the growth equation is about five times higher in the developing countries than in the developed countries.

Therefore, one of the main conclusions of the analyses of the human capital-growth relationship is the absence of homogeneity across countries. If economic, social and cultural characteristics of each country modify the relationship between human capital and growth, then the estimation of this relationship must be regional and to take into account the initial level of human capital. In order to include initial wealth of a country as factor in the econometric analysis, it is created a dummy variable which indicates if a country is rich or with medium wealth (dummy=1) or if it is poor (dummy=0), using the country classification made in the previous section.

The Effect of Health on Economic Development

Regarding the relationship between health and GDP per capita there is a strong relationship between them. All the models are very good with R^2 greater than 93% for SMC countries and greater than 75% for EU countries. The parameter coefficients are significant with a probability of 99%.

The parameter estimates of the regression models that describe the relationship between health and GDP per capita taking into account the initial level of wealth of a country are provided in Table 2.

The main conclusion provided by these models is that the effect of improvements in health on the growth of GDP per capita is more important for rich or medium wealthy SMC countries than for poor SMC countries.

An increase of 1 year in life expectancy at birth implies an increase in GDP per capita 3.5 times higher for rich or medium wealth SMC countries than for poor SMC countries (1470 [PPP] current international $ for rich and medium wealthy countries versus 401 [PPP] current international $ for poor countries). The intercept (GDP per capita for life expectancy at birth of 0 years) depends too on the initial wealth of a country. A minimum life expectancy at birth of 63.12 years in order to obtain a positive GDP per capita, for medium and rich SMC countries versus a minimum life expectancy at birth of 57.27 years in order to obtain a positive GDP per capita, for poor SMC countries.

The behavior of EU countries is different. The intercept does not depend on the initial wealth of the country and the effect of an increase of 1 year in life expectancy at birth is slightly higher (of 1.04 times) for rich or medium wealthy EU countries than for poor EU countries (Table 4).

The difference between rich and poor countries in the speed of GDP per capita growth with the improvements in Infant mortality rates is higher than the response at improvements in life expectancy. A decrease of 1 dead infant per 1000 live births implies an increase in GDP per capita 6 times higher for rich or medium wealthy SMC countries than for poor SMC countries (537.569 [PPP] current international $ for rich and medium wealthy countries versus 87.444 [PPP] current international $ for poor countries). For an infant mortality rate of 0 dead infant per 1000 live births, GDP per capita is 24151.56 (PPP) current inter-

Table 4. Life expectancy

Variables*(SMC countries)	N	R²	F	Model**
Dependent variable: LEB Independent variables: LR Dummy variable	28	0.696	28.63	LEB = 54.153 + 0.217·ALR + (18.033) (4.83) +2.936·Dummy (2.094)
Dependent variable: LEB Independent variables: SLE Dummy variable	29	0.767	42.85	LEB = 51.796 + 1.494·SLE + (18.772) (6.123) +4.808·Dummy (4.558)
Dependent variable: IMR Independent variables: LR Dummy variable	28	0.766	40.92	IMR = 107.485 – 0.978·LR - (9.26) (-5.64) -14.468·Dummy (-2.67)
Dependent variable: IMR Independent variables: SLE Dummy variable	29	0.784	47.169	IMR = 112.051 – 6.188·SLE - (9.63) (-6.012) - 23.32·Dummy (-5.242)
Dependent variable: LEB Independent variables: GDP Dummy variable	29	0.867	84.51	LEB = 60.668 + 0.002 ·GDP - (58.537) (8.097) – 0.001·GDP·Dummy (-5.487)
Dependent variable: IMR Independent variables: GDP Dummy variable	29	0.781	46.35	IMR = 72.85 – 0.007·GDP + (12.525) (-5.737) + 0.004·GDP·Dummy (3.764)
Dependent variable: ALR Independent variables: GDP Dummy variable	29	0.630	21.27	ALR = 46.247 + 0.004·GDP - (9.032) (4.023) – 450.125·GDP·Dummy (-2.67)
Dependent variable: SLE Independent variables: GDP Dummy variable	29	0.668	26.16	SLE = 7.22 + 0.001·GDP - (10.759) (6.001) – 0.001·GDP·Dummy (-4.888)

*Dummy=1 if a rich or medium wealthy country and Dummy=0 if a poor country; GDP = GDP per capita, PPP (current international $);
LR = Adult literacy rate (%), Total; SLE = School life expectancy (years), Primary to tertiary, Total

** The corresponding t-value is written under each regression coefficient

national $ for rich and medium wealthy SMC countries versus 8243.643 (PPP) current international $ for poor SMC countries.

Concerning EU countries, only the initial GDP per capita for an Infant mortality rate of no dead infant per 1000 live births depends on the initial wealth of country (22318.09 [PPP] current international $ for medium wealthy and rich countries, versus 17175.362 [PPP] current international $ for poor countries). A decrease of one dead infant per 1000 live births implies an increase in GDP per capita of 719.15 (PPP) current international $.

The Effect of Education on Economic Development

Concerning the relationship between education and GDP per capita there is a strong relationship between them for SMC countries but not for EU countries. The models are good with R² greater than 86%. The parameter coefficients are significant with a probability of 99%.

The parameter estimates of the regression models that describe the relationship between education and GDP per capita taking into account the initial level of wealth of a country are provided in Table 3.

An increase of 1% in adult literacy rate implies an increase in GDP per capita of 155.48 (PPP) current international $. The intercept depend on the initial wealth of the country.

An increase of 1 year in school life expectancy implies an increase in GDP per capita of 1193.87 (PPP) current international $. The intercept depend on the initial wealth of the country.

Other Relationships between Human Capital and Economic Development

In the previous sections, effects of education and health on economic development were treated as separate effects. This section describes the relationships between education and health and the impact of economic development on education and health.

The economic development and more important, the knowledge are factors which improve the health. For SMC countries, the relationships between these factors are validated and all the regression coefficients are significant with a probability of 99%.

The variation of life expectancy at birth explained by the variation of adult literacy rate or school life expectancy and initial wealth is lower than the variation explained of infant mortality rate by the same factors. An increase of 1% in adult literacy rate lowers the infant mortality rate with 1 year and an increase of 1 year in school life expectancy lowers the infant mortality rate with 6 years.

As for the impact of economic development on health, could be observed an inverse relation then for education. The variation of life expectancy at birth explained by the variation of GDP per capita and initial wealth is higher than the variation of infant mortality rate explained by the same factors. Therefore, the education is more important in decreasing the infant mortality rate

and economic development is more important in increasing life expectancy.

Since education is often subsidized by the state and in some countries compulsory for a certain minimum length of time, the economic development of a country has a direct effect on the educational level of a country.

For SMC countries, the relationships between these factors are validated and all the *regression coefficients* are significant with a probability of 99%.

For SMC countries, 66.8% of the variation of school life expectancy and 63% of the variation of adult literacy rate is explained by the variation of GDP per capita and initial wealth. The impact of GDP per capita on adult literacy rate is 1.5 times higher for poor countries then for rich and medium wealthy countries. The impact of GDP per capita on school life expectancy is 2 times higher for poor countries then for rich and medium wealthy countries.

INTERDEPENDENCIES BETWEEN HEALTH, EDUCATION, AND POVERTY WITH DIVERSITY OF DATASETS AND STATISTICAL TESTS TO TARGET DIRECTIONS OF ICT COORDINATION

The major assumption underlying this chapter is related to the aggregation of interdependencies throughout the countries analyzed in this panel. This says that the aggregation of the interconnections already observed at the level of households in different countries of the region is likely to occur in cross-sections of countries. If household data have shown the existence of interdependencies that captured the behavior of individuals and group ages with regard to health, education and poverty, there might be patterns through which household behavior is transmitted at the country and at the levels of the region. A series of regressions results are attempted in the following sections based on the World Bank database, the most recent UN data and on composite indices in addition to the use of regression analysis on Institutional profile data. An attempt is also made to assess Granger causality between variables.

In order to start the process of setting interdependencies at the regional level, it can be observed from the following graphs that GDP per capita and the other variables such as life expectancy at birth, mortality under age 5, physicians per 1000 people and female adult mortality entertain quadratic relationships. This implies a threshold that shows the likely effects of other variables. These variables are also related to the socio-economic area and include other series of explanatory factors. Figures 5-9 are devoted to confirming the existence of Preston's[3] (Preston, 1996; Fogel, 2004; Deaton, 2006) curves for the South Mediterranean countries considered.

Using World Bank Data

Health and Wealth Relationships

In a first set of regressions, the relationships between health measures represented by life expectancy at birth and by indices of mortality and wealth measured by GDP per capita are attempted over the 28 countries composing the South Mediterranean sample. The results attained show definitely that life expectancy at birth is strongly related to GDP per capita and its square implying that life expectancy at the level of this region of the world is directly under the effect of GDP per capita and that an increase (decrease) of 1 leads to a net increase (decrease) of life expectancy by 0.45. This same measure of wealth also explains the less than 5 percent mortality rate and an increase (decrease) of GDP by 1 unit decreases (increases) this variant of mortality by 0.74 units. The obtained result shows also the existence of a strong positive relationship between GDP and the number

of physicians per 1000 population. This explains the other results where female adult mortality, maternal mortality ratio, life expectancy at birth and others are explained either by per capita GDP or by the number of physicians. Table 5 introduces the most important relationships between variables related to health and wealth.

The introduction of the education sector into the system of relationship may be an important source for the explanation of further levels of interdependencies.

Education, Health, and Income

Using the other available sources of data for variables related to education, income, unemployment, and other health variables for the countries under study, a system of relationships have been estimated. The level of enrollment in primary school appears to be under the effect of both the health and wealth variables. It is also affected by poverty as measured by the human poverty index. However, the human development index is directly related to high enrollment. Poverty and bad health do negatively affect the level of enrollment at the primary school. Similarly, infant mortality rate is sensitive to both income and education. The levels of unemployment do affect infant mortality. Finally, the level of corruption as measured by CPI appears to be negatively related to income (see Table 6).

The central role of health requires larger supplies of different forms of direct and indirect services in this area to cover the expected increasing needs of the populations in different countries of the region. This requires that medical and paramedical coverage be enhanced at the levels of infrastructure and mainly human capital. Medical doctors and nurses besides health care technicians play a critical role in this process, through their knowledge and abilities but also through their numbers (stocks and flows). However, given the trends taking place internation-

Figure 5. Life expectancy at birth against GDP per capita, 28 countries

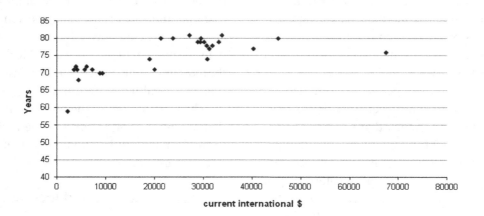

ally and with the likely impacts of the brain drain effects, it is important to account for, at least the risks related to the eventual existence of medical brain drain. This issue is covered in the following chapter.

Using the UN's Most Recent Database to Check for Consistencies with the above Estimations

Using again the seemingly unrelated equation system estimations method with the most recent UN-database for the South Mediterranean Countries, a system of equations is estimated to show that again, there are major interdependencies between health, education and economic sets of variables as published in the above database. As variables are expressed under logarithmic forms, elasticities can be directly set through the estimations.

Total fertility rate appears consequently to be highly responsive to be mainly responsive to the annual rate of urban population change with a corresponding elasticity of 0.635 with a significant impact of adult economic activity rate (elasticity of -1.47). To lesser degrees, the mortality rate of children under age of 5 years and the per capita income may also affect the level of fertility in

the overall sample of countries forming the SMC (*elasticities* of 2.03 and 0.22, respectively).

The maternal mortality rate appears to be sensitive to the mortality rate of children under five years (elasticity of 5.22) and to the share of rural population (elasticity of 1.19) implying that decreases (increases) in rural population contribute to decreases (increases) in maternal mortality.

School life expectancy appears to be mainly driven by infant mortality rate (elasticity of -0.22), adult unemployment rate (elasticity of 0.17) and to a lesser extent by youth literacy rate (elasticity of 1.97). But, the school life expectancy for men appear to be directly affected by the level of adult literacy rate (elasticity of 0.57) while that of women seems to be under the effects of adult illiteracy rate of women (0.45) and the life expectancy at birth of women (1.54).

Life expectancy at birth for men is statistically related to that of women (0.62) and to infant mortality rate (-0.06) while that of women is also related to life expectancy of men (0.07) besides the infant mortality rate (1.44).

The infant mortality rate seems to be more responsive to the mortality rate occurring under the age of five years (0.86) but also income as represented by GDP per capita (-0.06).

Figure 6. Mortality under 5 against GDP per capita, 28 countries

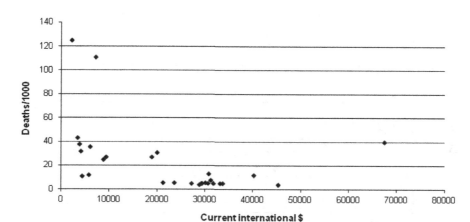

Figure 7. Physicians per 1000 population against GDP per capita, 28 countries

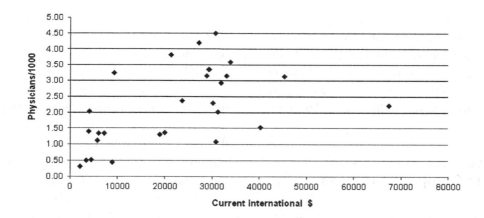

Mortality of children under the age of five seems to be mainly under the effect of adult unemployment rate (0.70).

The annual urban rate of population change appears to be highly sensitive to the total fertility rate (1.85) while the level of income varies with both the total school life expectancy (3.33) but mainly with the adult economic activity rate (14.43). This latter is also related to the income level (0.05) but also to adult unemployment rate (-0.11). The adult economic activity rate for women appears to be mainly under the effect of the total level of unemployment rate (-0.33).

The total literacy rate is mainly related to the total level of fertility (0.69). Only life expectancy of women does slightly affect their literacy (0.56) rate implying that there are different variables to which the literacy rates of men and women can be responsive. When accounting for the literacy rate of adult more sensitivity is mainly expressed

Figure 8. Female adult mortality rate against GDP per capita, 27 countries

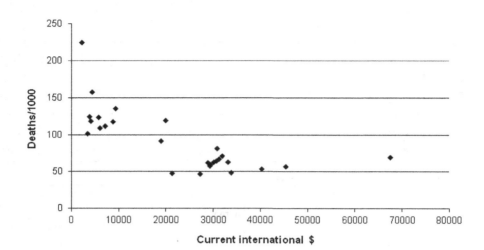

through the school life expectancy of men (0.47). When looking at the literacy rate of young women, this variable appears to be more sensitive to the school life expectancy of men (0.52) (see Table 7).

The above results are consistent with those that have been discussed earlier attained with the other databases.

Interdependencies Based on Aggregate Composite Indices

At this stage of the investigations, it appears important to see how aggregated composite indices developed for the countries of the region are related. The reason for this exercise is directly linked with the fact that The The *composite indices* provided by different independent sources may appear to not show clear interactions. The indices used include the Human Development Index (HDI) and the Human Poverty Index (HPI) as they are published by UNDP. It includes also the Economic Freedom Index (EFI) produced by the Heritage Foundation, the Knowledge Economic

Index (KEI) produced by World Bank Institute (WBI) with other indices related to the perception of the environment.

Table 8 shows again levels of interdependencies among these indices that are produced by different sources using different methods. These regressions show how corruption perception index can be improved (reduced) with more (less) improvements (reduction) in the human development and the economic freedom indices. In addition, human development is positively related to the environmental index but negatively related to human poverty. The other relationships show how the knowledge and poverty are negatively related. The estimated levels of elasticities (coefficients) are important (1 to 2) knowing that the scales used vary from 1 to 10 for CPI and from 0 to 1 for most of the other composite indices. For example, any improvement in the openness of the economy in the region would imply less corruption and more transparency as higher CPI indicates. Another improvement in HDI leads also to larger transparency. Improvements in the physi-

Figure 9. Maternal mortality ration against GDP per capita, 27 countries

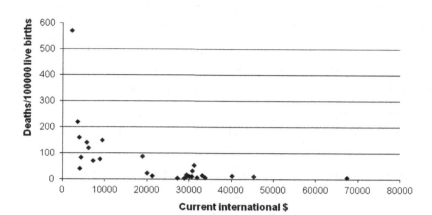

cal environment is also a source for the promotion of HDI and then of transparency. The promotion of education reduces poverty with an increase of the HDI and then of transparency.

Testing for Granger-Causality[4] using Country Time Series Data on Some Variables

With the above analyzes conducted both at the country and regional levels interdependencies have been identified among different variables at both country and regional levels. However, there remain several issues that need clarification. Among the important matters to be pursued, there is the direction of relationships between variables. One answer to this debate can be provided by testing for Granger-Causality between the variables considered. However, longer time series are available on few variables. The variables that have been selected are those of life expectancy at birth as representative of heath and the remittances of migrants and the share of trade in GDP in Algeria, Egypt, Turkey, and Morocco besides the primary and secondary enrollment in the case of Morocco only. One, two, and three lags have been used to

test for Granger causality. This is achieved through running unrestricted and restricted regressions between each two couple of variables that are found to have enough observations and that represent respectively health, economics, and education. In this context and for each couple of variables an F-statistic test has been performed. This is to test for the hypothesis H0 (the explanatory variable does not Granger cause the dependent variable again HA (the explanatory variable does cause in the Granger sense, the dependent variable). The results of these tests are introduced respectively as they are summarized below and in Table 9 under one lag, two lags and three lags knowing that the number of observations in each annual series has been lower than 30. It is recognized though that at least two limitations may affect the attained results. The first one is directly related to the number of variables in the categories health, economics, and education while the second is the length of the time series.

The results achieved under the above limitations are considered respectively under the 10, 5 and 1 percent probabilities. It seems that life expectancy at birth as representation of health does cause in the Granger sense the share of trade

Table 5. Most important relationships between variables related to health and wealth

	R^2	Obs.
$Ln\left(Life \text{ Exp at Birth}\right) = \underset{(2.04)}{1.82} + \underset{(2.44)}{0.47} Ln\left(\text{GDP per capita}\right) - \underset{(-2.12)}{0.02} Ln\left(\text{GDP per capita}\right)^2$	0.73	28
$Ln\left(Under \text{ 5 mortality rate}\right) = \underset{(6.47)}{9.78} - \underset{(-4.79)}{0.74} Ln\left(\text{GDP per capita}\right)$	0.47	28
$Ln\left(Physicians \text{ per 1000}\right) = -\underset{(-4.42)}{4.53} + \underset{(5.02)}{0.53} Ln\left(\text{GDP per capita}\right)$	0.49	28
$Ln\left(\text{GDP per capita}\right) = \underset{(43.05)}{9.20} + \underset{(4.29)}{1.02} Ln\left(Physicians \text{ per 1000}\right)$	0.50	28
$Ln\left(Under \text{ 5 mortality rate}\right) = \underset{(16.82)}{3.17} - \underset{(-4.84)}{0.99} Ln\left(\text{Physicians per 1000}\right)$	0.47	28
$Ln\left(Life \text{ Exp at Birth}\right) = \underset{(426.64)}{4.26} + \underset{(7.65)}{0.08} Ln\left(\text{Physicians per 1000}\right)$	0.69	28
$Ln\left(Life \text{ Exp at Birth}\right) = \underset{(344.02)}{4.27} + \underset{(6.61)}{0.09} Ln\left(\text{Physicians per 1000}\right)$	0.70	28
$Ln\left(Life \text{ Exp at Birth}\right) = \underset{(208.52)}{4.46} - \underset{(-7.42)}{0.06} Ln\left(\text{Under 5 mortality rate}\right)$	0.68	28
$Ln\left(Female \text{ adult mortality rate}\right) = \underset{(18.14)}{7.94} - \underset{(-8.06)}{0.36} Ln\left(\text{GDP per capita}\right)$	0.72	27
$Ln\left(Maternal \text{ mortality ratio}\right) = \underset{(11.02)}{14.96} - \underset{(-8.55)}{1.19} Ln\left(\text{GDP per capita}\right)$	0.74	27

in GDP for Algeria only under the 10% probability. Otherwise, no Granger causality has been established for Algeria under one lag. With two lags, trade appears to be Granger causing health as measured by life expectancy at birth both at 10% and at 5% probabilities. The same result is attained under 3 lags but only with a 10% level of significance. No causation has been attained for Egypt under one-lagged models. However, under two lags, life expectancy at birth working appears to be Granger causing under the 5% significance level. This is confirmed again under the three lagged models. For Turkey, life expectancy seems also to be causing life expectancy at 1% significance level with one and three lagged models. The most important results that are at-

tained are related to Morocco where education represented by enrollment at the primary school level appears to be Granger causing life expectancy. This is confirmed for both primary and secondary enrollment when using two and three lagged models. Tables 9-11 introduce respectively the details by country and for each couple of regressions.

Besides the limitations related to the absence of microeconomic and time series data and in addition to the difficulty of the determination of causality under Granger tests, other difficulties are related to the choices and trade-offs made by individuals and households over different socio-economic components (Fukuda-Parr, 2007; Gaertner, 2008).

Table 6. Level of corruption as measured by CPI related to income

Education, Health, and Income/Poverty		
$Ln\left(\%\text{ Enrolment primary}\right) = \underset{(5.21)}{6.14} - \underset{(-2.64)}{0.20}\left[Ln\left(Low\text{ birth weight}\right)\right] - \underset{(-2.08)}{0.07}\left[Ln\left(GNI\right)\right]$	0.64	17
$Ln\left(\%\text{ Enrolment primary}\right) = \underset{(6.51)}{7.21} - \underset{(-2.94)}{0.23}\left[Ln\left(Low\text{ birth weight}\right)\right] - \underset{(-2.04)}{0.10}\left[Ln\left(HPI\right)\right]$	0.46	17
$Ln\left(\text{Infant Mortality}\right) = \underset{(-2.39)}{-0.23}\left[Ln\left(Income\right)\right] - \underset{(-2.46)}{0.26}\left[Ln\left(\%\text{ Education}\right)\right]$	0.84	13
$Ln\left(\%\text{ Enrolment primary}\right) = \underset{(20.51)}{5.67} - \underset{(-3.26)}{0.18}\left[Ln\left(Low\text{ birth weight}\right)\right] + \underset{(2.06)}{0.26}\left[Ln\left(HDI\right)\right]$ $- \underset{(-2.94)}{0.07}\left[Ln\left(GNI\right)\right]$	0.58	17
Health, Income, and Unemployment		
$Ln\left(\text{Infant Mortality}\right) = \underset{(-3.49)}{-0.21}\left[Ln\left(Income\right)\right] + \underset{(3.21)}{1.29}\left[Ln\left(Unemployment\right)\right]$	0.86	13
$Ln\left(\text{Unemployment}\right) = -\underset{(-9.02)}{3.40} - \underset{(-2.98)}{0.54}\left[Ln\left(Poverty\text{ rate}\right)\right]$	0.39	15
Income, Education, and Corruption		
$Ln\left(\text{Income}\right) = -\underset{(-2.80)}{7.90} + \underset{(6.39)}{5.76}\left[Ln\left(\text{CPI}\right)\right]$	0.84	13

Regressions Based on Institutional Profiles

Institutional Profiles are sets of data about the institutional characteristics of developing, in transition and developed Countries produced by the Ministry of Economic Finance and Industry, France. This data used here pertains to 2006.

While the best appreciations are set at level 4, the lowest level is 0. In this context, only few variables attain levels above 2.5 in the region. A905 and D801 as they refer respectively to the appreciation of equity in the access to basic public services (education, health, water, and electricity) and to the net migration flow of non qualified labor are the ones that are above average. While the standard deviations are not high meaning that countries of the region have almost similar levels, D801 and D802 have higher dispersions. All

the other appreciations of training of the elites, professional training, and openness to foreign expertise, social mobility in relation to hiring and to the situation of the young school graduates are not well appreciated (see Table 12).

The descriptive statistics related to all the detailed components included are introduced in the appendix. They show that A905, A9050, A9051, A9052, A9053, D8001, and D90011 are above average.

The *correlation table* shows that the appreciation of equity of access to basic services (A905: education, health, water and electricity) is highly correlated with net migration flow of non qualified labor (D801: net migration flows of non qualified labor of men and women) (level of correlation: 0.47) and with the perception of social mobility (D901: hiring and promotion) (level of correlation: 0.55). The perception of the training of elites

Table 7. Seemingly unrelated equation system estimations based on the most recent UN database for the south Mediterranean countries (t-stat between parentheses)

Regression	R^2
V1= 2.030 V9 + 0.635 V12 + 0.221 V14 – 1.469 V15 (2.089) (3.369) (2.037) (-2.382)	0.89
V2= 5.225 V9 + 1.188 V11 (2.135) (4.498)	0.96
V3= 1.968 V21 + 0.170 V24 – 0.218 V8 (2.052) (2.583) (-2.690)	0.86
V4= 0.568 V18 (3.186)	0.87
V5= -6.080+ 1.539 V7 + 0.449 V20 (-2.542) (2.281) (2.264)	0.75
V6= 1.86 + 0.620 V7 – 0.057 V8 – 0.007V14 (5.497) (9.468) (-4.988) (-1.748)	0.99
V7= -2.063 + 0.066 V8 + 1.436 V6 (-2.756) (2.711) (9.468)	0.98
V8= 0.912 + 0.855 V9 – 0.064 V14 (2.234) (17.149) (-2.226)	0.99
V9= 0.698 V24 (4.339)	0.68
V12= 1.853 V1 (2.884)	0.85
V14= -62.285 + 3.333 V3 + 14.434 V16 – 0.195 V17 (-4.692) (3.300) (4.430) (-0.235)	0.77
V15= 3.894 + 0.47 V14 – 0.114 V24 (14.746) (2.181) (-2.918)	0.94
V17= 4.584 – 0.052 V14 – 0.330 V24 (5.129) (-0.705) (-2.501)	0.68
V18= 2.661 + 0.691 V3 (6.106) (3.933)	0.56
V20= 3.262 + 0.564 V5 – 0.124 V8 (3.703) (2.120) (-1.355)	0.69
V21= 3.293 + 0.470 V4 (6.842) (3.603)	0.83
V23= 3.096 + 0.524 V4 (4.514) (2.821)	0.80

V1: Total Fertility Rate, **V2**: Maternal Mortality Ratio, **V3**: Total "School Life Expectancy (in years)," **V4**: Men "School Life Expectancy (in years)," **V5**: Women "School Life Expectancy (in years)," **V6**: Life Expectancy at Birth "Men," **V7**: Life Expectancy at Birth "Women," **V8**: Infant Mortality Rate, **V9**: Under 5 Mortality Rate, **V10**: Population Distribution (%) 2008 "Urban," **V11**: Population Distribution (%) 2008 "Rural," **V12**: Annual Rate of Population Change (%) 2005-2010 "Urban," **V13**: Annual Rate of Population Change (%) 2005-2010 "Rural," **V14**: Per Capita GDP (US$), **V15**: Adult (15+) Economic Activity Rate "Total," **V16**: Adult (15+) Economic Activity Rate "Men," **V17**: Adult (15+) Economic Activity Rate "Women," **V18**: Adult (15+) Literacy Rate "Total," **V19**: Adult (15+) Literacy Rate "Men," **V20**: Adult (15+) Literacy Rate "Women," **V21**: Youth (15-24) Literacy Rate "Total," **V22**: Youth (15-24) Literacy Rate "Men," **V23**: Youth (15-24) Literacy Rate "Women," **V24**: Adult (15+) Unemployment Rate "Total," **V25**: Adult (15+) Unemployment Rate "Men," **V26**: Adult (15+) Unemployment Rate "Women," **V27**: Improved Drinking Water Coverage (%) "Total," **V28**: Improved Drinking Water Coverage (%) "Urban," **V29**: Improved Drinking Water Coverage (%) "Rural," **V30**: Improved Sanitation Coverage (%) "Total," **V31**: Improved Sanitation Coverage (%) "Urban," **V32**: Improved Sanitation Coverage (%) "Rural"

Table 8. Levels of interdependencies among indices that are produced by different sources using different methods

Regression	R^2
CPI= -4.411 + 1.045 HDI + 1.486 IEF (-3.3.5) (3.099) (4.608)	0.748
HDI= -2.675 – 0.110 HPI + 0.334 ENV (-3.555) (-2.674) (3.972)	0.905
ENV= 8.398 + 1.556 HDI (101.608) (7.197)	0.799
KEI= -0.374 HPI (-3.668)	0.943
HPI= 2.209 IEF – 1.515 KEI (2.251) (-6.336)	0.826

(D500) is independent from all other perceptions. A similar result is attained for the perception of openness to foreign expertise (D800). The net migration flow of qualified labor D802 is also not related to the other perceptions (D802), while the non-qualified labor (D801) is correlated with social mobility of university graduates (D902). Finally, the perception of social mobility in relation to hiring and promotion (D901) is correlated with the other component that is social mobility of university graduates (D902). The details results are introduced in the first table in the appendix to this chapter.

Further details can be obtained when observing the correlation matrix between each of the disaggregated components of the way different variables are perceived. The perception of access to public schools (A9050) is linked with the perception of access to basic health services (A9051) and with the perception of the local of the training of elites (A9060). Access to health is found to be related only to the net migration flow of non-qualified women (D8011). The perception of access to water (A9052) appears to be related to access to electricity (A9053), to social mobility in the public sector (D9010) and with the attractiveness of enterprises to hiring graduates (D9022). The perception of access to electricity (A9053)

is related to social mobility (D9010) and to the attractiveness of enterprises to hiring graduates (D9022). The perception of the locations where elites are trained (A9060) seems to account for the perceptions of professional training and satisfaction of enterprise needs (D5001) and negatively to the access of foreign human resources in local enterprises (D8000). The "perceptions of the social roles of the training systems" (A9061) is not related to any of the other variables while the professional training of adults (D5000) is viewed in relation to "the professional training and enterprise needs: D5001" and to the "consistency between training and job market: D9021." "Enterprise needs and professional training: D5001" is negatively related to "foreign expertise in local enterprises: D8000," to "social mobility in public services: D90010" and to the relationship between training and job market: D9021." The "hiring of foreign expertise in local enterprises: D8000" and the "hiring of foreign enterprises in foreign firms: D8001" are not related to any of the other variables. Similarly, the "net migration flow of qualified men and women D8020 and D8021" besides the "consistency of the training systems and the job market D9021" do not correlate with any of the other variables. The net migration flow of non-qualified male labor D8010 is related to the same variable related to female labor D8011, to the variable representing qualified male labor D8020 and to the perception of the unemployment rate by young graduates D9020. The net migration flow of non-qualified female labor D8011 correlates with the perception of the unemployment rate by young graduates D9020. Social mobility in the private sector D9011 is also related to this latter variable and to attractiveness of enterprises to hiring of graduates D9022. Finally, the perception of the unemployment rate by young graduates D9020 is related to D9022 as defined above.

The above results as indicated in the second table in the appendix to this chapter, express the existence of interdependencies among the way

Table 9. One lagged variables

		F-Calculated	H0 10%	H0 5%	H0 1%
Egypt	LEB LWR	0.000	Accept	Accept	Accept
	LEB LTR	0.000	Accept	Accept	Accept
	LWR LEB	**1.860**	Accept	Accept	Accept
	LTR LEB	2.865	Accept	Accept	Accept
Turkey	LEB LWR	**0.000**	Accept	Accept	Accept
	LWR LEB	**7.680**	Reject	Reject	Accept
Morocco	LEB/LPSS	26.000	Reject	Reject	Reject
	LEB/LSS	0.000	Accept	Accept	Accept
	LEB/LWRS	3.333	Reject	Accept	Accept
	LEB/trade	0.000	Accept	Accept	Accept
	LPSS/LEB	0.000	Accept	Accept	Accept
	LSS/LEB	0.510	Accept	Accept	Accept
	LWR/LEB	7.780	Reject	Reject	Reject
	Trade/LEB	3.850	Reject	Accept	Accept
Algeria	LEB/trade	0.000	Reject	Accept	Accept
	Trade/LEB	3.940	Reject	Accept	Accept

Table 10. Variables with two lags

		F-Calculated	H0 10%	H0 5%	H0 1%
Egypt	LEB LWR	3.667	Reject	Accept	Accept
	LEB LTR	3.667	Reject	Accept	Accept
	LWR LEB	5.923	Reject	Reject	Accept
	LTR LEB	2.013	Accept	Accept	Accept
Turkey	LEB LWR	12.000	Reject	Reject	Reject
	LWR LEB	4.904	Reject	Accept	Accept
Morocco	LEB/LPSS	5.750	Reject	Reject	Accept
	LEB/LSS	5.750	Reject	Reject	Accept
	LEB/LWRS	0.000	Accept	Accept	Accept
	LEB/trade	0.000	Accept	Accept	Accept
	LPSS/LEB	2.300	Accept	Accept	Accept
	LSS/LEB	0.632	Accept	Accept	Accept
	LWR/LEB	4.083	Reject	Accept	Accept
	Trade/LEB	1.825	Accept	Accept	Accept
Algeria	LEB/trade	5.250	Reject	Reject	Accept
	Trade/LEB	0.053	Accept	Accept	Accept

Table 11. Variables with three lags

		F-Calculated	H0 10%	H0 5%	H0 1%
Egypt	LEB LWR	0.000	Accept	Accept	Accept
	LEB LTR	0.000	Accept	Accept	Accept
	LWR LEB	**5.431**	Reject	Reject	Accept
	LTR LEB	2.865			
Turkey	LEB LWR	**7.000**	Reject	Reject	Accept
	LWR LEB	**4.971**	Reject	Reject	Accept
Morocco	LEB/LPSS	3.333	Reject	Accept	Accept
	LEB/LSS	3.000	Reject	Accept	Accept
	LEB/LWRS	3.333	Reject	Accept	Accept
	LEB/trade	0.000	Accept	Accept	Accept
	LPSS/LEB	1.667	Accept	Accept	Accept
	LSS/LEB	0.543	Accept	Accept	Accept
	LWR/LEB	2.966	Reject	Accept	Accept
	Trade/LEB	1.457	Accept	Accept	Accept
Algeria	LEB/trade	3.000	Reject	Accept	Accept
	Trade/LEB	1.466	Accept	Accept	Accept

Table 12. Descriptive statistics

	N	Minimum	Maximum	Mean	Std. Deviation
A905	13	1.0	4.0	2.865	.9471
A906	13	1.0	3.1	2.089	.7212
D500	13	1.0	3.5	1.437	.7127
D800	13	1.0	4.0	2.501	.9071
D801	13	.0	4.0	2.077	1.5516
D802	13	.0	4.0	1.534	1.2833
D901	13	1.4	3.4	2.420	.4754
D902	13	1.0	3.3	2.020	.8024
Valid N	13				

different variables are perceived in the sample composing the institutional profile of 2006 in the South Mediterranean countries.

The aggregate results show that interdependencies are not only occurring at the level of objective socio-economic variables but also in the way economic agents appreciate these variables.

These subjective appreciations within the scale 0 to 4 with 0 being the lowest level of assessment, the different components appear to be inter-related. This is clearly expressed through the set of regressions introduced in Table 13. The subjective appreciation of access to basic public goods appears to be related to the level of appreciation of access to health care and to the assessment of social mobility. While access to education seems to be driven mainly by the levels of healthcare to some level (quadratic term in the equation). Further explanations are provided in the following regressions that all confirm the links between education, health care and other variables that relate to economic performance (see Table 13).

All the results attained at this level of analysis of these subjective data reveal also that interdependencies do exist even when looking at subjective aggregate data. Are these indications related to the persistence of microeconomic interdependencies even when aggregation takes places? The quantitative aggregated data analyzed and discussed earlier seem to be confirming that the microeconomic interdependencies observed at the level of countries are well expressed also at the level of the region.

CONCLUSION

This chapter shows that for SMC countries the economic development depends on the improvements in education and health, as well as on the initial wealth of a country. There are some differences between SMC countries and EU countries. No direct relationship between the level of education and economic development could be seen and the relationship between health and economic development is different from SMC countries.

The regression analysis of different clusters concerning the potential relationships between education, health, and income measurements helps to come up with the following conclusions.

First, the use of aggregate data such as the "world cluster" to illustrate relationships, without taking care of the different economic, social, regional, and development specificities, leads to contradictory findings. The example of the regression analysis of the children out of primary school illustrates the ineffectiveness of aggregate data since the results of world countries completely contradicts the results of five sub-clusters. Data from sub-clusters, in contrast, improves the efficiency and helps detect the level of significance existing between the GDP per capita and both health and education.

Second, the GDP per capita impact on improving education is not very significant. In fact, the overall conclusion that could be driven from the regression analysis of the education and income indicators is that the relationship significance of GDP per capita is not considerable. In other words, the improvement of education within different clusters does not necessarily require an economic involvement or an increase in the income of the population. The single argument in favor of the importance of the GDP per capita for ameliorating the level of education concerns the literacy rates in middle-income countries (mainly SMC, major oil net exporters, and high and medium human development). In general, arguments other than income should be studied in order to enhance education.

Third, in contrast to education, the interpretations of regression tables for health and income indicators proved that GDP per capita is the key for most clusters. The enhancement of health in different clusters can only occur if it is accompanied by an amelioration of the income level of the population. Alternatively, low human development countries need to focus on measures other than GDP per capita to determine a significant relationship with health issues. The main point of low human development countries' health indicators is that the relationship significance varies from year to year. This "instability" can be explained by the rise of new factors that alter health, more than the GDP per capita would do, within a particular period.

In the second part, regression, correlation, and granger-tests have been the main techniques used on different data. The first set of data is mainly that of the World Bank and that was described in the previous chapter. The second is the most recent database of the UN. The third set is composed of the composite indices provided by different international organizations. The last set is the 2006 institutional profile data of the French Ministry of Finance.

Table 13. Regressions of health, education, and poverty components as appreciated within the survey

Regression outputs	R^2	N
A905 on D901, A9051, D800, D500, A9051 sq A905= -2.98 A9051sq + 3.49 A9051 + 0.65 D901 (-2.85) (3.38) (3.20)	0.87	12
A9050 on A9051sq, A9051 A9050= 2.90 A9051 – 2.05 A9051sq (3.06) (-2.16)	0.83	12
A9051 on A9052, A9050, A905 A9051= 2.40 A905 – 1.58 A9052 (3.07) (2.40)	0.88	12
A905 on D901, A9051, D800, A9051sq A905= -2.81 A9051sq + 3.33 A9051 + 0.55 D901 (-2.79) (3.34) (3.43)	0.86	12
A9050 on D901, A9051, D800, A9051sq A9050= -2.66 A9051sq + 3.41 A9051 (-3.30) (4.27)	0.91	12
A905 on D901, A9051, D800, D500, A9051sq A905= -2.98 A9051sq + 3.49 A9051 + 0.65 D901 (-2.85) (3.38) (3.20)	0.87	12
A905 on D901, A9051, D800, A9051sq A905= -2.81 A9051sq + 3.33 A9051 + 0.32 D901 (-2.79) (3.34) (3.43)	0.86	12
A9050 on D901, A9051, D800, A9051sq A9050= -2.66 A9051sq + 3.41 A9051 (-3.30) (4.27)	0.91	12
D500 on D901 D500= 0.63 D901 (2.67)	0.39	12

Definition of Variables: A905: Fairness in accessing public goods: education, health, water and electricity; A9050: Access to primary and secondary schooling; A9051: Access to basic health system; A9052: Access to water; A9053: Access to electricity; A906: Training of elites; A9060: Location of training of elites; A9061: Are the training systems for elites closed or open to be source of social mobility; D500: Professional training; D5000: Professional training of adults; D5001: Enterprise needs and professional training; D800: Foreign participation to professional training; D8000: Foreign expertise in local enterprises D8001: Foreign expertise in foreign enterprises D801: Net migration of non qualified labor; D8010: Net migration non qualified males; D8011: Net migration non qualified females; D802: Net migration skilled labor; D8020: Net migration skilled men; D8021: Net migration skilled females; D901: Social mobility through hiring and promotion; D9010: Social mobility through hiring and promotion public sector; D9011: Social mobility through hiring and promotion private sector; D902: Social mobility of university graduates; D9020: Unemployment of university graduates relative to average; D9021: Adaptation of training to market needs; D9022: Levels of enterprise interests to university graduates.

The overall results attained at every level of the analysis are the high magnitude of interdependencies among all sets of variables related to health, education, and poverty. Health and education appear to have an important driving effect for these interdependencies.

This is shown with the analysis of World Bank data as well as with the new UN database. The representative variables of health, education, and poverty seem to entertain higher levels of interdependencies meaning that any change in one of the variables affects the others. This is confirmed again through the analysis of some composite indices where clear relationships have been estimated. Furthermore, even the subjective appreciations of achievements in different variables related to health, education and economic activities have appeared to show interdependencies.

The results attained so far at the regional and aggregated levels appear to be referring to the real situations faced by households in different countries. This latter has already been shown through the results shown in the previous chapter with the analysis of household data.

However, given the type of data used at both country and regional levels, it has been very hard to account for some issues that are crucial to this study. These are tackled in the following chapter.

REFERENCES

Azariadis, C., & Drazen, A. (1990). Threshold externalities in economic development. *The Quarterly Journal of Economics*, *105*(2), 501–526. doi:10.2307/2937797

Barro, R. J. (1991). Economic growth in a cross-section of countries. *The Quarterly Journal of Economics*, *106*(2), 407–443. doi:10.2307/2937943

Deaton, A. (2006). *Global patterns of income and health: Facts, interpretations and policies.* Retrieved from http://www.wider.unu.edu/events/wider-annual-lecture-2006-announcement.htm

Fogel, R. W. (2004). *The escape from hunger and premature death, 1700–2100: Europe, America, and the third world.* Cambridge, UK: Cambridge University Press. doi:10.1017/CBO9780511817649

Fukuda-Parr, S. (2007). Human rights based approach to development – Is it rhetorical repackaging or a new paradigm? HD Insights. *HDR Networks, 7.*

Gaertner, W. (2008). Individual rights versus economic growth. *Journal of Human Development and Capabilities*, *9*(3), 389–400. doi:10.1080/14649880802236607

Preston, S. H. (1996). *American longevity, past, present and future.* Syracuse, NY: Syracuse University.

ENDNOTES

[1.] This first part is mainly based on the analysis conducted within the framework of FEMISE Project (FEM32-01).

[2.] Principal component analysis is a statistical method based on the decomposition of an original variable into its main components. Principal Component Analysis (PCA) is a mathematical procedure that uses an orthogonal transformation to convert a set of observations of possibly correlated variables into a set of values of linearly uncorrelated variables called principal components. The number of principal components is less than or equal to the number of original variables. This transformation is defined in such a way that the first principal component has the largest possible variance (that is, accounts for as much of the variability in the data as possible), and each succeeding component in turn has the highest variance possible under the constraint that it be orthogonal to (i.e., uncorrelated with) the preceding components. Principal components are guaranteed to be independent only if the data set is jointly normally distributed. PCA is sensitive to the relative scaling of the original variables.

[3.] Preston's curves refer to the existence of quadratic relationships between a dependent and an independent variable. Under a convex relationship, the relationship appears to be increasing before it starts to decrease while the opposite is observed under a concave relationship. This can happens with higher values of the independent variable such that one may think about the existence of a linear relation between variables while this is in fact a quadratic one. This can be misleading in data analysis.

4. Granger causality refers to the relationship between for example two variables on which time series data are available. The test consists in series of regressions under different lags and the use of the estimated sum of squared residuals in F-tests. One retains in this regression all lagged values of x that are individually significant according to their t-statistics, provided that collectively they add explanatory power to the regression according to an F-test.

APPENDIX

Table 14. Mean values of selected indicators of health, education and economic development, MENA and EU countries

Region	MENA			EU		
Year	1995	2000	2004	1995	2000	2004
GDP per capita, PPP (current international $)	8124.6	9153.06	10881.22	15615.03	20615.25	24509.07
Life expectancy at birth, total (years)	68.69	70.76	71.84	74.52	75.94	76.80
Adult literacy rate (%). Total	67.53	73.95	78.98	-	-	97.18
Mortality rate, infant (per 1,000 live births)	39.23	30.72	27.65	8.68	6.56	5.73
School life expectancy (years). Primary to tertiary. Total	10.94	10.43	11.63	14.98	15.10	15.47

Table 15. Mean values of selected indicators of health, education, and economic development, 2004

	MENA	EU	ROW	Oil exporters and OPEC countries	Developed countries	Developing countries	Underdeveloped countries	All countries
GDP per capita, PPP (current international $)	10881	24509	7277	13476	22319	5038	1369	10391
Life expectancy at birth, total (years)	72	77	64	69	77	65	47	66
Adult literacy rate (%). Total	79	97	78	83	94	83	52	80
Mortality rate, infant (per 1,000 live births)	28	6	50	36	8	42	99	44
School life expectancy (years). Primary to tertiary. Total	12	15	11	12	15	12	7	12

Table 16. Regression models for MENA countries

Variables	n	R²	F	Model
Dependent variable: School life expectancy (years). Primary to tertiary. Total (SLE) Independent variable: GDP per capita, PPP (current international $) (GDP)	35	0.42	23.65	SLE = -6.93 + 2.05·ln(GDP) (-1.86) (4.86)
Dependent variable: Adult literacy rate (%). Total (LR) Independent variable: Life expectancy at birth, total (years) (LEB)	45	0.63	72.59	LR = -100.95 + 2.44·LEB (-4.97) (8.61)
Dependent variable: School life expectancy (years). Primary to tertiary. Total (SLE) Independent variable: Life expectancy at birth, total (years) (LEB)	40	0.77	129.00	SLE = -91.85 + 24.31·ln(LEB) (-10.12) (11.36)
Dependent variable: Life expectancy at birth, total (years) (LEB) Independent variable: GDP per capita, PPP (current international $) (GDP)	45	0.69	97.98	LEB = 18.68 + 5.90·ln(GDP) (3.55) (9.90)
Dependent variable: Mortality rate, infant (per 1,000 live births) (IMR) Independent variable: GDP per capita, PPP (current international $) (GDP)	45	0.69	94.63	MR = 251.88 - 25.00·ln(GDP) (12.00) (-9.73)
Dependent variable: Mortality rate, infant (per 1,000 live births) (IMR) Independent variable: Adult literacy rate (%). Total (LR)	45	0.72	115.04	MR = 373.812 - 80.93·ln(LR) (11.563) (-10.726)

Note: Under each regression coefficient it is written the corresponding t-value

The Relationship between Economic Development Variables and Health and Education Variables

Figure 10.

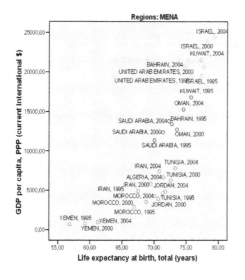

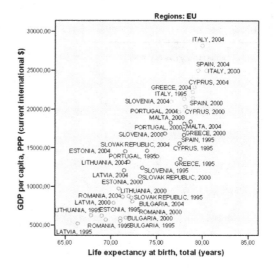

Figure 11.

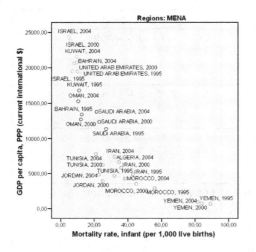

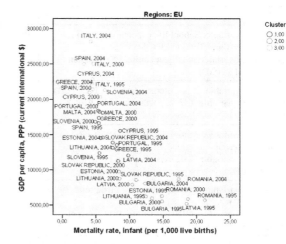

Figure 12.

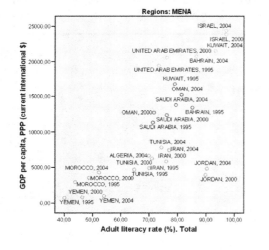

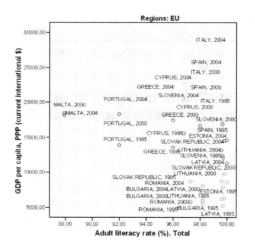

Figure 13.

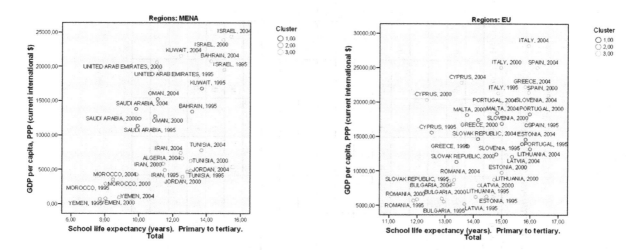

Table 17. Correlations of aggregate perceptions (institutional profiles 2006)

	A905	A906	D500	D800	D801	D802	D901	D902
A905	1	0	0	0	.746**	0	.555*	0
A906		1	0	0	0	0	0	0
D500			1	0	0	0	0	0
D800				1	0	0	0	0
D801					1	0	0	.684**
D802						1	0	0
D901							1	.585*
D902								1

Table 18. Correlations between perception components (institutional profiles 2006) South Mediterranean countries

	A9050	A9051	A9052	A9053	A9060	A9061	D5000	D5001	D8000	D8001	D8010	D8011	D8020	D8021	D9010	D9011	D9020	D9021	D9022
A9050	1	.918**	0	0	.557*	0	0	0	0	0	0	0	0	0	0	0	0	0	0
A9051		1	0	0	0	0	0	0	0	0	0	.611*	0	0	0	0	0	0	0
A9052			1	.982**	0										.561*				.670*
A9053				1	0										.639*				.636*
A9060					1	0	0	.571*	-.568*	0	0	0	0	0	0	0	0	0	0
A9061						1	0												
D5000							1	.702**	0									.644*	0
D5001								1	-.644*	0					.600*			.583*	0
D8000									1	0									0
D8001										1	0								0
D8010											1	.805**	.613*	0	0	0	.728**	0	0
D8011												1	0	0	0	0	.659*	0	0
D8020													1	0	0	0	0	0	0
D8021														1	0	0	0	0	0
D9010															1	0	0	0	0
D9011																1	.698**	0	.568*
D9020																	1	0	.843**
D9021																		1	0
D9022																			1

Section 2
Interdependencies and ICTs per Sector

Chapter 5
ICTs and Socioeconomic Performance with Focus on ICTs and Health

ABSTRACT

This chapter shows how interconnections do exist within the same sector and how ICTs can provide useful coordinating functions in the sector of health care. This is based on how e-health and other technological variants have been developing around the world and how these are promoting further access to the overall chain of health care. An overall quantitative assessment of the relationships between variables related to health and independent variables representing ICTs are established using multiple regression. The attained results show that statistically significant relationships do globally exist between health improvements and further access to information technologies. These relationships are promising for ensuring further use of advanced technologies in the area of health care in general. While there are variations between countries, the great inputs from advanced technologies in health care appear to be globally promising. Coordination between different players in this area is in the process of showing enhanced outputs at the level of health care and its related channels.

INTRODUCTION

In order to emphasize the role and likely impacts of ICTs on health and how ICTs can be used for enhancing the benefits from coordination, three major steps are pursued in this chapter. The first one focuses on the trends that are affecting ICTs in relation to the socioeconomic performance. Then more specifics are discussed in relation to the health care systems worldwide, in the context of developing countries with focus on MENA economies. The last part of this chapter is devoted to showing the relationships between health and ICTs.

DOI: 10.4018/978-1-4666-3643-9.ch005

ICT ROLE AND IMPACT ON SOCIOECONOMIC PERFORMANCE

Information and Communication Technologies (ICTs) refer to technologies that allow communication along with the electronic acquisition, processing, and broadcast of information. ICTs have an impact on businesses in both developed and developing countries. New opportunities emerge from the use of ICTs such as the design and delivery of digital goods and margin and revenue increase by accessing foreign markets directly. In the pursuit of development, sectors interact and share knowledge and techniques. These interdependencies among sectors need to be coordinated in order to achieve better progress. For instance, the economic performance influences and is impacted by performances in health and education sectors. In addition, there are variations between countries and regions in benefiting from these interdependencies. Therefore, this chapter focuses on the importance of coordinating ICTs to benefit from the variations by sector and by country and region (developed versus developing, especially MENA) in promoting development.

This collaboration has to do with the way ICTs can be helpful in education, health, social and economic performances and how they are used to coordinate interdependencies within and between these sectors. This chapter explains how ICTs and related technologies have been means to improve the lives of people and compares between the era of limited ICTs access and the era of reduced digital divide and improved access to ICTs, including the enhancement of old functions and the creation of new ones such as e-commerce, e-health, e-education, e-tourism, e-finance and e-trade. Developed economies are assumed to benefit more from these ICTs than developing ones. It also seems that the MENA region has the potential of performing better.

Literature Review

Information and Communication Technology (ICT), through radio, television, and print media, have been important in many developing countries. In recent years new ICTs, including Smartphones and Internet-associated applications have become accessible to larger populations worldwide. ICTs have been helping developing countries deal with different health, social and economic problems. ICTs are assumed to have a potential role in eliminating extreme poverty, achieving universal compulsory education and gender equality and fighting against serious diseases, by enhancing information accessibility and allowing communication.

However, disparities between countries still exist and poor and rural populations often do not have access to new ICTs. According to reports, OECD countries have the highest access to new ICTs, followed by South Asian and some African countries, including South Africa. Manochehri, Al-Esmail, and Ashrafi, (2012) stated that ICTs have an important impact on businesses in developed and developing countries in terms of productivity and economic growth. Burke (2010) reported the existence of important benefits from having websites, including the introduction of new customers and additional sales for firms. Other studies found that Arab countries still fall behind developed ones both in ICT spending (Nour, 2008) and in the lack of means needed to succeed in projects made to promote growth through IT transformation (El-Shenawy, 2010). In addition, Richardsson et al. (2006) identified five main areas of ICT applications to support enterprises and rural development, which include the economic development of products, community development, research and education, small and medium enterprises development, and media networks. The effect of ICTs also differs inside regions. The diffusion of ICT in OECD countries currently differs considerably since some of them have invested more or have began investing in ICTs earlier than other countries (OECD, 2003). This investment refers to establishing the infrastructure or networks for the use of ICT and providing productive equipment and software to businesses (Richardsson, et al., 2006). Galliano et al. (2008) found that there is a gap in the intensity of ICTs' usage between industrial French firms that are located in rural areas and those located in urban zones. The authors stated that two elements result from the geographic isolation that are the difficult access to information and the complicated mode of coordination with eternal partners, given their distance.

Piatkowski (2003) has already established the link between ICTs and company competitiveness. The author found that ICT platforms, including personal computers, mobiles and Internet, provide more visibility to businesses, offer more information to small enterprises, allow enterprises to overcome trade barriers and facilitate financial transactions. The private sector was encouraged to invest in an ICT infrastructure and use ICTs as a means of competitive advantage to conduct business. This can take the form of commercially driven connectivity, software, technology, e-commerce, and online transactions (Clift, 2003).

Manochehri et al. (2012) established a positive link between ICT investments and labor productivity. They stated that the most important benefits of ICTs come from their effective use, especially in enterprises that are structured to use these technologies. The ICT revolution in the US has stimulated enterprise restructuring and has modified the terms of competition: US enterprises have become more efficient in getting value from their ICT activities, given that spending in the US has jumped to 5.4% in 2010 according to Pettey and Tudor (2011).

It has been reported that investment in basic telecommunications in Africa resulted in a positive impact on economic, political, and institutional development. Shirazi (2008) has also established a link between ICTs (the Internet) and a rapid democratization in regions such as the Middle East. A recent example of such view has been witnessed recently through events such as the "Arab Spring" in Egypt, Libya, Syria, Tunisia, Yemen, and other Middle Eastern countries.

Adewoye and Akanbi (2012) pointed out to problems that delay the development of the SMEs sector in Nigeria, including obsolete technologies and machineries, lack of access to modern technology, lack or limited access to information on raw materials, management support and technical advisory services, financial problems and poor economic condition. Some of these problems can be resolved by applying ICTs to bring about sustainable economic development. According to Richardsson et al. (2006), Nigerian companies can use ICTs in online services for information, monitoring and consultation and transaction and processing (e-commerce).

Rallet and Torre (1999) found that there are factors impacting the diffusion of ICT. These factors include coordination mechanisms in innovative and research activities and the geographical proximity of economic agents to develop innovation activities. It has been reported that geographical proximity is beneficial if the nature of the activities is characterized by tacit knowledge. Thus, the less tacit knowledge is (later stages of the development process), the less the need for physical proximity. In addition, it is argued that ICTs can increase the possibilities of remote coordination since they are a means of turning tacit knowledge into codified knowledge.

Ssewanyana and Busler (2007) reported that the adoption and use of ICTs have an impact on business processes, even though disparities between developed and developing countries do exist. Internet usage in the developed world was 8 times that of developing countries in 2004 (ITU, 2011). ICTs have transformed the way businesses are conducted by introducing the concept of 'Networked economy' that links businesses with suppliers, internal manufacturing processes, shippers and customers in real-time. From a Ugandan case study, the adoption and usage of ICTs by enterprises in developing countries are said to follow the same pattern as the developed ones and only differ in the level of usage and adoption.

Method and Data

To assess the impacts of ICTs on economic and social performance data, some indicators were gathered especially from the World database (The World Bank) and the International Telecommunications Union (ITU) database to try to link ICT variables with health, education and economic indicators. Linear regressions were conducted to identify links and relationships between these indicators. Only countries included in the Middle East and North Africa (MENA) region are considered in this study. These include Bahrain, Egypt, Iran, Iraq, Israel, Jordan, Kuwait, Lebanon, Libya, Morocco, Oman, Qatar, Syria, Tunisia, Turkey, United Arab Emirates, and Yemen.

Among the ICT indicators used, there is the number of Internet users who are people with access to the worldwide network and the investment in telecoms with private participation (current US$) which is the value of telecom projects that have reached financial closure and directly or indirectly serve the public, including operation and management contracts with major capital expenditure, green-field projects, and divestitures. There are also the ICT goods imports and exports, which include telecommunications, audio and video, computer and related equipment; electronic components; and other ICT goods where software is excluded. In addition, ICT service exports include computer and communications services (telecommunications and postal and courier services) and information services (computer data and news-related service transactions).

The health, education and economic data was respectively represented by the total health expenditure, the total life expectancy at birth, the adult total literacy rate (as % of people ages 15 and above), GDP (current $US), and GDP per capita (current $US). The total health expenditure is the sum of public and private health expenditure. It covers the provision of health services (preventive and curative), family planning activities, nutrition activities, and emergency aid designated for health but does not include provision of water and sanitation. Life expectancy at birth is the number of years a newborn infant would live if prevailing patterns of mortality at the time of its birth were to stay the same throughout its life. The adult literacy rate is the percentage of people ages 15 and above who can, with understanding, read and write a short, simple statement on their everyday life. GDP at purchasers' prices is the sum of gross value added by all resident producers in the economy plus any product taxes and minus any subsidies not included in the value of the products. Data are in current US dollars. GDP per capita is gross domestic product divided by mid-year population.

Results

The indicators used in this chapter are listed in the Appendix (Tables 4, 5, 6, and 7) under their raw and natural logarithmic forms. The results of the regression analyses conducted are shown in Tables 1 and 2.

Discussion

It has been indicated in the literature that the share of ICT in investment is a core indicator of ICT diffusion. From the first set of results, it is observed that an increase in the economic performance, measured by GDP per Capita in the MENA region can lead to an increase in investment in telecommunications at a decreasing rate.

Table 1. Impact of economic and social development on ICTs

Equation	R²	Obs.
$\ln\left(Internet\,Users2010\right) = \underset{(-0.928)}{-5.295} + \underset{(3.557)}{0.807^*}\ln\left(GDP2009\right)$	0.46	17
$\ln\left(Internet\,Users2010\right) = \underset{(-1.432)}{-6.265} + \underset{(5.401)}{0.983^*}\ln\left(GDP2009\right) - \underset{(-3.376)}{0.567^*}\ln\left(HEPC2009\right)$	0.70	17
$\ln\left(InvInTelecoms2010\right) = \underset{(-0.874)}{-1.127} + \underset{(0.770)}{0.447^*}\ln\left(HEPC2009\right) - \underset{(2.569)}{0.746^*}\ln\left(GDP2009\right)$	0.59	10
$\ln\left(InvInTelecoms2010\right) = \underset{(0.189)}{1.633} + \underset{(2.126)}{0.727^*}\ln\left(GDP_{PC}2009\right)$	0.39	9

Table 2. Effects of ICTs on economic and social development

Equation	R²	Obs.
$\ln\left(GDP2010\right) = \underset{(5.85)}{14.08} + \underset{(4.86)}{0.75^*}\ln\left(Internet\,Users2009\right)$	0.68	13
$\ln\left(HEPC2010\right) = \underset{(0.24)}{0.65} + \underset{(2.19)}{0.40^*}\ln\left(InvestmentInTelecom2009\right) - \underset{(-1.22)}{0.22^*}\ln\left(Internet\,Users2009\right)$	0.45	9
$\ln\left(GDPperCapita2010\right) = \underset{(1.90)}{3.94} + \underset{(2.01)}{0.21^*}\ln\left(InvestmentInTelecom2009\right)$	0.37	9
$\ln\left(GDP2010\right) = \underset{(4.28)}{9.67} + \underset{(7.01)}{0.79^*}\ln\left(InvestmentInTelecom2009\right)$	0.88	9

Indeed, previous studies have shown that higher levels of ICT investments do not necessarily lead to better business performance than lower levels.

The results also show a positive relationship between economic performance (GDP) and the number of Internet users. An increase in GDP can lead to an increase in the number of Internet users but at a decreasing rate. However, an increase in health expenditures per capita by one point of percentage can trigger a decrease in the natural logarithm of the number of Internet users by 0.57 points.

Other indicators tested during the empirical analysis did not show any impact on the investment in ICT, number of Internet users, ICT goods for import, ICT goods for export or ICT service exports. These include the total adult literacy of ages 15 and above and life expectancy at birth. In addition, health expenditures per capita, GDP, GDP per capita, and total life expectancy at birth did not seem to affect the ICT goods imports, ICT goods exports, and ICT service exports.

The second set of results studies the impact of ICTs on the economic and social developments. It is observed that an increase in Internet users can lead to an increase in GDP at a decreasing rate. The same result appears when an increase in telecommunications investment occurs. In addition, a small increase in investment in telecommunications seems to lead to a slow increase in GDP per capita. The increase in telecommunications' by one percentage point leads to the increase in health expenditures per capita by 0.4 points of percentage.

This first part discusses ICTs' impact on businesses in North Africa and Middle Eastern countries. From the results, it appears that new economic and social opportunities emerge from the increased use of ICTs. At the same time, it seems that the enhanced economic and social development, notably in relation to health and GDP, leads to an improved use of information and communication technologies. A future development of this chapter can be focused on the need to coordinate interdependencies among sectors in order to achieve better progress. Variations between countries and regions in benefiting from these interdependencies are also subjects to be discussed further. This chapter focuses on proving the importance of ICTs in the economic and social developments as well as the effect of improved social and economic conditions on the usage of ICTs. These latter are helpful in education, health, social and economic performances. This chapter provided some explanations on how ICTs and related technologies can be means to enhance the lives of people. In addition, the chapter demonstrates that the development of MENA countries' economic and social conditions can be explained by the improved usage of ICTs and related technologies. According to the results, these countries seem to have the potential to perform better.

NEW TRENDS OF ICTS IN HEALTH

The Information and Communication Technologies (ICTs) have known a tremendous evolution in the last decade. The evolution consists of the emergence of broadband, smartphones and a multibillion-dollar social media industry that involves, for instance, blogs, Facebook, Twitter,

Youtube, and LinkedIn (Ratzan, 2011). All these media contribute to sharing information, promoting for diversity, and connecting people all around the globe. As different sectors such as education and economy have been benefiting from these technologies nowadays, the health sector does not make the exception.

Major Roles of ICTs in Health

The labels may differ from m-Health to e-Health to tele-Health, but they are all referring to using the ICTs in favor of health and all its aspects (Ebikeme, 2011). M-health is among the few areas in health communication that have generated success over limited time. This is the use of mobile devices to exchange health information. The increase in mobile phones and related messaging systems is also among the factors of m-health development (Sherry & Ratzan, 2012).

M-health refers to the use of mobile applications for healthcare. It is considered by Qiang, Yamamichi, Hausman, and Altman (2011) as young and promising, for the well-being of people. To the authors, Mobile applications can lower costs and improve the quality of healthcare. It can shift behavior to strengthen prevention to improve health outcomes over the long term. This is considered to be at the crossroad between health, technology, and finance.

This study assesses the current state of m-health in the developing world with extensive case studies from Haiti, India, and Kenya. In addition, it identifies emerging trends, risks, and opportunities in the m-health.

In a relatively very recent contribution, Al-Shorbaji (2012) starts with a listing of the benefits achieved in health sciences before discussing the knowledge gap that is still underway. The author recognizes how health science library and networks have been promoted to support medical education, medical research, and other uses. The contribution also indicates how the MEDLINE plus and PubMed have been providing further health care knowledge to different users. To the author these efforts have also contributed to enhance e-learning in the area of health. Self-medication and e-pharmacies have also been expanded but some risks are still prevailing in relation to the illegal websites offering pharmaceutical services. The role of the Telemedicine is also emphasized to be the successful provision of health care services when most of the time distance is a critical factor. This is becoming important with the development of series of services from Telemedicine: tele-surgery, tele-pathology, tele-radiology, tele-dermatology, and others. Besides the above contributions, mobile health is also introduced by the author as a source of successfully provided services. The development of health call centers, toll-free emergencies, and mobile telemedicine is expressed through the expansion of the new mobile health services. The chapter addresses also the progress achieved in electronic health with the development of electronic health recording, patient education and safety, Internet protocol television and social media and Web applications.

The amount of data produced is growing at a high rate: 55 new clinical trials, 1260 articles indexed in MEDLINE, and 5000 papers published in the biomedical sciences on a daily average (Lyman & Varian, 2003). Thus, it is becoming crucial to improve the health of communities and strengthen their health systems. These systems include the management system, the infrastructure, the diagnostic, the pathology, the treatments, the monitoring, the pharmaceuticals, etc.

The questions to be raised would be how are the developed countries benefiting from the ICTs in the health sector? How do the results differ from a country to another? And how can the developing countries benefit from these ICTs to contribute to their empowerment and reduce the poverty rate, especially in the MENA region?

ICTs are defined as tools that facilitate communication and the processing and transmission of information by electronic means; meanwhile,

health is defined as a complex interaction of biomedical, social, economic, and political determinants (Chetley, 2006). According to WHO (World Health Organization), the use of ICTs in health is not necessarily about technology (Dzenowagis, 2005) but more about reaching some desired outcomes. Among these outcomes, there is: making better treatment decisions by health workers, providing higher quality and safer care in hospitals, making informed choices when it comes to the patients' own health, making the governments more responsive to health needs and the policy makers more aware of health risks, simplify access to the information and knowledge for better health, and supporting the development of effective, efficient and equitable health systems by national and local information systems.

It is important to differentiate between the e-health and the conventional health care. When talking about e-health, it is more about the advanced technologies and the sophisticated tools used not just to treat patients but also used to develop medicine, analyze, and predict diseases. On the other hand, the use of ICTs in the conventional health is not eliminated as doctors and nurses can use software and newly developed machines in their daily work. However, they would need much more work to be able to use e-health: a change at the level of the practice habits, the long-term perspective of medicine, and the networking at a global level.

In the recent decades, many countries around the world are increasing investments in healthcare information technology on a national basis to increase efficiency of services, while improving the quality and safety of care. However, most of the MENA region countries still face challenges at different levels (Vital Wave Consulting, 2011). These challenges would be the shortage in terms of funding, equipments, and supplies; the insufficiency in terms of the quantity of skilled health care workers; the lack of education about prevention and treatment of preventable diseases as well as the lack of health systems infrastructure linking between the rural and urban centers.

The developed countries have reached outstanding results when it comes to using ICTs in the health sector. In fact, they were able to make sure that the e-Health applications developed so far can be maintained financially, operationally, and legally in the long term. Besides, some countries set common then national roadmaps aiming to develop e-Health systems and services as well to reinforce the individual good practices. An example of such action would be the Mobile Alliance for Maternal Action launched in India, South Africa, and Bangladesh to help mothers make rational decisions when it comes to pregnancy and childbirth (Ratzan, 2011). The citizens' awareness of the importance of ICTs in maintaining their good health has been increasing. In 2001, 86% of adults in the United States with access to the Internet had consulted it for health-related information, and 55% of primary care physicians in Germany and 90% in the United States used it (Kwankam, 2004).

In Europe, there is the European Commission that provides policymakers and program managers with accurate information on a regular basis by conducting studies on the issues likely to affect the policymaking. These include the exchange of good practices in e-Health, how to address common challenges, patient identity in e-Health, legal, and regulatory aspects of e-Health, and the impact of ICT on patient safety and risk management in healthcare.

In the United States, Google came up with an online surveillance system in 2008 in order to track flu outbreaks using the searches individuals have been doing. As a result, Google system was 1 to 2 weeks faster than the Centers for Disease Control and Prevention in predicting the flu levels in the country (Ratzan, 2011).

In Kenya, some doctor started using Personal Digital Assistants (PDAs) to help them manage their patients' data and treatments and stay up to date with that, and some workers in Kijabe Hospital use these PDAs to access up-to-date information about HIV, malaria, abdominal pain, and typhoid fever, among others, besides their diagnosis and treatment (Ebikeme, 2011).

In Peru, there are multiple mobile platforms to track the disease outbreaks, especially those like Chagas, Dengue, and Leishmaniasis, and the data collected allow a faster medical.

In India, the Space Research Organization connects 22 super specialty hospitals and 78 rural and remote health centers, all over the country using geo-stationary satellites.

On the other hand, the same technological evolution is taking place in few other developing countries. Recent numbers show that there are 5 billion wireless subscribers; more than 70% of them live in low to middle income countries (Ebikeme, 2011). The average penetration rates of mobile phones and Internet in the developing countries are greater than those recorded five years ago in the industrialized world proving that the catching-up is happening faster with the new ICTs (Kwankam, 2004). The Internet plays an academic role of a local training provider in the developing countries, and it is considered as a partial solution to the "brain drain" of health workers (Fraser & McGrath, 2000).

The developing countries can benefit more from the ICTs in many ways. By linking the health information to the mobile communication, disease prevention, wellness, monitoring, and treatments services can be improved. Additionally, different sectors such as governmental agencies, academics, private sector, and actors in civil society should provide their perspectives, resources and contribution to e-Health projects based on their expertise (Ratzan, 2011). The key idea is that "More can be done with less" (Ebikeme, 2011), for instance, by simply using a mobile phone as a diagnostic tool as well and as a mean to transmit patients' data remotely. The goals from using an ICT should meet those of treatment compliance, education, data collection, and remote monitoring.

ICTs and Health in Different Economies with Focus on MENA Countries

Countries in the MENA region are not benefiting from a quick growth in ICTs, when it comes to using those technologies in healthcare. People mostly use them for social, academic or business purposes, and less likely for healthcare purposes. In 2010, the MENA ICT Forum that took place for the first time in Jordan with the gathering of scientists, and policy-makers to analyze the existing visions and put together strategies for future growth of ICTs. However, by consulting the agenda of the forum, the health sector is not covered, or is not given much of an importance. There was also a workshop in Casablanca, Morocco with the theme "Innovation in HealthCare Technology Workshop" organized by the Arab Administrative Development Organization to discuss the Hospitals Information Systems (HIS), the performance management including the key performance indicators, the policies and procedures, the emergency management, and the staff training, as well as the remote monitoring and the interactive services. Through these efforts and others, the concept of using ICTs in health in the MENA region is still more a topic of discussion than of application.

In the United States of America, the Knowledge for Health Organization (K4Health) developed the K4Health e-Toolkits. They are, actually, electronic libraries of resources on a particular health topic developed by technical experts. These e-Toolkits are designed especially for health program managers, service providers, and policy makers in the health sector. Recently, they have developed one on the Adolescents Living with HIV (ALHIV) according to the organization's website (www.k4health.org).

In South Africa, a National Health Care Management Information System (NHC/MIS)

was designed to cover medical records, patient registration, billing, and scheduling modules in select hospitals in all 9 provinces (Littlejohns, et al., 2003). They also developed patient's smart cards which includes ID Verification; blood group; allergies; donor status; last 10 diagnoses, treatment, prescriptions; and medical aid. Back in 1998, the South African District Health Information System (DHIS) was launched in all provinces. It was the first systematic data-gathering tool used to identify public health issues. In fact, it enabled all the 4153 public clinics in the country to collect information on 10 national health indicators. Since the model was effective, it has been exported to other countries, including Mozambique and Cuba. Another successful project in South Africa is the Cell-Life project backed by Vodacom which consists of software and data management systems that allow clinic workers to use their mobile phones to monitor patients' HIV treatment and spot health problems before they become life-threatening (Kahn, 2004). From the previous trials and experience with ICTS in health in South Africa, there seems to be a need to involve users in the planning and design of the system, build information cultures, strengthen capacity of users, and focus on the benefits of the system, rather than the technology (Littlejohns, Wyatt, & Garvican, 2003).

In Australia and in 2011, Hewlet-Packard won a contract to supply and maintain ICT services to a portion of South Australia's new $2.1 billion digital Royal Adelaide Hospital (RAH). The main objective is to design, build, and maintain the hospital's ICT infrastructure for the facility throughout its construction, and it is scheduled to be completed by 2016. It will also operate and maintain the ICT systems for the following 30 years (Herrick, 2011). Besides, there is a project of a new 800-bed hospital that would be the first recipient of HP's "version 2.0 digital hospital solutions" and would include software applications that link conventional building engineering systems to the communications systems and their mobile devices.

According to the Center for Strategic & International Studies (Halamka, 2011), after the disasters of the great earthquake, Tsunami, and Fukushima nuclear plant crisis, the healthcare IT program in Japan will take some drastic measures to improve the health care using highly developed technologies. To name some of these projects, the country encourages the adoption of Electronic Health Records (EHR) in hospitals and provider offices, the use of public Internet to transmit and share electronic records safely and following the security standards and patient privacy, and the adoption of some international standards such as Clinical Document Architecture (CDA), Continuity of Care Document (CCD), and Continuity of Case Record (CCR). Another positive alternative suggested by the United States of America is to create a national healthcare identifier to link records and to create easily a national emergency care database and to decentralize the implementation programs at the prefecture levels to help staff and providers to easily plan, install and use electronic health records successfully.

ICT strategic intent can be measured by three main factors: the published strategy documentation, the actual progress in the implementation of ICT strategies, and the presence of technology-building initiatives and Research and Development (R&D) institutes (Dutta & Coury, 2002).

According to the World Markets Research Centre in 2002, in many Arab countries, the speed of the introduction of Internet access devices is increasing rapidly. Individually, Arabian Gulf states display ICT and Internet penetration levels comparable to the West. The United Arab Emirates penetration rate of almost 30 percent at the end of 2001 is higher than the European average. The European IP association ranked the United Arab Emirates as the 20th in the global Internet host penetration, with a population-to-host ratio of 37, placing it above Israel and six places below the United Kingdom (Dutta & Coury, 2002).

In Jordan, the Information Technology Association of Jordan (int@j) was founded in the year 2000 (www.intaj.com) with the mission to advance and promote the constituents it represents in both, the local and global markets. The key challenges of the ICT sector in the country consist of the low Internet penetration levels due to the supply and the demand for Internet access that remain low as well as the minimal level of R&D by global standards. In fact, Jordanian ICT companies, the academic sector, and the Government do not invest in R&D at a consistent level with a mature internationally competitive industry. Another stumbling block is the gap between academia and industry as Jordanian universities do not produce enough ICT graduates with the competencies required to sustain growth in the industry while the industry actually needs to communicate its skill needs, better cultivate talent, and facilitate a smooth labor market for ICT professionals. One more challenge would be the difficulty to attract and retain ICT experts in Jordan. It needs to be more competitive to sustain high-value industry productivity and growth.

A survey entitled "Media Access and Use in Southern Sudan" conducted in 2007 showed that in Southern Sudan, the radio was the main source of information for the population as a whole with 59% of respondents citing the radio as a source of information more than all other forms of media. On the other hand, mobile phones do not have such high rates of usage as radio because of 30% coverage rates. Nonetheless, the mobile phone network has expanded considerably since 2005 and is predicted to keep expanding in the years to come.

The Government of Yemen according to (GOPA, 2005) has not yet reached the stage of harmonizing or standardizing IT infrastructure and IT systems. One of the major targets tackled by the government is an IT-based unified and standardized Human Resource (HR) procedure.

The development of ICT solutions in Morocco has achieved great significance as both the public and private sector have understood its importance in building a strong economic infrastructure. It has a modern phone system; with the national network nearly 100% digital using fiber-optic links, and Internet access is readily available but still expensive.

In Qatar, ICT Qatar is working in collaboration with other government agencies, telecommunications providers, content providers, property developers and consumers to build a high-speed broadband network in the country (www.ictqatar. qa). The Qatar National Broadband Network (QNBN) is planning to connect all individuals and businesses to a fiber broadband network by 2015. As a result, Qatar now ranks among the top three in the Arab world in basic ICT indicators such as the numbers of computer users, Internet users, mobile telephone, fixed telephone lines, and broadband Internet subscribers.

As far as Egypt is concerned, the country takes the digital age seriously and its Ministry of Communications and Information Technology, MCIT, was formed specifically to facilitate Egypt's transition into the global information society. With a relatively modern and large phone system (over 10 million fixed and 10 million mobile phone lines), the government has been launching initiatives around e-Government, e-Learning, e-Business, e-Health, e-Culture, and has been promoting investments in the sector. Internet access is readily available and cheap.

According to www.grace-network.com, Africa's top performer in ICTs is Tunisia. While its ICT sector is poorly performing in comparison to second placed South Africa, Tunisia has come through leaps and bounds in the last twenty years. The government has given ICT the priority by encouraging the improvement of technologies and turning them into the major vectors of Tunisia's

social and economic development. Along with this, Tunisia has implemented a multidimensional strategy centered on modernizing its physical infrastructure by setting up a complimentary legal and statutory framework bearing in mind that the requirements for new ICT in higher education is closely related to innovating and creative scientific research.

After these few examples from different, we can come up with few prescriptions to improve ICTs in the MENA region (Dutta & Coury, 2002). The actions to be taken can be to create a common Arab ICT strategy aligned with national ambitions, to proceed towards technological sovereignty (autonomy in choices, control of national destiny, and technological development), to increase the competitiveness of the telecommunications industry, to recognize, attract, and build human capital, to reduce the digital divide and attenuate its effects offers benefits beyond ICT penetration, such as fostering social cohesion and producing a new generation of national leaders, and last but not least to stimulate Arabic content for more user-friendly applications.

A critical mass of professional and community users of ICTs in health has not yet been reached in developing countries. Many of the approaches being used are still at a relatively new stage of implementation, with insufficient studies to establish their relevance, applicability or cost effectiveness (Martínez, Rodrigues, & Infante, 2001).

MENA Countries and Achievements in E-Health

"ICT" Health is a healthcare technology company that provides innovative and powerful life care solutions that transform care delivery. In the Middle East, more than 100 hospitals have benefited from the company's deployed solutions. "ICT" Health currently has clients in Saudi Arabia, UAE, Qatar, Bahrain, India, and Africa, as well as in the United States of America. The company has strategic partnerships with global majors including Oracle, Hewlett Packard, Stryker, Hitachi, and Gambro, which helped it explore the best practices applicable to the healthcare sector. There are a number of pilot projects that have demonstrated improvements such as a 50% reduction in mortality or 25-50% increases in productivity within the healthcare system (Greenberg, 2005).

In Jordan int@j successfully diffused ICT into other sectors: Health, Pharmaceuticals, Energy, etc by conducting events and workshops to introduce ICT and ICT Enabled services to these sectors. The main advancement programs to the industry avail capital and finance and carry out human resources development initiatives. According to the same source, the strategic motives and key solutions of ICT in the health sector in Jordan are well set.

One of the main projects in Tunisia is the e-Disabled Project (World Bank, 2008) from which 3000 disabled students benefited from regular access and usage of the computer laboratories and software out of a target population of 10,000 so far. The project could also provide computer laboratories in schools for disabled children to have access to multilingual Arabic/French/Sign language software reinforcing school curriculum. Apart from the computer labs in the schools, 24 centers have been funded throughout Tunisia offering Internet access to the disabled population at large, including access to government services. Each center is equipped with hardware and software to allow citizens with disabilities (physical, intellectual, or auditive) to access content online. In 2007, the first group of these centers served over 500 disabled Tunisians in their Internet research and interactions with government services. By 2009, the full disabled schoolchildren population was covered. Another accomplishment in the country was the use of ICTs in the field of prevention against Sexually Transmitted Diseases (STD) AIDS training on February 2010 in Hammamet organized by the regional division of the Nabeul-Based National Family and Population Board targets hospital staff as well as all parties concerned.

In Oman, ICT Health has successfully installed its tightly integrated Web-based Picture Archival and Communications System (PACS) at Oman's Khoula Hospital on 2010. This system will allow staff across the facility to store, retrieve, distribute and present stored images and to access and update the hospital's tightly integrated "Al Shifa Hospital Information System and Radiology Information System" (HIS-RIS) through voice recognition, with much faster reporting times and accuracy. The system will allow staff using PACS to benefit from 40 terabytes (TB) of storage required to store all of the hospital's data for the next three years. The CEO of ICT Health, Gautam Dey, stated: "The Ministry of Health (MoH) in Oman, which provides around 80% of the country's healthcare, is committed to using technology solutions and services that are relevant, efficient and that empower staff members to provide the best possible level of care. For this reason, Oman has been voted as one of the top ten countries for healthcare in the world. According to him, the expectations of Al Shifa system were met since the lost/duplication of patients Records were eliminated; the completeness of Patients records was ensured thanks to warnings in case of incomplete Patients records; and the problems related to unreadable handwritings of Patients Records (major cause of medical errors) were eliminated. In addition to these achievements, the hospitals could reach a percentage of 60% of time saving on medical personnel and could have a better management and control of Medical resources (Alerts before expiry of medications, etc), a better communication with patients, resulting in better management of treatment to the satisfaction of Patients (e.g.: SMS), and more transparency in the health care processes.

In Egypt, the ministry of health developed a "National Network for Citizen Health Treatment by the Government" which encourages the use of ICT to create a national network for treatment at the expense of the State through establishment of an integrated information system (Web-based) to link Specialized Medical Councils and government hospitals that provide treatment services to the citizens to achieve a means of Web (TIGA, 2011). The Government of Egypt and its Ministry of Health have established several e-Health programs to bring better diagnostic and health services to a wider segment of the Egyptian society (IST Africa Consortium, 2011). Among these programs: the Emergency Medical Call Center and Ambulance Service, the National Network for Citizen Health Treatment, the Information System Units in Governmental Hospitals, the National Healthcare Capacity Building Project, the Pilot Project for Hospital Automation, the Women's Mobile Health Unit Project, the Integrated National Health Record System, and the IT Health Master Plan.

Algeria reports (www.who.int) that more than half of the listed actions to promote an enabling environment for ICTs in the health sector have been taken and are rated as moderately effective. The establishment of the "Health Algeria" network, a tool for data collection and exchange among the different actors in the health sector, is rated as the most effective action to date. The most significant challenges in this field have been strengthening the ICT infrastructure and expanding the Health Algeria network to certain regional and local areas where there is a lack of infrastructure.

As long as the United Arab Emirates are concerned, Imtac Technologies, an established UAE based IT services provider, announced in January 2009 the launch of ICT HEALTH, a new entity that will operate out of Dubai Healthcare City in a press release. It also plans to launch a series of integrated solution offerings based on the software-as-a-service (SAAS) framework along with transaction fee-based pricing models. With over 2.5 billion USD of healthcare claims estimated to be processed annually in Dubai alone, ICT HEALTH will play a key role in executing the new service to support the region's healthcare sector. Gautam Dey, the Chief Operating Officer of Imtac Technologies claimed: "ICT HEALTH

has been established with the aim of driving exponential growth in the healthcare market in the UAE. Our solution, in addition to being efficient, will bring about transparency and reduced costs while enhancing internal processes across companies operating in this sector."

According to the WHO, the policies related to ICTs in the health sector are still poor and need to be backed up by more support from the government.

The ICTQATAR continues to support the Supreme Council of Health's efforts to further digitize healthcare systems and records. Enhancing healthcare through better prevention, detection, diagnosis and treatment resulted in improved electronic data storage and sharing from which the public would benefit. From another perspective, the Supreme Health Council and Hamad Medical Corporation have begun efforts to build a unified health records system, and 500 employees, including doctors, nurses and therapists have already been trained in how to use the system. 4 of 12 hospitals have already fully integrated the system, and it is now the standard for all new hospitals in Qatar. Of Qatar's healthcare providers, 15.6 percent have health-related websites and only 3.1 percent offer transactional services—compared to a community of healthcare professionals and residents who are proficient in Internet use. Nearly 76 percent of physicians in Qatar were connected to an online health professionals' network as of the third quarter of 2008. In comparison, 57 percent of nurses, and 70 percent of allied health professionals were connected to such networks. Iran established the Centre for Knowledge Management, Leadership Development and e-Health on 26 July 2005 to enhance knowledge management in the Ministry of Health and Medical Education and for building capacity to use ICTs in health to develop management and leadership skills (www.who.int). Some of its objectives are to act as a national gateway for creation of awareness and access to international resources, to develop and maintain a national observatory of e-health activities and projects, to implement in collaboration with other ministries and institutions the Health Academy project for health education of young population through ICT, to conduct systematic monitoring and evaluation of work performed in KMC and provide feedback to stakeholders, and finally to manage, operate and coordinate the work of the Crisis Room in response to needs and for emergency preparedness.

In Yemen, GOPA has started a project in Yemen the main purpose of which is to restructure the organization and the management systems of the Ministries of Public Health and Population (MPHP).

Saudi Arabia has devoted important resources to health care. The country launched an e-health project in 2006 where different players are involved including universities. The King Abdulaziz Medical City symbolizes this involvement in new health care where ICTs will play an important role. Saudi Arabia announced also a five years plan on 2010 by the ministry of health (Alyemeni, 2011).

A survey completed in 2006 by WHO revealed that over 910 health facilities existed in South Sudan.

In Egypt, ICTs will be used to enable mothers of disabled children to combat the stigmatization. Using ICTs, women will be encouraged to connect with each other to communicate about their experiences and support each other and store information and knowledge to empower themselves.

Meaningful use of ICTs for health is not about the amount of hardware and software used but more about: improving quality safety efficiency, reducing health disparities, engaging patients and families in their health care, improving care coordination, improving population and public health, ensuring adequate privacy and security protections for personal health information. The lessons learned and to be applied in the coming projects of ICTs in health would be to keep the technology simple, relevant and local; to build on what is there and being used; to involve users in the design; to strengthen capacity to use, work

with and develop effective ICTs; to introduce greater monitoring and evaluation, particularly participatory approaches; to include communication strategies in the design of ICT projects; and to continue to research and share learning about what works, and what fails.

DATA AND TESTING OF LINKS BETWEEN HEALTH AND ICTS

As a follow-up to the literature review, health and ICTs appear to be interrelated with ICTs providing important prospects for the improvements of health care at its different stages. This part is an attempt for assessing the existence of quantitative relationships between health and ICTs. For that purpose, data and variables are first identified before proceeding with regressions, their results, and discussion.

Variables and Data

World Development Indicators (WDI) based on 167 countries from 2002 to 2010 are used. The variables included are divided into three main categories: Health indicators, and ICT indicators that are:

H1: Life expectancy at birth (years) of both sexes

H2: Infant mortality rate (probability of dying by age 1 per 1000 live births) of both sexes

H3: Under-five mortality rate (probability of dying by age 1 per 1000 live births)

H4: Adult mortality rate (probability of dying between 15 and 60 years per 1000 population)

H5: Prevalence of tuberculosis (per 100 000 population)

H6: Incidence of tuberculosis (per 100 000 population per year)

H7: Total fertility rate (per woman)

H8: Immunization, DPT (% of children ages 12-23 months)

ICT1: Mobile cellular subscriptions (per 100 people)

ICT2: Telephone lines (per 100 people)

ICT3: Internet users (per 100 people)

The first category includes life expectancy at birth, the annual population growth, the mortality rate for infants under 5 per 1000 infant, the DPT immunization (percentage of children between 12 and 23 months), and the total percentage of health expenditure in GDP. The second category includes the mobile cellular subscriptions per 100 people, the telephone lines per 100 people, the Internet users per 100, the percentage of ICT goods imports from the total goods imports, the ICT Development Index (IDI) and rank. The last category includes life expectancy at birth, the net income in the US$, and the percentage of primary completion rate at schools of a relevant age group.

Testing for the Relationships between Health and ICTs

This is achieved through multiple regression analysis where health variables are regressed on the ICT variables. This is a sample of 167 countries where several regressions are conducted. A sub-set of regressions are selected on the basis of lack of autocorrelations, absence of multicolinarity and endogenity. The final regressions selected are in Table 3 with variables as defined before.

Discussion

From these regressions, life expectancy at birth appears to be statistically and significantly related to Internet use in years 2000 and 2009. The levels of sensitivity of this variable (H1) are respectively 0.005 and 0.020. This means that a 1% increase in the use of Internet will have positive impacts of 0.025 in total. This does not mean causality but this reveals links between the independent variables and life expectancy. In the same way infant mortality (H2) benefits from access to Internet with respective sensitivities of -0.170 and -0.180 (total of -0.350) in 2009 and 2000. The "under five" mortality rate (H3) is also positively affected by ICTs as the estimated coefficients for 2000 and 2009 are consecutively -0.190 and -0.210. Regarding the prevalence of diseases as represented for tuberculosis (H5), the estimated coefficients are -0.12 and -0.20 for 2000 and 2009. The incidence of Tuberculosis (H6) is also positively affected by ICTs since the estimated coefficients are of -0.130 and -0.076 for 2000 and 2009, respectively. Concerning the total fertility

Table 3. Results of regressions

	Constant	H4	ICT32009	ICT32000	R^2
H1	5.140 (83.860)	-0.190 (-17.860)	0.020 (3.870)	0.005 (1.320)	0.880
H2	-0.900 (-1.650)	0.850 (9.002)	-0.170 (-3.770)	-0.18 (-5.680)	0.840
H3	-0.740 (-1.340)	0.890 (9.230)	-0.210 (-4.430)	-0.19 (-5.690)	0.850
H5	-2.110 (-2.160)		-0.200 (-2.430)	-0.12 (-2.050)	0.710
H6	-3.840 (-4.070)	1.620 (9.890)	-0.130 (-1.640)	-0.076 (-1.350)	0.710
H7	0.430 (1.420)	0.190 (3.59)	-0.160 (-6.220)	-0.03 (-1.660)	0.680

rate (H7), the estimated coefficients for 2000 and 2009 are, consecutively, -0.160 and -0.030. These results show that the statistics of measurements related to the variables H1 to H7 do entertain statistically significant links with ICT variables as represented by the Internet values of access. This does not mean that causality is tested as this is not a relevant exercise.

CONCLUSION

The objective assigned to this chapter is attained with the overview of the roles and impacts of ICTs on the socioeconomic performance and with the assessment of the relationships between ICTs and health. The results show that important impacts are prevailing both globally and at the level of the health sector. In addition, the trends taking place in the health area have been also emphasized. This is achieved trough looking first, at the trends characterizing the world development of new health system and its evolution under the impulse of ICTs.

There are important initiatives that are undertaken by both developing and developing economies in the area of mobilizing ICTs for health care purposes. Series of conferences and workshops have been held during the past few years to promote linkages between different health care components with more intensive use of ICTs. International organizations as well as some countries, including some rich developing ones are investing in the realization of health care platforms and in e-health. These efforts appear to be globally expressed in the quantitative linkage between different health and ICT components around the world. Further efforts are still needed to ensure that all countries and locations are benefiting from these new developments.

REFERENCES

Adewoye, J. O., & Akanbi, T. A. (2012). Role of information and communication technology investment on the profitability of small medium scale industries – A case of Sachet water companies in Oyo state, Nigeria. *Journal of Emerging Trends in Economics and Management Sciences*, *3*(1), 64–71.

Altuwaijri, M. (2010). Supporting the Saudi e-health initiative: The master of health informatics programme at KSAU-HS. *East Mediterr Health*, *16*(1), 119-124. Retrieved from http://sahi.org.sa/article_details.php?article_id=6

Alyemeni, R. M. (2011). Five year program to transform healthcare delivery in Saudi Arabia. *Saudi Arabia Ministry of Health*. Retrieved from http://www.himss.org/content/files/MiddleEast10_presentations/CS1_MohammedAlYemeni.pdf

Burke, K. (2010). The impact of internet and ICT use among SME agribusiness growers and producers. *Journal of Small Business and Entrepreneurship*, *23*(2), 173–194.

Chetley, A. (2006). Improving health, connecting people: The role of ICTs in the health sector of developing countries. *InfoDev*. Retrieved from http://www.asksource.info/pdf/framework2.pdf

Clift, S. (2003). E-democracy, e-governance and public net-work. *Publicus Articles*. Retrieved from http://www.publicus.net/articles/edempublicnetwork.html

Dutta, S., & Coury, M. E. (2002). *ICT challenges for the Arab world*. Retrieved from http://zunia.org/uploads/media/knowledge/Chapter_08_ICT_Challenges_for_the_Arab_World.pdf

Dzenowagis, J. (2005). *Connecting for health: global vision, local insight.* Geneva, Switzerland: World Health Organization.

Ebikeme, C. (2011). ICT 4 NTDs. *End the Neglect.* Retrieved from http://endtheneglect.org/2011/09/ict-4-ntds/

El-Shenawy, N. (2010). ICT measurement: Egypt's experience. In *Proceedings of the First Workshop of the Regional Project, ICT Indicators and Capacity Building for ICT Measurement in Arab Region.* Amman, Jordan: Ministry of Communication and Information Technology.

Elias, C. J. (2009). Policies and practices to advance global health technologies. *Center for Strategic and International Studies.* Retrieved from http://csis.org/files/media/csis/pubs/090420_elias_policiespractices.pdf

Europe's Information Society. (2010). Completed studies on ehealth issues. *ICT for Health.* Retrieved from http://ec.europa.eu/information_society/activities/health/studies/published/index_en.htm

Fraser, H. S. F., & McGrath, S. D. (2000). Information technology and telemedicine in sub-Saharan Africa. *British Medical Journal, 321*(7259), 465–466. doi:10.1136/bmj.321.7259.465

Galliano, D., Lethiais, V., & Soulié, N. (2008). Faible densité des espaces et usages des TIC par les enterprises: Besoin d'information ou de coordination? *Revue d'Economie Industrielle, 121*, 41–64.

GOPA. (2005). The challenges of ICT projects in developing countries: Yemen. *GOPA Worldwide Consultants.* Retrieved from http://gopa.de/index.php?id=45&type=98&L=1&L=1&tx_ttnews[cat]=2&tx_ttnews[pS]=1104534000&tx_ttnews[pL]=31535999&tx_ttnews[arc]=1&tx_ttnews[tt_news]=25&tx_ttnews[backPid]=47&cHash=95b4b8d95d

Greenberg, A. (2005). *ICTs for poverty alleviation: Basic tool and enabling sector.* Stockholm, Sweden: ICT for Development Secretariat.

Halamka, D. J. (2011). Addressing Japan's healthcare challenges with information technology. *Center for Strategic International Studies.* Retrieved from http://csis.org/files/publication/110830_Halamka_AddressingJapanHealthcare_Web.pdf

Herrick, C. (2011). HP wins ICT deal for royal adelaide hospital. *CIO Magazine.* Retrieved from http://www.cio.com.au/article/401373/hp_wins_ict_deal_royal_adelaide_hospital/?utm_campaign=&utm_medium=idg.to-twitter&utm_source=twitter.com&fpid=1&utm_content=awesm-publisher&fp=16

Int@j. (2007). *National ICT strategy of Jordan 2007-2011.* Retrieved from http://www.intaj.net/sites/default/files/National-ICT-Strategy-of-Jordan-2007-2011.pdf

IST-Africa Consortium. (2011). *Overview of ICT initiatives in Egypt.* Retrieved from http://www.ist-africa.org/home/default.asp?page=doc-by-id&docid=5185

ITU. (2011). ICT data and statistics. *ITU World Telecommunication Indicators Database.* Retrieved from http://www.itu.int/ITUD/ict/statistics/index.html

K4health. (2011). *Adolescents living with HIV (ALHIV).* Retrieved from http://www.k4health.org/toolkits/alhiv

Kahn, T. (2004). Mobile phones keep track of HIV treatments. *SciDev.Net.* Retrieved from http://www.scidev.net/News/index.cfm?fuseaction=readNews&itemid=1625&language=1

Kelly, T. (2011). ICT in health: The role of ICTs in the health sector in developing countries. *InfoDev*. Retrieved from http://www.infodev.org/en/Project.38.html

Kwankam, S. Y. (2004). What e-health can offer. *Bulletin of the World Health Organization, 82*(10). Retrieved from http://www.scielosp.org/scielo.php?pid=S004296862004001000021&script=sci_arttext

Littlejohns, P., Wyatt, J. C., & Garvican, L. (2003). Evaluating computerized health information systems: Hard lessons still to be learnt. *British Medical Journal, 326*(7394), 860–863. doi:10.1136/bmj.326.7394.860

Lyman, P., & Varian, H. R. (2003). *How much information?* Berkeley, CA: University of California at Berkeley. Retrieved from http://www.sims.berkeley.edu/research/projects/how-much-info-2003/

Manochehri, N., Al-Esmail, R., & Ashrafi, R. (2012). Examining the Impact of information and communication technologies (ICT) on enterprise practices: A preliminary perspective from Qatar. *The Electronic Journal on Information Systems in Developing Countries, 51*(3), 1–16.

Martínez, A., Rodrigues, R. J., & Infante, A. (2001). *Bases metodológicas para evaluar la viabilidad y el impacto de proyectos de telemedicina.* Madrid, Spain: Universidad Politécnica de Madrid/Pan American Health Organization.

MedPac. (2004). Information technology in health care. *Report to The Congress: New Approches in Medicare.* Retrieved from http://www.medpac.gov/publications%5Ccongressional_reports%5CJune04_ch7.pdf

Ministry of Health. (2012). Oman. *Health Care Information System (Al Shifa).* Retrieved from http://unpan1.un.org/intradoc/groups/public/documents/un-dpadm/unpan039615.pdf

Nour, S. S. (2008). *The use and economic impacts of ICT at the macro-micro levels in the Arab gulf countries.* Paper presented at the Fifth GLOBEL-ICS Academy, TaSTI, University of Tampere. Tampere, Finland.

OECD. (2003). *ICT and economic growth – Evidence from OECD countries, industries and firms.* Paris, France: OECD Publishing.

Office of Technology Assessment. (1982). *Medical technology under proposals to increase competition in health care.* Washington, DC: US Government Printing Office.

Parliamentary Office of Science and Technology. (2006). ICT in developing countries. *Postpone, 261.*

Pettey, C., & Tudor, B. (2011). *Gartner says worldwide IT spending to grow 5.1 percent in 2011.* Retrieved from http://www.gartner.com/it/page.jsp?id=1513614

Piatkowski, M. (2003). *The contribution of ICT investment to economic growth and labor productivity in Poland 1995-2000.* Retrieved from http://ideas.repec.org/p/wpa/wuwpdc/0308002.html

Qiang, C. Z., Yamamichi, M., Hausman, V., & Altman, D. (2011). *Mobile applications for the health sector.* Washington, DC: World Bank.

Rallet, A., & Torre, A. (1999). *Which need for geographical proximity in innovation networks at the era of global economy?.* Unpublished.

Ratzan, S. C. (2011). Health communication: Beyond recognition to impact. *Journal of Health Communication, International Perspectives, 16*(2), 109-111. Retrieved from http://dx.doi.org/10.1080/10810730.2011.5523

Richardson, P., & Kraemmergaard, P. (2006). Identifying the impacts of enterprise system implementation and use: Examples from Denmark. *International Journal of Accounting Information Systems, 7*(1), 36–49. doi:10.1016/j.accinf.2005.12.001

Sherry, J. M., & Ratzan, S. C. (2012). Measurement and evaluation outcomes for mhealth communication: Don't we have an app for that? *Journal of Health Communication, 17*(1), 1–3. doi:10.1080 /10810730.2012.670563

Shirazi, F. (2008). The contribution of ICT to freedom and democracy: An empirical analysis of archival data on the Middle East. *The Electronic Journal on Information Systems in Developing Countries, 35*(6), 1–24.

Sorenson, C., Drummond, M., & Kanavos, P. (2008). *Ensuring value for money in health care: The role of health technology assessment in European Union.* Cornwall, UK: World Health Organization.

Ssewanyana, J. K., & Busler, M. (2007). Adoption and usage of ICT in developing countries: Case of Ugandan firms. *International Journal of Education and Development using Information and Communication Technology, 3*(3), 49-59.

TIGA. (2011). *ICTs in health.* Retrieved from http://repository.uneca.org/tiga/?q=node/36

Vital Wave Consulting. (2011). *New incubation labs boost mobile innovation in the developing world.* Retrieved from http://vitalwave.blogspot. com/2011/06/new-incubation-labs-boost-mobile. html

Warner, K. E. (1990). Wellness at the worksite. *Health Affairs, 9,* 263–279. Retrieved from http:// content.healthaffairs.org/content/9/2/63.citati doi:10.1377/hlthaff.9.2.63

WHO. (2006). *Building foundations for e-health.* Report of the WHO Global Observatory for eHealth. Retrieved from http://www.who.int/goe/ data/country_reput ort/dza.pdf

WHO. (2009). *WHO eastern Mediterranean region: Lebanon.* Retrieved from http://www.who. int/goe/publications/atlas/lbn.pdf

World Bank. (2008). Social inclusion through ICT for Tunisian disabled. *Health in Middle East and North Africa.* Retrieved from http://web.world-bank.org/archive/website01055/WEB/0__CON-8.HTM

World DataBank. (2012). *World development indicators (WDI) & global development finance (GDF).* Retrieved from http://databank.world-bank.org/ddp/home.do

World Health Organization. (2010a). *10 facts on nutrition.* Retrieved from http://www.who.int/ mediacentre/factsheets/fs172/en/

World Health Organization. (2010b). *Integrated prevention into health care.* Fact Sheet #172. Retrieved from http://www.who.int/mediacentre/ factsheets/fs172/en/

Zhenwei, C. Q., Masatake, Y., Hausman, V., & Altman, D. (2011). *Mobile applications for the health sector.* Washington, DC: World Bank. Retrieved from http://siteresources.worldbank.org/ informationandcommunicationandtechnologies/ Resources/mHealth_report.pdf

APPENDIX

Table 4.

Country Name/ 2010	Internet Users	HEPC 2009	GDP pc 2009	GDP 2009	TLEB 2009
Bahrain	694009.2500	770.6236	17608.8298	20595000000.0000	75.0238
Egypt, Arab Rep.	21691776.0000	113.6203	2370.7111	188980000000.0000	72.9753
Iran, Islamic Rep.	9616571.9000	287.1472	4525.9486	331010000000.0000	72.7519
Iraq	791789.7750	200.4147	2096.8511	65193000000.0000	68.4860
Israel	4985164.8000	2004.3223	26102.3506	195390000000.0000	81.5049
Jordan	2351146.2600	373.2879	4242.1537	25092000000.0000	73.2897
Kuwait	1046799.9900	1578.7510	41364.6893	109460000000.0000	74.6047
Lebanon	1310555.0700	617.1315	8321.3707	34925000000.0000	72.4088
Libya	889715.6800	427.2364	9957.4904	62360000000.0000	74.7531
Morocco	15656191.9000	151.5131	2827.8186	90908000000.0000	71.8646
Oman	1725109.7000	520.3793	17280.0972	46866000000.0000	73.1246
Qatar	1435175.0900	1612.1451	61531.6921	98313000000.0000	78.0976
Syrian Arab Republic	4224995.4400	95.4403	2691.5977	53935000000.0000	75.7026
Tunisia	3856983.7100	242.5503	4168.9368	43522000000.0000	74.6000
Turkey	28969975.8000	575.4900	8553.7415	614550000000.0000	73.6967
United Arab Emirates	5859118.2000	1704.0598	38959.8122	270330000000.0000	76.5736
Yemen, Rep.	2970485.4800	63.4004	1077.2401	25130000000.0000	65.0305
Middle East & North Africa (all income levels)	96625274.0000	306.3408	5823.3642	2186100000000.0000	72.4873
Middle East & North Africa (developing only)	69363777.2000	189.2905	3268.2816	1064200000000.0000	72.0013
OECD members	844430192.0000	4185.6377	33407.9107	41053000000000.0000	79.3238
World	2038644960.0000	900.0732	8520.2518	58074000000000.0000	69.6272

Table 5.

Country Name/ 2010	Ln(Internet Users)	Ln(HEPC 2009)	Ln(GDP pc 2009)	Ln(GDP 2009)	Ln(TLEB 2009)
Bahrain	13.4502406	6.64720009	9.77615575	23.7483093	4.31780579
Egypt, Arab Rep.	16.8924438	4.73286191	7.77094524	25.9649287	4.29012059
Iran, Islamic Rep.	16.0789984	5.65999502	8.41758247	26.5254294	4.28705439
Iraq	13.5820512	5.30038866	7.648192	24.9006133	4.22663006
Israel	15.421977	7.60306129	10.1697806	25.9982724	4.40066287
Jordan	14.6704135	5.92235	8.35282637	23.9458284	4.29441951
Kuwait	13.8612484	7.36438929	10.6301829	25.4188506	4.31220393
Lebanon	14.0859613	6.42508207	9.02658227	24.2764604	4.28232723
Libya	13.6986572	6.05733754	9.20608035	24.856197	4.31419098
Morocco	16.566377	5.02067202	7.94726086	25.2331183	4.27478427
Oman	14.3608012	6.25455796	9.75731067	24.5705596	4.29216497
Qatar	14.1767974	7.38532093	11.0273076	25.311424	4.35795914
Syrian Arab Republic	15.2565287	4.55850061	7.89789022	24.7110368	4.32681199
Tunisia	15.165396	5.49120906	8.33541631	24.4965331	4.31214051
Turkey	17.1817705	6.35522189	9.05412406	27.1441625	4.29995746
United Arab Emirates	15.5835097	7.44076882	10.5702859	26.3229275	4.3382525
Yemen, Rep.	14.904236	4.14946995	6.98215763	23.9473317	4.17485583
Middle East & North Africa (all income levels)	18.3863509	5.72469811	8.66963342	28.4131307	4.2834117
Middle East & North Africa (developing only)	18.0548753	5.24328284	8.09201963	27.6932757	4.27668379
OECD members	20.5541726	8.33941434	10.416548	31.3458743	4.37353794
World	21.4355512	6.80247614	9.05020117	31.6927407	4.24315576

Table 6.

Country Name/ 2010	Investment in Telecoms 2010	Health Exp PC 2009	GDP pc 2009	GDP 2009	Life Birth 2009
Egypt, Arab Rep.	2113000000	113.620268	2370.71111	1.89E+11	72.9752683
Iran, Islamic Rep.	486000000	287.147214	4525.94861	3.31E+11	72.7518537
Iraq	456000000	200.414688	2096.85105	6.52E+10	68.4860488
Jordan	301000000	373.287909	4242.1537	2.51E+10	73.2896585
Morocco	1124000000	151.51309	2827.81855	9.09E+10	71.8646341
Syrian Arab Republic	65000000	95.44027	2691.59766	5.39E+10	75.702561
Tunisia	966000000	242.550288	4168.93675	4.35E+10	74.6
Turkey	1682980000	575.490023	8553.74145	6.15E+11	73.6966585
Yemen, Rep.	59000000	63.4003858	1077.24014	2.51E+10	65.0304634
Middle East & North Africa (developing only)	5854000000	189.290494	3268.28162	1.06E+12	72.0012722

Table 7.

Country Name/ 2010	Ln(Investment in Telecoms 2010)	Ln(Health Exp PC 2009)	Ln(GDP 2009)	Ln(GDP pc 2009)	Ln(Birth 2009)
Egypt, Arab Rep.	21.4713746	4.73286191	25.9649287	7.77094524	4.29012059
Iran, Islamic Rep.	20.0017192	5.65999502	26.5254294	8.41758247	4.28705439
Iraq	19.9380034	5.30038866	24.9006133	7.648192	4.22663006
Jordan	19.5226208	5.92235	23.9458284	8.35282637	4.29441951
Morocco	20.8401596	5.02067202	25.2331183	7.94726086	4.27478427
Syrian Arab Republic	17.9898978	4.55850061	24.7110368	7.89789022	4.32681199
Tunisia	20.6886744	5.49120906	24.4965331	8.33541631	4.31214051
Turkey	21.2438319	6.35522189	27.1441625	9.05412406	4.29995746
Yemen, Rep.	17.893048	4.14946995	23.9473317	6.98215763	4.17485583
Middle East & North Africa (developing only)	22.490391	5.24328284	27.6932757	8.09201963	4.27668379

Chapter 6
ICTs, Youth, Education, Health, and Prospects of Further Coordination

ABSTRACT

Despite the important role of youth, large portions of this group are often marginalized. Among the most common tools to promote youth in developing countries are ICTs. This chapter investigates the use of ICTs for youth promotion in developing countries. The first section examines the relationships between ICTs and youth in education, health, employment, and governance. The following section investigates the main concerns related to ICTs and youth in developing countries, mainly in Africa, Asia, and the Arab region. The last section of the chapter deals with the potential provided by ICTs in promoting further coordination. Each of these sections uses statistical evidence about the relationships between ICTs and the youth access to education, health, and to further social networks.

INTRODUCTION

The category of "youth" does not represent a simple quantitative dimension defined only by age. This group holds a complex, multi-dimensional set of socio-economic, demographic, and cultural factors that have as much to do with lifestyle as with chronology (Weiner & Rumiany, 2007). A demographic investigation might help to understand the significance of youth in the developing world. By considering those within the age range of 15

to 25 years (Based on United Nations statistical principles), statistics indicate that 1.2 billion of the world population are within that range. This young population is a fast-growing group, especially in Africa and most countries of the Middle East. In Asia, young people constitute over 61% of the world's youth population (Nahleen, 2006).

Still, nowadays the global impact of the youth population is not limited to its demographic significance. In the past, youth used to live in isolation like all other age groups, making it difficult

DOI: 10.4018/978-1-4666-3643-9.ch006

to affect change on them or their communities. Globalization along with Information and Communication Technologies (ICTs), are gradually changing this rigid landscape. In this context, ICTs became not only a tool, but a medium over which social, political and economic transformations occur all over the world. The last Arab revolutions or the so called "Arab Spring" is good evidence of the above stated assumption.

It is generally accepted that youth are the main producers and consumers of ICTs. As a result, the interaction between ICTs and youth provides a useful perspective when analyzing simultaneous changes produced in societies and economies. In fact, youth become more important change agents not only because they know how to use ICTs and may learn faster than adults, but also because they are more receptive and easily adaptable to change. The Global Forum on Youth and ICTs for Development held in Geneva in 2007 highlighted this issue. The objective of the Forum was to the use of youth creativity and dynamism in the exploitation of ICTs for the benefit of their peers and communities in advancement of the United Nations Millennium Development Goals (GAID, 2009).

In the past, information was assumed to flow from parents to youth, and eventually among youth themselves. However, with ICTs, the flow of information has been reversed, which established a new dynamic in social and family relations. This, in turn, leads to a larger change within societies. ICTs have also affected the flow of information within schools.

Therefore, while school is considered a closed and unidirectional institution of knowledge, the Internet offers unlimited information open to everyone. In sum, it seems possible to foster development by stimulating the interaction between youth and ICTs. In this regard, initiatives such as the Global Forum on "Youth and ICT for Development" are essential as they place the topic of youth and ICTs on the international community agenda. Even though, while addressing the issue of youth

and ICTs, it is important to bear in mind that the needs, requirements, hopes and expectations of the youth can vary tremendously from one region to another and from one country to another.

The first part of this chapter discusses ICTs and youth in relation to different fields; mainly education, health, employment, and governance. The second part of the chapter also investigates the phenomenon in different regions of the developing world. The final part deals with prospects from coordination through the use of ICTs.

ICTS AND YOUTH IN DIFFERENT SECTORS

This part looks at the relationships between youth, education, health, employment, and governance, respectively.

ICT and Education

Several studies suggest that achieving economic growth and ensuring competitiveness in the global economy is highly associated with investments in ICTs and quality education (OECD, 2005). While the number of educated youth grew significantly in recent years, knowledge about the use of ICTs in schools is still insufficient. The World Youth Report (2007) suggests that the current generation of youth is assumed to be the best educated so far. Even though a big number of children are not in school and an equally large number among this group are illiterate.

In a recent publication, Unwin (2012) emphasizes the most important directions of the services provided by the Web to the educational processes. The author shows how the unconnected learners are an important challenge that can be solved under special arrangements. The educational content while necessary is described to suffer from the multiplicity of operators. This issue can be solved if learners are given the possibilities of selection and choice. New means are recognized as necessary to promote both the use of the Web and the efficiency of users. Among the means, the chapter insists on the local features needed to enhance learning effectiveness.

Statistics indicate that adoption of ICTs has dramatically increased in developing countries in the last decade. However, developing educated societies does not only require providing computers and Internet connectivity, as is the case in several developing countries. More attention has to be given to issues related to curriculums requirements, continuous teacher training to be updated with new developments in ICTs, constant maintenance of hardware, and availability of new software. Concern therefore, must not be based only on hardware but also on "cost of ownership" (The Global e-Schools and Communities Initiative, 2011).

E-learning, which involve both teaching computer skills and using those skills for distance learning, is one of the most common innovative educational tools of the 21st century. Even though, this kind of education faces plenty of issues in developing countries. Previous implementation of e-learning in these countries faced issues such as the lack of computer labs in schools and universities, a high demand for technical support and maintenance, a need for higher investments in wireless technology, crucial reforms of curricula, and finally the need for training of teachers to ensure a better quality and sustainability of education programs (Nahleen, 2006).

The Global e-Government Readiness Report (2005) suggests that the lack of education and technical skills broadens the gap in economic and social opportunities. The report suggests, as well, that in most developing countries, only a small group dominates the use of the Internet and other ICTs, namely those with higher levels of educational skill. Many governments now recognize the need to focus on strategies to increase access to ICTs and improve the quality of education.

However, it has been shown by many studies that societies with low levels of literacy and formal education are most likely to lack computer and technical skills. This suggests that initiatives to improve the use of ICTs in such countries must be accompanied by educational reforms to enhance probabilities of success. Otherwise, fewer people will benefit disproportionately from the ICTs reforms, while groups with lower levels of education will continue to struggle to attain even the basic levels of education.

Overview of ICTs and Education

Education is the transmission of knowledge, the training towards critical thinking, the acquisition of skills, and the construction of shared values and habits (Assar & Franzoni, 2009). Conventional education or learning is administered through educational institutions (schools and universities) where students interact directly with their professor by the means of face-to-face interaction (Kamsin, 2005). On the other hand, E-learning is the introduction of emerging multimedia technologies and Internet technologies to conventional learning in order to facilitate it and improve its quality by making remote resources and knowledge more accessible (Debande & Ottersten, 2004). Those multimedia technologies include, but are not limited to, video conferencing, online testing, e-books and online discussion forums (Kamsin, 2005). According to Kamsin (2005), "it is now feasible to offer remote students full, interactive participation in a class that would previously have been restricted to students who were attending locally" (p. 79). the increasing interest in such distance education is rooted in the growth of the technologies that maintain an open two-way communication channel for dialogue within the educational platform they support (Hodgson, 2008). Besides that, E-learning targets students encountering troubles or having constraints in attending traditional classrooms. This can be caused by distance, personal issues, and responsibilities and in some cases some restraints. The concept of the Virtual Classroom goes along with e-learning as it means a physical separation of the student and his professor. The elements necessary for a proper functioning of virtual classrooms are live broadcasts, interactive videos, and electronic mails (e-mail). Thanks to this electronic networking, students can have access to learning resources and through the use of e-mail; they can interact with their friends, professors, and even technical staff in case it is needed. Thus, virtual classrooms foster an interactive environment enabling students to exchange their ideas and communicate with the relevant parties (Kamsin, 2005).

Young people in general have been indoctrinated into adopting technological advances within today's change-sustaining society (Beastall, 2006). With the convenient access to repositories of information made available via the Internet, the need for change in the fashion of teaching and learning mechanisms is further developed (Hodgson, 2008). Conventional education, by remaining fixed around a narrow curriculum, alienates students from the educational system (Beastall, 2006). However, conventional education still makes a case for itself in that, rather than conveying more information, it gives it precise meaning using real life discussions and interactions that add body language to the mix and thus reduces misunderstanding possibilities (Kamsin, 2005).

Due to the extensive exposure of the newer generations to ICTs, a new learning style based more on acquiring knowledge through digitized means such as the Internet has been developed. This shift has upset the former student-teacher dynamic in which teachers have monopolies over knowledge as they are recognized to be the only knowledge holders (Beastall, 2006). Therefore, according to Beastall (2006, p. 5), "today's students and teachers are not compatible, with teaching and learning styles frequently conflicting." This incompatibility is often referred to as "digital divide" (Sutherland-Smith, Snyder, & Angus, 2003).

In the European Union, e-learning is regarded as enhancing the individual's ability to manage and be at the heart of his own learning process, which shifts the role of teachers to advisors and guidance providers (Hodgson, 2008). Of course, putting the student at the centre of his own learning process is at a thin line between being a steep slope or a revolution in the educational pedagogy. In other words, it could mean that the student will learn better from selectively tackling different subjects at his own pace based on his or her acquired knowledge and skills. In which case, the student will be able to waste less time on the material he or she is already familiar with in order to focus on the things they are less knowledgeable about. On the other end of the stake, students faced with the flexibility offered by ICTs might find themselves lost in the absence of the proper pedagogical support to guide them.

Sarkar (2012) highlights the role of ICTs in higher education for the 21st century. In particular, he argued that ICTs have impacted educational practice in to date in quite small ways but that the impact will grow considerably in years to come and that ICTs will become a strong agent for change among many educational practices. It is evident from the study that use of ICT in education is increasing very rapidly in various states of India. One of the most common problems of using Information and Communication Technologies in education is to base choices on technological possibilities rather than educational needs. In developing countries where higher education is fraught with serious challenges at multiple levels, there is increasing pressure to ensure that technological possibilities are viewed in the context of educational needs. The use of ICTs in education lends itself to more student-centered learning settings and often this creates some tension for both some teachers and students. However, with the world moving rapidly into digital media and information, the role of ICTs in education is becoming more and more important and this importance will continue to grow and develop in the 21st century. Thus, the author suggests that ICTs in higher education is not a technique for educational development but also a way of socio-economic development of the nation.

Is e-learning or ICT applied to education a complement or substitute to conventional education?

E-learning can be conveniently associated with four important components: the necessary infrastructure equipment required for the implementation of this type of learning, relevant educational content, training programs for teachers and dialogue at all levels (Debande & Ottersten, 2004). However, light has been shed more on the first component being the main driving force that tilts the balance in favor of e-learning. In fact, according to Beastall (2006), "the introduction of ICT has not been complemented by increased levels of effective professional development for teaching staff in the pedagogy of ICT across the curriculum" (p. 6).

The absence of adequate pedagogical support is not an indicator of the teaching body's reluctance to adopt ICT in teaching. Teaching staff recognizes the importance of ICT in educating young people (Beastall, 2006). However, and in parallel, people (including the e-learning providers) understand that there are some things that cannot be taught solely by e-learning (Pailing, 2002). If a student were to take a course such as appraisal interviews online, he would miss on the opportunity of practicing real life role-play that requires the face-to-face interaction of at least two people in front of a professional trainer (Pailing, 2002).

The advantages of e-learning reside in the pedagogical approach used to implement it (MacKeogh, 2003). According to Beastall (2006), "the use of technology is not enough; it has to be based on an understanding of its pedagogical value" (p. 28). Most of the time, introducing ICT is believed to promote interactivity. People automatically accept this interactivity, but for the learning, mandatory responses should be built in the pedagogy of e-learning (MacKeogh, 2003).

In places such as the secluded Western Australia and remote and hard to reach places in the UK and Norway, distance e-learning delivers the promise to educate diverse populations on a large geographical scale (Valentine, 2002). However, on solid ground, and for most cases, the technological education tools are still used, for the major part, to solely present information instead of delivering it (Beastall, 2006). Thus, even in countries such the United Kingdom where the use of ICT is relatively effective, it still has not reached its full potential and remains purely a complement to traditional education. Regardless of the advantages allowed by distance learning, many problems associated to this kind of education exist. These problems include the quality of instruction, hidden costs, misuse of technology, and the attitudes of professors, students, and administrators (Valentine, 2002).

What is the cost (tangible—infrastructure, and human resources development) of introducing ICTs to education? How do they compare to the value added?

Rio Salado College, a community college located in Arizona has been able to cut its operating costs by 34 percent compared to similar colleges thanks to its nationally known successful distance-learning program (Scarafiotti, 2003). The tuition for the e-learning program is similar to face-to-face courses and serves twenty-one thousand students on a yearly basis, which is approximately half of the college enrollment (Scarafiotti, 2003).

According to the Technology Costing Methodology for assessing the costs of an e-learning program, the variables that mostly influence the cost of e-learning are human resources costs relating to what instructors do and to their payment (Scarafiotti, 2003). The need for full time faculty chairs to come up with the pedagogy and design of online courses, to train and evaluate the adjunct faculty, and to establish the policies of the program as to give the best results increases the cost of e-learning (Scarafiotti, 2003). However, since the cost of having adjunct faculties teach a three-credit course is 69 percent lower than having a full-time professor for the same purpose, Rio Salaso is capable of administering good programs at lower costs and with minimal human resources costs (Scarafiotti, 2003).

Moreover, e-learning introduces various technology tools and resources applied to education. In order to acquire such tools, associated costs must be allocated. Contrary to traditional education where the instructor is the only person responsible for designing the course, e-learning requires additional costs related to Web technicians and programmers, content designers, course testers, graphic artists, and others (Scarafiotti, 2003). Therefore, the cost of developing e-learning programs can only be justified on large-scale basis. In such a case, the program's recipients can increase in number without increasing the overhead incurred by the university (Valentine, 2002).

What are the variables affecting the successful implementation of ICT in developed countries?

In the case of Rio Salado College in Arizona, the reason behind the success of the e-learning program is the appointment of more than four hundred adjunct professors and twenty-seven faculty chairs working full time exclusively for the e-learning programs (Scarafiotti, 2003). In other words, one of the major reasons behind the success of an e-learning program is having faculty with proper training and expertise specifically for the learning methods associated with e-learning. Therefore, the proper implementation of an e-learning program has to be done in three steps: first, the infrastructure, then the content and instructors' training (Debande & Ottersten, 2004).

For e-learning to emulate the higher-order learning offered at the university level, it has to contain the brain stimulators contained in a university setting, rather than it being simple transfer of knowledge. Therefore, a successfully implemented e-learning program has to include tasks such as: description, explanation, prediction, argumentation, and evaluation of the findings usually involved in problem solving and acquiring

abstract university-level knowledge (MacKeogh, 2003).

The above-mentioned skills can also be partly developed by children through their use of computer programs in creating concrete computer models that are extremely hard to simulate otherwise, and use these models to reflect about the concepts (Beastall, 2006). The use of ICT in learning via software allows students in such cases to play around with variables and have a clear idea about the effect of each on the final result.

In the United Kingdom, the Department for Education and Skills (DFES) instructs the teaching body on a specialist to specialist basis to use ICT through the Hands-on Support model (Beastall, 2006). This model allows the teaching body to innovate in teaching and learning, especially that it provides for a better understanding for the reason and way in which ICT complement the school curriculum (Beastall, 2006).

Another factor behind the wider inclusion of ICT in learning and education at the level of the European Union is the political attention given to this kind of learning. In fact, the political rhetoric of education in the European Union stresses the importance of digital literacy in the scope of lifelong learning for all individuals, which naturally lead to better chances of adaptation to the information society (Hodgson, 2008).

Can the outcome of exclusive e-learning be controlled?

Exclusive e-learning as offered by Rio Salado College also includes all other student services normally found on campus, offered online and via the phone (Scarafiotti, 2003). These services include: advising, counseling, enrollment services, the bookstore, tutoring, help desk, and library services (Scarafiotti, 2003).

Why are ICT stalling in developing countries? Are there exceptions?

An approach to analyzing the multiple reasons behind the stagnation of ICT in developing countries could be to establish a contrast or confrontation with the reasons at the root of their success in other places of the world. As mentioned earlier, in order for ICT to widely penetrate schools and universities, a massive investment has to be made towards acquiring technological equipment and teacher training programs (Debande & Ottersten, 2004). Indeed, e-learning relies heavily first and foremost on technologies and technological tools. Developing countries have a considerable issue building, maintaining, and utilizing ICT for educational purposes (Assar & Franzoni, 2009).

However, even if developing countries no longer had an issue acquiring the infrastructure for ICT based learning, the availability of adequate human resources will continue hindering the development of e-learning: "evaluations show that even in the countries which seem to have the most number of computers, implementation of ICT in the school and the curriculum has not yet succeeded" (Debande & Ottersten, 2004, p. 34).

Other difficulties arising for developing countries include the absence of standards and standardization leading to the use of different systems, the duplication of efforts, and the waste of the technological resources even when available (Assar & Franzoni, 2009).

The problems facing the advancement of education in developing countries in general are: "The underserved regions of the world face many constraints in delivering education to the right people at the right time. Budgets are always tight, educational material is unavailable, human resources for teaching are scare and the best teachers rarely want to work in remote rural areas" (Assar & Franzoni, 2009). These factors seem to actually encourage the use of ICT for delivering education and providing equal opportunities for marginal groups (Assar & Franzoni, 2009). Realistically speaking, on the other hand, teachers in developing countries have little exposure to ICT and their use (Assar & Franzoni, 2009).

The costs related to the acquisition of both hardware and software needed to adopt ICT into education, the lack of sufficient telecommunication networks, the need for additional maintenance

for facilities is another discouraging and inhibiting factor, especially considering the low per capita income and the low standards of living (Assar & Franzoni, 2009).

The initiatives aiming to implement ICT-based education in developing countries are usually poorly coordinated and spend outrageous amounts on holding conferences to discuss policy issues that have already been discussed on other grounds (Unwin, 2008). Adding to the poor coordination is the flow of these policy discussions from top government down, thus giving more importance to the available supply rather than the demand of the marginalized and the poor (Unwin, 2008). Political policies are often more concerned about responding to the poor's basic needs (Assar & Franzoni, 2009).

In addition, the available ICT technology is developed to target more Westernized regions. Most of the ICT initiatives received much criticism for failing to adapt a Western-born and grown technology to a cultural context of disadvantaged countries (Unwin, 2008). ICT projects applied to education are actually more likely to succeed in developing countries when properly customized to reflect the local culture and conditions (Assar & Franzoni, 2009).

What are the impacts of this stagnation?

South American countries and places like Jakarta are turning towards e-learning in order to reach students who live in regions that are hard to reach (Valentine, 2002).

Some developing countries have expressed their need to adopt state run e-learning and distance learning in order to make up for the lack of physical space to host institutional education (Valentine, 2002).

With the advent of globalization and a rising emphasis worldwide on technology, fluency with information and communication technologies have increasingly become vital in the workplace. Therefore, the majority of ICT studies have concentrated on private and public adult education programs and the resulting economic effects.

There is a more recent trend concerning both ICT implementation and study: the matriculation of the lower levels of education into ICT awareness and use. It is not only a goal of preparing students for the work force, but also an effort to "engage students in higher-order thinking" (Lim, 2007, p. 21). However, these emphases are not necessarily mutually exclusive. A variety of case studies have been conducted to measure the global and regional spread of ICT.

Naturally, developed and developing countries approach the issue of ICT differently. The Lisbon European Council, in an effort to institute a plan to create a viable and technology-savvy economy, emphasized the importance of training the European youth to work in the digital age (Jeskanen-Sundström, 2003). It proposed to measure this variable by identifying the "number of computers per 100 students in primary, secondary, and tertiary education" (Jeskanen-Sundström, 2003).

Looser interpretations have merely measured access to relevant technologies. In one European study, the Czech Republic was able to claim that 69% of students in secondary education had access (no information about primary education was given). France was listed at 25% of primary school students and 72% of secondary school students, and Italy was at similar levels. New Zealand, Canada, and Iceland had close to 100% of secondary school students with access, though primary school access varied between 55% and 95%. The country with the highest level of access overall was Iceland (CERI, 2000). In more specific terms, the ratio of students-to-computers was the smallest in Canada, New Zealand, and Denmark at 12 or fewer secondary school students per computer and greatest in the Czech Republic and Hungary at 35 students per computer. These access patterns are not uniformly reflected in the amount of time students spend using ICT in the classroom, particularly the Internet: despite the higher ratio, 60% Hungarian secondary school students used the ICT sources a few times a week, compared to 70% of high-access Swedish and Canadian students (OECD, 2002).

Therefore, it is not only access that determines the educational usage of ICT. For the majority of the countries that received poor scores in educational usage, the reason was due to outdated or broken computers—however, very few claimed it was due to a lack of knowledge (OECD, 2002).

Ireland is an exception to this general pattern. While it had an above-average student-computer ratio at nine-to-one, and the usage was fairly comparable at fewer than 70%, the reason for the lack of usage was "low levels of confidence in computer use" (Cosgrove, Zastrutzki, & Shiel, 2005). This was partially attributed to the lack of Internet connectivity. The Irish government attempted to address this problem by instituting a funded program to help connect the schools to broadband connections. However, after a three-year period the frequency of student use had failed to increase (Cosgrove, et al., 2005).

As a non-European developed nation, Singapore offers an interesting perspective on ICT. In 1997, the government of Singapore implemented the MP1 ICT-education plan, aiming to increase the level of integration in schools (Lim, 2007). It concentrated on primary and secondary school systems, creating lessons involving basic and more complex ICT resources that facilitated "the shift of learning from information receiving towards finding, collating, and synthesizing relevant information…providing a greater degree of independent learning" (Lim, 2007, p. 16). It was largely successful, due to the heavy government support and the high amounts of interconnectivity between teachers of ICT-based courses, as well as the emphasis on flexible knowledge-gathering rather than task-oriented lessons (Lim, 2007).

The situation is more unsteady in the MENA region and, due to the lack of efficient data-collecting mechanisms concerning ITC, data is sparse. Access to the Internet has increase drastically in the past ten years, though interestingly it is an increase concentrated heavily within the youthful portion of the population (La Cava, Rossotto, & Paradi-Guilford, 2011). The rates of Internet access are significantly affected by education level. Of those who only received up to primary or secondary education, only 7% have access to the Internet, compared to 60% of university graduates (La Cava, et al., 2011). Highly developed and wealthy regions have much better statistics: the UAE has Internet access in 93% of its schools, with 84% of the student population taking advantage of the access (U.S.-Arab Chamber of Commerce, 2011). ICT development in many sectors of the MENA is stymied by poor levels of overall education. Morocco has attempted to address this by building 400 computer centers and providing free Internet access to youth clubs (U.S.-Arab Chamber of Commerce, 2011). Saudi Arabia has also been emphasizing ICT education, providing funds within its Five-Year Development plan for ICT education in primary and secondary schools (U.S.-Arab Chamber of Commerce, 2011). In Oman, agreements were signed in 2009 with the Microsoft Partners in learning program to supply training and materials oriented towards increasing ICT awareness in primary and secondary schools (U.S.-Arab Chamber of Commerce, 2011). Bahrain implemented similar programs in 2005 to great success—however, it must be noted that Bahrain has a much higher rate of enrollment for secondary education than the rest of the MENA region, providing a friendlier educational atmosphere for ICT programs (U.S.-Arab Chamber of Commerce, 2011).

Egypt, with literacy rates of less than 60%, is a prime example of a developing MENA nation's approach to ICT education. National policy indicates a goal of technologic advancement of primary and secondary schools, desiring one computer lab for every 15 classes in a school (World Bank, 2007). It also seeks to provide an online-education system, complete with tests and classes, and to train the teachers of these schools to properly instruct the students in ICT (World Bank, 2007). As of 2006, 69.7% of primary and secondary schools in Egypt have computer labs with Internet access. Interestingly, a slight majority of primary schools have access over secondary schools. (World Bank, 2007).

Quantitative Evidence about the Links between Education and ICTs

Therefore, it can be stated that ICT access and knowledge in primary and secondary educational systems has come under increased political and social scrutiny world-wide. The developed areas remain in the statistical lead, though Europe is falling behind more innovative and aggressive approaches of some Asian countries. The MENA and Arab regions are beginning to recognize the need for a technological revolution and early education in ICT, but are hindered by more basic and pervasive educational problems.

From the results of the regression displayed in Table 1, it is noticed that the primary enrollment (P) is positively affected by the percentage of mobile phones (Mobile) and the percentage of Internet users (Intusers) as their sensitivity ratios are consecutively 0.211 and 0.211. However, this does not imply that a causality effect exists. The secondary enrollment also shows positive results driven by the percentage of mobile phones as well as the percentage of Internet users, their respective coefficients are of 0.312 and 0.312. Regarding the tertiary enrollment, the sensitivity coefficients are of 2.142. Finally, for the educational expenditure, it is also highly affected by both the percentage of Internet users and the percentage of mobile phones as they exhibit coefficients of 5.820.

ICTs and Health

The focus on youth and health has become essential nowadays. The World Health Organization besides other international institutions do frequently address and emphasize the wellbeing of youth as a major issue, mainly with the growth of common health problems and life threatening diseases. The World Youth Report of 2007 indicates that over 10 million young people, mostly in Africa and Asia, were living with HIV/AIDS. This led to higher investments by health organizations and the UN since improving youth health leads to poverty reduction, and contributes significantly to reducing

Table 1. Regression

	Constant	Mobile	Intusers	ICTimp	Exp	R^2
P	0.676 (1.380)	0.211 (2.683)		-0.094 (-0.972)	0.158 (0.553)	0.483
	0.676 (1.380)		0.211 (2.683)	-0.094 (-0.972)	0.158 (.553)	0.483
S	0.565 (0.685)	0.312 (2.517)		-0.224 (-1.468)	0.218 (0.472)	0.457
	0.565 (0.685)		0.312 (2.517)	-0.224 (-1.468)	0.218 (.472)	0.457
T	2.495 (2.616)	0.417 (2.142)		-0.232 (-1.104)	-0.743 (-1.313)	0.219
	2.495 (2.616)		0.417 (2.142)	-0.232 (-1.104)	-0.743 (-1.313)	0.219
Exp	1.409 (21.689)	0.303 (5.820)		0.106 (1.319)		0.619
	1.409 (21.689)		0.303 (5.820)	0.106 (1.319)		0.619

child mortality (World Youth Report, 2007). One of the tools used to reduce such diseases are ICTs.

Advances in information and computer technologies in the last decades have led to the development of the health sector. Laufman (2002) demonstrated that new ICTs helped in better understanding basic physiologic, pathologic processes, and diagnosis through new imaging and scanning technologies. Even though, such technological development requires a higher responsibility of practitioners, managers, and policy-makers in order to assess the suitability of these new technologies (Hofmann, 2002). Reliable information and communication are highly important in health practices. Using appropriate technologies can increase the quality and the reach of health through better health care systems and public health processes. According to WHO (2004), "health technologies are evidence-based when they meet well defined specifications and are validated through controlled clinical studies or rest on a widely accepted consensus by experts" (p. 102). Many reviews indicate that ICTs have plenty of applications in health care. This suggests that policy makers should consider higher investments in technologies used in the health sector. Governments are also responsible for the training

of medical staff about the use of ICTs for medical purposes, mainly in developing countries where technical skills are still very low.

ICTs are used in many areas of health communication, including decision and social support, health promotion, knowledge transfer; and the delivery of services (Suggs, 2006). With regard to health issues that affect the youth, the e-networking has proved to be an effective way of finding information on health-related issues. This technology also helps young people to obtain relevant information in situations where the nature of the subject matter is embarrassing. E-networking is also a tool of sharing information and personal experiences among different youth groups and even across borders. The Nairobi-based African Youth Parliament, a network of young people in more than 45 countries committed to African development, is a good evidence of the last assumption.

The use of ICTs in the health sector also provides opportunities to connect health researchers, and therefore allow access to a wider range of information on several health topics. The increased linkage between communities, patients, and frontline health workers is an essential tool for diseases prevention. The use of ICTs also plays a crucial role in changing perceptions of diseases such as HIV/AIDS. A survey conducted in 2002 to assess the ICT needs and requirements to address health and HIV/AIDS issues in developing countries (mostly in Africa), highlighted that the application of ICTs at the community level has proved to be the most important and effective prevention component in any HIV/AIDS strategy (WHO, 2004). The survey results suggest also that ICTs release the highest benefits when used to improve access to information and education and communication tools for rural health care workers, where the lack of information and ICTs is remarkable.

Quantitative evidence about the links between ICT components and health dimensions has been introduced in the previous chapter that focuses on health and ICTs.

ICTs and Employment

Youth unemployment has become one of the biggest developmental challenges in almost every country in the world in recent years. The UN estimates that 88 million among the youth are currently unemployed, with highest rates in Western Asia and Africa (WHO, 2005). The International Labor Organization (ILO) estimates that about 80% of the world unemployed youth are in developing countries and economies. The organization indicates as well that youth unemployment in these economies is growing annually at more than 15% (Global Youth Entrepreneurship Forum, 2006).

Until now, efforts by governments to promote job creation in developing countries both in the private and public sectors are still insufficient. Such countries still rely on the injection of external foreign investment and external expertise to accelerate economic growth. While, little or no attention is given to the development of skills and entrepreneurial capabilities among youth, which can play a crucial role to promote long term and sustainable economic growth.

The current educational systems are producing more graduates and therefore more job seekers,

which makes the situation even more complex. These systems do not all the time produce highly qualified people with skills as required by multinationals. As a result, the role of globalization in terms of opening up markets for the youth in developing countries is negligible in many cases. Statistics indicate that more than 20 percent of firms in countries such as Algeria, Bangladesh, Brazil, China, Estonia, and Zambia, rate poor education and work skills among their workforce as one of the main obstacles facing the functioning of their operations.

Nahleen (2006) cites the Youth Employment Network (YEN) initiative, developed by the UN in collaboration with the World Bank and ILO, as highlighting four areas for national action. These include employability with the need for more investments in education, professional training, and Long Life Learning. It also accounts for the provision of the same opportunities to men and women (equal opportunities). The promotion of entrepreneurship at different stages of education and jobs is the third pillar. Employment creation by the economy is the last element that emphasizes sound macroeconomic and local policies.

ICTs and Governance

Engagement of youth in society and in governing issues that are of importance to their lives is crucial to the promotion of this demographic group. Contributing to and influencing the decision-making process for the development of ICTs initiatives, that take into consideration both short and long-term impact on society and communities. It is also important to ensure that the use of ICTs is for the enhancement of youth lives and to be aware of the dangers of misuse of such technologies.

Empowerment of youth is still considered as an idea and not yet a policy. This empowerment principally involves the exclusion of economic barriers and the creation of a more equitable society. It should, as well, provide more opportunities to citizens to participate in the political system and in the process of decision-making (Nahleen,

2006). Relatively, several neglected communities try to integrate youth by developing creative ways of using ICTs, individually and collectively. The use of such technologies reinforces the democratic involvement of youth by providing them a greater opportunity to express their individual political will. These innovative models of engagement are creating communities that are more equitable and unbiased.

REGIONAL CONCERNS

Development challenges usually differ among the different geographic areas. This is mainly due to differences in political, economic, demographic, social, and cultural issues. Even though, the geographic location is not the only factor affecting development within the same geographic region, it is impossible to generalize about certain issues such as poverty and economic growth, gender equity and technological progress (The World Bank, 2006). This might explain the fact that almost 80% of the world's population has had little or no access to telephones and to the Internet. In this chapter, discussions of regional issues are meant to highlight some of the challenges faced by the youth with regard to ICTs.

The African Context

Africa is the continent with the largest number of young people, with 50% of the population below the age of 18 (African Youth Report, 2009). However, this demographic group is still marginalized and need the most basic means of life in the continent, including education, employment, Health, and so on. Relatively, ICT penetration in Africa is still very low and has made little relative progress compared to other developed countries. The Key factors limiting both access and inclusion are shortages of telecommunication infrastructure and education. Of the entire population of Africa, only about 2% use the Internet compared to 68% in North America and 37% in Europe (African

Youth Report, 2009). Other factors leading to poor access to ICTs in Africa include poor electricity infrastructure, limited power distribution, inadequate road and rail network and heavy import tax on computers and cell phones.

The educational infrastructure, which is poorly funded in many parts of Africa, is also one of the main obstacles of ICTs penetration in Africa. The educational systems suffer from many problems such as irrelevant school and university curricula, lack of qualified and skilled teachers, lack of access to books and materials, and an inadequate number of educational facilities. Another obstacle for youth promotion is the conflicts and wars that stretched all over the continent (Angola, Democratic Republic of Congo, Rwanda and Uganda, Ethiopia, Sudan, and Somalia). Finally, one of the most serious challenges facing youth in the continent is HIV/AIDS. The number of young people affected by this disease is shocking, which led governments and international organizations to give more importance to fighting and preventing the rate of infections than to ICTs and youth promotion.

The Asian Context

The large populations and geography of Asia pose a particular set of challenges and opportunities within the continent. Large populations imply a larger tension on resources and on the delivery of basic services, such as in education and health. Even though, countries such as China, India, Malaysia, and the Philippines have achieved outstanding steps in economic growth. This growth is not equitable for all countries since several Asian countries live in extreme poverty.

The economies of East Asia, for example, are characterized by high economic growth due to the large numbers of youth in the work force (about 450 million, World Bank, 2007). However, the youth population in such countries is set to decline in the coming years, which might have negative consequences on the current economic growth rates. Another concern is related to youth access to basic services, particularly for those from ethnic groups and marginalized populations.

With regard to education, even with the considerable investments in this sector, issues about schools capacity and the quality of university studies still arise. Youth employment is still a major concern. The increased number of university graduates requires higher job opportunities within Asian countries, which is not the case all the time. Additionally, access to and use of ICTs varies significantly from one country to another among the youth. Therefore, while 53% of youth in China have access, only 12% in Indonesia use these technologies.

The number of young people is about 400 millions, which makes up about 30% of all youth in developing countries. If effectively employed, such large numbers constitute an excellent opportunity for economic growth in the region. However, a remarkable portion of firms in developing countries report that inadequate skills and education of workers are major obstacles to their operations. The problem is not only the number of schools and educational institutions, but also the quality of education at all levels. Finally, a common challenge for youth in the region is the lack of access to information and their lack of participation in key life decisions. This might lead to disconnection, frustration, or even aggressive behavior by the youth toward individuals and society.

The Arab Nations Context

The last revolutions in the Arab world raised many issues related to youth in these nations. This demographic group proved their ability to move and to change political and economic situations. The revolutions also showed a number of issues and problems facing youth in Arab societies.

The situation of Arab states' economies over the last two decades trends include reasons for both concern and optimism. Concern is mainly about the weak growth performance throughout the region, which led to a slow progress in poverty alleviation and greater income gap. As a result, almost 11.5 million people in the region live in poverty for the reason that the region's population growth rate has outpaced that of its economies (Haq, 2005). Even though, despite the slow growth, some human development indicators show impressive development, with considerable gains made in the delivery of health and education services. One of the main reasons for the weak growth in these states is the inability of governments to transform the growth in human capital into higher productivity. This is mainly due to low rates of return on education, and high rates of unemployment (above 13 percent), mainly among the educated youth.

To get out of this situation, Arab governments are urged to make more investments to provide the youth with income generating and entrepreneurial opportunities. These governments also need to create incentives and favorable market conditions for the private sector, as a source of jobs for youth. That will also imply greater access to and use of ICTs in order to integrate global markets.

BENEFITS FROM SOCIAL NETWORKS AND CASES

This part addresses the potential benefits from social networks and introduces some cases.

Potential for ICTs and Social Networks

Based on the country data information as provided by World Internet Statistics (2009, 2010, 2011), the number of Facebook users as an example of social media, appears to be mainly related not only to the number of computers and the Internet users but also to the level of human development of the country (HDI). This overall regression over world countries (Table 2) shows that developing and low HDI economies have less access to facebook in comparison with developed countries of higher HDI. In this regression, both the effects of the number of computers and the Internet users are positive.

When regressing the number of Facebook users over a narrower sample formed of Arab and Eastern European countries, the most important driver appears to be the number of Internet users besides an effect related to the level of human development. These results are shown in Table 3.

When the number of countries is narrowed further to the Arab countries only, the Internet users variable is the only effect that is statistically significant as shown in Table 4.

The same regression is conducted on the set of East European Economies (EEE). It shows again the prevalence of the number of Internet users. This is introduced in Table 5.

However, the statistical impacts of the variables appear to be different when comparing Arab and EEE countries. These effects are definitely higher in the Arab countries relative to EEE as shown in Table 6 using Chow Test.

Cases Cited in the Literature

Selling Telephone-Based Services (Grameen Bank)

The accessibility to mobile phone networks in many low and middle income countries create plenty of opportunities for young people. One option to take advantages of this technology is to purchase a mobile phone via a micro credit program and to earn income by providing low cost phone calls to others. One good example is the story illustrated below about a 16-year-old schoolgirl in rural India that was published in Business Week Online in 1999.

The Grameen Village Pay Phone Program (VPP) illustrates more the potential of mobile phones to create low-income earning opportunities for youth. With 1170 Grameen branches in Bangladesh and 105 micro credit organizations in 34 countries operating on the same Grameen model, the Grameen Bank is considered a pioneer of small loans to the poor. The Village Pay Phone program makes it possible for borrowers to buy a mobile phone, and then to make the telephone available for others in the village to pay for phone calls, to send Short Message Services (SMS) and to receive incoming calls. In 2000, the Grameen Village Pay Phones was operating in more than 2,000 villages in Bangladesh, with an average of 100 additional villages connected each month. The Grameen phones are used for multiple purposes. So, farmers use them to find out where they can get the best prices for their crops, assistance workers use them to better coordinate disaster response measures, and finally villagers are use the phones to communicate with local government officials.

The Grameen Telecom is a good example of the use ICTs for youth promotion. The potential of Grameen Telecom as an income generator has been appreciated by many organizations and investment companies, which attracted higher investments to the project. The World Bank's International Finance Corporation has invested

Table 2. Log Facebook users on different independent variables overall

Independent Variables	Coefficients	t stat	R²
Constant	1.111	3.010	0.810
Log Computers	0.260	2.520	
Log Cell phones	0.155	1.160	
Log Internet connection	-0.084	-0.846	
Log Internet users	0.472	3.056	
Log HDI	1.613	3.476	

Table 3. Log Facebook users on different independent variables: Arab+ EEE

Independent Variables	Coefficients	t stat	R²
Constant	0.143	0.184	0.805
Log Computers	0.113	0.899	
Log Cellphones	-0.073	-0.324	
Log Internet connection	-0.356	-1.694	
Log Internet users	1.256	5.267	
Log HDI	2.132	2.038	

Table 4. Log Facebook users on different independent variables: Arab countries

Independent Variables	Coefficients	t stat	R²
Constant	-0.714	-0.695	0.844
Log Internet users	1.046	6.572	

US$50 million in the project. The Norwegian company Telenor has also invested $25 million, and the Soros Economic Development Fund invested $10.6 million.

Young People as "Information Intermediaries"

The prevalent use of the English language on Internet has created a need for more work to enable non-English speakers to make effective use of it. To do this, information intermediaries are the ones responsible for interpreting internet information into local contexts. In most cases, young people perform this role. For example, in Sri Lanka and Mongolia, local populations have gained access to information on the Internet through community radio networks. Radio stations use intermediaries to search for information in the Internet, transform it to their local context, and then broadcasts the information in their language (ILO, 2001).

Another option for youth to take advantage of their skills in information technology is to develop simple websites in local languages. In India, the Swaminathan Foundation has set up Village Knowledge Centers, which create special websites to provide a variety of locally relevant information to citizens. Relatively, the Warana Nagar rural network project, in Maharashtra State in India, allows villagers to use 'facilitation booths' to access agricultural, medical, and educational information on the Internet. The project includes 10 computer servers, two small opening terminals (VSATs), and about 165 personal computers (ILO, 2001).

Opportunities for E-Commerce-Based Entrepreneurship in Remote Communities (Greenstar India)

Another good income generating opportunity for young people in India are the centers of the Los Angeles-based Greenstar Foundation. The foundation set up self-contained, solar-powered community centers in isolated areas on the West Bank, India, Jamaica, and Ghana. The centers offer Internet connection, health facilities, tele-medicine, distance-learning equipment, and a business center through which traditional cultural products can be sold via Internet. These projects mainly target areas without electricity in order to create job opportunities for youth and to sell

Table 5. Log Facebook users on different independent variables: EEE

Independent Variables	Coefficients	t stat	R²
Constant	0.482	0.413	0.678
Log Computers	0.104	0.642	
Log Internet users	0.807	3.548	
Log HDI	1.771	0.752	

Table 6. Comparison of Arab and EEE countries using the chow test

Dependent Variable	K	SSR (Arab+EEE)	SSR(Arab)	SSR(EEE)	Chow test
Log Facebook users	2	1.768	0.673	1.462	7.874

cultural products in digital formats to pay for the hardware and connections needed without the need for external funding.

The implementation of the Greenstar project in India is relatively new compared to the other countries where the Greenstar centers are already implemented. One good example of the use of cultural products as a financing source for the project is the Bedouin music available on the Greenstar Foundation website. Therefore, more than 40 compressed music files, made in a Bedouin village on the West Bank, a mountain village in Jamaica and a tribal village in central India, are available on the website. Such music is meant to make the money needed to finance the Greenstar centers.

Tele-Centers as Income Generators for Young People

Tele-centers are considered as a main job creation tool in many developing countries. The UNESCO has produced a user-friendly manual on how to set up several different types of community-based Tele-centers (Jensen & Esterhuysen, 2001). The manual is aimed at telecom operators, NGOs, community groups, local government, and small entrepreneurs. This guide outlines how to set up four types of Tele-centers, mainly micro Tele-centers,

Mini Tele-centers, Tele-centers, and full service Tele-centers. These centers provide a variety of services and lead to the creations of thousands if not millions of IT-related job opportunities. In India, The Ministry of Information Technology plans to convert over 6,000,000 Public Call Offices (PCOs) into public 'Tele-Info-Centers' that offer a variety of services, such as Internet browsing, fax, e-mail and long distance phone calls (Lobo, 2000).

Tele-centers or Internet kiosks offer a good entrepreneurship opportunity for youth since they involve lower start-up costs. For example, in India, equipment costs are about $10,000 and the telecom service provider's investment in a telephone line is about $ 1,000 (Mitter & Millar, 2001). Hence, young people, particularly those with good IT knowledge, can benefit from this entrepreneurship opportunity.

Income Generation through Cable Television (Grameen Micro-Credits)

Another ICT self-employment opportunity for young people is through acquiring satellite antennas to provide villagers with paid access to cable television. Cable TV systems have been installed in many developing regions to provide access to TV channels from a satellite, typically for a fee. The most remarkable current example is India, where cable TV systems have spread in urban neighborhoods to deliver programming from AsiaSat (Hudson, 2001).

The Newsletter of the Grameen Foundation (2000) indicates that a micro credit case study from India indicated that a loan of 80,000 taka ($1,569) was sufficient for a Grameen borrower to purchase two satellite antennas. These two antennas were able to supply an eight TV channel service to 30 houses at a fee of 200 taka per month per connection hence generating income of an average of 12,500 taka ($245) per month.

Government's Role in Promoting ICT Related Entrepreneurship: Promoting "Technopreneurship" in Singapore

'Technopreneurship 21' (T21) is a program launched by the Singapore Government to promote entrepreneurship in a variety of ways. One aspect of the program is to introduce a greater weight on entrepreneurship in the education system in order to encourage creativity, risk taking. Box 4 illustrates a similar program that was implemented in Ugandan schools (CIDA, 2000). The T21 also encourage start-ups through a $1 billion venture fund to support both local and foreign entrepreneurs attracted to Singapore.

Another main factors leading the Economic Development Board of Singapore to set up the 'Technopreneur' program is to surpass the difficulties faced by the high-tech start-ups. In this context, the board provides loss insurance to a maximum investment of S$3 million for start-ups. The program also includes other initiatives to help young investors, such as the Technopreneur Home Office Scheme. This plan makes it easier for technology entrepreneurs to use their residential locations as home offices, and therefore reduce their costs.

Finally, in order to encourage more ICT start-ups under the Technopreneurship program, the Economic Development Board of Singapore, in association with private sector partners such as Ernst and Young and the Singapore Venture Capital Association, has instituted the Phoenix prize. This Award recognizes entrepreneurs who have failed formerly and then achieved success, either through a new technology venture, or via using technology. The Phoenix Award aims to encourage more entrepreneurs to take necessary risks and persist in achieving their goals despite failures.

CONCLUSION

With an increasingly globalized world, the impact of ICTs on individuals and on societies is becoming more and more important. Such impact transformed ICTs form a luxury tool to a necessity for the development and growth of societies and economies. Younger generations are most affected by ICTs since they are the best users of these technologies.

Today, the role of young people in shaping their societies is becoming increasingly evident. The recent Arab revolutions are good evidence of the last hypothesis since Arab youth were the leaders of the revolutions in revolutionized countries.

Youth are the main producers and consumers of ICTs. Therefore, this demographic group became a more important agent of change not only because they know how to use ICT or because they may learn faster than adults, but also because they are more adaptive to change. This suggests that ICTs can be used for a better empowerment and promotion of youth especially in developing countries where a large part of this group is still marginalized.

This chapter relates the use of ICTs to youth promotion in developing countries. Therefore, it started by analyzing the relationship between ICTs and youth in several sectors, mainly education, health, employment, and governance. The chapter investigated, as well, the main concerns related to ICTs and youth in developing countries, mainly in Africa, Asia, and the Arab region. The last section of the chapter dealt with real case studies related to the use of ICTs for youth promotion in some developing markets. Such case studies indicate that ICTs could be an effective tool for job creation and for the promotion and empowerment of youth in such markets.

REFERENCES

African Youth Report. (2009). *Expanding opportunities for and with young people in Africa.* Retrieved from http://www.uneca.org/ayr2009/AfricanYouthReport_09.pdf

Beastall, L. (2006). Enchanting a disenchanted child: Revolutionizing the means of education using information and communication technology and e-learning. *British Journal of Sociology of Education*, *27*(1), 97–110. doi:10.1080/01425690500376758

Canadian International Development Agency. (2000). *Grameen telecom's village phone programme in rural Bangladesh: A multi-media case study final report.* Retrieved from www.telecommons.com/villagephone/finalreport.pdf

Center for Education Research and Innovation. (2000). *ICT: School innovation and the quality of learning: Progress and pitfalls.* Retrieved from http://www.oecd.org/dataoecd/24/38/1957030.pdf

Cosgrove, J., Zastrutzki, S., & Shiel, G. (2005). A survey of ICT in post-primary schools. *Irish Journal of Education*, *36*, 25–48. Retrieved from http://www.jstor.org/stable/30077502

Debande, O., & Ottersten, E. K. (2004). Information and communication technologies: A tool empowering and developing the horizon of the learner. *Higher Education. Management and Policy*, *16*(2), 31–61.

Franzoni, A. L., & Assar, S. (2009). Student learning styles adaptation method based on teaching strategies and electronic media. *Journal of Educational Technology & Society*, *12*(4), 15–29.

GAID Committee of eLeaders for Youth and ICT. (2009). *Youth and ICT for development best practice.* Retrieved from http://unpan1.un.org/intradoc/groups/public/documents/gaid/unpan036084.pdf

Global e-Government Readiness Report, UN-DESA. (2005). *From e-government to e-inclusion.* Retrieved from http://unpan1.un.org/intradoc/groups/public/documents/un/unpan021888.pdf

Global Youth Entrepreneurship Forum. (2006). *Discussion summary and agenda for action.* Retrieved from http://www.youthbusiness.org/PDF/GFYEDiscussionSummary.pdf

Haq, T. (2005). *Labor markets and youth employment in the Arab states.* Retrieved from http://www.un.org/esa/socdev/unyin/workshops/256,1,LabourMarkets&YouthEmploymentintheArabStates

Hodgson, V. E. (2008). Learning spaces, context and auto/biography in online learning communities. *International Journal of Web Based Communities*, *4*(2), 159–172. doi:10.1504/IJWBC.2008.017670

Hofmann, B. (2002). Is there a technological imperative in health care? *International Journal of Technology Assessment in Health Care*, *18*(3), 675–689.

Hudson, H. (2001). *The potential of ICTs for development: Opportunities and obstacles.* Background Paper. New York, NY: World Employment Report 2001.

ILO. (2001). *Generating decent work for young people: An issues paper*. New York, NY: ILO.

Jensen, M., & Esterhuysen, A. (2001). The community telecentre cookbook for Africa recipes for self-sustainability: How to establish a multi-purpose community telecentre in Africa. *UNESCO*. Retrieved from http://unesdoc.unesco.org/images/0012/001230/123004e.pdf

Jeskanen-Sundström, H. (2003). ICT statistics at the new millennium: Developing official statistics: Measuring the diffusion of ICT and its impact. *International Statistical Review, 71*(1), 5–15. Retrieved from http://www.jstor.org/stable/1403870 doi:10.1111/j.1751-5823.2003.tb00181.x

Kamsin, A. (2005). Is e-learning the solution and substitute for conventional learning? *Journal of the Computer. Internet and Management, 13*(3), 79–89.

La Cava, G., Rossotto, C., & Paradi-Guilford, C. (2011). Information and communication technologies (ICT) for youth in Mena: Policies to promote employment opportunities. *Arab World Brief, 1*, 1-5. Retrieved from http://www.aicto.org/fileadmin/user_upload/Youth.pdf

Laufman, H. (2002). Are engineer's unsung heroes of medical progress? *The Historic Physics. Engineering in Medicine, 36*(5), 325–334.

Lim, C. P. (2007). Effective integration of ICT in Singapore schools: Pedagogical and policy implications. *Educational Technology Research and Development, 55*(1), 83–116. Retrieved from http://www.jstor.org/stable/30221231 doi:10.1007/s11423-006-9025-2

Lobo, A. (2000). Taking IT to the villages. *ZDNet India, 6*.

MacKeogh, K. (2003). *Student perceptions of the use of ICTs in European education: Report of a survey*. Dublin, Ireland: Oscail - Dublin City University. Retrieved from http://www.oscail.ie/academic/picture.php

Mitter, S., & Millar, J. (2001). *The impact of ICT on the spatial division of labor in the service sector*. Geneva, Switzerland: ILO.

Nahleen, A. (2006). *Youth and ICT as agents for change*. New York, NY: The Global Alliance for ICT and Development, UNDESA.

Organization for Economic Co-Operation and Development. (2002). *ICT in education and government*. Retrieved from http://www.oecd.org/dataoecd/34/36/2771146.pdf

Pailing, M. (2002). E-learning: Is it really the best thing since sliced bread? *Industrial and Commercial Training, 34*(4), 151–155. doi:10.1108/00197850210429138

Report, W. Y. (2007). *Young people's transition to adulthood: Progress and challenges*. Retrieved from http://www.un.org/esa/socdev/unyin/documents/wyr07_complete.pdf

Sarkar, S. (2012). The role of information and communication technology (ICT) in higher education for the 21st century. *The Science Probe, 1*(1), 30–40.

Scarafiotti, C. (2003). A three-prong strategic approach to successful distance learning delivery. *Journal of Asynchronous Learning Networks, 7*(2), 50–55.

Suggs, L. S. (2006). A 10-year retrospective of research in new technologies for health communication. *Journal of Health Communication, 11*(1), 61–74. doi:10.1080/10810730500461083

Sutherland-Smith, W., Snyder, L., & Angus, L. (2003). The digital divide: Differences in computer use between home and school in low socio-economic households. *Educational Studies in Language and Literature, 3*, 5–19. doi:10.1023/A:1024523503078

Unwin, T. (2008). Survey of e-learning in Africa. *UNESCO Chair in ICT for Development*. Retrieved from http://www.elearning-africa.com/

Unwin, T. (2012). Education. In Sadowsky, G. (Ed.), *Accelerating Development Using the Web: Empowering Poor and Marginalized Populations*. New York, NY: World Wide Web Foundation.

U.S.-Arab Chamber of Commerce. (2011). *US-Arab trade line*. Retrieved from http://www.nusacc.org/assets/library/15_trdln1110kbe.pdf

Valentine, D. (2002). *Distance learning: Promises, problems, and possibilities*. Retrieved from http://distance.westga.edu/~distance/ojdla/fall53/valentine53.html

Weiner, A., & Rumiany, D. (2007). A new logic of reducing the global digital divide in sub-Saharan Africa: From obstacles to opportunities. *ATDF Journal, 4*(1), 14–21.

World Bank. (2006). *Equity and development*. Retrieved from http://siteresources.worldbank.org/INTWDR2006/Resources/477383-127230817535/082136412X.pdf

World Bank. (2007). *Survey of ICT and education in Africa: Egypt country report Egypt: ICT in education in Egypt*. Washington, DC: World Bank.

World Health Organization. (2004). *Ehealth for health-care delivery: Strategy 2004-2007*. Retrieved from http://www.who.int/eht/en/EHT_strategy_2004-2007.pdf

World Health Organization. (2005). *Health and the millennium development goals*. Retrieved from http://www.who.int/mdg/publications/mdg_report/en/index.html

Chapter 7
Women Empowerment and ICTs in Developing Economies

ABSTRACT

The revolution in Information and Communication Technologies (ICTs) has vast implications for the developing world; yet this revolution is associated with several issues. One of the main issues is the gender digital divide that has been widely growing in these economies. The absence of clear knowledge about the ways gender inequality and ICTs are impacting each other remain a main issue of ICTs and women. This chapter examines some issues and challenges related to women and ICTs in developing economies. The chapter discusses some potential uses of ICTs for women empowerment. Finally, real case studies of the use of ICTs for women empowerment in developing countries are introduced to show that local development projects can benefit from technological support.

INTRODUCTION

One of the central forces that shape the 21st century are the new Information and Communication Technologies. These technologies impact living, learning, work, communication, and also leisure time. These relatively new tools with their continuous improvements have the potential to enable individuals, groups, and societies through addressing economic, cultural, and social challenges with greater efficiency and attainment.

Despite the fact that ICTs and the Internet offer large opportunities for human development and empowerment in many areas, such technologies are considered one of the key contributing input to the reduction of social and economic disparities across different social and economic groups (Ben, 2012). The gender gap is one of the most significant sources of inequalities in the era of this digital revolution, mainly in developing countries. Throughout the world, women face serious challenges that are not only economic but also social

DOI: 10.4018/978-1-4666-3643-9.ch007

as well as cultural obstacles that limit or prevent their access to use and benefit from ICTs.

There is a higher understanding and awareness about the challenges faced by women. It is also pervasively known that the most important ones reside in access to education and to the opportunities that could be provided by ICTs. These are important steps towards transforming the digital divide into a digital opportunity that all could access and use. Involving and engaging universal access to information is a direct step toward the promotion of social and economic progress and thus ensuring better development. Women represent a central economic force in most developing countries. Economies are becoming increasingly information-driven. Accordingly, the issues of women's access to and use of ICTs are becoming more and more important in both developed and developing economies. With the multiplicity of digital platforms and ICT applications with their likely positive implications on employment, education, and other areas of life, women need more incentives and policy frameworks to support and advance the elimination of the digital gap characterizing gender in developing economies.

Rakow (1986) is among the earliest researchers that dealt with gender and ICTs. This author considers that the use of telephones by women generates high levels of benefits not just to these women but also to their families and related. The study recognizes that the telephone plays an important function in women's lives as a way of maintaining long-distance communications with family and friends, and a way of reducing domestic isolation. This has had implications on phone businesses through the identification of women as attractive targets for marketing agencies and telecommunication operators.

Other studies have focus on ICTs as a basic entrepreneurial tool for women empowerment (Shade, 2002). However, a wide range of scholars have paid attention to the critical role of ICTs in gender empowerment. Kramarae (2004) argues that enabling women to have access to ICTs would be a good strategy for providing new voices, values, and vision into the traditional discussions of communication and technology, and their role in gender empowerment.

There are several factors that can affect women use of ICTs. Johnson (2012) defines technophobia (or fear of technology), computer illiteracy, and poverty as the most important reasons for gender divide. The author suggests as well that the gender divide could be treated from a sociological side through reducing barriers to access ICTs using proximity to ICTs or Internet connectivity, or mental such as the ability to understand or use ICTs. According to this author, marginalization in the utilization of technology occurs with women spread over different income levels, age groups and literacy levels. An ethnographic study conducted in a middle-class locality in Chennai, in South India in 2006 about the use of ICTs suggests that fear and prejudice from ICTs (mainly Internet) and the belief that new ICTs are not for them are key reasons to explain the Internet penetration rate in this region. These factors are emphasized in Faulkner and Lie (2007).

Women presence in decision-making structures in the ICT sector is still very low. Equitable access to ICTs and the independence in receiving and producing information are central to the construction of an Information Society for all and to women empowerment.

Hafkin (2012) shows how mobile cellular operators have undertaken high-profile efforts to encourage "Bottom of the Pyramid" (BoP) women to adopt telephony. Examples of promising initiatives are discussed. These include also the support of entrepreneurial activities of women. The benefits from these developments are reported to be very high. Series of studies and reports are stressing these benefits and encouraging investments in these directions.

This chapter examines some issues and challenges related to women and ICTs in developing economies. It discusses also some potential uses of ICTs for women empowerment. Finally, real case studies of the use of ICTs for women empowerment in developing countries are illustrated. Four sections are introduced with the last one devoted to some promising cases about the roles of ICTs in the empowerment of women.

FRAMEWORKS SHOWING DEPRIVATION OF WOMEN

This part of the current chapter introduces series of dimensions that show the extent of deprivation faced by women in series of areas with the attempts of measurement.

Deprivation of Girls and Women

The best contribution in this area is that of Osmani and Sen (2003). They looked at the interconnections between gender inequality and maternal deprivation, on the health of coming generations. Women's deprivation in nutrition, healthcare, and others at any age affects negatively society in the form of ill health of current and future children but also of future adults. Maternal deprivation "adversely affects the health of the fetus, which in turn leads to long-term health risks that extend not just into childhood but into adulthood as well." However, differences have been identified in the ways children and adults experience the consequences via fetal deprivation. According to the authors, gender inequality leads to a double loss that aggravates both regimes of diseases and thus raising the economic cost of "overlapping health transition."

Another contribution took the same avenue through focusing on why "Nutrition of Women and Adolescent Girls" matters (Ransom & Elder, 2003). Malnutrition as both under-nutrition and deficiencies related to absence of micronutrients is an ill health caused by poor food regime intake and its interactions with infectious and other poor health and social conditions. This is affecting the well-being of millions of women and adolescent

girls around the world. Although malnutrition's effects on this group have been recognized for decades, there has been little measurable progress in addressing the specific nutritional problems of women and adolescent girls. Ignorance about the symptoms of malnutrition, such as the lethargy and depression caused by iron deficiency, may be dismissed as "normal" or unimportant, further exacerbating the problem. Adequate nutrition is especially critical for women because affects not only the own health of undernourished women but also that of their children. Children of malnourished women are more likely to face cognitive impairments, short stature, lower resistance to infections, and a higher risk of disease and death throughout their live. Women in general express higher levels of health vulnerability relative to men. According to medical and specialized studies, this vulnerability is higher under poverty and absence of education. Socio-cultural factors and gender disparities increase women's chances of being malnourished. Globally, 50 percent of all pregnant women are anemic, and at least 120 million women in less developed countries are underweight. Research shows that being underweight hinders women's productivity and can lead to increased rates of illness and mortality. In some regions, the majority of women are underweight (South Asia, 60 percent of women are underweight). Many women who are underweight are also stunted, or below the median height for their age. Stunting is a known risk factor for obstetric complications such as obstructed labor and the need for skilled intervention during delivery, leading to injury or death for mothers and their newborns. It also is associated with reduced work capacity. Adolescent girls are particularly vulnerable to malnutrition because they are growing faster than at any time after their first year of life. They need protein, iron, and other micronutrients to support the adolescent growth spurt and meet the body's increased demand for iron during menstruation. Adolescents who become pregnant are at greater risk of various complications since they may not yet have finished growing. Pregnant adolescents who are underweight or stunted are especially likely to experience obstructed labor and other obstetric complications. There is evidence that the bodies of the still-growing adolescent mother and her baby may compete for nutrients, raising the infant's risk of low birth weight (defined as a birth weight of less than 2,500 grams) and early death.

Gender Empowerment Measure

Gender Empowerment Measure (GEM) as developed by UNDP has been showing consistently lower values for its different components that measure the participation of women (parliament, management and administration, technical and professional jobs). In 2002, the GEM values for Morocco, Mauritania, Turkey, and Egypt were respectively 0.421, 0.410, 0.312, and 0.260. During the same year, the GEM of Norway and Finland attained 0.837 and 0.803. The most values attained by this index in 2007/2008 are 0.325, 0.129, 0.263, and 0.298 for Morocco, Yemen, Egypt, and Turkey, respectively.

This low level of the index indicates that women are not fully engaged in their respective economies. This is an important signal for the limited social, political, and economic inclusion for most of the women in the countries of this region. While improvements in women social and familial status were promoted in Tunisia and more recently in Morocco, most women and mainly those in poor neighborhoods and in rural areas. They suffer from poor health, limited education besides poverty.

Women and ICTs

A large set of publications and reports have addressed the potential benefits from expanding the access to ICTs with major focus on the trends related to gender and access of women to the different ICT components. Some authors have linked the concept of missing women* to the potential role of ICTs. Among these latter authors, Gillard et al. (2008) can be cited as a good representative. In this chapter the authors discuss the omission of women in the work of Walsham and Sahay (2005) about research on information systems in developing countries. The newer chapter addresses the substantial gender and development literature that demonstrates the centrality of gender in understanding of information systems in developing countries. The relationship among gender, Information and Communication Technologies (ICTs) and globalization illustrate how changes in the global economy impact on and are influenced by changing gender identities and roles.

Miller et al. (2010) have shown that women are contributing to the promotion of science. The analysis is based on a panel data of scientists in some developing countries. However, the gains to productivity with access to ICTs and higher education have not reduced the gender gap in this career.

Youngs (2012) considers women's relationship to Information and Communication Technologies (ICTs) and finds that it is important to look at the historically embedded gender inequalities that exist in the areas of science and technology as well as examining the creative and entrepreneurial uses of ICTs in which women around the world are engaged. The picture of globalization and ICTs and women's lives is highly complex, reflecting structural problems but also new dynamics that have contributed to empowering women and global women's movements.

Gurumurthy (2010) describes an important experiment related to women and ICTs. The author shows how women have been able to use ICTs to adjust to new forms of information, organization and empowerment. The discussion of some myths reveals that there is no clear cut about women and access to tele-centers but debates are still prevailing about access and use of ICTs by the poor.

In an interesting report on women and ICTs in India, Malhotra, Kanesathan, and Patel (2012) finds series of empirical facts about the engagement of women in using ICTs and promoting entrepreneurial activities. The analysis of the experiences of some NGOs is very instructive about the progress made by women in different regions of India. Allison and Gomez (2012) attempted to identify benefits and constraints of ICTs on women. The authors identify that individual women gain more self-esteem with women less isolated with access to markets and to health information. Collectively, women are also more empowered with improved economic situation, health, education, cultural transformation and capacity building. Toyama, Karishma, Pal, Joyojeet, and Srinivasan (2005) have placed emphasis on the gender divide and its impacts on women in accessing ICTs.

CHALLENGES AND ISSUES

The implied challenges and related issues are discussed in this part of the chapter.

Ensuring women access to ICTs has several benefits on both women and society. For women, having resources and access to new information and communication technologies lead to women promotion and empowerment. For society as a whole, ICTs offer vast possibilities for poverty alleviation, overcoming women's isolation, improving governance, and advancing gender equality. Even though, this prospective can only be realized if the factors leading the current gender digital divide are well identified and addressed.

Women's access to ICTs is not simply a matter of whether using a computer that is connected to Internet. Other issues are to be considered when evaluating women's use of ICTs. Taking into consideration their social roles, women are generally more aware than men of the social, economic, and environmental needs of their own communities. Hence, ensuring women access to new technologies can lead to a better use of ICTs in addressing societies' problems, fighting poverty, and opening up possibilities of access to a global

pool of knowledge. A good example is the role that ICTs can play fighting AIDS and saving or improving lives of many women (and men) facing the related hazards of this disease in Asian and African countries (Ben, 2012).

Socio-Cultural and Institutional Barriers

Generally, in both developed and developing countries, women have less access than men to ICT facilities. There are several barriers that limit women's access participation in the Information Society. One of the most pervasive problems limiting women's access to ICTs is "technophobia," or fear of technology (Johnson, 2012). Women have generally limited relationships with technology and machines as a result of the old believe that t machines and technology are a man's domain and are not for women and girls. This generates a gender bias in attitudes towards studying or using information technology, which leads to discouraging girls from studying science and technology, either by parents or teachers' biases.

In several developing countries, girls are encouraged to get married at an early age or to get a job rather than pursuing further studies (Primo, 2003). In many of these countries, there is a social preference for boy children, and investing in boys' education is usually made at the expense of girls, who are required to help in home daily tasks for all or part of the school day. As a result, fewer women enter into the science and technology fields and therefore a limited number of women scientists and technologists exist in academia and in research and development. Gender biases against women in some universities and research institutes in developing countries also influence the level of women's participation in university and research institutions. Relatively females in developing countries have greater difficulty finding employment in science and technology professions and therefore have less access to supervisory positions in such fields.

Access and Control Issues

In many developing countries women's access to and control over ICTs is inferior to that of men. One of the main reasons is the fact that Infrastructure is largely concentrated in urban areas, while the majority of women in several developing countries are located in remote and rural areas. Therefore, females in such countries have no access to ICTs and therefore no control over them. This suggests that the development of infrastructure should take into consideration decisions about locations of facilities that provide access to remote and rural areas, where there higher portions of women. Ramilo (2001) suggest that the starting point in building infrastructure is policy, so women advocates have to get involved in policy areas to ensure a higher access to ICTs by women.

Another access issue is related to the low penetration rates in developing countries by both genders. Statistics show that one-third of the world's population has never made a phone call, and less than one-fifth has experienced the Internet (Primo, 2003). These figures illustrate the lack of telecommunications service to poor and rural peoples in different countries, of whom a great number are women. Women's access and use of ICTs is related to several factors, among which are literacy and education, geographic location (North or South, rural or urban), and social class.

Finally, the way in which ICTs are used in some developing countries can also be considered as a gender issue. Research has shown that most women in developing countries make restricted use of ICTs, limiting themselves to email and email discussions, generally for networking purposes. Relatively, very few women, in developing countries, have used ICTs for business development, educational purposes, or for information to improve the quality of life of either themselves or their families (such as health and nutritional information). Hence, developing the technical skills of women in these countries is to be considered for a better use of ICTs.

Education, Training, and Skills Development

Statistics indicate that 870 million of the world's populations are illiterate, of which two-thirds are women (Primo, 2003). They indicate, as well, that the world's lowest literacy rates among women are found in African countries. Women in such countries face several challenges in pursuing their studies mainly due to the lack of time to attend classes, family responsibilities, and socio-cultural practices that rate girls' education as less important. Accordingly, though the gender gap in primary and secondary school enrolment started to decrease in recent years, girls still represent 60 percent of the 100 million growing up without access to basic education. 95 percent of these out-of-school children reside Sub-Saharan Africa, southern Asia, and the Arab States. In Central and Eastern Europe, there is less concern about girls' enrolment in primary and secondary school, yet many concerns were raised about the limited access to higher education mainly because of the higher costs of IT training and professions.

Literacy, language, and computer skills are central skills to take advantage of ICTs for development initiatives. Information literacy is mainly the ability to evaluate different sets of information and to apply it into real-life contexts. The remoteness and limited experience of women in developing countries means that they are less likely to have these skills. Thus, Women and girls with less requisite skills are more likely to be excluded from local initiatives. Another issue resides in the fact that a high proportion of women in developing countries live in rural areas, which means that they are less likely than men to access computers and benefit from ICTs. In view of that, the UNESCO place literacy and basic education for girls and women as central concerns. Following the World Education Forum (Dakar, 2000), the UNESCO defined the six Dakar goals of its work the period between 2002-2007, among which a 50 percent reduction in female illiteracy and the elimination of gender disparities at primary and secondary levels. Efforts to ensure women's access to technical and scientific education have also been intensified. Green and Adam (1998) have already insisted on similar matters.

Language Issues

Though the high penetration rates among populations all over the world, the language issue remains one of the main obstacles facing Internet users. While millions of people are able to access information and meet with people from around the world, other minorities are excluded from these services just because they do not speak Internet languages, mainly English. A great portion of these excluded minorities are women. For a great number of women, lack of proficiency in international languages is a major problem, even for educated women in Eastern Europe, Latin America, and French-speaking Africa. The problem of language is not limited to English; the majority of poor women in the world do not speak the languages that dominate the Internet, mainly French, German, Japanese, and Chinese. The shortage of those languages limits those women from the benefits they are able to draw by the use of ICTs.

Cost, Time, and Mobility

Due to shortages in telecommunication infrastructures, national and international connectivity in many developing countries is still limited and expensive. In rural areas, there are limited incentives to extend connectivity infrastructure for the fact that it requires huge investments (Gurumurthy, 2006). Another reason for the shortages in infrastructures in remote areas is the fact the majority of villages and small towns in developing countries are characterized by lower population densities, poverty, and geographical distance from established telecommunications networks, so investments to extend the technical infrastructure are very limited. These technical challenges together with telecommunications policies and regulations lead to highly priced services, which limit the ability of poor communities, mainly women, to access these technologies.

Equipment and connection costs are generally excessive in developing countries compared to developed nations. In 2001, Monthly Internet access charges amounted to 1.2% of average monthly income for the typical user in the US compared with 278% in Nepal, 191% in Bangladesh and 60% in Sri Lanka (Primo, 2003). Generally, the majority of communications facilities are associated with expensive costs. Accordingly, high portions of developing countries populations, especially women, are less likely to have money to buy televisions, radios, or to access them when they wish, particularly when the household technology is controlled by someone else (typically a husband or father). Women might also not have the disposable income needed to pay for information services, particularly when other needs have higher priority.

Regarding time, women might have several responsibilities simultaneously, mainly working women. In addition to their responsibilities at work, women, in developing countries, are generally responsible for housework and children. This leads to a minor use of ICTs and connectivity by women who have less time left to seek out ICT connections or spend time online than men. Primo (2003) conducted a study in several countries about ICTs use by women. The study suggests that women use ICTs for communication (mainly email) and electronic banking, while men spend time browsing the Internet, downloading software, and reading newspapers. Women's greater family and nurturing responsibilities mean that they usually have less time, and less choice, when it comes to spending their money. Even community access, often seen as the key to Internet diffusion in the developing world, may be outside the financial reach of many women.

In most developing countries, women's liberty and mobility is not the same of that of men. This leads women to not be able to travel unaccompanied, so mobility for women constitutes another obstacle for their integration in the information society. This lack of mobility is chief cause of the limited access of women to new ICTs, especially with the absence of connectivity in rural areas, where women account for a high portion of the population.

Gender Segregation and Employment

ICTs create plenty of opportunities of employment for women, especially in the service industries. Women's skills and abilities have made them preferred employees for certain kinds of work, particularly in banking, telecommunications industries, and insurance. However, Men are more likely to be found in the high-paying, while low-paid ICT jobs are generally occupied by women. This suggests that countries should adopt policies that promote science and technology education for all, and that do not limit this kind of education for men. Countries such as Brazil, India, and Malaysia are good examples of technology education promotion, and women in these countries made inroads into skilled jobs such as software programmers or computer analysts. Even though, the majority of these women are from privileged backgrounds, and the numbers remain relatively low.

ICT developments also reproduce gender inequalities present in the broader fabric of society. Tele-working or working from home is always promoted as being more convenient for women child-care and home responsibilities. The issue is that even highly-skilled women might opt for this choice especially if they are married, with broaden the gap between men and women in ICTs high-skills professions. Statistics show that women in Malaysia and India are more likely to opt for home-based work, even when it is skilled (ITU World Telecommunication Development Report, 2002). Call centers are among the most important sources of employment in the last decades,

especially for women. In the United Kingdom, 67 percent of call center employees are women. In 2007, India exceeded a million women employees in call centers (United Nations the World's Women, 2000). The physical separation of these jobs is also due to the higher bargaining powers of women doing tele-work.

Women are generally paid 30 to 40 percent less than men for comparable work. The 2001 ILO report reveals that women under-represented in ICTs employment in both developed and developing countries. The ILO report also that in addition to the pay inequalities that exist between those who have ICT skills and those who do not, men are better paid in these jobs.

POTENTIAL USES OF ICTS FOR WOMEN EMPOWERMENT

In this section, the focus is placed on the likely roles of ICTs to promote the inclusion and empowerment of women.

Networking and Advocacy to Promote Gender Equality

ICTs gave people opportunities to interconnect, network, and cooperate on a more global scale than was previously possible. For individuals, Internet has been a good universe for self-expression and for building connections. ICTs also facilitated building a more inclusive society that enables all clusters to communicate, to network, and to influence policy makers. For women, the Internet has provided subversive territory in which to stress their identity and to defend their human rights. Networking and connectivity provides also an opportunity for women's organizations to mobilize the international public opinion against discriminatory acts against women in several parts of the world. A good evidence of the last assumption is the Asian Human Rights Commission. This organization contacted progressive several international women's rights groups about the phenomenon of 'honor' killings in Asia and posted several reports about the occurrence on their websites.

Information sharing and dialogues through email, online newsletters, and List Serves between women from the North and South and among women in the South have also enabled collaboration on a global scale to promote the agenda of gender equality (Moorti & Ros, 2003). Of particular interest to the cause of gender equality are the advocacy efforts of groups of men. The White Ribbon Campaign in Canada, initiated by a group of men, among other strategies, uses the Internet, CD ROM, and printed materials to mobilize men to denounce violence against women (www.whiteribbon.ca).

Building Women's Capacity

Several organizations consider building women's capacities to access and use ICTs accessible as a priority. Such associations provide general training in ICTs for ICT-related jobs to women at a first level. Then, women in the job market are being supported for skill enhancement, career growth, and greater work efficiency. Pursuing women with limited access to ICTs is a central to ensure that they are equal beneficiaries of technology. In 2003, the United Nations Development Program (UNDP), in accordance with the Women's Affairs Ministry in Afghanistan, launched the first series of computer training centers for Afghani women. The courses offered by the centers taught basic accounting and word-processing skills to government and NGO employees (Abirafeh, 2003). Another good example of programs that builds women capacity is The WIRES project (www. ceewauwires.org). The program targeted women entrepreneurs in small-scale businesses in several regions in Uganda. The women were provided entrepreneurial information repackaged in simple, ready-to-use formats, in local languages. Through this project, women have been able to access ICTs and get information related to markets, prices, credit services, and trade-support services (www. digitaldivident.org).

Building women's capacity in decision-making structures through ICTs can bring extraordinary gains for women. The "Women Mayors' Link is a project developed in the 12 countries in South-Eastern Europe (Gurumurthy, 2004). The network has been developed to reinforce women mayors' leadership skills, and for a regional and international exchange of best practices in similar projects. Communication was mainly accomplished via emails and websites in order to strengthen the cooperation between women mayors and local women's networks to improve the quality of life of women and children in local communities. These initiatives have been a success, so they need to be replicated elsewhere, mainly in developing countries.

Using ICTs to build women's capacity can also help NGOs working with women to become more effective. The Women's Electronic Network Training Workshop program seeking to provide women's NGOs in the Asia-Pacific region to use new ICTs in their work. The WENWT strategy contributes to both a higher effectiveness of NGOs at local levels and also a diversification and democratization of online spaces.

Diffusion of Rights-Based Information for Women

New ICTs have been used by gender-equality organizations all over the world to publish and propagate rights-based information. The communication of these ideas is mainly done through websites, e-magazines, and email. In some developed countries, websites provide support to women seeking help on domestic violence. For example, www.ndvh.org provides online assistance related domestic violence for different states in the USA. Another example is the Femmigration website (www.femmigration.net) which provides support, and complaints service to help women migrants to the EU who may be tricked into prostitution and other sexual abuse (Youngs, 2002).

Several NGOs worldwide use ICTs to disseminate information and to contribute to the debate on gender equality and rights. Yet, access to and participation in the platforms available on Internet for shaping the rights discourse is related to many factors. First, because of infrastructure, culture, and language issues, the majority of women in the world do not have access to new ICTs, which limits this gender from participating in these platforms. Second, though media are used extensively by feminist groups in developing countries, they are used mainly for information dissemination and not to defend women rights and to discuss gender-equality issue. Tele-centers can also be used to disseminate information supporting the social and political empowerment of feminist groups. Issues such as violence, religious law, on workers' rights (for example, minimum wages), and citizenship rights can be discussed Finally, Educational institutions, Governments, and NGOs must take a lead in this process, especially in rural areas.

ICTs as Amplifiers of Women's Voices and Perspectives

ICTs constitute a low-cost tool to communicate and publish women issues, experiences, and perspectives. The Deccan Development Society in South India is a good example of the ICTs for women promotion. Throughout this project, socially disadvantaged women have used radio and video to document and disseminate traditional farming practices, to influence policy makers, and to publicize their community-based development work. Such development activities reflect the recording of women of their own history and the recognition of their knowledge (Pavrala, 2000).

ICTs can be also a domicile for free discussions and debates about ways to promote women. A good example is Wikigender, on online discus-

sion launched by Wikipedia From 3-10 February 2012. Wikigender hosted its first online discussion. Wikigender gathered views on how can access to ICTs promote opportunities for women and girls. In particular, the main idea discussed in this online discussion is the ways in which social networks can promote gender equality. Registration and participation in the discussion was made via Disqus, Twitter, or Facebook, so all social networks were included in this discussion. Another advantage of this online discussion is the free access, so participants needed just to have an account in one of the social networks previously cited to take part of the discussion.

Further Benefits and Sometimes Constraints

There is a very interesting paper by Jacobsen (2011). It has the benefit of relating ICTs and gender equity, to the broader economic, social, and technological contexts. The author considers the potential role of various transformative general-purpose technologies in affecting gender equity. The particular technologies considered at length and contrasted are four network technologies: electricity and water provision on the one hand, and the newer information and communications technologies of the Internet and mobile phones on the other.

Available evidence on the effects of transformative technologies, both historically and in recent developing country contexts, is surveyed. The results indicate difficulties in finding cleanly measurable factors due to the complex nature of the effects of the technologies, as well as the containment of many effects in the household/nonmarket sector rather than the market sector. However, there is some optimism regarding continued expansion of electrification and the use of mobile phones in particular for improving women's empowerment.

In the case of water, it was not clear that the freed up time was available for remunerated uses, but it is possible that additional productivity in the household sector occurred. Electricity provision appeared more promising for increasing remunerated activity on the part of women, perhaps because it is both substitutable for physical labor and complementary to a wider range of production activities. Internet services did not appear substitutable for physical labor but was significant for reducing transactions costs on information flows, albeit the Internet is only lightly utilized to date by female entrepreneurs in low-income countries. Mobile phones, however, appear to be useful in all four ways, reducing the physical labor of travel to discover information (including fruitless trips to get supplies or meet customers which could then be avoided), reducing the costs of money and transfer, and increasing the ability of women entrepreneurs to coordinate their family and work lives. Given their relatively low cost relative to the other infrastructures and their multiple uses, it is not surprising that they have proved so popular and reached such high infiltration levels in many societies. Significantly more research needs to be carried out in evaluating both the overall effects and the gender-differentiated effects of these transformational technologies. The lack of both carefully crafted case study evaluations and larger statistical studies for the contemporary cases (as opposed to the historical studies) is notable. However, the multiple possible effects of truly general-purpose transformational technologies make it hard to isolate their effects from the other related effects that occur simultaneously or in short order. Thus how much of economic growth and changes in gender equity can be credited to any one, or any set, of technologies may be ultimately unanswerable given the holistic nature of transformation. This is small comfort for development researchers looking for payback on particular innovations, but the danger is overlooking the larger transformational effects by over-focusing on the smaller, more easily measurable changes. In addition, a capabilities framework for considering economic development would argue that the very ubiquity of

these technologies is reason enough to advocate for their extension to all members of any society where they are widespread so as to allow for full participation of both genders in the fundamental interactions of the society.

Beena and Madhu (2012), consider that education is the engine of change. Information and communications are closely linked to the mechanism that affects change. To the authors, socially, most Indian women are still tradition bound and are in disadvantageous position. ICTs are emerging as a powerful tool for women empowerment in a developing country like India.

The sample size of the research was 200 by no. of trainees and 30 by no of instructors of different Governmental and Nongovernmental Organizations of Jaipur district. Researcher used random sampling technique to select the sample for the study. The data was collected with the help of self-constructed questionnaire. The analysis of mean and graphical representation used for the analysis of data indicated that the Age group, Marital status, Educational level had significant effect on different variable of women empowerment like self-confidence, self-awareness, independence, and feeling of freedom. The study can be used to create awareness among women for the improvement of their live. This research concluded that the information and communication technology empower a women in various areas like social, educational, personal, psychological, political, technological and economical.

Miller, Duque, and Shrum (2012) present the analysis of gender differences in productivity using panel data on scientists in low-income countries (540 researchers from Ghana, Kenya, and Kerala [India]). The same survey is conducted in 2001 and 2005. Gender inequality in science as it has taken on new significance is the main purpose of this research. The mobile telephone, e-mail, and the World Wide Web, technologies that facilitate global processes, are argued to possess the potential to change the way knowledge is produced by removing constraints of time and place from professional activities. These ICT instruments are central to this study. Results indicate very few gender disparities in outcomes at either period of the study with the exception of productivity in international journals. The authors show that substantial gains in access to technology and higher education by women have not reduced the gender gap on this important career dimension.

Gurumurthy (2006) claims that ICTs are providing new economic and social opportunities. Their use, however, continues to be governed by existing power relations whereby women frequently experience relative disadvantage. Amid this inequality are individuals and organizations that are working to use ICTs to further gender equality. These are the issues addressed by the BRIDGE Cutting Edge Pack on Gender and ICTs. The first section of the paper consists of extracts from the Overview Report in the Pack. It describes ways in which women have been able to use ICTs to support new forms of information exchange, organization, and empowerment. The second section, taken from the textbox 'Telecentres: Some Myths,' describes three assertions which frequently lead to problems in all forms of investment in development-related information exchanges with poor or less powerful groups, not only those relating to tele-centres and women.

Chew, Levy, and Ilavarasan (2011) present as a response to the increasing need for rigorous impact assessment in ICT4D. This research examines whether ICTs enable microenterprise growth, to what degree, and under what conditions. Two models chosen to predict relationships between antecedents of ICT access, ICT use, and business growth are selected. Using data collected through a multistage probability survey of women micro-entrepreneurs in Mumbai, India, the models are tested. Both models predict a statistically significant, but limited causal relationship between access to ICTs (as the independent variable) and business growth (as the dependent variable). The theoretical model and the analytical techniques suggest that future research should pay greater attention to the specific factors that mediate the impact of ICTs on the growth of very small businesses.

Olga and Mendez (2011) present a case of the gender digital divide in the use of mobile phones in a small community of Latino immigrant farm workers in Southeast Ohio in the US. Contrary to the findings of previous studies that rural women around the world are using Information and Communication Technologies (ICTs) for empowerment, this research reveals that immigration status interacts with gender and class identities such that Latina immigrant women who work in horticulture nurseries face limits of access, use, and distribution of knowledge for their own purposes and needs. The findings suggest that mobile phones are not inherently empowering to women, and under specific circumstances such as undocumented migration, they can serve as a device that strengthens hierarchical power relations between women and men.

Reyes and Asinas (2011) assess the outcome of the tenth Young Women Leaders Conference held on 27 September 2010 at Miriam College, Philippines. The Workshops revealed that young women continue to face traditional structural barriers that inhibit them from actively participating in political debate and public life. However, they have created new spaces for asserting varied (re) conceptions of citizenship and gender justice, often mediated by rapidly changing information and communication technologies. Likewise, they are increasingly on the move: the face of labor migration in the Philippines is that of a young woman. How then might migration change our understandings of citizenship? Many young women in the Philippines are engaged in 'everyday revolutions' in spaces where imaginations, alternative visions, and voices are emerging and merging.

Debbie Goh (2012) discusses the use of Third World feminist epistemology as theory and method in gender digital divide research to establish the consciousness of Appalachian women left behind in the information society and to enable them define how information and communication technologies can be used effectively and meaningfully to improve their situations. This chapter draws from findings of an ethnographic study that examines how women in West Virginia negotiate the complexity of their identities as mothers, wives, and workers, alongside the structural factors that create the conditions for them to engage in computer learning and use. It also discusses how non-economic concerns become central in discussions about their experiences and lives and identifies opportunities that will help them transcend their marginalized positions. Despite efforts to introduce Information and Communication Technologies (ICTs) to women, Internet access rates for women do not always rise in relation with national Internet penetration rates.

Pillai and Shanta (2011) deal with the integration of gender in policies relating to information and communication technology to empower socially excluded poor women as producers of this technology. It examines an interventionist ICT policy undertaken by Kudumbasree (an innovative women-based participatory program) to empower poor women. The central part of the investigation is a survey of Kudumbasree supported micro enterprises scattered across the states to understand the nature and characteristics of the enterprises, activity pattern, and performance. The attained results show that given the levels of basic literacy in the state, engendering ICT for poor women, is feasible, but with the provision of the right organizational support.

Women and Access to Internet Based on Information from the International Telecommunication Union (ITU)

The ITU has been working together with national country statistical offices from developing countries around the world to improve the availability and quality of statistics on ICT access and use by households and individuals. Gender-disaggregated data collected through official surveys are nationally representative, reliable, and can be compared among countries and over time. They provide an important input for policymaking, especially since the inclusion of socioeconomic and demographic variables—including age, income levels, educational attainment, etc.—provide in-depth information on the use of ICTs by men and women. By 2010, 72 countries out of ITU's total membership (192) had been collecting ICT use data through official surveys. Thirty-four developing economies had collected ICT use data between 2008 and 2010 and most of these countries collect data on Internet users disaggregated by gender. The charts in Figure 1 show the percentage of Internet users, by gender, for European countries and non-European countries, for the latest available year (2008-2010) (see Figure 1).

CASES FROM DEVELOPING COUNTRIES

The real cases are finally the best way to show how women have been benefiting from ICTs. The use of this method here in this chapter compensates for the fact that the other chapters did not have real cases. Some of these cases are discussed directly in this part.

Nabanna: A Successful Story of Empowerment

The "Networking Rural Women and Knowledge," a UNESCO project in Nabanna, India, makes use of databases, intranet portals and Web based partnerships to promote poor women (Jain, 2004). The use of these ICT tools was made in local language, and stress was made on building a framework for information sharing, content creation, and Web-based partnership with organizations in other regions. The purpose of the project is to build

Figure 1. Percentage of internet users, by gender, non-European economies, 2008-2010 (source: ITU statistics, http://www.itu.int/ict/statistics)

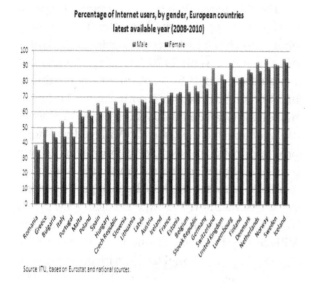

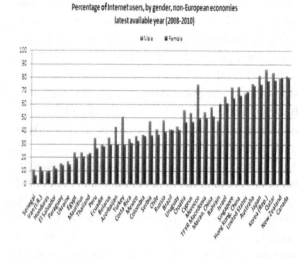

information networks for local women via providing facilities and training at five ICT centers in Baduria, Rudrapur, Taragunia, Arbelia, and Punda.

The project enabled a group of sixty 20-40 years old to access to control information and communication technology through the use of ICTs. Through the Nabanna Network, women share local information as well as information about the other groups obtained via meetings or newsletter. For instance, women in Baduria exchanged information related to income generating activities, specific education projects, microfinance, and health. Accordingly, young educated women have gained access to and control of ICTs, while less educated and older women gained a higher access to information. Therefore, Women in Baduria have enhanced the performance of their activities through ICTs.

In its report for 2004, the UNESCO defined the following changes in women's agency thanks to the Nabanna project:

- A greater respect gained both at the family level and at community level.

- A higher confidence than before while approaching the job market, and therefore, the program helped them to find jobs and to increase their income.
- Use of more innovative computers programs, such as Paintbrush in WindowXP.
- An increase in the income of local income and an enhancement of solidarity among the community feminist groups.

Rural Women, Green Cooperatives, and the Adoption of E-Business in Asia

The huge development of ICTs worldwide and the higher use e-commerce in the recent years encouraged the women's green cooperatives in the Asian and Pacific region to benefit from these new technologies. E-business application enables increased opportunities for promoting their business, developing marketing channels, and creating networks with customers. E-business enables also such farmers to reduce the time period in which purchase, inventory and pricing decisions are made

(Meera, et al., 2004). Even in the poorest nations, using ICTs is can lead to significant enhancements in agricultural information and communication systems and business operations. For instance, mobile phones might be used by farmers to verify the market prices of their products and to fix the transportation and the mechanisms necessary for sale of their products. Radio programs can also be used for a rapid sharing and dissemination of information about weather that might affect agricultural products (UN, 2007).

The use of ICTs in agriculture has become, for many researchers, necessary for social and economic empowerment of farmers, particularly women. While, others argue that in developing countries where gender-specific constraints are prominent, the limited access of women to ICTs might deepen even more gender inequities. They suggest that simple tools such as the telephone, fax, and e-mail can be easily used and incorporated in the activities of rural women's green cooperatives as a first step for the implementation of ICTs strategies. By applying these tools to their business activities, rural women can better benefit from new technologies and participate in today's information society. Relatively, Free and low cost e-mail services are easily accessible since women need only to have access to the Internet. Finally, via computer networks, business processes in women's green cooperatives, such as ordering, transactions, fulfillment of orders and delivery of goods might be achieved more effectively and in a shorter time.

The Grameen Phone Project

The accessibility to mobile phone networks in many low-and middle-income countries create plenty of opportunities for young people. One option to take advantages of this technology is to purchase a mobile phone via a micro credit program and to earn income by providing low cost phone calls to others. One good example is the story illustrated below about a 16-year-old schoolgirl in rural India that was published in Business week Online in 1999.

The Grameen Village Pay Phone Program (VPP) illustrate more the The potential of mobile phones to create low-income earning opportunities for youth. With 1170 Grameen branches in Bangladesh and 105 micro credit organizations in 34 countries operating on the same Grameen model, the Grameen Bank is considered a pioneer of small loans to the poor The Village Pay Phone program makes it possible for borrowers to buy a mobile phone, and then to make the telephone available for others in the village to pay for phone calls, to send Short Message Services (SMS) and to receive incoming calls. In 2000, the Grameen Village Pay Phones was operating in more than 2,000 villages in Bangladesh, with an average of 100 additional villages connected each month. The Grameen phones are used for multiple purposes. So, farmers use them to find out where they can get the best prices for their crops, assistance workers use them to better coordinate disaster response measures, and finally villagers are use the phones to communicate with local government officials.

The Grameen Telecom is a good example of the use ICTs for youth promotion. The potential of Grameen Telecom as an income generator has been appreciated by many organizations and investment companies, which attracted higher investments to the project. The World Bank's International Finance Corporation has invested US$50 million in the project. The Norwegian company Telenor has also invested US$25 million, and the Soros Economic Development Fund invested US$10.6 million.

Web for Small Home-Based Businesses in India, Latin America, and Africa

ICTs can also as a tool for the promotion and women small businesses in developing countries. A successful example of ICTs application in small enterprises is the use of smart cards by Indian women milk collectors in Rajasthan. The smart cards are used to note the quality, fat proportion, and sales of milk to distributors. The cards are also used as a tool to increase profits through the elimination of middlemen, which generally associated with extra costs.

Another success in this context is the Tortasperu, a nationwide network of housewives that sell Peruvian baked goods to expatriates over the Internet in Latin America (Mitter, 2003). This network is an example of a profitable opportunity for women work at home while taking care of their children.

The same model has been simulated in Africa through several initiatives. The Ethiopia's virtual gift shop is a successful example of the model. In this virtual shop, traditional Ethiopian costumes, food items, and spices produced by women are sold over the Internet. Another replication of the model is found in the Middle East, where handicrafts made by women artisans of Morocco, Tunisia, Lebanon, Egypt, and Jordan are sold in a virtual shop called "elsouk" (Mitter, 2003). The main advantage of these businesses is low capital and skill requirements. Another advantage of the Web for small home-based businesses is that networking businesses provide equitable opportunities for men and women. Finally, through these businesses, women have the potential to earn income from home while raising a family, which makes Internet an attractive working tool for women. Yet, as discussed earlier, there are still many barriers for women use of ICTs for entrepreneurship in developing countries.

Call Centers

Starting the 1970s, multinational corporations started to move factories and production centers to developing countries, where unskilled or low-skilled workers are more available. The preferred labor force, especially in service industries, are often female, and a large body of literature has examined this phenomenon (Jauhari, 2004; Toyama,

et al., 2005). Routine tasks like data entry, transcription, tele-phone sales, and consumer service can now easily be done, and are more convenient for women. For employers, recruiting women for such positions is cheaper and cost saving.

Call centers provide a wide range of telephone and occasionally Internet services. Some are owned entirely by international companies such as IBM or American Express; others are independent and contract with multiple foreign companies. Many call centers are quite large, with up to 2500 seat telephone and even more (Mattingly, 2005). Therefore, they provide thousands of job opportunities for women especially in developing where labor cost is lower.

A successful example of call centers recruiting women in developing countries is the international leader in the call center field, Webhelp. This French group is installed in Morocco, French, and Romania, and employs more than 7500 employees in these countries. In Morocco, Webhelp 10 sites installed in Rabat and Fez and employs more than 1000 employees, of which the majority. This call centers, in addition to other call centers, created thousands of job opportunities for women with a certain level of education, or at least those communicating in French.

CONCLUSION

Ensuring equitable access to ICTs and autonomy to receive and produce information relevant are critical issues for women. Therefore, this gender, which constitutes the majority in most societies, needs to be involved in decision making related to ICTs in order to fully participate in its growth and impact. Access and costs are of the main barriers for ICT use, so it is of the utmost importance to engage women and gender advocates in policies and regulations related to ICTs. Such policies should take into consideration the integration of women, particularly rural and poor women. So, gender must be considered from the start of project design. Only when these considerations are taken into account, the ICT policies and projects will properly address the gender digital divide and further contribute to women's economic empowerment.

The potential of ICT for women in developing countries is highly dependent upon their levels of technical skill and education. Integration of women in the information society in countries with higher illiteracy rates is quite difficult. Hence, governments and NGOs need to take into consideration the promotion of education in such countries for a better access of women to new technologies.

It is important to recognize that ICTs by itself cannot answer all the obstacles facing women's development, yet they can bring new information resources and can open new communication channels for marginalized communities. Last but not the least, when policies and programs that address the improvement of women access to and control over ICTs, they should take into consideration the demographic characteristics of each society in order to ensure that the objectives set by the programs are achieved. As UN studies have indicated, though the costs of using ICTs for development may be high, not using them at all may prove to be costlier.

REFERENCES

Abirafeh, L. (2003). *Afghan women: One year later – Creating digital opportunities for Afghan women.* Retrieved from http://www.developmentgateway. org/node/134111/sdm/docview?docid=427938

Allison & Gomez. (2012). Gender and public access ICT. In Gomez (Ed.), *Libraries, Telecentres, Cybercafes, and Public Access to ICT: International Comparisons.* Hershey, PA: IGI Global.

Beena, M., & Mathur, M. (2012). Role of ICT education for women empowerment. *International Journal of Economics and Research*, *3*(3), 164–172.

Ben, R. (2012). Gendering professionalism in the internationalization of information work. In *Globalization, Technology and Gender Disparity: Social Impacts of ICTs* (pp. 51–69). Hershey, PA: IGI Global. doi:10.4018/978-1-4666-0020-1. ch005

Debbie, G. (2012). *Who we are and what we want.* Retrieved from http://www.tandfonline. com/loi/rics20

Faulkner, W., & Lie, M. (2007). Gender technology and development. *Technology and Development*, *11*(2), 157–177.

Gillard, H., Howcroft, D., Mitev, N., & Richardson, H. (2008). Missing women: Gender, ICTs and the shaping of the global economy. *Information Technology for Development*, *14*(4), 262–279. doi:10.1002/itdj.20098

Green, E., & Adam, A. (1998). Online leisure: Gender, and ICTs in the home. *Information Communication and Society*, *1*(3), 291–312. doi:10.1080/13691189809358971

Gurumurthy, A. (2004). *Gender and ICT's. Overview Report.* Sussex, UK: Institute of Development Studies.

Gurumurthy, A. (2006). Promoting gender equality? Some development-related uses of ICTs by women. *Development in Practice*, *16*(6), 611–615. doi:10.1080/09614520600958298

Gurumurthy, A. (2010). Understanding gender in a digitally transformed world. *IIT for Change Think Piece.* Retrieved from http://www.itforchange.net/

Hafkin, N. (2012). Gender. In Sadowsky, G. (Ed.), *Accelerating Development Using the Web: Empowering Poor and Marginalized Populations.* New York, NY: World Wide Web Foundation.

ILO. (2001). *The ILO's world employment report 2001.* Retrieved from http://isearch.babylon. com/?q=The+2001+ILO+report&babsrc= SP_def&affID=101587

ITU. (2002). *ITU world telecommunication development report*. Retrieved from http://www.itu.int/pub/D-IND-WTDR-2002/en

ITU. (2003). *ITU world telecommunication development report*. Retrieved from http://www.itu.int/pub/D-IND-WTDR-2003/en

ITU. (2004). *ITU world telecommunication development report*. Retrieved from http://www.itu.int/pub/D-IND-WTDR-2004/en

ITU. (2005). *ITU world telecommunication development report*. Retrieved from http://www.itu.int/pub/D-IND-WTDR-2005/en

ITU. (2006). *ITU world telecommunication development report*. Retrieved from http://www.itu.int/pub/D-IND-WTDR-2006/en

ITU. (2007). *ITU world telecommunication development report*. Retrieved from http://www.itu.int/pub/D-IND-WTDR-2007/en

ITU. (2008). *ITU world telecommunication development report*. Retrieved from http://www.itu.int/pub/D-IND-WTDR-2008/en

ITU. (2009). *ITU world telecommunication development report*. Retrieved from http://www.itu.int/pub/D-IND-WTDR-2009/en

ITU. (2010). *ITU world telecommunication development report*. Retrieved from http://www.itu.int/pub/D-IND-WTDR-2010/en

ITU. (2011). *ITU world telecommunication development report*. Retrieved from http://www.itu.int/pub/D-IND-WTDR-2011/en

Jacobsen, J. P. (2011). The role of technological change in increasing gender equity. *ACSPL Working Paper Series, 1.*

Jain, S. (2004). *ICTS and women's empowerment: some case studies from India.* Retrieved from http://www.ifuw.org/seminars/2007/jain.pdf

Jauhari, V. (2004). *Information technology, corporate business firms and sustainable development: Lessons from cases of success from India.* Paper presented at the International Seminar on e-Commerce and Economic Development. New-Delhi, India.

Johnson, V. (2012). The gender divide: Attitudinal issues inhibiting access. In *Globalization, Technology Development, and Gender Disparity: Social Impacts of ICTs.* Hershey, PA: IGI Global. doi:10.4018/978-1-4666-0020-1.ch009

Kramarae, C. (2004). Do we really want more control of technology? In Foss, K., Foss, S., & Griffin, C. L. (Eds.), *Readings in Feminist Rhetorical Theory.* Thousand Oaks, CA: Sage.

Malhotra, A., Kanesathasan, A., & Patel, P. (2012). Connectivity how mobile phones, computers and the internet can catalyze women's entrepreneurship India: A case study. *ICRW Publications.* Retrieved from http://www.icrw.org/publications/connectivity-how-mobile-phones-computers-and-internet-can-catalyze-womens-entrepreneurs

Mattingly, D. (2005). Indian women working in call centers: Sites of resistance. In *Globalization, Technology Development, and Gender Disparity: Social Impacts of ICTs.* Hershey, PA: IGI Global.

Meera, S. N., Jhamtani, A., & Rao, D. U. M. (2004). Information and communication technology in agricultural development: A comparative analysis of three projects from India. *ODI.* Retrieved from http://www.odi.org.uk/agren/papers/agrenpaper_135.pdf

Miller, B. P., Duque, R., & Shrum, W. (2012). Gender, ICTs, and productivity in low-income countries panel study. *Science, Technology & Human Values, 37*(1), 30–63. doi:10.1177/0162243910392800

Mitter, S. (2004). *Globalization and ICT: Employment opportunities for women.* New York, NY: United Nations Commission on Science and Technology for Development.

Moorti & Ros. (2003). Editors' introduction: Gender and the information society. *Feminist Media Studies*, *3*(3), 345–388. doi:10.1080/1468077032000166568

Olga, P., & Mendez, G. (2011). Gender digital divide: The role of mobile phones among Latina farm workers in southeast Ohio. *Gender, Technology and Development*, *15*(1), 53–74. doi:10.1177/097185241101500103

Osmani, S., & Sen, A. (2003). The hidden penalties of gender inequality: Fetal origins of ill-health. *Economics and Human Biology*, *1*, 105–121. doi:10.1016/S1570-677X(02)00006-0

Pavrala, V. (2000). Voices from the margins, voices for change. *A Journal on Communication for Development, 4*(2). Retrieved from http://bsfs.georgetown.edu/files/Thesis_Joelle_Thomas.pdf

Pillai, P. M., & Shanta, N. (2011). ICT and employment promotion among poor women: How can we make it happen? Some reflections on Kerala's experience. *Indian Journal of Gender Studies*, *18*(1), 51–76. doi:10.1177/097152151001800103

Primo, N. (2003). Gender issues in the information society. In *UNESCO Publications for the World Summit on the Information Society*. New York, NY: UNESCO.

Rakow, L. (1986). Rethinking gender research in communication. *The Journal of Communication*, *36*, 11–36. doi:10.1111/j.1460-2466.1986.tb01447.x

Ramilo, G. (2002). *Issues, policies and outcomes: Are ICT policies addressing gender equality?* Retrieved from http://www.unescap.org/wid/04widresources/11widactivities/01ictegm/backgroundpaper.pdf

Ransom, E. I., & Elder, L. K. (2003). *Nutrition of women and adolescent girls: Why it matters*. Washington, DC: Population Reference Bureau.

Reyes, M., & Asinas, A. (2011). Locating young women in a plethora of issues: Reflections from the tenth young women leader's conference 2010. *Gender and Development*, *9*(3), 423–439. doi:10.1080/13552074.2011.625674

Shade, L. R. (2002). *Gender and community in the social construction of the internet*. New York, NY: Peter Lang.

Toyama, K., Karishma, K., Pal, D. M., Joyojeet, S. S., & Srinivasan, J. (2005). *PC kiosks trends in rural India*. Retrieved, May 2006, from http://www.globaldevelopment.org/papers/

UNCTAD. (2010). *Information and communication report, 2010*. New York, NY: UNCTAD.

UNESCO. (2000). *World education forum*. Retrieved from http://www.unesco.org/education/efa/wef_2000/

UNESCO. (2004). *In movement, UNESCO salutes women video artists*. Retrieved from http://unesdoc.unesco.org/images/0014/001495/149531eo.pdf

United Nations. (2007). *Guidebook on developing women's entrepreneurship in green cooperatives in the Asian and Pacific region*. New York, NY: United Nations.

Walsham, G., & Sahay, S. (1999). GIS for district-level administration in India: Problems and opportunities. *Management Information Systems Quarterly*, *23*(1), 39–66. doi:10.2307/249409

Youngs, G. (2002). Closing the gaps: Women, communications and technology. *In Development*, *45*(4), 23–28. doi:10.1057/palgrave.development.1110400

Youngs, G. (2012). Globalization, information and communication technologies, and women's lives. In *Globalization, Technology Diffusion and Gender Disparity: Social Impacts of ICTs*. Hershey, PA: IGI Global. doi:10.4018/978-1-4666-0020-1.ch003

Chapter 8
ICTs and Coordination for Poverty Alleviation

ABSTRACT

In recent decades, calls for poverty alleviation have increased significantly in both developed and developing countries. Relatively, ICTs have been viewed as offering helpful tools for poverty reduction. This chapter investigates access to ICTs in the context of poverty, in both developed and developing countries. Based on a sample of 40 countries (20 developing and 20 developed countries), several statistical tests have been performed with promising results obtained. It is first shown that people in developing countries have less access to ICTs relative to those in developed countries. Second, it is also proven that the use of Internet is positively affected by the literacy rate within a country. The higher the literacy rate, the higher the number of Internet users in a country. The third result conveys that countries with higher GDP per capita ensure higher access to ICTs for their populations. Finally, this chapter proposes that populations of countries with higher poverty rates have less access to ICTs.

INTRODUCTION

This chapter is organized in four sections. The first one attempts to show how the poor faces major interdependencies in needs of goods and services. This prepares for the second section that discusses how ICTs could be linked with poverty in order to help satisfy the existing needs and their interactions. The third section introduces a methodological set up for testing series of hypotheses related to the effects of ICTs on series of poverty dimensions. The results of these tests are introduced and discussed in the last section.

HIGH INTERDEPENDENCIES OF THE NEEDS OF THE POOR

Individuals and groups face major interdependencies for the satisfaction of their needs for goods and services. However, the poorest segments face more constraints and risks for attainment of their basic requirements. Table 1 shows the large set of needs and their likely independencies in the context of poverty. The variety of needs is to be satisfied under series of monetary and non-monetary pressure and constraints. Incomes are low, prices that are higher than for other groups besides other risks

DOI: 10.4018/978-1-4666-3643-9.ch008

related to growth and development of needs. This first part attempts to underline the main features of poverty through looking at the multiplicity of needs, their interdependencies, but also the pressures of constraints and risks. The framework introduced in Table 1 to show the areas of needs and the risks faced by the poor, is also used later in chapter 10 to show the levels of coordination needed among series of players. For each sector of material and immaterial needs, the requirements related to access (entry), necessary transactions (transaction and maintenance), besides constraints and opportunities (opportunities) in addition to the risks (risks) are introduced in Table 1.

Several studies have dealt with the issue of poor households paying higher costs for services and basic facilities. Each study tries to look at the possible reasons behind the higher costs incurred by poor people while selecting goods and services. The studies retained in this chapter are those dealing with the high costs incurred by the poor to access health care, care for children, education, water, energy, transportation, housing, judicial and credit systems. Some studies pointed out clearly that access to food, clothing, and other items is more expensive for the poor than it is for the households with higher income.

A study performed in the United States revealed that rural poor households pay food prices that are 2.5 percent higher than other rural households and 3.1 percent higher than suburban households. According to the same study, these rural poor households face higher prices because they have a limited access to supermarkets located in the suburbs of urban areas and because they cannot afford to buy large quantities for which discounts are often offered. Poor households, faced with limited income, are obliged to buy small quantities from grocery stores; which turns out to be more expensive than buying large quantities from supermarkets (Kaufman, 1999).

Similarly, another study about the analysis of grocery store availability and food prices disparities was conducted within the Minneapolis and St. Paul metropolitan areas. The results of the study revealed that the poor pay slightly more for food in the grocery market and in non-chain stores and that the poor have less access to chain stores. According to the study, the factor contributing to the higher grocery costs in poor neighborhoods is that large chain stores, where prices tend to be lower, are not located in these neighborhoods (Chung & Myers, 1999).

When poor households face higher prices for services and even for some goods like food, a risk of long-term impoverishment takes place. In the framework of equity and health sector reforms conducted by the World Bank, user fees for public services have been introduced in many developing countries since the publication of the "World Bank Policy 1987." The introduction of user fees has covered the health sector in some developing countries and this new health policy has led to the "medical poverty trap." This medical poverty trap occurs because increases in out-of-pocket expenses for medical care drive some families below the poverty line and aggravate the poverty level of those that are already poor. The user fees recommended, widens the gap between the rich and the poor. This is justified by the facts that even if they pay the same fees, the poor incur some hidden costs like the costs coming from marginalized education or buying non equilibrated food (Whitehead, Dahlgren, & Evans, 2001).

Another study tackled the out-of-pocket health care spending by lower income Medicaid beneficiaries. It was estimated in the study that the beneficiaries with incomes below the poverty level and who did not receive Medicaid spent 50% of their income out-of-pocket for health care. The beneficiaries with incomes between 100% and 125% of the poverty level spent only 30% of their income out-of-pocket for healthcare. It clearly appears that out-of-pocket healthcare spending for lower income Medicare beneficiaries is a burden for the poor (Gross, Gibson, Corea, Caplan, & Brangan, 1999).

Access to education is another need for which the lower-income households bear high costs. School attendance creates an opportunity cost

Table 1. Variety of needs and poverty

	Entry	Transaction and maintenance	Opportunity	Risks
Food	- Constrained by liquidity; - Buy at a very retail; - Limited access to wholesale markets; - Constrained by storage, risks, and markets.	- Travel distance; - Location of grocery and chain stores; - Availability of wanted items; - Storage costs	- Limited income spent on other expenditures - Time spent in the operation of purchasing	- Nutritional risks related to the non equilibrium of dietary food; - Risks associated with health
Clothing	- Constraint of income; - Location of chain and grocery stores	- Travel distance; - Availability of alternatives; - Storage and cleaning costs	- Limited income for other expenditures;	- Health infection problems
Education	- Constrained by income; - Satisfaction of other needs; - Time allocated to schooling	- Travel distance; - Availability of education; - Location of education centers; - Maintaining the flow of education	Foregone Payoffs from other activities	- Shortages of inputs; - Employment possibilities; - Long term impoverishment
Health	- Constrained by income; - Competition of needs; - Degree of illness and the type of health problems; - User fees for public services	- Travel distance; - Availability of healthcare; - Availability of alternatives; - Maintaining the flow of health care	Time spent to look for health care	- Health problems aggravation; - Long term impoverishment - Aggravation of the current poverty level.
Energy	- Affordability to be connected to the electricity system; - Constrained by income; - Obligation to buy other energy means from local shops and in small quantities.	- Travel Distance; - Existence of other energy means and the possibility to obtain them - Availability of substitutes; - Repair and maintenance of energy equipment	- Outcomes from other activities; - Time spent on obtaining other energy means; - Impact on work or study at night	- Fire and wood collection risks; - Health infection risks; - Long term impoverishment.
Water	- Affordability to be connected to the piped water system; - Constraint of income;	- Travel distance; - Availability of water supply; - Availability of other free means of water supply - Repair and maintenance of water equipment	- Time spent for water collection; - Physical efforts to collect water from unpiped sources	- Health effects of water collection; - Possibility to attract diseases; - Long term impoverishment
Housing	- Inability to pay high rents; - Constraint of income	- Availability of housing opportunities; - Travel distance between work and home; - Cleaning, painting, and repairing	- Time spent to look for shelter; - Lost income because of low productivity impacted by living conditions.	- Incidence of ill health and infection because of poor living conditions
Transportation	- Constraint of income; - Inability to buy a personal vehicle; - Access of public transportation	- Travel distance; - Availability of transportation means; - Maintaining the flow of transportation	Lost income from other activities that can be performed during the lost time	- Health infection problems; - Transportation is not always insured (absenteeism).

continued on following page

of foregone income that poor households might need. Compared to high-income people, the poor allocates less time to schooling and are less able to increase their human capital (Sylwester, 2002). From these two findings, it is clear that poor households incur high costs in the education of their children because they forgo the payoffs derived from sending their kids to work.

Table 1. Continued

	Entry	Transaction and maintenance	Opportunity	Risks
Judicial system	- Limited information, - Location of the court systems in cities, - Illiteracy, - Fuzzy property rights	-Travel time, -Complexity of mechanisms, - Costs related to lodging and food when away; - Follow up of the judicial conflict	Lost income from other activities that can be performed during the lost time	Risks of losing the case and other risks related to new conflicts
Credit System	- Amount to be borrowed; - Guaranty required; - Availability of financial institutions; - Availability of individual lenders; - Very high interest rates.	- Costs related to loan files; - Transportation costs; - Follow up of the credit mechanism	Lost income from other activities that can be performed during the lost time	Insolvability of the grantee and incapability to pay back the loan and interests

Low-income families not only incur higher costs for food, health care, and education, but they also face high charges to ensure care for their children with disabilities and chronic illnesses. The results of a study investigating private costs related to children's disabilities in poor families indicate that low-income families with special-needs incur both out-of-pocket expenses and foregone earnings (Lukemeyer, Meyers, & Smeeding, 2002). Out of the sample chosen, 20% of families with special-needs incurred total monthly costs exceeding $ 100. It is clear that households with disabled members face additional expenditures.

Poor households living in rural areas also face high costs for water. These households are often not connected to piped water system. They use water from tanker trucks, streams, rivers and lakes. However, it generally costs much more for households to buy water from tanker trucks than to pay fees for the piped water (Grusky, 2001). These higher costs of water incurred by poor households can be justified by implicit costs of water collection. Water collection seems to be a heavy burden for households because they have to spend time, physical efforts and their health is affected looking for water (Thompson & Porras, 2002).

Studies have shown evidence that housing and health issues are interrelated. Being unable to pay high rents, low-income households find themselves obliged to look for less expensive housing which is always associated with poor quality conditions. Poor households turn out to live in poor physical conditions and environmentally hazardous buildings and neighborhoods. The poor living conditions can be seen as an exposure to bad weather conditions, heath issues, noise, poor air quality, and overcrowding and can negatively impact productivity and schooling. As a result of these poor housing conditions, additional costs are generated for poor households who are confronted with health deterioration (Ambrose, 2002).

In the absence of modern sources of energy, poor households use wood, gas, coal or paraffin for cooking, heating, and lighting. These resources can be very expensive and increase the risks of fire or health infection, implying high costs of energy to poor households. Using wood for cooking is very expensive because it takes a long time to collect wood (this time can be used to generate other income) and it is always very dangerous knowing that the collection is performed in forests and very far areas ("How does energy affects people's lives in rural communities?"). The use of paraffin is also expensive for poor households because they have to buy it from local shops and in small quantities. The cost of paraffin in local shops is always higher because of the margins added to the original price by several dealers before it reaches the households. Another example to illustrate the higher costs of energy faced by poor households is lighting. Poor households often use candles for lighting and candles are expensive, especially if they are bought one at a time and can cause fires. It is also difficult to work or study at night if there are no proper lights. All these add up to the costs of energy incurred by low-income households living in poor neighborhoods.

Transportation costs incurred by poor individuals and households are also high. These people, even if they live in rural areas, need to travel or transport goods from their countryside to the city. The first hidden cost is the time lost while moving from the place of living to the national road or the highway system. The additional cost does not end when reaching the national road or the highway but the risks of not finding means of transportation, the additional waiting time required, and the uncertainties associated with waiting add up to make these poor households and individuals bear high costs. The same thing applies for the transportation of goods and products from production zones to distribution and selling points (Kim, 1999). Within the same framework, welfare recipients and deprived segments of the society face higher costs when searching for employment. This is due to the travel time and distance between their living places and job locations (Sawicki & Moody, 2000).

The judicial and credit systems are two other services for which poor individuals and households incur higher costs compared to other households.

For the judicial systems, poor households face higher costs because of the lack of information needed to resolve conflicts and because of illiteracy given the complexity of the judicial mechanism. In addition, courts are located in major cities and poor households have to travel from their place of residence to these cities. This process causes additional travel and accommodation costs for the poor when they are far from their homes. The payoffs of other opportunities foregone and the risk of losing the case or creating new conflicts also add up to increase the costs to the poor.

Poor households and individuals also face higher costs when willing to contract loans. Because of higher expected risks, lenders may demand collateral and guaranties or charge high interest rates. The availability of financial institutions and individual lenders willing to conduct credit with poor households and individuals is another factor that leads to high costs of credit. Because the majority of lenders are located in major cities, the poor has to move to the bank. This creates some other expenses. Credit file expenses also add up to increase the costs associated with credit granting. In addition, the risk of insolvability of borrowers is seen as a risk that may aggravate their poverty level.

Poor households and individuals are exposed to high-income risk. This risk is originated from frequent climatic and economic policy shocks that increase the vulnerability of households to severe hardships. Examples of these shocks include but not limited to poor harvest due to drought and floods and unexpected additional expenses encountered because of variations in economic policies imposed by the country. However, as pointed out in many studies held in this framework, the nature and types of shocks vary in time and intensity depending on the efforts of developing countries to deal with such issues. It is this variation that determines the level of impact and the policies developed by poor individuals to overcome these shocks (Dercon, 2002).

Dercon (2002) also pointed out that there are two types of income risks faced by poor individuals and households. Given their aggregate nature, common risks impact all the individuals in a given community or region. Idiosyncratic or individual risks affect a particular member of the society.

The concept of vulnerability of the poor comes from the notion that deprived segments are more sensitive to shocks that threaten their livelihood and survival. An assessment of the vulnerability of the poor in Guatemala has found that natural disasters and agricultural related shocks and to a lesser extent economic shocks have more impact on poor households and individuals relative to the rich segments of society. The number of shocks to which the poor are exposed also increases their vulnerability. The poor are not exposed to only one shock during a given period of time. The study held in Guatemala has pointed out that more than half of the households chosen in the sample have reported that they have experienced more than one shock during the previous 12 months (Tesliuc & Lindert, 2002).

Another study differently tackled the concept of vulnerability of the poor to natural shocks. This study has defined vulnerability as the probability that poor individuals will fall below the poverty line and focused on variations in consumption patterns as the source of this vulnerability. Some households tend to be poor because of the high variance in their consumption or because they have some specific characteristics that constrain them to decrease their mean consumption and therefore oblige them to stay below the poverty line. Rainfall shocks in Ethiopia were found to impact consumption significantly because of the positive and high elasticities between rainfall shocks and consumption. Rainfall shocks do not affect consumption directly. But through the income effect, rainfall shocks cause variations in consumption patterns of poor people who therefore become exposed to the fall below poverty line (Dabalen & Poupart, 2002).

Even if economic, natural, and political shocks are the determinants of the vulnerability to poverty, there are some factors that impact the influence of these disasters. Geographical location is one of these factors. In 1997, poor households in agro-climatic regions suffered from consumption poverty less likely than households living in the arid and semi-arid areas. The age and the number of children are other factors determining the degree of vulnerability to poverty. Still in Kenya, communities with more children aged between 8 and 15 years were more vulnerable than communities comprising households with younger children (Christiaensen & Subbarao, 2004).

It is widely known from studies on poverty that, at the macro-economic level, disasters or crises tend to reduce the level of income and magnify the risk or the probability that the poor will become poorer. However, the study held about households in Argentina for the period 1995-2002 has concluded that income variability or risk loses its utility in the measurement of poverty when households are disaggregated into different groups. In other words, income risk is not uniform among all the households. This conclusion was reached after calculating the risk-adjusted income of different groups of households.

Lower levels of variability in income are observed in households with better-educated members. But households with informal workers and unemployed or inactive members tend to experience higher levels of income variability (Cruces, 2002).

Poverty was dissociated from "vulnerability to poverty" in a study held in Indonesia. Poverty is seen to be a stochastic phenomenon because people who are poor today may not be poor tomorrow and non-poor people of today risk to fall in poverty tomorrow. This stochastic behavior of poverty should be taken into account by policy makers to implement policy interventions that are "forward looking" to fight poverty. In other words, policy interventions should not concentrate only on the poor of today but also the likely people to be poor in the future. One of the main findings of the study is that poverty is distinguished from "vulnerability to poverty." Using data from Indonesia, 22% of the population in Indonesia is found to be poor while 45% of the population is observed to be "vulnerable to poverty." The other finding shed light on the difference in the distribution of poverty and vulnerability among different segments of society. This difference should be considered by policy makers to implement both poverty alleviation programs to reduce vulnerability and poverty prevention programs to fight poverty. Finally, the study tackled the sources of vulnerability for different segments of society. For instance, consumption volatility is the main source of vulnerability to poverty in urban and more educated segments while low mean income devoted to consumption makes less educated households living in rural areas vulnerable to poverty (Chaudhuri, Jalan, & Suryahadi, 2002).

Poverty and vulnerability to natural and economic shocks are interrelated. Empirical studies have concluded that poverty is the leading source of vulnerability to shocks experienced by poor households because poverty distracts them from the necessary means to resist to such shocks. But it is not only poverty that reinforces vulnerability, but sensitive exposure to shocks also paves the way to poverty. This link exposes poor households throughout the world into two disadvantages. The first disadvantage is related to the difficulty in generating income while the second disadvantage is concerned with the sensitivity to economic, political, and natural shocks (Morduch, 1999).

Ligon and Schechter (2002) tackled the concept of vulnerability with a different perspective. The measure of vulnerability is proven to be linked to many factors: current measures of poverty, exposure to aggregate risk, exposure to idiosyncratic risk, unexplained risk, and some standard error. The sources of uncertainty or risk magnifying vulnerability to poverty besides the current levels of poverty impact both the current and future welfare of households. Indeed, the loss in welfare of households is associated with poverty and with any possible source of uncertainty or risk. The effect of poverty and risk on reducing welfare is the focus of the study held in Bulgaria in 1994. This study estimated the effect of changes in different sources of risk on welfare and highlighted the role of education to reduce vulnerability. In the sample chosen, welfare would increase by 14% if inequality is eliminated and by 3% if aggregate risk is eliminated. The effect of eliminating idiosyncratic risk on welfare is also significant even if it is small in magnitude

compared to aggregate risk. Besides, education is proven to be the primordial way to reduce vulnerability to poverty. Households with more educated members are significantly lass poor and significantly less vulnerable to both aggregate and idiosyncratic risks (Ligon & Schechter, 2002).

Adverse economic shocks, believed to increase the vulnerability to poverty, can be easily transferred among geographical borders because of the dynamic environment characterized by its random and stochastic behaviors. Because of this easy transfer of economic shocks, social protection policies should be implemented all over the world to protect households from the adverse effects of poverty. This protection approach should be future oriented and should focus on identifying not only the poor of today but also the ones candidates to fall below the poverty line in the future. This sensitivity to adverse economic shocks and other sources of risk such as natural disasters and climate conditions determines the vulnerability to poverty, which can be dealt with by establishing consumption insurance schemes (Skoufias, 2002).

All the segments of the community or region may be exposed to poverty risks. For elders, poverty risks are shaped by their work history constrained by education, labor union coverage and professional jobs held, and influenced by their accumulated capital and experience. Individuals with high education acquire intellectual and industrial capital and experience that allow them to hold high pay occupations, engage in full time positions, and benefit from the coverage of labor unions defending their rights. All these education driven benefits prevent highly educated individuals, in their older age, from moving into poverty. For example, older men who had less than high school education in the United States were 16 times more likely to become poor than older man who had more than high school education and held union, professional, or managerial jobs. This is justified in the study by the fact that highly educated individuals are more likely to have held professional occupations and had high earnings throughout their career besides management and decision making skills paving them the way to plan their retirement. As a result, these people are far away from falling into the poverty range (McLaughlin & Jensen, 2000).

Poverty risks are aggravated by the inefficient and bad distribution of benefits derived from social protection programs targeting the poor. The benefits of these programs supposed to target the most deprived segments of society turn out to be captured by other segments. There are even some programs that concentrate on poor people, but the rate of coverage is very low and this has a little impact on the process of poverty alleviation (Ravallion, 2002).

Depending on the type and the degree of severity of the costs faced, households develop strategies to overcome them and reduce the long-term impoverishment risks. Public strategies and economic policies aim at smoothing and ensuring a constant trend in the level of income because the variation in income level is the source of risks for them. There are even some strategies that help poor individuals and households to earn a higher income and therefore reduce the exposition to crises and shocks. Nevertheless, whether they aim at increasing or ensuring a constant level of income, they can be divided into two risk-management and risk-coping strategies. Risk-management strategies deal with the riskiness of the income process and aim at smoothing the level of income while risk coping strategies attempt to smooth consumption and attempt to overcome the income risk (Dercon, 2002).

Faced with variations in the income level, poor households adopt risk-management strategies that attempt to influence the component of income. Income diversification, one of the risk-management strategies, deals with diversifying the sources of income. The reasoning behind income diversification is that when income is earned from more than one activity, the income risk is reduced because the mean income is maintained. According to Dercon

(2002), combining two income sources (correlation coefficient less than 1) with the same mean and variance reduces the income risk. However, the income diversification strategy is difficult to implement leading to its ineffectiveness in some cases. Different activities, which the poor can undertake, are not conducted at the same time of the year and may be positively correlated. The timing of activities and their positive correlation reduce the usefulness of diversification. Entry constraints also impact the effectiveness of income diversification strategy because poor households and individuals lack high levels of capital that will allow them to undertake high-return activities (Dercon, 2002).

The income skewing strategy also attempts to reduce the income risk; but the process is different. Income skewing strategy points out that poor households should engage in low risk and low return activities. Even if these activities earn a lower return, the income level is smoothed because there is a lower uncertainty that poor individuals will lose their jobs categorized as low risk jobs (Dercon, 2002).

The second type of strategies stressed by Dercon (2002) is the risk-coping strategies that are devoted to ensure consumption smoothing and reduce the consequences of income risk. One of these strategies is self-insurance through savings. Households, willing to maximize their expected utility over time and having an infinite planning horizon, prefer to accumulate or save assets in good years to be used in bad years. However, even with preference and planning, households are impatient to consume at the present time; which leads to fluctuations in savings but more smoothing in consumption (Dercon, 2002).

In addition to self-insurance strategy, informal risk-sharing arrangements between ethnic groups, neighborhood groups, community groups, or family networks can be used to reduce the effects of income risk and save poor individuals and households from long-term impoverishment.

In these risk-sharing arrangements, households or individuals tend to support others when their income situation is good with the hope to receive support from others when their income situation gets bad. The risk-sharing arrangements are similar to an insurance system founded by the members of the community to reduce the vulnerability of poor individuals to severe shocks (Dercon, 2002).

Finally and based on series of surveys conducted in different countries of the world, Barnerjee and Duflo (2006) characterized the main issues that underline poverty. Table 2 summarizes most of the characteristics of the poor. Again, interdependencies appear at different levels.

POVERTY AND ICTS

Starting the early 1990s, calls for fighting poverty have increased significantly in both developed and developing countries. Several plans and strategies for poverty alleviation have been launched either by governments or non-government and associations. In 1990, the World Bank's World Development Report reviewed poverty reduction and revealed that poverty has become a transformed concept, having previously been marginalised within the Bank. Alongside, the United Nations Development Programme (UNDP) published the first Human Development Report. This report made poverty and poverty reduction a worldwide issue. Ten years later, and based on earlier international development targets, the Millennium development goals were officially established following the Millennium summit of 2000, where all present world leaders adopted the United Nations Millennium Declaration. The MDGs were made to apply the idea that every individual has the right to dignity, freedom, equality. Therefore, they set targets and indicators for poverty reduction in order to achieve the declaration's objectives on a set of fifteen-year timeline (Hulme, 2009). Therefore, The MDGs focus on the major areas of human

development that are boosting human capital, improving infrastructure, and increasing social, economic, and political rights, with a higher focus on increasing basic standards of living. Hence, one might notice that the major objective of MDGs is oriented toward poverty alleviation worldwide.

Nwakanma (2012, p. 11) considers that "challenges to the effective use of the Web for social and economic development in developing countries are all linked to poverty." While poverty alleviation is a goal, its constituent elements hamper the achievement of this goal, at least from the ICT perspective. The author refers to a study on "Ten Good Reasons Why the Internet Bypasses the Poor." The illiteracy, the limit of Web-content, the language barrier, the non-adapted software, the reduced connectivity in rural areas, the reduced mobility of the poor, the opportunity cost of time, the cost of access to the Web, limited knowledge about the potential benefits besides other reasons. The needs of the poor are necessary to be part of the contents to be provided.

In recent decades, there has been a growing evidence of the role that ICTs can play in development enhancement. Relatively, the UN Millennium Declaration emphasized on partnerships with the private sector in order to ensure that the benefits of new technologies are available to all. In spite of this enabling potential role, ICTs still have to be widely extended to support developing countries in addressing development problems via innovative solutions that are both effective and easily applicable. The United Nations Development Programme (UNDP) recognised the importance of a partnership approach that can take advantage of the role of ICTs development both as an enabler of development as well as an enhancer of capacity development at both individual and societal levels. In its development strategy, there is a focus on the use of ICTs to effectively contribute to the achievement of the MDGs, particularly those related to education, health, environment, equity, gender, and poverty reduction (Hulme, 2009).

Table 2. Characterization of the poor and paradoxes from Barnerjee and Duflo (2006)

Area of Decision	Main Characteristics	Paradoxes
Family	■ High number of children ■ High fertility rate ■ Low average age of children	More children drive more consumption and thus limited allocation for other household operations under constrained budget. Access to cigarettes and other practices reduces the budget but also affects health.
Food and consumption	■ Revenu increases directly used in food consumption ■ Large consumption of cigarettes and others ■ Large expenditures in ceremonies	
Assets & Property	■ Revenu increases devoted to acquisitions of radios and TV ■ In rural areas, land not in excess of 2 hectares. ■ Micro-enterprises with limited inputs, bicycles, sewing machines	Poor households may not invest in new inputs for their micro-business..
Health and Well-being	■ Health problems not monitored. ■ Prevalence of under-nutrition..	While knowing the negative impact of malnutrition, only limited efforts are made regarding allowing more resources to better food and health monitoring. This affects also labor productivity.
Education	■ L'investissement dans l'éducation représente une part négligeable du budget ■ Large drop-out from education at early ages	Poor households may prefer immediate returns rather than those that might be related to education. Children may consequently be encouraged to work.
Employment and entrepreneurship	■ Micro-enterprises at a small scale with chronic liquidity problems, ■ Large share opt for microenterprises ■ Lack of specialized skills ■ Several jobs during the year ■ Short run migration to other places for employment	Multiplication of revenue generating activities may be against specialization and mobilization of their small savings towards improvement of their micro-business.
Financial markets	■ Heavy indebted, ■ Use of informal credit markets ■ High prices and higher interests are charged	Formal and semi-formal savings can ber liable sources in comparison with access to informal market with high interest rates.
Savings	■ Savings at home outside banks ■ Hard to save because of consumption tentations ■ Small amounts saved	
Insurance	■ No formal insurance system ■ Social insurance systems in case of hazards	
Land and Housing	■ Difficulty of evidence about property rates in case of land or housing. ■ Difficulty of formal sales and transfers	
Infrastructures	■ Acces to water, electricity and road are limited in most rural areas relative to cities, ■ Rural schools, hospitals and other public facilities of limites quantity and quality mainly in rural areas.	

Selection by the author from Banerjee and Duflo (2006)

There are different views regarding the role of ICTs in poverty alleviation. The first view believes that ICTs have the potential to fight rural and urban poverty and promote sustainable development (Samiullah & Rao, 2000). However, this can only be achieved if ICTs are appropriately implemented and made to address the different needs of urban and rural people. The authors argue that successful use of ICTs can only be achieved in the existence of enabling atmosphere and circumstances, such as the free flow of information, the participation of the private sector and NGOs, access by women, and capacity building.

While it seems obvious that telecommunications contribute to an efficient functioning and growth of economies, ICTs may be a cause, an outcome, and a sign of development. Kenny, Navas-Sabater, and Qiang (2000) argue that econometric studies have showed increasing evidence of a causal relationship between telecommunications development and economic development; however, this can be explained by the high returns on investment in the telecommunications sector. Other studies have extended these relationships to other indicators, such as social development, cost savings for industry, and increased transport efficiency. Internet has been widely discussed at the micro-economic level as a tool providing a good opportunity to firms and entrepreneurs to reduce costs, increase market share, and achieve economies of scale.

The second view believes that ICTs are simply a channel for information exchange and dissemination (Heeks, 1999). However, Heeks (1999) argues that information exchange and dissemination are both essential for development. For this reason, the availability of information sources for the poor is an area that has been addressed for many years. Despite this interest, even when information is available, poor populations do not get access to it either due to poor infrastructure, ignorance, or illiteracy. Wresch (1996) suggest four information problems that are usually faced by the poor: geographic isolation, lack of communication channels, language problems, and lack of computer systems. Communication channels and computer systems are directly ICT related constraints. In the case of geographic isolation, the key message is that electronic channels are used to complement face-to-face contact, not to replace it. The telephone, for example, is the main medium used for communication, but there are many places where telephone lines do not exist. Hence, ICTs can play an important role in poverty alleviation, but it should be accompanied by other means and strategies.

Therefore, as with any tool, ICTs has the potential to initiate either a positive or a negative change,

depending on how it is implemented. This suggests that both successes and failures in applying ICTs to the problems of poverty need to be examined, so that ICTs can be used more effectively. Relatively, assessment and evaluation of previous projects can be of great importance to decisions makers. This research chapter incorporate cases studies as well as issues related to applying ICTs for poverty alleviation purposes in several sectors worldwide. The chapter analyse also ICTs links to countries poverty indicators via a study that incorporate a sample of 40 countries, from which 20 are belong to the developing world while the other 20 are relatively developed countries. The study's results reveal several interesting results. First, people in developing countries have less access to ICTs relative to those in developed countries. The study argues also that the use of Internet is positively affected by the literacy rate within a country. Finally, the results convey populations of countries with higher rates of poverty (lower GDP per Capita and higher poverty rates) have less access to ICTs. Mathison (2005) has largely discussed the dividends that are obtained from ICTs in a context of poverty.

This chapter discusses the role of ICTs in poverty reduction. It is organised into four sections. The first section is a literature review of ICTs application for poverty alleviation. The literature review includes case studies of ICTs applications as well as issues related to ICTs application for poverty reduction. The second section is Methodology, which include a statistical study relating ICTs to poverty indicators. The next section is based on results and discussions while the last section is a conclusion.

Case Studies from Literature

As stated earlier, some views support the implementation of ICTs for poverty alleviation, while others do not agree with this view. There are several success stories that highlight the need for optimism on what the poor could achieve by having access to information technologies. Other stories suggest that ICTs implementation should be supported by other strategies to avoid failures.

The following case studies include ICTs uses for poverty alleviation in different sectors all over the world. They aim at showing how ICTs have been supporting poverty alleviation in series of places and initiatives.

Banking: The Grameen Bank

One of the most cited banking success stories in developing countries is that of the Grameen bank. Notable works in this respect include Camp and Anderson (1999) and Lawson and Meyenn (2000). The Grameen Bank (GB) of Bangladesh is a village-based micro-finance organization. This small financing organization changed the lives people in many villages in Bangladesh via ensuring access to the telephone. The Grameen Bank offered women in villages loans to buy cellular phones that they rent to other villagers on a commercial basis. The GB refers to these phones as 'Village Pay Phones' (VPPs). The effects of VPPs can be considered from two perspectives: sellers of services (telephone owners or women), who had an investment opportunity to improve their economic situation, and buyers of services (villagers), who had a higher access to mobile phones which was not unaffordable before. Hence, the GB can be considered as a success story of the implementation of ICTs to reduce poverty.

Agriculture: ICTs and Farmers

In developing countries, the incomes of millions of people depend heavily on agriculture. One of the major problem faced by many farmers and small entrepreneurs reside in the lack of communication channels to have an idea about prices travelling to markets to sell products. This leads farmers to rely on middlemen who take advantage of the poor communication facilities. Munyua (2007) suggest that small farmers suffer from poor market infrastructures, insufficient marketing experience,

and a lack of agricultural know-how. Relatively, accurate and well-timed market information can reduce transaction and travel costs. De Silva (2008) suggests that cost of information in Seri-lanka is estimated at 11% of the total cost of farmers from the time of growing to the time of selling.

Jenson's (2007) study on the fish prices in India provides a good evidence of the micro-economic impact of ICTs (mainly mobile phones) in this sector. He argued that the arrival of mobiles brought significant and immediate reductions in price volatility and waste amounts in the fishing system. In Kenya, The DrumNet is a network of rurally located farm business support centres in 5 Kenyan provinces. This network delivers agricultural extension, loans facilities, and marketing services to small farmers with the aim of increasing their farm productivity, their access to markets, and the efficiency with which they conduct business (Giné, 2005). Although there were some good results, very few had a clear idea of what they expect ICT to do for them, which makes it difficult for to modify products and services. Hence, shortages of skills might be a main obstacle to ICTs implementation for poverty alleviation.

Health: ICT Applications in Developing Countries

While early efforts in the use of ICT in healthcare gave diverse outcomes, there, actually, an extensive enthusiasm about the role ICT can play in the health sector (Elder & Clarke, 2007). One of the main factors leading to this increasing enthusiasm is the rise in the use of mobile devices that can help in providing important health services in developing countries. The technology of mobile phones is considered as more advantageous for e-health due to their prevalence and relative affordability. Idowu, Ogunbodede, and Idowu (2003) illustrate how Nigerian doctors use mobiles to communicate with each other across different parts of a large hospital, and to take action to urgent situations even when they are offsite. Lester, Lee, and Lambert

(2006) evaluate the use of mobiles in facilitating information flows for AIDS intervention programs. They suggest that for mobile phones to play an effective role for health improvement, many issues are to be addressed. Illiteracy and localization are among the main obstacles faced in developing countries. This leads to a limited use of Mobiles and ICTs for health improvement (Kaplan, 2006).

Greenberg (2005) studied ICTs as a basic tool for poverty alleviation. He suggested two cases studies of ICTs application for health improvement. The first program is the RESCUER, which was applied in Uganda. The second program is the TEHIP, a Canadian International Development Research Centre (IDRC) program in collaboration with the Tanzania Ministry of Health running from 1994 to 2004. The results of this program suggest that it is impossible to make rational decisions on how to allocate healthcare budgets and resources without reasonably accurate statistics. These accurate statistics might be achieved only through the effective use of ICTs.

Another good example of ICTs application for poverty alleviation is the radio and TV health programs that treat diseases and respond to the questions of the audience. These programs can be considered as good mechanism to improve health within poor populations. Therefore, the poor audience can minimize the costs of medical doctors' prescription to a call price in order to have a medical recommendation. Relatively, poor people with access to Internet can have information about all diseases just by navigating on Internet. In this way, patients might not need to visit the medical doctors, or at least they can be well informed before visiting a medical specialist, which lead to decreasing his costs.

Distance Education

In recent decades, the use of distance learning has become increasingly popular in both developed and developing. Such learning method has proved to be efficient in many occasions. Relatively, this method has been widely used as a tool to fight illiteracy and poverty in remote areas. Green and Deutsch (2002) examined distance learning for women in several commonwealth countries. They suggest that in the African region, most Commonwealth countries have been using mainly print-based distance learning, often supported by radio broadcasts and audio/videocassettes for formal education for decades. The distinguished exception is the African Virtual University that uses satellite channels to provide courses through videoconferencing to university campuses in 11 countries. With regard to the Asian Commonwealth countries, radio, television, and audio/videocassettes have been used to support both formal and non-formal education for decades. While, New ICTs started to be used in few countries. This suggests that old technologies are more prevalent in distance learning than the new ones, as was suggested in previous sections.

In Morocco, for example, the TV and Radio programs that have been launched almost a decade ago to fight illiteracy constitute a good example of ICTs use for poverty alleviation. These programs might be useful for poor populations in cities and also in remote areas where access to schools and to education is relatively harder. This example supports the hypothesis that old technologies are used more frequently in developing countries for distance learning.

The use of mobile telephony in education is a relatively new area, even for developed Countries. Most of the research exploring the feasibility and potential benefits of using mobiles for distance learning in this domain is still at a very early stage (Traxler & Leach, 2006). Ramos (2006) examined a case study about Technology-Supported Distance Education via is a project that explores the potential of ICTs and distance non-formal education in order to achieve the mandate of the Water, Sanitation, and Hygiene (WASH) in an effective and sustainable manner. The SMS technology, among other ICT tools, was used to enhance the delivery of relevant information through distance non-formal education strategies. The project results were important since it contributed to improved lives of the targeted people in terms of empowerment of the community. This case study suggests also that the SMS technology could be a viable technology for delivering distance education courses, mainly in countries where SMS usage is higher.

Issues Related to ICT Use for Poverty Alleviation

Less Access to ICTs by the Poor

Though the international efforts to use ICTs in poverty reduction, the usage of these technologies and access to them is still very low in many regions of the world, mainly in poor countries (global knowledge Partnership, 2005). Based on a comparative study about the number of telephone lines, Internet users and personal computers in 16 developing countries in Asia, GKP suggests that of the 16 countries discussed, nine have less than one Internet user per 100 people. These results suggest that the poorest people in Asia presently have low access to the Internet. Despite the fact that poor populations have minor access to Internet, technology remains an essential tool for poverty reduction especially when applied appropriately and sensitively (GKP, 2005).

As a direct medium to delivering information to the poor, 'old' technologies like radio and television have the potential to achieve far wider outreach at a lower cost than the new technologies, to which access is still low by poor population (GKP, 2005). However, comparison of different ICTs should take into consideration both outreach and cost considerations. Whereas radio might achieve a broader audience, it is a uni-directional. Therefore, for a higher outreach, listeners need to be aware of programming schedules. On the other hand, Internet, telephones, or mobile phones are multi-directional channels that can be used to

transmit multi-media data. As well, information is available to recipients whenever they choose to access it.

Development vs. Poverty Reduction

Previous literature suggests that development and poverty reduction are not synonymous (Spence, 2003). Hence, it is possible for a country to develop while the poverty situation remains static. On the other hand, it is important to note that no country has been successful in reducing poverty without achieving development in its broad sense. This suggests that human development is clearly central to poverty reduction. Spence (2003) suggest that growth and development are necessary but not sufficient for poverty reduction. He suggests also that ICTs are important for pro-poor strategies and investments. These ICTs need to be integrated with social and economic development strategies (mainly among information, science, education, health, economy, finance, rural development, etc.). Such strategies are not all the time oriented toward poverty reduction. Consequently, ICT strategies need to seriously address poverty reduction, equity, and social development.

Lack of Support by Governments

One of the main obstacles facing ICTs implementation in poor countries is the lack of governments support. Opoku and Mensah (1998) conducted a study on current ICT initiatives in Africa and the role of policies in this process. They suggest that several initiatives to improve interconnectivity and networking in the continent have been undertaken either by the private sector or by the donor community. Yet, very few have been initiated or supported by African governments. In discussing the role of policies, the authors focus on the need for private investment in the ICT industry and greater liberalization of the telecommunications sector. In another study, de Boer and Walbeek (1998) designed a project to bridge the information gap between the North and the South. The project focused on ways to improve the application of telematics (defined as a combination of tele-communications and informatics) in developing countries. They used questionnaires to assess and quantify the current situation of telematics in six countries including Burkina Faso, Ethiopia, and Zimbabwe. The results suggest that the telematics sector was characterized by small and weak organizations with committed employees. The main threats were in the weak telecommunications infrastructure, limited energy supply, and restrictive laws.

Difficulty to Use Technology

Despite the wide availability and use of technology in developed countries, good technology implementations in developing countries are often difficult and costly. Many implementation projects fail and many that are successful exceed their original budgets. Most developing countries suffer from shortages in funds and skills. Mayer (2000) discusses the challenges facing the implementation of ICT networks and services in rural areas. One of the main recommendations of Mayer for a good application of ICTs in such areas is the promotion and the development of low-cost information among low-skilled populations. An older study by Kling (1996) suggests that computerization is also the source of problems. The author notes that computers are harder to work and this lead lowering access to these technologies.

With regard to accepting a particular technology, issues such as access, cost, teaching functions, organizational issues, and speed afforded to change are important issues (Rajesh, 2003). In addition to the factors mentioned above, once a technology is selected, other factors are to be taken into consideration by policy makers. A good Management of ICTs requires extensive training. In many developing countries, there is a shortage of staff to train manpower in new technology. As well, constant retraining of manpower to adapt

with changing technology is also costly. These often act as constraints before the smooth growth of ICT. At last, Maintenance of equipment also needs sufficiently trained staff, high quality replacement parts and machine friendly attitude from the users.

Cultural Factors

Language is one of the major factors facing the application of ICTs by many developing countries. The radio and TV programs, computer software and the printed texts are produced in different countries bearing different cultural backgrounds. Consequently, such tools may fail to impress the recipients in another country. With regard to cultural patterns, there are two groups of policy makers. Policy makers can be Pro-implementation or Anti-implementation (Rajesh, 2003). According to the nature and characteristics of a culture, people might be either in favor of implementing technology or to reject it. A good example is the Japanese people who have over the years built up a reputation of being quick to adapt and implement new technologies. Developing countries are generally known for their resistance to change. Relatively, the adoption of ICTs in such countries is generally harder.

METHODOLOGICAL SETUP FOR EMPIRICAL EVIDENCE

Most arguments related to poverty focus on insufficient nutrition, inadequate shelter and so on. Even though, literature has started to argue that lack of access to Information and Communications Technologies (ICTs) is an element of poverty. Kenny (2001) discusses the use of ICTs in poverty alleviation in relation to poor people's limited access to ICTs. Actually, while researchers believe that ICTs have the potential to combat rural and urban poverty and foster sustainable development (Samiullah & Rao, 2000). Others suggest that ICTs are simply a channel for information exchange and dissemination (Heeks, 1999). These technologies might be efficient only if appropriately deployed and made to address the differential needs of urban and rural people. successful ICT interventions can only be achieved if there is an enabling environment, the participation of the private sector and NGOs, the free flow of information, access by all society ingredients, and capacity building (Islam, 2005).

This chapter investigates the relationship between ICT integration and poverty on a sample of 40 countries. The sample is divided into two groups: a group composed of 20 of developed countries and another that is constituted of 20 developing countries. Several assumptions are to be tested through statistical analyses. First, the chapter tests the hypothesis that there is higher access to ICTs in developed countries than in developing countries. This hypothesis is tested using three ICTs, fixed phone, mobile phone, and Internet. The second hypothesis relate literacy rate to Internet use. Internet was selected since it requires some skills not like fixed or mobile phone. This hypothesis suggests that countries with higher literacy rates have higher number of Internet users. The third hypothesis suggests that countries with higher GDP per Capita have higher access to ICTs. The last hypothesis suggests that countries with lower poverty rates have higher rates of ICTs use. The sources used include Central Intelligence Agency website, UNESCO website, World Bank website, and other sources.

RESULTS AND DISCUSSION

These results are related to series of hypotheses formulated in relation to the role of ICTs in different series of contexts. These results are introduced and discussed in relation to each hypothesis.

Hypothesis 1: New ICT Use in Developed vs. Developing Countries

This hypothesis suggests that people in developing countries have less access to new technologies than those in developed countries. To test this hypothesis, comparison of access to three technologies is made, mainly fixed phone, mobile phone, and Internet. Hence, three hypotheses are developed and tested through t-tests.

Hypothesis 1.1

The first hypothesis suggests that people in developing countries have less access to fixed line phones than in developed countries, so that:

H0: People in developed and in developing countries have equal access to fixed line phones.
H1: People in developing countries have less access to fixed line phones than those in developed countries.

In order to test this hypothesis, an independence t-test is used on a sample composed of 40 countries, 20 developing countries and 20 developed ones.

Results

As shown in Table 3, the P-value is smaller than Alfa (P-value = 0 < 0.05), which suggest that the null hypothesis (H0) is rejected and confirm that people in developing countries have less access to fixed line phones than those in developed countries

Hypothesis 1.2

Similarly, the second hypothesis suggests that people in poorer countries have less access to mobile phones. This leads to two hypotheses:

H0: People in developed and in developing countries have equal access to mobile phones.

H1: People in developing countries have less access to mobile phones than those in developed countries.

Results

As indicated in Table 4, the p-value is smaller than 0.05, hence the null hypothesis is rejected and there is enough statistical evidence that people in developing countries have less access to mobile phones than those in developed countries.

Hypothesis 1.3 `

The third hypothesis suggests that people in developing countries have less access to Internet than those in industrial countries as:

H0: People in developed and in developing countries have equal access to Internet.
H1: People in developing countries have less access to Internet than those in developed countries.

Results

The results of Table 5 are similar to Tables 3 and 4, so they suggest that people in developing countries have less access to Internet than those in developed countries.

The results of the three hypotheses show that in general people in developing countries have less access to ICTs relative to those in developed countries. This can be explained by several factors including financial situation and literacy differences. The next hypothesis tests the relationship between literacy rate and Internet penetration within developed and developing countries.

Hypothesis 2: Literacy Rate vs. Internet Use

Previous literature suggests that people with higher levels of education are more likely to use Internet. Based on this assumption, this hypothesis suggests that countries with higher literacy have higher access to education have higher Internet

Table 3. T-test output for fixed phone penetration in developed countries vs. developing countries

		Levene's Test for Equality of Variances		t-test for Equality of Means						
									95% Confidence Interval of the Difference	
		F	Sig.	t	df	Sig. (2-tailed)	Mean Difference	Std. Error Difference	Lower	Upper
Fixed_line_penetration	Equal variances assumed	8,771	,005	16,274	38	,000	,40450	,02486	,35418	,45482
	Equal variances not assumed			16,274	25,226	,000	,40450	,02486	,35333	,45567

Table 4. T-test output for mobile phone use in developed countries vs. developing countries

		Levene's Test for Equality of Variances		t-test for Equality of Means						
									95% Confidence Interval of the Difference	
		F	Sig.	t	df	Sig. (2-tailed)	Mean Difference	Std. Error Difference	Lower	Upper
mobile_penetration	Equal variances assumed	2,106	,155	8,368	38	,000	,72036	,08608	,54610	,89463
	Equal variances not assumed			8,368	36,894	,000	,72036	,08608	,54593	,89480

penetration rates. Therefore, literacy rate affect positively the number of Internet users in a country. To test this hypothesis, a simple regression is used, with literacy rate as an independent variable, and Internet penetration (number of Internet users/ the population size) as a dependent variable. A sample of 40 countries (20 developed countries and 20 developing countries) is used for this test.

Therefore, the null and alternative hypotheses are as follows:

H0: Literacy rate is not related to Internet penetration within countries.
H1: Literacy rate is positively related to Internet penetration.

Results

The regression results (as shown in Table 6) suggest that Internet penetration is positively affected by the literacy rate within a country. This confirms the previous assumptions suggesting that Internet is mostly used by people with higher literacy levels. Even though, literacy rate might

not be the only factor leading to higher Internet penetration, other factors might be also leading to such higher Internet use in countries with higher literacy rates.

Hypothesis 3: GDP per Capita vs. New ICT Use

This hypothesis suggests that poorer people have less access to new technologies. Hence, people in countries with higher GDP per Capita have higher access to new technologies. In order to test this assumption, the GDP per Capita effect on access to three ICTs is examined, as in the first hypothesis. These ICTs are fixed phone, Mobile phone, and Internet. Therefore, three hypotheses are developed and tested:

Hypothesis 3.1: GDP per Capita vs. Fixed Phone Use

This hypothesis suggests that GDP per Capita has a positive effect on fixed phone penetration in a country. In other words, a higher GDP per

Table 5. T-test output for internet penetration in developed countries vs. developing countries

Independent Samples Test

		Levene's Test for Equality of Variances		t-test for Equality of Means						
									95% Confidence Interval of the Difference	
		F	Sig.	t	df	Sig. (2-tailed)	Mean Difference	Std. Error Difference	Lower	Upper
internet_penetration	Equal variances assumed	1,310	,260	15,280	38	,000	,6596009	,0431679	,5722121	,7469896
	Equal variances not assumed			15,280	34,918	,000	,6596009	,0431679	,5719580	,7472437

Table 6. Regression output for internet penetration vs. literacy rate

Model		Unstandardized Coefficients		Standardized Coefficients	t	Sig.
		B	Std. Error	Beta		
1	(Constant)	-,551	,105		-5,250	,000
	literacy_rate	1,238	,129	,842	9,602	,000

a. Dependent Variable: Internet_penetration

Capita in a country lead to a higher access to fixed phones. So the null and alternative hypotheses are as follows:

H0: GDP per Capita (poverty indicator) is not related to fixed line phone use.
H1: GDP per Capita (poverty indicator) is positively related to fixed line phone use.

Results

As shown in Table 7, the regression results indicate that the GDP per Capita has a positive effect on fixed line use. Therefore, countries with higher GDP per Capita have higher access to fixed line phones.

Hypothesis 3.2: GDP per Capita vs. Mobile Phone Use

This hypothesis test the relationship between GDP per Capita and mobile phone use in the countries included in our sample. So that, the null and alternative hypotheses are as follows:

H0: GDP per Capita (poverty indicator) is not related to mobile phone use.
H1: GDP per Capita (poverty indicator) is positively related to mobile phone use.

Results

As shown in Table 8, the regression results suggest that the GDP per Capita has a positive effect on mobile phone use. Therefore, countries with higher GDP per Capita have higher access to mobile line phones.

Hypothesis 3.3: GDP per Capita vs. Internet Use

This hypothesis suggests that countries with higher GDP per Capita have higher access to Internet with:

H0: GDP per Capita (poverty indicator) is not related to Internet use.
H1: GDP per Capita (poverty indicator) is positively related to Internet use.

Results

The results of Table 9 suggest that the GDP per Capita has a positive effect on Internet use. So, countries with higher GDP per Capita have higher access to Internet.

Overall, the regression analyses performed above suggest that countries with higher GDP per Capita, ensure higher access to ICTs for their populations.

Hypothesis 4: Poverty Rates vs. ICT Use

This hypothesis suggests that higher poverty rates within a country lead to a low access to ICTs by the country's population. Three linear regressions are performed to test poverty rate effect on fixed phone use, mobile phone use, and Internet use.

Hypothesis 4.1: Poverty vs. Fixed Phone Use

This first hypothesis suggests that countries with higher poverty have lower fixed phone penetration rates with:

H0: Poverty rates within countries is not related to fixed phone use.
H1: Poverty rate within countries is positively related to fixed phone use.

Results

The regression results (as shown in Table 10) indicate that the poverty percentage in a country has a negative effect on fixed line phone use. Therefore, countries with higher rates of poverty have less access to fixed phones by citizens.

Table 7. Regression output for fixed phone penetration vs. GDP per capita

Model		Unstandardized Coefficients		Standardized Coefficients	t	Sig.
		B	Std. Error	Beta		
1	(Constant)	1,051	2,014		,522	,605
	GDP_per_Capita	,001	,000	,925	14,956	,000

a. Dependent Variable: Fixed_line_penetration_percentage

Table 8. Regression output for mobile phone penetration vs. GDP per capita

Model		Unstandardized Coefficients		Standardized Coefficients	t	Sig.
		B	Std. Error	Beta		
1	(Constant)	38,550	6,155		6,263	,000
	GDP_per_Capita	,002	,000	,817	8,740	,000

a. Dependent Variable: mobile_penetration_percentage

Table 9. Regression output for internet penetration vs. GDP per capita

Model		Unstandardized Coefficients		Standardized Coefficients	t	Sig.
		B	Std. Error	Beta		
1	(Constant)	2,008	2,585		,777	,442
	GDP_per_Capita	,002	,000	,956	20,047	,000

a. Dependent Variable: Internet_penetration_percentage

Table 10. Regression output for fixed phone penetration vs. poverty rates

Model		Unstandardized Coefficients		Standardized Coefficients	t	Sig.
		B	Std. Error	Beta		
1	(Constant)	44,215	3,597		12,292	,000
	poverty_percentage	-,785	,107	-,765	-7,317	,000

a. Dependent Variable: Fixed_line_penetration_percentage

Table 11. Regression output for mobile phone use vs. poverty rates

Model		Unstandardized Coefficients		Standardized Coefficients	t	Sig.
		B	Std. Error	Beta		
1	(Constant)	123,137	6,547		18,809	,000
	poverty_percentage	-1,689	,195	-,814	-8,649	,000

a. Dependent Variable: mobile_penetration_percentage

Hypothesis 4.2: Poverty vs. Mobile Phone Use

This hypothesis suggests that countries with higher poverty rates have less access to the mobile phone technology with:

H0: Poverty rates within countries is not related to mobile phone use.

H1: Poverty rate within countries is positively related to mobile phone use.

Results

The results of Table 11 indicate that there enough evidence to reject the null hypothesis, which suggest that the poverty rate in a country has a negative effect on mobile phone use. Therefore, countries with higher rates of poverty have less access to mobile phones

Hypothesis 4.3: Poverty vs. Internet Use

This last hypothesis conveys that higher poverty rate in country lead to lower access to Internet in this country. Therefore, the null and alternative hypotheses are as follows:

H0: Poverty rates within countries is not related to Internet use.

H1: Poverty rate within countries is positively related to Internet use.

Results

The regression analysis (as shown in the Table 12) indicates that the poverty percentage in a country has a negative effect on Internet use. Therefore, countries with higher rates of poverty have less access to the Internet.

On the whole, the 3 regression analyses performed in this section suggest that countries with higher poverty rates have less access to ICTs. In other words, wealthy countries ensure higher access to ICTs for their populations and have consequently higher potential for higher benefits.

CONCLUSION

This chapter investigates the relationship between ICTs use and poverty on a sample of 40 countries. The sample is divided into two groups: a group composed of 20 of developed countries and another that is constituted of 20 developing countries. Several assumptions are tested through statistical analyses, and interesting results were established. The first result suggests that people in developing countries have less access to ICTs relative to those in developed countries. The second test indicates that the use of Internet is positively affected by the literacy rate within a country. Therefore, the higher the literacy rate, the higher the number of Internet users in a country. The third result conveys that countries with higher GDP per Capita ensure higher access to ICTs for their populations. The final result demonstrates

Table 12. Regression output for Internet penetration vs. poverty rates

Model		Unstandardized Coefficients		Standardized Coefficients	t	Sig.
		B	Std. Error	Beta		
1	(Constant)	76,758	5,551		13,827	,000
	poverty_percentage	-1,369	,166	-,802	-8,271	,000

a. Dependent Variable: Internet_penetration_percentage

that populations of countries with higher rates of poverty have less access to ICTs. On the whole, the study made suggest that people in developed countries have generally better access to ICTs than those in developing nations.

In recent decades, there has been a growing evidence of the role that ICTs can play in development enhancement in both developed and developing countries. In spite of this enabling potential role, ICTs still have to be widely extended especially in developing countries. ICTs have been also viewed as an efficient tool to fight poverty. Yet, there are different views regarding the role of ICTs in poverty alleviation. The first view suggests that ICTs have the potential to fight poverty and promote sustainable development (Samiullah & Rao, 2000). This can only be achieved, according to the authors, only if ICTs are appropriately implemented and made to address the different needs of urban and rural people. The other vision conveys that ICTs are simply a channel for information exchange and dissemination (Heeks, 1999).

REFERENCES

Ambrose, P. (2002). *The cost of poor housing, urban regeneration and non-housing outcomes*. Paper presented at the HSA Conference, Housing Policies for the New UK. York, UK.

Banerjee, A. V., & Duflo, E. (2007). The economic lives of the poor. *The Journal of Economic Perspectives, 21*(1), 141–167. doi:10.1257/jep.21.1.141

Camp, L. J., & Anderson, B. L. (1999). *Grameen phone: Empowering the poor through connectivity*. Retrieved from http://www.telecommons.com/villagephone/Camp_article12_99.htm

Chaudhuri, S., Jalan, J., & Suryahadi, A. (2002). *Assessing household vulnerability to poverty from cross-sectional data: A methodology and estimates from Indonesia*. New York, NY: Columbia University.

Christiaensen, L., & Subbarao, K. (2004). Towards an understanding of household vulnerability in rural Kenya. *Journal of African Economies, 14*(4), 520–558. doi:10.1093/jae/eji008

Chung, C., & Myers, S. L. (1999). Do the poor pay more for food? An analysis of grocery store availability and food price disparities. *The Journal of Consumer Affairs, 33*, 276–296. doi:10.1111/j.1745-6606.1999.tb00071.x

Dabalen, A., & Poupart, N. (2002). *Vulnerability to rainfall shock in Ethiopia*. Ann Arbor, MI: University of Michigan.

De Boer, S. J., & Walbeek, M. M. (1998). *Bridging the telematics gap in developing countries: Research bits for development policy*. Twente, The Netherlands: University of Twente. Retrieved from http://ubalpha.civ.utwente.nl/cgi-bin/nph wwwredir/cat.dinkel.utwente.nl:1694/X?%5CTOO+S2+7

De Silva. Ratnadiwakara, & Soysa. (2008). *Transaction costs in agriculture: From the planting decision to selling at the wholesale market: A case-study on the feeder area of the Dambulla dedicated economic centre in Sri Lanka*. Ottawa, Canada: IDRC.

Dercon, S. (2002). Managing income risk of the poor. *Research Observer, 17*(2), 237–265.

Elder, L., & Clarke, M. (2007). Past, present and future: Experiences and lessons from telehealth projects. *Open Medicine, 1*, 3. Retrieved from http://www.openmedicine.ca/article/viewArticle/191/98

Giné, X. (2005). DRUMNET case study. *The World Bank*. Retrieved from http://siteresources. worldbank.org/DEC/Resources/DrumnetCaseStudy.pdf

Green, L., & Trevor-Deutsch, L. (2002). *Women and ICTs for open and distance learning: Some experiences and strategies from the commonwealth*. Retrieved from http://www.col.org/colweb/webdav/site/myjahiasite/shared/docs/Women and ICTs.pdf

Greenberg, A. (2005). *ICTs for poverty alleviation: Basic tool and enabling sector*. Stockholm, Sweden: ICT for Development Secretariat.

Gross, D. J., Alecxih, L., Gibson, M. J., Corea, J., Caplan, C., & Brangan, N. (1999). Out-of-pocket health spending by poor and near-poor elderly medicare beneficiaries. *Health Services Research, 34*(1), 241–254.

Grusky, S. (2001). Privatization tidal wave: IMF/world bank water policies and the price paid by the poor. *Multinational Monitor, 22*(9).

Heeks, R. (1999). Information and communication technologies, poverty and development. *Development Informatics Working Paper Series*. Retrieved from http://www.man.ac.uk/idpm/idpm_dp.htm#devinf_wp

Hulme, D. (2009). *The millennium development goals (MDGs): A short history of the world's biggest promise*. Manchester, UK: The University of Manchester.

Idowu, B., Ogunbodede, E., & Idowu, B. (2003). Information and communication technology in Nigeria: The health sector experience. *Journal of Information Technology Impact, 3*(2), 69–76.

Islam, K. B. (2005). *National ICT policies and plans towards poverty reduction: Emerging trends and issues*. New York, NY: United Nations.

Jenson, R. T. (2007). The digital provide: Information (technology), market performance and welfare in the south indian fisheries sector. *The Quarterly Journal of Economics, 122*(3), 879–924. doi:10.1162/qjec.122.3.879

Kaplan, W. A. (2006). Can the ubiquitous power of mobile phones be used to improve health outcomes in developing countries? *Globalization and Health, 2*(9), 1–14.

Kaufman, P. (1999). Rural poor have less access to supermarkets, large grocery stores. *Rural Development Perspectives, 13*(3), 19–26.

Kenny, C. (2001). Information and communication technologies and poverty. *TechKnowLogia*. Retrieved from http://www.techknowlogia.org/

Kenny, C., Navas-Sabater, J., & Qiang, J. (2000). ICTs and poverty. *The World Bank*. Retrieved from http://www.worldbank.org/poverty/strategies/srcbook/ict0829.pdf

Kim, S. (2000). Urban development in the United States, 1690-1990. *Southern Economic Journal, 66*(4), 855–880. doi:10.2307/1061533

Kling, R. (1996). *Computerization and controversy: Value conflicts and social choices*. San Diego, CA: Academic Press.

Lawson, C., & Meyenn, N. (2000). *Bringing cellular phone service to rural areas: Grameen telecom and village payphones in Bangladesh*. Retrieved from http://rru.worldbank.org/Documents/PublicPolicyJournal/205lawson.pdf

Lester, B. T., Ma, L., Lee, O., & Lambert, J. (2006). Social activism in elementary school education: A science, technology, and society approach to teaching global warming. *International Journal of Science Education, 28*, 315–339. doi:10.1080/09500690500240100

Ligon, E., & Schechter, L. (2002). *Measuring vulnerability*. Berkeley, CA: University of California.

Lukemeyer, A., Meyers, M. K., & Smeeding, T. (2002). Expensive children in poor families: Out-of-pocket expenditures for the care of disabled and chronically ill children in welfare families. *Journal of Marriage and the Family, 62*, 399–415. doi:10.1111/j.1741-3737.2000.00399.x

Mathison, S. (2005). *ICT for poverty reduction in Asia: Digital dividends for the poor*. New York, NY: Global Knowledge Partnership.

Mayer, R. (2000). *Challenges to implementing ICT networks and services*. Paper presented at the Rural Areas' Village Power Conference. Washington, DC. Retrieved from http://www.rsvp.nrel. gov/vpconference/vp2000/telecom_workshop/ telecom_rebecca_mayer.pdf

McLaughlin, D. K., & Jensen, L. (2000). Work history and U.S. elders' transitions into poverty. *The Gerontologist, 40*(4), 5–16. doi:10.1093/ geront/40.4.469

Morduch, J. (1999). Between the state and the market: Can informal insurance patch the safety net? *The World Bank Research Observer, 14*(2), 187–207. doi:10.1093/wbro/14.2.187

Munyua, H. (2007). *ICTs and small-scale agriculture in Africa: A scoping study*. Ottawa, Canada: IDRC.

Nwakanma, N. (2012). Culture. In Sadowsky, G. (Ed.), *Accelerating Development Using the Web: Empowering Poor and Marginalized Populations*. New York, NY: World Wide Web Foundation.

Opoku, & Mensah, A. (1998). ICT initiatives and the role of policies in southern Africa. In *Information and Communication Technology and Development*. Rawoo Publication.

Rajesh, M. (2003). A study of the problems associated with ICT adaptability in developing countries in the context of distance education. *Turkish Online Journal of Distance Education, 5*(1). Retrieved from http://tojde.anadolu.edu.tr/ tojde10/articles/Rajesh.htm

Ramos, A. (2006). *Technology-supported distance education (Philippines)*. Retrieved from http://www.idrc.ca/panasia/ev-55758-201-1-DO_TOPIC.html

Ravallion, M. (2002). *Targeted transfers in poor countries: Revisiting the trade-offs and policy options*. Washington, DC: The World Bank. doi:10.2139/ssrn.1754444

Samiullah, Y., & Rao, S. (2000). *Role of ICTs in urban and rural poverty reduction*. Paper presented at the MoEF-TERI-UNEP Regional Workshop for Asia and Pacific on ICT and Environment. Delhi, India. Retrieved from http://www.teri.res. in/icteap/present/session4/sami.doc

Sawicki, D. S., & Moody, M. (2000). Developing transportation alternatives for welfare recipients moving to work. *Journal of the American Planning Association. American Planning Association, 66*(3), 306–318. doi:10.1080/01944360008976109

Skoufias, E. (2002). *Consumption insurance and vulnerability to poverty: A synthesis of the evidence from Bangladesh, Ethiopia, Mali, Mexico, and Russia*. New York, NY: International Food Policy Research Institute. doi:10.1080/09578810500066498

Spence, R. (2003). *Information and communications technologies (ICTs) for poverty reduction: When, where and how?* Washington, DC: IDRC.

Sylwester, K. (2002). A model of public education and income inequality with a subsistence constraint. *Southern Economic Journal, 69*(1), 144–158. doi:10.2307/1061561

Tesliuc, E. D., & Lindert, K. (2002). *Vulnerability: A quantitative and qualitative assessment.* Washington, DC: World Bank.

Thompson, J., & Porras, I. T. (2002). Thirty years of change in water use in east Africa. *Appropriate Technology, 29*(2), 69–85.

Traxler, J., & Leach, J. (2006). Innovative and sustainable mobile learning in Africa. In *Proceedings of the IEEE 4th International Workshop on Wireless, Mobile and Ubiquitous Technologies in Education.* Los Alamitos, CA: IEEE Computer Society.

Whitehead, M., Dahlgren, G., & Evans, T. (2001). Equity and health sector reforms: Can low income countries escape the medical poverty trap? *Lancet, 358,* 833–836. doi:10.1016/S0140-6736(01)05975-X

Wresch, W. (1996). *Disconnected: Haves and have-nots in the information age.* New Brunswick, NJ: Rutgers University Press.

Section 3
Socioeconomic Issues and Policies

Chapter 9
The Triple Helix as a Model for Coordination with Potential for ICTs

ABSTRACT

Promising frameworks have been developed to ensure that different players can have benefits from economic and social activities with high levels of interdependencies. Among these frameworks, the triple helix model constitutes an interesting model that accounts for interactions and ensures coordination of tasks. This chapter focuses on both the elements of the framework and its applications. A special focus is placed on knowledge diffusion in MENA and Arab countries. The usefulness of the triple helix coordinating process is clearly shown to be a way of accounting for interferences and interdependencies. The implicit idea is that further requirements of coordination under this model need further use of ICT tools.

INTRODUCTION

This chapter is devoted to showing how the triple helix framework can be useful in coordinating research, innovation, and education functions among at least three major players: universities, government, and industry. As such, the triple helix model is introduced to show its coordinating features. While this presentation is mainly focusing on the role of the triple helix framework in the diffusion of knowledge, it indicates how different players could coordinate and monitor their actions and programs. This is intended for applications in the area of health, education, and socioeconomic outcomes. It is also proposed for generalization to series of development programs where several players intervene. The role of ICTs is likely to be a major enhancer of the efficiency of the overall coordination system. The triple helix model with its ICTs counterpart can be also useful in coordinating socioeconomic development projects and programs. The chapter is written mainly on the basis of previous findings from the literature. It focuses on Arab countries and the efforts invested in R&D.

DOI: 10.4018/978-1-4666-3643-9.ch009

The chapter introduces the triple helix framework and discusses its applications with a focus on the Arab World.

THE TRIPLE HELIX FRAMEWORK

Knowledge diffusion models have evolved through time to account for both production-transfer processes and the related agents or institutions. These models are useful frameworks that ensure strategies and means for the enhancement and acceleration of knowledge for development through its production and transfers. They are useful for countries and localities besides the sectors that are behind these processes. As such, they account for the interferences between sectors and different players. These include policy, knowledge, and applications. As the focus of this book is on health, education and socioeconomic outcomes, these can really benefit from the framework provided by the triple helix.

Viale and Etzkowitz (2005) provide an excellent historical background about single, double and triple helices as they have been used to describe and analyze knowledge related processes. To these authors, the single helix relates to the insulated individual inventor, during the first industrial revolution where the knowledge is mainly tacit. With more explicit knowledge, this previous stage is replaced during the second industrial revolution by the double helix as a representation of the weak relationships between the industry and the university where the first one is not fully following a scientific path, while the second not completely adhering to an industrialization process. As in Carayol (2003), cognitive integration between science and technology contribute to the generation of major needs of societies. Governments and public organizations have to intervene to facilitate knowledge production, diffusion, and financial support. Three institutional spheres are then involved under the triple helix framework. Besides, ICTs play a major role in the enhancement of the general coordination system. In fact,

the Internet use is very effective in facilitating and enhancing a new paradigm in development, Knowledge Networks. These networks gather institutions and people from all around the world and from all the categories of the society for the sake of the discovery of new knowledge and its use for the improvement of nations (Cukor & McKnight, 2001). The quadruple helix accounts also for the roles played by civil society as the fourth institutional player in the creation and diffusion of knowledge for development (Carayannis & Campbell, 2012). With the inclusion of other institutions and key actors in this process, the game becomes larger and some authors talk about Nth-Helix (Leydesdorff, 2012). However, major theoretical and empirical debates are still occurring at this level.

Etzkowitz and Zhou (2006) have discussed this matter already. They consider that the debate over the Triple Helix model has focused on the question of whether there is a fourth helix. Various candidates have been suggested, such as labor, venture capital, the informal sector, and civil society. However, introduction of a fourth helix might cause a triadic model to lose its creative dynamic. Nevertheless, an expanded model is required to incorporate a critical dimension. To resolve this paradox, we propose a Sustainability Triple Helix of university-public-government as a complement to the Innovation Triple Helix of university-industry-government. This introduces a missing element into the model, while retaining its dynamic properties.

Carayannis and Campbell (2012) discuss the diversity of models that could be mobilized. The traditional Triple Helix innovation model focuses on university-industry-government relations. The Quadruple Helix innovation systems bring in the perspectives of the media-based and culture-based public, as well as that of civil society. The Quintuple Helix emphasizes the natural environments of society, also for knowledge production and innovation. Therefore, the quadruple helix contextualizes the triple helix, and the quintuple helix the quadruple helix. Features of the quadruple helix are: culture (cultures) and innovation culture (innovation cultures); the knowledge of culture and the culture of knowledge; values and lifestyles; multiculturalism, and creativity; media; arts and arts universities; and multi-level innovation systems (local, national, global), with universities of the sciences, but also universities of the arts.

The Triple Helix concept is comprised of three basic elements. These include (1) a more prominent role for the university in innovation with industry and government in a knowledge–based society, (2) a movement toward collaborative relationships among the three major institutional spheres, in which innovation policy is increasingly an outcome of interaction rather than a prescription from government, and (3) in addition to fulfilling their traditional functions, each institutional sphere also "takes the role of the other" performing new roles as well as their traditional function.

Institutions taking non-traditional roles are viewed as a major potential source of innovation in "innovation." Industry operates in the Triple Helix as the locus of production with government as the source of contractual relations that guarantee stable interactions and exchange, the university as a source of new knowledge and technology and the generative principle of knowledge-based economies.

Consequently, the most dominant approach is focusing on the triple helix model and its variations as it has been applied to series of situations in both developed and developing economies.

This spiral represents the engagement of three players which are university, industry and government. A better view of the interferences appears when looking at a two-dimensional representation (Figure 1) where three circles are intersecting to show the levels of interdependencies.

This illustrates how coordination can be ensured overall the system but also at the level of each component. At the level of universities, different entities can already ensure coordination to benefit from their interferences. The same applies for industry and for the government entities. These collaborations are desired to ensure the full yield

expected from the mobilization of the triple helix framework. Depending on the multiplicity of interests related to the issue at hand, international players and NGOs can be part of the overall framework. This could reduce the game to three players or can also be expanded to four, five or even more under quadruple, quintuple helix models.

To ensure the monitoring and follow-up of this process, information is highly needed especially under complex issues. This shows that different means provided under ICTs are useful for the success of the implementation of the triple helix process.

Davcev and Gómez, (2010) discuss with a series of authors, the topic of "ICT Innovations 2009." This book provides a collection of papers from the First International Conference on ICT Innovations held in September 2009, in Ohrid, Macedonia. The authors emphasize that ICT has enlarged its horizons and it is practiced under multidisciplinary contexts. This trend is recognized as introducing new challenges to theoretical and technical approaches. To the authors, the most important sets of benefits from using ICTs reside in the new ways of working made possible. To the authors, "Complexity, uncertainty and scaling issues of real world problems as well as natural phenomena in ecology, medicine and biology demanding ICT assistance create challenging application domains for artificial intelligence, decision support and intelligent systems, wireless sensor networks, pervasive and ubiquitous computing, multimedia information systems, data management systems, Internet and Web applications and services, computer networks, security and cryptography, distributed systems, GRID and cloud computing." The applications to the major gains in education and in health are clearly described in some chapters of this book.

Earlier, Sage and Rouse (1999) recognized the potential of ICTs to businesses and organizational practices. The authors refer to examples from the financial world where small changes in interest rate in one location imply large effects on stock

Figure 1. A two dimensional representation of the triple helix framework

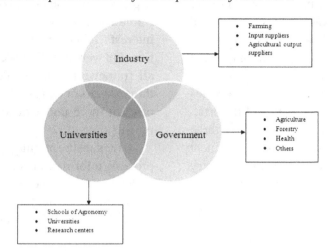

markets in other places. This information change is described by the authors as a source of changes in markets and marketing operations. It is also seen by the authors as leading to changes in managerial practices. New opportunities and challenges are generated and need to be captured by the new managerial practices. Finally, the authors consider that ICTs have created new informational systems that need to be captured by the way knowledge is managed at all levels of each economy. This chapter discusses interactions and intersections between organizations, information technology and information systems, and the ways in which the creative use of information systems changes organizational environments.

Sage (1999) has discussed the information and knowledge issues in relation to sustainable development. The author refers to the fulfillment of human needs through the simultaneous socioeconomic, technological, and environmental achievements. This framework is likely to ensure the needs for health, education, and more sustainable development. Information and knowledge technologies are important means to ensure the occurrence of this system.

As the triple helix framework applies to series of situations where there is a diversity of players over multiple resources, the above applications can also be expanded to the more general area

of interferences between knowledge and development. Shinn (2002) has already insisted on the capacity of the triple helix to deal with new production of knowledge.

APPLICATIONS OF THE TRIPLE HELIX FRAMEWORK

The above framework has been largely applied to series of countries, starting with the developed ones, series of regions and sectors worldwide.

Jensen and Tragardh (2004) critically examine the positive narrative surrounding the Triple Helix concept as a model for development in all kinds of regions. They claim that existing and problematic structural preconditions should be taken into consideration when applying the Triple Helix concept in weak regions. Empirically, they base their paper on two longitudinal case studies in Sweden, where government is trying to break the negative trends in weak regions by initiating Triple Helix-like programs. However, due to poor preconditions, such initiatives tend to fail. Thus, a negative narrative can be related about Triple Helix cooperation when applied in weak regions.

Merle (2006) analyzes the relationship between science and policy through looking at the political discourses about the use of knowledge. The findings underline the importance of knowledge utilization as useful for policy conduct and analysis.

Fogelberg and Thorpenberg (2012) recognize the importance of the players in knowledge production and diffusion and that convergence of interests of these partners is key for development. The case of Sweden is used to illustrate the potential and limits of the triple helix model. They establish that policies for regional innovation in Sweden rely on the view of different groups of actors. One recent organizational expression of this view is the development of innovation policy and development organizations known as 'Arenas.' These organizations were modeled on the Triple Helix innovation theory, which is known for promoting innovation as collaboration between industry, university, and policy. This chapter analyses the historical development of two such Arenas, which were created by public and private actors in two Swedish cities. The study used a historical case-study approach, combined with interviews with project management and project workers, to highlight the difficulties in stabilizing broad collaboration patterns. Lawler (2011) consider mainly the university, the industry, and the government as the main players in research and innovation.

Carayannis and Campbell (2012) consider that developed and developing economies alike face increased resource scarcity and competitive rivalry. In this context, science and technology appear as an essential source of competitive and sustainable advantage at national and regional levels. In the economic development context, Information and Communication Technologies (ICTs) allow for the creation of new jobs, new industry and service sector opportunities and a more skilled workforce. This is done through a smooth flow of information and enhancement of international trade, mainly advanced technologies (Cukor & McKnight, 2001). However, the key determinant of their efficacy is the quality and quantity of entrepreneurship-enabled innovation that unlocks and captures the benefits of the science enterprise in the form of private, public, or hybrid goods. Linking basic and applied research with the market, via technology transfer and commercialization mechanisms, including government–university–industry partnerships and capital investments, constitutes the essential trigger mechanism and driving force of sustainable competitive advantage and prosperity. In this volume, the authors define the terms and principles of knowledge creation, diffusion, and use, and establish a theoretical framework for their study. In particular, they focus on the "Quadruple Helix" model, through which government, academia, industry, and civil society are seen as key actors promoting a democratic approach to innovation through which strategy development and decision-making are exposed to feedback from key stakeholders, resulting in socially accountable policies and practices.

Natário, Couto, and de Almeida (2012) analyze the dynamics of the triple helix model in less favored regions, examining the role of three spheres: universities, firms, and government. They identify profiles of behavior in terms of triple helix model performance from the firm's perspective and recognize key factors for successful innovation dynamics in a less favored region of Portugal. A brief bibliographic revision regarding development of the triple helix model in the innovation process is followed by a description of the role of the helixes and the presentation of a model, after which the hypotheses are defined for testing. The methodology consists of a survey involving companies in a less favored region of Portugal and the application of multivariate statistical analysis "k-means clusters" to detect behavioral patterns in terms of performance and dynamics of the triple helix model from the firm's viewpoint. In order to verify the hypotheses, tests of multiple average differences are used to assess the unique characteristics of each cluster and the independent test of Chi-square. The results point to the existence of a positive relationship between the dynamics of the triple helix model in terms of different types and objectives to innovate. This is with regard to introducing new products as well as ecological innovation and their efforts to improve communications relative to the obstacles to innovate—explicitly, the lack of information and geographical location, the companies' innovation performance, and the level of cooperation and interaction with the university producing benefits for them in obtaining additional financial resources and prestige for the researcher, including obtaining information for the education process. In this light, Balasubramanian et al. (2009) argue about the fact that ICTs have contributed greatly to the enhancement of the university-industry partnership and technology transfer.

MacGregor, Marques-Gou, and Simon-Villar (2010) explore the readiness for the quadruple helix in 16 European innovation systems located in medium-sized cities. The role of local and regional actors who are mainly policy makers within each innovation system is emphasized. The findings indicate that the attained results are transferable to other medium and small sized cities faced with further competition and scale threats. However, Meyer and Leydes (2006) insist mainly on the power of the triple helix model.

Kaukonen and Nieminen (1999) have pioneered discussions on the science and technology system particularly. Two perspectives have been visible, one emphasizing the transitory changes in the modes of knowledge production, the other focusing on the institutional integration of the S&T system (Triple Helix). The article analyzes the development of the Finnish S&T system and policy as a national case from the point of view of the Triple Helix thesis. It concludes that both perspectives—systemic transition and integration—are essential for understanding recent changes in S&T, but do not yet cover the whole range of relevant issues. In addition, one should take into account the spatial, or international, dimension of S&T, which is crucial especially when viewed from a small country perspective. Furthermore, it is important to consider the cognitive dimension of S&T, as the socio-cognitive diversity of research fields affects their specific role in the transformation processes.

Other applications are expanded to cover diversities of economies in the developing world.

In *Theory and Practice of Triple Helix Model in Developing Countries: Issues and Challenges* by Saad (2005), the author uses practical cases and experiences from Africa, Latin America, and Asia with the examination of the best practices pursued. This book is a considered by the author as a response to the growing awareness about the needs for policy shifts from traditional technology shifts to a more sustainable approach to the role for technology and innovation in development. The book explores the triple helix system of innovation based on the dynamics of the interactive relationships between government, industry and universities in the creation, dissemination and sharing of knowledge. A major point addressed by the author is the extent to which the "triple helix" system of relationships between university, industry, and government can enhance the effectiveness of universities in developing countries as agents of innovation, industrialization, and sustainable development. Indeed, among the various strategies of the European Commission, ICT cluster is considered to be among the policy instruments that endorse development towards sustainability. (Kaivo-Oja & Stenvall, 2011).

Other authors have looked at the dynamics of the collaboration of university, industry, and government. The study maps these emergence dynamics of the knowledge base of innovations of Research and Development (R&D) by exploring the longitudinal trend within the networked research relations in Bangladesh using a triple helix model. They use data on publications, the social sciences and the arts and humanities for analysis of science indicators and the patent data with the patent success ratio as a measure of innovation within TH domains. The findings show that the network dynamics have varied considerably according to the R&D policies of the government. The collaboration patterns of co-authorship relations in the SCI publications prominently increased, with some variation, from 1996 to 2006.

Nevertheless, inter-institutional collaboration was negatively influenced by the national Science and Technology (S&T) research policies in the last 5 years due to their evaluation criteria. Finally, the findings reveal that the R&D system of Bangladesh is still undergoing a process of institutionalizing S&T and has failed to boost its research capacity for building the knowledge base of innovations by neglecting the network effects of TH dynamics. Merle (2006) has expanded the triple helix model to include social sciences. Furthermore, the triple helix approach applies also for sectors of the economy, regions, and cities. They also apply to a specific technology.

Haneul, Huang, Furong, Bodoff, Junghoun, and Young Chan (2011) analyze the agricultural innovation systems in Korea and China with comparisons from the perspective of triple helix innovation. The qualitative analysis is based on information about agricultural scientific publications from 1990 to 2010 and patent information from 1980 to 2010. By calculating transmission of uncertainty that indicates collaboration of industry, government, and university, the authors track the dynamics of the units comprising the triple helix. In addition, they analyze topics in scientific publications and patents in order to compare the areas of focus in the two countries. The findings reveal both commonalities and differences between the two countries, thus providing knowledge and insights into the agricultural sector.

Creative industries have also benefited from the application of the triple helix model. The study by Colapinto and Porlezza (2010) is one example. The authors focus on theoretical approaches to explain the current paradigm shift in innovation and knowledge production and use: the Triple Helix model (and its developments) and the systems theory. The Creative Enterprise Australia is analyzed according to the theoretical approaches shown. The chapter sheds new light on the evolving role of knowledge pointing out the overlapping relationships between all actors involved, the interpenetration of systems, and

the prominent appointment of the media as an interpretative framework of the convergence of the depicted theories.

Rao, Xian-Fe, and Piccaluga (2012) consider that the triple helix theory stresses co-evolution and interaction among governments, enterprises and universities, and is paid great attention to, by governments, universities and enterprises worldwide. The purpose of this chapter is to investigate the role that Chinese government R&D investments play in the interaction between enterprises and universities. Based on provincial panel data of Chinese universities from 2004-2010, the impact of government R&D investments on patent technology transfer activities of Chinese universities is studied by empirical analysis. More specifically, the chapter examines the impact of both Chinese government R&D funding and national R&D programs on the number and the revenue of patent technology transfer contracts. The study finds that the amount of government R&D funding and the number of 973 Programs in one region have significantly increased the number and the revenue of patent technology transfer contracts in that region. Moreover, the number of National S&T Pillar Programs, 863 Program, and National Natural Science Foundation Program are also determinants of the number of patent technology transfer contracts. This chapter studies government's role in university-enterprise patent technology transfer activities in a Chinese context. It reveals a government-dominant position to promote patent technology transfer activities in the Chinese triple helix model. It also provides a reference for decision makers in governments, industries, and universities.

Rodrigues and Melo (2012) discuss the role of the triple helix model (THM) from the view of it, being widely used as a source of inspiration for policies and programs aimed at fostering innovation. This is evolving across the range of policymaking geographical scales, as well as independently of the geographies of context that determine different framework conditions for promoting innovation. This article questions the extent to which the THM provides a solid conceptual basis for development policies, particularly at the local level. It does this by exploring the experience of a Portuguese small municipality, in which the development policy effort is not only guided by the model itself, but is also targeted at the materialization of local 'triple helices.' The authors take advantage of their direct involvement in the local policymaking exercise and confront their observations of the change dynamics evolving in the municipality with the 'endless transitions' that are at the very core of the THM.

Simon and Maquès (2012) discuss the necessary public support of the triple helix R&D collaboration in the context of Europe. For that, they emphasize the role of the fourth pillar that is the organizations that benefit from public and private sector funds. To the authors, these organizations are likely to facilitate the complex collaboration among triple helix partners. These types of units are analyzed in Holland, Spain and Sweden.

Lopez-Vega and Ramis-Pujol (2006), in their paper, discuss the Mediterranean System of Innovation (MSI) and expose the results of an interactive work with 25 different innovation delegates from northern and southern Mediterranean countries. The study uses the literature of National Systems of Innovation in order to study the different methods Mediterranean countries use to move forward their innovation capacity. The results demonstrate the most relevant enabling and blocking methods for innovation as well as proved that R&D support is to some extent changing to services and business models. Lastly, it insisted on the need of a solid well-defined innovation strategy in order to be able to improve the current capabilities.

THE CASE OF ARAB COUNTRIES

The Arab world still need further applications of the triple helix approach in order to promote sustainable inclusion of knowledge as driver and engine of economic growth. It is observed that only few studies are available about the situation and prospects of the Arab economies. Besides the one cited above and related to Saudi Arabia, there are other research papers that shed light on some features related to the knowledge economies. Kohl and Hashemi (2011) after noting the deficiencies in knowledge generation, acquisition and use in relation to development, they focus on the roles that could be played by Science Parks. The case of the UAE is largely used to underline the managerial changes that can be necessary to generate the desired direct effects and spillovers needed for development. Al Suqri (2011) focuses on Oman. Using qualitative data through email and face-to-face interviews, the author analyzes the barriers preventing users from access to knowledge and to overcome them.

In another paper, Hanafi (2011) looks at the barriers to the production of social knowledge. The author attempts to show how the university system and the system of social knowledge production influence elite formation in the Arab East (in Egypt, Syria, the Palestinian territory, Jordan, and Lebanon). The author focuses on the compartmentalization of scholarly activities, the demise of the university as a public sphere and the criteria for publication that count towards promotion. Universities have often produced compartmentalized elites inside each nation-state and they do not communicate with one another. In addition, the author discusses the publication process in these countries with either elite that publish globally but perish locally or elite that publish locally and perish globally. The article pays special attention to elite universities.

Shin, Jeung, and Yangson (2011) analyze the research productivity of Saudi academics using the triple-helix model. In the analysis, they combine domestic and international collaboration of university and industry. According to the analysis, research collaboration in Saudi Arabia which is measured by the triple-helix, is found to be uncertainty (negative t-value) while scientific productivity has been dramatically increasing since the late 2000s. The triple-helix collaboration does not quite differ between domestic collaboration and "domestic and international" collaborations. In our further analysis, we found that technological development was not based on scientific research in Saudi Arabia; rather, the technological development relies on prior technology (patent references). From that point, Saudi Arabia's current long-term strategic plan to develop a scientific base for a knowledge-based industry is well aligned to the current contexts of Saudi Arabia.

Khatib, Tsipouri, Bassiakos, and Haj-Daoud (2012) analyze knowledge, research, and innovation as of crucial importance for the competitiveness of the Palestinian economy. The authors conduct and analyze a community innovation survey on two major industrial sectors: the quarrying and stone fabrication besides the food and beverages sector. Very promising indicators and high innovative potentials are shown in both sectors. Employment, export, and revenues are clearly improved in innovative enterprises. Lack of cooperation between the industrial sector and the higher education and research and development institutions is found to be a major problem that should be tackled in order to strengthen the enterprises' ability to innovate.

Djeflat (2007) discusses the issue of the governance of territorial systems in Maghreb countries. The shift of Maghreb Countries (MC) to liberal economic systems has been going on for many years pushing the public sector to give place to the private one. Everyone knows that opening-up could not be reached with the absence of well-organized innovation systems. Due to the faced challenges and the approaching deadline of opening up of nations to the economies to the world, Maghreb authorities are more and more revolving to more decentralized means of innovation with the objective of making all the parties participate in the innovation process. In fact, three directions are being followed at the same time. The first direction consists of treating the issue of innovation at the local or territorial level, the second one deals with the involvement of higher

number of actors and third relates to adoption of a new mode of governance of this system. Those three elements make what is called the Territorial Innovation System (TIS). Djeflat (2007) discusses the interrelationships of knowledge and innovation networks at the territorial level. Throughout his study, Djeflat (2007) looks at the impact and effectiveness of the governance strategies in creating the territorial innovation system by the means of intermediate institutions. Finally, the study aims at determining the principal actors and elements of the governance reform involved in filling the innovation processes. To be able to do that, the study focused on the realization of an in-depth analysis of different case studies from various regions of the countries studied, through the gathering of a considerable amount of data and interviews. Djeflat (2007) used three criteria into consideration while running his research: the regional context, the industrial/technological sector and finally the firm dimension.

The results of the study demonstrate the fact that networking is the dominant characteristic of the TIS in the Italian case. However, the presence of a number of deficiencies cannot be denied (Corti, 2005). It was noticed that the interviewed parties have weak relationships with the other district firms. In addition, those parties do not have a co-marketing policy with the suppliers and have a general strategic policy of buying technologies. Further, only one party and its major customers have set up a common R&D program of new products and only one party controls the raw materials in an individual way, instead of using a network method. Besides, only one firm is considered as the corporate of the district, and thus is regarded as the network leader. Thus, a percentage of 5-6% of the sales of the entire district results from one party. Concerning the role of intermediate institutions, it was demonstrated throughout the study, that those institutions do not interact sufficiently with the local universities. The local administrations are incapable of supporting the district firms about logistic and infrastructural problem solving. According to Djeflat (2007),

"The corporate governance policy explains to a large extent the weaknesses of the trading relationships inside the district between the actor leader and the other firms not shared." Concerning the Maghreb Countries, it was shown that local productive systems do not provide any foundation for TIS. For instance, in Morocco, they cannot be even regarded as local productive systems. To Djeflat (2007) "In Morocco, they cannot be even be considered as local productive systems even if their development led to a real transformation of their territory through employment creation and the upgrading of the productive capacity of several local units to become amongst the most efficient agricultural units in the country."

Oukil's (2011) study discusses the issue of technology-based entrepreneurship with the specific case of the Middle East and North Africa region. It focuses on the importance of technology-based entrepreneurship as a way to achieve industrialization and technological progress. This study first starts by discussing the context of entrepreneurship in MENA countries. Then, it moves to highlight the particular engagement of the private sector in rushing the drive toward the technological entrepreneurship in the region. The study is based on a scheme realized by the Organization for Economic Cooperation and Development (OECD) that ranks industries depending on their degree complexity and knowledge intensity. The study uses secondary data drawn from the business website Bloomberg.com. The analysis of the results demonstrates the increasing interest of MENA countries in both entrepreneurship and technological developments. However, a lack of the needed educational measures is noticed. To cope with this situation, decision makers are making considerable efforts in order to boost both the public and private sector to make innovation initiative and to place an appropriate focus on entrepreneurship learning for all.

Many studies demonstrate the positive impact of technology and innovation including scientific, technological, and organizational knowledge on the enhancement of the needed productivity supporting progress and competitiveness (Freeman, 1991; Koster, 2008; Morrison, 2006; Solow, 1956; Tejinder, 2010). In fact, the move from underdevelopment to industry-based development requires both technological progress and innovation. Countries of the MENA region have a large variety of possibilities in order to enhance their technological progress, either through importing foreign technology, or through the development of local technologies.

After conducting the study, the results show that the late emergence of entrepreneurship in Arab countries is explained by two set of factors that can be divided to objective factors and subjective ones. The objective factors comprise the pre-entry flaws, the unstable position of entrants, lack of survival tools, and the lack of knowledge on the steps and processes on how to exit. Concerning the subjective factors, they do include conservatism, culture, and education. Moreover, from the surveys conducted in the study on some Arab countries, it was found that younger generations with sciences and engineering degrees and higher levels of local or foreign educations are more and more motivated to start new businesses and explore the entrepreneurial opportunities. The results show that 'in a survey of 1.4 million Arab youth, 94% surveyed were interested in working for themselves. In Kuwait, 28% of youth are planning on starting their own business in the next 12 months, and 32% in Saudi Arabia' (Aramex.com).

According to Faris, El Hawari, and Ihsan (2009), the level of technology is now among the indicators of progress and living standards. In the case of MENA countries, the figures indicate that an increasing number of private businesses invest heavily in advanced high tech industries (Oukil, 2011). Table 1 from Oukil (2011) shows the efforts of both public and private sectors in the industrialization process, showing the evolution of MENA countries in the "technopreneurship" development that includes the knowledge intensive industries sector.

In addition, there is significant evidence showing that countries of the MENA region have reached considerable progresses in terms of industrialization and growth processes. It is also proved that efforts pertaining to this subject were not only made in the public sector, but in the private sector as well. Another determinant of success in starting businesses is certainly education (Naude, Gries, Wood, & Meintjies, 2008). One disparity between Arab countries and other ones that succeeded in reaching higher growth rates is the specific attention given to entrepreneurship and technopreneurship education. Developed countries focus on formally institutionalized programs on entrepreneurship. Those programs are offered at different levels and time periods. Besides, developed countries offer some programs "Non-degree training" to individuals with weak educational backgrounds.

A good listing of the most important institutions and agencies in the MENA region that promote entrepreneurship can be found in Oukil (2011).

Entrepreneurship education in the MENA region is still at an early phase, and only very few universities offer courses on this subject. Even if those courses are kind of obligatory in some business schools in some countries such as Oman, Jordan, and the United Arab of Emirates, the schools of science and engineering do not benefit from this opportunity of learning about the entrepreneurial skills. Courses where students learn how to raise capital, innovation processes, protect intellectual property and act as entrepreneurs should be taught to all students, regardless of their field of study.

The international, national, and regional efforts for the effective promotion of a knowledge economy that is based on functional relationships between series of players in the related areas appear up to now, to be not fully successful in bridging the gap between these countries and the rest of

the world. The Gulf countries appear to be more advanced than the others but major investments are still needed to cope with the requirements of the triple helix framework. Table 1 shows the main players to be considered in the promotion of R&D in Arab countries.

The hosting of an academy of sciences is another indication of how the above players can ensure the attainment of further progress towards R&D. The situation in Arab countries (Table 2) shows that some countries have had academies for a long time.

It can be observed from the above that Arab countries have institutions that are either limited in number (Algeria, Egypt, Lebanon) or exist under the need of further coordination (Morocco, Libya, Kuwait). Some of these institutions have existed for a long time. Assumptions about limited institutional efficiency for the promotion of research are likely to be formulated.

As said in the UNESCO 2010 report, research is shown to be linked to series of bureaucracies mainly related to the higher education. The report shows that, in eight Arab countries, the ministries of higher education and scientific research are responsible for R&D. In another five countries, councils and government academies assume this role. This function falls to universities and research centers in four Arab countries, to ministries of education in three and to the ministry of planning in one. Only seven Arab countries or territories out of 22 have a national academy of sciences or play host to a supranational academy. This is an astounding fact, as academies of sciences, being strong advocates of science and impartial advisory bodies have been at the vanguard of scientific endeavor in advanced countries such as the USA, UK, and France for centuries. They are also part of the landscape in economically emerging economies such as Brazil, China, India, Malaysia, and Mexico.

Research and development in the Arab world has also been benefiting from initiatives developed

Table 1. Government bodies responsible for R&D policies and co-ordination in the Arab world, 2006 (source: UNESCO Report, 2010)

Algeria: *Ministry of Higher Education and Scientific Research*
Bahrain: *Centre for Studies and Research*
Egypt: *Ministry of State for Scientific Research*
Iraq: *Ministry of Higher Education and Scientific Research*
Jordan: *Ministry of Higher Education and Scientific Research and Higher Council for Science and Technology*
Kuwait: *Kuwait Foundation for the Advancement of Sciences, Institute for Scientific Research And University/Research Center*
Lebanon: *National Council for Scientific Research*
Libya: *Higher Education and Research Secretary, Jamahiriya General Planning Council and National Authority for Scientific Research*
Mauritania: *Ministry of National Education*
Morocco: *Hassan II Academy of Sciences and Technologies, Ministry of National Education, Higher Education, Staff-Training and Scientific Research, Permanent "Interministrial" Commission of Scientific Research and Technological Development, National Centre for Scientific and Technical Research, Coordination Council of Higher Education and Institutions outside Universities*
Oman: *Research Council*
Palestine: *Ministry of Higher Education, Autonomous R&D Unit at Ministry of Planning Territories*
Qatar: *Secretariat General, Council of Ministers*
Saudi Arabia: *King Abdul Aziz City for Science and Technology*
Sudan: *Ministry of Education and Scientific Research*
Syria: *Higher Council for Sciences and Ministry of Higher Education*
Tunisia: *Ministry of Higher Education, Research and Technology*
UAE: *University of United Arab Emirates and Emirates Ministry of Agriculture*
Yemen: *Ministry of Higher Education and Scientific Research*

with international organizations. Some of these initiatives are discussed below under series of initiatives for the region but also under specific country projects. These are discussed under the following headings.

The NECTAR Initiative

Launched by UNESCO's Regional Bureau for Science in the Arab States in Cairo (Egypt) in June 2011, the Network for the Expansion of Converging Technologies in the Arab Region (NECTAR) is in charge of monitoring that Arab countries be able to embrace the knowledge economy and sustainable development through strengthening their capacity for innovation.

The UNESCO Science Report (2010) has placed emphasis on the fact that university research in the Arab world is only academic, even though higher education is considered as engine for discovery and innovation. Innovation is further hindered by the weak linkages between academia

and industry. In addition, universities are not focusing on the features of the knowledge economy. This report does also show the gap between the skills needed by businesses and those produced by Arab universities.

The development of partnerships between academia and industry with emphasis on new technologies is the main goal of NECTAR. Plans are consequently set to reorient academia towards problem solving and removal of barriers between disciplines. These constraints are identified to be limiting innovation in the Arab world. For instance, Nanotechnology is at the crossroads of a large range of disciplines (biology, chemistry and physics, materials science, engineering and computer science). It is one of the fastest-growing fields in science, with applications ranging from health care to microelectronics, renewable energies, and water purification, but nanotechnology research is still limited in the Arab world.

Nectar has now three centers of excellence. The first centre is affiliated with the Science and

Table 2. Arab countries hosting a national or supranational academy of science, 2009

Egypt: *Academy of Scientific Research and Technology founded in 1948 and Egyptian Academy of Sciences founded in 1944*   **Iraq**: *Iraq Academy of Sciences founded in 1944*   **Jordan**: *Islamic World Academy of Sciences founded in 1986*   **Lebanon**: *Arab Academy of Sciences 2002*   **Morocco**: *Hassan II Academy of Sciences and Technology founded in 2006*   **Palestine**: *Palestine Academy of Sciences and Autonomous Technology 1997*   **Sudan**: *Sudan National Academy of Science 2006*

Technology Center for Excellence of the Egyptian Ministry of Military Production. The second is within the Faculty of Engineering at Khartoum University and the third is situated in the "École normale supérieure de l'enseignement technique" in Rabat (Morocco), part of Mohamed V–Souissi University. Other centers of excellence are planned in Bahrain, Iraq, Jordan, and Syria plan to establish their own units.

The UNISPAR Initiative

Since 2002, UNISPAR has focused on capacity-building and technical assistance in the governance of science and technology parks.

The expected results from the above network are supported by the promotion of science parks that aim first at developing stronger partnerships and linkages between universities and industry. This includes small and medium-sized enterprises for promoting innovation, engineering education, North-South cooperation with gender mainstreaming, maintenance, and related areas for technological development. The second aim is to enhance human resources, including the training of engineers in the transfer of research results, the maintenance of equipment and related areas, and the development of stronger networking of technology for development, sponsored by industry with UNESCO support.

These contributions of UNESCO are supported by collaboration with the international professional organizations such as the World Technopolis Association (WTA) and the International Association of Science Parks (IASP).

This is now attracting international development agencies like the Korean International Co-operation Agency (KOICA). In September 2006, UNESCO, KOICA and Daejeon Metropolitan City signed a five-year agreement to help developing countries manage science and technology parks in such areas as biotechnology and ICTs. As part of this agreement, international training workshops are being organized annually for park managers. The project is also developing regional networks.

Special Country Supports

UNESCO and Iraq launched an initiative to help rebuild the country's intellectual infrastructure and begin the transition towards a knowledge-based economy via the development of a Science, Technology, and Innovation (STI) policy.

Once an engine of innovation in the Middle East, Iraq is dependent on imported technology today, after years of isolation and conflict. There are modest signs of recovery, however. Iraqi scientists authored 55 scientific papers in 2000 but 184 in 2008, according to the UNESCO Science Report 2010, mostly in clinical medicine. The share of papers authored within international collaboration also grew, from 27% to 45%.

The major tasks will be to pilot a comprehensive assessment of research infrastructure across the country. The task force will be composed of national and international government experts, scientists, academics, and entrepreneurs. They will articulate policy priorities over a 12-month period within a consultation intended to foster a national dialogue on ways in which science, technology, and innovation can spur economic growth and improve the quality of life in Iraq. They will examine mechanisms for encouraging technology transfer and private sector engagement, identifying the needs of researchers and innovators, channeling funding in line with regional and local priorities. Once policy priorities are identified, the program will provide a comprehensive national STI policy.

Government priorities for research over the next four years have already been outlined in the Ministry of Planning's five-year plan. These include capacity-building, information technology, agriculture, environment, and water resources besides renewable energy.

These above initiatives and projects need to be leading to promising R&D policies given the large arrays of needs expressed in the Arab economies. An analytical review of different related publications is introduced to show how these steps and experiences have been analyzed by different types of authors.

Government Policies under the Triple Helix Approach

Chouchane, Mamtani, Al-Thani, Al-Thani, Ameduri, and Sheikh (2011), in their paper, argue about the fact that medical technology has known lately significant advances and the new discoveries in biomedical research have the needed potential to enhance human health in a considerable way. Due to this new trend, many economies in the Arab Gulf regions, namely Qatar are placing huge investments on establishing new centers in biomedical research. However, many challenges are faced when it comes to the establishment of these new kind of centers dedicated to biomedical research. In fact, as one of the major challenges, one could mention the low profile of medical centers and their insignificant endowments in the region. To overcome these constraints, Qatar Foundation for Education, Science, and Community Development has been able to attract six branch campuses of American centers of higher

education in Qatar. One important example of those growing institutions is the Weill Cornell Medical College in Qatar of Cornell University, which is the first and only medical institution in Qatar. The discoveries allowed by this program have the potential to influence public policy in a positive way and thus reduce premature mortality.

The role of universities has long been recognized as main suppliers of basic scientific knowledge for industrial innovation throughout their research and related activities. Universities are usually seen as one of the major contributors to the wealth creation and economic development (Dooley & Kirk, 2007). In the Tunisian context, higher education and scientific research represent pillars to the knowledge-based society. Indeed, the Tunisian tertiary education faces challenges of cooperating positively with the economic, social, and technological changes and trends (Eleventh Tunisian Development Plan, 2011). Bouhamed, Bouraoui, and Chaabouni (2010), in their paper, explore the different initiatives taken by the Tunisian University so that it can be able to enhance socio-economic development. This study explores two approaches. These are a triple helix model focusing on the role of the university in knowledge-based economies and the development of the entrepreneurial university. This latter three has three responsibilities: teaching, research, and service through the different entrepreneurial initiatives. From this perspective, universities contribute positively to the nation's economic development throughout the creation of scientific centers, business incubation and advanced training programs that enhance the cross-institutional mobility of both people and businesses (Gunasekara, 2006). The study also emphasized the third role of the university as a main contributor to the development but not from the perspective of the triple helix model. Instead, it focuses on the placing a strong focus on the teaching and research missions. As a result, this mechanism allows for a stronger regional focus on student recruitment and needs, shaping regional networking, entrepreneurial initiatives, and finally, regionally targeted teaching and research (Gunasekara, 2006). The empirical study is mainly based on both qualitative and quantitative data collected about the Sfax University (DU). The analysis of the findings demonstrate the fact that some knowledge capitalization and hybrid, boundary-spanning mechanisms are developed by the Tunisian government for the sake of enhancing SU capacity in social economic development throughout, encouraging the mobility of researchers between research parks and production firms, creation of Sfax technopark that enhances a suitable environment for the transfer and sharing of technological knowledge, and the establishment of business incubators.

The important role of knowledge is now advocated by a various number of academics, business, and policy sources. In fact, the knowledge-based economy is characterized by its continuous need for learning in order to allow organizations to renovate and cope with the current competition (Lundvall, 2002).

The main objective of the authors, Bouraoui, Bouhamed, and Chaabouni (2010) behind this study is to investigate the inter-organizational learning implemented by different Tunisian pharmaceutical companies throughout various cooperative agreements including: north-south, south-north, and firm-university cooperation. The main reason behind this study is to explore the relevance of the pharmaceutical company alliance capability in managing its portfolio of cooperation by considering the particularity of each agreement. The empirical research is based upon a Tunisian pharmaceutical company (AL-PHA). The results obtained show and demonstrate the degree to which inter-organizational learning differs among companies and university partners. The findings demonstrate the fact that collaboration with pharmaceutical companies represents a main enabler of the transfer of knowledge required for the production of medicines. It is also proved that the collaboration with universities are short-term relations that aspire to attain some scientific

activities needed by ALPHA caused by the shortage in some technological resources.

Oukil's (2011) paper about the technology-based entrepreneurship deals with the case of the Middle East and North African region (MENA). In this study, the author stresses the importance of technology-based entrepreneurship as a means to achieve industrialization and technological development. First, the paper describes the environment of entrepreneurship in the developing economies of the MENA region. The paper uses the method developed by the Organization for Economic Cooperation and Development (OECD) of ranking economies depending on their degree of complexity and on the power of their knowledge. In fact, the author, throughout this paper, proposes another approach of dealing with the issue of technological development. The empirical research is based on secondary data gathered from the business website Bloomberg. The findings demonstrate that entrepreneurship and technological advancements is the subject of a growing attention in the MENA regions. However, the supportive educational measures needed for the latter are either missing or weak. The support of this idea is the fact that the private sector is as active as the public sector when it comes to the processes relative to the industrialization and technological development.

Arab countries are currently struggling to incorporate the international business and close the gaps with the rest of the world in the quickest way. The main problem behind this issue is that the policies pertaining to Arab countries lack many important features. In order to gain a competitive advantage and reach growth and competitiveness, huge investments and business creation are needed. Many scholars argue about the strong necessity of changes in management and government along with the improvement of the business culture through education. Said Oukil (2011) centers his study on the case of Arab countries, using secondary data and relevant academic researches. The results of his research show that many challenges are facing the Arab countries that should be encountered to be able to move forward.

The UN Arab Human Development Reports included a number of indicators that demonstrate the slow progress towards the development of knowledge economies in the Arab region and stressed the role of the intensification of knowledge acquisition as a main key to success. David McGlennon's paper discusses the major developments in research, and innovation performance in the GCC since the early 2000s, studies the different trends in higher education, with the specific cases of Qatar and the United Arab Emirates (UAE), and finally suggested ways of improving the current situation. Indeed, the latest international indicators relative to research capacity did not show any progress for GCC countries. The appropriate example revealing this situation is the fact that the 2006 World Bank Knowledge Economy Index demonstrated that all GCC countries are rated under the world average for the indices relative to both innovation and education, with the only exception of the UAE and Bahrain.

The role of Business and Technology incubators is of a major importance in the development of innovation and new business development structures of national economies. These incubators differ in the way they function and influence national development programs depending on the region.

Hedner, Almubaraki, Busler, and Abouzeedan (2011), in their study, investigated the different roles of business and technology incubators in two different regions of the world, particularly, the Gulf Cooperation Council (GCC) countries, and Kuwait, Bahrain, Qatar, UAE and Saudi Arabia and some countries of Europe. The study also discussed the existing management methods that enable the functioning of daily activities of these institutes. Finally, the paper discussed the important contribution of these business and technology incubators in the nation's regional growth.

The need for different technologies enabling the production of energy, materials, products and services at the local level, is growing progressively with the economic diversification of GCC countries. Many conditions including the geographical location, demographic trends, health and education challenges and rapid expansion and diversification of GCC countries represent significant socio-economic basis for national science and technologies policies and rules necessary for the development of national research, development and innovation capacity and making sure they cope with the local needs. According to Wilson and O'Sullivan, (2011), the adoption of diversification will allow the youth of the GCC region to have a diversified set of employment options. To be able to do that, a number of initiatives need to be taken including an adequate investment in research and development, employment of highly skilled labor, financial support, appropriate rules and legislation, the ease of access to both scientific and technological information, and finally the implementation of a socio-economic strategy to make sure that the results of research and development cover the different sector of the diversifying nations.

CONCLUSION

The objective of this chapter is to show how interdependencies between education, research, and businesses could be considered under the triple helix framework. After the introduction of the model and its applications with a focus on Arab Countries, the discussion is pursued to underline the potential of this model. Interferences between series of players are among the features that are tackled with focus on knowledge features. Research and development appear to be the main features discussed in this presentation. However, the framework is suggested to provide means for coordination between the players identified for the coordination of health, education, and socio-economic development. Within this framework, a large demand for ICT is expected to be developed also as means of coordination. This is likely to happen in all sectors including education, health, and economic activities. As the number of players grows, the need for coordination and for the help of ICT increases.

As developed above, business networks can also benefit from the triple helix framework especially with the development of internationalization, global markets, and different forms of localizations. However, local development can also gain further, as public and private players from different spheres need to coordinate their actions to support the objectives of achieving higher outcomes to the population.

The applications of the triple helix framework have been showing progress in different countries but the implementation of real schemes in relation to the results shown is still underway. It is expected though that developing economies are more advanced in this area. Developing countries are still proceeding with this scheme. Arab countries are also in this case.

Depending on the sector of the economy, the interdependencies are often identified and lead to participatory approaches where all the players are not often on the same footing of knowledge. ICT are often used to bridge the gaps and ensure better contributions to the achievement of these advancements. However, more can be done to enhance the interactions between different players.

REFERENCES

Al-Suqri, M. N., & Lillard, L. L. (2011). Barriers to effective information seeking of social scientists in developing countries: The case of Sultan Qaboos University in Oman. *Journal of Library and Information Science*, *1*(2), 86–99.

Aramex.com. (2010). *A publicly listed company trading on the Dubai stock exchange (DFM) and was founded by Fadi Ghandour in 1982*. Retrieved February 24, 2010, from http://www.aramex.com/news/item.aspx?id=b72adf8f-8e65-4966-b2a6-3ed841d90f1d

Balasubramanian, K., Clarke-Okah, W., Daniel, J., Ferreira, F., Kanwar, A., & Kwan, A. (2009). *ICTs for higher education: Background paper from the commonwealth of learning*. Paper presented at the UNESCO World Conference on Higher Education. New York, NY.

Bouhamed, A., Bouraoui, N., & Chaabouni, J. (2010). *The role of Tunisian universities in regional development*. Paper presented at the Triple Helix Conference 2010. Madrid, Spain.

Bouraoui, N., Bouhamed, A., & Chaabouni, J. (2010). *Alliance capability in Tunisian pharmaceutical industry*. Paper presented at the VIII Triple Helix International Conference on University, Industry and Government Linkages. Madrid, Spain.

Carayannis, E. G., & Campbell, D. F. J. (2012). Mode3 knowledge production in quadruple helix innovation systems: Twenty-first-century democracy, innovation, and entrepreneurship for development. *Springer Briefs in Business*, *7*, 1–63.

Carayol, N. (2003). Objectives, agreements and matching in science-industry collaborations: Reassembling the pieces of the puzzle. *Research Policy*, *32*, 887–908. doi:10.1016/S0048-7333(02)00108-7

Chouchane, L., Mamtani, R., Al-Thani, M. H., Al-Thani, A. A., Ameduri, M., & Sheikh, J. I. (2011). Medical education and research environment in Qatar: A new epoch for translational research in the Middle East. *Journal of Translational Medicine*, *9*(16).

Colapinto, C., & Porlezza, C. (2011). Innovation in creative industries: From the quadruple helix model to the systems theory. *Journal of the Knowledge Economy, 1*(3), 173–190.

Corti, E. (2005). *Intermediate institutions for the growth of governance processes in the Mediterranean partner countries*. The Ingomed Study. Maghtech/ISSM.

Cukor, P., & McKnight, L. W. (2001). *Knowledge, networks, and development*. Working Paper 4193-01. Cambridge, MA: MIT Press.

Davcev, D., & Gómez, J. M. (2010). *ICT innovations 2009*. Berlin, Germany: Springer. doi:10.1007/978-3-642-10781-8

Djeflat, A. (2007). *The governance of territorial innovation systems (TIS) and the role of intermediate institutions in Maghreb countries*. Paper presented at GLOBELICS-RUSSIA-2007: Regional and National Innovation Systems for Development, Competitiveness and Welfare: The Government-Academia-Industry Partnership (theory, problems, practice and prospects). Saratov, Russia.

Etzkowitz, H., & Zhou, C. (2006). Triple helix twins: Innovation and sustainability. *Science & Public Policy, 33*(1), 77–83. doi:10.3152/147154306781779154

Faris, W. F., El Hawari, Y., & Ihsan, S. I. (2009). Technology transfer: Challenges and perspective Arab world as a case study. *International Journal of Arab Culture. Management and Sustainable Development, 1*(2), 195–207.

Fogelberg, H., & Thorpenberg, S. (2012). Regional innovation policy and public-private partnership: The case of triple helix arenas in western Sweden. *Science and Public Policy. Science & Public Policy, 39*(3), 347–356. doi:10.1093/scipol/scs023

Freeman, C. (1991). Networks of innovators: A synthesis of research issues. *Research Policy, 20*(5), 499–514. doi:10.1016/0048-7333(91)90072-X

Gunasekara, C. (2006). Reframing the role of universities in the development of regional innovation systems. *The Journal of Technology Transfer, 31*(1), 101–113. doi:10.1007/s10961-005-5016-4

Hanafi, S. (2011). University systems in the Arab east: Publish globally and perish locally vs publish locally and perish globally. *Current Sociology, 59*(3), 291–309. doi:10.1177/0011392111400782

Haneul, K., Huang, M., Furong, J., Bodoff, D., Junghoun, M., & Young Chan, C. (2011). Triple helix in the agricultural sector of northeast Asian countries: A comparative study between Korea and China. *Scientometrics, 90*(1), 101–120.

Hedner, T., Almubaraki, H., Busler, M., & Abouzeedan, A. (2011). Business and technology incubators and their role in Europe in comparison to the GCC countries: An analysis of current affairs. In *Innovation and Entrepreneurship*. Gothenburg, Sweden: University of Gothenburg.

Jensen, C., & Tragardh, B. (2004). Narrating the triple helix concept in weak regions: Lessons from Sweden. *International Journal of Technology Management, 27*(5), 513–530. doi:10.1504/IJTM.2004.004287

Kaivo-oja, J., & Jari Stenvall, J. (2011). The cloud university platform: New challenges of the co-operation in the European university system. *European Integration Studies, 5*, 39–44.

Kaukonen, E., & Nieminen, M. (1999). Modeling the triple helix from a small country perspective: The case of Finland. *The Journal of Technology Transfer, 24*(2/3), 173–183. doi:10.1023/A:1007851321496

Khatib, I. A., Tsipouri, L., Bassiakos, Y., & Haj-Daoud, A. (2012, February). Innovation in Palestinian industries: A necessity for surviving the abnormal. *Journal of the Knowledge Economy*, 63-78.

Kohl, H., & Al Hashemi, H. (2011). Science parks as main driver for the development of national innovations systems in resources-driven economies! The importance of intellectual capital management for sustainable manufacturing: Advances in sustainable manufacturing. In *Proceedings of the 8th Global Conference on Sustainable Manufacturing, GCSM 2010*. Berlin, Germany: Springer.

Koster, S. (2008). Entrepreneurship and economic development in a developing country. *Journal of Entrepreneurship*, *17*(2), 137–173. doi:10.1177/097135570801700202

Lawler, C. (2011). The capitalization of knowledge: A triple helix of university-industry government. *Studies in Higher Education*. Retrieved from http://www.tandfonline.com/loi/cshe20

Leydesdorff, L. (2012). The triple helix, quadruple helix and …an n-tuple of helices: Explanatory models for analyzing the knowledge-based economy? *Journal of the Knowledge Economy*, *3*(1), 25–35. doi:10.1007/s13132-011-0049-4

Lopez-Vega, H., & Ramis-Pujol, J. (2006). Connecting the Mediterranean system of innovation: A functional perspective. *EuroMed Journal of Business*, *6*(1), 46–62. doi:10.1108/14502191111130307

Lundvall, B.-A. (2002). *Innovation, growth and social cohesion: The Danish model*. London, UK: Edward Elgar Publishers.

MacGregor, S. P., Marques-Gou, P., & Simon-Villar, A. (2010). Gauging readiness for the quadruple helix: A study of 16 European organizations. *Journal of the Knowledge Economy*, *33*(1), 77–83.

McGlennon, D. (2006). *Building research capacity in the gulf cooperation council countries: Strategy, funding and engagement*. Paper presented at Le Colloque Mondial du Forum de l'UNESCO sur l'Enseignement Supérieur, la Recherche et la Connaissance. Paris, France.

Merle, J. (2006). Utilization of social science knowledge in science policy: Systems of innovation, triple helix and VINNOVA. *Social Sciences Information. Information Sur les Sciences Sociales*, *45*(3), 431–462. doi:10.1177/0539018406066535

Meyer, M., & Leydes, L. (2006). Triple helix indicators of knowledge-based innovation systems. *Research Policy*, *35*(10), 1441–1449. doi:10.1016/j.respol.2006.09.016

Morrison, J. (2006). *International business environment: Global and local marketplaces in a changing world*. New York, NY: Palgrave MacMillan.

Naude, W., Gries, T., Wood, E., & Meintjies, A. (2008). Regional determinants of entrepreneurial start-ups in a developing country. *Entrepreneurship & Regional Development*, *20*(2), 111–124. doi:10.1080/08985620701631498

Oukil, M. S. (2011). A development perspective of technology-based entrepreneurship in the Middle East and North Africa. *Annuals of Innovation & Entrepreneurship, 2*(6000).

Rao, K., Xian-fe, M., & Piccaluga, A. (2012). The impact of government R&D investments on patent technology transfer activities of Chinese universities: From the perspective of triple helix theory. *Journal of Knowledge-based Innovation in China*, *4*(1), 4–17. doi:10.1108/17561411211208730

Rodrigues, C., & Melo, A. (2012). The triple helix model as an instrument of local response to the economic crisis. *European Planning Studies*. doi:10.1080/09654313.2012.709063

Saad, M., & Zawdie, G. (2005). From technology transfer to the emergence of a triple helix culture: The experience of Algeria in innovation and technological capability development. *Technology Analysis and Strategic Management*, *17*(1), 89–103. doi:10.1080/09537320500044750

Sage, A. P. (1999). Sustainable development: Issues in information, knowledge, and systems management. *Information Knowledge Systems Management*, *1*(3/4), 185–224.

Sage, A. P., & Rouse, W. (1999). Information systems frontiers in knowledge management. *Business and Economics. Information Systems Frontiers*, *1*(3), 205–219. doi:10.1023/A:1010046210832

Shin, J. C., Jeung, L., & Yangson, K. (2011). Knowledge-based innovation and collaboration: A triple-helix approach in Saudi Arabia. *Scientometrics*, *90*(1), 311–326. doi:10.1007/s11192-011-0518-3

Shinn, T. (2002). The triple helix and new production of knowledge: Prepackaged thinking on science and technology. *Social Studies of Science*, *32*(4), 599–614.

Simon, A., & Marquès, P. (2012). Public policy support to triple helix R&D collaborations: A European model for fourth pillar organizations. *Innovation, Technology, and Knowledge Management*, 79-93.

Solow, R. (1956). A contribution to the theory of economic growth. *The Quarterly Journal of Economics*, *70*(1), 65–94. doi:10.2307/1884513

Tejinder, S. (2010). Role of innovation in growth of countries: Perspectives of innovations. *Economics and Business*, *4*(1), 15–17.

Viale, R., & Etzkowitz, H. (2005). *Third academic revolution: Polyvalent knowledge: The "DNA" of the triple helix*. Paper presented at the 5th Triple Helix Conference-The Capitalization of…. New York, NY.

Wilson, K., & O'Sullivan, E. (2011). *Shaping the gulf national innovation systems*. Paper presented at the Gulf Research Meeting 2011. Cambridge, UK.

Chapter 10

Socioeconomic Reforms, Human Development, and the Millennium Development Goals with ICTs for Coordination

ABSTRACT

The Millennium Development Goals (MDGs) is an international effort engaging all countries and mainly the developing ones towards the reduction of health, education, and other deficits by 2015. Information and Communication Technologies (ICTs) have contributed to this global undertaking through the creation of further coordination, evaluation, and monitoring. Their roles can be expanded to better coordinate local and national actions with the overall international efforts. Based mainly on previous findings from available literature, the present chapter illustrates how ICTs have been promoted to ensure these coordination functions.

INTRODUCTION

The results attained in the previous chapters show clearly the extent and magnitude of the levels of interdependencies between different series of socio-economic variables at both regional and country levels. This strengthens the validity of the multidimensional approach to poverty and to wealth as supported by the empirical analyses conducted using a series of variables pertaining to economic, social and other dimensions. The interdependencies assessed within this framework

show also that further and meaningful gains can be implicitly expected from the existence and from the consideration of these relationships. Economic and social policies that have been pursued in different developing regions and in each of the countries can therefore benefit from more integration and coordination at local, national, regional and international levels. Major reforms have been undertaken to cover economic, education and health policies besides the further move in democratization in different regions. However, these reforms have not addressed the depth of

DOI: 10.4018/978-1-4666-3643-9.ch010

integration and further coordination among different public organizations and institutions in the economic and social spheres and sectors. Even the development of non-governmental agencies and the inclusion of private sectors in social policies do still appear to be sector specific and is not all the time fully contributing to the transversal nature of the policies that are needed by the populations. While transversal and interdependent needs are easily understood and well perceived by every individual, especially in situation of poverty, these perceptions and signs of the necessary gains from interdependencies are not expressed at the global and macroeconomic levels. Besides that, there are still missing factors and needs that are not identified by individuals that are in situation of vulnerability and poverty. These missing signals and still hidden components, lead to socio-economic policies that suffer from imperfections and inefficiencies with regard to the achievement of social goals focusing on poverty alleviation. Social policies and related poverty programs have been most of the time treated as another sector that compete with the other traditional public sectors. Coordination with other economic and social players (NGOs) can also be conducted within this type of framework increasing thus the likely gains that can be attained from issuing and strengthening transversal policies.

With the amount and the quality of social and economic investigations related to interdependencies among different sectors in different economies and with the specific focuses on the roles of education and health, a large body of knowledge has been accumulated with most of the outcomes of this literature having been reviewed. As a consequence of these accumulations, integrated international policies have been promoted and have led to the Millennium Development Goals (MDGs). These goals were set on the basis of multidisciplinary approach of poverty as it was conceived at that time from a macroeconomic perspective with the prospect of producing homogeneous and internationally comparable monitoring systems.

However, poverty has been occurring under several dimensions that have not been all the time identified as further missing components still have to be revealed. These deficits in both the limitations of the macroeconomic frameworks and the means to pursue measurements are likely to be among the factors that have limited the attainment of some goals in some countries. The further missing dimensions of poverty may also have had negative impacts on the attainment of the objectives. Further research is then needed to overcome the difficulties of not achieving partially or totally the planned goals. However, the MDG policies constitute a framework that embodies higher level of integration and coordination of policies that account not only for income poverty but also for health, education, and other components.

Human development policies are sets of strategic and practical means devoted at the level of each country and region to the assessment of the progress made in monitoring social issues that include poverty and other social deficits. The national programs and strategies need further coordination and integration in order to capture and achieve realistic results.

However, few countries are pursuing localized policies and programs that are globally coordinated at the national and international levels. The multiplicity of players including the role of NGOs besides the involvement of the private and public sectors have often led to inefficiencies.

There are two major inter-related levels at which economic and social policies accounting for interdependencies between health, education, and economic performance are promoted. The first level is international and is led by organizations such as United Nations, World Bank and others. The second level is directly related to the country with and without localized actions. In the context of this work, the first level has been playing a leading role in promoting national programs that have been focusing on interdependencies. The Millennium Development Goals (MDG) and the Human Development Programs are the most important frameworks that have been developed during the last years and that are still benefiting from further improvements (United Nations, 2003).

The major question addressed in this chapter is related to the link between ICTs and the MDGs. Otherwise, how ICTs can better help coordinate the eight goals of the MDGs at different levels to ensure major attainments by 2015?

After a brief discussion of the MDGs, the focus is placed on ICTs and MDGs at different levels.

The eight Millennium Development Goals (MDGs) are interdependent objectives that were set in 1990 by most governments under the leadership of the United Nations. Most goals are expected to be attained by 2015. Each goal is translated into targets to ensure the monitoring and evaluation of the achievements using 1990 as a reference year.

Developing countries have been showing variations in the levels of achievements of MDGs. Large variations across economies and within the same country have been observed. The persistence of urban-rural disparities besides gender differences do still exist. Studies report that the relative poor performance in achieving the goals can be directly related to the low economic growth observed throughout the world regions during 1990-2011.

LITERATURE REVIEW

Several authors have attempted to analyze the role of Information and Communication Technologies (ICTs) in relation to the attainment of the Millennium Development Goals (MDGs), globally, in developing economies and in some regions of the World. The number of contributions has been increasing since 2003. The international meetings besides the region forums devoted to the progress towards MDGs have often accelerated the rate of questioning of ICTs in relation to MDGs. The papers have been considering ICTs in general but specific insights have been placed also on the roles of mobile technologies and Internet in the achievement of the MDGs. While some pa-

pers focused on the overall MDGs, others have analyzed particular goals such as those related to health and education.

For instance, the question analyzed by Ngwenyama, Andoh-Baidoo, Bollou, and Morawczynki (2006) focuses on the relationship between ICTs, Health, Education and Development with applications to five Western African Countries over the period 1997-2003. The results show that ICTs do provide a key solution to achieve development but will not lead to the attainment of the full goals unless investments are pursued in health and education. These results indicate that the infrastructure for education and health care and ICTs infrastructure are complementary for development. The study emphasizes that placing a large amount of investment in ICTs projects without investing proportionally in health and education infrastructure does not result in development.

According to the authors, the existing relationship between education and economic development has long been recognized; however, education is more important and can be an engine for ICTs promotion. In this sense, without education, none of the benefits allowed by ICTs could be achieved. Besides, the study considers that the lack of basic health for the population makes development suffer from the long-term cost of simple contagious illnesses. In addition, education is highly linked to health in the sense that one needs education to learn about and avoid diseases such as HIV-AIDS and to guard against others. Thus, poor health and education leads to a decreasing productivity.

Similarly, the question analyzed by Kivunike, Ekenberg, and Danielson (2009) focus on the perceptions of the role of ICTs on the quality of life. The authors use Sen's approach defining the indicators of the quality of life that include: social opportunities, economic facilities, and political freedoms. An investigation of the impact of ICTs on these local indicators was conducted. It was concluded that centering the attention on ICTs without taking into consideration the social, economic, and political elements could result in missed opportunities and misused resources.

Other authors place more emphasis on the sole role of ICTs in promoting development. Mikre (2011) provides insights about the positive effects of ICTs on development, with a focus on education. The author considers that ICTs allow for the endorsement of changes in working conditions, usage, and sharing of relevant information. To this author, education is the field where this influence is clear and significant. ICTs have impacts on the teaching and learning approaches as they enhance active, collaborative, integrative, and evaluative learning environment. Furthermore, ICTs adoption and usage in developing countries foster the training of faculty in new skills, techniques, and modern pedagogies. Thus, high investments on ICTs infrastructure in schools along with creating networks do reduce the existing gaps between the quality of education in urban and rural regions. Besides, the author considers that the major challenges of ICTs implementation in education systems are mainly linked to policy, planning, infrastructure, learning content and language, capacity building and financing. Indeed, the development of any country is built upon the quality of education presented to the nation. This chapter also considers that ICTs, regardless of their limitations, have a great role in this context. To the author, computers and Internet are important tools to promote education and thus development.

Similarly, in an article extracted from the Journal of Information Technology for Development about the role of ICTs in education, Assar, El Amrani, and Watson (2010) consider that the underserved regions of the world are struggling to deliver education to the right people at the right time. They actually suffer from limited budgets dedicated to educational programs, unavailable educational material, scarcity of human resources for teaching, and instructors unwilling to work in rural areas. All these problems have encouraged the adoption and usage of ICTs to deliver education and training for workers. The authors consider that the implementation of ICTs in education in developing countries is considered to be a challenge since it is currently difficult to picture future learning environments that are not supported by a particular type of ICTs. ICTs implementation in the education sector is of a great importance in the sense that these technologies provide educational resources access to the underserved and geographically and culturally disadvantaged. In addition, ICTs implementation in education has often been considered as a tool toward educational change in the sense that it improves the learning results and the skills of learners, and prepares them for the information society. In addition, these programs will allow over passing the concept of the digital divide that concerns the existing gap between those who utilize technology and those who do not.

In his article about the importance of ICTs to development, Qureishi (2011) states that Information and communication technologies usage contribute to development through facilitating the access to new markets, improved competitiveness, and access to information. To the author, an effective use of ICTs can maximize profits, through achieving higher returns and carrying lower costs. Simultaneously, those unable to use ICTs are being excluded from the economic and social practices of globalization. The studies in this topic look at new approaches that allow the investigation of the effects of ICTs on development. By taking into consideration the economic and social processes of globalization, they examine the adoption of those ICTs and evaluate the impacts of this implementation on prevailing over the disparities within the studied countries.

Mazen, Sherah, and Johnston (2009), in their article, talk about the adoption of Inter-Organizational Systems (IOS) by a number of organizations as a tool of managing their business operations across the supply chain. The authors discuss the low adoption rate of IOS in the Gulf region and relative existing challenges related to doing business with organizations using IOS.

In the same track, Carte, Dharmasiri, and Travis (2011) focus on the IT capabilities in relation to development. The authors consider that ICTs can serve as a valuable economic development tool given their omnipresence and ubiquity in much of the developed world. Developing countries suffer from the lack of IT skills, language obstacles, and illiteracy, making the adoption and usage of ICTs difficult. The results of the study propose a hybrid-learning program aiming to improve IT skills and awareness.

The essay, extracted from the International Telecommunication Union Study (2010), places a high emphasis on the role of ICTs on the achievement of MDGs. As the study reveals, ICTs increase the access to market information, create employment, and thus increase wealth. Besides, ICTs usage increases skills and productivity leading to higher incomes. In addition, ICTs contribute to the achievement of MDG2, about achieving universal primary education through increasing supply of trained instructors and enhancing distance learning that helps greatly in educational and literacy programs in rural areas. As for MDG3 (goal 3) that aims to promote gender equality and empower women, ICTs deliver programs targeted to gender equality and empowerment of women. Moreover, ICTs help in the achievement of MDG4, 5, 6 linked to the health issue through increasing access of rural caregivers, enhancement of the delivery of basic training for health employees and improving information sharing on diseases. Furthermore, to ensure environment stability, ICTs allow resource management, energy saving, and pollution reduction. Finally, ICTs play an important role in creating a global partnership for development.

Similarly, Kundishora's (2010) article on the impact of ICTs on socio-economic and development and thus on MDG's achievement, explores the different means by which ICTs contribute greatly to the achievement of Millennium Development Goals (MDGs). The author indicates that a proper usage of information enabled by ICTs is a key driver to socio-economic development. MDG's attainment is accelerated through a proper usage of ICTs. To the author, an appropriate use of ICTs enables the reduction in the existing gap between developing and developed countries.

An article on the impact of ICTs on MDG, by Kabanda (2011) links the solution to poverty and hunger to knowledge. The author considers in his study ICTs to be enablers of the production and sharing of knowledge, and thus the attainment of MDGs. Indeed, given the strong correlation between the GDP growth and ICTs indicators, ICTs can be considered as a tool of economic growth. The article explores the ways in which ICTs increase the productivity, which consists of better communication and networking at lower costs, digitalization of production and distribution, new trade opportunities enabled by e-commerce, access to information and knowledge, and finally growing competitiveness.

Another study by the UNDP (2011) on democratic governance focuses on the role of Mobile technologies in development (2011). To the author, mobile technologies are proposing new channels of communication between people and governments. In fact, these technologies allow for a larger access to public information and essential services. A significant number of people are rushing toward the use of these technologies in an everyday basis. Recent studies claimed that ICTs could be used by everyone by 2015 and allow for the achievement of the targets. The study emphasized that, in a global population of approximately seven billion people, the number of mobile phone subscriptions amounts to 5.4 billion, which is very surprising. The mobile phone penetration rate in low-income and low middle-income countries is 45 percent and 76 percent, respectively. Consequently, mobile technologies are starting to have a significant impact on all aspects of human development. The study indicates that the use of those technologies are now influencing positively democratic governance and other development fields including education, health, agriculture, employment, crisis avoidance and the environment. As an example, it is proven that larger mobile subscription contributes significantly to higher economic growth as shown in Vodafone studies (UNDP, 2011). Furthermore, mobile technologies offer important means allowing people to connect with public and governmental institutions, which reinforce the demand side of governance. Promoting service deliverance and reform within main governing institutions, including public administrations, parliaments, and systems of justice, creates new prospects for open governance. The study considers that mobile technologies allow citizens to get rid of intermediaries who take monetary advantages for helping in the transactions, and thus enhancing the service delivery. The study focuses also on the role played by mobile technologies in the fight against poverty through increasing service delivery prospects in fields such as health care, agriculture, employment, and education.

Another study in this context, by the United Nations ICT Task Force (2003), about the role of information and communication technologies in the achievement of MDGs, examines a matrix that links ICTs to the eight spheres of Millennium development goals in order to explain the significance of ICTs in reaching MDGs. The results of the matrix show that first ICTs contribute significantly to the abolition of severe poverty and hunger. In fact, many ICTs projects aim to eradicate extreme poverty and hunger. Data collection covers the actual ICTs programs, uses, and applications initiated by all the social parties with the state, NGOs, and the private sector in trying to eradicate poverty and hunger within developing countries. Besides, ICTs usage has a strong impact on the attainment of universal primary education. Indeed, figures illustrating children's usage of ICTs in classrooms represent an important indicator showing ICTs progress. On the other hand, ICTs access and usage contribute to the promotion of gender equality and the empowerment of women. Actually, ICTs generate important opportunities

for bridging the gender divide and supporting the empowerment of women in developing countries. An assessment of past, present, and future contributions of ICTs as they are linked to gender will provide an indication of what has been done, what is done currently, and what needs to be stressed on in order to use information technologies in the best possible way to achieve women's social, political, and economic empowerment. In addition, the measurement of the ICTs impact on the reduction of child mortality, improvement of maternal health and the fight against HIV/AIDS, Malaria and other major diseases has been proved difficult. This is mainly because of the presence of other factors impacting the health. As a result, the study suggests the use of "surrogate endpoints" such as better exchange of information and better management of health systems. Furthermore, ICTs can enhance the sustainable environmental management by improving the response systems, assisting environmental activism, and allowing for more efficient resource usage. Indicators showing these impacts will be around the content, prevention and monitoring of environmental disasters, improved efficiency and resource management, and ICTs initiatives related to the environment.

The article Byrne, Nicholson, and Salem (2011) about the influence of information communication technologies on ICTs looks at some specific illustrations showing the role of information and communication technologies as enablers of the millennium development goals' achievement. To the authors, attaining the MDGs is not only related to progress toward targets, but is more linked to incorporating the social and cultural dimensions of development and also implementing the opportunities allowed by ICTs usage.

Bernardi and DeChiara (2011), in their article about ICTs and the health information systems, investigate the history of the reform of the information systems on HIV/AIDS according to a number of institutional logics and priorities. The main aim of this article is to have a deep understanding of these inconsistencies and examine their impact on the implementation and evaluation of the HIV/AIDS programs and initiatives.

In the same context, Ivar, Kossi, Titlestad, Tohouri, and Braa (2009), in their article about the integration of health information systems, examine the influence of ineffective and unpredictable health information systems for managing and examining the health sector capacity to attain the MDGs. An analysis of the cases of four countries (South Africa, Zanzibar, Sierra Leone, and Botswana) was conducted. Indeed, it was concluded that technical solutions are necessary in aligning the various political parties and enabling integration; however, these solutions need to be developed within the varying framework of an evolving health information system for the sake of attaining the level necessary to achieve the MDGs.

Major Findings from Global, Regional, and National Engagement in Human Development

Health, education, unemployment, and poverty are deficits that prevail in the region. These deficits are the sources of the low performance of most countries of the region. Besides, the data provided yearly by World Human Development reports, special reports focusing on the Arab World have also shown the extent and importance of such social deficits. Most of the information provided below is obtained from these reports. Morocco has produced a human development report that covers the situation of the past 50 years (RDH50). Besides these reports, national human development reports are also available.

The evaluation of national health systems of 191 countries indicated that Kuwait, Qatar, and the United Arab Emirates scored the best among Arab countries in terms of goodness (ranking between 26 and 30) while Libya and United Arab Emirates scored the best in terms of fairness (ranking between 3 and 22). Indeed, the performance of

health care systems, in terms of fairness, depends heavily on geographical locations of the patients (UNDP, 2002). Besides, health care is not evenly distributed between countries and even within countries. The rural population is less likely to access health care than its urban counterpart. The lack of resources and the lack of transportation impede health care development in rural areas. It has also been recognized that illiteracy is another problem that prevents rural population from accessing health care facilities (UNDP, 2002). Life expectancy at birth differs from one country to another depending mainly on income level of the country. The United Arab Emirates have higher life expectancy reaching 77.9 years (UNDP, 2005). Since 1956, life expectancy at birth in Morocco, has jumped from 47 years of age in beginning 1960s to 71 years of age today (72.5 years for females and 68.5 years for males) (RDH 50, 2006). On average, the indicator of life expectancy at birth in Arab countries has significantly increased from 52.1 years in 1970s to 66.5 years in the first five years of the new century. This average is slightly higher than the average indicator for developing countries (64.9 years) and lower than the one of middle-income countries (70.1 years) (UNDP, 2005).

Studies have found that disease and disability reduce life expectancy by 5 to 11 years. Life expectancy is reduced by 9 years due to disability in almost one third of Arab countries. In fact, countries with high survival rates do not always have low disability rates. Kuwait, Qatar, and Oman are examples of countries with low mortality rates that lose more than 9 years in disability. Years of life lost to disease in these countries are higher than the average international standard, for comparable countries, which is 6 to 7 years. Internationally, 20% of adults suffer from a longstanding illness or disability (UNDP, 2002).

Arab women are even more likely to have disabilities at birth and lose more years to disease than men. "The proportion of females reporting long-standing illness exceeds that of males by more than 6 percent and can be up to 8.5 percent higher." For women, the number of years lost to disease is not necessarily related to income-level but to differences in lifestyle and gender discrimination (UNDP, 2002).

In Morocco, the health system has known a considerable improvement since independence (Martin, 2008). The Moroccan government has improved primary health care, training medical and paramedical personnel, and has facilitated access to health services. The current number of health care establishments exceeds 2460 compared to 394 in 1960. The country has a resident-to-bed ratio of 1 bed for 1000 residents. The doctor-to-resident ratio increased from 1 doctor for 12,120 residents in 1967 to 1 doctor for 1900 residents in 2004 (RDH 50, 2006).

In Egypt, Bahrain, Jordan, and Tunisia, there is a high degree of ill health among the old age population. More than 50% of the elderly have health problems. Almost 30% of these people perceive their health conditions to be very poor (UNDP, 2002).

Other causes that affect health are tobacco/ alcohol/drug use and road accidents. Studies have shown that tobacco use is quite high in the region and there is an increasing trend of women smoking. In 1998, around 182,000 people died from tobacco use. Alcohol and drug use is also spreading at a high pace among young people (UNDP, 2002).

Infant Mortality Rate (IMR) and under-five mortality in Arab countries range from 1.02% to 7.53% and 2% to 10%, respectively (UNDP, 2002). The Global Human Development Report 2002 states that Arab countries have made a rapid improvement in reducing infant and under-five mortality. They reduced under-five mortality from 20% in 1970 to 6% in 2002. The lowest rate of infant mortality was recorded in Qatar while the highest rate is in Yemen. The lowest rate of under-five age mortality is the one of Bahrain,

Kuwait, Qatar, and United Arab Emirates, while the highest rate was shown in Mauritania, Sudan, Yemen, and Iraq (after the Gulf War). Oil-rich countries, in general, experience lower rates of mortality because they improved their health system to increase life expectancy and decrease child mortality.

Nevertheless, there are other middle-income Arab countries that have known a rapid progress too. Tunisia was one of the 10 countries that made the fastest improvement in raising life expectancy and Yemen did a remarkable progress in decreasing under-five mortality (UNDP, 2002). Morocco succeeded in decreasing infant mortality from 14.9% (17% in rural areas and 10% in urban areas) in 1962 to 4.79% (5.67% in rural areas and 3.86% in urban areas) in 2004 thanks to children vaccination campaign (RDH50, 2006). The Global Human Development Report 2003 adds that "Egypt achieved the largest reduction in under-five mortality rates, from around 10% to 4%. However, other countries are being left behind. In Iraq the under-five mortality rate almost tripled in the 1990s, to 13%."

Maternal mortality is another serious health challenge facing Arab countries. More than half of the Arab countries have a Maternal Mortality Ratio (MMR) higher than 75 per 100,000 live births and almost a third of the countries have an MMR of 200 per 100,000 live births (UNDP, 2002). The Global Human Development Report 2002 states that lifetime chance of dying in pregnancy or childbirth is 1 in 55 among SMC compared to 1 in 157 and 1 in 283 in Latin American/Caribbean and East Asia/the Pacific, respectively. Gulf countries have shown lower rates of maternal mortality. Kuwait and United Arab Emirates were able to decrease their MMR to only 5 per 100,000 live births. Other countries like Saudi Arabia, Qatar, and Oman, can also be considered in the lower level of maternal mortality compared to the rest of the Arab world. Their MMRs range between 10 and 20 per 100,000 live births. However, these countries did not reach yet the low level of maternal mortality of countries with "comparable command over economic resources" (UNDP, 2002).

Another health problem that is starting to threaten the Arab world is AIDS. Albeit Arab countries have reported relatively lower levels of HIV/AIDS, the virus is spreading among the population at high pace. On average, Arab states have only 0.3% of the population carrying HIV while developing countries have an average of 1.3% and middle-income countries have an average of 0.8% (UNDP, 2005).

Some countries, however, enjoy better economic capabilities but suffer from significant nutritional problems such as Egypt, Morocco, Kuwait, Syria, Saudi Arabia, Libya, Oman, and United Arab Emirates. Having levels of stunting between 15% and 25%, these countries are considered to be "richer than developed" (UNDP, 2002). In Yemen, the percentage of underweight children rose from 30% in 1992 to 46% in 1997 (UNDP, 2003).

The second challenge facing the Arab world is education. Knowledge and education constitute the road to development in the era of globalization. Since the middle of the twentieth century, Arab countries have made a significant progress in fighting illiteracy. Illiteracy rate among Arab adult decreased from 60% in 1980 to 43% in 1990s (UNDP, 2002). In 2004, the average literacy rate in the Arab world reached 69.9%, but this rate is still lower than the average literacy rate in the developing countries, which is 78.9%. These rates are lower in Arab countries than the average rates in developing countries where 71.7% of women are literate and the rate of literate women represents 84% of that of men (UNDP, 2006). Some countries like Jordan and Palestine have succeeded in increasing literacy among women reaching 85% literacy rate. Other countries, however, like Morocco, Yemen, Sudan, Mauritania, and Sudan have a literacy rate of women lower than 50% (UNDP, 2005).

According to UNDP (2002), the number of illiterate people is still increasing to the extent that Arab countries embark upon the twenty-first century burdened by over 60 million illiterate adults, the majority of whom are women. More disparities are identified in rural areas where women and the poor are very unlikely to reach higher education levels. This is mainly due to the low enrolment rates in basic education of these categories of society. The UNDP report adds that illiteracy among males in the Arab world will persist at least until 2025 while illiteracy among females is expected to continue to exist until 2040. Morocco has one of the highest illiteracy rates in the world. Despite the small and slow improvement noted in this domain, the number of illiterate Moroccans, in absolute terms, more than doubled between 1960 and 2004. It increased from 6 million to 12.8 million persons (RDH50, 2006).

Since 1980, the number of students enrolled in the three levels of education (primary, secondary, and tertiary) has substantially increased from 31 million to reach 56 million in 1995. This increase was much higher in 1980s than in the first five years of 1990s. In the Arab world, the proportion of children enrolled in primary level reached 77% during the 1990s compared to 79% in South Asia and more than 90% in East Asia/Pacific, Latin American/Caribbean, and CIS (UNDP, 2003). In Morocco, the same indicator jumped from 17% in the mid 1950s to 47% in 1964 before it reaches 92% in 2004 (RHD50, 2006). In the mid 1990s, the average enrolment rates, in Arab countries, for the secondary (54%) and tertiary levels (13%) exceeded the average enrolment rates of developing countries (49% in secondary level and 9% in tertiary level) (UNDP, 2002). The number of students enrolled in primary and secondary levels in Morocco moved from 366,000 in 1956 to 5.8 million in 2004 (RDH50, 2006). Among Arab states, only one country has achieved universal primary education while six countries are still on track and four countries are far behind (UNDP, 2002).

Although females have lower access to education in most countries of the Arab world, there are some exceptions in certain regions. Jordan, Lebanon, Palestine, and oil-producing countries have a higher enrolment rates for females than for males. Still, Arab countries are lagging far behind industrialized countries in terms of education and enrolment. The average enrolment rate in industrialized countries, in the same period, was 106% for second level and 60% for the third level. These levels of education, which were reported for 1995, are not expected to be reached by Arab countries until 2030 (UNDP, 2002).

Based on the finding of UNESCO report of 2005, "the Arab child on average is provided with 0.4 years of pre-schooling compared to 1.6 years in Latin America and the Caribbean, 1.8 years in Central and Eastern Europe and 2.2 years in North America and Western Europe." Arab countries have an enrolment rate at the pre-schooling level lower than 20%. Saudi Arabia, Oman, Djibouti, Algeria, and Yemen have the lowest pre-schooling enrolment rates of only 5% while UAE, Kuwait, and Lebanon have the highest rates reaching 70%. Most countries rely on private institutions and women organizations to provide this level of education with "a belief that the support of small children is considered basically a women's issue and not a public priority" (UNDP, 2005).

Gender inequality has been reduced at this level of education since female enrolment rates is at least 90% of male enrolment rates in most Arab countries except Morocco, Yemen, and the Comoros (UNDP, 2005). The Global Human Development Report 2002 describes Arab countries' performance in decreasing gender inequality in primary education to be the best in the world while Sub-Saharan Africa's performance is the lowest. Only one Arab country has achieved gender equality in primary education while twelve are still on track and one country is far behind.

The last deficit to be tackled is poverty. The analysis of poverty in Arab countries is limited by the lack of comprehensive and comparable data sets, reluctance of some official sources to provide data, irregular patterns in data collection, and publication at the level of the individual country. As a result, poverty and income indicators in Arab countries are underestimated.

In 1999, The GDP of all Arab countries combined did not exceed $531.2 billion, which is less than the GDP of one European country like Spain ($595.5 billion) (UNDP, 2002). The Global Human Development Report 2003 states that the annual per capita income growth during 1990s in the SMC was 1% while the percentage point reduction in poverty was -0.1%. Concerning the real GDP, its average growth between 1975 and 1998 was slightly higher (3.3%) than the world average (2.9%). However, this period of time was marked by a strong economic growth in the region along with a very high demographic growth of 2.8%. Hence, the real per capita income during this period knew a very small increase of 0.5% per year compared to 1.3% as global average (UNDP, 2002). The Global Human Development Report 2005 confirms that most Middle Eastern countries and Latin American countries experienced a minor increase in average income.

This situation of quasi-stagnation reflects deterioration in the average standard of living in Arab countries compared to the rest of the world. In terms of GDP growth, Arab countries lagged behind Latin America and Caribbean (1% growth), South Asia (3%), and East Asia and Pacific (5.9%).

Previous studies on the available data for the period 1970-2000 have shown that "SMC have had the lowest regional incidence of extreme poverty in recent years, with less than 2.5 percent of the population living on or below the $1/day income level for dire poverty adopted for the Millennium Development Goals." The study explains that this situation may be due to "egalitarian income-distribution practices and to the ability of the region's poor to capitalize on periods of economic growth, particularly between 1970 and 1985" (UNDP, 2002).

Although the region is considered to have one of the lowest poverty rates in the world, it has one of the lowest drops in the percentage of extremely poor people. The percentage of people in SMC living on less than $1 a day has barely changed in the 1990s (from 2.4% in 1990 to 2.3% in 1999) while the same indicator has moved considerably in other regions like East Asia and the Pacific (from 27.6% to 14.2%). The number of extremely poor people in the Arab world moved from 6 million to 7 million in the period 1990-1999 (UNDP, 2002).

Despite the low proportion (2.4%) of Arabs living below $1 a day in the period 1990-2001, some countries like Yemen had a significantly high percentage of extremely poor people reaching 15.7% (UNDP, 2003). In Morocco, The rate of relative poverty dropped from 56% in 1960 to 14.2% in 2006. "However, due to the demographic growth, the absolute number of poor people remained at an average of 5 million; three quarters of whom live in rural areas." Indeed, 4 million Moroccans live in extreme poverty (spending less than 3,235Dhs annually in urban areas and less than 2,989Dhs in rural ones) and 25% of the population spends less than 4,500dhs annually. Poverty in Morocco is usually more present among women, children, youth, and people with special needs (RDH50, 2006).

According to the UNDP, a study on seven Arab countries has found that the ratio of the income share of the richest to the poorest population is relatively low; meaning that inequality in income distribution is low in the region. The average ratio of income share in the Arab world is 10% compared to 24.6% in Mexico, 19.3% in Kenya, and 14.2% in Turkey. This can be explained by the role of migration and remittances in terms of sending money to their households and helping create new jobs. A less optimistic picture has been given by an ESCWA study showing an increase of the income share ratio in Egypt, Iraq, and Jordan. In Egypt, for instance, the ratio of richest/poorest in the period 1980-1990 has increased from 27% to 28%. Other countries like Yemen had a rural household income less than two-thirds the one of their urban counterparts in 1992.

The Arab human Development Report of 2003 revealed an increase in poverty and inequality in income distribution in the region. In the 1990s, the rate of poverty in Egypt varied between 30% and 40% making poverty in Egypt alone constitute 10% of the total rate in the Arab world. During the same period, poverty rates in the region varied from "21% in Jordan to 30% in Yemen, 45% in Djibouti, and 85% in the Sudan." In Palestine, almost three-fourths of the population lives in poverty with an income of less than US $2 a day.

The Arab Human Development Report of 2005 indicates that "the spread of income poverty generally leads to women's disenfranchisement in the areas of parliamentary participation, professional and technical employment, and control of economic resources." Poverty, hence, widens marginalization and disempowerment of women. A study done on Morocco, Tunisia, Egypt, Jordan, and Yemen has shown that there is no evidence of "feminization of poverty." The same report adds that under situations of poverty, "women have the least access to food, health, education, training and opportunities for employment and other needs." Based on income and expenditure indicators, poverty levels are not higher among women than among men. However, when considering women's limited access to capacities (health, knowledge, and income), human poverty levels are proved to be higher among women.

"Poverty is the antithesis of human development depriving people of the opportunity to acquire capabilities and to utilize them effectively to achieve a descent life" (UNDP, 2004). Low income or expenditure and failure to meet basic needs are just few aspects of poverty. It is the inability to access and control all human, physical, financial, and social assets that define "human poverty" as synonymous to powerlessness (UNDP, 2002). Among the 103 developing countries, Palestine, Qatar, Jordan, and Lebanon ranked in the top 20 in the Human Poverty Index list with HPI-1 ranks of 7, 10, 11, and 18, respectively. Mauritania is the Arab country that had the lowest rank (79) among developing countries (UNDP, 2003).

The attempts made by both international, regional and national organizations to account for the interdependencies of health, education and socio-economic performance, have also been made by different segments of civil society. This latter engagement has been taken earlier and ahead of governments because of the nature of actions of non-governmental organizations. They pursue fieldwork where links between health, education, and poverty are most of the time easy to observe in localized situations. However, the weaknesses in both accounting fully for the interdependencies and the performance of the economies under study have been related to the limitations in the type of governance pursued and the participation of the population to the design, implementation, and evaluation of health, education and other economic programs (Akala & El-Saharty, 2006). Through the change in the demographic profile, with the new epidemiological trends and the new life styles, new types of pressures induced new attitudes. Higher demand for health care with consequences on education and the performance of the economies of the region have been expected. The interdependencies between health, education, and economic performance do require public and private responses that account for the nature and magnitudes of these demands. The present study has placed emphasis on the relationships between health, education, and economic performance in order to show how both sector and multi-sector development are necessary to capture the changes in population needs that are more integrated. As emphasized in Akala and El-Saharty (2006) and in other publications by international organizations, the region has the means and the potential

to respond effectively to the health challenges and their effects on each economy in the region.

The results attained so far have shown largely the existence of patterns of interdependencies among socioeconomic, health and education variables. These interdependencies would have been certainly captured better with further microeconomic data. However, with the available information, the relationships between different variables related to health, education, poverty, and economic performance of the region have been assessed. Furthermore and most of the time, the magnitudes interdependencies are too important that economic and social policies in the region of study cannot omit the potential gains from these interactions. The implied economic, political, and social policies are required consequently to be more integrated while accounting for different sector and global policies.

This section starts with reviewing the reforms undertaken before tackling the issues of sector policies and integration respectively in the second and third parts.

Domestic Social and Economic Policies: Overall Political, Economic, and Social Reforms

The region has been traditionally characterized by its limited integration with the world economy, the predominance of public sectors, and limited private investment (Mitha, 2007). Besides their closed economies and the substantial state intervention, countries of the region faced major challenges in different sectors. This includes the effects of rapid urbanization, attraction of foreign investment, restoring economic growth, controlling demographic growth, improving the education system, decreasing unemployment rate, building democracy, saving natural resources, and ensuring food at accessible prices (Richards, 2001). By the middle of the 1980s, the region has experienced many changes and reforms that are described below as political, economic, and social.

Political Reforms

Some countries in the region have been witnessing wars, conflicts, and tensions causing economic losses and also lack of coordination among economic, political and social players. Even within this difficult environment, economic, political, and social reforms have been undertaken (Poortman, 2006). However, different authors have identified the limiting factors that negatively can affect the outcomes of these reforms (Mitha, 2007). Among these factors, excessive regulations, corruption, and lack of transparency are largely cited. The responses provided in this area include regular open elections, extension of the number of political parties and unions besides the number and the areas covered by civil society with emphasis on the development of media. While these are internal and domestic responses to initiate further freedom in these societies, external events and pressures have also contributed to these changes. Almost all countries in the region have been concerned with the adhesion to new international arrangements suggested by international and regional organizations.

Economic and Financial Reforms

In their evaluation of the economic reforms undertaken in the region, Dasgupta, Hamilton, Pagiola, and Wheeler (2001) have identified important moves related to achieving economic stabilization by lessening inflation rates, reducing black market in exchange rates, reducing government spending and government deficit, and closing the balance-of-payments gap. As can be observed from the index of economic freedom (Heritage Foundation reports, 2000 and 2007), Egypt, Jordan, Morocco, and Tunisia were among the top countries in macroeconomic stabilization. However, the countries in this region have been described as late reformers in comparison with Latin American and East Asian countries. They have also shown signs of limited integration to world markets (Page, 2003). Privatization and liberalization may have also contributed to increasing unemployment (Bellin, 2004) because of the limited time response of the private sector and the economy.

Besides, the region appears to be among those economies that are lagging in the three areas considered in the competitiveness index. Other more qualitative studies confirm that the region had slower rates of reforms (Cameron & Rhein, 2005). Most countries in the region engaged in privatization programs with the progressive reduction of the role of the public sector in some productive sectors of the economy. Egypt and Morocco led this process that started in the 1990s with a larger diversified portfolio for Morocco (Kikeri & Nellis, 2002). Series of public monopolies were reformed with partial or total involvement of the private sector. This process has concerned manufacturing, banks, telecommunication, energy besides sectors like tobacco and cement. The proceeds have been engaged in public provision of infrastructure and other development projects. They attained the overall level of 18.9 billion US dollars for the period 1990-2003 but this level is still limited in comparison with other regions in the world (Nells, 2006).

But the impacts of these economic reforms have appeared to be limited (Nabli & Véganzounès-Varodakis, 2004). It is further shown that the political economy in the region exhibits constraints that may reduce the extent of these reforms (Nabli, et al., 2004).

Social Reforms

While social policies were important components of public policies before the area of structural adjustments, these policies have not been given the priority with the beginning of the political and economic reforms (Richards, 2001; Dolorez, 1996). The social reforms have been introduced later with the pressure of international organizations and with the development of Non government organizations. These reforms have focused mainly on poverty reduction, participation, gender issues, and focus on the youth and children. However, a clear orientation on human development is not fully considered in all the countries of the region. Some countries started to work on improving women rights while lagging behind the traditional status of women (Arab Human Development Report, 2004).

Other social reforms concern health care, childcare, and poverty reduction. Some reforms are also achieved through income transfers pensions, social security payments and insurance. Actually, the World Bank initiated some reform programs focusing on social protection and human development. In addition, some countries initiated improvements in the education system in terms of quality and coverage besides health-care services.

Need of Further Policy Coordination and Integration

The Overall Framework for Integration

The current framework introduces major directions of coordination that appear to be critical in relation to poverty alleviation in the region of study. The framework starts with the insistence on the participation of the population and their representatives (non-governmental agencies and elected institutions). With the other players that include central and local governments, private businesses and the NGOs, policy formation, selection and implementation is taking place to meet the basic needs of the population. These needs are viewed in relation to the constraints and risks facing the choices of individuals and groups. The summary of needs, constraints and risks besides the directions of policy recommendations (shown in Table 1), introduces some examples that help understand the necessary dynamics needed for more coordination and integration. The MDGs constitute the best opportunity for ensuring this integration of needs besides ensuring adequate

supplies. ICTs are important tools for the acceleration of this process as they provide further means for monitoring and management of the attainment of the goals at levels of localities, countries, regions and the world.

The framework used in chapter 9 to underline the needs and risks faced by the poor is again used here to show the variety of players and the types of coordination and policies to be emphasized (see Table 1).

Strengthening Social Policies towards Further Inclusion of Women

The implementation of transversal and integrated policies requires specific sector policies that include economic, health, education and employment policies for the region and for each country. It is well known that a large body of publications and reports has been devoted to the diagnosis and the necessary changes that are needed in the region.

Series of documents including those of the "Population Reference Bureau" including Roudi-Fahimi and Moghadam (2003) offer sound arguments for the role of policies focusing on further inclusion of women. The above study shows that further benefits can be attained through women's education. This is based on the evidence that there are links between education and fertility and employment as the structures of the economies and the conservative culture in the region lead to lower levels of women education than in other places with similar income levels. Education is linked to fertility, as education is the most important determinant of age at first marriage and age at first birth in these countries. Furthermore, educated women are more likely to use reproductive health and family planning information and have smaller family size. Education also affects health as women with more education have healthier families. The remaining concerns are that illiteracy remains high in some of these countries, that there are still large gender gaps in literacy and school enrollment and that the quality of education is low and led to mismatch

Table 1. Interconnections of population needs and requirement of further policy coordination and integration

	Constraints	Risks	Players	Coordination and Integration of Policies
Food	- Constrained by liquidity; - Buy at a very retail; - Limited access to wholesale markets; - Constrained by storage, risks, and markets. - Travel distance; - Location of grocery and chain stores; - Availability of needed items; - Storage costs - Limited income spent on other expenditures - Time spent in the operation of purchasing	-Nutritional risks related to the diet requirements; - Risks associated with health	Government, Local government, Public Agencies, Private businesses, Non-governmental organizations, Unions & Political parties.	- Production and trade, - Quality control, - Needs of special groups, - Special regions, - Health, -Education -Security -Economy & Finance
Clothing	- Constraint of income; - Location of chain and grocery stores - Travel distance; - Availability of alternatives; - Storage and cleaning costs - Limited income for other expenditures;	- Health infection problems	Government, Local government, Public Agencies, Private businesses, Non-governmental organizations, Unions & Political parties.	-Quality control, -Production, -Trade, -Health, -Education -Security -Economy & Finance
Education	- Constrained by income; - Satisfaction of other needs; - Time allocated to schooling - Travel distance; - Availability of education; - Location of education centers; - Maintaining the flow of education - Foregone Payoffs from other activities	- Shortages of inputs; - Employment possibilities; - Long term impoverishment	Government, Local government, Public Agencies, Private businesses, Non-governmental organizations, Unions & Political parties.	-Education, -Health, -Employment, -Social and youth, -Sports -Security -Economy & Finance
Health	- Constrained by income; - Competition of needs; - Degree of illness and the type of health problems; - User fees for public services - Travel distance; - Availability of healthcare; - Availability of alternatives; - Maintaining the flow of health care - Time spent to look for health care	- Health problems aggravation; - Long term impoverishment - Aggravation of the current poverty level.	Government, Local government, Public Agencies, Private businesses, Non-governmental organizations, Unions & Political parties.	-Health, -Housing, -Infrastructure, -Family, -Social, -Employment, -Education, -Sports -Security -Economy & Finance
Energy	- Affordability to be connected to the electricity system; - Constrained by income; - Obligation to buy other energy means from local shops and in small quantities. - Travel Distance; - Existence of other energy means and the possibility to obtain them - Availability of substitutes; - Repair and maintenance of energy equipment - Outcomes from other activities; - Time spent on obtaining other energy means; - Impact on work or study at night	- Fire and wood collection risks; - Health infection risks; - Long term impoverishment.	Government, Local government, Public Agencies, Private businesses, Non-governmental organizations, Unions & Political parties.	-Energy, - Forests, - Commerce, - Housing, -Health, -Education, -Water -Security -Economy & Finance

continued on following page

Table 1. Continued

		Constraints	Risks	Players	Coordination and Integration of Policies
Water		- Affordability to be connected to the piped water system; - Constraint of income; - Travel distance; - Availability of water supply; - Availability of other free means of water supply - Repair and maintenance of water equipment - Time spent for water collection; - Physical efforts to collect water from unpiped sources	- Health effects of water collection; - Possibility to attract diseases; - Long term impoverishment	Government, Local government, Public Agencies, Private businesses, Non-governmental organizations, Unions & Political parties.	-Water, - Energy, -Health, -Agriculture, -Environment, -Infrastructure -Security -Economy & Finance
Housing		- Inability to pay high rents; - Constraint of income - Availability of housing opportunities; - Travel distance between work and home; - Cleaning, painting, and repairing - Time spent to look for shelter; - Lost income because of low productivity impacted by living conditions.	- Incidence of ill health and infection because of poor living conditions	Government, Local government, Public Agencies, Private businesses, Non-governmental organizations, Unions & Political parties.	-Housing, -Infrastructure, -Water, -Energy, -Environment, -Health, -Education -Security -Economy & Finance
Transportation		- Constraint of income; - Inability to buy a personal vehicle; - Access of public transportation - Travel distance; - Availability of transportation means; - Maintaining the flow of transportation - Lost income from other activities that can be performed during the lost time	- Health infection problems; - Transportation is not always insured (absenteeism).	Government, Local government, Public Agencies, Private businesses, Non-governmental organizations, Unions & Political parties.	-Transportation, -Energy, -Water, -Commerce, -Infrastructure, -Health, -Security -Economy & Finance
Judicial system		- Limited information, - Location of the court systems in cities, - Illiteracy, - Fuzzy property rights - Travel time, - Complexity of mechanisms, - Costs related to lodging and food when away; - Follow up of the judicial conflict. - Lost income from other activities that can be performed during the lost time	Risks of losing the case and other risks related to new conflicts	Government, Local government, Public Agencies, Private businesses, Non-governmental organizations, Unions & Political parties.	-Justice -Education -Infrastructure -Human Rights -Security -Economy & Finance
Credit System		- Amount to be borrowed; - Guaranty required; - Availability of financial institutions; - Availability of individual lenders; - Very high interest rates. - Costs related to loan files; - Transportation costs; - Follow up of the credit mechanism - Lost income from other activities that can be performed during the lost time	Insolvability of the grantee and incapability to pay back the loan and interests	Government, Local government, Public Agencies, Private businesses, Non-governmental organizations, Unions & Political parties.	-Economy & Finance - Banking - Security -Education
Employment		-Qualification and education, -Age, -Health, -Gender, -Wage, -Other benefits	-Related to the enterprise, -Related to employees, - Related to the economic environment	Government, Local government, Public Agencies, Private businesses, Non-governmental organizations, Unions & Political parties.	-Industry and commerce, -Employment, -Economy & Finance, -Education, -Health, -Insurance, -Security.

between the labor market needs and graduates skills. Policies emphasizing the inclusion of girls and women in education are likely to generate the outcomes needed to accelerate development. While sector policies are also needed, they may not be sufficient, as transversal policies are needed to sustain the reduction of income gaps and gender differences (Roudi-Fahimi, 2004).

CONCLUSION

It is definitely clear that the situation of the poorer segments of the population can improve if further policy coordination and integration is pursued. The directions of further coordination appear to have been provided by the international framework that accounts on achieving MDGs by 2015. It is also provided by the orientations focusing on human development. The recent reforms undertaken seem to be mainly focusing on economic and political components while accounting for social components as a residual sector that should be considered with the implementation of reforms. The overall policy schemes that are driven by both international organizations and by the domestic reforms, cannot lead to the needed policy integration if not based on ownership and domestic generalization of these policies to different country locations. Furthermore, specific transversal policies focusing on women, children and older segments of the population need further strengthening. More inclusive health and education policies with gender and rural focus can be promising in the region. Preventing and accounting for the existence of handicapped segments of the population are also dimensions that require inclusion within the socially coordinated policy packages.

REFERENCES

Akala, A., & El-Saharty, S. (2006). Public-health challenges in the Middle East and North Africa. *Lancet, 367*(9515), 961–964. doi:10.1016/S0140-6736(06)68402-X

Assar, S., El Amrani, R., & Watson, R. (2010). ICT and education: A critical role in human and social development. *Information Technology for Development, 16*, 151–158. doi:10.1080/026811 02.2010.506051

Bellin, E. (2004). *The political-economic conundrum: The affinity of economic and political reform in the Middle East and North Africa. Carnegie Paper*. Pittsburgh, PA: Carnegie University.

Bernardi, R., & DeChiara, F. (2011). ICTs and monitoring of MDGs: A case study of Kenya HIV/AIDs monitoring and evaluation in a donor multi-agency context. *Information Technology for Development, 17*(1), 1–3. doi:10.1080/0268 1102.2010.511699

Byrne, E., Nicholson, B., & Salem, F. (2011). Information communication technologies and the millennium development goals. *Information Technology for Development, 17*(1), 1–3. doi:10 .1080/02681102.2010.513825

Cameron, F., & Rhein, E. (2005). *Promoting political and economic reform in the Mediterranean and Middle East*. Retrieved from http://www.esiweb.org/pdf/esi_turkey_tpq_id_28.pdf

Carte, T. A., Dharmasiri, A., & Travis, P. (2011). Globalization in development: Do information and communication technologies really matter? *Information Technology for Development, 17*(4), 289–305. doi:10.1080/02681102.2011.604083

Dasgupta, S., Hamilton, K., Pagiola, S., & Wheeler, D. (2008). Environmental economics at the world bank. *Review of Environmental Economics and Policy, 2*(1), 4–25. doi:10.1093/reep/rem025

Dolorez, T. (1996). The dynamics of domination. *University of California*. Retrieved from http://www.jstor.org/view/00943061/di974042/97p07327/0

Farzaneh, R. F. (2004). *Progress toward the millennium development goals in the Middle East and North Africa. Policy Brief*. New York, NY: Population Reference Bureau.

Farzaneh, R. F., & Moghadam, V. M. (2003). *Empowering women, developing society: Female education in the Middle East and North Africa. Policy Brief*. New York, NY: Population Reference Bureau.

Heritage Foundation. (2010). *Heritage foundation annual report, 2010*. New York, NY: Heritage Foundation.

ITU. (2010). *Relevance and impact of ICTs to the MDGs*. International Telecommunication Union Study. Retrieved from http://www.itu.int

Ivar, S. J., Kossi, E., Titlestad, O., Tohouri, R., & Braa, J. (2009). Comparing strategies to integrate health systems following a data warehouse approach in four countries. In *Proceedings of the 10th International Conference on Social Implications of Computers in Developing Countries*. IEEE.

Kabanda, G. (2011). Impact of information and communication technologies (ICTs) on the millennium development goals (MDGs). *Journal of African Studies and Development, 8*, 154–170.

Kamel Nabli, M., & Véganzonès-Varoudakis. (2004). *Reform complimentaries and economic growth in the Middle East and North Africa*. Washington, DC: World Bank.

Kikeri, S., & Nellis, J. (2002). *Privatization in competitive sectors: The record to date*. Research Working Paper. Unpublished.

Kivunike, F., Ekenberg, L., & Danielson, M. (2009). Investigating perception of the role of ICT toward the quality of life of people in rural communities in Uganda. In *Proceedings of the 10th International Conference on Social Implications of Computers in Developing Countries*. IEEE.

Kundishora, S. (2010). *An overview on the impact of ICTs on socio-economic development*. New York, NY: Millennium Development Goals and Society.

Martin, M. C. (2008). *Individual and collective resources and health in Morocco*. UNU-WIDER Research Paper. Unpublished.

Mazen, A., Sherah, K., & Johnston, R. B. (2009). Investigating IOS adoption maturity using a dyadic approach. *International Journal of e-Collaboration, 5*(2), 43–60. doi:10.4018/jec.2009040103

Mikre, F. (2011). The roles of information communication technologies in education. *Ethiopian Journal of Education & Schooling, 6*(2).

Mitha, F. (2007). Economic reform in the Middle East and North Africa (MENA). In The *Selected Works of Farooq A Mitha*. Gainesville, FL: University of Florida. Retrieved from http://works.bepress.com/farooq_mitha/1

Nells, J. (2006). *Privatization: A summary assessment*. Working Paper 87. New York, NY: Centre for Global Development.

Ngwenyama, O., Andoh-Baidoo, K., Bollou, F., & Morawczynki, O. (2006). Is there a relationship between ICT, health, education and development? An empirical analysis of five western African countries from 1997-2003. *The Electronic Journal on Information Systems in Developing Countries, 23*(5), 1–11.

Page, J. (2003). *Structural reforms in the Middle East and North Africa*. Retrieved from http://www.yemenembassy.org/economic/Reports/WEF/Page_62_78_Structural_Reforms.pdf

Poortman, C. (2006). Reforms in the MENA region. *World Bank*. Retrieved from http://go.worldbank.org/CEX1H34N30

Qureishi, S. (2011). Globalization in development: Do information and communication technologies really matter? *Information Technology for Development*, *17*(4), 249–252. doi:10.1080/026 81102.2011.610142

RDH50. (2012). *RDH general report: 50 ans de développement humain & perspectives 2025*. Retrieved from http://www.rdh50.ma/Fr/pdf/general/RG-FR.pdf

Richards, A. (2001). The political economy of economic reform in the Middle East: The challenge to governance. *University of California*. Retrieved from http://sccie.ucsc.edu/documents/working_papers/2001/challenge_econreform.pdf

Strauss, J., & Duncan, T. (1998). Health nutrition and economic development. *Journal of Economic Literature*, *36*(2), 766–817.

United Nations Development Program. (2011a). *Human development reports*. Retrieved from: http://hdr.undp.org/en/

United Nations Development Program. (2011b). *Arab human development reports*. Retrieved from http://arab-hdr.org/

United Nations Development Program. (2011c). *Mobile technologies and empowerment: Enhancing human development through participation and innovation*. Retrieved from http://undpegov.org

United Nations ICT Task Force. (2003). *Using information and communication technologies to achieve millennium development goals*. New York, NY: United Nations.

Chapter 11
Social Deficits, Social Cohesion, and Prospects from ICTs

ABSTRACT

This chapter investigates the multiplicity of the social deficits occurring in most Arab countries. It also assesses the extent and magnitude of such deficits and looks at their interactions. Further needs for human development and social cohesion[1] are discussed as means and policies that can alleviate these shortages and create new avenues for enhanced and coordinated development. The Millennium Development Goals pursued by developing countries, represent a promising framework that is targeting 2015 for the attainment of the objectives. This chapter identifies the main directions of social deficits as they relate to health, education, and poverty, with a focus on the Arab economies. The potential provided by the Information and Communication Technologies (ICTs) in the coordination of the alleviation of the social deficits are also discussed. ICTs are then recognized as important sources for the improvement of identification, extent, and the use of the policy tools for poverty reduction. The framework of social cohesion is also placed in parallel with human development through a discussion of policies needed to reduce deprivation.

INTRODUCTION

The adoption of the Millennium Development Goals (MDGs) in 2000 has generated major changes in social cohesion policies in both developed and developing countries.

In developing economies, poverty and exclusion are both rural and urban with major interconnections that are driven by rural migration and inappropriate inclusion in urban areas. The social policies that were pursued before in these economies were found to be limited and inefficient complements to the economic policies pursued (OECD, 2008). But, with the publication of the first World Development Report as analyzed by Hopkins (1991) shows that following the consequences of structural adjustment policies, developing economies have been invited to pursue further social policies and to engage in human development programs. The pursuit of MDGs has been an opportunity for developing countries to reduce their social deficits through the promotion

DOI: 10.4018/978-1-4666-3643-9.ch011

of targeted social policies that are integrated with the economic policies pursued with major focus on the monitoring of the overall outcomes in each economy. In this process and in the context of southern Mediterranean countries, a large set of questions can be formulated in relation to the extent of implementation of these targeted policies, their monitoring, and adjustments processes. The extent of further inclusion of the poorest and marginalized segments is also an important dimension that accompanies the economic reforms that have been taking place in these economies.

These different dimensions are analyzed in this chapter as follows:

- Rural migration as determinant of poverty and exclusion,
- Further determinants of poverty and exclusion,
- Global outcomes under the on-going social policies,
- Interdependencies of deficits and need of social cohesion policies.

These issues are also discussed in relation to the inputs from ICTs for coordination purposes.

The determinants of poverty in the southern Mediterranean region appear to be different from those that are behind the poverty in the EU economies. The share of rural population in most of these countries (except some Gulf countries) is relatively higher than that in Europe and the overall population growth is also relatively high. Furthermore, the level of industrialization is still low in the southern Mediterranean economies. This implies that job creation is far below the labor supply; i.e. the youngest segments, both educated and non-educated people, have less economic opportunities in most of the southern Mediterranean economies. These factors are respectively reviewed before tackling the occurrence of human and social deficits.

RURAL MIGRATION AND URBAN IMPLICIT EXCLUSION AS DETERMINANTS OF POVERTY AND EXCLUSION

While poverty in developed economies has mainly an urban origin as it is related to the degradation of the living and earning conditions of certain segments of the population, most developing economies are mainly concerned with the rural dimension of poverty besides its urban expressions. In developing countries, poverty appears to have both rural and urban dimensions. Given the weight of rural population in the above economies and the state of urbanization and the low development of manufacturing industries, the rural origin of poverty appears to be dominating.

The Likely Factors that Drive Poverty and Social Exclusion

Macroeconomic policies have been and are still biased against rural areas. Prior contributions have shown the extent of the effects of macroeconomic policies on the agricultural and rural sectors (Krueger, Schiff, & Valdès, 1988). Even with the liberalization and openness of these economies, the implicit discrimination against agriculture has not been fully eliminated (Kym & Valenzuela, 2006). Market imperfections through depressed price and incomes are also among the factors that generate rural poverty (Dutta & Mishra, 2004). Furthermore, unfavorable weather conditions are also among the major reasons that have to be added to explain the high level of rural poverty (Ravaillon, 2006). Besides the economic impacts that generate the economic side of rural poverty, the education and health systems and in rural areas are also major factors that support multidimensional rural poverty (Mude, Barrett, McPeak, & Doss 2003; Ulubaşoğlu & Cardak, 2006). The lack of infrastructure and the quality of education (Loury, 1981) contribute to the limitation of education in rural areas. Rural migration decisions are also motivated by the need to better educate children in rural areas (Mude, et al., 2003). Several case studies have shown these effects in Mexico (McKenzie & Rapoport, 2006) and in Albania (Germenji & Swinnen, 2005).

Poverty is then exacerbated because rural poverty leads to urban poverty with urban conditions of living generating and accelerating urban poverty in a developing context. This transfer is ensured by rural migration that promotes urban poverty with the creation of informalities as supported by different versions of Harris and Todaro (1970). The context of southern Mediterranean region is highly concerned with the role of rural migration and its urban implications (Reiffers, 2003). Nissanke and Thorbecke (2005) introduce the links between policy debates and the components related to development with focus on poverty.

Empirical Evidence about the Rural Origin of Poverty and Social Exclusion

Based on these results, it can easily be stated that rural migration in relation to degraded urban conditions for both jobs and living lead to further poverty. This type of poverty is multidimensional as it includes employment, income, and education. Table 1 provides evidence about these issues as estimated for the southern Mediterranean countries (different sources).

The rural rates of migration as annual percentage of the total population impose high pressure on cities in these economies. The high pressure of migrants and the low capability of inclusion in cities, imply that significant levels of poverty are also observed in urban areas. In comparison with developed economies, the rural migration component is very low which implies that poverty is mainly an urban phenomenon. As said above, while poverty is mainly urban in developed economies, it is both rural and urban in developing countries and in southern Mediterranean economies. These trends are mainly observed in the Arab countries.

Different reports including those related to human development studies focusing on the Arab world have identified a series of social and human development deficits that are introduced in the following section.

FURTHER DETERMINANTS OF POVERTY AND EXCLUSION IN THE ARAB WORLD

While rural migration is an issue, other related factors are also the origin of poverty and exclusion in the region. As rural migration adds to the urban population, the demographic factors through the high level of fertility have a series of consequences on the Arab world economies. Figure 1 shows how the demographic conditions that emphasize the situation of gender lead to higher fertility and to higher demand for schooling; thus, imposing both high levels of both skilled and unskilled labor that

Table 1. Rural migration and urbanization rate

Country	Rural Migration Rate in Percent	Urbanization Rate in percent
Jordan	0.014 to 0.04	0.823
Libya	0.003 to 0.005	0.848
Lebanon	0.001 to 0.003	0.866
Yemen	0.006	0.273
Algeria	0.004 to 0.007	0.633
Tunisia	0.002	0.653
Syria	0.004	0.506
Oman	0.004	0.715
Morocco	0.003 to 0.007	0.587
Turkey	0.003 to 0.005	0.673
Egypt	0.001	0.428
Mauritania	0.001	0.404

Sources: Diverse national and international sources with averages indicated for rural migration. Sources include also different reports of World Urbanization Prospects (United Nations).

is introduced in the job markets annually. Either the labor flow or stocks are too high that they cannot be absorbed given the investment regimes and the rates of industrialization of the Arab economies. Some reports and publications talk about the "youth quick" in relation to the large number of young people concerned. The excess labor supply with increasing local unemployment leads to further emigration of both skilled and unskilled labor. The emigration of skilled labor lowers then the chances of investments and valuation of local new opportunities that favor again emigration. This entertains and expands the vicious circle of poverty in the region.

Unemployment and lack of income can be an important source of poverty. According to the above framework, it is the consequence of the economic situation that is prevailing in the job markets. The limited levels of investments and the relative low level of economic performance due to reduced development of manufacturing and service industries lead to a demand for jobs that is largely below the labor supply. The labor supply is determined by a series of factors that account directly for the annual rates of graduation from schools and the demographic pressure placed on the economy.

The highest unemployment rate was observed in Algeria (30%) in 2001, followed by Morocco (24%), then Tunisia (16%). Both Syria and Yemen attained 12%. The lowest rate (less than 10%) was registered in Oman, Egypt, Lebanon Saudi Arabia, Kuwait, and U.A.E. These rates have been increasing over the period 2001-2009 as they have attained in 2005: 12.90% in Algeria, 8.70% in Egypt, 13% in Jordan (2009), 20% in Mauritania (2004), 10% in Morocco (2009), 15% in Saudi Arabia, 19% in Sudan (2002), and 9% in Syria (2008). All available studies recognize the high rate of unemployment to be between 10 and 20% with highest rates applying to new entrants and to the youngest segments of the population. In 2000, first-time job seekers represented 95% of the total unemployed in Egypt. In Yemen, this rate attained 65%, 52% in Morocco, and finally less than 30% in Jordan.

Educated workers are increasingly concerned with these high unemployment rates with women being more affected than men even if their share in the labor markets has been increasing (Bilgin & Ismihan, 2008). Within these same countries, unemployed persons with higher education attained 32% in Jordan, 16% in Algeria, 12% in Egypt, and 8% in Morocco. As for unemployed persons with secondary education, the highest rate was registered in Egypt with 68% and the lowest rate was in Jordan with 15%. This rate represented 33% for Tunisia, 22% for Morocco, and 20% for Algeria.

Women unemployment rate attained a maximum of 30% in Algeria and a minimum of 8% in Yemen. This rate registered 28% in Morocco, 21% in Jordan, and 15% in Tunisia.

The growth of labor force in Arab countries increased over the years. It was at a rate of 3% during the period 1970-1980, 3.2% during the period 1980-1990 and attained 4% during the period 1980-1990. During the last decade 2000-2010, this rate decreased to attain 3.7%. During the 1970-1990 period, the highest rate was 3.3%, observed in both Morocco and Tunisia, and the lowest rate was in Egypt (2.3%).

This situation changed during the period 1990-2000; Morocco and Tunisia registered respectively the lowest rates with 2.6% and 2.7% when Jordan attained the highest rate of 5.2%.

This situation of unemployment has been engendering incentives for emigration with an increasing trend for the departure of skilled labor. The number of Arab graduates that migrate for overseas jobs annually is 70,000. Citing statistics obtained from the Arab League, ILO, UNESCO, and other Arab and international organizations, it noted that about 100,000 scientists, doctors and engineers leave Lebanon, Syria, Iraq, Jordan, Egypt, Tunisia, Morocco, and Algeria annually. Seventy percent of the scientists do not return home, while about 50 percent of doctors, 23

Figure 1. Relationships between social and economic variables in the region

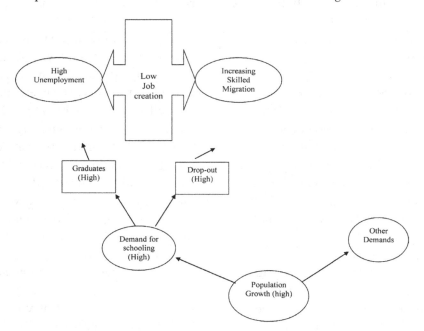

percent of engineers, and 15 percent of scientists move to Europe, the US, and Canada.

As in El-Hamidi and Wahba (2006), many factors are contributing to the explanation of such a high unemployment rates in the Arab Countries.

An important study about "Why Has Unemployment Rate in Algeria been higher than in MENA and Transition Countries" (Kpodar, 2007) has looked at factors that explain the high unemployment rate in Algeria during the 1995-2005 period. The results of the study suggested that slower labor productivity growth increased the differential relative to the sample average. In contrast, positive terms of trade shocks resulting from rising oil prices led to a decrease in the gap. Neither labor market regulation nor the tax wedge seemed to be more harmful to Algeria than to other countries. The author suggested some actions that could be considered to improve employment in Algeria. For instance, he proposed that the Algerian government pursue growth-enhancing policies that will create conditions for enough long-term

employment to attract the growing work force and reduce unemployment. He also suggested setting structural reforms to increase productivity and promoting financial development, trade liberalization, private investment, and human capital accumulation. Other suggestions include that the private sector and investments should be the main engine of job creation.

Another interesting paper (Pissarides, Véganzonès, & Varoudakis, 2005) tried to assess the links between human capital and growth in the MENA region. The empirical results attained show the low levels of returns to education, the low level of human capital valuation in the context of large unemployment in the region.

Different macroeconomic indicators show the current on-going trend in the Arab countries. It can be expected that this situation can be worsened in relation to the current economic and financial crisis. The migration of skilled labor is expected to continue and can thus affect the prospects of future growth and development in these countries.

EXTENT OF SOCIAL DEFICITS

At the beginning of the third millennium, most Arab countries decided to take the lead and confront the different challenges they have been facing. Many reforms and initiatives have been undertaken. Nevertheless, true economic and social development cannot be reached without building human development.

Health, education, employment, and poverty are the major deficits that the region suffers from. Although the last half of the century witnessed an important progress in terms of human development, there is still much to do to reach the international benchmark (AHDR, 2002).

Deficits in Healthcare

Based on The World Health Report 2000, assessments of national health systems are made based on two determinants of performance: goodness and fairness. Goodness or responsiveness is the extent to which a health system responds to people's expectations. Fairness is the extent to which the system responds to the needs of all citizens equally, with no discrimination. A study evaluating national health systems of 191 countries indicated that Kuwait, Qatar and the United Arab Emirates scored the best among Arab countries in terms of goodness of their system (ranking between 26 and 30) while Djibouti, Libya, and United Arab Emirates scored the best in terms of fairness (ranking between 3 and 22). Mauritania, Sudan, and Syria fare the worst among Arab states in terms of fairness in financial contributions. Indeed, the performance of health care systems, in terms of fairness, depends heavily on the geographical locations of patients (AHDR, 2002).

Health care is not evenly distributed between Arab countries and even within countries. There are remarkable disparities in health care access within countries depending on citizens' location. The rural population is less likely to access health care than its urban counterpart. The lack of resources and transportation (geographical isolation) impede health care development in rural areas. Illiteracy and culture are another problem that prevents rural citizens from accessing health care facilities. Many rural citizens still opt for traditional treatments to cure their diseases. The only country which does not face disparities in health care access between its urban and rural areas is Syria (AHDR, 2002).

Measurement of overall health is usually based on life expectancy and longevity. Life expectancy at birth differs from a country to another depending mainly on the income level of the country. Djibouti has a life expectancy at birth of only 52.7 years while United Arab Emirates have a higher life expectancy reaching 77.9 years (HDR, 2006). Since the independence of Morocco, life expectancy indicator has jumped from 47 years of age in early 1960s to 71 years of age today (72.5 years for females and 68.5 years for males) (HDR50, 2006). On average, the indicator of life expectancy at birth in Arab countries has significantly increased from 52.1 years in the 1970s to 66.5 years in the first five years of the 21st century. This average is slightly higher than the average indicator for developing countries (64.9 years) and lower than the one of middle-income countries (70.1 years) (HDR, 2006).

Arab women live at least as much as Arab men do. "The difference between the two sexes is 2.5 years or less in around two thirds of the countries; for the remainder, the difference is between 3 and 3.5 years." This suggests that women's health should be improved because the global average difference is around 4 years and in some developed countries it can reach 11 years. The low difference in life expectancy between genders in the region can be explained by the high maternal mortality rates (AHDR, 2002).

Studies have found that diseases and disability reduce life expectancy by 5 to 11 years. Life expectancy is reduced by 9 years due to disability in almost one third of Arab countries. In fact, countries with high survival rates do not always have low disability rates. Kuwait, Qatar, and Oman are examples of countries with low mortality rates that lose more than 9 years in disability. Years of life lost due to diseases in these countries are higher than the average international standard, for comparable countries, which is 6 to 7 years. Internationally, 20% of adults suffer from a longstanding illness or disability (AHDR, 2002).

Arab women are even more likely to have disabilities at birth and lose more years due to disease than men. "The proportion of females reporting long-standing illness exceeds that of males by more than 6 percent and can be up to 8.5 percent higher." For women, the number of years lost to disease is not necessarily related to income-level but to differences in lifestyle and gender discrimination (AHDR, 2002).

In Morocco, the health system has known a considerable improvement since the independence. The state worked on improving primary health care, training medical and paramedical personnel, and facilitating citizens' access to health services. The current number of health care establishments exceeds 2460 compared to 394 in 1960. The country hosts 120 hospitals with a resident-to-bed ratio of 1 bed for 1000 residents. The doctor-to-resident ratio increased from 1 doctor for 12,120 residents in 1967 to 1 doctor for 1900 residents in 2004 (RDH50, 2006).

In Egypt, Bahrain, Jordan, and Tunisia, a study showed a considerable degree of ill health among the old age population. More than 50% of the elderly suffer from sight problems and have difficulty walking. Almost 30% of these people perceive their health conditions to be very poor. Most elderly experience morale problems and high depression (AHDR, 2002).

According to the WHO, health is defined as "a state of complete physical, mental, and social well-being." Besides physical health problems, Arab population suffers from mental and psychological issues that negatively affect their well-being. In Arab countries, individuals' relationship with the state and society is shaped by exclusion, lack of esteem, and marginalization. These conditions lead to permanent psychological pressure among citizens, which causes physical and psychological illnesses. Examples of problems that psychological pressure can bring are hormonal imbalance, immune system failure, and nervous breakdowns (AHDR, 2004).

Although health conditions vary widely from a country to another, there are some areas where improvement is definitely needed. The major challenges in the health sector are preventive care, primary care, infant, child, and maternal mortality.

Preventive care and primary care are not given enough attention by most Arab countries. Arab health systems tend to emphasize on curative care and hospitalization (generally in the secondary and tertiary levels). Budget allocations and health sector expenditures show that focusing on curative care, rather than preventive care, increases costs and fail to lower diseases recurrence. To increase their level of health and well-being, Arab countries need to focus more on investing in and introducing preventive care programs (AHDR, 2002).

Cultural and behavioral change is also important in preventing many diseases and reaching better health. Examples of cultural behaviors that cause health problems in the region are marriage between close relatives, early marriage, and female circumcision. Other behaviors that can be avoided to reduce health problems are alcohol drinking, tobacco/drug use and respecting road and traffic signs to avoid road accidents. Studies have shown that tobacco use is quite high in the region and there is an increasing trend of women smoking. In 1998, around 182,000 people died from tobacco use. Alcohol drinking and drug use is also spreading at a high pace among the young (AHDR, 2002).

As also reported in the FEM 32-01 report (2008), Infant Mortality Rate (IMR), and under-five mortality in Arab countries range from 1.02% to 7.53% and 2% to 10%, respectively (AHDR,

2002). The Global Human Development Report 2002 states that Arab countries have made a rapid improvement in reducing infant and under-five mortality. They reduced under-five mortality from 20% in 1970 to 6% in 2002. The lowest rate of infant mortality was recorded in Qatar while the highest rate is in Yemen. The lowest rate of under-five age mortality is the one of Bahrain, Kuwait, Qatar, and United Arab Emirates while the highest rate was shown in Mauritania, Djibouti, Somalia, Sudan, Yemen, and Iraq (after the Gulf War). Oil-rich countries, in general, experience lower rates of mortality because they improved their health systems to increase life expectancy and decrease child mortality.

Nevertheless, there are other middle-income Arab countries that have known a rapid progress too. Tunisia was one of the 10 countries that made the fastest improvement in raising life expectancy and Yemen did a remarkable progress in decreasing under-five mortality (AHDR, 2002). Morocco succeeded in decreasing infant mortality from 14.9% (17% in rural areas and 10% in urban areas) in 1962 to 4.79% (5.67% in rural areas and 3.86% in urban areas) in 2004 through children vaccination campaigns (HDR50, 2006). The Global Human Development Report 2003 recognized that "Egypt achieved the largest reduction in under-five mortality rates, from around 10% to 4%" and that other countries are lagging on this health component.

Arab women suffer high rates of mortality and morbidity related to their reproductive health. In most Arab countries, more than 80% of women are attended by trained personnel when giving birth. However, many Arab women in less developed countries like Somalia, Yemen, and Mauritania still deliver their newborns without the assistance of any trained personnel. For instance, in Yemen the percentage of women that are medically assisted during their child delivery does not exceed 25% (AHDR, 2005). On average, Arab states have a lower percentage of birth attended by skilled health personnel (70%) than comparable middle-income countries (88%) but higher than

the average percentage of developing countries (59%) (HDR, 2006).

Another health issue that is related to women is female genital mutilation.

Besides diseases that have existed in the Arab world for a long time, there are new kinds of diseases that are increasingly spreading in the recent decades. For instance, Morocco faces both "poor country diseases" and "rich country diseases" (HDR50, 2006).

The spread of urban lifestyle among Arab countries has helped them reduce the rate of viral, bacterial, and parasitical diseases but caused an increase in chronic diseases such as cancer, diabetes, hypertension, and heart disease. Obesity is another issue that started perturbing the health of Arabs. Arab countries have greater number of women suffering weight issues than men while comparable countries face exactly the opposite (AHDR, 2005).

Another health problem that is starting to threaten the Arab world is AIDS. Albeit Arab countries have reported relatively lower levels of HIV/AIDS, the virus is spreading among the population at a high pace. On average, Arab states have only 0.3% of the population carrying HIV while developing countries have an average of 1.3% and middle-income countries have an average of 0.8% (HDR, 2006).

According to AHDR, 2005, women represent 50% of people carrying HIV in the region and research has shown an increasing trend of females catching the virus. Indeed, the probability of contracting the disease among females—between 15 and 24 years—is twice the probability of their counterparts. Some of the reasons behind this trend are the poor health care provided to women, the low level of empowerment of women, some cultural practices like female circumcision, illiteracy, the lack of awareness about the disease and the methods of prevention, and the prevailing culture of silence surrounding sexuality.

The budget for health services was cut by more than 90% while it was more than $500 million in 1989. Malnutrition became a public health problem after the embargo. From 1991 to 1996, the percentage of children under five with chronic malnutrition increased from 18% to 31%, the percentage of children with underweight malnutrition moved from 9% to 26%, and the percentage of children with acute malnutrition has reached 11% (AHDR, 2002).

During the last 50 years, Morocco suffered and still suffers from three major deficits in the health sector. First, the coverage of health services is still insufficient. The capacity of hospitals is small and the percentage of the population covered by insurance does not exceed 16%. Second, inequality in health care access exists between urban and rural citizens. Urban population enjoys, on average, 6 more years of life than rural population. Infant Mortality Rate (IMR) in rural areas is twice that of urban ones. The IMR in some regions is close to the rate recorded in the beginning of 1970s. Third, the country has high rates of child and maternal mortality. During the period 2003-2004, 47 under-five children in 1000 child births died compared to an average of 9 in Spain. In other terms, Morocco's rate of under-five mortality is 5.2 times more than Spain's. Maternal mortality rate is 227 per 100,000 births compared to 20 in developed countries (HDR50, 2006).

Health achievements are not perfectly correlated with the level of income. There are social, cultural, and other factors that shape the effectiveness of health care systems. Gender discrimination, education level, poor management, political stability, and the priority given to health investments are all key determinants of the development of health care systems in Arab countries. For instance, the level of health expenditure to GDP shows that Arab countries lag far behind comparable middle-income countries. Most Arab states spend between 3% and 4.5% of GDP on health while comparable countries spend 5.7% on average (AHDR, 2002). On average, Arab states spend $86 per capita which is lower than the average expenditure of middle income countries ($95 per capita) (HDR, 2005). Furthermore, there is a remarkable disparity in the distribution of medical personnel between urban and rural areas and rich and poor regions. Many countries in the region started undertaking some reforms in the health sector that focus mainly on two objectives: containing costs and increasing efficiency (AHDR, 2002).

Deficits in Education

Education spending can also be considered as an indicator for the level and situation of education in Arab countries. Beginning 1985, Arab states reduced their investment in the education sector. Although expenditure in the education sector rose from $18 billion in 1980 to $28 billion in 1995, the rate of increase after 1985 was much slower than that of the period 1980-1985. This pattern was the opposite of the international pattern of education spending. Education expenditure as a percentage of GNP is an indicator in which Arab countries scored higher than developing and developed countries in the period 1980-1985 (AHDR, 2002).

A better and more effective educational indicator is per capita expenditure in education. Here again, there was an important rise in this indicator between 1980 and 1985 while there was a decline after 1985. This diminishing marginal rate of education spending was due to the macroeconomic difficulties that faced the region in this period along with the structural adjustment programs adopted by MENA countries, which restrain government spending (AHDR, 2002). According to the 2001 Global Human Development Report, in 1997, Middle Eastern countries had an average public education spending per pupil of $584 and a percentage of 22% of GNP per capita compared to an average of $194 and a percentage of 16% in developing countries. The Middle East comes second in the ranking of regions' average public education spending. The region was surpassed by advanced countries in terms of spending per pupil in public education ($5,360) but it scored slightly higher in terms of education spending as percentage of GNP than these countries (21%).

Education systems in Arab countries are usually separated into two "unrelated parts: very expensive private education, enjoyed by the better-off minority, and poor quality government education for the majority. Unfortunately, private tuition has become indispensable in order to obtain high grades on public qualifying examinations for enrolment in higher education." As a result, some disciplines that are expected to result in a better career have become "the preserve of financially privileged groups." Thereby, education is no more the means for social advancement; it rather became "a means of perpetuating social stratification and poverty" (AHDR, 2002).

Albeit Arab countries have witnessed some quantitative improvements in education, they faced a reverse trend in the quality of education. Education systems in Arab countries face a very serious problem of declining quality. This decline has been indicated by the high failure and repetition rates. The real output of education has also declined as levels of knowledge achievement have decreased and analytical and innovative capacity has deteriorated (AHDR, 2002).

According to RDH50, during the 1980s, the Moroccan education system witnessed a serious and long crisis marked by "academic failures, the relapse of the dropouts into illiteracy and functional illiteracy, a decrease in civic behavior and critical thinking skills, unemployment of college graduates, and lack of basic skills…" In an attempt to improve the education system in Morocco, many shifts and reforms were undertaken. These reforms were ineffective and might have contributed to "producing graduates ill-prepared for the changes and demands of the modern economy and society. The system ended up producing schools of varying levels whose individual performance keeps decreasing the farther they are away from large urban areas."

The incompatibility of education system and local job market in Arab states has led to decreased productivity, increased unemployment, and distorted wage structure. Hence, education is not enhancing social advancement in the region; it is rather impeding any kind of human development (AHDR, 2002). The AHDR (2003) has identified some factors that reduced educational quality such as the weak education policies, the poor working conditions for instructors, and the inadequate educational methodologies (AHDR, 2003).

Early education is the most important level of education in a person's life because this is the stage of life where the child's brain is the most flexible and the most sensitive to its surroundings. Unfortunately, "in some Arab countries, the quality of education provided in many kindergartens in the region does not fulfill the requirements for advancing and developing children's capabilities in order to help socialize a creative and innovative generation." Most pre-school systems teach children reading and writing but give little attention to their integrated growth. Kindergartens lack the facilities and the free space needed for enhancing children's self-confidence by playing, expressing themselves, making choices, and making decisions. Other factors that unfavorably affect pre-school systems in Arab countries are teachers' capabilities, poor curricula, overcrowded classes, and the indifferent quality of teacher training. For instance, many Arab teachers lack motivation because of the low salaries and the other jobs they need to take to ensure certain standard of living (AHDR, 2003).

Based on the findings of the UNESCO report of 2005, the Arab child on average is provided with 0.4 years of pre-schooling compared to 1.6 years in Latin America and the Caribbean, 1.8 years in Central and Eastern Europe and 2.2 years in North America and Western Europe. Arab countries have an enrolment rate at the pre-schooling level lower than 20%. Saudi Arabia, Oman, Djibouti, Algeria, and Yemen have the lowest pre-schooling enrolment rates of only 5% while UAE, Kuwait, and Lebanon have the highest rates reaching 70%. Most countries rely on private institutions and women organizations to provide this level of education with "a belief that the support of small children is considered basically a women's issue and not a public priority" (AHDR, 2005).

With an enrolment rate fluctuating between 95% in Syria and 50% in Djibouti, primary education is another aspect of education where great disparities exist among Arab countries as well as genders. Gender inequality has been reduced at this level of education since female enrolment rate is at least 90% of male enrolment rate in most Arab countries except Morocco, Yemen, and the Comoros (AHDR, 2005). The 2002 Global Human Development Report describes Arab countries' performance in decreasing gender inequality in primary education to be the best in the world while Sub-Saharan Africa's performance is the lowest. Only one Arab country has achieved gender equality in primary education while twelve are still on track and one country is far behind. However, the cultural, social, and economic factors that exist in most developing countries are still affecting gender inequalities. The paper by Osmani and Sen (2003) cited in series of chapters in this book, has both the theoretical and mainly the practical grounds on which discrimination against females, is still observed in series of economies. The directions of gender discrimination and inequality have been discussed in series of publications and reports.

This is also expressed in schooling at the secondary level as female enrolment rate is lower than in the primary level. In most Arab countries, less than 80% of girls attend secondary level except in Qatar, Bahrain, Jordan, and Palestine. This rate does not exceed 20% in Djibouti and Mauritania. In Yemen and Djibouti, the rate of female attending secondary level is only 46% and 69%, respectively. Indeed, the only reason hampering females' attendance in secondary school is poverty while the reasons related to males' attendance include other factors. Girls, generally, tend to study majors of service-oriented professions such as nursing while boys prefer industrial, agricultural, and vocational education (AHDR, 2005).

In higher education, twelve countries have reached gender equality. These countries are Algeria, Bahrain, Jordan, Lebanon, Libya, Oman, Qatar, Kuwait, UAE, Saudi Arabia, Tunisia, and Palestine. In Kuwait, Qatar, and UAE females attend higher education more than males do. However, it is important to note that large number of men study abroad which might explain some discrepancies in the data reported. Countries that have reported the lowest rates of female enrolment in higher education (less than 10%) are Djibouti, Yemen, Sudan, Mauritania, and the Comoros (AHDR, 2005).

There are some gender inequalities, however, in women's access to engineering/technical education. At the University of Kuwait, for example, males are accepted in the engineering and petroleum studies on the basis of a grade point average of 67.9 while female students must achieve an average of 83.5 to be accepted. Despite some efforts to eradicate this discrimination, women studying engineering usually specialize in architecture or chemical engineering while men choose mechanics and electronics. These disparities exist even in medicine where men tend to study surgery while women go for gynecology, pediatrics and dentistry (AHDR, 2005).

Studies have shown that some Arab countries proved to have good quality of education in certain disciplines. Kuwait was the only country that participated in the "Third International Mathematics and Science Study, 1995" competing with 40 other countries, but it ranked at the end of the list of the participating countries. Four years later, other Arab countries participated in the Trends in Mathematics, and Science Study (1999). Tunisia was ranked 29th, Jordan was ranked 32nd, and Morocco was the 37th on the list. Singapore topped the mathematics list while Taiwan topped the science list (AHDR, 2003). Other studies have found that Morocco, Jordan, and Algeria have a higher quality of public education services than private systems.

An overall picture of education level in the Arab world shows that Arab countries have an "adult literacy rate of 67 percent compared to a global average of 79 percent; a combined school enrolment ratio of 60 percent compared to 64 percent; and average years of schooling of 5.2 compared to 6.7 years" (AHDR, 2002).

The Global Human Development Report 2005 adds that in Arab and African countries, girls receive 1 year less of education than boys on average while in South Asia this difference reaches 2 years. In order to improve their education systems, Arab countries need to focus on three areas: enhancing human capabilities, building strong synergy between education and the socio-economic system; and creating a program for education reform at the pan-Arab level. Some of the important points needed to build an effective education system are: making the individual the central to the learning process, encouraging creativity and the spirit of challenge, helping students cope with a future of uncertainty, and enabling all children to have access to education with equal opportunities (AHDR, 2002).

Income Deficits and Unemployment

The third major deficit facing the Arab world is unemployment. Although data on employment are difficult to find, it can still be assumed that unemployment is increasing all over the region. "Most countries suffer from double-digit unemployment and that regional hot spots, such as Algeria, Iraq and the occupied Palestinian territory, suffer from much higher rates." Employment has been affected mainly by the slow or negative growth experienced by Arab countries (AHDR, 2002).

Some countries like Saudi Arabia are characterized by segmented labor markets with differential wages. Nationals are paid higher wages than non-nationals, which makes private employers prefer recruiting migrants. To absorb the unemployed national workforce, Gulf governments try to hire these people in the public sector. However, the low economic growth (1.2%) and the high population growth (4.3%) make governments unable to create enough job opportunities for all nationals. As a result, Gulf-countries government policies try to limit labor exports (AHDR, 2002).

The decline in labor exports aggravates unemployment in middle-income countries that used to benefit from their labor migration as an

"employment cushion." Moreover, the decline in migration to Europe and the United States after 09/11 attacks contributes to an increase in unemployment rates within middle-income countries. Other obstacles to employment are the traditional and dysfunctional labor market as well as labor-market intermediation in the Arab region. Stabilization and structural adjustment programs aiming to reduce government spending have led many MENA countries to decrease their investments in expending public sector job opportunities (AHDR, 2002).

There are, actually, different faces of unemployment in Arab countries. Unemployment, defined as under utilization of labor, includes three categories: open unemployment (job seekers are unable to find work), visible underemployment (employees working less than a fixed time), and invisible underemployment (employees' productivity is low, under-using their abilities, do not earn enough to satisfy their basic needs). Invisible unemployment, although not given enough attention, usually results from an inadequate education system causing poverty and low productivity at the global economy level (AHDR, 2002).

The demand for jobs in Morocco has recorded an average annual increase of 2.3% between 1960 and 2003. Unemployment rate has shifted from 9.4% in 1960 to 10.7% in 1982 before it reaches 16% in 1994 along with an annual increase of unemployed people reaching 57,000. After 1994, unemployment rate decreased to 11.2%. The job market has known an average annual increase in job offers of 152,000 in the period 1971-1981, a drop to 137,000 job offers between 1982 and 1994, and a jump to 217,000 in 1995-2003. Mainly present among women, urban citizens, youth, and graduates, unemployment in Morocco is usually due to the rapid demographic growth (4% annually among urban population), rural migration, the lack of enterprise creation, government intervention, and the inadequacy of education system with the job market. In 2002, unemployment rate was 30.8% among high school graduates and 34.4% among university graduates. Moreover, the number of women job seekers has tripled during the period 1960-2003. In 2003, unemployment rate was 25.4% among women compared to 17.4% among men. The Young population (15-24 years old) experience high unemployment rate, which is equivalent to 34.5% compared to 20.2% among adults (over 24 years old) (RDH50, 2006).

In general, women in the Arab region do not have the same job opportunities, job conditions, and wages as men. Albeit the great increase in women's share in economic activity – 19% compared to 3% for the world- between 1990 and 2003, economic participation of Arab women is still the lowest in the world. The percentage of Arab women participating in economic activity does not exceed 33.3% while the same average percentage in the world is 55.6%. Furthermore, female participation is only 42% of males', which is considered to be the lowest rate in the world with a global average of 69% (AHDR, 2005).

In fact, female unemployment rate exceeds that of men in almost two thirds of Arab states and it is more than the double in half of these countries. For the first decade of the 21st century, the annual growth rate in the Arab work force is estimated at 3.5% while the one of female work is estimated at 5% percent (AHDR, 2005).

The low participation of women in economic life can be explained by the different kinds of discrimination that women face in the Arab region. There are, for example, some laws, which hamper women economic participation despite their claim for women "protection." Examples of these laws are personal status and labor legislation which require women to get father's or a husband's permission to work, travel or borrow from financial institutions (AHDR, 2005).

Another form of discrimination concerns wages. In the private sector, men are paid higher wages than women. Women feel forced to work in the public sector because they give equal pay and work conditions. However, with the implementation of structural adjustments, most Arab countries are decreasing their job offerings in

the public sector. "The wage gap between men and women increases as their level of education decreases." For instance, in Jordan, earnings of female university graduates are 71% those of their males' counterparts while earnings of women with basic education are only 50% those of men with the same education level. For illiterate women, their earnings represent less than 33% of illiterate men (AHDR, 2005).

In times of economic recession, female workers are the first to be fired. For instance, in the first half of 1990s, a period characterized by a slow growth, the number of working women has significantly decreased in Egypt, especially in the private sector. Surprisingly, during the same period, the number of working men experienced an increase. Women continue to be underprivileged even when economic conditions improve. They are, actually, the last to be hired in times of economic expansion (AHDR, 2005).

Implications on Poverty

Poor people are less likely to participate in civil and political society because they tend to focus on meeting their basic needs rather than contributing in the public sphere. As the poverty and income distribution inequalities are rising, the weaker social group is growing among Arab countries. This growing lower class impedes the societal transformation needed to create a free and well-governed society (AHDR, 2004).

Arab states are urged to take serious measures to limit the spread of poverty among their population, promote human dignity, and fight the non-income aspects of poverty such as powerlessness and exclusion. Reducing human poverty and attaining social justice require the implementation of some mechanisms like increase in expenditure on education and health. Such expenditures are considered to be investments in humanity (AHDR, 2005).

Overall, the Arab world lags behind in many indicators but has shown a significant progress in many sectors. According to the Human Development Report 2001, Arab countries made the fastest progress in health and education. "Since the early 1970s life expectancy at birth has improved by 14 years and the infant mortality rate by 85 per 1,000 live births, and since 1985 the adult literacy rate has risen by 15 percentage points—faster progress than in any other region."

INTERDEPENDENCIES OF DEFICITS AND NEED OF SOCIAL COHESION POLICIES[2]

Previous studies (Driouchi, Zouag, & Boboc, 2009) have shown extensively the interdependencies existing among diverse components that form the needs and that are shown to constitute deficits. These components include health, education, and economic conditions where poverty is not only related to income but also to knowledge and health. Furthermore, the obtained results have shown that education plays an important causal role in the determination of health and economic conditions that is income poverty (Driouchi, et al., 2009). These interdependencies have been shown to take place both at the household level and at the aggregate (Driouchi, et al., 2009). This section is an attempt to show how different variables interfere in the determination of the larger need for integrated policies at both local and national levels.

The eight Millennium Development Goals (MDGs) are interdependent objectives that were set in 2000 by most governments under the leadership of the United Nations. Most goals are expected to be attained by 2015. As it can be seen from the following table, each goal is translated into targets in order to ensure the monitoring and evaluation of the achievements using 1990 as a reference year.

The region under investigation has been showing variations in the levels of achievements of MDGs. Large variations across countries and within the same country have been observed. The persistence of urban rural disparities besides

gender differences do still exist. Studies report that the relative poor performance in achieving the goals can be directly related to the low economic growth observed throughout the region during the period 1990-2011. The social deficits that are still observed show that global and local economic and social policies could be accelerated and fine-tuned towards social cohesion. The experiences accumulated by some developed countries appear to be promising in both targeting and combating deprivation locally and globally. The roles of NGOs are important in providing instruments and means to ensure alleviation at local and regional levels. Further details are provided in the endnotes of this chapter. These introduce to social cohesion policies and to the deprivation approach as it has been developing through the theory and practice in the developed economies.

PROSPECTS FROM ICTS AND SOCIAL COHESION POLICIES

It is observed in many areas around the world, that local communities, mainly in poor neighborhoods have been showing signals of solidarity and collective action. This covers social, economic, and financial matters to support needs of individuals and groups. As such, they express the social capital that prevails in the community and that sustains the existing level of social cohesion. This is shown when individuals and groups in the community are facing difficulties and losses. These are also mobilized when public goods and services are concerned. These traditions have been maintained with the development of a social cohesion that is using information and communication technologies. Different components of ICTs have been described through their supportive functions to social cohesion and community development. Series of publications address community development, the enhancement of the roles of governments and the public-private partnership as framework that produce superior outcomes with ICTs.

There have been series of reports and publications dealing with the roles of ICTs in promoting social cohesion and poverty alleviation. Most of the relevant contributions are recent.

The first work cited here, is that by Lahusen (2013) where the emphasis is first placed on the effects of the European integration and enlargement on social cohesion. The author finds that Europe is by series of institutions that distributed between regions and social groups. The second finding is related to the commitment for social cohesion with its economic and social implications. These two types of findings are then opposed to the prevalence of segregation between regions and groups. The author recognizes the existence of underprivileged and marginalized locations and human groups. Advanced technologies and mainly ICTs can play an important function in reducing these social cohesion gaps.

Rocha and Neer (2012) look at the issue of local employment of youth and inclusion in Argentina. They discuss the existence of initiatives for the development of talents, social cohesion, and inclusion through the mobilization of resources that include human capital and also technologies. The role provided to ICTs in training of talents, monitoring of projects and inclusion of inputs from different players to ensure sustainability. Public-private partnerships are underlined to be the key features for successful coordination and mobilization of means.

El-Haddadeh and Weerakkody (2012) assess the impact of alternative socially innovative public initiatives on social cohesion. The purpose is to describe to evaluate the effect that alternative socially innovative service initiatives have, in facilitating social cohesion. However, advanced technologies are again important to ensure the necessary inputs and the required coordination to ensure successful projects leading to further social cohesion.

The above publications represent just a few examples of research that has been developed these last years to ensure and to strengthen social cohesion both locally and globally. They show that major prospects are to be attained under the efficient use of advanced technologies and especially of Information and Communication Technologies. Under these technologies, the media appear to have an important role. However, some other papers have been stressing the role of ICTs explicitly in relation to communities and to social cohesion.

In the paper by Thapa, Sein, and Sæbø (2012), the authors explore how ICT can lead to human development in Sen's capability approach. This research is a response to the critique that Sen views capabilities only of the individual. The authors incorporate the societal level by adding collective capabilities. They propose also how ICTs help to create and promote the capabilities of communities. These lead to development through collective action. A qualitative case study of an ICT initiative in a remote mountain region of Nepal is used for illustration. The empirical findings support the above proposition where also developing collective capabilities also simultaneously enhanced individual capabilities. This is a contribution to theory by showing that not just the characteristics of social capabilities as way to promote collective action but also means to promote individuals.

The monitoring of New Zealand's Computers in Homes (CIH) has been researched since its inception in 2000 by Craig and Williams (2011). The paper traces the inter-relationship between the research findings over the course of a decade and the evolution of CIH practice in low-income communities. One, a large-scale study, is being conducted at a national level, and includes every new participant in the CIH scheme throughout the country using an online survey to provide baseline data. A second small-scale case study is being conducted in one urban CIH primary school community that has recently launched the scheme for 31 of its families. It aims to further explore previous findings about the relationship between social support and community Internet, by assessing the value of social media for parents in building a sense of community belonging. The authors address the potential for social media to engage CIH participants in making sense of their own Internet experience and thus in owning their own research. After finding the positive effects, the authors suggest the use of social media to further promote social cohesion.

Zhang and Elin (2012) address the concepts of community and online community and discuss the characteristics of a community in relation to traditional definitions. They apply a space and place perspective as a framework for the definition of traditional offline communities and for developing online communities that can be made operational. The methods and quantitative measures of social network analysis are suggested as means for investigating the nature and function of communities. These can be used to quantify the types of subjective social phenomena generally associated with communities.

Magro (2012) focuses on e-government with the advent of Web 2.0 technologies. The paper reviews the recent literature concerning Web 2.0, social media, social networking, and how it has been used in the public sector. Observations include topics such as the evolution of social media case studies in the literature, the progress of social media policies, strategies over time, and social media use in disaster management as this is an important role for government. Other observations include the lack of a tangible goal for e-government, and the needs of change are still in government perceptions and resource management to ensure the success in the use of social media.

Aguilera, Guillot, and Rallet (2012) discuss the relationship between the spread of communication tools and the physical mobility of individuals in relation to the fixed telephone, the development of the Internet and especially e-commerce. The spread of individual and such as the mobile phones, have recently generated new interest in the fields of transportation economics, geography and sociology. This article discusses the main topics from the debate between complementarity and substitution besides interactions with the spatio-temporal organization of daily activities. Several issues are then introduction for further research.

Broadbent and Papadopoulos (2012) stress the increasing evidence that the lack of access to Information and Communication Technology (ICT) that severely limits education, employment and economic prospects. This paper utilizes the context of an innovative ICT project in Melbourne to discuss the challenges of connecting disadvantaged communities both in is development and in its assessment. In a community with very low social capital, engagement in a community, takes time, commitment and practice. The paper describes also the process of the research in this community while emphasizing that the objectives of community can be met with the inclusion of the stakeholders that enable change.

De Bailliencourt, Beauvisage, Granjon, and Smoread (2011) show how the new means of communication become integrated into the personal communication practices and a third of the French population utilizes ICTs in their interpersonal exchanges. Taking into account age cohort effects in the adoption of the most advanced modes of interaction and the progress of ICT equipment penetration rate, the paper expect larger access rates. However, the social network mechanisms of the adoption of specific interpersonal communication tools indicate that multiple tool usages can be facilitated and hindered by relational factors. The authors observe that intensive use of multiple communication services is connected to communication practices.

However, Gomez and Pather (2012) in discussing the evaluation of Information and Communication Technologies (ICT) in development activities explore the experiences of ICT evaluation in the broad business environment. The authors draw the parallel between ICT and ICT for Development (ICTD) environment. They motivate the need for a fundamental paradigm shift in ICTD evaluation. They argue that it is not sufficient to use quantifiable benefits of ICT. The authors discuss the intangible benefits such as empowerment, self-esteem, and social cohesion that are more important for development. Consequently, more exploration of the theoretical and methodological grounds is needed.

Mobile communication has become a common phenomenon in most parts of the world. Ling and Horst (2012) consider that there are indeed more mobile subscriptions than there are people who use the Internet. For many people outside of the metropolitan areas of Europe and North America, this is literally their first use of electronically mediated interaction. This preface to the special issue of New Media and Society examines mobile communication in a communication sheds light upon notions of information, appropriation and development and how it is challenging, and in many cases changing, notions of gender. While the mobile phone reshapes development and micro dynamics of gendered interactions, it is not necessarily a revolutionary tool. Existing power structures may be rearranged, but they are nonetheless quite stable. The analysis of mobile communication in the global south helps understand the rise of innovative practices around information and communication technologies and, in turn, enables us to develop theory to understand these emergent empirical realities.

Mehruz (2012) explores the concept of social capital and its role to sustain IT adoption and use in micro-enterprises. It is based on a review of the literature about social capital, IT adoption and micro-enterprises, and sustainable development. The author suggests the existence of a gap in understanding of what is known about social capital as it impacts micro-enterprise activities and subsequently sustainability. The author concludes by discussing both the importance of social capital as well as some arguments against it for sustaining micro-enterprises. In addition,

research issues that need to be addressed in this domain are also highlighted.

Dzorgbo, Duque, Ynalvez, and Shrum (2012) focus on mobile telephony and its rapid diffusion in India. However, the studies on social impacts are scarce. The authors use network surveys of separate groups in Kerala residents in 2002 and in 2007 to examine the shifts in mobile usage patterns and social relationships. Results show near saturation of mobiles among both the professionals and nonprofessionals sampled besides a decrease in the number of social linkages across tie types and physical locations. They also indicate a shift towards friends and family but away from work relationships in the core networks. These results are interpreted as supporting a bounded solidarity.

Sharma (2012) focuses on the role of education in promoting development through future generations. The author starts first with recognizing the impossibility of imagining future learning environments without Information and Communication Technologies (ICTs). The author observes also that the current widespread diffusion and use of ICT especially by the digital generation, will affect the complete learning process today and in the future. For countries like India, ICTs have the potential for increasing access to improving the relevance and quality of education. ICT may deliver significant educational benefits by providing tools for the teaching and learning process and enhancing the skills needed with further reliance on ICTs. This research is in support of the promotion of the further integration of ICTs in education for improving and empowering quality of learning, leading to the economic development of India.

However, other issues are also included in the social cohesion process with an active role of ICTs. Raquel and Osório (2012) focus on ageing population with strategies adopted by different countries to encourage older workers remain longer in the labor force. This is away to keep them healthy, active and independent. This requires the involvement of older adults in an increasingly global, technological, and digital contemporary society. The authors consider that this is inducing challenges for education and lifelong learning, especially to older people with limited digital skills. These are examples of social challenges that could be resolved through ICTs. This generates further social cohesion that includes young and older segments of the population.

CONCLUSION

From the above discussion, it appears that the poverty determinants in the Arab region are today directly related to income poverty and the high unemployment rate. This is to be connected with the high demographic pressure imposed by population growth and rural migration to both cities inside each economy but also internationally. The educational sector plays an important role in producing high flows and stocks of graduates as well as unemployed labor, even if the educational sector benefits from large investments. In the sense of employment, education appears to be inefficient in creating promising jobs. In addition, the health sector and its related means for social financial and social support may also affect the overall social but also economic performance through labor productivity and the competitiveness of each economy. To face this situation, governments have engaged in human development programs and in attempts to achieve the MDGs but to what extent can these countries attain outcomes similar to those attained by those economies that are strengthening policies under the principle of social cohesion? Further analysis of the experiences such as those launched by Egypt, Morocco, and Syria is needed to provide the direction of response to the above question. It appears from the above discussion that social cohesion policies as they need to apply to remote locations but also to urban neighborhoods are promising directions to be emphasized.

REFERENCES

Aguilera, A., Guillot, C., & Rallet, A. (2012). Mobile ICTs and physical mobility: Review and research agenda. In Hsiao, C. M., & Liao, Y.-P. (Eds.), *Transportation Research Part A: Policy and Practice* (pp. 664–672). London, UK: Elsevier. doi:10.1016/j.tra.2012.01.005

Bilgin, M., & Ismihan, N. (2008). An analysis of the unemployment in selected MENA countries and Turkey. *Journal of Third World Studies*, 25(2), 189.

Broadbent, R., & Papadopoulos, T. (2012). Getting wired@collingwood: An ICT project underpinned by action research. *Community Development Journal*, 47(2), 248–265. doi:10.1093/cdj/bsq061

Carstairs, V., & Morris, R. (1989). Deprivation: Explaining differences in mortality between Scotland and England and Wales. *British Medical Journal*, 299, 886–889. doi:10.1136/bmj.299.6704.886

Craig, B., & Williams, J. (2011). Research informing practice: Toward effective engagement in community ICT in New Zealand. *The Journal of Community Informatics, 7*. Retrieved from http://ci-journal.net/index.php/ciej/article/view/792/811

De Bailliencourt, T., Beauvisage, T., Granjon, F., & Smoreda, Z. (2011). Extended sociability and relational capital management: Interweaving ICTs and social relations. In Ling, R., & Campbell, S. (Eds.), *Mobile Communication: Bringing Us Together or Tearing Us Apart?* New York, NY: Transaction Publishers.

Deutsch, J., & Silber, J. (2008). The order of acquisition of durable goods and the measurement of multidimensional poverty. *Quantitative Approaches to Multidimensional Poverty Measurement*. Retrieved from http://www6.bwl.uni-kiel.de/phd/downloads/schneider/ss06/paper_silber2.pdf

Driouchi, A., Zouag, N., & Boboc, C. (2009). Interdependencies of health, education and poverty: The case of south Mediterranean economies. *Estudios De Economia Applicada, 27*(2), 523–544.

Dutta, S., & Coury, M. E. (2002). *ICT challenges for the Arab world*. Retrieved from http://zunia.org/uploads/media/knowledge/Chapter_08_ICT_Challenges_for_the_Arab_World.pdf

Dzorgbo, D. B., Duque, R. B., Ynalvez, M. A., & Shrum, W. M. (2012). Are mobile phones changing social networks? A longitudinal study of core networks in Kerala. *New Media & Society, 13*(3), 391–410.

El-Haddadeh, R., & Weerakkody, V. (2012). Evaluating the impact of alternative socially innovative public sector service initiatives on social cohesion (ALLIANCE): A research note. *Transforming Government: People, Process, and Policy, 6*(3), 283–299. doi:10.1108/17506161211251272

El Hamidi, F., & Wahba, J. (2006). *The effects of structural adjustment on youth unemployment in Egypt*. Paper presented at the ERF Twelfth Annual Conference Proceedings. Cairo, Egypt.

FEM 32-01. (2008). *Interdependencies of health, education and poverty in south Mediterranean economies: Towards new economic & social policies*. FEMISE Scientific Reports. FEMISE.

Germenji, E., & Swinnen, J. (2005). Human capital, market imperfections, poverty, and migration: Evidence from Albania. *Research Group on Food Policy, Transition & Development*. Retrieved from http://ideas.repec.org/p/lic/licosd/15705.html

Gomez, R., & Pather, S. (2012). ICT evaluation: Are we asking the right questions? *The Electronic Journal on Information Systems in Developing Countries, 50*(5), 1–14.

Hopkins, M. (1991). Human development revisited: A new UNDP report. *World Development, 19*(10), 1469–1473. doi:10.1016/0305-750X(91)90089-Z

Kpodar, K. (2007). *Why has unemployment in Algeria been higher than in MENA and transition countries?* IMF Working Paper, WP/07/210. Washington, DC: IMF.

Krueger, A. O., Schiff, M., & Valdès, A. (1988). Agricultural incentives in developing countries: Measuring the effects of sectoral and economy wide policies. *The World Bank Economic Review, 2*(3), 255–271. doi:10.1093/wber/2.3.255

Kym, A., Martin, W., & Valenzuela, E. (2006). The relative importance of global agricultural subsidies and market access. *World Trade Review, 5*, 357–376. doi:10.1017/S1474745606002916

Kym, A., & Valenzuela, E. (2006). *Do global trade still harm developing country farmers?* World Bank Policy Research Working Paper 3901. Washington, DC: World Bank.

Lahusen, C. (2013). European integration, social cohesion, and political contentiousness. In *Economic and Political Change in Asia and Europe, 2013* (pp. 31–52). Berlin, Germany: Springer. doi:10.1007/978-94-007-4653-4_3

Ling, R., & Horst, A. (2011). Mobile communication in the global south. *New Media & Society, 13*(3), 363–374. doi:10.1177/1461444810393899

Loury, G. C. (1981). Intergenerational transfers and the distribution of earnings. *Econometrica, 49*(4), 843–867. doi:10.2307/1912506

Mack, J. (1985). *How poor is too poor? Defining poverty*. Retrieved from http://www.poverty.ac.uk/sites/default/files/how_poor_is_too_poor_0.pdf

Magro, M. (2012). A review of social media use in e-government. *American Scientist*, 2(2), 148–161.

Martin, M. C. (2008). *Individual and collective resources and health in Morocco*. UNU-WIDER Research Paper. Unpublished.

McKenzie, D., & Rapoport, H. (2006). *Can migration reduce educational attainment?* World Bank Policy Research Working Paper 3952. Washington, DC: World Bank.

Mehruz, K. (2012). Exploring social capital in sustaining IT adoption and use in micro-enterprises. In *Proceedings of the Southern Association for Information Systems Conference*. Atlanta, GA: Southern Association for Information Systems.

Mude, A. G., Barrett, C. B., McPeak, J. G., & Doss, C. (2003). Educational investments in a spatially varied economy. *Economica*, 74(294), 351–369. doi:10.1111/j.1468-0335.2006.00538.x

Nissanke, M., & Thorbecke, E. (2005). Channels and policy debate in the globalization-inequality-poverty nexus. *World Development*, 34(8), 1338–1360. doi:10.1016/j.worlddev.2005.10.008

Nolan, B., & Whelan, T. C. (2011). *Resources, deprivation, and poverty*. Oxford, UK: Oxford University Press. doi:10.1093/acprof:oso/9780199588435.001.0001

ODPM. (2004). *The English indices of deprivation 2004: Summary* (Revised ed.). Retrieved from http://www.communities.gov.uk/documents/communities/pdf/131209.pdf

OECD. (2008). *Politiques sociales, prestations et questions sociales*. Retrieved from http://www.oecd.org/topic/0,3373,fr_2649_33933_1_1_1_1_37419,00.html

Pampalon, R., & Guy, R. (2000). Deprivation index for health and welfare planning in Quebec. *Chronic Diseases in Canada*, 21(3), 104–114.

Pissarides, C. A. Véganzonès, & Varoudakis, M. A. (2005). *Labor markets and economic growth in the MENA region*. London, UK: London School of Economics and CERDI, CNRS, Université d'Auvergne.

Raquel, M. P., & Osório, A. (2012). Lifelong learning, intergenerational relationships and ICT: Perceptions of children and older adult: Elderly, education, intergenerational relationships and social development. In *Proceedings of 2nd Conference of ELOA and Digital Inclusion in Society*. ELOA.

Ravallion, M. (2006). *Inequality is bad for the poor. Background Paper to 2006 World Development Report, Equity and Development*. New York, NY: United Nations.

RDH50. (2012). *RDH general report: 50 ans de développement humain & perspectives 2025*. Retrieved from http://www.rdh50.ma/Fr/pdf/general/RG-FR.pdf

Reiffers, J. L. (2003). *Rapport du FEMISE 2003 sur le partenariat Euro-Méditerranéen*. Retrieved from http://www.defi-univ.org/REIFFERS-Jean-Louis,2311

Rocha, H., & Neer, N. (2012). *Local youth employment and inclusion in Argentina: A public-private initiative for the development of talents, social cohesion and inclusion*. Retrieved from http://ssrn.com/2097880

Sharma, V. (2012). The influence of ICTs in improving and empowering the quality of education system in developing countries like India. *Golden Research Thoughts*, 2(2). Retrieved from http://www.aygrt.net

Thapa, D., Sein, M. K., & Sæbø. (2012). Building collective capabilities through ICT in a mountain region of Nepal: Where social capital lead to collective action. *Journal of Information Technology, Information Technology for Development*, 18(1).

Townsend, P. (1979). *Poverty in the United Kingdom: A survey of household resources and standards of living.* Harmondsworth, UK: Penguin.

Townsend, P. (1987). Deprivation. *Journal of Social Policy, 16*(2), 125–146. doi:10.1017/S0047279400020341

Ulubaşoğlu, M. A., & Cardak, B. A. (2006). International comparisons of rural-urban educational attainment data and determinants. *European Economic Review, 51*(7), 1828–1857. doi:10.1016/j.euroecorev.2006.11.003

UNDP. (2002). Arab human development report 2002: Creating opportunities for future generations. *Regional Bureau of Arab States.* Retrieved on July 9th, 2007, from http://www.nakbaonline.org/download/UNDP/EnglishVersion/Ar-Human-Dev-2002.pdf

UNDP. (2003). Arab human development report: Building a knowledge-society. *Regional Bureau of Arab States.* Retrieved on July 9th, 2007, from http://www.miftah.org/Doc/Reports/Englishcomplete2003.pdf

UNDP. (2004). Arab human development report: Towards freedom in the Arab world. *Regional Bureau of Arab States.* Retrieved on July 9th, 2007, from http://www.pogar.org/publications/other/ahdr/ahdr2004e.pdf

UNDP. (2005). Arab human development report: Towards the rise of women. *Regional Bureau of Arab States.* Retrieved on July 9th, 2007, from http://www.auswaertigesamt.de/diplo/de/Aussenpolitik/Kulturpolitik/DialogIslam/HumanDevelopRep2005.pdf

Zhang, Y., & Bolton, G. E. (2012). *Social network effects on coordination: A laboratory investigation.* Retrieved from http://ssrn.com/102139/ssrn.2000974

KEY TERMS AND DEFINITIONS

Human Deprivation Approach, Social Cohesion Approach: The approach of deprivation started in 1980 in Great Britain following a long tradition related to the monitoring of social inequalities mainly in the health sector. Several empirical measures have been developed during the last ten years in the United Kingdom. These indices have been expanding to cover social situations in other countries. The deprivation approach is based on the assessment of needs relative to the basic requirements that are not covered. Mack (1985) added the identification of the on-going living conditions rather than income and expenditures. This approach follows the basic idea of Townsend (1979) who focused on the fact that poverty is also related to needs that are not socially satisfied but well perceived (Deutsch & Silber, 2008). Peter Townsend (1987) identified deprivation as related to a disadvantage that is observable when comparing an individual or household in the local or a larger community. This approach was initiated in Britain in 1980s in relation to health inequalities. However, as needs are interrelated, other components have been included. They include employment, consumption, housing, education, and others. An index is used to include variables that locate individuals and households relative to the majority. The following four criteria were developed using the 1991 census as the basis of Townsend index (Unemployed aged above 16 in the labor force, Household Room occupation rate, Car ownership rate, and House ownership). A second type of deprivation index was developed by Carstairs and Morris (1989). This is also based on 4 variables where 3 are the same as in Townsend's index. The fourth variable refers to the belongings to low social group instead of house ownership. The third index that was developed earlier by Jarman (1983) was called the

Score of Under-privileged Areas. This index was re-introduced in 1984 to assess the local demand for health services. Nolan and Whelan (2011) discuss the deprivation issue and show the usefulness of ensuring knowledge about local deprivation as means to support development actions. Other contributions include that of Pampalon and Guy (2000). Practical details are shown in ODPM – Office of Deputy Prime Minister (2004) reports.

Theory and Practice of Social Cohesion: The promotion of social cohesion within European states is made following an open method of co-ordination. The European council fixes common objectives and guidelines. These are transformed into national policies that are built in accordance with the country needs and resources with the design of a monitoring strategy. While the policies are executed at a national level, they are evaluated using Laeken indicators. Those Laeken indicators were developed by the European council as a set of common European statistical indicators. They were specifically defined and structured as indicators to measure social results rather than the means used to achieve them. These indicators are based on a classification given to each component. Laeken indicators are formed of 21 variables that are divided as primary and secondary indicators. They cover income, employment, education, and health. Income is composed of series of measures and deals with low income, since a lack of monetary resources in a market economy reduces access to a range of goods and services. Six indicators are devoted to employment, since participation in the labor market is considered an important factor in social inclusion. The share of early school leavers not in education or training (indicator 9) focuses on young persons aged 18 through 24 and gauges the efficiency of a country's educational system, as well as the ability of a society to combat poverty and improve social cohesion. The only indicator in the health category is life expectancy at birth, which combines a number of factors ranging from socio-economic status to access to health care.

ENDNOTES

1. This chapter uses some of the material the author developed in another paper that looks at social cohesion with comparisons between European and South Mediterranean countries. Part of this material is published in a FEMISE report dealing with social cohesion in collaboration with CESPI, Italy.

2. Social cohesion policies are related to those prevailing in most countries of Europe. They are monitored both in local territories and at the national levels. They aim at including those leaving under socially difficult conditions. There is a large set of publications related to the issue of social cohesion policy mainly by OECD.

Chapter 12
Risk Factors, Health, Education, and Poverty:
Can ICTs Help[1]?

ABSTRACT

Other complicating and risk factors are introduced to show the extent of interdependencies between health and education. The situation of women and children, besides the series of risks and uncertainties faced, impose more advanced coordination schemes. Accounting for these risks can ensure good conditions for the use of different ICT components. New means and strategies for mobilizing ICTs[2] either for databases or software tools and empirical analyses are also important when considering the process of accounting for interdependencies. However, the enhancement of literacy in each economy appears to be conditioning the success of Internet penetration.

INTRODUCTION

While the above microeconomic and macroeconomic sections have shown the existence of important interdependencies among the components related to health, education and poverty, there are also important factors that can be considered as sources of risks if not included. These factors prevail at both supply and demand sides of health, education, and employment. The problem of migration of skilled labor with its relationship to education, poverty and to the overall social, economic, and political conditions is a major example of the risks that are faced by developing economies and the region. Besides short, medium, and long term effects of the risks related to migration of skilled labor, there are other risks related to longer terms impacts. These include environmental risks besides the structural trends that relate to the population characteristics. The role played by gender is likely to directly affect children, labor productivity, education, and health. In this chapter, a special focus is placed on brain drain, gender issues and rural versus urban trends. The issues discussed in this chapter show that ICTs can help only if conditions of access to different services are ensured and that women would constitute the main targets of development policies.

DOI: 10.4018/978-1-4666-3643-9.ch012

This chapter focuses first on gender inequality. This is followed by showing how rural urban interconnections are likely to affect development. The effects of disabilities constitute the third issue tackled. The availability of skilled labor through the case of medical doctors is then discussed to show how this limits the provision of health services. All these issues are introduced to show how these limiting factors could be major sources of risks in identifying, planning, and monitoring of health, education, employment, and income policies. They need to be considered while assessing interdependencies. Most of these issues are introduced and discussed within the context of MENA countries. These are taken as a case study for other countries that may exhibit similar social deficits. All these factors lead to questions related to how ICTs can be useful to help address and focus on these different risks. This is introduced in part 2 after a review of all sources of risks facing the economies.

SOURCES OF RISKS AND INTERDEPENDENCIES

Series of issues are discussed in relation to their importance in shaping the social performance and affecting the interdependencies between health, education, and economic factors. Different sources of risks and uncertainties could affect the social performance at local, national, and regional levels. The major sources discussed here include the likely effects of global climatic changes, the impacts of international economic crises, risks related to specific sectors besides all endogenous risks inherent to individuals and groups. The objective behind addressing these issues is to underline the most important social features that may generate complex effects on social performance when these factors are not emphasized in local and national social policies.

Climatic Risks

These risks are present and do affect localities, regions and economies, especially if they are under vulnerable natural resource conditions. This is the case of most South Mediterranean countries and mainly the Arab economies. Several publications and reports do exist to show that the signals related to climatic change and to the gradual increase in warming. These signals are not in favor of those economies that are geographically located under naturally stressed environments. External natural stresses are likely to transmit its effects to individuals and groups in the economy through affecting activities related to natural capital, human capital, physical capital, and financial resources. The best representations of these mechanisms are found in the UNCTAD (2010) information and communication report 2010. According to the set of relationships shown in the cited diagrams, the livelihoods of individuals and groups, mainly those that are under precarious conditions, are drastically affected by the degradation of climatic conditions.

Among a large array of publications about the effects of climatic change on agriculture and rural areas and the possible solutions promised by ICTs, Kumar and Singh (2012) can be cited. The authors consider that even if rural development is among the public priorities, the rate of penetration of ICTs is relatively slow. The main reasons rely on the lack of infrastructure, limited awareness of local officials about the usefulness of ICTs and the multiplicity of local languages. However, the large potential from ICTs can be very promising. This includes the introduction of new alternatives and options to cope with very highly variable agriculture. The changing climatic conditions are likely to be compensated with the development of new activities that both help agriculture and non-agriculture in vulnerable settings.

International Risks and Macroeconomic Risks

Using data on volatility, Norman, Ranciere, Serven, and Ventura (2007) found that transmission of volatility to consumption is more important in developing countries. Increased volatility is shown to be harmful to growth in developing economies as transmission takes place in the overall economy.

In the same way, the above authors show how developing countries have high levels of volatility of output gap and overall regulation index. These indicate how international risks can be transmitted to the economies with major effects on different categories of agents and on the macro-economy. In addition, risks generated within a specific sector are likely to be diffused in the same way. This shows how each economy is vulnerable and how developing countries are more sensitive to these risks.

Price, Income, and Environmental Risks

The higher costs of services and access to facilities incurred by poor people can be seen as a paradox because besides the low income, the total costs implicitly paid for services are high. Poor people have to incur travel distance costs moving from one area to another to get goods or services. Also, and given their limited resources, poor households do not have a wide range of options from which they can choose.

This restriction in choices is a major reason leading to higher costs incurred by the poor. In addition to travel distance and restriction in choice, the waiting time and the transaction costs also increase the burden of higher costs to low-income households.

Poor households and individuals are exposed to high-income risk. This risk originates from frequent climatic and economic policy shocks that increase the vulnerability of households to severe hardships. Examples of these shocks include but not limited to, poor harvest due to drought and floods and unexpected additional expenses encountered due to variations in economic policies imposed by the country. However, as pointed out in many studies held in this framework, the nature and types of shocks vary in time and intensity depending on the efforts of developing countries to deal with such issues. It is this variation that determines the level of impact and the policies developed by poor individuals to overcome these shocks (Dercon, 2002). Dercon (2002) also pointed out that there are two types of income risks faced by poor individuals and households. Given their aggregate nature, common risks impact all the individuals in a given community or region. Idiosyncratic or individual risks affect a particular member of the society. The concept of vulnerability of the poor comes from the notion that deprived segments are more sensitive to shocks that threaten their livelihood and survival. An assessment of the vulnerability of the poor in Guatemala has found that natural disasters and agricultural related shocks and to a lesser extent economic shocks have more impact on poor households and individuals relative to the rich segments of society. The number of shocks to which the poor are exposed also increases their vulnerability. The poor are not exposed to only one shock during a given period of time. The study held in Guatemala has pointed out that more than half of the households chosen in the sample have reported that they have experienced more than one shock during the previous 12 months (Tesliuc & Lindert, 2002).

Another study differently tackled the concept of vulnerability of the poor to natural shocks. This study has defined vulnerability as the probability that poor individuals will fall below the poverty line and focused on variations in consumption patterns as the source of this vulnerability. Some households tend to be poor because of the high variance in their consumption or because they have some specific characteristics that constrain them to decrease from their mean consumption and therefore oblige them to stay below the poverty line. Rainfall shocks in Ethiopia were found to impact consumption significantly because of the positive and high elasticities between rainfall shocks and consumption. Rainfall shocks do not affect consumption directly. Nonetheless, rainfall shocks cause variations in consumption patterns of poor people who therefore become exposed to the fall below poverty line through the income effect (Dabalen & Poupart, 2002).

Even if economic, natural, and political shocks are the determinants of the vulnerability to poverty, there are some factors that impact the influence of these disasters. Geographical location is one of these factors. The age and the number of children are other factors determining the degree of vulnerability to poverty. Still in Kenya, communities with more children aged between 8 and 15 years were more vulnerable than communities comprising households with younger children (Christiaensen &Subbarao, 2001).

It is widely known from studies on poverty that, at the macro-economic level, disasters or crises tend to reduce the level of income and magnify the risk or the probability that the poor will become poorer. However, the study held about households in Argentina for the period 1995-2002 has concluded that income variability or risk loses its utility in the measurement of poverty when households are disaggregated into different groups. In other words, income risk is not uniform among all the households. This conclusion was reached after calculating the risk-adjusted income of different groups of households.

Lower levels of variability in income are observed in households with better-educated members. But households with informal workers and unemployed or inactive members tend to experience higher levels of income variability (Cruces, 2002).

Accounting for Gender Inequality and Transmission Channels

This is based mainly on data and outcomes already introduced in chapter 8 when discussing the issues of women in poverty. Keeping in mind the two bio-economic models discussed in the first part of chapter 8, the current section is devoted to underlying how risks that can originate in the demographic and biological profile, could be transmitted to the spheres of education, health and employment. The situation of women in the MENA region with series of regressions that are also shown in chapter 8, are introduced and reinterpreted to indicate how risks can be transmitted.

Health and Urbanization

Based on WHO data on some health related variables, the estimated relationships have shown that urbanization is an important driver for the enhancement of medically controlled birth of children (Table 1).

It is a 1% change in urbanization that produces a similar level of realization in births attended by skilled medical staff. Otherwise, the maternal and infant mortality rates are still high in the region. They appear also to be inter-related and that a 1-point reduction in maternal mortality rate leads to 0.44 reductions in infant mortality. However, the increasing rate of urbanization can reduce drastically the maternal mortality rate in these regions. Other related results are included in the Table 2.

Definition of variables: BASHP: Births attended by skilled health personnel %; IMR: Infant mortality rate per 1000; MMR: Maternal mortality rate 1 per 10000; LRMD: Lifetime risk maternal death 1 in; TFR: Total fertility rate; URBR: Urbanization rate %.

While the above results confirm the important role of women in the determination of different health, education and other socio-economic deficits, the case study of Morocco using aggregate data on dropout from different school levels, does underline the magnitude of global interdependencies. This is again strengthened using cross section data on South Mediterranean countries. In these two exercises, data from different sources are used. In terms of nutrition, the variables used stand for the percentage of under-fives (2000-2006) suffering from underweight – moderate and severe, Vitamin A supplement coverage rate (6-59 months) 2005 – at least one dose (%), Vitamin A supplement coverage rate (6-59 months) 2005 – full coverage (%), percentage of children (2000-2006) who are breastfed with complementary food (6-9 months), percentage of infants with low birth weight 1999-2006 and percentage of households

consuming iodized salt 2000-2006. Concerning health, the indicators used are the percentage of population using improved drinking-water sources 2004 (urban and Total), percentage of new-born protected against tetanus, 1-year-old children immunized (2006) against Tuberculosis (corresponding vaccine is BCG), infant mortality rate (per 1000 live births), maternal mortality ratio (per 100 000 live births), life expectancy at birth – total (years), general government expenditure on health as percentage of total expenditure on health (% health), total expenditure on health as percentage of gross domestic product (Health exp), and total fertility rate 2006 (per woman). This report also uses a Moroccan local indicator

Table 1. Urbanization and health variables

Country	Maternal mortality ratio (per 100 000) [Lower estimate-upper estimate]	Lifetime risk of maternal death (1 in)	Total fertility rate	Births attended by skilled health personnel (%)	Infant mortality rate (per 1000)	Urbanization (%)
	MMR	LRMD	FR	BASHP	IMR	URB
Algeria	0.140	0.005	2.500	0.920	3.500	0.633
Bahrain	0.028	0.001	2.500	0.990	0.900	0.965
Egypt	0.084	0.003	3.300	0.694	2.600	0.428
Iran	0.076	0.003	2.100	0.896	3.200	0.669
Iraq	0.250	0.015	4.800	0.721	10.200	0.669
Jordan	0.041	0.002	3.500	0.995	2.300	0.823
Kuwait	0.005	0.000	2.400	1.000	1.000	0.983
Lebanon	0.150	0.004	2.300	0.930	2.700	0.866
Libya	0.097	0.004	3.000	0.944	1.800	0.848
Mauritania	1.000	0.071	5.800	0.569	7.800	0.404
Morocco	0.220	0.008	2.800	0.626	3.800	0.587
Oman	0.087	0.006	3.800	0.947	1.000	0.715
Qatar	0.007	0.000	3.000	1.000	1.000	0.954
Saudi	0.023	0.002	4.100	0.930	2.200	0.810
Syria	0.160	0.008	3.500	0.700	1.500	0.506
Tunisia	0.120	0.003	2.000	0.898	2.100	0.653
Turkey	0.070	0.002	2.500	0.830	2.800	0.673
Emirates	0.054	0.002	2.500	1.000	0.700	0.767
Yemen	0.570	0.053	6.200	0.216	8.200	0.273

Table 2. Regression outputs based on data from Table 1

Regressions	R²	Observations
BASHP= 0.16 + 0.96 URB (2.52) (7.82)	0.78	19
IMR= 1.94 + 0.44 MMR (7.31) (4.62)	0.56	19
TFR= 1.95 + 0.14 LRMD (8.27) (3.54)	0.42	19
MMR= 4.49 + 1.02 LRMD – 1.10 TFR (16.03) (35.94) (-8.53)	0.99	19
MMR= -3.90 -1.88 URBR + 0.75 IMR (-13.17) (-2.59) (2.38)	0.69	19
IMR= 2.71 + 0.35 LRMD (2.75) (2.56)	0.59	19
BASHP= 0.49 – 0.19 IMR – 0.49 TFR (2.18) (-2.06) (-2.23)	0.56	19

which is the distribution of the number of disease cases subject to vaccination per region (2006) published by the "Direction de l'Epidémiologie et de la lutte Contre les Maladies (DELM)," Ministry of Health, Morocco. This indicator represents the incidence rate per 100,000 inhabitants and the diseases are Measles, Tetanus, Whooping Cough, Poliomyelitis, Diphteria, Tuberculosis, Typhoid, Viral Hepatitis, Bilharziose, Paludism, and Leishmaniose. The average disease cases number per region is then computed and used in the regressions.

Health and Education

The education indicators used are the primary school enrolment ratio 2000-2006 – net male, primary school enrolment ratio 2000-2006 – net female, primary school attendance ratio (2000-2006) net male, drop out % rate primary, youth (15-24 years) literacy rate 2000-2006 (Female), primary school enrolment (% gross), secondary school enrolment (% gross), and percentage of central government expenditures (1995-2005) on education. Other indicators related to the dropout rate from primary (per year, 6 years), secondary (per year, 3 years), and tertiary schools (per year, 3 years) per region for female and total (Ministry of Education, Morocco).

Concerning the explanation of dropout in the case of Morocco, regression results show clearly the relationships between the rate of failure and dropout from schools and the levels of poverty and health. The first set of outputs explains the dropout rate at the level of primary schooling. Children leave school because of health problems (measured by average frequency of diseases in a region) and poverty (measured by region). The elasticity of loss relative to health is 0.81 meaning that a 1% change in average disease leads to 0.81% change in dropout. Otherwise, to decrease dropout from school by 0.81%, health needs to be improved such that the frequency of diseases be reduced by 1%. Similarly, a 1% change in poverty leads to 0.56% change in dropout, meaning that reduction of poverty by 1% reduces the drop-out from primary school by 0.56%. In case of simultaneous health and poverty improvements, the result is 1.37% reduction in dropout. Girls appear to have the leading role in this process because the corresponding elasticities are higher. These results are again confirmed when looking at the effect of age. It seems that health conditions and poverty affect the drop out at all levels of the primary school with poverty only affecting the dropout of girls in 2nd and 3rd years. For the college level poverty seems to have an important influence on the drop out for both males and females. However, the effects of poverty are getting lower in general and for females especially implying that other factors do affect the dropout rate (Table 3).

Transmission to Education

The second set of regression results confirms the role of health and mainly that of women on education. In this context, health has been measured by weight, nutrition, vaccination, maternal mortality, and health expenditures. All these variables show their appropriate links with dependent variables related to different dimensions of education. These include school enrolment, female literacy, dropout, and public expenditures on education. Different regression results are introduced in Table 4.

The Effects of Rural and Urban Interconnections

At the exception of Bahrain, Kuwait, and Qatar that are mainly urban, the other countries have lower but intermediate urbanization rates. These include Saudi Arabia, Jordan, Lebanon, United Arab Emirates, and Oman. The remaining countries are still having important rural population and economy. These countries are Mauritania, Yemen, Libya, Tunisia, Algeria, Morocco, Egypt, and Turkey. The socio-economic situation in these latter countries is exacerbated by the deficits originating from rural areas. These deficits are expressed by the limited availability of infrastructure and the difficulties of access to basic facilities. Rural emigration can be understood as the consequence of the socio-economic deficits prevailing in rural areas but also among the causes of urban degradation and poverty.

The socio-economic degradation of rural areas with its consequences on both rural and urban population has been extensively discussed in series of publications. The role of adverse macroeconomic policies has been discussed by Krueger, Schiff, and Valdès (1988). Liberalization policies have not often generated major changes in the direction of biases affecting rural areas (Boussard, Gérard, & Piketty, 2005; Anderson, Martin, & Van der Mensbrugghe, 2006). Other contributions have placed emphasis on the role of agricultural market imperfections and their effects on prices and revenues (Dutta & Mishra, 2004). Such pressures on agriculture and rural areas do accelerate rural migration and intensify the level of poverty (Ravaillon, 2006).

Within the above framework, South Mediterranean Countries and mainly those with important rural areas are pursuing agricultural liberalization policies with focus on larger reduction of government intervention. Rural development in this region and mainly in North Africa, Egypt and Turkey is the central component of any strategy that leads to improving living conditions and the well-being of the societies. The significance of agricultural reforms in countries stems not only from the need to reduce poverty (estimated 70% of poverty is in rural areas when those areas cover about 43% of the population) but also to increase the attractiveness of rural regions.

Tunisia, Lebanon, Egypt, Turkey, and Morocco are intensively engaged in these policies by dismantling the state commodity marketing monopolies and continuous reduction of tariffs. Some sector models have been indicating that these policies have not often been in favor of rural areas. Producers of cereals and livestock products in the region could suffer significant losses from trade liberalization. This characterizes the processes of degradation of rural areas with an increase in urban poverty. It is not in favor of economic and social development. Health, education and other basic needs are consequently affected and a more general situation of deprivation is observed.

Table 5 is devoted to characterizing the predominance of rural versus urban living conditions and styles in the region. The first column of data is based on the estimated rate of rural migration as calculated over 1990-2006 data. It is the change in rural population adjusted for natural rural population growth and reported to total population for each country.

The second column shows that the urbanization rate is generally between 0.3 and 0.7 for the North African region and for Syria and Turkey. Otherwise, this rate is around and above 0.8 as this is the case of Kuwait, Bahrain, and Qatar. However, the highest rates of rural migration are in Jordan, Sudan, and Yemen. Mauritania and Egypt with

Table 3. Education, health, and dropout regressions

Interdependencies: Case of Morocco)	R²	Obs.
Drop Out from Primary, Poverty & Health		
$Ln\left(\text{Total primary drop out, M \& F}\right) = - \underset{(-2.99)}{0.81}\left[Ln\left(\text{Average Diseases}\right)\right] + \underset{(3.97)}{0.56}\left[Ln\left(\text{Poverty rate}\right)\right]$	0.63	15
$Ln\left(\text{Total primary drop out, Female}\right) = - \underset{(-3.32)}{0.92}\left[Ln\left(\text{Average Diseases}\right)\right] + \underset{(4.56)}{0.66}\left[Ln\left(\text{Poverty rate}\right)\right]$	0.69	15
$Ln\left(\text{Drop out from 1st year, primary, M \& F}\right) = \underset{(2.68)}{0.48}\left[Ln\left(\text{Poverty rate}\right)\right]$	0.38	15
$Ln\left(\text{Drop out from 1st year, primary, Female}\right) = \underset{(2.78)}{0.56}\left[Ln\left(\text{Poverty rate}\right)\right]$	0.45	14
$Ln\left(\begin{array}{l}\text{Drop out from 2nd}\\ \text{year, primary, M \& F}\end{array}\right) = - \underset{(-2.17)}{1.03}\left[Ln\left(\text{Average Diseases}\right)\right] + \underset{(3.02)}{0.84}\left[Ln\left(\text{Poverty rate}\right)\right]$	0.56	14
$Ln\left(\text{Drop out from 2nd year, primary, Female}\right) = \underset{(3.43)}{1.04}\left[Ln\left(\text{Poverty rate}\right)\right]$	0.56	14
$Ln\left(\text{Drop out from 3 rd year, primary, M \& F}\right) = \underset{(2.42)}{0.57}\left[Ln\left(\text{Poverty rate}\right)\right]$	0.45	14
$Ln\left(\text{Drop out from 3 rd year, primary, Female}\right) = \underset{(3.03)}{0.60}\left[Ln\left(\text{Poverty rate}\right)\right]$	0.48	15
$Ln\left(\text{Drop out from 4 th year, primary, M \& F}\right) = - \underset{(-2.83)}{0.99}\left[Ln\left(\text{Average Diseases}\right)\right]$	0.46	15
$Ln\left(\begin{array}{l}\text{Drop out from 4 th}\\ \text{year, primary, Female}\end{array}\right) = - \underset{(-2.70)}{1.12}\left[Ln\left(\text{Average Diseases}\right)\right] + \underset{(2.49)}{0.54}\left[Ln\left(\text{Poverty rate}\right)\right]$	0.48	15
$Ln\left(\begin{array}{l}\text{Drop out from 5 th}\\ \text{year, primary, M \& F}\end{array}\right) = - \underset{(-3.67)}{0.98}\left[Ln\left(\text{Average Diseases}\right)\right] + \underset{(2.52)}{0.35}\left[Ln\left(\text{Poverty rate}\right)\right]$	0.58	15
$Ln\left(\begin{array}{l}\text{Drop out from 5 th}\\ \text{year, primary, Female}\end{array}\right) = - \underset{(-3.56)}{1.03}\left[Ln\left(\text{Average Diseases}\right)\right] + \underset{(2.74)}{0.41}\left[Ln\left(\text{Poverty rate}\right)\right]$	0.58	15
$Ln\left(\begin{array}{l}\text{Drop out from 6 th}\\ \text{year, primary, M \& F}\end{array}\right) = - \underset{(-2.06)}{0.96}\left[Ln\left(\text{Average Diseases}\right)\right] + \underset{(3.80)}{0.93}\left[Ln\left(\text{Poverty rate}\right)\right]$	0.57	15
$Ln\left(\begin{array}{l}\text{Drop out from 6 th}\\ \text{year, primary, Female}\end{array}\right) = - \underset{(-2.28)}{1.07}\left[Ln\left(\text{Average Diseases}\right)\right] + \underset{(4.24)}{1.04}\left[Ln\left(\text{Poverty rate}\right)\right]$	0.62	15

continued on following page

Table 3. Continued

Interdependencies: Case of Morocco)	R²	Obs.
Drop Out from College & Poverty		
$Ln\left(\text{Drop out from college, Total, M \& F}\right) = -\underset{(-2.01)}{0.93} + \underset{(4.37)}{0.35}\left[Ln\left(Poverty \text{ rate}\right)\right]$	0.60	15
$Ln\left(\text{Drop out from college, Total, Female}\right) = -\underset{(-2.41)}{1.02} + \underset{(4.03)}{0.30}\left[Ln\left(Poverty \text{ rate}\right)\right]$	0.57	15
$Ln\left(\text{Drop out from 1 st year, college, M \& F}\right) = \underset{(4.53)}{0.55}\left[Ln\left(Poverty \text{ rate}\right)\right]$	0.61	15
$Ln\left(\text{Drop out from 1 st year, college, Female}\right) = \underset{(4.79)}{0.60}\left[Ln\left(Poverty \text{ rate}\right)\right]$	0.64	15
$Ln\left(\text{Drop out from 2 nd year, college, M \& F}\right) = \underset{(3.11)}{0.81}\left[Ln\left(Poverty \text{ rate}\right)\right]$	0.45	15
$Ln\left(\text{Drop out from 2 nd year, college, Female}\right) = -\underset{(-2.36)}{1.50} + \underset{(2.68)}{0.30}\left[Ln\left(Poverty \text{ rate}\right)\right]$	0.37	15
$Ln\left(\text{Drop out from 3 rd year, college, M \& F}\right) = \underset{(4.10)}{0.25}\left[Ln\left(Poverty \text{ rate}\right)\right]$	0.59	15
$Ln\left(\text{Drop out from 3 rd year, college, Female}\right) = -\underset{(-2.30)}{0.75} + \underset{(3.29)}{0.19}\left[Ln\left(Poverty \text{ rate}\right)\right]$	0.50	15
Drop Out from High School & Poverty		
$Ln\left(\text{Drop out from High School, Total, M \& F}\right) = \underset{(2.61)}{0.41}\left[Ln\left(Poverty \text{ rate}\right)\right]$	0.35	15
$Ln\left(\text{Drop out from High School, Total, Female}\right) = \underset{(2.08)}{0.26}\left[Ln\left(Poverty \text{ rate}\right)\right]$	0.25	15
$Ln\left(\text{Drop out from 3 rd year of High School, M \& F}\right) = \underset{(2.05)}{0.39}\left[Ln\left(Poverty \text{ rate}\right)\right]$	0.27	15
$Ln\left(\text{Drop out from 3 rd year of High School, Female}\right) = \underset{(2.00)}{0.52}\left[Ln\left(Poverty \text{ rate}\right)\right]$	0.26	15

both relatively low rural migration and low urbanization show the predominance of rural living conditions. North African countries express intermediate figures for both rural and urbanization rates.

Martin (2008) in studying the perception that rural women in Morocco have of their health shows that better access to own as well as to collective resources contributes to the creation of capabilities to maintain a decent health status which supports the association between Socioeconomic Status (SES) and health. This also highlights the complexity of the mechanisms associating the two. Here, notions such as freedom, governance and equity all take part in explaining of the link and all have relevance in terms of policy implications.

The results of the study emphasize the importance of jointly tackling (meaning here simultane-

Table 4. Assessment of interdependencies between health and education variables

Interdependencies	R^2	Obs.
$Ln\begin{pmatrix}\text{Pr}imary\text{ school enrolment}\\\text{ratio (2000- 06), net Male}\end{pmatrix} = \underset{(12.12)}{7.19} - \underset{(-4.57)}{0.21}\begin{bmatrix}Ln\begin{pmatrix}Underweight\\\text{moderate \& severe}\end{pmatrix}\end{bmatrix} - \underset{(-4.14)}{0.65}\begin{bmatrix}Ln\begin{pmatrix}\text{Vitamin A supplement}\\\text{at least one dose (\%)}\end{pmatrix}\end{bmatrix}$	0.62	20
$Ln\begin{pmatrix}\text{Prim. sch. enrolm. ratio}\\\text{(2000- 06), net Female}\end{pmatrix} = \underset{(8.51)}{6.82} - \underset{(-4.31)}{0.27}\begin{bmatrix}Ln\begin{pmatrix}\text{\% under 5 (2000- 06) suffering}\\\text{from underweight mod. \& sev.}\end{pmatrix}\end{bmatrix} - \underset{(-2.46)}{0.53}\begin{bmatrix}Ln\begin{pmatrix}Vitamin\text{ A supplement}\\\text{at least one dose (\%)}\end{pmatrix}\end{bmatrix}$	0.53	20
$Ln\begin{pmatrix}\text{Pr}im.\text{ sch. enrol. ratio}\\\text{(2000- 06), net Male}\end{pmatrix} = \underset{(32.62)}{3.97} + \underset{(7.84)}{0.34}\begin{bmatrix}Ln\begin{pmatrix}\text{Vitamin A}\\\text{supplement Full}\end{pmatrix}\end{bmatrix} - \underset{(-3.38)}{0.10}\begin{bmatrix}Ln\begin{pmatrix}Underweight\\\text{mod. \& sev.}\end{pmatrix}\end{bmatrix}$	0.83	20
$Ln\begin{pmatrix}\text{Prim. sch. attendance ratio}\\\text{(2000- 2006), net Male}\end{pmatrix} = \underset{(2.16)}{0.25}\begin{bmatrix}Ln\begin{pmatrix}\text{Improved Drinking-}\\\text{water sources}\end{pmatrix}\end{bmatrix} + \underset{(4.18)}{0.65}\begin{bmatrix}Ln\begin{pmatrix}\text{Immun. vaccines}\\\text{"BCG"}\end{pmatrix}\end{bmatrix}$	0.80	20
$Ln\begin{pmatrix}\text{Prim. sch. attendance ratio}\\\text{(2000- 2006), net Male}\end{pmatrix} = \underset{(2.35)}{0.33}\begin{bmatrix}Ln\begin{pmatrix}\text{Improved Drinking-}\\\text{water sources}\end{pmatrix}\end{bmatrix} + \underset{(3.58)}{0.59}\begin{bmatrix}Ln\begin{pmatrix}\text{Immun. vaccines}\\\text{"BCG"}\end{pmatrix}\end{bmatrix}$	0.81	20
$Ln\left(\text{Infant mortality under 5}\right) = \underset{(5.40)}{19.53} - \underset{(-2.09)}{1.82}\left[Ln\left(Female\text{ literacy}\right)\right] - \underset{(-2.57)}{1.90}\left[Ln\left(Nb\text{ Tetanos}\right)\right]$	0.59	17
$Ln\left(\text{Drop out}\right) = \underset{(3.39)}{16.72} - \underset{(-2.45)}{1.89}\left[Ln\left(Health\text{ expenditures}\right)\right] - \underset{(-3.23)}{3.15}\left[Ln\left(\%\text{ Health}\right)\right]$	0.56	13
$Ln\left(\%\text{ Enrolment secondary}\right) = \underset{(2.30)}{4.29} - \underset{(-2.51)}{0.05}\left[Ln\left(Maternal\text{ mortality (100000 births)}\right)\right]$	0.72	19
$Ln\left(\%\text{ of children (2000- 2006) breastfed with complementary (6- 9 months)}\right) = \underset{(3.10)}{1.98}$ $+ \underset{(2.28)}{0.46}\left[Ln\left(Gov.Exp.\text{ on Education}\right)\right] + \underset{(2.67)}{0.18}\left[Ln\left(Household\text{ Iodized Salt Consump.}\right)\right]$	0.37	20
$Ln\left(\text{Health Exp}\right) = \underset{(3.82)}{5.34} + \underset{(3.14)}{0.33}\left[Ln\left(\%\text{ Education}\right)\right] - \underset{(-3.99)}{0.95}\left[Ln\left(\%\text{ Health}\right)\right]$	0.72	14

ously but also in a coordinated manner) individual, family, communal or regional mediators of socio economic status will lead to health improvements. Any intervention that increases individual and collective wealth and capabilities may render the environment more prone to produce health. The public investments undertaken have to take into account not only the health objective but also the socio economic status and the population vulnerability factors. In addition, public resources invested in one sphere of activity, particularly in education, will have positive spillovers in health.

The question asked by Martin is whether or not the availability and access to public health resources can reduce health inequalities and compensate for lower income. Including variables linked to the level and type of social and economic services and infrastructure in an economy in evaluating health is seldom done even in developed country studies. In the developing countries, what is sometimes done is to analyze the impact of infrastructure directly linked to the risk of disease transmission (potable water, sanitation, electricity, health services).

Table 5. Rural migration and urbanization rates

Country	Rural Migration	Urbanization Rate
Jordan	0.014	0.823
Libya	0.005	0.848
Lebanon	0.003	0.866
Yemen	0.006	0.273
Algeria	0.004	0.633
Tunisia	0.002	0.653
Syrian	0.004	0.506
Oman	0.004	0.715
Morocco	0.003	0.587
Turkey	0.003	0.673
Egypt	0.001	0.428
Mauritania	0.001	0.404

Martin adopted a production approach to estimate the capacity of women at given levels of vulnerability to produce health with both own resources and collective ones available.

As a measure of the availability of collective resource, the author uses the availability of public goods and services. The measures are density of primary schools and health centers per capita. Their proximity encourages their use.

The results support the expected relations between the individual's variables and the perception of health. The results referring to the availability of collective resources show that the communes with a high density of schools seem to report better perceptions of health than communes with low density of schools.

Analyzing the interactions between individual and collective resources the author shows that the women's health is associated with the communes characteristics but also with the individual resources that the women have at their disposal. For example, if the available collective resources are too expensive for the poorest women these resources will be used essentially by wealthy women. Further, the presence of public resources seems more strongly linked with the health of poor women than wealthy ones.

The Aggravating Effects of Disabilities

Among the important sources dealing with handicaps and disabilities in the region, there is a note by the World Bank. From this note, the data reported are based on the information provided by Metts (2004) and used in the World Bank note. This information about disabled population in the region is not precise and may concern 10 to 27 million people in 2002 for a total population of 250 million. Egypt and Iran seem to have the highest figures in the region (Table 6).

The literature on the relationship between poverty and disability in developing countries tends to be limited but seems to clearly be stating that poverty and disability are well related in the region. In addition, disability appears to be an important source that can lead to poverty. It is also clearly established that the vulnerable segments of the population are likely to be suffering more from disabilities. Children, old people, and women, especially in poor and rural areas are expected to suffer more from disabilities and handicaps. Rebecca and Moore (2003) show how

Table 6. Disabled population figures

Disabled Population Estimates, 2002		
	Low Estimate	High Estimate
Algeria	1,158,100	3,098,700
Djibouti	7,000	69,300
Egypt	2,608,500	6,979,500
Iran	2,519,700	6,741,900
Iraq	725,200	1,940,400
Jordan	196,100	524,700
Lebanon	133,200	356,400
Morocco	1,113,700	2,979,900
Syria	510,600	1,366,200
Tunisia	358,900	960,300
West Bank & Gaza	125,800	336,600
Yemen	193,000	1,910,700
Total	9,649,800	27,264,600

Source: Metts (2004).

the relationships between poverty and disabilities can be viewed and how the interdependent effects should be considered when looking at poverty alleviation.

Accidents, different hazards besides the prevalence of marriages contracted between close family members within the limits imposed by religion, appear to be the major sources of physical and mental disabilities and handicaps.

While further socio-economic and medical studies are needed for the region, the available investigations show that accidents at different stages of life that are related to different hazards, conflicts but also to the likely effects of consanguinity are the most important sources of handicaps and then of poverty.

The causes of disability in the region are also related to the socio-economic and demographic changes with the increasing share of the aging population, job-related injuries, and different accidents. The increases in non-communicable diseases and the stress-related mental health problems are also important sources. These disabilities are then major sources for the development of distressed living conditions in different countries in the region. Different types of accidents including those on roads and others besides those related to smoking and other practices have led to individual and group difficulties. It is certain that the on-going conflicts in the region are also among the sources of current observed handicaps. Studies from Yemen and Egypt indicate higher rates of disability for boys that could be related to higher mortality of disabled girls (Abu-Habib, 1997). The UNDP site indicates that the disability rate in the region varies from 0.5% to 4.4% and is higher for males in comparison with females. But these figures are too old that further monitoring of disabilities is needed (Table 7).

Other studies have attempted to reveal the extent of consanguinity in the region. While this is pervasive in other places in the world, the likely implied burden of this practice is likely to be dominating among the poor households. Fur-

ther investigations are needed to clarify the causal relationships between consanguineous marriage, disabilities, and poverty.

The available literature shows that the extent of consanguinity in the region is not to be neglected even though sound economic, cultural, and social reasons are behind it. But, these patterns are likely to affect to some extent, the level of disability and its social and economic consequences. As shown in Table 8, the rate of first cousin marriage varies from the lowest 18% and 20% (Lebanon, Morocco, and Egypt, respectively) to 41% to 43% (Saudi Arabia, Libya, and Mauritania, respectively). The other countries show rates that are between 20 and 34% (Table 8).

Among the investigations devoted to the issues of consanguinity in the region, Bener and Alali (2004) dealt with the case of Qatar. They found that the degree of consanguinity between each

Table 7. Rates of disability per country

Disability Rate based on most recent surveys				
Country	Year	Total	Male	Female
Algeria	1992	1.2	1.4	1.1
Bahrain	1991	0.8	0.8	0.8
Egypt	1996	4.4		
Gaza	1996	2.1	2.3	1.8
Iraq	1977	0.9	1.1	0.7
Jordan	1994	1.2	1.5	1.0
Kuwait	1980	0.4	0.5	0.4
Lebanon	1994	1.0	1.2	0.8
Libya	1995	1.7	2.0	1.3
Mauritania	1988	1.5	1.5	1.5
Morocco	1982	1.1	1.2	1.1
Oman	1993	1.9	2.0	1.8
Qatar	1986	0.2	0.1	0.3
Sudan	1993	1.6	1.8	1.4
Syria	1993	0.8	1.0	0.6
Tunisia	1994	1.2	1.5	1.0
Turkey	1985	1.4	1.7	1.1
Yemen	1994	0.5	0.6	0.5

Table 8. Rate of marriage with first cousin

Country	Percent of ever-married women (15 to 49 years old) who married a first cousin
Algeria	22
Bahrain	24
Djibouti	25
Egypt	20
Jordan	26
Kuwait	26
Lebanon	18
Libya	43
Mauritania	43
Morocco	19
Palestine	28
Oman	34
Qatar	34
Saudi Arabia	41
Syria	29
Tunisia	24
UAE	24
Yemen	31

Sources: League of Arab States, Pan-Arab Project for Child Development: Arab Mother and Child Health Surveys (Lebanon and Libya 1995, Morocco 1996/97) and Pan-Arab Project for Family Health (Syria and Tunisia 2001, Algeria Djibouti 2002, Morocco 2003/2004, and Yemen 2003); Council of Health Ministers of GCC States, Gulf Family Health Surveys (Bahrain, Oman, and United Arab Emirates 1995, Kuwait and Saudi Arabia 1996, Qatar 1998); ORC Marco, Demographic and Health Surveys (Mauritania 2001/2002, Jordan 2002, and Egypt 2003) and Palestinian Central Bureau of Statistics' special Tabulations of the 2004 Palestinian Demographic and Health Survey. H.Rashad, M.Osman, and F.Roudi-Fahimi, 2005. Marriage in the Arab World. Population Reference Bureau (PRB)

female and her spouse in the studied sample was high (54%) and that the dominant type of consanguineous marriage was between first cousins (35%). Furthermore, the consanguinity rate in Qatar appeared to have increased from 42% to 54% in one generation. Another study looked at the case of Turkey (Fisiloglu, 2002). This investigation showed that consanguineous marriage was preferred as important social and economic benefits are ensured to the family and to the group.

Other studies (Donbak, 2004) have looked at the consanguinity problem in a region of Turkey. The main results are that the region is experiencing a high rate of consanguinity that is around 31% on average and that there are needs for reduction to benefit the health quality of the population.

Table 9, as introduced in Tabutin and Shoumaker (2005), shows that consanguinity cannot be neglected when observing the relationships of marriages in South Mediterranean countries. It shows that marriage between first cousins attains a maximum of 36% in Saudi Arabia and a minimum of 15% in Turkey. The other countries have rates varying from 22% in Algeria (2002) to 35 in Egypt (1995).

Marriages between other relatives is less marked but still present with a maximum of 36% in Palestine (1995) and a minimum of 4% in Egypt (1995) and Iran (1995). The other rates in the other countries vary between 6% in Yemen (1997) and 23% in Koweit (1987).

Table 9. Marriage between cousins

Country	Date of the survey	First cousins	Other relatives	no link	Total
	1970	23	9	68	100
	1986	27	11	62	100
Algeria	2002	22	11	67	100
Saudi Arabia	1987	36	22	42	100
	1991	31	7	62	100
	1995	35	4	61	100
Egypt	2000	32	6	62	100
Iran	1991	25	4	71	100
Jordan	2002	26	17	57	100
Koweit	1987	30	23	47	100
Palestine	1995	30	36	34	100
Tunisia	1995	28	12	60	100
Turkey	1993	15	8	77	100
Yemen	1997	34	6	60	100

Sources: national reports

In Morocco, this type of marriage exists also as shown in Talbi, Khadmaoui, Soulaymani, and Chafik (2007). Consanguinity rate attains a maximum of 32.9% in Khouribga and a minimum of 18.2% in Safi. Table 10 shows also that high sickness rates within consanguineous marriages are observed with a maximum of 71.05% in El Jadida and a minimum of 53.85% in Khouribga. Consanguinity health related problems vary from 33.33% in Safi and 66.67% in Settat.

Another study (Noujai & Lfarakh, 1999) has already shown the role played by consanguineous marriages in the determination of socio-economic characteristics of families in Morocco. Further studies are needed to show the links between types of marriages, health, and eventually handicaps.

Table 10. Child development index 1990-2006

Country	Child Development Index		
	1990–94	1995–99	2000–06
Algeria	13.55	12.63	6.57
Bahrain	..	5.76	4.51
Egypt	16.94	12.66	7.61
Iraq	11.18	17.52	..
Jordan	8.01	8.17	6.84
Kuwait	..	9.1	9.89
Lebanon	..	8.9	10.23
Mauritania	50.12	32.03	29.69
Morocco	26.35	19.62	11.01
Oman	21.44	14.25	15.7
Qatar	..	6.83	5.16
S.Arabia	..	9.1	9.89
Syria	10.73	9.66	6.4
Tunisia	..	7.7	4.54
Turkey	20.01	15.25	7.12
U.A.E.	..	12.94	9.61
Yemen	40.37	42.03	33.32

Source: The Child Development Index Holding governments to account for children's wellbeing (2008) by Save the Children 1 St John's Lane London EC1M 4AR UK

The Issue of Children in the Region

The importance and extent of the issues related to children in the region is discussed here in relation to the new index related to child development indicator.

The Child Development Index (CDI) produced by "Save the Children UK" is composed of three indicators covering the wellbeing of children in 88, 118, and 137 countries, respectively, for the periods 1990-94, 1995-99, and 2000-06.

The components included in the CDI measure deprivation in health, nutrition, and schooling. Within a scale of 0-100, the lowest values show low levels of deprivations while higher scores indicate serious levels of deficits. These components include:

- **Health:** The under-five mortality rate (the probability of dying between birth and five years of age, expressed as a percentage on a scale of 0 to 340 deaths per 1,000 live births),
- **Nutrition:** The percentage of under the age of five years, who are moderately or severely underweight,
- **Education:** The percentage of primary school-age children who are not enrolled in school.

The overall Child Development Index is the simple average of the three components for each period under review and for each country.

Table 10 introduces the levels of CDI for countries in the study region for the three successive periods.

For the period of 1990-94, the highest value of 50.12 is observed in Mauritania with the lowest for Jordan 8.17. For the period 1995-99, the highest and lowest values are respectively Yemen and Bahrain (42.03 and 5.76). The highest value for the period 2000-06 is for Yemen 33.32 while the lowest score is for Bahrain and Tunisia (4.51 and 4.54). However, all these countries have had a decrease of their CDI. The means for all countries are respectively 21.87, 14.36, and 11.13 while the corresponding standard deviations are 13.70, 9.50, and 8.47. The maximal values are 50.12, 42.03, and 33.32 while the minimal ones are 8.01, 5.76, and 4.51.

This shows that the levels of CDI in the region are still high in comparison with developed economies but large variability in this index characterizes the region even though an increasing trend is observed for each country and overall.

Migration of Medical Skilled Labor

The new economics of skilled labor emigration from developing countries has been providing new evidence to support the existence of human capital gains not only in the destination but also in the source countries. However, there has been no final position with regard to the magnitude of the potential gains and losses achieved by the countries' source of emigration because remittances and skills may not be complements (Ranis, 2007). In addition, when accounting for risk aversion, gains in education in countries of the origin of migrants are reduced and losses can be experienced (Driouchi, Baudassé, Boboc, & Zouag, 2007). This brings back the issue of brain drain that has prevailed earlier. The emigration of medical doctors and nurses given the shortage experienced in developed countries helps understand the extent and magnitude of its socio-economic implications. While the brain drain can affect all the sectors in different economies, it is crucial for the area of health given its interdependencies with education and other socio-economic dimensions. This emigration constitutes an important risk for the supply of health care staff both quantitatively and qualitatively. South Mediterranean countries can suffer from this risk even if drastic health care plans and actions are developed without addressing the issue of brain drain.

This section introduces the main issues related to the problem of brain drain in general with a specific focus on its effects on health and related sectors in the context of South Mediterranean countries.

Brain Drain and Overall Migration of Skilled Labor

Important results have been attained when looking at the issue of brain drain. Some authors have developed models and assessments of human capital gains and losses over different economies (Beine, Docquier, & Rapoport, 2001, 2003, 2006; Docquier & Rapoport, 2003, 2005, 2007; Docquier, Lohest, & Marfouk, 2005, 2007; Docquier & Sekkat, 2006; Docquier, Lindsay, Lowell, & Marfouk, 2007). Besides showing the existence of brain gains, the findings include also the factors that affect migration and the magnitude of human capital gains and losses. Given the multiplicity of factors that have an impact on human capital gains and losses in the countries source of skilled labor migration, domestic, regional and international policies need further investigations and more practical evidence (Docquier & Sekkat, 2006). In this process, series of contributions are still developing (Schaeffer, 2005; Chakraborty, 2006; Hung-Ju, 2006).

Based on the data of Docquier and Marfouk for the year 2000, the emigration rates of different labor skills in some South Mediterranean countries show levels that vary from 0 to 9.4%. Highly skilled labor can represent up to 38.6% of the total emigration. This is generally a high rate compared to the total average shown in the first row of Table 11. OECD countries appear to be among the major recipients of this emigration. These higher rates show that the likelihood of brain drain is very high for the region (Table 11).

This high level of emigration rate is critical for engineers, medical doctors, and nurses besides other types of technicians. The following paragraph is devoted to medical doctors.

Migration of Medical Skilled Labor

The "Medical Brain Drain" is a new panel data on physicians' emigration rates (1991-2004) developed by Frédéric Docquier and Alok Bhargava (2006). This dataset is recognized by the authors as a product of the Trade Team – Development Research Group, is part of a larger effort in the group to measure the extent of the brain drain as part of the International Migration and Development Program. According to this database, the South Mediterranean countries have shown in 2004 high levels of emigration of emigration of medical doctors. The main countries of destination are UK, USA, France, Canada, Germany, Belgium, Australia, Italy, Sweden, Switzerland, and Austria.

In 2004, the emigration of medical doctors rates for different countries of the region are shown in Table 12. The total emigration rate related to all destinations ranges from 0.1 to 12 percent. The lowest rates occur in Oman, Saudi Arabia, and Mauritania while the highest levels are attained by Iraq, Lebanon, Syria, Sudan, and Morocco. Intermediate levels are recognized for the remaining countries with values between 2 and 4 percent (Table 12).

Even though the rate in 2004 appears to be high, the trends expressed over the period 1991-2004 appear to be promising (constant or decreasing) for most of the countries in the region. The countries show increasing rates are Algeria, Iraq, Libya, and Bahrain. All other countries have either constant or decreasing annual trends. The decreas-

Table 11. Emigration rates of low, medium, and highly skilled

	Rate of emigration				Working-aged residents (in thousand)				Emigrants (OECD)			
	Low	Medium	High	Total	Low	Medium	High	Total	Low	Medium	High	Total
TOTAL	1.1%	1.8%	5.4%	1.8%	1880775	945844	360614	3187233	21511670	17107447	20403327	59022443
Algeria	4.6%	2.1%	9.4%	4.5%	9669	2557	822	13048	466467	55820	85537	607824
Egypt	0.2%	0.8%	4.6%	0.9%	18701	7434	3131	29266	46382	58048	149432	253861
Libya	0.5%	0.6%	2.4%	0.9%	1032	750	471	2253	4849	4854	11441	21144
Morocco	6.8%	8.1%	17.0%	7.6%	10635	2034	691	13361	773685	180313	141168	1095166
Sudan	0.1%	0.7%	6.9%	0.3%	11163	1198	252	12613	8442	8897	18789	36127
Tunisia	5.1%	3.8%	12.5%	5.4%	3574	799	274	4648	192846	31939	39350	264135
Maurita-nia	0.8%	3.6%	11.8%	1.2%	917	46	19	982	7398	1707	2556	11662
Bahrain	0.5%	1.0%	4.9%	1.3%	189	130	46	364	1017	1270	2351	4638
Iraq	1.3%	4.0%	11.1%	2.7%	6497	1560	758	8816	85838	65505	95086	246429
Jordan	1.0%	2.4%	7.2%	2.8%	923	671	421	2015	9685	16513	32768	58966
Kuwait	0.5%	0.9%	7.1%	1.8%	563	537	206	1306	2774	4706	15785	23266
Lebanon	9.4%	11.1%	38.6%	15.0%	911	625	220	1756	94613	77963	138214	310789
Oman	0.0%	0.0%	0.6%	0.1%	575	394	139	1108	276	194	791	1261
Qatar	0.1%	0.2%	2.5%	0.5%	183	125	44	352	246	247	1128	1621
Saudi Arabia	0.0%	0.1%	0.9%	0.2%	4854	3329	1169	9352	2232	3656	10738	16626
Syria	0.9%	2.3%	6.1%	1.9%	4087	1254	805	6146	36326	28947	51851	117124
Turkey	5.7%	4.9%	5.8%	5.6%	25742	4572	2816	33130	1556811	237729	174043	1968583
Emirates	0.1%	0.1%	1.0%	0.2%	864	593	208	1665	530	498	2119	3146
Yemen	0.1%	1.2%	6.0%	0.4%	4968	533	112	5614	7053	6678	7218	20949

ing trends even if statistically significant are still low. Lebanon and Syria besides Jordan and Egypt have shown important reduction in their rates of emigration of physicians. Figure 1 introduces the country comparisons.

Table 13 confirms the 1991-2004 trends for each country included in the sample. The first observation is that the decreases are low. The second observation is that these trends are obtained from net emigration rates and may also be related to other factors that are outside the willingness of these countries to retain their medical doctors (Table 13).

However, the emigration rate has to be viewed with the domestic availability of medical doctors. When this latter variable is measured by the number of physicians per 1000 people for each country, large variations can be noticed. Figure 2 shows how Lebanon has been leading both annually and throughout the study period 1991-2004 with almost 3.5 doctors for 1000 people. It is followed by Egypt that attains a level above 2 doctors for the same number of people. The other countries are largely below 2 doctors per 1000 people with most of them being between 1 and 1.5 (Figure 2).

Nevertheless, the most important element in this analysis is the trend pursued by each country with regard to the domestic availability of doctors. Table 14 shows the annual trends for each country. These trends are most of the time statistically different except between Sudan and Mauritania that are both characterized by low annual trends. Iraq is also an exception as it shows a negative annual trend. However, the highest rate of annual improvement is attained by Lebanon (0.16) that is followed by United Arab Emirates (0.10), Qatar (0.09), Egypt (0.08), Jordan (0.06), Kuwait (0.06), Oman (0.05), Syria (0.05), and Bahrain (0.04). The other countries have lower and slower annual changes ranging from 0 (Saudi Arabia and Libya) to 0.03 (Turkey). In addition, the remaining countries have annual rates of 0.01 (Tunisia, Mauritania, and Sudan) and 0.02 (Algeria and Morocco). The estimated rate for Yemen is lowest of all as it is only 0.005.

Also all the countries in the sample have statistically significant intercepts that are generally high at the exception of Yemen, Sudan and Mauritania (Table 14).

From the above descriptive statistical analyzes, it can be inferred that there are variations among countries in the South Mediterranean region with regard to the likely effect of medical brain drain. All these countries have significant emigration rates of physicians. In 2004, countries such as Iraq, Syria, Lebanon, Libya Jordan, Sudan, Morocco, and Jordan had emigration rates of physicians higher than 7 percent, which is not the case of Mauritania (0.6%), Oman (0.13%), and Saudi Arabia (0.8%) that can be considered as an exception, the other countries in the sample have rates that are between 2 and 4 percent.

However, over the period 1991-2004, the annual trends estimated for the rate of emigration and for the number of physicians per 1000 people, show signals that are in favor of Reduction Brain Drain (RBD), Increase Brain Drain (IBD), and Constant Brain Drain (CBD). Table 15 summarizes the country ranking with respect to each variable. It clearly suggests that accounting for both variables shows that Lebanon, Emirates, Jordan, Syria, Morocco, Egypt, Kuwait, Qatar and Turkey have been pursuing a strategy of net brain drain reduction. Sudan is also in the above category but the rates of improvements are slower. Countries like Tunisia while improving its number of physicians could also benefit from further reduction of its emigration rate. While Algeria is benefiting from the increase of its medical stock, it is facing the increase of the emigration rate. On the other extreme, Libya and Iraq have appeared to be faced with the medical brain drain (Table 15).

The emigration of medical skilled labor affects also the domestic availability of nurses and technicians. The available documents and publications show that the South Mediterranean countries are also concerned by this type of emigration. With the limited number of reports and studies dealing with the specific determinants of nurse emigration, it is assumed that the overall economic, social and

Table 12. Emigration rates of physicians in south Mediterranean countries 2004

	Physicians' emigration rates in %											
COUNTRY	**Total**	**USA**	**UK**	**CAN**	**FRA**	**GER**	**BEL**	**AUS**	**ITA**	**SWE**	**SWI**	**AUT**
Algeria	0.0423	0.0011	0.0001	0.0008	0.0323	0.0004	0.0058	0	0.0005	0.0004	0.0008	0
Bahrain	0.0205	0.006	0	0.0086	0	0	0	0.0058	0	0	0	0
Egypt	0.0226	0.0123	0.0008	0.0012	0.0002	0.0008	0.0002	0.0041	0.0009	0.0003	0	0.0005
Iran	0.0633	0.0226	0.0011	0.0014	0.0007	0.0177	0.0007	0.0022	0.0013	0.0103	0.0001	0.0048
Iraq	0.1243	0.0309	0.0084	0.006	0.0007	0.011	0.0008	0.0124	0.0021	0.0292	0.0003	0.0043
Jordan	0.0662	0.0267	0.0021	0.0007	0.0003	0.0168	0.0009	0.0014	0.0146	0.0009	0.0002	0.0017
Kuwait	0.0214	0.0062	0.0003	0.0104	0	0	0	0.0021	0.0003	0.0021	0	0
Lebanon	0.0974	0.0508	0.0001	0.0093	0.0057	0.0054	0.005	0.006	0.0099	0.004	0.0004	0.0008
Libya	0.0794	0.0056	0.0073	0.0091	0	0.0171	0.0008	0.0007	0.0291	0.0013	0.0001	0.0011
Mauritania	0.0058	0	0	0	0	0	0.0033	0	0	0.0025	0	0
Morocco	0.0702	0.0023	0	0.0006	0.0159	0.0043	0.0439	0.0003	0.0016	0.0008	0.0004	0.0002
Oman	0.0013	0.0003	0	0	0	0	0	0.001	0	0	0	0
Qatar	0.0282	0	0	0	0	0	0.0282	0	0	0	0	0
Saudi Arabia	0.0077	0.0012	0.0001	0.0049	0	0.0007	0	0.0002	0.0002	0	0	0.0004
Sudan	0.0971	0.024	0.0141	0.002	0.0005	0.0104	0.0002	0.0077	0.0012	0.0024	0.0002	0.0011
Syria	0.1048	0.0543	0.002	0.0021	0.0076	0.0182	0.0015	0.0019	0.0098	0.0039	0.0001	0.0032
Tunisia	0.0453	0.0019	0.0001	0	0.0065	0.0029	0.021	0	0.0109	0.0011	0.0004	0.0003
Turkey	0.0231	0.0051	0.0002	0.0004	0.0001	0.0092	0.0046	0.0007	0.0003	0.0007	0.0003	0.0012
United Arab Emirates	0.0449	0.0012	0.0002	0.0426	0	0	0	0.0004	0	0.0005	0	0
Yemen	0.0194	0.0014	0.0012	0.0005	0	0.0108	0	0.0026	0.0006	0	0.0002	0.0019

political environment of the region do have a major impact on the decisions to emigrate. Given the number of female nurses in the overall stock of medical staff, the status of women in the region may also play an important role in these decisions. This adds more pressure on the domestic medical training system and relates consequently the problem to the necessary reforms of education in these countries. Research and medical research are also important inputs for the enhancement of the efficiency of the health system. This is again constrained by the brain drain of medical staff including researchers.

The risk related to brain drain is an important issue to be considered when formulating and implementing integrated economic and social policies devoted to the enhancement of the well-being of the populations in the region.

ICTS OFFERING TOOLS FOR RISK MINIMIZATION

A good contribution to answering this question resides in analyzing the effects of ICTs, mainly in developing economies where the major sources discussed in the first part of this study, are more prevalent. In this part, two examples of publications are considered. One relates to the overall developing countries situation and the other is related to a local case study. These two papers are selected to be representatives of the categories of issues needed in this section.

The global paper selected and that cover developing countries is that of Baliamoune-Lutz (2003). This paper examines the relationships between ICT components and development indicators. Among the clearly established results, this research has identified that personal computers and Internet

Figure 1. Comparisons of emigration of medical doctors between countries

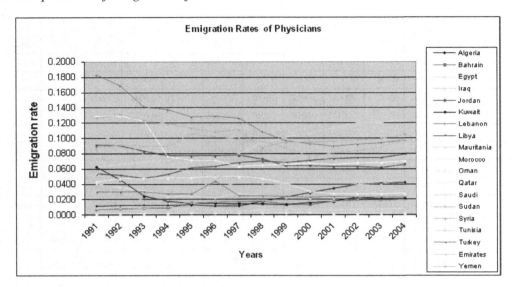

hosts do have a positive link with the per capita income measure. This says that income measures can be seen in relation to at least one ICT component. However, as poverty is a local process, large array of papers have been developing to show how the enhancement of levels of introduction of ICTs and local development are related. This is shown in specific poverty alleviation projects.

The paper on local development is that of Modise, Lekoko, and Thobega (2012). It introduces a case of a development project "Lentswe La Oodi Weavers" in a rural village in Botswana. Its objective is the socio-economic empowerment for women and of the community. This project shows that ICTs work best for local communities when adapted to local lifestyles. "The women who started the project almost 30 years ago did not have any formal education and achieved their dignity in their own communities as women who are independent and have empowered themselves for better livelihoods and sustainable income, meager as it may be." The women in this community are shown to be boosting their weaving productivity also through the use of ICTs. The chapter identifies also that the acquisition of further skills is highly needed. The areas to be strengthened are

those of management, marketing and sales. Here again ICTs can play an important role.

But, if no clear relation is established between ICTs and education as in Baliamoune-Lutz (2003), it is though clearly established that ICT components entertain positive relationships with literacy. This implies that access to basic reading and counting skills is likely to enhance the use of different ICT components.

The most recent research on the issues related to ICTs and development, have been showing very promising results.

Checchi, Loch, Straub, Sevcik, & Meso (2012) insist on the missing elements in the existing research on ICTs in relation to national policies. The paper uses stakeholder theory to suggest new perspectives for ICTs in relation to the stages of development in a given country.

Rizk and Kamel (2012) describe the evolution of the ICT sector in Egypt with an emphasis on national ICT strategy development and deployment as an integral element of Egypt's overall development process within the context of an emerging economy and the various growing potentials ICT offers for its socioeconomic development. The experience in Egypt demonstrated the impact of

Table 13. Annual trends of emigration rates of physicians

Country	R²	Intercept	t-stat Intercept	Coeff	t-stat coeff	Observations
Algeria	0.84	0.005	1.860	0.003	8.000	14
Bahrain	0.78	0.008	7.550	0.001	6.590	14
Egypt	0.61	0.033	16.720	-0.001	-4.330	14
Iraq	0.96	0.060	24.960	0.005	17.140	14
Jordan	0.88	0.088	46.880	-0.002	-9.240	14
Kuwait	0.29	0.035	5.600	-0.002	-2.230	14
Lebanon	0.86	0.160	27.210	-0.007	-8.410	14
Libya	0.90	0.050	29.560	0.002	10.370	14
Mauritania	0.39	0.008	12.050	0.000	-2.770	14
Morocco	0.55	0.110	12.410	-0.005	-3.850	14
Oman	0.09	0.002	6.150	0.000	1.200	14
Qatar	0.66	0.053	17.870	-0.002	-4.870	14
Saudi A.	0.34	0.010	12.370	-0.002	-2.470	14
Sudan	0.06	0.094	22.240	-0.001	-0.860	14
Syria	0.64	0.125	29.280	-0.003	-4.630	14
Tunisia	0.17	0.047	35.590	0.000	-1.580	14
Turkey	0.30	0.032	12.810	-0.001	-2.260	14
Emirates	0.71	0.084	13.230	-0.005	-5.390	14
Yemen	0.28	0.025	10.280	-0.001	-2.190	14

Figure 2. Physicians per 1000 people in MENA 1991-2004

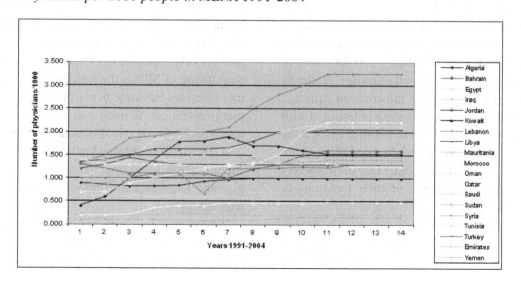

Table 14. Country annual trends in number of physicians per 1000 people

	R squared	Intercept	t-stat constant	Coefficient	t-stat coefficient	Observations
Algeria	0.70	0.84	40.12	0.02	5.31	14
Bahrain	0.58	1.04	13.57	0.04	4.11	14
Egypt	0.71	1.32	12.59	0.08	5.49	14
Iraq	0.79	0.61	86.72	-0.01	-6.80	14
Jordan	0.93	1.38	37.86	0.06	12.60	14
Kuwait	0.35	1.01	5.31	0.06	2.56	14
Lebanon	0.95	1.37	16.97	0.16	15.43	14
Libya	0.02	1.31	49.78	0.00	-0.51	14
Mauritania	0.63	0.08	7.12	0.01	4.51	14
Morocco	0.77	0.24	8.89	0.02	6.40	14
Oman	0.68	0.85	12.27	0.05	5.01	14
Qatar	0.72	1.06	8.84	0.09	5.53	14
Saudi A.	0.00	1.43	33.50	0.00	0.12	14
Sudan	0.77	0.08	11.84	0.01	6.40	14
Syria	0.87	0.87	21.58	0.05	9.09	14
Tunisia	0.35	0.62	23.29	0.01	2.54	14
Turkey	0.48	0.94	14.18	0.03	3.36	14
Emirates	0.87	0.94	10.36	0.10	8.84	14
Yemen	0.33	0.17	10.76	0.005	2.45	14

ICT; however, its effect on societal transformation is not yet completed. A need exists to revisit the newly emerging role that ICT can play in the 21st century that goes beyond socioeconomic development and growth. ICT strategy development and implementation must cater to the different needs of the community while realizing universal access in terms of ICT literacy and its effective utilization for developmental purposes. Building the ICT infrastructure and information structure in the development process must be coupled with concrete projects and initiatives that engage the society at large with its multiple stakeholders from public, private, government, and civil society organizations irrespective of their locations or background.

Onyije and Briggs (2012) show how ICTs constitute a new pattern for research and innovation policies. The conjecture is discussed in connection with academic production and policy initiatives in the area of ICT. Such pattern is considered as a possible answer to the problem of Marginalization. In addition, some examples in relation to the role of ICTs in reducing marginalization are provided by the authors; they cover ICT as Solution for the Marginalized through E-Governance, E-Health, and poverty alleviation. They also include the monitoring of MDGs through progress measurement besides advancements in inclusion of the marginalization. Women and also all those that have special needs could benefit from the inputs of ICTs. These could also further benefit from the support of the innovative use of existing technologies and the creation of more multi-stakeholder partnerships.

Perry and Jaggernath (2012) mention the prevalence of violence against women in South Africa and critically examines the impacts of this

Table 15. Ranking of countries

Emigration rates of physicians			Number of physicians per 1000 people		
	Coeff			Coeff	
Lebanon	-0.007	RBD	Lebanon	0.16	RBD
Morocco	-0.005	RBD	Emirates	0.1	RBD
Emirates	-0.005	RBD	Qatar	0.09	RBD
Syria	-0.003	RBD	Egypt	0.08	RBD
Jordan	-0.002	RBD	Jordan	0.06	RBD
Kuwait	-0.002	RBD	Kuwait	0.06	RBD
Qatar	-0.002	RBD	Oman	0.05	RBD
Saudi	-0.002	RBD	Syria	0.05	RBD
Egypt	-0.001	RBD	Bahrain	0.04	RBD
Sudan	-0.001	RBD	Turkey	0.03	RBD
Turkey	-0.001	RBD	Algeria	0.02	RBD
Yemen	-0.001	RBD	Morocco	0.02	RBD
Mauritania	0	CBD	Mauritania	0.01	RBD
Oman	0	CBD	Sudan	0.01	RBD
Tunisia	0	CBD	Tunisia	0.01	RBD
Bahrain	0.001	IBD	Yemen	0.005	RBD
Libya	0.002	IBD	Libya	0	CBD
Algeria	0.003	IBD	Saudi A.	0	CBD
Iraq	0.005	IBD	Iraq	-0.01	IBD

Table 16. Internet penetration rate and literacy in African, Asian, and MENA countries

Countries	Number of countries	coefficient	t-statistics	R^2
Africa	49	2.26	5.15	0.36
Asia and MENA	38	3.23	3.08	0.21
All	87	2.91	7.12	0.37

violence on the efforts to meet the Millennium Development Goals (MDGs). The authors contribute to the existing knowledge on the links between violence and the eight MDG goals to suggest the necessity for promoting gender equality. Under this equality, MDGs can be better achieved.

Dodson, Sterling, and Bennett (2012) examine forty articles published in the *Journal of Information Technologies and International Development* (ICTD) to advance the debate about the effectiveness of ICTD initiatives at a particularly important point in the history of the discipline. The authors conclude that top-down, technology-centric, goal-diffuse approaches to ICTD contribute to unsatisfactory development results as supported by 2003-2010 data.

Based on World Internet Statistics and UNESCO, regressions analysis is conducted on African, Asian, and MENA besides all together to show how the literacy rates prevailing in each country are likely to be helping drive access to ICTs. Intuitively, this is to say that acquiring the basic skills is conditioning the access to ICTs. It is also known from previous chapters that access to ICTs can also help improve literacy, as they are series of means provided by new information technologies to enhance education in general (previous chapter on youth and education). The results of the regression between ICTs and literacy rates in the selected developing countries are provided in Table 16. The only ICT variable that produced promising results is Internet penetration with both dependent and independent variables expressed under their logarithmic forms (Table 16).

With the number of observations as shown above, each set of countries, the regressions of different ICT components are exhibiting statistically significant coefficients for the literacy rate variable. These coefficients are high and positive meaning that the enhancement of literacy rates in these countries does help the level of Internet penetration. While the estimated coefficients appear to be respectively 2.26 and 3.23 for Africa and Asia (including MENA), their comparisons show no statistical significance under a t-test (1.98).

These results confirm the other findings shown in different chapters of this book, but the current results clearly indicate that illiteracy is an important constraint facing Internet penetration and thus further access to benefits from ICTs.

Picot and Lorenz (2010) in their book *ICT for the Next Five Billion People: Information and Communication for Sustainable Development* attempt to address the issue of the next five billion people that need to access the Internet. The authors in this book refer to the potential users that are mainly from emerging countries where economic barriers to access are to be eliminated with new approaches to infrastructure development and provision of services. The authors consider that this access is likely to create new conditions for the promotion of welfare and reduction of poverty as Internet services help get further education, better health and enhanced living conditions. All the chapters in this book attempt addressing the main issues related to the role of Internet and

enhanced economic lifestyles. All the chapters converge to showing the role of ICTs for the poor at large scale with enhanced links to markets and services. The underserved areas and locations are also benefitting from good treatment in this book. Emerging markets with the role of m-payment, m-health besides the development of other mobile applications are also extensively discussed. Enterprise incubation, virtual transactions besides new business models are discussed. This applies also to community centers and the use of advanced but simple technologies to attain the needs of the population in series of locations and situations.

CONCLUSION

This chapter focuses on some special topics that are directly related to the magnitude and extent of interdependencies of health, education, and poverty. These issues cover brain drain, gender, rural/urban besides the situation of children, handicaps, and medical doctors. Further results are consequently attained from the above concerns.

If interdependencies of health, education, and income were an important matter in the region of study, important risks as that of brain drain and other might affect the supply of adequate health care and education under the pressure of limited human resources. These limitations are again emphasized when focusing on the role of women and children with their central economic and social roles in different economies. In the context of SMCs and mainly MENA, further improvements are needed in relation to the inclusion of women in these economies and societies given the potential gains that each country can attain. Under the pressure of rural versus urban interconnections, both men and women suffer relatively from higher levels of deficits in rural areas but urbanization does not reduce these deficits if decent inclusion policies were absent. While handicaps originate not only from genetic concerns, these latter appear to be important and require further identification and communication with the poor segments of the population. Illiteracy is identified to be a major constraint for the attainment of higher social benefits. It also affects the potential benefits from ICTs[3].

REFERENCES

Abu Habib, L. (1997). *Gender and disability: Women's experiences in the Middle East.* Oxford, UK: Oxfam Professional.

Anderson, K., Martin, W., & Van Dder Mensbrugghe, D. (2006). Would multilateral trade reform benefit sub-Saharan Africans? *Journal of African Economies, 15.*

Baliamoune-Lutz. (2003). An analysis of the determinants and effects of ICT diffusion in developing countries. *Information Technology for Development, 10,* 151–169. doi:10.1002/itdj.1590100303

Beine, M., Docquier, F., & Rapoport, H. (2001). Brain drain and economic growth: Theory and evidence. *Journal of Development Economics, 64*(1), 275–289. doi:10.1016/S0304-3878(00)00133-4

Beine, M., Docquier, F., & Rapoport, H. (2003). *Brain drain and LDC's growth: Winners and losers. IZA DP No. 819.* Washington, DC: The Institute for the Study of Labor.

Beine, M., Docquier, F., & Rapoport, H. (2006). *Brain drain and human capital formation in developing countries: Winners and losers.* Louvain, Belgium: Université Catholique de Louvain. doi:10.1111/j.1468-0297.2008.02135.x

Bener, A., & Alali, K. A. (2004). *Consanguineous marriage in a newly developed country: The Qatari population.* Al Tarfa, Qatar: University of Qatar. doi:10.1017/S0021932004007060

Boussard, J. M., Gérard, F., & Piketty, M. G. (2005). *Libéraliser l'agriculture? Théorie, modèles et réalité.* Montpellier, France: Cirad.

Chakraborty, B. S. (2006). Brain drain: An alternative theorization. *The Journal of International Trade & Economic Development, 15*(3), 293–309. doi:10.1080/09638190600871602

Checchi, R. M., Loch, K. D., Straub, D., Sevcik, G., & Meso, P. (2012). National ICT policies and development: A stage model and stakeholder theory perspective. *Journal of Global Information Management, 20*(1), 57–79. doi:10.4018/jgim.2012010103

Christiaensen, L., & Subbarao, K. (2004). Towards an understanding of household vulnerability in rural Kenya. *Journal of African Economies, 14*(4), 520–558. doi:10.1093/jae/eji008

Cruces, G. (2002). *Risk-adjusted poverty in Argentina: Measurement and determinants.* London, UK: London School of Economics. doi:10.1080/00220380701526329

Dabalen, A., & Poupart, N. (2002). *Vulnerability to rainfall shock in Ethiopia.* Ann Arbor, MI: University of Michigan.

Dercon, S. (2002). Managing income risk of the poor. *Research Observer, 17*(2), 237–265.

Docquier, F., Lindsay Lowell, B., & Marfouk, F. (2007). *Measuring brain drain by gender.* IZA Discussion Paper 3235. Unpublished.

Docquier, F., Lohest, O., & Marfouk, A. (2007). Brain drain in developing regions (1990-2000). *The World Bank Economic Review, 21*(2), 193–218. doi:10.1093/wber/lhm008

Docquier, F., & Rapoport, H. (2003). Ethnic discrimination and the migration of skilled labor. *Journal of Development Economics, 70*(1), 159–172. doi:10.1016/S0304-3878(02)00081-0

Docquier, F., & Sekkat, K. (2006). *Brain drain, what do we know?* Working Paper No.31. Paris, France: Agence Française de Développement.

Dodson, L. L., Sterling, R., & Bennett, J. (2012). Considering failure: Eight years of ITID research. In *Proceedings of the Fifth International Conference on Information and Communication Technologies and Development*, (pp. 56-64). IEEE.

Donbak, L. (2004). Consanguinity in Kahramanmaras City, Turkey, and its medical impact. *Saudi Medical Journal, 25*(12), 1991–1994.

Driouchi, A., Baudassé, T., Boboc, C., & Zouag, N. (2007). *New economics of brain drain and risk aversion: Theory and empirical evidence.* Orleans, France: Laboratoire d'Economie d'Orléans.

Dutta, I., & Mishra, A. (2004). *Corruption and competition in the presence of inequality and market imperfections.* Delhi, India: Delhi School of Economics.

Fisiloglu, H. (2002). Consanguineous marriage and marital adjustment in Turkey. *The Family Journal (Alexandria, Va.), 9*(2), 215–222.

Hung-Ju, C. (2006). International migration and economic growth: A source country perspective. *Journal of Population Economics, 19*(4), 725–748. doi:10.1007/s00148-005-0023-1

Krueger, A. O., Schiff, M., & Valdès, A. (1988). Agricultural incentives in developing countries: Measuring the effects of sectoral and economy wide policies. *The World Bank Economic Review, 2*(3), 255–271. doi:10.1093/wber/2.3.255

Kumar, A., & Singh, K. M. (2012). *ICT for agricultural development under changing climate.* New Delhi, India: Narendra Publishing House.

Martin, M. C. (2008). *Individual and collective resources and health in Morocco.* UNU-WIDER Research Paper. Unpublished.

Metts, R. L. (2004). *Background paper prepared for the disability and development.* Washington, DC: World Bank.

Modise, O. M., Lekoko, R. N., & Thobega, J. M. (2012). Socio-economic empowerment through technologies: The case of tapestry at Lentswe la Oodi Weavers in Botswana. In Lekoko, R. N., & Semali, L. M. (Eds.), *Cases on Developing Countries and ICT Integration: Rural Community Development.* Hershey, PA: IGI Global.

Nagla, R., & Sherif, K. (2012). ICT strategy4development: Public-private partnerships—The case of Egypt. *International Journal of Strategic Information Technology and Applications.* Retrieved from http://www.igi-global.com/article/ict-strategy4development-public privatepartnerships/67351

Norman, L., Ranciere, R., Serven, L., & Ventura, J. (2007). Macroeconomic volatility and welfare in developing countries: An introduction. *The World Bank Economic Review, 21*(3), 343–387. doi:10.1093/wber/lhm017

Noujai, A., & Lfarakh, A. (1999). *Enquête nationale sur la santé de la mère et de l'enfant.* Morocco: Service des Etudes et de l'Information Sanitaire.

Onyije, L., & Briggs, F. (2012). Technology solution for the marginalized. *European Scientific Journal, 8*(13), 71–80.

Perry, E. C., & Jaggernath, J. (2012). Violence against women, vulnerabilities and disempowerment: Multiple and interrelated impacts on achieving the millennium development goals in South Africa. *Agenda: Empowering Women for Gender Equity, 26*(1), 20–32.

Picot, A., & Lorenz, J. (2010). *ICT for the next five billion people information and communication for sustainable development.* Berlin, Germany: Springer. doi:10.1007/978-3-642-12225-5

Ranis, G. (2007). *Migration, trade, capital and development: Substitutes, complements and policies.* Washington, DC: Economic Growth Center.

Ravallion, M. (2006). Looking beyond averages in the trade and poverty debate. *World Development, 34*(8), 1374–1392. doi:10.1016/j.worlddev.2005.10.015

Rebecca, Y., & Moore, K. (2003). Including disabled people in poverty reduction work: Nothing about us, without us. *World Development, 31*(3), 571–590. doi:10.1016/S0305-750X(02)00218-8

Schaeffer, P. (2005). Human capital, migration strategy, and the brain drain. *The Journal of International Trade & Economic Development, 1*(3), 319–335. doi:10.1080/09638190500203344

Tabutin, D., & Schoumaker, B. (2005). *La démographie du monde arabe et du moyen-orient des années 1950 aux années 2000: Synthèse des changements et bilan statistique*. Paris, France: Institut National d'Etudes Démographiques.

Talbi, J., Khadmaoui, A., Soulaymani, A., & Chafik, A. (2007). Study of consanguinity in Moroccan population: Influence on the profile of health. *Anthropology, 15*, 1–11.

Tesliuc, E. D., & Lindert, K. (2002). *Vulnerability: A quantitative and qualitative assessment*. Washington, DC: World Bank.

UNCTAD. (2010). *ICTs, enterprises and poverty alleviation*. New York, NY: United Nations.

ENDNOTES

1. Risks and uncertainties are important elements to be considered in decision making but also when accounting for interdependencies. This chapter claims that there are many sources of risks and uncertainties that face coordination. ICTs can though provide tools and means to enrich the decision making process at local, national and regional levels. However, the major sources of risks as they relate to the situation of women, children, the old segments of the population as well as those with disabilities are very important. The availability of knowledge resources including medical doctors is an important issue in the case of the countries analyzed.

2. Given the expected large effects of different sources of risks and uncertainty, it is very important to ensure that data related to gender, children, hospitals, medical doctors, as well as to accidents, diseases, school outcomes, and others be monitored through the use of adequate ICT supports. The Geographic Information Systems (GIS) are very important tools to be included in the gathering, monitoring, and use of these data. Among the ICT tools, computers, telecommunication means, as well as other devises are necessary for enhancing knowledge about the issues raised in this chapter. Appropriate software for the analysis is also part of the ICT tools needed.

3. This chapter does not discuss extensively the issue of gender inequality but introduces the main features that relate to the position of women in different societies mainly those of the South Mediterranean area with a focus of MENA. According to series of reports, it is also clear that the Arab countries are among those that exhibit larger deficits in the inclusion of women. However, the matter introduced by the reference used indicates clearly that there are important risks of transmitting discrimination against women to newer future generations. If these discriminations persist now, they affect current nutrition and health of current children and generate consequently unfavorable impacts on future children. The perpetual transmission of these deficits is likely to eliminate women. This approach has also been supporting the theses related to missing women.

Chapter 13
Implications of the Findings and Prospects for Further Coordination

ABSTRACT

This last chapter summarizes the most important findings from the previous chapters of this book. It places emphasis on fragmentation and scatted decisions as likely sources of economic and social inefficiencies when externalities or interdependencies are present. Coordination, including government interventions, is underlined to be the means for re-establishing economic and social benefits. In this context, new technologies and especially ICTs can be important inputs for better coordination and enhancement of the levels of the overall social benefits. However, further research is needed to identify the levels of causality besides all the factors that influence the access to health, education, and socioeconomic outcomes in different contexts and situations. The economies in the South Mediterranean Countries (SMC), Middle East, and North Africa, besides the Arab countries are shown having to account for further interdependencies between health, education, and the socioeconomic situations. The roles and impacts of ICTs are found to be promising for the achievement of higher socioeconomic performances.

INTRODUCTION

This last chapter builds on the knowledge accumulated from previous chapters and sections. This is devoted to the extension of the attained results and conclusions. It is based on the existence of important interdependencies that need to be accounted for, at the levels of individuals, households, areas, countries, and regions. The role of ICTs has appeared to provide useful coordinating tools to promote further welfare and development.

The issues dealt with here include all the results attained in each previous chapter. Besides the outcomes related to interdependencies, the other issues such as health, gender, urbanization in relation to rural migration and a number of

DOI: 10.4018/978-1-4666-3643-9.ch013

demographic features related to handicaps are considered.

These findings are here looked at, from the viewpoint of their development implications. The need of further multidisciplinary approaches to better assess the links between socioeconomic status and health and to analyze the effects of exogenous risks and uncertainties appears to be a high priority issue. Further implications are related to the perception and implementation of poverty alleviation processes in global and local contexts besides the clear need for transversal economic and social policies. These different levels of implications are respectively reviewed in this last chapter.

Finally, the limitations and the constraints faced are introduced besides some future directions for research as related to the area of interdependencies of health, education, and economic performance, and their impact on the intergenerational transmission of poverty. These areas of both theoretical and empirical interests are expected to become necessary with the acceleration and generalization of further economic and social development in South Mediterranean countries, MENA and Arab economies.

FINDINGS AND IMPLICATIONS

This part summarizes the most important results attained. Achievements include the results that are directly related to the topic at hand. As fragmentation is most of the time found to be inducing inefficient outcomes in the presence of externalities and interdependencies, coordination is then provided as a corrective measure. While it is recognized in the economic literature, that government intervention is the major way to reduce market failures, coordination in general can re-establish the economic and social optima. However, new technologies can provide important inputs for this coordination.

Emphasis is also placed on the role of local development in relation to the existence of interdependencies and on the central importance of health and education. The need for further transversal and horizontal economic and social policies is also discussed.

Overall Accomplishments

This includes the data gathered, the frameworks used both theoretical and empirical besides the results attained.

The Data Gathered

This book has tried to use different sets of data. The data include information that is published by international organizations and by countries. However, most of the data used are from international organizations. Three subsets of socioeconomic data are from the World Bank and the United Nations. They concern the variables that are directly related to the study. Some specific data related to school dropouts and consumption expenditures are from Morocco.

The Need of Furthering Multidisciplinary Approaches

It is clear from this book that different dimensions have been covered but it is felt throughout the conduct of this work, that many aspects are still missing. Their inclusion may have improved the results. While the contribution of economics and statistics appears to be dominating, that of other social scientists and technologists would have enhanced the overall level of achievement. The need of health care, education, and expertise in behavioural sciences and culture appears to be also important in determining further links among different variables and dimensions. The complex nature of the living condition of people in the special context of South Mediterranean countries would have required larger teams composed of different specialists that could contribute to the clarification of other dimensions not included in this book.

While this shows the limits of this work, it also underlines, the level of effort invested. In this sense, the existing literature and reports compiled include contributions from different disciplines. This exercise is facilitated with the publications of demographers, medical doctors, and sociologists besides other specialists that look at theories and applications related to interdependencies. This contribution is also made easier with series of reports by international organizations. Some databases produced internationally for different countries are also instrumental in the conduct of this work.

The Findings Attained

The results attained at both country and regional levels show clearly that major interdependencies exist between health, education, other socioeconomic status, and economic performance. They are exacerbated when not identified in poor contexts and poorer countries. Knowledge about these interdependencies is likely to be an important source that can show both the impact of favourable and unfavourable economic and social conditions. The situation of women and especially those in poor urban neighbourhoods and in rural areas is at the same time critical but can become an engine for the promotion of development in the region.

As the driving role of education and health is largely underlined, access of women to both education and health can have larger positive consequences on the promotion of the South Mediterranean economies. The needed improvement in education to ameliorate health status appears to be very important. Both men and women need to reach relatively high levels of education for health improvement to occur. Interestingly, education has however rapid impact on health behaviour

as even small improvements in education lead to important health behavioural change.

The rate of dropout from primary and secondary schools, at least in the context of the Moroccan economy, is definitely related to poverty and to the health and nutrition. The increase of the level of education and the elimination of illiteracy require that more global actions be undertaken. Girls are more affected by the high level of dropouts implying that the situation of women in the future may not be easily improved if no action is taken. Other variables that explain this high rate of school attrition for girls can be those described in the literature. They relate to early marriage and low level of education.

Other vulnerable segments such as the handicapped, children, and the old can also value better access to health and education. The likely impacts of an improved access of women in the analyzed economies are expected to generate higher positive social effects given the multiplicity of their roles in households and in these economies. The mechanisms of transmission are supported by the estimated levels of interdependencies but also by the social positions occupied by women. Under these considerations, supplies of education and health in different locations are likely to accelerate the engines of economic and social improvements. These supplies can start with the provision of minimal education (literacy) and minimal health (health protection) but need to recognize that a rapid increase in the number of years of education is also important.

These supplies are likely to suffer from the shortages of human resources that can provide and implement the supplementary minimal programs. Among the constraints, the brain drain of medical staff can have delaying effects if no further policies are introduced to reduce the negative impacts of this type of emigration in the region.

The strength and importance of interdependencies between socioeconomic status and health and the specificities of different categories of the population call for the necessary involvement of not only the public and private sectors but also the populations through nongovernmental organizations.

Other indirect results from this book can be underlined. They include methodological benefits related to the promotion of further multidisciplinary approaches to tackle socioeconomic issues in the region. They also concern the deepening of the understanding of poverty, the effects of hazards and the role of early warnings besides the importance of local and proximity development.

Detailed Results as Obtained in Each Chapter

Detailed results can be related to the conclusions attained at the level of each of the previous chapters considered in this book. The results can be grouped under three major headings that follow the three parts composing the document. The first group of chapters (1 to 4) or section I introduce frameworks and theories devoted to show how fragmentation and need for coordination of interdependencies can be provided. It also addresses the empirical issues related to the assessments of interdependencies in the context of MENA and Arab Countries.

The second group focuses on the expression of interdependencies in relation to the sectors of heath, youth and education, women and poverty (chapters 5 to 9). A special emphasis on the promising contributions of ICTs for each of the sectors is underlined.

The third group of chapters (10 to 12) discusses special issues related to interdependencies of health, education, and socioeconomic policies.

Chapter 1

As this chapter looked to the social costs of fragmentation and anti-commons from the standpoint of developing economies, an important emphasis has been placed first on showing how different authors have dealt with this question. Furthermore, cases have been used to underline the impacts of fragmentation and anti-commons on economic and social development. A special focus is placed on the situation of developing economies, mainly in relation to the new issues raised by the new technologies and institutions that are highly desired in developing economies. Health and agriculture with the needs of the poorest segments of the population are chosen to illustrate the effects of fragmentation and scattering. A simplified theoretical model is used to underline the differences between commons, anti-commons and different market structures. The "Doing Business" data are also mobilized to test empirically for the effects of fragmentation and anti-commons on enterprise creation. The results show that, in developing countries, as the number of procedures and the required time for enterprise creation increase the costs related to the stages considered by the dataset. The attained results confirm the validity of the theoretical model used but also the likelihood of the effects of fragmentation and anti-commons on developing economies. The need of a balance between fragmentation and coordination is definitely in favor of coordination but such a balance resides the continuous awareness about the monitoring of economies and society in order to identify areas where interventions are necessary. The identification of the types of coordination requires also that research be continuously mobilized with instruments requiring continuous updates.

This first chapter has finally prepared to the following ones. The coming chapters address the extent of coordination and interdependencies and the need for assessment. This is related the interactions between health, education and the economy at local and regional contexts of the South Mediterranean, MENA and Arab countries. Through these first chapters, readers are first prepared to the demand side for coordination and tools. Information and Communication Technologies (ICTs) as a set of means devoted to the enhancement of the management and coordination of interfaces between large series of functions and players are then introduced.

Chapter 2

Even if interconnections between health, education, and economic outcomes are intuitively well known by individuals and households, these interdependencies need to be identified and assessed at different levels of aggregation. The expression of these interdependencies helps for a better perception of the role of ICTs in coordinating the interferences of health, education, and economic outcomes.

The empirical applications underlined above are showing the importance of the magnitude of these interdependencies in different economic and social contexts. The central role of the theory that accounts for the different types of assets such as health, knowledge, social capitals, and traditional economic wealth appears to be promising. It introduces a framework that helps understand the foundations of deficits in different components of wealth. This includes the definitions and expressions of poverty. This has also shown how health is a major component in the wealth of individuals and countries as a whole, that is, health can be a major source that ensures economic activities through labor productivity. This relationship can then be enhanced with the other types of assets such as knowledge and social capital.

Attempts to test empirically for interdependencies have been also discussed. They indicate that major steps have been made to investigate the magnitude of the likely gains to be attained when accounting for interdependent and integrated policies. While causality has not yet been established, major progress is expected in this area.

The assessments that have been achieved so far have been expanded through the works of international organizations as well as through the inputs of some individual pioneers. Further

investigations are needed, given the deficit of knowledge existing on series of related issues and the types of specialists needed to cover the missing dimensions.

Chapter 3

This chapter is mainly based on a description of the general methodological guidelines that are used in some of the following chapter. It also shows how a theoretical model is often needed to guide the empirical analysis, the inclusion of relevant variables besides the types of data needed. This chapter includes the introduction of a theoretical model that indicates how empirical investigations need to be carried out. It also introduces the empirical methods that are likely to be applied. Variables and data are also discussed with focus on the SMC countries. The methodologies underlined and mobilized in the next chapter do also account for simple regression analysis besides the introduction of simultaneous equations with seemingly unrelated errors.

Different types of variables and sub-variables are described depending on the sources of information used. Data are mainly related to cross-sections of countries in the region as published by alternative sources.

This clearly establishes the need of software, databases, and other information as necessary ICT components for the conduct of the analysis of interdependencies between health, education and other wealth variables.

Chapter 4

This chapter shows that for SMC countries, economic development depends on the improvements in education and health, as well as on the initial wealth of a country. There are some differences between SMC countries and EU countries. No direct relationship between the level of education and economic development could be seen and the relationship between health and economic development is different from SMC countries.

The regression analysis of different clusters concerning the potential relationships between education, health, and income measurements helps to come up with the following conclusions.

First, the use of aggregate data such as the "world cluster" to illustrate relationships, without taking care of the different economic, social, regional, and development specificities, leads to contradictory findings. The example of the regression analysis of the children out of primary school illustrates the ineffectiveness of aggregate data since the results of world countries completely contradicts the results of five sub-clusters. Data from sub-clusters, in contrast, improves the efficiency and helps detect the level of significance existing between the GDP per capita and both health and education.

Second, the GDP per capita impact on improving education is not very significant. In fact, the overall conclusion that could be driven from the regression analysis of the education and income indicators is that the relationship significance is not statistically significant. In other words, the improvement of education within different clusters does not necessarily require an economic involvement or an increase in the income of the population. The single argument in favor of the importance of the GDP per capita for ameliorating the level of education concerns the literacy rates in middle-income countries (mainly SMC, major oil net exporters, and high and medium human development). In general, other arguments than income should be studied in order to enhance education.

Third, in contrast to education, the interpretations of regression tables for health and income indicators proved that GDP per capita is the key for most of clusters. The enhancement of health in different clusters can only occur if it is accompanied by an amelioration of the income level of the population. Alternatively, low human development countries need to focus on other measures

than GDP per capita to determine a significant relationship with health issues. The main point of the low human development countries' health indicators is that the significance of the relationship varies from year to year. This "instability" can be explained by the rise of new factors that alter health, more than the GDP per capita, would do, within a particular period.

In the second part, regression, correlation, and granger-tests have been the main techniques used on different data. The first set of data is mainly that of World Bank and that was described in the previous chapter. The second is the most recent database of the UN. The third set is composed of the composite indices provided by different international organizations.

The overall results attained at every level of the analysis are the high magnitude of interdependencies among all sets of variables related to health, education, and poverty. Health and education appear to have an important driving effect for these interdependencies.

This is shown with the analyzes of World Bank data as well as with the new UN database. The representative variables of health, education, and poverty seem to entertain higher levels of interdependencies meaning that any change in one of the variables affects the others. This is confirmed again through the analysis of some composite indices where clear relationships have been estimated.

The results attained so far at the regional and aggregated levels appear to be referring to the real situations faced by households in different countries. However, given the type of data used at both country and regional levels, it has been very hard to account for some the issues that are crucial to this study.

Chapter 5

The objective assigned to this chapter is attained with the assessment of ICTs in relation to socioeconomic performance and with the determination of the impact of ICTs on health related components. A large description of the development of ICTs related health services is also pursued.

There are important initiatives that are undertaken by both developing and developing economies in the area of mobilizing ICTs for health care purposes. Series of conferences and workshops have been held during the past few years to promote linkages between different health care components with more intensive use of ICTs. International organizations as well as some countries, including some rich developing ones are investing in the realization of health care platforms and in e-health. These efforts appear to be globally expressed in the quantitative linkage between different health and ICT components around the world. Further efforts are still needed to ensure that all countries and locations are benefiting from these new developments.

Chapter 6

With an increasingly globalized world, the impact of ICTs on individuals and on societies is becoming more and more important. Such impact transformed ICTs form a luxury tool to a necessity for the development and growth of societies and economies. Younger generations are most affected **by** ICTs since they are the best users of these technologies.

Youth are the main producers and consumers of ICTs. Therefore, this demographic group became a more important agent of change not only because they know how to use ICT or because they may learn faster than adults, but also because they are more adaptive to change. This suggests that ICTs can be used for a better empowerment and promotion of youth especially in developing countries where a large part of this group is still marginalized.

This chapter relates the use of ICTs to youth promotion in developing countries. Therefore, it analyzes the relation between ICTs and youth in several sectors, mainly education, health, employ-

ment, and governance. It investigates, as well, the main concerns related to ICTs and youth in developing countries, mainly in Africa, Asia, and the Arab region. The last part of the chapter deals with real cases studies related to the use of ICTs for youth promotion in some developing markets. Such case studies indicate that ICTs could be an effective tool for job creation and for the promotion and empowerment of youth in such markets.

Chapter 7

Ensuring equitable access to ICTs and autonomy to receive and produce information relevant are critical issues for women. Therefore, gender issues which need to be investigated in relation to their roles in decision-making. The central focus is in the interdependencies between health, education, and socioeconomic outcomes. ICTs play and have high potential in ensuring coordination with a central role given to women. Access and costs are of the main barriers for ICT use, so it is of the utmost importance to engage women and gender advocates in policies and regulations related to ICTs. Such policies should take into consideration the integration of women, particularly rural and poor women. So, gender must be considered from the start of project design. Only when these considerations are taken into account, the ICT policies and projects will properly address the gender digital divide and further contribute to women's economic empowerment.

The potential of ICT for women in developing countries is highly dependent upon their levels of technical skill and education. Integration of women in the information society in countries with higher illiteracy rates is quite difficult. Hence, governments and NGOs need to take into consideration the promotion of education in such countries for a better access of women to new technologies.

It is important to recognize that ICTs cannot answer all the questions facing women's development, yet they can bring new information resources and can open new communication channels for marginalized communities. Policies and programs addressing the improvement of women access and control over ICTs, should take into consideration the demographic characteristics of each society in order to ensure that the objectives set by the programs are achieved. As UN studies have indicated, though the costs of using ICTs for development may be high, not using them at all may prove to be costlier.

Chapter 8

This chapter investigates the relationship between ICTs use and poverty on a sample of 40 countries. The sample is divided into two groups: a group composed of 20 of developed countries and another that is constituted of 20 developing countries. Several assumptions are tested through statistical analyses, and interesting results were established. The first result suggests that people in developing countries have less access to ICTs relative to those in developed countries. The second test indicates that the use of Internet is positively affected by the literacy rate within a country. Therefore, the higher the literacy rate, the higher the number of Internet users in a country. The third result conveys that countries with higher GDP per Capita ensure higher access to ICTs for their populations. The final result demonstrates that populations of countries with higher rates of poverty have less access to ICTs. On the whole, the study made suggest that people in developed countries have generally better access to ICTs than those in developing nations.

In recent decades, there has been a growing evidence of the role that ICTs can play in development enhancement in both developed and developing countries. In spite of this enabling potential role, ICTs still have to be widely extended especially in developing countries. ICTs have been also viewed as an efficient tool to fight poverty. Yet, there are different views regarding the role of ICTs in poverty alleviation. The first view suggests that ICTs have the potential to fight poverty and promote

sustainable development (Samiullah & Rao, 2000). This can only be achieved, according to the authors, only if ICTs are appropriately implemented and made to address the different needs of urban and rural people. The other vision conveys that ICTs are simply a channel for information exchange and dissemination (Heeks, 1999).

Chapter 9

The objective of this chapter is about showing how interdependencies between education, research, and businesses can be considered under the triple helix framework. After the introduction of the model and its applications with a focus on Arab Countries, the discussion is pursued to underline its potential. Interferences between series of players are among the features that are tackled. Within this framework, a large demand for ICT is expected to be developed also as means of coordination. This is likely to happen in all sectors including education, health, and economic activities. As the number of players, grows as the need for coordination and for the help of ICT is needed.

As developed above, business networks can also benefit from the triple helix framework especially with the development of internationalization, global markets, and different forms of localizations. However, local development can gain better as public and private players from different spheres need to coordinate their actions to support the objectives of achieving higher outcomes to the population.

The applications of the triple helix framework have been showing progress in different countries but the implementation of real schemes in relation to results are still underway. It is expected though that developing economies are more advanced in this area. Developing countries are still proceeding with this scheme. Arab countries are also in this case.

Depending on the sector of the economy, the interdependencies are often identified and lead to participatory approaches where all the players are not often on the same footing of knowledge. ICT are often used to bridge the gaps and ensure better contributions to the achievement of advancements. However, more can be done to enhance the interactions between different players.

Chapter 10

It is definitely clear that the situation of the poorer segments of the population can improve if further policy coordination and integration is pursued. The directions of further coordination appear to have been provided by the international framework that accounts on achieving MDGs by 2015. It is also provided by the orientations focusing on human development. The recent reforms undertaken seem to be mainly focusing on economic and political components while accounting for social components as a residual sector that should be considered with the implementation of reforms. The overall policy schemes that are driven by both international organizations and by the domestic reforms, cannot lead to the needed policy integration if not based on ownership and domestic generalization of these policies to different country locations. Furthermore, specific transversal policies focusing on women, children and older segments of the population need further strengthening. More inclusive health and education policies with gender and rural focus can be promising in the region. Preventing and accounting for the existence of handicapped segments of the population are also dimensions that require inclusion within the socially coordinated policy packages.

Chapter 11

From the above analyzes and discussion, it appears that the poverty determinants in the Arab region are today directly related to income poverty and the high unemployment rate. This is to be connected with the high demographic pressure imposed by population growth and rural migration to both cit-

ies inside each economy but also internationally. The educational sector plays an important role in producing high flows and stocks of graduates as well as unskilled labor, even if the educational sector benefits from large investments. In the sense of employment, education appears to be not efficient. To face this situation, governments have engaged in human development programs and in attempts to achieve the MDGs but to what extent can these countries attain outcomes similar to those attained by those economies that are strengthening policies under the principle of social cohesion? Further analysis of the experiences such as those launched by Egypt, Morocco, and Syria is needed to provide the direction of response to the above question.

Chapter 12

This chapter focuses on some special topics that are directly related to the magnitude and extent of interdependencies of health, education, and poverty. These issues cover the brain drain, the gender, the rural/urban besides the situation of children, handicaps, and medical doctors. Further results are consequently attained from the above concerns.

If interdependencies of health, education, and income were an important matter in the region of study, important risks as that of brain drain and other might affect the supply of adequate health care and education under the pressure of limited human resources. These limitations are again emphasized when focusing on the role of women and children with their central economic and social roles in different economies. In the context of SMCs and mainly MENA, further improvements are needed in relation to the inclusion of women in these economies and societies given the potential gains that each country can attain. Under the pressure of rural versus urban interconnections, both men and women suffer relatively from higher levels of deficits in rural areas but urbanization does not reduce these deficits if decent inclusion policies were absent. While handicaps originate not only from genetic concerns, these latter appear to be important and require further identification and communication with the poor segments of the population. Illiteracy is identified to be a major constraint for the attainment of higher social benefits. It also affects the potential benefits from ICTs.

Gains towards Understanding and Evaluating Poverty Alleviation Programs

The knowledge of the extent of interdependencies and their incorporation in the design of poverty alleviation program can largely benefit the vulnerable and deprived people in the society and can raise social cohesion.

Two important issues are considered below to show the level of likely gains to be attained when accounting for interdependencies. It is well known that poverty has never benefited from the attention of policy makers until recently as it was a taboo and that household survey data are either not conducted or not shared in most of these countries (Farrukh, 2006). It is also common knowledge that income poverty measures lead to showing that the region has poverty levels that are below those prevailing in other countries, but the existence of such a hall even in the oil producing and exporting countries needs major attention. There are though major variations among countries and within countries as is revealed by the data collected in countries such as Algeria, Morocco, Tunisia, Egypt, and Yemen. However, further knowledge need to be added, especially that in relation to the non-income components, in order to enrich the knowledge about poverty in the region. Applied research on these matters on the region needs to be accelerated in order to provide more detailed supports to economic and social policies. Two major issues can be discussed

in relation to the findings contained in the present report. They include the effects of incidental risks, those hazards and exogenous shocks and the missing dimensions that need to be included in the context of poverty alleviation.

Effects of Incidental Risks and Poverty

The existence of these interdependencies at the household level in each country of the region can also be a major source of vulnerability and can lead to the intergenerational transmission of deprivation when accounting for different risks and uncertainties that can affect any element of chain of poverty causation.

Even when historically, means of adjustments have been developed and implemented in these cases, further attention is to be devoted to the poor segments of the population. Higher vulnerabilities are expected to exist among women, girls, children, handicapped and older segments of the population in this region. The social status of each member of these segments is such that any degradation in one of the elements of the interdependent chain does affect the other components. Health accidents, deaths, sudden unemployment and job loss, price increase, among others do drastically affect the survival of households.

Current economic and development literature show consistently the impact of low income on the limited choices available to the poor. The accumulated evidence underlines the difficulty and sometimes the impossibility of poor segments of the population to access basic services that are provided by the public and private sectors. It is also widely accepted that these facts are largely observed in developing economies and in the region under study, given the extent of income poverty, illiteracy, market imperfections, and the absence of safety nets.

This says that poor individuals and households face the dilemma of both low income and consequently implicit high costs of access to basic goods and services. These goods and services include education, health care, housing, water, energy, transportation, credit markets, legal systems, and courts, besides others. However, this implicit high cost of access is not only faced at the level of basic services but also at the acquisition of food, clothing, and other necessary goods. This is easily understood when accounting for the competitive needs and the pressure placed on a limited income especially in an environmental context with relatively higher fertility levels even though a decrease in the number of children has been observed in recent international population surveys.

Under these pressures, occasional risks and uncertainties do affect the overall capacity of households, especially those vulnerable and poor segments. The impacts of such risks are exacerbated by the interdependencies between economic, social, health and educational situations of households. Further studies developed by World Bank, UNDP, and other organizations are still pointing out several new issues that are to be addressed in the region in order to reduce the likely impacts of not just income poverty but multidimensional one.

Effects of Hazards and Other Exogenous Sources of Deprivation

As different variables and sub-variables appeared to be largely interconnected, different favourable and unfavourable exogenous factors are likely to induce positive and negative effects on the situation of individual and households at the level of different localities, countries and the region.

These risks and uncertainties do induce highly unexpected negative effects on the most vulnerable segments of the population. Epidemics, natural hazards, and also economic crises besides unfavourable policies are likely to generate new supplementary burdens of deprivations among the poorest and the most vulnerable segments of the population.

The investigations undertaken in this study have been showing the high level of vulnerabilities of women in general and mainly those in rural areas. Women are consequently likely to suffer more from any unexpected exogenous shock. Children as well as older people are also in the same category. While the previous analyzes did not look precisely at the situation of children and oldest segments of the population, it is expected that these categories do also suffer from the negative impacts of any hazard because their vulnerable situation at the level of the household, in each country and in all the South Mediterranean economies.

While medium term strategies can be developed by the vulnerable segments of the population to adapt to shocks that are progressive, those that are sudden have more critical and sometimes detrimental impacts. This is experienced in the region with the adjustments to droughts through rural migration and the development of non-agricultural activities during low rainfall and unfavourable weather conditions. However, sudden natural shocks such as floods and earthquakes have contributed to generate further losses, mainly in poor areas and among the poorest segments of the population.

The relative high frequency of conflicts and wars in some parts of the South Mediterranean region is also a source of important damages that affect the region and mainly the poorest segments of the populations. This has generated important flows of refugees and an important stock of displacements and population re-allocation in this region of the world. Under these types of circumstances, education and health besides the requirements of daily life become crucial with the growth of such natural and human hazards.

The Importance of Missing Dimensions of Poverty

The results attained in this study show also how larger series of variables on which no data are available, may have important explanatory powers in the extent and magnitudes of the levels of interdependencies. The on-going household surveys as well as the aggregate databases do not account for series of missing variables that may have important roles in identifying sources and extent of social and economic deficits. The missing information is now being tackled in series of projects (Alkire & Foster, 2008; Alkire, 2008, 2007) that recognize also that poverty has determinants that vary with households, regions and countries. For international comparisons, larger lists of poverty and deprivation components have to be added with a subsequent index for poverty assessments.

The identification of these missing variables is likely to contribute not just to understanding of local deprivation but also the overall programs and measurement of poverty at the global levels. Besides the issue of missing women that has been extensively addressed in the literature of human development (Osmani & Sen, 2003) and that can be an important issue in the South Mediterranean region, other hidden information can be useful in understanding poverty in the context of the countries composing the region. Even with the lack of rigorous knowledge about economic data, the countries of the region appear to have relatively low levels of income poverty and vulnerability as assessed by international organizations. But these levels do not all the time show the real extent of poverty as this latter is multidimensional and includes larger series of components that are not addressed most of the time for different reasons, including that of the perception of poverty by researchers and practitioners of development.

The South Mediterranean region with the different countries composing it appears to show that large sets of variables can be introduced. The interdependencies assessed mainly at the levels of households in Morocco, Turkey, and Egypt support the existence of variables that are not currently in the databases. While examples of missing variables are already suggested in the literature (Solava & Alkire, 2007), a series of components seem to

be extensively behind poverty. This is the case of physical and social mobility and of variables related to the dimension of social capital and to the dominating culture in the region.

Physical mobility can be related to health issues (physical and mental) and can be a major source of absence and limited expression of capacity in movement and access to different goods and services at different and further distances. Even under a high level of supply of infrastructure, human mobility is directly related to the capacity to undertake movements and be capable of accessing facilities that are at given distances.

In the region and mainly in its rural areas, the situation of infrastructure is such that those with some health difficulties may not be relatively mobile. In addition, the lack of information and the high level of illiteracy may also be behind the limited mobility. It is then clear that the vulnerable segments of the population are likely to be of limited mobility. Women, children, old people, and handicapped besides those that are forced to be mobile within limited distances (prisons, refugee's camps) are segments that can be relatively immobile in the region.

The region can be also suffering from lack of social mobility as individuals are not all the time provided access to new and higher levels of employment, housing, and access to better opportunities during their life spans. The interdependencies between socio economic status and health plays a role in this but the existing social, cultural, and political implicit barriers of access and change of situations deprive individuals and large population segments from participation to the overall sharing of the outcomes of development.

The Central Role of Education and Health in Poverty Alleviation Programs

Even with limited time series data on variables related to health, education, and poverty, both education and health have appeared to be important engines to promote development in South Mediterranean countries.

Important variations have appeared throughout countries with education having an important driving role in Morocco but with more emphasis placed on health in the cases of Turkey and Egypt.

The existing interdependencies shown under both country and regional analyzes, underline the importance of health and education in driving the economies and societies in the South Mediterranean region. Specific country results related to the likely determination of the continuation of schooling have shown the importance of the health and economic conditions in staying or leaving school. The rate of school dropout has appeared to be higher for girls at both primary and secondary levels in the case of Morocco. Variables directly related to health and nutrition besides economic components appeared to have major influences on school continuous attendance by children. As indicated in other publications, the dropout from school can be related to the alternative of employment of children and to the early marriage of girls. This is pervasive in the regions even under the trend of increasing age of marriage and the constraints placed against the employment of children.

In traditional activities such as agriculture and handicrafts, learning opportunities are provided for some years before formal inclusion in these professions. However, some studies are questioning these types of learning on the ground that these are non-paid activities provided to children rather being real learning experiences. Major attempts to create better conditions for maintaining and increasing the number of children in schools have been made. They include the provision of public and communal transportation, food, and housing. These actions are really accounting for the existence of major interdependencies but they need acceleration and development in order to further promote larger schooling.

Social new arrangements have also been provided in some countries in the region to ensure that girls can attend schools by increasing the age of marriage. However, again social practices and sometimes cultural values are still constraining these new social trends. The opening up of job markets for girls and women besides the promotion of the status of women through creating further incentives for their inclusion into the administrative, political, and economic life are under way but the indices such as the Gender Empowerment Measure still indicate low performances for the countries of the region.

Importance of Transversal Policies with Further Coordination and Integration

It is now clearly established that transversal policies and further coordination and integration of different sectors of the economy and society are likely to generate further positive effects on development. While the tradition of sector policies is important, that of transversal and horizontal approaches appears to be more promising for the process of inclusion and expansion of development.

The average picture of an economy and society in the South Mediterranean region indicates more closed and more centralized systems of decision making with a prominent role of Governments. All decisions and programs are expected to go through a public system of institutions where central ministries and parliaments play a central role. Social activities and poverty alleviation programs are also conducted most of the time on the same principles and practices. In almost all countries of the region, there are ministries of education and health with representations in different localities but most of the decisions related to health, education, employment and economic affairs are centrally taken.

On the other hand, households in different localities and regions in every country live and perceive the interdependencies that exist between different components that affect their daily living conditions. The needs of mainly those that are under stressed economic and social conditions are normally assumed to be considered within the framework of the locality, the region and the administrative entity to which they belong, but most of the time more resources and more administrative power is needed from the central entities.

The local representations require more resources and instruments to supply the needed services. Education and health as well as other sectors are most of the time under the respective central authorities. Further, these programs may not be consistent with the features and characteristics of a given region of implementation.

Coordination and integration within the horizontal and vertical meanings have been discussed for the South Mediterranean region over the last years implying that the development and furthering of this approach have been accelerated. The orientation for the achievement of the MDGs and the development of human development programs has been among the incentives that have pushed countries to achieve further integration. However, this external means require further adoption within countries to promote local and global development. The reforms undertaken and the changes taking place in the economic, social, and political spheres while necessary are not sufficient if these reforms do not include further coordination and integration including that with different localities.

STRENGTHENING LOCAL DEVELOPMENT

This book and its findings indicate implicitly that there are different interdependent levels that can address and sustain development especially in its territorial components.

Consistency between global or macroeconomic and the needs of the populations cannot be achieved if microeconomic concerns are not addressed both locally and globally. This also says that local development matters and might be the

most important determinant of global development. That is why regions and localities in South Mediterranean countries have to be the engines of development.

The need for focus on local development has been observed for most of the countries composing the region under study. Most of these countries appear to be more centralized even though major political, social, and political reforms have been undertaken. Within the context of a centrally harmonized local development, the interdependencies between health, education and economic performance can be the most important determinants in comparison with sector driven and centralized development.

Locally conducted poverty alleviation programs have the merit of accounting for household and local specificities, including the types of needs and deprivations rather than on global frameworks that define poverty and the average target population.

Further drivers including political, economic, and social components can be mobilized efficiently in different countries of the region. The shift that is taking place in the United Arab Emirates and other traditional golf oil exporting countries can be examples of trends that can be developed in the entire region. These means are required to account for health and education besides the economic and financial components. The ownership of technologies that appeared from the report as directly related to the socioeconomic components is likely to constitute a major engine in enterprise and job creation.

STRENGTHENING ENTERPRISE AND JOB CREATION

Health and education are the two most important forms of human capital. In the context of globalization both are strongly needed for individuals to perform in the job market and to achieve competitiveness of both small and large enterprises.

Their interdependencies with employment make the required improvement even more pressing.

In South Mediterranean countries, as in a lot of developing economies, the creation of jobs has become more and more dependent on the development of small new and medium businesses. Such a relation is becoming essential for allowing self-employment and creating jobs through the mobilization of small investments supported by different public and banking programs. Such a strategy has been accelerated in the region, since 2000 with mainly the increase in the unemployment of young and skilled labor. These programs are also enhanced with the contributions of large businesses that have developed special programs and instruments, which facilitate the level of small enterprise creation through outsourcing for example.

In a context of globalization and of evolution towards knowledge intensive products, proceeds and services, the competitiveness of all enterprises is realized through their technological leveling and the reinforcement of their innovation capacity. This is more confirmed given that obsolescence of knowledge and know-how that occurs at a higher speed in comparison with past periods. The creation and development of enterprises and job opportunities, although essential in a growth and development process, becomes more demanding in terms of new knowledge and innovations. The most important way that is also the most promising is the one that consists in creating enterprises centered on benefit yielding innovations but most of these enterprises that are adapted to future markets are not yet created.

Nevertheless, during their education, students address series of domains that are often generators of ideas in terms of general knowledge but also in terms of enterprise creation practice and creation. Unfortunately, the last part is seldom valued in the education mechanisms despite trainings and projects. Trainings also are not mobilized in a functional manner. These facts would explain among others, why enterprise creation is not the major concern of schools and universities' graduates in the region of study. In the contrary, job research, namely in the public sector, remained the major expectation of many graduates despite the changes made at the level of the job market structures since 1990. Such prospect that was reinforced by the education system itself, among others, was progressively replaced by expectations more related to jobs created by the private sector. However, such concerns in terms of hiring have been quickly faced with the sector's limits and with the global dynamics of the economy.

Despite the fact that investment is the most important means for job creation, new enterprise creation is the first source of self-employment before constituting a recruitment center. The self-employment related researches progressively showed the promising character of the creation process of a new type of enterprise. This latter would be integrated in the education and applied research logic, while facing the concerns about market needs in terms of innovating products and services. Another asset is related to investment extent, enterprise size, and jobs and functions mobilized. Such integration is likely to create growth and progress regarding market concerns and satisfaction of needs. The examples offered by the new information technologies in the South Mediterranean countries and elsewhere, show clearly the effects of this integration in different areas. These examples confirm the importance of start-ups and small enterprises not only in terms of job creation but also regarding the creation of new wealth in the economy. This wealth accounts not only for the economic and financial components in the locality but also for the infrastructure and for the provision of the needs of the local population. This includes health and education. This is also strengthened through necessary synergies with large enterprises but also with the public sector and with non-governmental agencies.

It is thus a matter of choosing new strategies aiming at the pursuit of new avenues through the mobilization of human resources able to identify and promote new ways but also to produce through the creation and promotion of enterprises. In a more practical way, it is a matter of creating favorable conditions so that students, by their graduation at most, can develop innovating enterprises. It is thus necessary that the education system accompany these students along the duration of the program in order to help them generate ideas and projects. The ideal case would be a process directly related to the valorization of achievements following applied researches conducted within education and training organisms. This is based on the existence of a deep relationship between education processes and investigations related to research and development. In the absence of such processes, the deep relationships held with existing enterprises and the accumulated experiences in different sectors, could supply more knowledge in terms of mechanisms able to constitute levers for innovating ideas among students. It is also necessary to install incubation processes likely to offer favorable conditions for the concretization of ideas through transforming them into promising enterprises. Finally, it is necessary to have access to mechanisms related to launching the enterprise within an incubator or directly in the production structure. These latter are functional clusters such as defined in economic literature and development reports.

Several studies and reports related to the implementation and to the launching strategies of technological clusters. This is the case of European Union countries, namely France, Belgium, Germany, and Luxembourg. Canada and the United States of America did not ignore this development strategy. Many international organizations and developed countries recommend the adoption of the strategy of clusters for developing countries. The literature in this subject is abundant and continues to develop during recent years. Some developing countries such as Turkey, Morocco, and Brazil continue their attempts for the promotion of local competitive clusters. The related theories have been developed by series of authors including Porter (1990), Lipsey (2002), Globerman (2001), Belleflamme, Picard, and Thisse (1999), Picard and Toulemonde (2004), Hutton (2004), and Monfort and Nicolini (2002), among others.

FINDINGS AND PROSPECTS FROM ICTS

The major objective of this chapter is to show how to conduct a study on the importance of interdependencies between health, education and the performance with focus on the South Mediterranean Economies (SMC). The motivation behind the achievement of such an objective is mainly related to the determination of the direction of the likely gains that each country can attain when accounting for integrated social and economic policies. In this exercise, health, and education systems are central.

Before pursuing how the empirical assessment of the interdependencies can be conducted, a brief literature search is conducted. It allows for the identification of the importance of the topic but also the recent nature of the questions addressed both in theory and empirically. Among the important directions revealed, there are the links between health and wealth, the importance of non monetary assets (knowledge and social capital) besides the impacts of globalization on health in developing economies as developed in the previous chapter.

The situation in the South Mediterranean countries has been characterized as being not fully accounting for these interdependencies, as the policy-making models pursued are sector oriented and based on the trends taking place mainly in developed economies. The SMC economies even though can gain from the knowledge about the interdependencies; they can also reduce the existing constraints to allow the population access to basic services.

The current study has also shown that interdependencies are not fully valued in this type of context as access to different components is governed differently. Given the extent and magnitude of education, health, and socio-economic deficits in the SMC economies, the identification of interdependencies generates new directions for more integrated economic and social policies that can also gain from the reduction of barriers to access to basic services such as health and education.

The results attained both in assessing different variables as well in revealing the relationships between different socio-economic components, have shown the extent of the likely gains that can be attained when accounting for more integrated policies. They also show the global constraints that limit access and then expression of full benefits from interdependencies. Furthermore, the limited access to health technologies and related knowledge reduces the level of research and education that could be devoted to enhancing local flows of information for the population to participate to different partial and global programs. The results show also that income poverty is not the major deficit but deficits in health and education are the main reasons for the absence of economic policies capable of generating socio-economic improvements that can create better conditions for access to the basket of the necessary services and goods in the region. Within the context of these economies, implicit discrimination has appeared to be among the major factors that affect these countries.

The results attained so far are mainly based on using panels of data covering the SMC at different periods of time. Both descriptive statistics and regression analysis are used to assess the direction of interdependencies. One specific piece of data related to drop out from different school levels has been used to investigate the link with health and economic variables in the 16 regions of Morocco, has been used. The microeconomic results based on the household data contained in the above surveys show consistently the existence of important interdependencies among economic,

social, health and education variables. However, these relationships are not fully considered in partial and global policy making in these economies. These interdependencies are consequently major sources of social gains at both sector and global levels. Also further international and regional strengthening of collaboration in the areas of education, health and related social areas is likely to enhance the level of services in each South Mediterranean economy.

In this overall process of looking at interdependencies between health, education and other socio-economic variables, it has appeared that the available technologies including ICTs can ensure further coordination. The inputs from ICTs intervene at all stages from analysis, to implementation, monitoring, and evaluation. Convergence with continuous development of ICT tools is providing promising and cheaper tools to ensure the needed coordination between players, actions, and territories.

LIMITATIONS AND NEED FOR FURTHER RESEARCH

Major limitations have appeared during the implementation of this research. These Limitations have concerned the scope, the coverage, and extent of this research. That is why progressive changes have been progressively operated. However, some of the limitations have helped identify new research avenues directly related to this study.

Limitations

The data limitations have contributed in reducing the scope and initial intentions placed on this work. While the geographical area of the South Mediterranean can be well delimited, the availability of information has imposed that the MSC include most of the time the Arab countries and Turkey as they have similar levels and patterns of development. These concerns are shared herein as limitations and warnings that need to be addressed in order to inform the readers about the limits within which this research was achieved. This also has shown the importance of future investigations related to the interdependencies between health, education, and poverty.

One of the important findings of the research on the link between socio economic status and health is that the children economic status and or the early life status have very important implications for adult health. The data available in the South Mediterranean Countries does not allow us to test for such hypothesis. Evidence however suggests that this result probably holds in this part of the world as well. We will need to develop alternative hypothesis to test for this important finding.

This book is not about the analysis of the sectors of health, education and economic performance and related sector policies in general and in the South Mediterranean economies. It is dealing with the interferences of health, education, and economic performance with their implied policies. This investigation is about the assessment of the interdependencies between health, education, and economic performance. It aims at showing the existence, the extent and the eventual policy implications.

Furthermore, the initial intent of this project was to look at the economic performance mainly for households faced with income poverty.

Future Research

The region needs more disciplinary and multidisciplinary research in the areas related to health, education, and poverty. These directions of research could be better located in the countries of the South Mediterranean region in universities and research centers. These investigations are likely to enrich the development programs that are undertaken in different countries and in the region. The central role of women is an example of research

area that is needed to support the promotion of gender issues in different areas. Governments, private initiatives, and non-governmental agencies can then enrich the content of their actions and programs. It is also the same for poverty alleviation and for related human development policies. Some research directions include:

- Missing specific poverty dimensions in the region,
- Causality and determinants of vulnerability and poverty in the context of the region,
- Socio-economics of health and health issues,
- Socio-economics of knowledge content and diffusion,
- Measurement and quantitative issues with shared databases and tools,
- Benchmarks within countries and between countries,
- Local development versus global development,
- Efficient means and institutions for the promotion of education,
- Public versus private supplies of health and education,
- Impacts of delays in reducing poverty and implications on North-South relationships.

CONCLUSION

This book has so far introduced the framework of fragmentation and coordination in relation to health, education, and socio-economic factors. It has shown how these interferences can be revealed through available data and how these interdependencies need to be well identified in order to enrich economic and social policies. This has shown also that ICTs have and can have more important roles to play in enhancing private and social benefits. As interdependencies have been identified to occur at different levels, territorial units need also to be considered as these forms the basis of development. The needs for microeconomic data as well as for other signals that relate to how decisions are made are among the necessary ingredients. Those lead to further research questions where both technologies and social sciences are invited to contribute.

REFERENCES

Alkire, S. (2008). *The capability approach: Mapping measurement issues and choosing dimensions*. OPHI Paper Working Series. OPHI.

Alkire, S., & Foster, J. (2008). *Counting and multidimensional poverty measurement*. OPHI Paper Working Series. OPHI.

Belleflamme, P., Picard, P., & Thisse, J. F. (1999). An economic theory of regional clusters. *Journal of Urban Economics*, *48*(1), 158–184. doi:10.1006/juec.1999.2161

Farrukh, I. (2006). *Sustaining gains in poverty reduction and human development in the Middle East and North Africa*. Portland, OR: Book News.

Globerman, S. (2001). *La localisation des activités à plus grande valeur ajoutée*. Bellingham, WA: Western Washington University.

Heeks, R. (1999). *Information and communication technologies, poverty and development*. Manchester, UK: IDPM. Retrieved from http://www.man.ac.uk/idpm/idpm_dp.htm#devinf_wp

Hutton, T. A. (2004). The new economy of the inner city. *Cities (London, England)*, *21*(2), 89–108. doi:10.1016/j.cities.2004.01.002

Lipsey, R. G. (2002). Some implications of endogenous technological change for technology policies in developing countries. *Economics of Innovation and New Technology*, *11*, 4–5. doi:10.1080/10438590200000003

Monfort, P., & Nicolini, R. (2002). Regional convergence and international integration. *Journal of Urban Economics*, *48*, 286–306. doi:10.1006/juec.1999.2167

Osmani, S., & Sen, A. (2003). The hidden penalties of gender inequality: Fetal origins of ill-health. *Economics and Human Biology*, *1*, 105–121. doi:10.1016/S1570-677X(02)00006-0

Picard, P., & Toulemonde, E. (2004). Endogenous qualifications and firms' agglomeration. *Journal of Urban Economics*, *55*(3), 458–477. doi:10.1016/S0094-1190(03)00075-5

Porter, M. (1990). The competitive advantage of nations. *Journal of Development Economics*, *37*(8), 1189–1213.

Samiullah, Y., & Rao, S. (2000). *Role of ICTs in urban and rural poverty reduction*. Paper presented at the MoEF-TERI-UNEP Regional Workshop for Asia and Pacific on ICT and Environment. Delhi, India. Retrieved from http://www.teri.res.in/icteap/present/session4/sami.doc

Solava, I., & Alkire, S. (2007). *Agency and empowerment: A proposal for internationally comparable indicators*. OPHI Paper Working Series. OPHI.

Compilation of References

Abirafeh, L. (2003). *Afghan women: One year later – Creating digital opportunities for Afghan women.* Retrieved from http://www.developmentgateway.org/node/134111/sdm/docview?docid=427938

Abu Habib, L. (1997). *Gender and disability: Women's experiences in the Middle East.* Oxford, UK: Oxfam Professional.

Acemoglu, D., & Johnson, S. (2006). *Disease and development: The effect of life expectancy on economic growth.* Cambridge, MA: MIT Press. doi:10.3386/w12269

Adams, P., Hurd, M., McFadden, D., Merril, A., & Ribeiro, T. (2003). Healthy, wealthy and wise? Tests for direct causal paths between health and socioeconomic status. *Journal of Econometrics, 112*(1), 3–56. doi:10.1016/S0304-4076(02)00145-8

Adewoye, J. O., & Akanbi, T. A. (2012). Role of information and communication technology investment on the profitability of small medium scale industries – A case of Sachet water companies in Oyo state, Nigeria. *Journal of Emerging Trends in Economics and Management Sciences, 3*(1), 64–71.

African Youth Report. (2009). *Expanding opportunities for and with young people in Africa.* Retrieved from http://www.uneca.org/ayr2009/AfricanYouthReport_09.pdf

Aguayo-Rico, A., Guerra-Turrubiates, I., & Montes, R. (2005). Empirical evidence of the impact of health on economic growth. *Issues in Political Economy, 14.* Retrieved from http://org.elon.edu/ipe/aguayorico%20final.pdf

Aguilera, A., Guillot, C., & Rallet, A. (2012). Mobile ICTs and physical mobility: Review and research agenda. In Hsiao, C. M., & Liao, Y.-P. (Eds.), *Transportation Research Part A: Policy and Practice* (pp. 664–672). London, UK: Elsevier. doi:10.1016/j.tra.2012.01.005

Akala, A., & El-Saharty, S. (2006). Public-health challenges in the Middle East and North Africa. *Lancet, 367*(9515), 961–964. doi:10.1016/S0140-6736(06)68402-X

Ali Abdel Gadir, A. (2007). Poverty in the Arab region: A selective review. In Ali Abdel Gadir, A., & Shenggen, F. (Eds.), *Public Policy and Poverty Reduction in the Arab Region.* Safat, Kuwait: The Arab Planning Institute.

Alkire, S. (2008). *The capability approach: Mapping measurement issues and choosing dimensions.* OPHI Paper Working Series. OPHI.

Alkire, S., & Foster, J. (2008). *Counting and multidimensional poverty measurement.* OPHI Paper Working Series. OPHI.

Allison & Gomez. (2012). Gender and public access ICT. In Gomez (Ed.), *Libraries, Telecentres, Cybercafes, and Public Access to ICT: International Comparisons.* Hershey, PA: IGI Global.

Al-Suqri, M. N., & Lillard, L. L. (2011). Barriers to effective information seeking of social scientists in developing countries: The case of Sultan Qaboos University in Oman. *Journal of Library and Information Science, 1*(2), 86–99.

Altuwaijri, M. (2010). Supporting the Saudi e-health initiative: The master of health informatics programme at KSAU-HS. *East Mediterr Health, 16*(1), 119-124. Retrieved from http://sahi.org.sa/article_details.php?article_id=6

Alyemeni, R. M. (2011). Five year program to transform healthcare delivery in Saudi Arabia. *Saudi Arabia Ministry of Health.* Retrieved from http://www.himss.org/content/files/MiddleEast10_presentations/CS1_MohammedAlYemeni.pdf

Ambrose, P. (2002). *The cost of poor housing, urban regeneration and non-housing outcomes.* Paper presented at the HSA Conference, Housing Policies for the New UK. York, UK.

Anderson, K., Foster, J., & Frisvold, D. (2004). *Investing in health: The long-term impact of head start.* Working Paper No. 04-W26. Nashville, TN: Vanderbilt University.

Anderson, K., Martin, W., & Van Dder Mensbrugghe, D. (2006). Would multilateral trade reform benefit sub-Saharan Africans? *Journal of African Economies, 15.*

Aoki, K. (1998). Neocolonialism, anticommons property, and biopiracy in the (not-so-brave) new world order of international intellectual property protection. *Indiana Journal of Global Legal Studies, 6*(1), 11–38.

Aramex.com. (2010). *A publicly listed company trading on the Dubai stock exchange (DFM) and was founded by Fadi Ghandour in 1982.* Retrieved February 24, 2010, from http://www.aramex.com/news/item.aspx?id=b72adf8f-8e65-4966-b2a6-3ed841d90f1d

Arayssi, M., Sarkis, J. K., & Mardini, R. U. (2006). The value of life: A new labor theory-based model. *Journal of Business Valuation and Economic Loss Analysis, 1*(1). doi:10.2202/1932-9156.1004

Assar, S., El Amrani, R., & Watson, R. (2010). ICT and education: A critical role in human and social development. *Information Technology for Development, 16,* 151–158. doi:10.1080/02681102.2010.506051

Australian Medial Association. (2002). *The links between health and education for indigenous Australian children.* Retrieved from http://ama.com.au/node/508

Ayodeji, A. F., & El-Saharty, S. (2006). Public-health challenges in the Middle East and North Africa. *Lancet, 367,* 961–964. doi:10.1016/S0140-6736(06)68402-X

Azariadis, C., & Drazen, A. (1990). Threshold externalities in economic development. *The Quarterly Journal of Economics, 105*(2), 501–526. doi:10.2307/2937797

Balasubramanian, K., Clarke-Okah, W., Daniel, J., Ferreira, F., Kanwar, A., & Kwan, A. (2009). *ICTs for higher education: Background paper from the commonwealth of learning.* Paper presented at the UNESCO World Conference on Higher Education. New York, NY.

Baliamoune-Lutz. (2003). An analysis of the determinants and effects of ICT diffusion in developing countries. *Information Technology for Development, 10,* 151–169. doi:10.1002/itdj.1590100303

Banerjee, A. V., & Duflo, E. (2007). The economic lives of the poor. *The Journal of Economic Perspectives, 21*(1), 141–167. doi:10.1257/jep.21.1.141

Bardasi, E., & Francesconi, M. (2003). The impact of a typical employment on individual wellbeing: Evidence from a panel of British workers. *Institute for Social and Economic Research.* Retrieved from http://www.iser.essex.ac.uk/pubs/workpaps/pdf/2003-02.pdf

Barro, R. J. (1991). Economic growth in a cross-section of countries. *The Quarterly Journal of Economics, 106*(2), 407–443. doi:10.2307/2937943

Beastall, L. (2006). Enchanting a disenchanted child: Revolutionizing the means of education using information and communication technology and e-learning. *British Journal of Sociology of Education, 27*(1), 97–110. doi:10.1080/01425690500376758

Beena, M., & Mathur, M. (2012). Role of ICT education for women empowerment. *International Journal of Economics and Research, 3*(3), 164–172.

Behrman, J. R., & Rosenzweig, M. R. (2004). Returns to birth weight. *The Review of Economics and Statistics, 86*(2), 586–601. doi:10.1162/003465304323031139

Beine, M., Docquier, F., & Rapoport, H. (2001). Brain drain and economic growth: Theory and evidence. *Journal of Development Economics, 64*(1), 275–289. doi:10.1016/S0304-3878(00)00133-4

Beine, M., Docquier, F., & Rapoport, H. (2003). *Brain drain and LDC's growth: Winners and losers. IZA DP No. 819.* Washington, DC: The Institute for the Study of Labor.

Beine, M., Docquier, F., & Rapoport, H. (2006). *Brain drain and human capital formation in developing countries: Winners and losers.* Louvain, Belgium: Université Catholique de Louvain. doi:10.1111/j.1468-0297.2008.02135.x

Belleflamme, P., Picard, P., & Thisse, J. F. (1999). An economic theory of regional clusters. *Journal of Urban Economics, 48*(1), 158–184. doi:10.1006/juec.1999.2161

Bellin, E. (2004). *The political-economic conundrum: The affinity of economic and political reform in the Middle East and North Africa. Carnegie Paper*. Pittsburgh, PA: Carnegie University.

Bener, A., & Alali, K. A. (2004). *Consanguineous marriage in a newly developed country: The Qatari population*. Al Tarfa, Qatar: University of Qatar. doi:10.1017/S0021932004007060

Ben, R. (2012). Gendering professionalism in the internationalization of information work. In *Globalization, Technology and Gender Disparity: Social Impacts of ICTs* (pp. 51–69). Hershey, PA: IGI Global. doi:10.4018/978-1-4666-0020-1.ch005

Berge, E., & Van Laerhoven, F. (2011). Governing the commons for two decades: A complex story. *International Journal of the Commons, 5*. Retrieved from http://www.thecommonsjournal.org/index.php/ijc/article/view/325/230 accessed 03 sept 2012

Bergstrom, T. (2010). The uncommon insight of Elinor Ostrom. *Scandinavian Journal of Economics*. Retrieved August 10, 2012, from http://works.bepress.com/ted_bergstrom/107

Bernard, P. (2006). *The lifecourse paradigm in research and in policy*. Paper presented at the First Symposium of the Population, Work and Family Collaboration. Ottawa, Canada. Retrieved from http://policyresearch.gc.ca/doclib/LC/PS_LC_Bernard_200603_e.pdf

Bernardi, R., & DeChiara, F. (2011). ICTs and monitoring of MDGs: A case study of Kenya HIV/AIDs monitoring and evaluation in a donor multi-agency context. *Information Technology for Development, 17*(1), 1–3. doi:10.1080/02681102.2010.511699

Bilgin, M., & Ismihan, N. (2008). An analysis of the unemployment in selected MENA countries and Turkey. *Journal of Third World Studies, 25*(2), 189.

Black, L., McTear, M., Black, N., & Harper, R., & Lemon. (2005). Evaluating the DI@l-log system on a cohort of elderly, diabetic patients: Results from a preliminary study. [Lisbon, Portugal: InterSpeech.]. *Proceedings of InterSpeech, 2005*, 821–824.

Bleakley, H. (2007). disease and development: evidence from hookworm eradication in the American south. *The Quarterly Journal of Economics, 122*(1), 73–117. doi:10.1162/qjec.121.1.73

Bloom, D. E., & Canning, D. (2000). The health and wealth of nations. *American Association for the Advancement of Science, 287*(5456), 1207–1209. doi:10.1126/science.287.5456.1207

Bloom, D. E., Canning, D., & Sevilla, J. (2004). The effect of health on economic growth: A production function approach. *World Development, 32*(1), 1–13. doi:10.1016/j.worlddev.2003.07.002

Bobonis, G. J., Miguel, E., & Sharma, C. P. (2006). Anemia and school participation. *The Journal of Human Resources, 41*(4), 692–721.

Boettke, P. Z., Caceres, W., & Martin, A. G. (2012). *Error is obvious, coordination is the puzzle*. Retrieved August 12, 2012, from http://ssrn.com/2004362

Bouhamed, A., Bouraoui, N., & Chaabouni, J. (2010). *The role of Tunisian universities in regional development*. Paper presented at the Triple Helix Conference 2010. Madrid, Spain.

Bouraoui, N., Bouhamed, A., & Chaabouni, J. (2010). *Alliance capability in Tunisian pharmaceutical industry*. Paper presented at the VIII Triple Helix International Conference on University, Industry and Government Linkages. Madrid, Spain.

Boussard, J. M., Gérard, F., & Piketty, M. G. (2005). *Libéraliser l'agriculture? Théorie, modèles et réalité*. Montpellier, France: Cirad.

Bozzoli, C., Deaton, A., & Quintana-Domeque, C. (2007). *Child mortality, income and adult height*. Retrieved from http://papers.nber.org/papers/w12966.pdf

Bridges, J. F. P., & Haywood. (2003). Theory verses empiricism in health economics. *The European Journal of Health Economics, 4*, 90–95. doi:10.1007/s10198-002-0162-1

Brinkley, G. L. (2011). *The macroeconomic impact of improving health: Investigating the causal direction*. Retrieved from http://trc.ucdavis.edu/glbrinkley/Docs/Causal.pdf

Broadbent, R., & Papadopoulos, T. (2012). Getting wired@collingwood: An ICT project underpinned by action research. *Community Development Journal, 47*(2), 248–265. doi:10.1093/cdj/bsq061

Buchanan, J. M., & Yoon, Y. J. (2000). Symmetric tragedies: Commons and anti-commons. *The Journal of Law & Economics*, *43*, 1–13. doi:10.1086/467445

Burchell, B., Lapido, D. K., & Wilkinson, F. (1999). Job insecurity and work intensification: Flexibility and the changing boundaries of work. *Joseph Rowntree Foundation*. Retrieved from http://www.jrf.org.uk/knowledge/findings/socialpolicy/849.asp

Burke, K. (2010). The impact of internet and ICT use among SME agribusiness growers and producers. *Journal of Small Business and Entrepreneurship*, *23*(2), 173–194.

Byrne, E., Nicholson, B., & Salem, F. (2011). Information communication technologies and the millennium development goals. *Information Technology for Development*, *17*(1), 1–3. doi:10.1080/02681102.2010.513825

Cameron, F., & Rhein, E. (2005). *Promoting political and economic reform in the Mediterranean and Middle East*. Retrieved from http://www.esiweb.org/pdf/esi_turkey_tpq_id_28.pdf

Camp, L. J., & Anderson, B. L. (1999). *Grameen phone: Empowering the poor through connectivity*. Retrieved from http://www.telecommons.com/villagephone/Camp_article12_99.htm

Canadian International Development Agency. (2000). *Grameen telecom's village phone programme in rural Bangladesh: A multi-media case study final report*. Retrieved from www.telecommons.com/villagephone/finalreport.pdf

Canavese, A. (2005). *Commons, anti-commons, corruption, and behavior*. Retrieved August 12, 2012, from http://escholarship.org/uc/item/09p2972h

Cantrell, R., Hettel, G., Barry, G., & Hamilton, R. (2004). Impact of intellectual property on nonprofit research institutions and the developing countries they serve. *Minnesota Journal of Law. Science & Technology*, *6*, 253–276.

Carayannis, E. G., & Campbell, D. F. J. (2012). Mode3 knowledge production in quadruple helix innovation systems: Twenty-first-century democracy, innovation, and entrepreneurship for development. *Springer Briefs in Business*, *7*, 1–63.

Carayol, N. (2003). Objectives, agreements and matching in science-industry collaborations: Reassembling the pieces of the puzzle. *Research Policy*, *32*, 887–908. doi:10.1016/S0048-7333(02)00108-7

Carstairs, V., & Morris, R. (1989). Deprivation: Explaining differences in mortality between Scotland and England and Wales. *British Medical Journal*, *299*, 886–889. doi:10.1136/bmj.299.6704.886

Carte, T. A., Dharmasiri, A., & Travis, P. (2011). Globalization in development: Do information and communication technologies really matter? *Information Technology for Development*, *17*(4), 289–305. doi:10.1080/02681102.2011.604083

Case, A., Fertig, A., & Paxson, C. (2003). *From cradle to grave? The lasting impact of childhood health and circumstance*. Retrieved from http://www.nber.org/papers/w9788

Center for Education Research and Innovation. (2000). *ICT: School innovation and the quality of learning: Progress and pitfalls*. Retrieved from http://www.oecd.org/dataoecd/24/38/1957030.pdf

Chakrabarty, R. P. (1989). *Multivariate analysis by users of SIPP micro-data files*. Washington, DC: U.S. Bureau of Census.

Chakraborty, B. S. (2006). Brain drain: An alternative theorization. *The Journal of International Trade & Economic Development*, *15*(3), 293–309. doi:10.1080/09638190600871602

Chakraborty, S., & Bhattacharya, J. (2012). *Fertility choice under child mortality and social norms. Staff General Research Papers 34911*. Ames, IA: Iowa State University.

Chakraborty, S., & Das, M. (2005). Mortality, human capital and persistent inequality. *Journal of Economic Growth*, *10*(2), 159–192. doi:10.1007/s10887-005-1670-5

Chang, W. W. (2012). *The economics of offshoring*. Retrieved from.

Chatterjee, M. (1990). *Indian women, their health, and economic productivity. Discussion Paper 109*. Washington, DC: The World Bank.

Chaudhuri, S., Jalan, J., & Suryahadi, A. (2002). *Assessing household vulnerability to poverty from cross-sectional data: A methodology and estimates from Indonesia.* New York, NY: Columbia University.

Checchi, R. M., Loch, K. D., Straub, D., Sevcik, G., & Meso, P. (2012). National ICT policies and development: A stage model and stakeholder theory perspective. *Journal of Global Information Management, 20*(1), 57–79. doi:10.4018/jgim.2012010103

Chen, W., Engineer, M., & King, I. (2006). *Choosing longevity with overlapping generations.* Dunedin, New Zealand: University of Victoria and University of Otago.

Chetley, A. (2006). Improving health, connecting people: The role of ICTs in the health sector of developing countries. *InfoDev.* Retrieved from http://www.asksource.info/pdf/framework2.pdf

Chouchane, L., Mamtani, R., Al-Thani, M. H., Al-Thani, A. A., Ameduri, M., & Sheikh, J. I. (2011). Medical education and research environment in Qatar: A new epoch for translational research in the Middle East. *Journal of Translational Medicine, 9*(16).

Christiaensen, L., & Subbarao, K. (2004). Towards an understanding of household vulnerability in rural Kenya. *Journal of African Economies, 14*(4), 520–558. doi:10.1093/jae/eji008

Chung, C., & Myers, S. L. (1999). Do the poor pay more for food? An analysis of grocery store availability and food price disparities. *The Journal of Consumer Affairs, 33*, 276–296. doi:10.1111/j.1745-6606.1999.tb00071.x

Clift, S. (2003). E-democracy, e-governance and public net-work. *Publicus Articles.* Retrieved from http://www.publicus.net/articles/edempublicnetwork.html

Coelho, M., Filipe, J., & Ferreira, M. (2009). *Tragedies on natural resources a commons and anti-commons approach.* Working Papers 2009/21. Lisbon, Portugal: Technical University of Lisbon.

Colapinto, C., & Porlezza, C. (2011). Innovation in creative industries: From the quadruple helix model to the systems theory. *Journal of the Knowledge Economy, 1*(3), 173–190.

Corti, E. (2005). *Intermediate institutions for the growth of governance processes in the Mediterranean partner countries.* The Ingomed Study. Maghtech/ISSM.

Cosgrove, J., Zastrutzki, S., & Shiel, G. (2005). A survey of ICT in post-primary schools. *Irish Journal of Education, 36,* 25–48. Retrieved from http://www.jstor.org/stable/30077502

Craig, B., & Williams, J. (2011). Research informing practice: Toward effective engagement in community ICT in New Zealand. *The Journal of Community Informatics, 7.* Retrieved from http://ci-journal.net/index.php/ciej/article/view/792/811

Cruces, G. (2002). *Risk-adjusted poverty in Argentina: Measurement and determinants.* London, UK: London School of Economics. doi:10.1080/00220380701526329

Cukor, P., & McKnight, L. W. (2001). *Knowledge, networks, and development.* Working Paper 4193-01. Cambridge, MA: MIT Press.

Cutler, D. & Lleras-Muney. (2012). *Education and health: Insights from international comparisons.* NBER Working Paper No. 17738. Washington, DC: NBER program.

Cutler, D., Lleras-Muney, A., & Vogl, T. (2008). *Socio economic status and health: Dimensions and mechanisms.* NBER Working Paper 14333. Washington, DC: NBER.

Cutler, D. M., & Lleras-Muney, A. (2006). *Education and health: Evaluating theories and evidence.* Washington, DC: National Bureau of Economic Research. doi:10.3386/w12352

Cutler, D., Miller, G., & Norton, D. (2007). *Evidence on early-life income and late-life health from America's dust bowl era.* Rochester, NY: University of Rochester. doi:10.1073/pnas.0700035104

Dabalen, A., & Poupart, N. (2002). *Vulnerability to rainfall shock in Ethiopia.* Ann Arbor, MI: University of Michigan.

D'Agostino, L. M., & Santangelo, G. D. (2012). *Does the global fragmentation of R&D activities pay back? The home region perspective.* Paper presented at the DRUID Academy. Cambridge, UK.

Dasgupta, S., Hamilton, K., Pagiola, S., & Wheeler, D. (2008). Environmental economics at the world bank. *Review of Environmental Economics and Policy*, *2*(1), 4–25. doi:10.1093/reep/rem025

Davcev, D., & Gómez, J. M. (2010). *ICT innovations 2009*. Berlin, Germany: Springer. doi:10.1007/978-3-642-10781-8

De Bailliencourt, T., Beauvisage, T., Granjon, F., & Smoreda, Z. (2011). Extended sociability and relational capital management: Interweaving ICTs and social relations. In Ling, R., & Campbell, S. (Eds.), *Mobile Communication: Bringing Us Together or Tearing Us Apart?*New York, NY: Transaction Publishers.

De Boer, S. J., & Walbeek, M. M. (1998). *Bridging the telematics gap in developing countries: Research bits for development policy*. Twente, The Netherlands: University of Twente. Retrieved from http://ubalpha.civ. utwente.nl/cgi-bin/nph wwwredir/cat.dinkel.utwente. nl:1694/X?%5CTOO+S2+7

De Silva. Ratnadiwakara, & Soysa. (2008). *Transaction costs in agriculture: From the planting decision to selling at the wholesale market: A case-study on the feeder area of the Dambulla dedicated economic centre in Sri Lanka*. Ottawa, Canada: IDRC.

Deardorff, A. V. (1998). *Fragmentation across cones*. Discussion Paper No. 427. Paper presented at a Conference on Globalization and International Trade. Bürgenstock, Switzerland.

Deardorff, A. V. (1998). *Fragmentation in simple trade models*. Discussion Paper No. 422. Paper presented in a Session on Globalization and Regionalism: Conflict or Complements? Chicago, IL.

Deaton, A. (2006). *Global patterns of income and health: Facts, interpretations and policies*. Retrieved from http:// www.wider.unu.edu/events/wider-annual-lecture-2006-announcement.htm

Deaton, A. (2003). Health, income, inequality and economic development. *Journal of Economic Literature*, *41*(1), 113–158. doi:10.1257/002205103321544710

Debande, O., & Ottersten, E. K. (2004). Information and communication technologies: A tool empowering and developing the horizon of the learner. *Higher Education. Management and Policy*, *16*(2), 31–61.

Debbie, G. (2012). *Who we are and what we want*. Retrieved from http://www.tandfonline.com/loi/rics20

DeJong, J., Shepard, B., Roudi-Fahimi, F., & Ashford, L. (2005). *Young adolescents' sexual and reproductive health and rights: Middle East and North Africa*. Washington, DC: Population Reference Bureau.

Depoorter, B., & Vanneste, S. (2004). *Putting humpty dumpty back together: Experimental evidence of anticommons tragedies*. Research Paper No. 04-53. Washington, DC: George Mason Law & Economics.

Depoorter, B., Bertacchini, E., & De Mot, J. (2008). Never two without three: Commons, anticommons and semicommons. *Social Science Research Network Electronic Paper Collection*. Retrieved August 12, 2012, from http://ssrn. com/abstract=1162189

Dercon, S. (2002). Managing income risk of the poor. *Research Observer*, *17*(2), 237–265.

Deutsch, J., & Silber, J. (2008). The order of acquisition of durable goods and the measurement of multidimensional poverty. *Quantitative Approaches to Multidimensional Poverty Measurement*. Retrieved from http://www6.bwl. uni-kiel.de/phd/downloads/schneider/ss06/paper_silber2. pdf

Ding, W., Lehrer, S. F., Rosenquist, J. N., & Audrain-McGovern, J. (2007). *The impact of poor health on education: New evidence using genetic markers*. Retrieved from http://post.queensu.ca/~lehrers/genes.pdf

Djeflat, A. (2007). *The governance of territorial innovation systems (TIS) and the role of intermediate institutions in Maghreb countries*. Paper presented at GLOBELICS-RUSSIA-2007: Regional and National Innovation Systems for Development, Competitiveness and Welfare: The Government-Academia-Industry Partnership (theory, problems, practice and prospects). Saratov, Russia.

Docquier, F., & Sekkat, K. (2006). *Brain drain, what do we know?* Working Paper No.31. Paris, France: Agence Française de Développement.

Docquier, F., Lindsay Lowell, B., & Marfouk, F. (2007). *Measuring brain drain by gender.* IZA Discussion Paper 3235. Unpublished.

Docquier, F., Lohest, O., & Marfouk, A. (2007). Brain drain in developing regions (1990-2000). *The World Bank Economic Review, 21*(2), 193–218. doi:10.1093/wber/lhm008

Docquier, F., & Rapoport, H. (2003). Ethnic discrimination and the migration of skilled labor. *Journal of Development Economics, 70*(1), 159–172. doi:10.1016/S0304-3878(02)00081-0

Dodson, L. L., Sterling, R., & Bennett, J. (2012). Considering failure: Eight years of ITID research. In *Proceedings of the Fifth International Conference on Information and Communication Technologies and Development,* (pp. 56-64). IEEE.

Dolorez, T. (1996). The dynamics of domination. *University of California.* Retrieved from http://www.jstor.org/view/00943061/di974042/97p07327/0

Donbak, L. (2004). Consanguinity in Kahramanmaras City, Turkey, and its medical impact. *Saudi Medical Journal, 25*(12), 1991–1994.

Doyle, O., Harmon, C., & Walker, I. (2005). *The impact of parental income and education on the health of their children. Institute for the Study of Labor, IZA DP No. 1832.* Washington, DC: Institute for the Study of Labor.

Driouchi, A., Baudassé, T., Boboc, C., & Zouag, N. (2007). *New economics of brain drain and risk aversion: Theory and empirical evidence.* Orleans, France: Laboratoire d'Economie d'Orléans.

Driouchi, A., Zouag, N., & Boboc, C. (2009). Interdependencies of health, education and poverty: The case of south Mediterranean economies. *Estudios De Economia Applicada, 27*(2), 523–544.

Dutta, S., & Coury, M. E. (2002). *ICT challenges for the Arab world.* Retrieved from http://zunia.org/uploads/media/knowledge/Chapter_08_ICT_Challenges_for_the_Arab_World.pdf

Dutta, I., & Mishra, A. (2004). *Corruption and competition in the presence of inequality and market imperfections.* Delhi, India: Delhi School of Economics.

Dzenowagis, J. (2005). *Connecting for health: global vision, local insight.* Geneva, Switzerland: World Health Organization.

Dzorgbo, D. B., Duque, R. B., Ynalvez, M. A., & Shrum, W. M. (2012). Are mobile phones changing social networks? A longitudinal study of core networks in Kerala. *New Media & Society, 13*(3), 391–410.

Ebikeme, C. (2011). ICT 4 NTDs. *End the Neglect.* Retrieved from http://endtheneglect.org/2011/09/ict-4-ntds/

El Hamidi, F., & Wahba, J. (2006). *The effects of structural adjustment on youth unemployment in Egypt.* Paper presented at the ERF Twelfth Annual Conference Proceedings. Cairo, Egypt.

El Naggar, D. (2007). Overview: Health sector brief. *The World Bank.* Retrieved from http://web.worldbank.org/Website/External/Contries/MENA/Extmnaregtophealth/0,contentMD K:20510402~menu PK:583116~pagePK:34004173~piPK:34003707~theSi tePK:583110,00.html

Elder, L., & Clarke, M. (2007). Past, present and future: Experiences and lessons from tele-health projects. *Open Medicine, 1,* 3. Retrieved from http://www.openmedicine.ca/article/viewArticle/191/98

El-Haddadeh, R., & Weerakkody, V. (2012). Evaluating the impact of alternative socially innovative public sector service initiatives on social cohesion (ALLIANCE): A research note. *Transforming Government: People, Process, and Policy, 6*(3), 283–299. doi:10.1108/17506161211251272

Elias, C. J. (2009). Policies and practices to advance global health technologies. *Center for Strategic and International Studies.* Retrieved from http://csis.org/files/media/csis/pubs/090420_elias_policiespractices.pdf

El-Shenawy, N. (2010). ICT measurement: Egypt's experience. In *Proceedings of the First Workshop of the Regional Project, ICT Indicators and Capacity Building for ICT Measurement in Arab Region.* Amman, Jordan: Ministry of Communication and Information Technology.

Etzkowitz, H., & Zhou, C. (2006). Triple helix twins: Innovation and sustainability. *Science & Public Policy*, *33*(1), 77–83. doi:10.3152/147154306781779154

Europe's Information Society. (2010). Completed studies on ehealth issues. *ICT for Health*. Retrieved from http://ec.europa.eu/information_society/activities/health/studies/published/index_en.htm

Evans, R. G. (2008). The undisciplined economist. *Health Policy (Amsterdam)*, *3*(4), 21–32.

Faris, W. F., El Hawari, Y., & Ihsan, S. I. (2009). Technology transfer: Challenges and perspective Arab world as a case study. *International Journal of Arab Culture. Management and Sustainable Development*, *1*(2), 195–207.

Farrell, D., Ghai, S., & Shavers, T. (2005). *The coming demographic deficit: How aging population will reduce global wealth*. Retrieved from http://mkqpreview1.qdweb.net/PDFDownload.aspx?ar=1588

Farrukh, I. (2006). *Sustaining gains in poverty reduction and human development in the Middle East and North Africa*. Portland, OR: Book News.

Farzaneh, R. F. (2004). *Progress toward the millennium development goals in the Middle East and North Africa. Policy Brief*. New York, NY: Population Reference Bureau.

Farzaneh, R. F., & Moghadam, V. M. (2003). *Empowering women, developing society: Female education in the Middle East and North Africa. Policy Brief*. New York, NY: Population Reference Bureau.

Faulkner, W., & Lie, M. (2007). Gender technology and development. *Technology and Development*, *11*(2), 157–177.

FEM 32-01. (2008). *Interdependencies of health, education and poverty in south Mediterranean economies: Towards new economic & social policies*. FEMISE Scientific Reports. FEMISE.

Fennell, L. A. (2011). Ostrom's law: Property rights in the commons. *International Journal of the Commons, Anti-Commons. Semi-Commons*, *5*(1), 9–27.

Fisiloglu, H. (2002). Consanguineous marriage and marital adjustment in Turkey. *The Family Journal (Alexandria, Va.)*, *9*(2), 215–222.

Fogelberg, H., & Thorpenberg, S. (2012). Regional innovation policy and public-private partnership: The case of triple helix arenas in western Sweden. *Science and Public Policy. Science & Public Policy*, *39*(3), 347–356. doi:10.1093/scipol/scs023

Fogel, R. W. (2004). *The escape from hunger and premature death, 1700–2100: Europe, America, and the third world*. Cambridge, UK: Cambridge University Press. doi:10.1017/CBO9780511817649

Franzoni, A. L., & Assar, S. (2009). Student learning styles adaptation method based on teaching strategies and electronic media. *Journal of Educational Technology & Society*, *12*(4), 15–29.

Fraser, H. S. F., & McGrath, S. D. (2000). Information technology and telemedicine in sub-Saharan Africa. *British Medical Journal*, *321*(7259), 465–466. doi:10.1136/bmj.321.7259.465

Freeman, C. (1991). Networks of innovators: A synthesis of research issues. *Research Policy*, *20*(5), 499–514. doi:10.1016/0048-7333(91)90072-X

Freudenberg, N., & Ruglis, J. (2007). Reframing school dropout as a public health issue. *Preventing Chronic Disease*, *4*(4). Retrieved from http://www.cdc.gov/pcd/issues/2007/oct/07_0063.htm

Fukuda-Parr, S. (2007). Human rights based approach to development – Is it rhetorical repackaging or a new paradigm? HD Insights. *HDR Networks, 7*.

Gaertner, W. (2008). Individual rights versus economic growth. *Journal of Human Development and Capabilities*, *9*(3), 389–400. doi:10.1080/14649880802236607

GAID Committee of eLeaders for Youth and ICT. (2009). *Youth and ICT for development best practice*. Retrieved from http://unpan1.un.org/intradoc/groups/public/documents/gaid/unpan036084.pdf

Galliano, D., Lethiais, V., & Soulié, N. (2008). Faible densité des espaces et usages des TIC par les enterprises: Besoin d'information ou de coordination? *Revue d'Economie Industrielle*, *121*, 41–64.

Gan, L., & Gong, G. (2007). *Estimating interdependence between health and education in a dynamic model*. Washington, DC: National Bureau of Economic Research.

Gerdtham, U. G., & Thgren, M. L. (2002). New panel results on co-integration of international health expenditure and GDP. *Applied Economics, 34*, 1679–1686. doi:10.1080/00036840110116397

Germenji, E., & Swinnen, J. (2005). Human capital, market imperfections, poverty, and migration: Evidence from Albania. *Research Group on Food Policy, Transition & Development.* Retrieved from http://ideas.repec.org/p/lic/licosd/15705.html

Gillard, H., Howcroft, D., Mitev, N., & Richardson, H. (2008). Missing women: Gender, ICTs and the shaping of the global economy. *Information Technology for Development, 14*(4), 262–279. doi:10.1002/itdj.20098

Giné, X. (2005). DRUMNET case study. *The World Bank.* Retrieved from http://siteresources.worldbank.org/DEC/Resources/DrumnetCaseStudy.pdf

Global e-Government Readiness Report, UNDESA. (2005). *From e-government to e-inclusion.* Retrieved from http://unpan1.un.org/intradoc/groups/public/documents/un/unpan021888.pdf

Global Youth Entrepreneurship Forum. (2006). *Discussion summary and agenda for action.* Retrieved from http://www.youthbusiness.org/PDF/GFYEDiscussionSummary.pdf

Globerman, S. (2001). *La localisation des activités à plus grande valeur ajoutée.* Bellingham, WA: Western Washington University.

Gollock, A. (2008). *Les implications de l'Accord de l'OMC sur les aspects de droits de propriété intellectuelle qui touchent au commerce (ADPIC) sur l'accès aux médicaments en Afrique subsaharienne.* (Thesis). Université Grenoble II. Grenoble, France.

Gomez, R., & Pather, S. (2012). ICT evaluation: Are we asking the right questions? *The Electronic Journal on Information Systems in Developing Countries, 50*(5), 1–14.

GOPA. (2005). The challenges of ICT projects in developing countries: Yemen. *GOPA Worldwide Consultants.* Retrieved from http://gopa.de/index.php?id=45&type=98&L=1&L=1&tx_ttnews[cat]=2&tx_ttnews[pS]=1104534000&tx_ttnews[pL]=31535999&tx_ttnews[arc]=1&tx_ttnews[ttnews]=25&tx_ttnews[backPid]=47&cHash=95b4b8d95d

Graff, G., Cullen, S., Bradford, K., Zilberman, D., & Bennett, E. (2003). The public and private structure of intellectual property ownership in agricultural biotechnology. *Nature Biotechnology, 21*, 989–995. doi:10.1038/nbt0903-989

Green, L., & Trevor-Deutsch, L. (2002). *Women and ICTs for open and distance learning: Some experiences and strategies from the commonwealth.* Retrieved from http://www.col.org/colweb/webdav/site/myjahiasite/shared/docs/Women and ICTs.pdf

Greenberg, A. (2005). *ICTs for poverty alleviation: Basic tool and enabling sector.* Stockholm, Sweden: ICT for Development Secretariat.

Green, E., & Adam, A. (1998). Online leisure: Gender, and ICTs in the home. *Information Communication and Society, 1*(3), 291–312. doi:10.1080/13691189809358971

Grimmelmann, J. (2012). *Three theories of copyright in ratings.* Retrieved from http://ssrn.com/2094523

Grimmelmann, J. (2010). The internet is a semi-commons. *Fordham Law Review, 78*, 2799–2842.

Grimm, M., & Harttgen, K. (2007). Longer life, higher welfare? *Oxford Economic Papers, 60*(2), 193–211. doi:10.1093/oep/gpm025

Gross, D. J., Alecxih, L., Gibson, M. J., Corea, J., Caplan, C., & Brangan, N. (1999). Out-of-pocket health spending by poor and near-poor elderly medicare beneficiaries. *Health Services Research, 34*(1), 241–254.

Grossman, M. (2005). *Education and nonmarket outcomes.* Washington, DC: National Bureau of Economic Research. doi:10.3386/w11582

Grusky, S. (2001). Privatization tidal wave: IMF/world bank water policies and the price paid by the poor. *Multinational Monitor, 22*(9).

Gunasekara, C. (2006). Reframing the role of universities in the development of regional innovation systems. *The Journal of Technology Transfer, 31*(1), 101–113. doi:10.1007/s10961-005-5016-4

Gupta, S., Verhoeven, M., & Tiongson, E. (1999). *Does higher government spending buy better results in education and health care?* Washington, DC: International Monetary Fund, Fiscal Affairs Department.

Gurumurthy, A. (2010). Understanding gender in a digitally transformed world. *IIT for Change Think Piece*. Retrieved from http://www.itforchange.net/

Gurumurthy, A. (2004). *Gender and ICT's. Overview Report*. Sussex, UK: Institute of Development Studies.

Gurumurthy, A. (2006). Promoting gender equality? Some development-related uses of ICTs by women. *Development in Practice*, *16*(6), 611–615. doi:10.1080/09614520600958298

Gwatkin, D. R., Rutstein, S., Kiersten, J., Eldaw, S., Wagstaff, A., & Amouzou, A. (2007). *Socio economic differences in health, nutrition, and population, Morocco (1992-2003/04)*. Washington, DC: The World Bank.

Gwatkin, D. R., Rutstein, S., Kiersten, J., Eldaw, S., Wagstaff, A., & Amouzou, A. (2007). *Socio-economic differences in health, nutrition, and population, Egypt (1995-2000)*. Washington, DC: The World Bank.

Gwatkin, D. R., Rutstein, S., Kiersten, J., Eldaw, S., Wagstaff, A., & Amouzou, A. (2007). *Socio-economic differences in health, nutrition, and population, Jordan (1997)*. Washington, DC: The World Bank.

Gwatkin, D. R., Rutstein, S., Kiersten, J., Eldaw, S., Wagstaff, A., & Amouzou, A. (2007). *Socio-economic differences in health, nutrition, and population, Turkey (1993, 1998)*. Washington, DC: The World Bank.

Gwatkin, D. R., Rutstein, S., Kiersten, J., Eldaw, S., Wagstaff, A., & Amouzou, A. (2007). *Socio-economic differences in health, nutrition, and population, Yemen (1997)*. Washington, DC: The World Bank.

Hafkin, N. (2012). Gender. In Sadowsky, G. (Ed.), *Accelerating Development Using the Web: Empowering Poor and Marginalized Populations*. New York, NY: World Wide Web Foundation.

Halamka, D. J. (2011). Addressing Japan's healthcare challenges with information technology. *Center for Strategic International Studies*. Retrieved from http://csis.org/files/publication/110830_Halamka_Addressing-JapanHealthcare_Web.pdf

Hall, B. H., & Harhoff, D. (2012). *Recent research on the economics of patents*. NBER Working Papers 17773. Washington, DC: National Bureau of Economic Research, Inc.

Hanafi, S. (2011). University systems in the Arab east: Publish globally and perish locally vs publish locally and perish globally. *Current Sociology*, *59*(3), 291–309. doi:10.1177/0011392111400782

Handa, S., & Neitzert, M. (1997). *Gender and life-cycle differentials in the impact of health on employment in Jamaica*. Outreach Division Discussion Paper No.16. Washington, DC: International Food Policy Research Institute. Retrieved from http://www.ifpri.org/divs/cd/dp/papers/commdp16.pdf

Haneul, K., Huang, M., Furong, J., Bodoff, D., Junghoun, M., & Young Chan, C. (2011). Triple helix in the agricultural sector of northeast Asian countries: A comparative study between Korea and China. *Scientometrics*, *90*(1), 101–120.

Haq, T. (2005). *Labor markets and youth employment in the Arab states*. Retrieved from http://www.un.org/esa/socdev/unyin/workshops/256,1,LabourMarkets&Youth EmploymentintheArabStates

Hardin, G. (1968). The tragedy of the commons. *Science*, *162*, 1243–1248. doi:10.1126/science.162.3859.1243

Hedner, T., Almubaraki, H., Busler, M., & Abouzeedan, A. (2011). Business and technology incubators and their role in Europe in comparison to the GCC countries: An analysis of current affairs. In *Innovation and Entrepreneurship*. Gothenburg, Sweden: University of Gothenburg.

Heeks, R. (1999). *Information and communication technologies, poverty and development*. Manchester, UK: IDPM. Retrieved from http://www.man.ac.uk/idpm/idpm_dp.htm#devinf_wp

Heller, M. A. (1998). The tragedy of the anti-commons: Property in the transition from Marx to markets. *Harvard Law Review*, *111*(3), 621–688. doi:10.2307/1342203

Heller, M., & Eisenberg, R. (1998). Can patents deter innovation? The anticommons in biomedical research. *Science, 280*(5364), 698–701. doi:10.1126/science.280.5364.698

Heritage Foundation. (2010). *Heritage foundation annual report, 2010.* New York, NY: Heritage Foundation.

Herrick, C. (2011). HP wins ICT deal for royal adelaide hospital. *CIO Magazine.* Retrieved from http://www.cio.com.au/article/401373/hp_wins_ict_deal_royal_adelaide_hospital/?utm_campaign=&utm_medium=idg.to-twitter&utm_source=twitter.com&fpid=1&utm_content=awesm-publisher&fp=16

Hodgson, V. E. (2008). Learning spaces, context and auto/biography in online learning communities. *International Journal of Web Based Communities, 4*(2), 159–172. doi:10.1504/IJWBC.2008.017670

Hoel, M. (2003). Efficient use of health care resources: The interaction between improved health and reduced health related income loss. *International Journal of Health Care Finance and Economics, 2,* 285–296. doi:10.1023/A:1022308217947

Hofmann, B. (2002). Is there a technological imperative in health care? *International Journal of Technology Assessment in Health Care, 18*(3), 675–689.

Holmes, C. C., & Adams, N. M. (2002). A probabilistic nearest neighbor method for statistical pattern recognition. *Journal of the Royal Statistical Society. Series B. Methodological, 64,* 295–306. doi:10.1111/1467-9868.00338

Hopkins, M. (1991). Human development revisited: A new UNDP report. *World Development, 19*(10), 1469–1473. doi:10.1016/0305-750X(91)90089-Z

Hoxby, C. (2007). Child mortality, income and adult height. *National Bureau of Economic Research.* Retrieved from http://www.nber.org/programs/ed/

Hudson, H. (2001). *The potential of ICTs for development: Opportunities and obstacles.* Background Paper. New York, NY: World Employment Report 2001.

Hulme, D. (2009). *The millennium development goals (MDGs): A short history of the world's biggest promise.* Manchester, UK: The University of Manchester.

Hung-Ju, C. (2006). International migration and economic growth: A source country perspective. *Journal of Population Economics, 19*(4), 725–748. doi:10.1007/s00148-005-0023-1

Hung, V. P., Macaulay, T. G., & Marsh, S. P. (2007). The economics of land fragmentation in the north of Vietnam. *The Australian Journal of Agricultural and Resource Economics, 51*(2), 195–211. doi:10.1111/j.1467-8489.2007.00378.x

Hurd, M., & Kapteyn, A. (2003). Health, wealth, and the role of institutions. *The Journal of Human Resources, 38*(2), 386–415. doi:10.2307/1558749

Hurd, M., & Kapteyn, A. (2005). Health, wealth and the role of institutions. In *Multidisciplinary Economics* (pp. 307–332). Washington, DC: RAND. doi:10.1007/0-387-26259-8_28

Hutton, T. A. (2004). The new economy of the inner city. *Cities (London, England), 21*(2), 89–108. doi:10.1016/j.cities.2004.01.002

Idowu, B., Ogunbodede, E., & Idowu, B. (2003). Information and communication technology in Nigeria: The health sector experience. *Journal of Information Technology Impact, 3*(2), 69–76.

ILO. (2001). *Generating decent work for young people: An issues paper.* New York, NY: ILO.

ILO. (2001). *The ILO's world employment report 2001.* Retrieved from http://isearch.babylon.com/?q=The+2001+ILO+report&babsrc=SP_def&affID=101587

Int@j. (2007). *National ICT strategy of Jordan 2007-2011.* Retrieved from http://www.intaj.net/sites/default/files/National-ICT-Strategy-of-Jordan-2007-2011.pdf

Islam, K. B. (2005). *National ICT policies and plans towards poverty reduction: Emerging trends and issues.* New York, NY: United Nations.

IST-Africa Consortium. (2011). *Overview of ICT initiatives in Egypt.* Retrieved from http://www.ist-africa.org/home/default.asp?page=doc-by-id&docid=5185

ITU. (2002). *ITU world telecommunication development report*. Retrieved from http://www.itu.int/pub/D-IND-WTDR-2002/en

ITU. (2003). *ITU world telecommunication development report*. Retrieved from http://www.itu.int/pub/D-IND-WTDR-2003/en

ITU. (2004). *ITU world telecommunication development report*. Retrieved from http://www.itu.int/pub/D-IND-WTDR-2004/en

ITU. (2005). *ITU world telecommunication development report*. Retrieved from http://www.itu.int/pub/D-IND-WTDR-2005/en

ITU. (2006). *ITU world telecommunication development report*. Retrieved from http://www.itu.int/pub/D-IND-WTDR-2006/en

ITU. (2007). *ITU world telecommunication development report*. Retrieved from http://www.itu.int/pub/D-IND-WTDR-2007/en

ITU. (2008). *ITU world telecommunication development report*. Retrieved from http://www.itu.int/pub/D-IND-WTDR-2008/en

ITU. (2009). *ITU world telecommunication development report*. Retrieved from http://www.itu.int/pub/D-IND-WTDR-2009/en

ITU. (2010). *ITU world telecommunication development report*. Retrieved from http://www.itu.int/pub/D-IND-WTDR-2010/en

ITU. (2010). *Relevance and impact of ICTs to the MDGs*. International Telecommunication Union Study. Retrieved from http://www.itu.int

ITU. (2011). ICT data and statistics. *ITU World Telecommunication Indicators Database*. Retrieved from http://www.itu.int/ITUD/ict/statistics/index.html

ITU. (2011). *ITU world telecommunication development report*. Retrieved from http://www.itu.int/pub/D-IND-WTDR-2011/en

Ivar, S. J., Kossi, E., Titlestad, O., Tohouri, R., & Braa, J. (2009). Comparing strategies to integrate health systems following a data warehouse approach in four countries. In *Proceedings of the 10th International Conference on Social Implications of Computers in Developing Countries*. IEEE.

Jacobsen, J. P. (2011). The role of technological change in increasing gender equity. *ACSPL Working Paper Series, 1*.

Jain, S. (2004). *ICTS and women's empowerment: some case studies from India*. Retrieved from http://www.ifuw.org/seminars/2007/jain.pdf

Jauhari, V. (2004). *Information technology, corporate business firms and sustainable development: Lessons from cases of success from India*. Paper presented at the International Seminar on e-Commerce and Economic Development. New-Delhi, India.

Jensen, M., & Esterhuysen, A. (2001). The community telecentre cookbook for Africa recipes for self-sustainability: How to establish a multi-purpose community telecentre in Africa. *UNESCO*. Retrieved from http://unesdoc.unesco.org/images/0012/001230/123004e.pdf

Jensen, C., & Tragardh, B. (2004). Narrating the triple helix concept in weak regions: Lessons from Sweden. *International Journal of Technology Management, 27*(5), 513–530. doi:10.1504/IJTM.2004.004287

Jenson, R. T. (2007). The digital provide: Information (technology), market performance and welfare in the south indian fisheries sector. *The Quarterly Journal of Economics, 122*(3), 879–924. doi:10.1162/qjec.122.3.879

Jeskanen-Sundström, H. (2003). ICT statistics at the new millennium: Developing official statistics: Measuring the diffusion of ICT and its impact. *International Statistical Review, 71*(1), 5–15. Retrieved from http://www.jstor.org/stable/1403870doi:10.1111/j.1751-5823.2003.tb00181.x

Johnson, O. E. G. (1970). A note on the economics of fragmentation. *The Nigerian Journal of Economic and Social Studies, 12*, 175–184.

Johnson, V. (2012). The gender divide: Attitudinal issues inhibiting access. In *Globalization, Technology Development, and Gender Disparity: Social Impacts of ICTs*. Hershey, PA: IGI Global. doi:10.4018/978-1-4666-0020-1.ch009

K4health. (2011). *Adolescents living with HIV (ALHIV)*. Retrieved from http://www.k4health.org/toolkits/alhiv

Kabanda, G. (2011). Impact of information and communication technologies (ICTs) on the millennium development goals (MDGs). *Journal of African Studies and Development, 8*, 154–170.

Kahn, T. (2004). Mobile phones keep track of HIV treatments. *SciDev.Net*. Retrieved from http://www.scidev.net/News/index.cfm?fuseaction=readNews&itemid=1625&language=1

Kaivo-oja, J., & Jari Stenvall, J. (2011). The cloud university platform: New challenges of the co-operation in the European university system. *European Integration Studies*, 5, 39–44.

Kamel Nabli, M., & Véganzonès-Varoudakis. (2004). *Reform complimentaries and economic growth in the Middle East and North Africa*. Washington, DC: World Bank.

Kamsin, A. (2005). Is e-learning the solution and substitute for conventional learning? *Journal of the Computer. Internet and Management*, *13*(3), 79–89.

Kapczynski, A., Crone, E., & Merson, M. (2003). Global health and university patents. *Science*, *301*, 1659. doi:10.1126/science.301.5640.1629

Kaplan, W. A. (2006). Can the ubiquitous power of mobile phones be used to improve health outcomes in developing countries? *Globalization and Health*, *2*(9), 1–14.

Kaufman, P. (1999). Rural poor have less access to supermarkets, large grocery stores. *Rural Development Perspectives*, *13*(3), 19–26.

Kaukonen, E., & Nieminen, M. (1999). Modeling the triple helix from a small country perspective: The case of Finland. *The Journal of Technology Transfer*, *24*(2/3), 173–183. doi:10.1023/A:1007851321496

Kelly, T. (2011). ICT in health: The role of ICTs in the health sector in developing countries. *InfoDev*. Retrieved from http://www.infodev.org/en/Project.38.html

Kennedy, D., & Michelman, F. (1980). Are property and contract efficient? *Hofstra Law Review*, *8*(711), 712–737.

Kenny, C. (2001). Information and communication technologies and poverty. *TechKnowLogia*. Retrieved from http://www.techknowlogia.org/

Kenny, C., Navas-Sabater, J., & Qiang, J. (2000). ICTs and poverty. *The World Bank*. Retrieved from http://www.worldbank.org/poverty/strategies/srcbook/ict0829.pdf

Khatib, I. A., Tsipouri, L., Bassiakos, Y., & Haj-Daoud, A. (2012, February). Innovation in Palestinian industries: A necessity for surviving the abnormal. *Journal of the Knowledge Economy*, 63-78.

Kikeri, S., & Nellis, J. (2002). *Privatization in competitive sectors: The record to date*. Research Working Paper. Unpublished.

Kim, S. (2000). Urban development in the United States, 1690-1990. *Southern Economic Journal*, *66*(4), 855–880. doi:10.2307/1061533

Kivunike, F., Ekenberg, L., & Danielson, M. (2009). Investigating perception of the role of ICT toward the quality of life of people in rural communities in Uganda. In *Proceedings of the 10th International Conference on Social Implications of Computers in Developing Countries*. IEEE.

Klerkx, P. (2012). Beyond fragmentation and disconnect: Networks for knowledge exchange in the English land management advisory system. *Land Use Policy*, *3*, 13–24.

Kling, R. (1996). *Computerization and controversy: Value conflicts and social choices*. San Diego, CA: Academic Press.

Knapp, D. (2007). *The influence of health on labor productivity: An analysis of European conscription data*. (Thesis). The Ohio State University. Columbus, OH.

Kohl, H., & Al Hashemi, H. (2011). Science parks as main driver for the development of national innovations systems in resources-driven economies! The importance of intellectual capital management for sustainable manufacturing: Advances in sustainable manufacturing. In *Proceedings of the 8th Global Conference on Sustainable Manufacturing, GCSM 2010*. Berlin, Germany: Springer.

Koster, S. (2008). Entrepreneurship and economic development in a developing country. *Journal of Entrepreneurship*, *17*(2), 137–173. doi:10.1177/097135570801700202

Kpodar, K. (2007). *Why has unemployment in Algeria been higher than in MENA and transition countries?* IMF Working Paper, WP/07/210. Washington, DC: IMF.

Kramarae, C. (2004). Do we really want more control of technology? In Foss, K., Foss, S., & Griffin, C. L. (Eds.), *Readings in Feminist Rhetorical Theory*. Thousand Oaks, CA: Sage.

Krueger, A. O., Schiff, M., & Valdès, A. (1988). Agricultural incentives in developing countries: Measuring the effects of sectoral and economy wide policies. *The World Bank Economic Review*, *2*(3), 255–271. doi:10.1093/wber/2.3.255

Kumar, A., & Singh, K. M. (2012). *ICT for agricultural development under changing climate*. New Delhi, India: Narendra Publishing House.

Kundishora, S. (2010). *An overview on the impact of ICTs on socio-economic development*. New York, NY: Millennium Development Goals and Society.

Kuziemsky, C., Weber-Jahnke, J., & Williams, J. (2012). Engineering the healthcare collaboration space. In *Proceedings of IEEE SEHC*, (pp. 51-57). Zurich, Switzerland: IEEE Press.

Kwankam, S. Y. (2004). What e-health can offer. *Bulletin of the World Health Organization, 82*(10). Retrieved from http://www.scielosp.org/scielo.php?pid=S00429686200 4001000021&script=sci_arttext

Kym, A., & Valenzuela, E. (2006). *Do global trade still harm developing country farmers?* World Bank Policy Research Working Paper 3901. Washington, DC: World Bank.

Kym, A., Martin, W., & Valenzuela, E. (2006). The relative importance of global agricultural subsidies and market access. *World Trade Review, 5*, 357–376. doi:10.1017/S1474745606002916

La Cava, G., Rossotto, C., & Paradi-Guilford, C. (2011). Information and communication technologies (ICT) for youth in Mena: Policies to promote employment opportunities. *Arab World Brief, 1*, 1-5. Retrieved from http://www.aicto.org/fileadmin/user_upload/Youth.pdf

Lahusen, C. (2013). European integration, social cohesion, and political contentiousness. In *Economic and Political Change in Asia and Europe, 2013* (pp. 31–52). Berlin, Germany: Springer. doi:10.1007/978-94-007-4653-4_3

Lambrinos, J. (1980). Health: A source of bias in labor supply models. *The Review of Economics and Statistics, 63*(2), 206–216. doi:10.2307/1924091

Laufman, H. (2002). Are engineer's unsung heroes of medical progress? *The Historic Physics. Engineering in Medicine, 36*(5), 325–334.

Lawler, C. (2011). The capitalization of knowledge: A triple helix of university-industry government. *Studies in Higher Education*. Retrieved from http://www.tandfonline.com/loi/cshe20

Lawson, C., & Meyenn, N. (2000). *Bringing cellular phone service to rural areas: Grameen telecom and village payphones in Bangladesh*. Retrieved from http://rru.worldbank.org/Documents/PublicPolicyJournal/205lawson.pdf

Lee, J., & Kim, H. (2007). A longitudinal analysis of the impact of health shocks on the wealth of elders. *Journal of Population Economics, 21*(1), 217–230. doi:10.1007/s00148-007-0156-5

Lester, B. T., Ma, L., Lee, O., & Lambert, J. (2006). Social activism in elementary school education: A science, technology, and society approach to teaching global warming. *International Journal of Science Education, 28*, 315–339. doi:10.1080/09500690500240100

Lewis, D. J., & Plantinga, A. J. (2007). Policies for habitat fragmentation: Combining econometrics with GIS-based. *Land Economics, 83*, 109–127.

Leydesdorff, L. (2012). The triple helix, quadruple helix and …an n-tuple of helices: Explanatory models for analyzing the knowledge-based economy? *Journal of the Knowledge Economy, 3*(1), 25–35. doi:10.1007/s13132-011-0049-4

Liao, W.-C. (2012). *Inshoring: The geographic fragmentation of production and inequality*. Singapore, Singapore: National University of Singapore.

Ligon, E., & Schechter, L. (2002). *Measuring vulnerability*. Berkeley, CA: University of California.

Lim, C. P. (2007). Effective integration of ICT in Singapore schools: Pedagogical and policy implications. *Educational Technology Research and Development, 55*(1), 83–116. Retrieved from http://www.jstor.org/stable/30221231doi:10.1007/s11423-006-9025-2

Lindhal, T. (2012). Coordination problems and resource collapse in the commons — Exploring the role of knowledge heterogeneity. *Ecological Economics Ecological, 79*, 52–59. doi:10.1016/j.ecolecon.2012.04.016

Ling, R., & Horst, A. (2011). Mobile communication in the global south. *New Media & Society, 13*(3), 363–374. doi:10.1177/1461444810393899

Lipsey, R. G. (2002). Some implications of endogenous technological change for technology policies in developing countries. *Economics of Innovation and New Technology, 11*, 4–5. doi:10.1080/10438590200000003

Littlejohns, P., Wyatt, J. C., & Garvican, L. (2003). Evaluating computerized health information systems: Hard lessons still to be learnt. *British Medical Journal*, *326*(7394), 860–863. doi:10.1136/bmj.326.7394.860

Lobo, A. (2000). Taking IT to the villages. *ZDNet India, 6*.

London Health Commission. (2004). *Sustainable local economies for health project*. Retrieved from http://www.londonshealth.gov.uk/RTF/SLEHP_guidance.doc

Lopez-Vega, H., & Ramis-Pujol, J. (2006). Connecting the Mediterranean system of innovation: A functional perspective. *EuroMed Journal of Business*, *6*(1), 46–62. doi:10.1108/14502191111130307

Loury, G. C. (1981). Intergenerational transfers and the distribution of earnings. *Econometrica*, *49*(4), 843–867. doi:10.2307/1912506

Lucas, A. O. (2005). International collaboration in health research. *Bulletin of the World Health Organization*, *83*(7), 481–560.

Lukemeyer, A., Meyers, M. K., & Smeeding, T. (2002). Expensive children in poor families: Out-of-pocket expenditures for the care of disabled and chronically ill children in welfare families. *Journal of Marriage and the Family*, *62*, 399–415. doi:10.1111/j.1741-3737.2000.00399.x

Lundvall, B.-A. (2002). *Innovation, growth and social cohesion: The Danish model*. London, UK: Edward Elgar Publishers.

Lyman, P., & Varian, H. R. (2003). *How much information?* Berkeley, CA: University of California at Berkeley. Retrieved from http://www.sims.berkeley.edu/research/projects/how-much-info-2003/

Lynch, W. J., Smith, G. D., Kaplan, G. A., & House, J. S. (2002). Income inequality and mortality: Importance to health of individual income, psychosocial environment, or material conditions. *British Medical Journal*, *320*(7243), 1200–1204. doi:10.1136/bmj.320.7243.1200

Maccini, S., & Yang, D. (2008). *Under the weather: Health, schooling, and economic consequences of famines on survivors: Evidence from China's great famine*. IZA Discussion Paper. Washington, DC: IZA.

MacGregor, S. P., Marques-Gou, P., & Simon-Villar, A. (2010). Gauging readiness for the quadruple helix: A study of 16 European organizations. *Journal of the Knowledge Economy*, *33*(1), 77–83.

Mack, J. (1985). *How poor is too poor? Defining poverty*. Retrieved from http://www.poverty.ac.uk/sites/default/files/how_poor_is_too_poor_0.pdf

MacKeogh, K. (2003). *Student perceptions of the use of ICTs in European education: Report of a survey*. Dublin, Ireland: Oscail - Dublin City University. Retrieved from http://www.oscail.ie/academic/picture.php

Magro, M. (2012). A review of social media use in e-government. *American Scientist*, *2*(2), 148–161.

Malhotra, A., Kanesathasan, A., & Patel, P. (2012). Connectivity how mobile phones, computers and the internet can catalyze women's entrepreneurship India: A case study. *ICRW Publications*. Retrieved from http://www.icrw.org/publications/connectivity-how-mobile-phones-computers-and-internet-can-catalyze-womens-entrepreneurs

Manochehri, N., Al-Esmail, R., & Ashrafi, R. (2012). Examining the Impact of information and communication technologies (ICT) on enterprise practices: A preliminary perspective from Qatar. *The Electronic Journal on Information Systems in Developing Countries*, *51*(3), 1–16.

Martin, M. C. (2008). *Individual and collective resources and health in Morocco*. UNU-WIDER Research Paper. Unpublished.

Martínez, A., Rodrigues, R. J., & Infante, A. (2001). *Bases metodológicas para evaluar la viabilidad y el impacto de proyectos de telemedicina*. Madrid, Spain: Universidad Politécnica de Madrid/Pan American Health Organization.

Mathison, S. (2005). *ICT for poverty reduction in Asia: Digital dividends for the poor*. New York, NY: Global Knowledge Partnership.

Mattingly, D. (2005). Indian women working in call centers: Sites of resistance. In *Globalization, Technology Development, and Gender Disparity: Social Impacts of ICTs*. Hershey, PA: IGI Global.

Mayer, R. (2000). *Challenges to implementing ICT networks and services.* Paper presented at the Rural Areas' Village Power Conference. Washington, DC. Retrieved from http://www.rsvp.nrel.gov/vpconference/vp2000/telecom_workshop/telecom_rebecca_mayer.pdf

Mayer-Foulkes, D. (2004). *The intergenerational impact of health on economic growth.* Paper presented at the Global Forum for Health Research, Forum 8. Mexico City, Mexico.

Mayer-Foulkes, D., Aghion, P., & Howitt, P. (2004). *The effect of financial development on convergence: Theory and evidence.* NBER Working Papers 10358. Washington, DC: National Bureau of Economic Research, Inc.

Mazen, A., Sherah, K., & Johnston, R. B. (2009). Investigating IOS adoption maturity using a dyadic approach. *International Journal of e-Collaboration, 5*(2), 43–60. doi:10.4018/jec.2009040103

McGlennon, D. (2006). *Building research capacity in the gulf cooperation council countries: Strategy, funding and engagement.* Paper presented at Le Colloque Mondial du Forum de l'UNESCO sur l'Enseignement Supérieur, la Recherche et la Connaissance. Paris, France.

McKenzie, D., & Rapoport, H. (2006). *Can migration reduce educational attainment?* World Bank Policy Research Working Paper 3952. Washington, DC: World Bank.

McKeown, T. (1979). *Medicine; health; diseases; public health; philosophy, medical; philosophy; causes and theories of causation.* Princeton, NJ: Princeton University Press.

McLaughlin, D. K., & Jensen, L. (2000). Work history and U.S. elders' transitions into poverty. *The Gerontologist, 40*(4), 5–16. doi:10.1093/geront/40.4.469

MedPac. (2004). Information technology in health care. *Report to The Congress: New Approches in Medicare.* Retrieved from http://www.medpac.gov/publications%5Ccongressional_reports%5CJune04_ch7.pdf

Meera, S. N., Jhamtani, A., & Rao, D. U. M. (2004). Information and communication technology in agricultural development: A comparative analysis of three projects from India. *ODI.* Retrieved from http://www.odi.org.uk/agren/papers/agrenpaper_135.pdf

Mehruz, K. (2012). Exploring social capital in sustaining IT adoption and use in micro-enterprises. In *Proceedings of the Southern Association for Information Systems Conference.* Atlanta, GA: Southern Association for Information Systems.

Merle, J. (2006). Utilization of social science knowledge in science policy: Systems of innovation, triple helix and VINNOVA. *Social Sciences Information. Information Sur les Sciences Sociales, 45*(3), 431–462. doi:10.1177/0539018406066535

Metts, R. L. (2004). *Background paper prepared for the disability and development.* Washington, DC: World Bank.

Meyer, M., & Leydes, L. (2006). Triple helix indicators of knowledge-based innovation systems. *Research Policy, 35*(10), 1441–1449. doi:10.1016/j.respol.2006.09.016

Miguel, E., & Kremer, M. (2004). Worms: Identifying impacts on education and health in the presence of treatment externalities. *Econometrica, 72,* 159–217. doi:10.1111/j.1468-0262.2004.00481.x

Mikre, F. (2011). The roles of information communication technologies in education. *Ethiopian Journal of Education & Schooling, 6*(2).

Miller, B. P., Duque, R., & Shrum, W. (2012). Gender, ICTs, and productivity in low-income countries panel study. *Science, Technology & Human Values, 37*(1), 30–63. doi:10.1177/0162243910392800

Ministry of Health. (2012). Oman. *Health Care Information System (Al Shifa).* Retrieved from http://unpan1.un.org/intradoc/groups/public/documents/un-dpadm/unpan039615.pdf

Mitha, F. (2007). Economic reform in the Middle East and North Africa (MENA). In The *Selected Works of Farooq A Mitha.* Gainesville, FL: University of Florida. Retrieved from http://works.bepress.com/farooq_mitha/1

Mitter, S. (2004). *Globalization and ICT: Employment opportunities for women.* New York, NY: United Nations Commission on Science and Technology for Development.

Mitter, S., & Millar, J. (2001). *The impact of ICT on the spatial division of labor in the service sector.* Geneva, Switzerland: ILO.

Modise, O. M., Lekoko, R. N., & Thobega, J. M. (2012). Socio-economic empowerment through technologies: The case of tapestry at Lentswe la Oodi Weavers in Botswana. In Lekoko, R. N., & Semali, L. M. (Eds.), *Cases on Developing Countries and ICT Integration: Rural Community Development*. Hershey, PA: IGI Global.

Monfort, P., & Nicolini, R. (2002). Regional convergence and international integration. *Journal of Urban Economics*, *48*, 286–306. doi:10.1006/juec.1999.2167

Moorti & Ros. (2003). Editors' introduction: Gender and the information society. *Feminist Media Studies*, *3*(3), 345–388. doi:10.1080/1468077032000166568

Morduch, J. (1999). Between the state and the market: Can informal insurance patch the safety net? *The World Bank Research Observer*, *14*(2), 187–207. doi:10.1093/wbro/14.2.187

Morrison, J. (2006). *International business environment: Global and local marketplaces in a changing world*. New York, NY: Palgrave MacMillan.

Morrisson, C. (2002). *Health, education and poverty reduction. OECD Development Centre Policy Brief No. 19*. Paris, France: OECD Development Centre.

Mudambi, R. (2008). *Location, control and innovation in knowledge-intensive industries. Discussion Paper 08-0430*. Philadelphia, PA: Temple University Fox School of Business.

Mude, A. G., Barrett, C. B., McPeak, J. G., & Doss, C. (2003). Educational investments in a spatially varied economy. *Economica*, *74*(294), 351–369. doi:10.1111/j.1468-0335.2006.00538.x

Munyua, H. (2007). *ICTs and small-scale agriculture in Africa: A scoping study*. Ottawa, Canada: IDRC.

Muysken, J., Yetkiner, I. H., & Ziesemer, T. (1999). *Health, labour productivity and growth. CCSO Working Papers 200015*. Groningen, The Netherlands: University of Groningen.

Nagla, R., & Sherif, K. (2012). ICT strategy4development: Public-private partnerships—The case of Egypt. *International Journal of Strategic Information Technology and Applications*. Retrieved from http://www.igi-global.com/article/ict-strategy4development-public privatepartnerships/67351

Nahleen, A. (2006). *Youth and ICT as agents for change*. New York, NY: The Global Alliance for ICT and Development, UNDESA.

Nash, M. (2001). Grains of hope. *Time*. Retrieved from www.time.com/time/asia/biz/magazine/0,9754,98034,00.html

Naude, W., Gries, T., Wood, E., & Meintjies, A. (2008). Regional determinants of entrepreneurial start-ups in a developing country. *Entrepreneurship & Regional Development*, *20*(2), 111–124. doi:10.1080/08985620701631498

Neal, K., Doye, D., & Brorsen, B. W. (2012). *Fragmentation of agricultural land parcels*. Paper presented at the Southern Agricultural Economics Association Annual Meeting. Birmingham, AL.

Nells, J. (2006). *Privatization: A summary assessment. Working Paper 87*. New York, NY: Centre for Global Development.

Ngwenyama, O., Andoh-Baidoo, K., Bollou, F., & Morawczynki, O. (2006). Is there a relationship between ICT, health, education and development? An empirical analysis of five western African countries from 1997-2003. *The Electronic Journal on Information Systems in Developing Countries*, *23*(5), 1–11.

Nissanke, M., & Thorbecke, E. (2005). Channels and policy debate in the globalization-inequality-poverty nexus. *World Development*, *34*(8), 1338–1360. doi:10.1016/j.worlddev.2005.10.008

Nolan, B., & Whelan, T. C. (2011). *Resources, deprivation, and poverty*. Oxford, UK: Oxford University Press. doi:10.1093/acprof:oso/9780199588435.001.0001

Norman, L., Ranciere, R., Serven, L., & Ventura, J. (2007). Macroeconomic volatility and welfare in developing countries: An introduction. *The World Bank Economic Review*, *21*(3), 343–387. doi:10.1093/wber/lhm017

Noujai, A., & Lfarakh, A. (1999). *Enquête nationale sur la santé de la mère et de l'enfant*. Morocco: Service des Etudes et de l'Information Sanitaire.

Nour, S. S. (2008). *The use and economic impacts of ICT at the macro-micro levels in the Arab gulf countries*. Paper presented at the Fifth GLOBELICS Academy, TaSTI, University of Tampere. Tampere, Finland.

Nwakanma, N. (2012). Culture. In Sadowsky, G. (Ed.), *Accelerating Development Using the Web: Empowering Poor and Marginalized Populations*. New York, NY: World Wide Web Foundation.

ODPM. (2004). *The English indices of deprivation 2004: Summary* (Revised ed.). Retrieved from http://www.communities.gov.uk/documents/communities/pdf/131209.pdf

OECD. (2003). *ICT and economic growth – Evidence from OECD countries, industries and firms*. Paris, France: OECD Publishing.

OECD. (2008). *Politiques sociales, prestations et questions sociales*. Retrieved from http://www.oecd.org/topic/0,3373,fr_2649_33933_1_1_1_1_37419,00.html

Office of Technology Assessment. (1982). *Medical technology under proposals to increase competition in health care*. Washington, DC: US Government Printing Office.

Olga, P., & Mendez, G. (2011). Gender digital divide: The role of mobile phones among Latina farm workers in southeast Ohio. *Gender, Technology and Development*, *15*(1), 53–74. doi:10.1177/097185241101500103

Onyije, L., & Briggs, F. (2012). Technology solution for the marginalized. *European Scientific Journal*, *8*(13), 71–80.

Opoku, & Mensah, A. (1998). ICT initiatives and the role of policies in southern Africa. In *Information and Communication Technology and Development*. Rawoo Publication.

Organization for Economic Co-Operation and Development. (2002). *ICT in education and government*. Retrieved from http://www.oecd.org/dataoecd/34/36/2771146.pdf

Osmani, S., & Sen, A. (2003). The hidden penalties of gender inequality: Fetal origins of ill-health. *Economics and Human Biology*, *1*, 105–121. doi:10.1016/S1570-677X(02)00006-0

Ostrom, E. (1990). *Governing the commons: The evolution of institutions for collective actions*. Cambridge, UK: Cambridge University Press. doi:10.1017/CBO9780511807763

Ostrom, E., & Schlager, E. (1992). Property rights regimes and natural resources. *Land Economics*, *68*, 249–262. doi:10.2307/3146375

Oukil, M. S. (2011). A development perspective of technology-based entrepreneurship in the Middle East and North Africa. *Annuals of Innovation & Entrepreneurship*, *2*(6000).

Page, J. (2003). *Structural reforms in the Middle East and North Africa*. Retrieved from http://www.yemenembassy.org/economic/Reports/WEF/Page_62_78_Structural_Reforms.pdf

Pailing, M. (2002). E-learning: Is it really the best thing since sliced bread? *Industrial and Commercial Training*, *34*(4), 151–155. doi:10.1108/00197850210429138

Pampalon, R., & Guy, R. (2000). Deprivation index for health and welfare planning in Quebec. *Chronic Diseases in Canada*, *21*(3), 104–114.

Parisi, F., Depoorter, B., & Schulz, N. (2005). Duality in property: Commons and anticommons. *International Review of Law and Economics*, *25*, 4–10. doi:10.1016/j.irle.2005.12.003

Parliamentary Office of Science and Technology. (2006). ICT in developing countries. *Postpone*, *261*.

Pavrala, V. (2000). Voices from the margins, voices for change. *A Journal on Communication for Development*, *4*(2). Retrieved from http://bsfs.georgetown.edu/files/Thesis_Joelle_Thomas.pdf

Perry, E. C., & Jaggernath, J. (2012). Violence against women, vulnerabilities and disempowerment: Multiple and interrelated impacts on achieving the millennium development goals in South Africa. *Agenda: Empowering Women for Gender Equity*, *26*(1), 20–32.

Pettey, C., & Tudor, B. (2011). *Gartner says worldwide IT spending to grow 5.1 percent in 2011*. Retrieved from http://www.gartner.com/it/page.jsp?id=1513614

Piatkowski, M. (2003). *The contribution of ICT investment to economic growth and labor productivity in Poland 1995-2000*. Retrieved from http://ideas.repec.org/p/wpa/wuwpdc/0308002.html

Picard, P., & Toulemonde, E. (2004). Endogenous qualifications and firms' agglomeration. *Journal of Urban Economics*, *55*(3), 458–477. doi:10.1016/S0094-1190(03)00075-5

Picot, A., & Lorenz, J. (2010). *ICT for the next five billion people information and communication for sustainable development.* Berlin, Germany: Springer. doi:10.1007/978-3-642-12225-5

Pillai, P. M., & Shanta, N. (2011). ICT and employment promotion among poor women: How can we make it happen? Some reflections on Kerala's experience. *Indian Journal of Gender Studies, 18*(1), 51–76. doi:10.1177/097152151001800103

Pissarides, C. A. Véganzonès, & Varoudakis, M. A. (2005). *Labor markets and economic growth in the MENA region.* London, UK: London School of Economics and CERDI, CNRS, Université d'Auvergne.

Poortman, C. (2006). Reforms in the MENA region. *World Bank.* Retrieved from http://go.worldbank.org/CEX1H34N30

Porter, M. (1990). The competitive advantage of nations. *Journal of Development Economics, 37*(8), 1189–1213.

Preston, S. H. (1996). *American longevity, past, present and future.* Syracuse, NY: Syracuse University.

Primo, N. (2003). Gender issues in the information society. In *UNESCO Publications for the World Summit on the Information Society.* New York, NY: UNESCO.

Psacharopoulos, G., & Patinos, H. P. (2002). *Returns to investment in education.* Policy Research Working Paper 2881. Retrieved from http://siteresources.worldbank.org/EDU-CATION/Resources/278200-099079877269/547664-1099079934475/547667-1135281504040/Returns_Investment_Edu.pdf

Qiang, C. Z., Yamamichi, M., Hausman, V., & Altman, D. (2011). *Mobile applications for the health sector.* Washington, DC: World Bank.

Qureshi, S. (2011). Globalization in development: Do information and communication technologies really matter? *Information Technology for Development, 17*(4), 249–252. doi:10.1080/02681102.2011.610142

Rajesh, M. (2003). A study of the problems associated with ICT adaptability in developing countries in the context of distance education. *Turkish Online Journal of Distance Education, 5*(1). Retrieved from http://tojde.anadolu.edu.tr/tojde10/articles/Rajesh.htm

Rakow, L. (1986). Rethinking gender research in communication. *The Journal of Communication, 36*, 11–36. doi:10.1111/j.1460-2466.1986.tb01447.x

Rallet, A., & Torre, A. (1999). *Which need for geographical proximity in innovation networks at the era of global economy?.* Unpublished.

Ramilo, G. (2002). *Issues, policies and outcomes: Are ICT policies addressing gender equality?* Retrieved from http://www.unescap.org/wid/04widresources/11widactivities/01ictegm/backgroundpaper.pdf

Ramos, A. (2006). *Technology-supported distance education (Philippines).* Retrieved from http://www.idrc.ca/panasia/ev-55758-201-1-DO_TOPIC.html

Ranis, G. (2007). *Migration, trade, capital and development: Substitutes, complements and policies.* Washington, DC: Economic Growth Center.

Ranjay, G., Franz, W., & Pavel, Z. (2012). The two facets of collaboration: Cooperation and coordination in strategic alliances. *The Academy of Management Annals, 6*, 531–583. doi:10.1080/19416520.2012.691646

Ransom, E. I., & Elder, L. K. (2003). *Nutrition of women and adolescent girls: Why it matters.* Washington, DC: Population Reference Bureau.

Rao, K., Xian-fe, M., & Piccaluga, A. (2012). The impact of government R&D investments on patent technology transfer activities of Chinese universities: From the perspective of triple helix theory. *Journal of Knowledge-based Innovation in China, 4*(1), 4–17. doi:10.1108/17561411211208730

Raquel, M. P., & Osório, A. (2012). Lifelong learning, intergenerational relationships and ICT: Perceptions of children and older adult: Elderly, education, intergenerational relationships and social development. In *Proceedings of 2nd Conference of ELOA and Digital Inclusion in Society.* ELOA.

Ratzan, S. C. (2011). Health communication: Beyond recognition to impact. *Journal of Health Communication, International Perspectives, 16*(2), 109-111. Retrieved from http://dx.doi.org/10.1080/10810730.2011.5523

Ravallion, M. (2002). *Targeted transfers in poor countries: Revisiting the trade-offs and policy options*. Washington, DC: The World Bank. doi:10.2139/ssrn.1754444

Ravallion, M. (2006). *Inequality is bad for the poor. Background Paper to 2006 World Development Report, Equity and Development*. New York, NY: United Nations.

Ravallion, M. (2006). Looking beyond averages in the trade and poverty debate. *World Development, 34*(8), 1374–1392. doi:10.1016/j.worlddev.2005.10.015

RDH50. (2012). *RDH general report: 50 ans de développement humain & perspectives 2025*. Retrieved from http://www.rdh50.ma/Fr/pdf/general/RG-FR.pdf

Rebecca, Y., & Moore, K. (2003). Including disabled people in poverty reduction work: Nothing about us, without us. *World Development, 31*(3), 571–590. doi:10.1016/S0305-750X(02)00218-8

Reiffers, J. L. (2003). *Rapport du FEMISE 2003 sur le partenariat Euro-Méditerranéen*. Retrieved from http://www.defi-univ.org/REIFFERS-Jean-Louis,2311

Report, W. Y. (2007). *Young people's transition to adulthood: Progress and challenges*. Retrieved from http://www.un.org/esa/socdev/unyin/documents/wyr07_complete.pdf

Reyes, M., & Asinas, A. (2011). Locating young women in a plethora of issues: Reflections from the tenth young women leader's conference 2010. *Gender and Development, 9*(3), 423–439. doi:10.1080/13552074.2011.625674

Richards, A. (2001). The political economy of economic reform in the Middle East: The challenge to governance. *University of California*. Retrieved from http://sccie.ucsc.edu/documents/working_papers/2001/challenge_econreform.pdf

Richardson, P., & Kraemmergaard, P. (2006). Identifying the impacts of enterprise system implementation and use: Examples from Denmark. *International Journal of Accounting Information Systems, 7*(1), 36–49. doi:10.1016/j.accinf.2005.12.001

Rocha, H., & Neer, N. (2012). *Local youth employment and inclusion in Argentina: A public-private initiative for the development of talents, social cohesion and inclusion*. Retrieved from http://ssrn.com/2097880

Rodrigues, C., & Melo, A. (2012). The triple helix model as an instrument of local response to the economic crisis. *European Planning Studies*. doi:10.1080/09654313.2012.709063

Rodriguez, E. (2002). Marginal employment and health in Britain and Germany: Does unstable employment predict health? *Social Science & Medicine, 55*, 963–979. doi:10.1016/S0277-9536(01)00234-9

Ross, C., & Mirowsky, J. (1995). Does employment affect health? *Journal of Health and Social Behavior, 36*, 230–243. doi:10.2307/2137340

Roudi-Fahimi, F. (2005). *Achieving the MDGs in the Middle East: Why improved reproductive health is key*. Washington, DC: Population Reference Bureau.

Roudi-Fahimi, F. (2007). *Gender and equity in access to health care services in the Middle East and North Africa*. Washington, DC: Population Reference Bureau.

Roudi-Fahimi, F., & Ashford, L. (2005). *Investing in reproductive health to achieve development goals, The Middle East and North Africa*. Washington, DC: Population Reference Bureau.

Saad, M., & Zawdie, G. (2005). From technology transfer to the emergence of a triple helix culture: The experience of Algeria in innovation and technological capability development. *Technology Analysis and Strategic Management, 17*(1), 89–103. doi:10.1080/09537320500044750

Sadowsky, G. (2012). Introduction. In Sadowsky, G. (Ed.), *Accelerating Development using the Web: Empowering Poor and Marginalized Populations*. New York, NY: World Wide Web Foundation.

Sage, A. P. (1999). Sustainable development: Issues in information, knowledge, and systems management. *Information Knowledge Systems Management, 1*(3/4), 185–224.

Sage, A. P., & Rouse, W. (1999). Information systems frontiers in knowledge management. *Business and Economics. Information Systems Frontiers, 1*(3), 205–219. doi:10.1023/A:1010046210832

Samiullah, Y., & Rao, S. (2000). *Role of ICTs in urban and rural poverty reduction*. Paper presented at the MoEF-TERI-UNEP Regional Workshop for Asia and Pacific on ICT and Environment. Delhi, India. Retrieved from http://www.teri.res.in/icteap/present/session4/sami.doc

Sandra, E. B., Devereux, P. J., & Salvanes, K. J. (2005). *From the cradle to the labor market? The effect of birth weight on adult outcomes*. Working Paper 11796. Washington, DC: NBER. Retrieved from http://www.nber.org/papers/w11796.pdf?new_window=1

Sarbib, J. L. (2002). *Meeting the public health challenges in the 21st century in the MENA/EM region*. Washington, DC: World Bank.

Sarkar, S. (2012). The role of information and communication technology (ICT) in higher education for the 21st century. *The Science Probe*, *1*(1), 30–40.

Sawicki, D. S., & Moody, M. (2000). Developing transportation alternatives for welfare recipients moving to work. *Journal of the American Planning Association. American Planning Association*, *66*(3), 306–318. doi:10.1080/01944360008976109

Scarafiotti, C. (2003). A three-prong strategic approach to successful distance learning delivery. *Journal of Asynchronous Learning Networks*, *7*(2), 50–55.

Schaeffer, P. (2005). Human capital, migration strategy, and the brain drain. *The Journal of International Trade & Economic Development*, *1*(3), 319–335. doi:10.1080/09638190500203344

Schieber, G., Maeda, A., & Klingen, N. (2007). Health reforms in the MENA region. *The World Bank Research Observer*, *13*(1), 123–131.

Schlager, E., & Ostrom, E. (2010). Property-rights regimes and natural resources: A conceptual analysis. *Land Economics*, *68*, 249–262. doi:10.2307/3146375

Schultz, T. P. (2005). *Productive benefits of health: Evidence from low-income countries*. New Haven, CT: Yale University.

Schuring, M., Burdorf, L., Kunst, A., & Mackenbach, J. (2006). *The effects of ill health on entering and maintaining paid employment: Evidence in European countries*. Rotterdam, The Netherlands: Department of Public Health, Erasmus MC. Retrieved from http://jech.bmj.com/cgi/content/full/61/7/597

Sen, A. (1998). Mortality as an indicator of economic success and failure. *Economic Journal. Revue Economique et Sociale*, *108*(446), 1–25.

Shade, L. R. (2002). *Gender and community in the social construction of the internet*. New York, NY: Peter Lang.

Shapiro. (2001). Navigating the patent ticket: Cross licenses, patent proofs and standard setting. In *Innovation Policy and the Economy*, (vol. 1, pp. 119-150). Cambridge, MA: MIT Press.

Sharma, V. (2012). The influence of ICTs in improving and empowering the quality of education system in developing countries like India. *Golden Research Thoughts*, *2*(2). Retrieved from http://www.aygrt.net

Sherry, J. M., & Ratzan, S. C. (2012). Measurement and evaluation outcomes for mhealth communication: Don't we have an app for that? *Journal of Health Communication*, *17*(1), 1–3. doi:10.1080/10810730.2012.670563

Shin, J. C., Jeung, L., & Yangson, K. (2011). Knowledge-based innovation and collaboration: A triple-helix approach in Saudi Arabia. *Scientometrics*, *90*(1), 311–326. doi:10.1007/s11192-011-0518-3

Shinn, T. (2002). The triple helix and new production of knowledge: Prepackaged thinking on science and technology. *Social Studies of Science*, *32*(4), 599–614.

Shirazi, F. (2008). The contribution of ICT to freedom and democracy: An empirical analysis of archival data on the Middle East. *The Electronic Journal on Information Systems in Developing Countries*, *35*(6), 1–24.

Simon, A., & Marquès, P. (2012). Public policy support to triple helix R&D collaborations: A European model for fourth pillar organizations. *Innovation, Technology, and Knowledge Management*, 79-93.

Skoufias, E. (2002). *Consumption insurance and vulnerability to poverty: A synthesis of the evidence from Bangladesh, Ethiopia, Mali, Mexico, and Russia*. New York, NY: International Food Policy Research Institute. doi:10.1080/09578810500066498

Smith, E. R. (1999). *Social identity and social cognition*. Oxford, UK: Blackwell Publishers.

Smith, H. E. (2000). Semi-common property rights and scattering in the open fields. *The Journal of Legal Studies*, *29*, 131–169. doi:10.1086/468066

Smith, H. E. (2005). Governing the tele-semi-commons. *Yale Journal on Regulation*, *22*, 289–314.

Smith, H. E. (2008). Governing water: The semi-commons of fluid property rights. *Arizona Law Review*, *50*, 445. Retrieved from http://nrs.harvard.edu/urn-3:HUL.InstRepos:dash.current.terms-ofuse#OAP

Solava, I., & Alkire, S. (2007). *Agency and empowerment: A proposal for internationally comparable indicators.* OPHI Paper Working Series. OPHI.

Solow, R. (1956). A contribution to the theory of economic growth. *The Quarterly Journal of Economics*, *70*(1), 65–94. doi:10.2307/1884513

Sommestad, L. (2001). Health and wealth: The contribution of welfare state policies to economic growth. In *Proceedings of the Expert Conference Best Practices in Progressive Governance, 2001.* Institute for Futures Studies.

Sorenson, C., Drummond, M., & Kanavos, P. (2008). *Ensuring value for money in health care: The role of health technology assessment in European Union.* Cornwall, UK: World Health Organization.

Spence, R. (2003). *Information and communications technologies (ICTs) for poverty reduction: When, where and how?* Washington, DC: IDRC.

Ssewanyana, J. K., & Busler, M. (2007). Adoption and usage of ICT in developing countries: Case of Ugandan firms. *International Journal of Education and Development using Information and Communication Technology*, *3*(3), 49-59.

Strauss, J., & Thomas, D. (1998). Health, nutrition, and economic development. *Journal of Economic Literature*, *36*(2), 766–817.

Suggs, L. S. (2006). A 10-year retrospective of research in new technologies for health communication. *Journal of Health Communication*, *11*(1), 61–74. doi:10.1080/10810730500461083

Suhrcke, M., McKee, M., Sauto Arce, R., Tsolova, S., & Mortensen, J. (2005). *The contribution of health to the economy in the European Union.* Retrieved from http://ec.europa.eu/health/ph_overview/Documents/health_economy_en.pdf

Sutherland-Smith, W., Snyder, L., & Angus, L. (2003). The digital divide: Differences in computer use between home and school in low socio-economic households. *Educational Studies in Language and Literature*, *3*, 5–19. doi:10.1023/A:1024523503078

Sylwester, K. (2002). A model of public education and income inequality with a subsistence constraint. *Southern Economic Journal*, *69*(1), 144–158. doi:10.2307/1061561

Tabutin, D., & Schoumaker, B. (2005). *La démographie du monde arabe et du moyen-orient des années 1950 aux années 2000: Synthèse des changements et bilan statistique.* Paris, France: Institut National d'Etudes Démographiques.

Talbi, J., Khadmaoui, A., Soulaymani, A., & Chafik, A. (2007). Study of consanguinity in Moroccan population: Influence on the profile of health. *Anthropology*, *15*, 1–11.

Tejinder, S. (2010). Role of innovation in growth of countries: Perspectives of innovations. *Economics and Business*, *4*(1), 15–17.

Tesliuc, E. D., & Lindert, K. (2002). *Vulnerability: A quantitative and qualitative assessment.* Washington, DC: World Bank.

Thapa, D., Sein, M. K., & Sæbø. (2012). Building collective capabilities through ICT in a mountain region of Nepal: Where social capital lead to collective action. *Journal of Information Technology, Information Technology for Development*, *18*(1).

The World Bank Group. (2012). *Doing business home.* Retrieved from http://www.doingbusiness.org/

Thompson, J., & Porras, I. T. (2002). Thirty years of change in water use in east Africa. *Appropriate Technology*, *29*(2), 69–85.

TIGA. (2011). *ICTs in health.* Retrieved from http://repository.uneca.org/tiga/?q=node/36

Tompa, E. (2002). The impact of health on productivity: Empirical evidence and policy implications. In *The Review of Economic Performance and Social Progress 2002: Towards a Social Understanding of Productivity, 2002*, (pp. 181-202). Retrieved from http://www.csls.ca/repsp/2/emiletompa.pdf

Townsend, P. (1979). *Poverty in the United Kingdom: A survey of household resources and standards of living.* Harmondsworth, UK: Penguin.

Townsend, P. (1987). Deprivation. *Journal of Social Policy, 16*(2), 125–146. doi:10.1017/S0047279400020341

Toyama, K., Karishma, K., Pal, D. M., Joyojeet, S. S., & Srinivasan, J. (2005). *PC kiosks trends in rural India.* Retrieved, May 2006, from http://www.globaldevelopment.org/papers/

Traxler, J., & Leach, J. (2006). Innovative and sustainable mobile learning in Africa. In *Proceedings of the IEEE 4th International Workshop on Wireless, Mobile and Ubiquitous Technologies in Education.* Los Alamitos, CA: IEEE Computer Society.

U.S.-Arab Chamber of Commerce. (2011). *US-Arab trade line.* Retrieved from http://www.nusacc.org/assets/library/15_trdln1110kbe.pdf

Ulubaşoğlu, M. A., & Cardak, B. A. (2006). International comparisons of rural-urban educational attainment data and determinants. *European Economic Review, 51*(7), 1828–1857. doi:10.1016/j.euroecorev.2006.11.003

UNCTAD. (2010). *ICTs, enterprises and poverty alleviation.* New York, NY: United Nations.

UNCTAD. (2010). *Information and communication report, 2010.* New York, NY: UNCTAD.

UNDP. (2002). Arab human development report 2002: Creating opportunities for future generations. *Regional Bureau of Arab States.* Retrieved on July 9th, 2007, from http://www.nakbaonline.org/download/UNDP/English-Version/Ar-Human-Dev-2002.pdf

UNDP. (2003). Arab human development report: Building a knowledge-society. *Regional Bureau of Arab States.* Retrieved on July 9th, 2007, from http://www.miftah.org/Doc/Reports/Englishcomplete2003.pdf

UNDP. (2004). Arab human development report: Towards freedom in the Arab world. *Regional Bureau of Arab States.* Retrieved on July 9th, 2007, from http://www.pogar.org/publications/other/ahdr/ahdr2004e.pdf

UNDP. (2005). Arab human development report: Towards the rise of women. *Regional Bureau of Arab States.* Retrieved on July 9th, 2007, from http://www.auswaertigesamt.de/diplo/de/Aussenpolitik/Kulturpolitik/DialogIslam/HumanDevelopRep2005.pdf

UNESCO. (2000). *World education forum.* Retrieved from http://www.unesco.org/education/efa/wef_2000/

UNESCO. (2004). *In movement, UNESCO salutes women video artists.* Retrieved from http://unesdoc.unesco.org/images/0014/001495/149531eo.pdf

United Nations Development Program. (2011). *Human development reports.* Retrieved from: http://hdr.undp.org/en/

United Nations Development Program. (2011). *Arab human development reports.* Retrieved from http://arab-hdr.org/

United Nations Development Program. (2011). *Mobile technologies and empowerment: Enhancing human development through participation and innovation.* Retrieved from http://undpegov.org

United Nations Development Programme. (2002). *Arab human development report.* New York, NY: UN.

United Nations Development Programme. (2003). *Arab human development report.* New York, NY: UN.

United Nations Development Programme. (2004). *Arab human development report.* New York, NY: UN.

United Nations Development Programme. (2005). *Arab human development report.* New York, NY: UN.

United Nations ICT Task Force. (2003). *Using information and communication technologies to achieve millennium development goals.* New York, NY: United Nations.

United Nations. (2007). *Guidebook on developing women's entrepreneurship in green cooperatives in the Asian and Pacific region.* New York, NY: United Nations.

Unwin, T. (2008). Survey of e-learning in Africa. *UNESCO Chair in ICT for Development.* Retrieved from http://www.elearning-africa.com/

Unwin, T. (2012). Education. In Sadowsky, G. (Ed.), *Accelerating Development Using the Web: Empowering Poor and Marginalized Populations*. New York, NY: World Wide Web Foundation.

Valentine, D. (2002). *Distance learning: Promises, problems, and possibilities*. Retrieved from http://distance. westga.edu/~distance/ojdla/fall53/valentine53.html

Velho, L. (2004). Agricultural biotechnology research partnerships in sub-saharan Africa: Achievements, challenges and policy issues. *Technology Policy Briefs*, *4*, 1–12.

Viale, R., & Etzkowitz, H. (2005). *Third academic revolution: Polyvalent knowledge: The "DNA" of the triple helix*. Paper presented at the 5th Triple Helix Conference-The Capitalization of…. New York, NY.

Vital Wave Consulting. (2011). *New incubation labs boost mobile innovation in the developing world*. Retrieved from http://vitalwave.blogspot.com/2011/06/new-incubation-labs-boost-mobile.html

Walsham, G., & Sahay, S. (1999). GIS for district-level administration in India: Problems and opportunities. *Management Information Systems Quarterly*, *23*(1), 39–66. doi:10.2307/249409

Warner, K. E. (1990). Wellness at the worksite. *Health Affairs*, *9*, 263–279. Retrieved from http://content.healthaffairs.org/content/9/2/63.citatidoi:10.1377/hlthaff.9.2.63

Weil, D. N. (2006). *Accounting for the effect of health on economic growth*. Retrieved from http://weblamp.princeton.edu/chw/papers/Weil_David_Accounting_for_the_Effect_of_Health on_Economic_Growth_Oct_2006.pdf

Weiner, A., & Rumiany, D. (2007). A new logic of reducing the global digital divide in sub-Saharan Africa: From obstacles to opportunities. *ATDF Journal*, *4*(1), 14–21.

Whitehead, M., Dahlgren, G., & Evans, T. (2001). Equity and health sector reforms: Can low income countries escape the medical poverty trap? *Lancet*, *358*, 833–836. doi:10.1016/S0140-6736(01)05975-X

WHO. (2006). *Building foundations for e-health*. Report of the WHO Global Observatory for eHealth. Retrieved from http://www.who.int/goe/data/country_reput ort/dza.pdf

WHO. (2009). *WHO eastern Mediterranean region: Lebanon*. Retrieved from http://www.who.int/goe/publications/atlas/lbn.pdf

Wichmann, T. (1995). *Food consumption and growth in a two sector economy*. Berlin, Germany: Technical University Berlin.

Wilson, K., & O'Sullivan, E. (2011). *Shaping the gulf national innovation systems*. Paper presented at the Gulf Research Meeting 2011. Cambridge, UK.

World Bank. (2006). *Equity and development*. Retrieved from http://siteresources.worldbank.org/INTWDR2006/Resources/477383-127230817535/082136412X.pdf

World Bank. (2007). *Survey of ICT and education in Africa: Egypt country report Egypt: ICT in education in Egypt*. Washington, DC: World Bank.

World Bank. (2008). Social inclusion through ICT for Tunisian disabled. *Health in Middle East and North Africa*. Retrieved from http://web.worldbank.org/archive/website01055/WEB/0__CON-8.HTM

World DataBank. (2012). *World development indicators (WDI) & global development finance (GDF)*. Retrieved from http://databank.worldbank.org/ddp/home.do

World Health Organization. (2004). *Ehealth for healthcare delivery: Strategy 2004-2007*. Retrieved from http://www.who.int/eht/en/EHT_strategy_2004-2007.pdf

World Health Organization. (2005). *Health and the millennium development goals*. Retrieved from http://www.who.int/mdg/publications/mdg_report/en/index.html

World Health Organization. (2010). *10 facts on nutrition*. Retrieved from http://www.who.int/mediacentre/factsheets/fs172/en/

World Health Organization. (2010). *Integrated prevention into health care*. Fact Sheet #172. Retrieved from http://www.who.int/mediacentre/factsheets/fs172/en/

Wresch, W. (1996). *Disconnected: Haves and have-nots in the information age*. New Brunswick, NJ: Rutgers University Press.

Xu, K., Evans, S. B., Kawabata, D., Zeramdini, R., Klavus, J., & Murray, C. (2003). Household catastrophic health expenditure: A multicounty analysis. *Lancet*, *362*, 111–117. doi:10.1016/S0140-6736(03)13861-5

Yamauchi, F. (2006). *Early childhood nutrition, schooling, and sibling inequality in a dynamic context: Evidence from South Africa*. FCND Discussion Paper 203. Washington, DC: FCND.

Youngs, G. (2002). Closing the gaps: Women, communications and technology. *In Development*, *45*(4), 23–28. doi:10.1057/palgrave.development.1110400

Youngs, G. (2012). Globalization, information and communication technologies, and women's lives. In *Globalization, Technology Diffusion and Gender Disparity: Social Impacts of ICTs*. Hershey, PA: IGI Global. doi:10.4018/978-1-4666-0020-1.ch003

Zhang, Y., & Bolton, G. E. (2012). *Social network effects on coordination: A laboratory investigation*. Retrieved from http://ssrn.com/102139/ssrn.2000974

Zhenwei, C. Q., Masatake, Y., Hausman, V., & Altman, D. (2011). *Mobile applications for the health sector*. Washington, DC: World Bank. Retrieved from http://siteresources.worldbank.org/informationandcommunicationandtechnologies/Resources/mHealth_report.pdf

About the Author

Ahmed Driouchi holds a PhD in Applied Economics from the University of Minnesota, USA. He also has a "Doctorate-ès-Sciences" with Major in Economics from the Hassan II Institute of Agronomy and Veterinary Medicine, Morocco. He has been conducting a series of projects with a large number of international and national organizations on a large array of economic issues (UNDP, World Bank, USAID, GTZ, FAO, ICARDA, IAAE, EIB, FEMISE, Go-Euromed, and others). He is currently Professor of Applied Economics at Al Akhawayn University and Dean of the Institute of Economic Analysis and Prospective Studies (IEAPS) (2005-now). This institute is created with the collaboration of the World Bank, the Moroccan Government, and Al Akhawayn University. The author is also the founding Dean of the School of Business Administration at Al Akhawayn University (1995-2005). He is also Professor of Economics at "National Agricultural School of Engineering, Meknes," Morocco, and the School of Business Administration at Al Akhawayn University, Ifrane. With focus on his major field of economics and emphasis on quantitative methods, the author is open on other disciplines. This multidisciplinarity is related to his educational career with his initial training in agricultural engineering and agricultural economics and his previous research in agriculture, bio-economics, risks, and their relations to economic development. His current work emphasizes the economics of knowledge for development with a focus on education, health, and poverty. The geographical area of research covers the Arab, MENA, and the Mediterranean economies with their relation to Europe. Different publications and scientific articles are produced by the author. In addition, the author spent several years looking at the economics of intellectual property rights and innovations. The most recent areas covered include market analyses of pharmaceuticals and patents, theory and applications, and a contribution on the migration of skilled labor. He suggested a new win-win framework for the migration of medical doctors. His active affiliation with FEMISE has been of great help to him in generating new ideas and innovative research outcomes.

Index

X

Y